# LIVES OF THE TUDOR AGE

LIVES BEFORE THE TUDORS

in preparation

LIVES OF THE TUDOR AGE

1485–1603

*by Ann Hoffmann*

LIVES OF THE STUART AGE

1603–1714

*Compiled by Laurence Urdang Associates*

LIVES OF THE GEORGIAN AGE

1714–1837

*Compiled by Laurence Urdang Associates*

LIVES OF THE VICTORIAN AGE

in preparation

★

Osprey Publishing Limited

*Series Editor:* ROGER CLEEVE

The biographies presented in these books are those
which during the periods covered attained their
peak of achievement. Cross-references are given to
the relevant volume where this distinction is not
obvious.

# LIVES

## OF THE

## TUDOR AGE

### 1485–1603

*by*
*Ann Hoffmann*

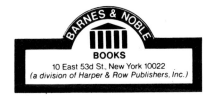

BARNES & NOBLE
BOOKS
10 East 53d St., New York 10022
(a division of Harper & Row Publishers, Inc.)

Published in the U.S.A. 1977 by Harper & Row Publishers, Inc.
Barnes & Noble Import Division

ISBN 0–06–494331–3

LC 76–15685

*Designed by Frederick Price*

Filmset and printed in Great Britain by
BAS Printers Limited, Wallop, Hampshire, England

# PREFACE

This volume contains 308 short biographies of men and women who were prominent in the Tudor age.

Selection has not been easy. Basically only those people who made some impact on the period, either on account of their birth status, or by their achievement or the fact that they were at the top of their profession or trade, have been included. A few entries have been added for those foreign nationals who had a lasting influence on English life and thought of the age. Inevitably there have had to be some omissions due to lack of space (the *Dictionary of National Biography* contains more entries for the same period under the first letter of the alphabet than the whole of this book).

Some personalities do not fall neatly into the Tudor period, but overspill into the early seventeenth century. The main factor in deciding in which volume of the series such people should figure has been the date of the peak of their achievement. Where appropriate, an entry will be found in the present volume giving cross-references to other volumes. The one exception is James VI of Scotland (James I of England), for whom there are two entries.

The biographies are arranged alphabetically under the surname of the person concerned, with cross-references from titles or, in the case of women, married names. References will be found in the Index to subsidiary persons mentioned in the text, as well as to those who have entries in this volume; the Classified Index groups the entries under status, professions, and occupations.

A selective bibliography appears at the end of each entry. It includes the standard life, where such a work exists, together with other worthwhile titles on the subject. The place of publication is listed only in the case of titles not published in London. Where no such books can be recommended, the reader should refer to the *Dictionary of National Biography*.

So far as is possible, an attempt has been made to give the details and locations of major portraits and engravings. Since the preparation of a comprehensive portrait section would involve research beyond the scope of this series, the iconographies should be regarded as a guide only. In particular, the locations of some original engravings are not known, but where these have been illustrated, the reader should refer to the acknowledgments for the sources of the photographs used.

*Sources:*

The *Dictionary of National Biography* is naturally the major source, although much of the information in it has been superseded by twentieth-century research.

The standard bibliographical work on the period is Conyers Read, *Bibliography of British History, Tudor Period, 1485–1603* (2nd edition, Oxford, 1959); this includes works published up to the end of 1956. A slighter volume, but no less useful, is the bibliographical handbook compiled by Mortimer Levine for the Conference on British Studies, under the title *Tudor England 1485–1603* (Cambridge, 1968), which covers material published before the end of August 1966. A more recent critical bibliography by G. R. Elton, *Modern Historians on British History 1485–1945* (London, 1970), contains a useful section on the sixteenth century and lists publications up to the end of 1969.

The official papers of the period have been printed in the *Calendars of State Papers*, Domestic and Foreign series, for the reigns of Henry VIII, Edward VI, Mary I, and Elizabeth I. Other relevant volumes are the *Calendar of State Papers relating to Scotland* and the *Calendar of State Papers relating to Ireland* for the same reigns; the *Calendar of State Papers, Venetian*, vols i-ix; *Calendar of State Papers relating to English Affairs, Rome*, vols i and ii; *Letters and State Papers relating to English Affairs, preserved principally in the Archives of Simancas*, vols i-iv.

The most useful general sources are:

J. B. Black, *The Reign of Elizabeth* (Oxford History of England, 2nd ed., Oxford, 1959).
G. R. Elton, *England under the Tudors* (2nd ed. 1974).
Michael Foss, *Tudor Portraits: Success and Failure of an Age* (1973).
K. Garvin (ed.), *The Great Tudors* (1935).
J. Hurstfield (ed.), *The Tudors* (Historical Association, 1973).
J. D. Mackie, *The Earlier Tudors, 1485–1558* (Oxford History of England, rev. ed., 1972).
Christopher Morris, *The Tudors* (1955).
A. L. Rowse, *The Elizabethan Renaissance: The Life of the Society* (1971).
A. L. Rowse, *The Elizabethan Renaissance: The Cultural Achievement* (1972).
A. L. Rowse, *The England of Elizabeth* (1950).
A. L. Rowse, *The Expansion of Elizabethan England* (1955).
J. A. Williamson, *The Tudor Age* (rev. ed. 1970).

*Iconographies:*
The principal published authority on portraits is Roy Strong, *Tudor and Jacobean Portraits* (2 vols, 1969). Other sources used include:

J. W. Goodison, *Catalogue of Cambridge Portraits*, vol. i (no later volumes yet available) (Cambridge, 1955).
Oliver Millar, *Tudor, Stuart and Early Georgian Pictures in the Royal Collection* (2 vols, 1963).
R. L. Poole, *Catalogue of Portraits in the University ... of Oxford* (3 vols, 1912–25).
David Talbot-Rice, *Edinburgh University Portraits* (1957).

*Abbreviations:*
These occur chiefly in the iconographies, where the practice followed has been to give each location in full the first time it occurs in each entry and to abbreviate it thereafter.

| | |
|---|---|
| B.M. | British Museum, London. |
| B.N. | Bibliothèque Nationale, Paris. |
| D.N.B. | Dictionary of National Biography. |
| H.M.C. | Historical Manuscripts Commission, London. |
| N.M.M. | National Maritime Museum, Greenwich. |
| N.P.G. | National Portrait Gallery, London. |
| R.T.H. | Radio Times Hulton Picture Library, London. |
| S.N.P.G. | Scottish National Portrait Gallery, Edinburgh. |
| V. & A. | Victoria and Albert Museum, London. |

*Dates:*
England did not adopt the Gregorian, or New Style, calendar until 1752. To avoid confusion, the method followed

here is that used by most modern historians. i.e. to take the beginning of the historical year as 1 January. Thus a date falling between 1 January and 24 March is written not, for example, as 22 February 1558/9, but as 22 February 1559.

*Acknowledgments:*
I am deeply indebted to Dr A. L. Rowse and Dr Neville Williams for their many valuable comments on my text. I also wish to express my gratitude to Mrs Susan Coltart and Mrs Pam Hollands, for their efficient typing from my much corrected drafts; to Mrs Pat Hodgson, who collected the bulk of the illustrations; and to Miss Alison Hodgson, for her meticulous editing and proof-reading. Most of all I would like to thank Mr Roger Cleeve, of Osprey Publishing Limited, for his patience and understanding throughout the many months that this volume has been in preparation.

A.H.

For ALEXANDRA AND MARGARET

# ILLUSTRATIONS

## WITH ACKNOWLEDGEMENTS

ix

**Albany, Duke of** (1481–1536), see Stewart, John.

**Alençon, François, Duc d'** (1554–1584), later Duc d'Anjou, suitor for the hand of Elizabeth I (q.v.).

Alençon was born at St Germain-en-Laye on 15 March 1554, the fourth and youngest surviving son of Henri II and Catherine de' Medici (q.v.). He was baptized Hercule François, but after the death of his eldest brother, François II, dropped the first name. An unattractive, difficult child, he was not greatly loved by his mother; but when Catherine's scheme for one of her elder sons (first Charles, then Henri) to marry the English Queen failed to come to fruition, in 1572 she urged Alençon to press his suit with Elizabeth. He was then seventeen years of age, the Queen thirty-eight. Negotiations were begun, and Elizabeth asked for time to reflect on the proposal; but nothing came of the matter.

The Duke first appeared on the political scene in France as leader of the party of *mécontents,* towards the end of the reign of his brother, Charles IX. In 1574, when his other brother, Henri, Duc d'Anjou (later Henri III), accepted the throne of Poland, Alençon succeeded to the dukedom of Anjou. (To avoid confusion, modern historical practice is to continue to refer to him under his earlier title, as here.) France, then in the throes of a series of religious wars, was fraught with intrigue on the part of the Guise, Bourbon, and Montmorency factions. For a time Alençon was kept

under arrest at the French Court, but in August 1575 he escaped and joined Henri de Bourbon, Prince de Condé, leader of the Huguenots. When the fifth war of religion was brought to an end in May 1576 by the Peace of Monsieur (named after the Duc d'Anjou), he was able to take possession of lands in Anjou and Touraine previously withheld from him by his brother; under the treaty the Huguenots were granted major concessions, including freedom of worship.

Alençon, outwardly reconciled with the King, nevertheless continued to intrigue against him. In the summer of 1578, intent on securing a kingdom for himself in the Netherlands, he offered to lead a Dutch revolt against their new governor, Don John of Austria; the States General proclaimed him their Defender of Liberties. At the same time Catherine de' Medici, who was sparing no effort to keep the peace between France and Spain, but had failed to persuade Philip II (q.v.) to give her youngest son a principality, urged Alençon to reopen marriage negotiations with Elizabeth.

Early in 1579 the Duke sent his friend Jean Simier to plead his cause with the Queen; as soon as he could get away from the Netherlands, where the formidable Duke of Parma had succeeded to the governorship on the death of Don John, Alençon himself visited the Queen at Greenwich. For three weeks that August he wooed her ardently, and she responded, kissing him in public, calling him by the pet name of her 'frog', and proclaiming her intention to marry him. Neither the Privy Councillors nor the English people were enthusiastic about the match, however; Elizabeth quarrelled with her Council over it, and although a preliminary marriage treaty was signed in November that year, no further steps were taken, in view of the Frenchman's obvious unpopularity in the country, particularly with the Puritans.

In August 1581 Alençon scored a major victory over Parma, taking Cambrai and forcing the Spaniards to retreat. That autumn he revisited England at Elizabeth's invitation; she received him as encouragingly as before, and the marriage negotiations were resumed. A new treaty was signed, but once more the arrangements petered out due to public mistrust of France and opposition from the Puritans. Three months later, Alençon returned to his duties in the Netherlands; marriage with the English Queen was never again mentioned. Elizabeth, it seemed, had put politics before her personal desires and, having failed to persuade Henri III to agree to an offensive alliance with England against Spain, showed no further interest in it.

Disappointed, Alençon now concentrated his ambitions on obtaining sovereignty of the Netherlands. In January 1582, soon after his return from England, he had himself proclaimed as Duc de Brabant and Comte de Flandres. Within the next twelve months, his utter incompetence as a military commander became apparent in a series of disastrous confrontations with Parma's forces; not surprisingly, there were quarrels between Alençon and the States General. Having failed to seize Antwerp in January 1583, in a campaign in which most of his men were brutally massacred, the Duke finally gave up; in June that year he returned home to France for good. The following summer he succumbed to a fever and died at Château-Thierry on 10 June 1584, naming the Protestant Henri de Navarre as his heir. Elizabeth is said to have been deeply affected by the news of his death.

Alençon's prolonged 'on-off' courtship of the English Queen was the source of much amusement and speculation throughout the courts of Europe for the best part of a decade. Elizabeth obviously had some feeling for her 'frog', but just how far it was politically motivated, historians can only conjecture. That the marriage, had it taken place, would have proved highly unpopular in the eyes of the English people, there is little doubt.

## Allen, William (1532–1594), cardinal.

William Allen was born in 1532 in Rossall, Lancashire, the second son of John Allen and his wife, Jane Lister. Educated initially at home, he entered Oriel College, Oxford, in 1547, taking his B.A. and becoming a fellow of the college in 1550, and his M.A. in 1554. His tutor at Oxford was an ardent Catholic, the Rev. Morgan Philipps.

In 1556 Allen was elected Principal of St Mary's Hall, Oxford, where he also became for a time proctor; about two years later he was appointed a canon of York. The accession of Elizabeth I (q.v.) in 1558 rendered his position as an uncompromising Catholic insecure, and in 1561 he decided to leave England; he settled at Louvain in France. Taking up residence at the university there, he became tutor to a young Englishman, Christopher Blount, who was later to be executed for participation in the rebellion led by the Earl of Essex (see Devereux, Robert) in 1601. Allen caught an infection from Blount and became so ill that he was advised by his doctors to return to England – which he did, in disguise, in 1562.

In the next few years he moved about between Lancashire, Oxford, and the household of the Duke of Norfolk (see Howard, Thomas, 4th Duke) in Norfolk, devoting his time to recovering lapsed Catholics; he refused to take an oath acknowledging Elizabeth as head of the English Church, and consequently the government viewed his activities with suspicion. In 1565 Allen's open opposition to the Queen's religious policy forced him to seek refuge on the Continent, from which he never returned. In 1567 he was listed by the Queen as one of those to be apprehended for 'contempt and obstinacy' on account of his recent treatise on Purgatory, written while he was at Louvain but not published until 1565.

Allen was ordained at Mechelen in 1567, and in that same year undertook his first journey to Rome, together with his former tutor, Morgan Philipps, and Dr Vendeville, Regius Professor of Canon Law at Douai, whom Allen persuaded to let him found a seminary for English students abroad. The plan was to give instruction in the Catholic religion to young Englishmen who would form a body of priests capable of restoring Catholicism in England. It received the approval of Pope Pius V, and in 1568 Allen rented a house at Douai and took in his first students. He met with considerable local opposition and was hampered at the outset by lack of funds, but having become a Bachelor of Divinity in 1569 and Regius Professor of Philosophy at Douai University the following year, he was able to give his salary to improve and enlarge facilities at the seminary. The situation was further improved by a grant from Pope Gregory XIII (q.v.) which made the new college financially independent, and in return Allen travelled to Rome to advise the Pope concerning the establishment of a similar institution in that city; it was agreed that some students would be sent from Douai to Rome as soon as the English College there was ready.

Allen returned to Douai from Rome in 1576 to find that an unhealthy situation had developed between his students and the Dutch Protestants, who were angry at the English taking, as they thought, the side of Philip II (q.v.) in the dispute between the Netherlands and Spain. In November Allen thought it wise to withdraw to Paris, where he began to make plans for the removal of the college to Rheims; this was effected in 1578.

In 1579 he was called on to make a third journey to Rome because of disputes that had arisen in the English College there between the students and the head; the main object of his visit, however, was to persuade the Society of Jesus to take over the College. While in Rome, Allen met and recruited Father Robert Parsons (q.v.) to help him organize Roman Catholic resistance to the Protestantism established in England by Elizabeth. It may have been Parsons's original idea that Jesuit priests should be sent to England for this purpose; in any event, he and Allen worked on the scheme together, and in 1580 the first mission, headed by Parsons and Edmund Campion (q.v.), was sent to England.

Allen remained in Rheims as head of the College until 1585, when as a result of ill-health he went to Spa for treatment. Later that year, having made a good recovery, he was able to travel again to Rome, probably having been summoned by Pope Sixtus V to take part in the revision of the Vulgate (Latin translation of the Bible). On 7 August 1587 he was made a cardinal at the request of Philip II, who counted on his support in England following the anticipated overthrow of Elizabeth after she had been defeated by the 'Great Enterprise' (Armada); the idea was that Allen would then go to England as Papal Legate and eventually become Archbishop of Canterbury, and even Lord Chancellor. In the meanwhile he was kept adequately supplied with money by the Pope and Philip, being granted an abbey in Calabria and the revenues from the archbishopric of Palermo.

Although initially Allen had confined his activities to promoting missionary work in England through his priests from Douai and Rheims, from about 1582 onwards he was involved in political intrigue. He corresponded with Mary, Queen of Scots (q.v.) and the Guises; he was a party to Parsons's plot to overthrow Elizabeth; and he wholeheartedly supported Philip in his invasion plans. The Cardinal's political writings, however, won him no admiration in England, from Catholics or Protestants: in 1587 he published a vicious letter attacking Elizabeth and defending the surrender by the English governor to the Spaniards of Deventer and another fort in the Netherlands, and a particularly offensive paper, issued in Antwerp just before the sailing of the Spanish Armada in 1588, entitled *An Admonition to the Nobility and People of England and Ireland, concerning the Present Warres.*

In 1589 Allen was made Apostolic Librarian. For some time he had been working on the revision of the Vulgate and also supervising the new English translation of the Bible by Gregory Martin, known as the Douai Bible, of which the New Testament had been published in 1582; the Old Testament would not appear until 1609, after Allen's death. Another of his projects was a revision of the writings of St Augustine, but this was never completed. Allen died on 16 October 1594; he was buried in the Holy Trinity Church attached to the English College in Rome.

Cardinal William Allen was in his day the most important English Catholic abroad. Regarded as a traitor by the Protestants, it can be said in his favour that he was motivated purely by his religious faith; his excursions into political intrigue were failures, and at the English Colleges at Douai and Rome he relied too much on the strength of his own personality and too little on an efficient organization for the future. Because so many years of his life were spent abroad, Allen never really understood his fellow countrymen.

L. Hicks, 'Cardinal Allen and the Society [of Jesus]', *The Month*, clx (1932), pp. 342–53, 528–36.

L. Hicks, 'Allen and Deventer (1587)', *The Month*, clxiii (1934), pp. 507–17.

L. Hicks, 'Cardinal Allen's admonition', *The Month*, clxxxv (1948), pp. 232–42; clxxxvi (1949), pp. 30–9.

T. F. Knox, 'Letters and Memorials of William Allen', in *Records of the English Catholics under the Penal Laws*, vol. ii (1882).

G. Mattingly, 'William Allen and Catholic Propaganda in England', *Travaux d'Humanisme et Renaissance*, xxviii (1957), pp. 325–9.

P. Ryan, 'Some Correspondence of William Allen, 1579–85, from the Jesuit Archives', *Catholic Record Society Miscellany*, vii (1911), pp. 12–105.

*Portrait*: oil, by unknown artist, sixteenth century: Ushaw College, Durham; engraving, by unknown artist: location unknown.

**Alleyn, Edward** (1566–1626), actor and founder of Dulwich College.

Edward Alleyn was born on 1 September 1566 at St Botolph's, Bishopsgate, in the City of London, where his father, described in the records as a 'yeoman of London', bought an inn the same year. He and his brother John, the only two of four sons to grow to manhood, grew up in the atmosphere of the inn, where groups of players frequently performed in the courtyard, and as boys they probably first learned the art of acting by taking some of the female parts.

Alleyn senior died when Edward was four years old, and when his mother remarried ten years later, he and John took over the joint management of the inn, combining inn-keeping with acting. John acted with Lord Sheffield's company and later with Lord Admiral Howard's, while Edward is known to have joined the Earl of Worcester's company before he was eighteen and later to have transferred to the Lord Admiral's company. At this date the latter company was one of those which hired the Globe Theatre, built by James Burbage (q.v.), as well as the Curtain and another playhouse at Newington Butts; from time to time they joined with Burbage's company, known as the Lord Chamberlain's, for whom William Shakespeare (q.v.) wrote exclusively. By the age of twenty-six Alleyn had played all the leading parts and had won acclaim for his interpretation of many roles, rivalled only by the contemporary Shakespearian actor, Richard Burbage

(q.v.), son of James. Having inherited his father's property on the death of his mother, he was able to spend lavishly on a theatrical wardrobe.

In October 1592 Alleyn married Joan Woodward, step-daughter of the theatrical manager and owner of the Rose playhouse, Philip Henslowe. Thereafter he became a partner in the latter's ventures, managing the company, selecting the plays and taking leading parts, while Henslowe controlled the financial side. Not long after his marriage Alleyn went on tour because of plague in London, but in the winter of 1593–4 he returned and for the next three years played at the Rose. After a brief retirement in 1597–8, he is said to have returned to the stage only at the express wish of Queen Elizabeth (q.v.). By this time he and Henslowe had acquired the lease of the Paris Garden and had been granted a licence for bear-baiting, which brought in a good income.

In 1594 the Lord Admiral's company and the Lord Chamberlain's went their different ways; after which date no Admiral's men performed in Shakespeare's plays. Then in 1600 Alleyn founded a new Lord Admiral's company, which played at the Fortune Theatre, built by Alleyn and Henslowe and opened in December that year; Alleyn was to manage this company until his final retirement from the stage in 1603. His last appearance was as the Genius of London and Thamesis in an entertainment produced by the City to welcome James I (see James VI of Scotland).

From the summer of 1605 onwards Alleyn began to negotiate for the manor of Dulwich, which he finally purchased from Sir Francis Calton in May 1606; over the next few years he bought other properties in the neighbourhood. He maintained his financial interest in the

Fortune and other playhouses and continued to live on Bankside until 1613, but in 1610 he sold his interest in the bear garden to Henslowe. Having no heir to inherit his estate, he had conceived the idea of establishing in Dulwich a college or charitable institution for the education of poor boys, and in order to set this in motion he now moved to Hall Place, Dulwich. A contract to build the college, which was to consist of a chapel, a schoolhouse and twelve almshouses, was signed on 17 May 1613.

For the next few years Alleyn devoted himself to this project and to the cultivation of his newly-acquired lands.

After Henslowe's death in 1616, he was again briefly involved in theatrical affairs and the management of the Paris Garden; he also had to defend his father-in-law's Will before the Lord Chancellor. Meanwhile on 1 September 1616 the new chapel at Dulwich was consecrated, and in 1619 a patent was granted for the foundation of the College of God's Gift (later Dulwich College). Under this foundation charter all the property pur-chased by Alleyn in Dulwich and else-where, including the Fortune Theatre, was granted to the college.

In December 1621 the Fortune was burned down. Alleyn immediately formed a syndicate to rebuild it, and the new playhouse was opened in 1623. In June that year he accompanied Inigo Jones (see *Lives of the Stuart Age*) to Southampton to make arrangements for the welcoming entertainment to be offered to the Infanta of Spain, bride-designate of Prince Charles, later Charles I (see *Lives of the Stuart Age*). Shortly afterwards Alleyn's wife Joan died; a few months later, in December 1623, he married Constance, daughter of the poet and Dean of St Paul's, John Donne (see *Lives of the Stuart Age*).

In the summer of 1626 Alleyn caught a chill while riding to York to inspect a property. He never regained his health and died at Dulwich on 25 November the same year. He was buried in the college chapel. Under his Will the college received his books, pictures, and musical instruments, as well as furniture and furnishings, horses and farm implements. Control of the college passed to two cousins, and in the ensuing years various members of the Alleyn (Allen) family held office as Warden and Master. James Allen, who was Master in 1721–46, founded the James Allen Girls' School.

Edward Alleyn was one of the greatest actors of the Elizabethan stage.

The *Alleyn Papers*, edited by J. Payne Collier, were published by the Shakespeare Society in 1843.

J. Payne Collier, *Memoirs of Edward Alleyn* (1844).
G. L. Hosking, *Life and Times of Edward Alleyn* (1952).
W. Young, *History of Dulwich College* (1889).

*Portrait*: oil, by unknown artist: Dulwich College Picture Gallery, London; copies elsewhere.

6

**Andrewes, Lancelot** (1555–1626), theologian and court preacher, successively Bishop of Chichester, Ely, and Winchester.

The son of a merchant who rose to be Master of Trinity House, Lancelot Andrewes was born at Barking in 1555. He was educated at Cooper's Free Grammar School, Ratcliffe, and at Merchant Taylors' School, from where he won a scholarship to Pembroke Hall, Cambridge. He was elected a fellow of his college in 1576 and was ordained as a deacon in 1580.

Soon after taking holy orders Andrewes was persuaded to act as chaplain to Henry Hastings, 3rd Earl of Huntingdon, who was then President of the North; while serving in this capacity he is said through his preaching to have won large numbers of northerners over to the Protestant religion. In 1589 he was rewarded by Sir Francis Walsingham (q.v.), who was instrumental in his being given the living of St Giles's, Cripplegate, as well as a prebend at St Paul's; he was also chosen to be Master of his old college at Cambridge, Pembroke Hall.

The ascetic life which Andrewes led at this time, combined with his rigorous preaching and lecturing, brought on a severe illness which endangered his life. He recovered and was appointed as chaplain to Archbishop John Whitgift (q.v.) and chaplain in ordinary to the Queen. Elizabeth I (q.v.) later offered Andrewes two bishoprics (Salisbury and Ely), but he refused them on account of her insistence that he should co-operate in effecting a reduction of the power of the Church in state affairs. He did, however, accept two appointments at Westminster during the last years of her reign: a prebend in 1597, and the office of Dean in 1601.

On the accession of James I (see James VI of Scotland) Andrewes rose rapidly in the Church as a result of the King's appreciation of his great learning and gifts as a preacher. He took part in the Hampton Court Conference of 1603–4 and played a prominent part in the preparation of the Authorized Version of the Bible, begun in 1607 and published in 1611. Lord Almoner in 1605, he was the same year persuaded to accept the see of Chichester; in 1609 he was made a Privy Councillor and was translated to Ely. He went with the King to Scotland in the summer of 1618, in order to persuade the General Assembly to accept the Five Articles of Religion introducing Anglican principles (i.e. episcopacy) into the Church of Scotland. In 1619 Andrewes was consecrated as Bishop of Winchester and, relinquishing the post of Lord Almoner, became Dean of the Chapels Royal, an office which he was to hold for the rest of his life. He died on 26 September 1626.

Lancelot Andrewes was one of the most learned theologians of his time. A master of rhetoric and an eloquent preacher of the old style, popular at court, he steadfastly defended Anglican doctrines at a period of considerable controversy within the Church, while criticizing the extreme viewpoints of both the Puritans and the Calvinists. Among his most celebrated sermons are those he preached on the anniversaries of the Gunpowder Plot of 1605 (see Fawkes, Guy, in *Lives of the Stuart Age*); a full bibliography of his sermons will be found in the Welsby biography listed below. His writings, few of which were published during his lifetime, fill eight volumes in the *Library of Anglo-Catholic Theology* (1841–54).

Florence M. G. Evans, *Lancelot Andrewes* (1952).
Paul A. Welsby, *Lancelot Andrewes, 1555–1626* (1958).

*Portrait*: oil, by unknown artist: Bodleian Library, Oxford.

**Angus, 6th Earl of** (?1489–1557), see Douglas, Archibald, 6th Earl.

**Angus, 8th Earl of** (1555–1588), see Douglas, Archibald, 8th Earl.

**Anjou, Duc d'** (1554–1584), see Alençon, François, Duc d'.

**Anne Boleyn** (?1507–1536), second Queen consort of Henry VIII (q.v.) and mother of Elizabeth I (q.v.).

Anne was the second daughter of Sir Thomas Boleyn (q.v.), later Earl of Wiltshire and Ormonde, and his wife, Elizabeth Howard, daughter of the Earl of Surrey. There is a confusion about Anne's birth: some writers state that she was born as early as 1501–2, but 1507 is more generally accepted as the year of her birth. She spent her early childhood at the family home of Hever Castle, near Edenbridge, Kent.

In 1514 Anne accompanied her elder sister to France. Mary Boleyn had been appointed maid-of-honour to Mary Tudor (q.v.), Louis XII's bride, but Anne, at the age of seven, being too young for royal service, was sent to be educated in the house of a French nobleman known to her parents. When her father visited the French court in 1519 he secured a place for her as maid-of-honour to Queen Claude, wife of François I. By the end of 1522, however, she was back in England and living at the court of Henry VIII, where Sir Thomas was rising rapidly in favour.

By all accounts the dark-haired Anne was no beauty. The contemporary Italian diarist Sanudo recorded that she was 'not one of the handsomest women in the world ... of middling stature, swarthy complexion, long neck, wide mouth, bosom not much raised ... eyes, which are black and beautiful and take great effect'. Her enemies referred to disfigurements such as a swelling on her neck, a wart, and a sixth finger on her right hand; none of these are borne out by later portraits, however, and they were undoubtedly exaggerated.

Anne's charm lay in her vivacious, sparkling wit and the flirtatious 'French ways' she had acquired abroad. She was extremely *chic*, whereas the Queen was dowdy. She had many ardent admirers at court, including the elder Sir Thomas Wyatt (q.v.) and Henry Percy, heir to the Earl of Northumberland, who sought her hand in marriage. She was apparently on the point of marrying Percy when Cardinal Wolsey (q.v.), at the King's command, intervened. It soon became clear that Henry had fallen deeply in love with her himself. Precisely when this momentous attraction came about is uncertain—the King's love letters to Anne, written in his own hand, are undated—but it must have been some time between 1525 and 1527. Henry, increasingly disenchanted with his marriage to the ageing Catherine of Aragon (q.v.), and desperately aware of the need for a legitimate male heir, first began seriously to contemplate a divorce in 1527. Historians have long pondered as to which came uppermost in the royal order of priorities, love for Anne or the desire for a son, and whether or not Henry's infatuation with her pre-dated his decision to extricate himself from Catherine. It is clear that Anne had no intention of yielding to the King's desires until she could be sure of the crown.

Once proceedings for the divorce were under way, Anne became the King's mistress. By July 1531, when Henry finally separated from Catherine, they were living together openly. In September the following year Henry made her Marquess (not Marchioness, as usually stated) of Pembroke, and in October 1532 she accompanied the King on a visit to France. Public disgust turned to unconcealed fury when at Easter 1533 it became known that they had been secretly married on 25 January.

Anne was already pregnant. Since it was vital that the new heir should be legitimate, the divorce proceedings had to be speeded up, and on 28 May Archbishop Cranmer (q.v.) pronounced that the King's marriage to Catherine was null and void and declared Anne to be his lawful wife. She was crowned on 1 June and, a little over two months later, in the first week of September, at Greenwich, gave birth to a daughter, the future Elizabeth I.

The King's disappointment was intense. His passion for Anne was in any case beginning to cool, and by 1534 he had switched his affections to Jane Seymour (q.v.). Anne, bitterly jealous, showed herself to be spiteful and arrogant; through her behaviour she made many enemies at court, particularly on account of her maliciousness towards Catherine and her daughter, the Princess Mary (see Mary I). Had she produced a son, the marriage—and Anne's life—might have been saved; certainly so long as Catherine lived there was no danger, as the King's second marriage could hardly be annulled without implying that the first was valid. In the event, having suffered one miscarriage in 1534, Anne gave birth to a stillborn male child on 29 January 1536. Catherine had died three weeks previously.

Henry now sought a means to get rid of his wife in order to be free to marry Jane Seymour. He appointed a commission to inquire into the matter of the Queen's 'treason', and on 2 May Anne was arrested and sent to the Tower. A few days later she was indicted before a grand jury on the charge of adultery with no less than five men, including her own

brother, Lord Rochford. On 12 May four of her reputed lovers were found guilty of high treason, and three days later Anne was brought before a tribunal of twenty-six peers presided over by her uncle, the Duke of Norfolk (see Howard, Thomas, 3rd Duke) as Lord High Steward. Not a single witness was called, and although Anne professed her innocence, both she and her brother were condemned unanimously. Events now moved swiftly. On 17 May the Queen's 'lovers' were executed, and that same day Cranmer pronounced her marriage to be invalid. Anne's own execution had to await the arrival of an executioner hastily summoned from Calais (decapitation by the sword being previously unknown in England, although customary in France). Two days later, on 19 May 1536, she was beheaded on Tower Green.

The impact of Anne Boleyn on the course of English history is far-reaching. To say that she was the cause of the Reformation is too strong; nevertheless, had Henry VIII not fallen in love with her when he did, there might have been no divorce and no break from Rome. Wolsey blamed her for his fall. Norfolk once referred to her as 'a great whore', but Anne's guilt as an adulteress has never been proved to the satisfaction of historians. The fact remains that she and five men were sent to their deaths because their king wished to take a new wife.

Marie-Louise Bruce, *Anne Boleyn* (1972).
Hester W. Chapman, *Anne Boleyn* (1974).
P. Friedmann, *Anne Boleyn, a chapter of English history, 1527–1536* (2 vols; 1884).
H. W. Trovillion (ed.), *Henry VIII's love letters to Anne Boleyn* (rev. ed. 1945).

*Portraits:* oil on panel, Anne about 1535, by unknown late-sixteenth-century artist: National Portrait Gallery, London; oil, by unknown artist, probably contemporary: Mrs K. Radclyffe; oil on panel, by unknown artist: Viscount Mountgarret; other versions in the Royal Collection, Windsor, National Gallery of Ireland, and elsewhere. N.B. According to Roy Strong, the drawing by Holbein formerly in the Earl of Bradford Collection at Weston Park, now in the British Museum, is of doubtful authenticity so far as the sitter is concerned, but it has traditionally been indentified as Anne Boleyn.

**Anne of Cleves** (1515–1557), fourth Queen consort of Henry VIII (q.v.).

Anne was born on 22 September 1515,

the second daughter of John, Duke of Cleves. Her upbringing was a narrow one, and she had few accomplishments apart from needlework; she spoke no language other than German, her mother tongue. Plain and ungraceful, her one redeeming attribute seems to have been a gentle temperament.

In 1538 Anne became a pawn in the project formulated by Thomas Cromwell (q.v.) to counter a possible Catholic attack on England by an alliance with the German Lutherans. Cromwell's suggestion that Henry should make a political marriage with Anne was not well received by the King, but as the Emperor Charles V (q.v.) and François I of France were seen to be moving towards a closer understanding he was persuaded of the wisdom of the match, and in January 1539 reluctantly gave his consent to the opening of negotiations. Anne's father died a month later; her brother William, the new Duke, allied with the Lutherans although not himself a Lutheran, but like Henry a follower of the Erastian view of state supremacy in ecclesiastical affairs, was already involved in a bitter quarrel with Charles over the duchy of Gelderland. Since Henry had no wish to provoke the Emperor unduly, the negotiations proceeded very slowly. The treaty was eventually signed at Düsseldorf on 4 September and at Hampton Court on 6 October 1539, following a rumour that Charles was planning to march through France to Ghent to put down a rebellion there.

Anne landed at Deal on 27 December 1539. When Henry met his bride at Rochester a few days later, he was shocked to find her far removed from the beauty Cromwell had made her out to be and quite unlike the flattering picture painted by Holbein which he had been sent. According to Cromwell, he took an instant dislike to her. Nevertheless an official reception to welcome the new Queen to London was held at Shooters Hill, and they were married at Greenwich on 6 January.

The marriage was soon a political embarrassment. The Emperor, having suppressed Ghent, was now threatening Cleves; furthermore, the alliance with France was breaking up. Henry saw that his union with the 'Flanders mare' (as he privately called his wife) had been totally unnecessary, and since it was now distasteful to him, he sought to free himself from it. Cromwell, discredited, was executed in June 1540. On 9 July Convocation declared the marriage null and void, and the annulment was confirmed by Parliament a few days later. The ex-Queen consort was pensioned off with lands to the value of £4,000 a year, on condition that she remained in England.

Anne accepted her fate calmly, even cheerfully. She was accorded precedence over all the ladies at court after the wife and daughters of the King and was soon reported to be wearing a new dress every day. She spent the rest of her life in happy retirement, emerging occasionally for an appearance at court, and died at Chelsea on 16 July 1557, at the age of forty-two.

*Portraits:* miniature, on an ivory box, by Holbein: Victoria and Albert Museum, London; oil, by Holbein: Louvre, Paris; oil, Flemish school (similar to portrait at Louvre): St John's College, Oxford.

**Anne of Denmark** (1574–1619), Queen consort of James VI of Scotland, later James I of England, see *Lives of the Stuart Age.*

**Arran, 1st Earl of** (?1477–1529), see Hamilton, James, 1st Earl.

**Arran, 2nd Earl of** (d. 1575), see Hamilton, James, 2nd Earl.

**Arran, 3rd Earl of** (?1530–1609), see Hamilton, James, 3rd Earl.

**Arran, Earl of** (d. 1595), see Stewart, James, Earl of Arran.

**Arthur** (1486–1502), Prince of Wales, eldest son of Henry VII (q.v.) and Elizabeth of York (q.v.).

Arthur was born on 20 September 1486 and christened at Winchester Cathedral, the Earl of Oxford and the Earl of Derby (see Stanley, Thomas, in *Lives Before the Tudors*) standing as godfathers. At the age of three he was made Prince of Wales.

Information is scanty, but it seems that Arthur was never a strong child. His father engaged the best private tutors for him, including Bernard Andréas, the blind poet laureate and historian, who recorded that by the age of fifteen the Prince was familiar with the chief Greek and Latin authors.

Negotiations for his betrothal to Catherine of Aragon (q.v.), which had begun when Arthur was only two years

old, reached a satisfactory conclusion in 1500, and the fifteen-year-old Catherine arrived in England in October 1501. The marriage took place at St Paul's Cathedral, London, on 14 November, after which the Prince and Princess of Wales set up court at Ludlow. They were considered too young to cohabit, and when Arthur died suddenly on 2 April 1502 the marriage had not been consummated.

See titles listed in this book under Henry VII.

*Portraits:* engraving, by unknown engraver, after unknown sixteenth-century artist: location not known. N.B. There is a portrait in the Royal Collection at Windsor, but the authenticity of the sitter has been questioned.

**Arundel, 12th Earl of** (?1511–1580), see Fitzalan, Henry.

**Ascham, Roger** (1515–1568), humanist, scholar, and author.

Ascham was born at Kirby Wiske, near York, some time in 1515. He received his early education in the household of Sir Anthony Wingfield, where he first came into contact with the classics and also developed a love of sport, especially archery. At the age of fourteen he entered St John's College, Cambridge, where he distinguished himself in classics and became Greek reader in 1538. At this period enthusiasm for the classics was at its height, and Ascham played an important role in the development of Greek studies at the university. In 1545 he published the first book on archery in English, a treatise written in dialogue under the title of *Toxophilus*.

In 1548 Ascham was appointed tutor to the Princess Elizabeth (see Elizabeth I) in succession to one of his former pupils, William Grindal. While admiring the Princess's intellectual ability, Ascham did not take to life in her service; he quarrelled with her steward and eventually

with Elizabeth herself, and finally resigned in order to take a post as secretary to Sir Richard Morison, English Ambassador to Charles V (q.v.) from 1550 to 1553.

After several years with Morison at Augsburg, Ascham returned to England and was appointed Latin secretary to the already ailing Edward VI (q.v.). When Mary (see Mary I) became Queen shortly afterwards, she desired him to continue in that post; it was a mark of her esteem for his scholarship not only that he was re-appointed, but that he received her special permission to continue in his Protestantism. In 1558, at the start of yet another reign, Ascham became private tutor to his erstwhile pupil, now Queen Elizabeth, a post which he held until his death ten years later.

The last years of Ascham's life were devoted chiefly to writing *Scholemaster*, which was published by his widow in 1570. In this work he put forward (for those days) enlightened views on education. He criticized the prevailing discipline and held that pupils should be attracted to learning through gentle persuasion on the part of their teacher; he also spoke out forcibly against idle attendance at court and Italian travel.

William Camden (q.v.), in his *Annales* published in 1568, wrote of Ascham's poverty and his addiction to gambling and cock-fighting. How far the latter charge is true is not known, but it seems that the scholar suffered greatly from ill-health and found it difficult to make ends meet. He had married in 1554 and had three sons; when he died in 1568 he was survived by his widow and two sons.

Roger Ascham, although a devoted and first-class Greek scholar, from his university days had all the patriotic zeal of the humanists of the age; he fought for the use of the English language and through his writings he contributed appreciably to the development of an English prose style. In the preface to *Toxophilus* he stressed that he was writing 'Englishe matter in the Englishe tongue for Englishe men'. He also pleaded in the same work that sport (such as archery) should be regarded as an important part of a boy's education.

*The English Works of Roger Ascham*, edited by W. Aldis Wright and published at Cambridge in 1904, includes the texts of *Toxophilus* and *Scholemaster*.

L. V. Ryan, *Roger Ascham* (Stanford, Calif., 1963).

**Aske, Robert** (d. 1537), leader of the Pilgrimage of Grace.

Born at about the turn of the century, Robert Aske came from a family of Yorkshire gentry with lands at Aughton in the East Riding. At one time he was in the service of the Earl of Northumberland.

In 1527 Aske was admitted to Gray's Inn. He subsequently became a respected London lawyer, gaining a reputation for oratory. He is said to have had only one eye, but tremendous physical stamina which enabled him to go without food or sleep for long periods.

When, in October 1536, the people of the East Riding of Yorkshire rose in protest against the Reformation legislation being enforced by Henry VIII (q.v.), Aske assumed the leadership of the insurgents. The discontent that had been smouldering for some time in the north of England was directed principally against the dissolution of the monasteries and the rise of 'new men' such as Thomas Cromwell (q.v.). At the beginning of the month rioters at Louth, in Lincolnshire, had attacked Cromwell's commissioners; although this rising was quelled by 19 October, it triggered off the Yorkshire rebellion, which was soon to spread throughout the northern counties

and to go down in history as the Pilgrimage of Grace.

Rallying his followers at Wighton Hill on 13 October, Aske gave them the name of 'Pilgrims'; each man was made to take a form of oath. York was occupied on the 16th, and from that city proclamations were issued, as a result of which some 30,000 men mustered at Doncaster. Among Aske's supporters were Edward Lee, Archbishop of York, and Baron Darcy of Templehurst (see Darcy, Thomas), who surrendered Pomfret Castle (Pontefract) on 21 October.

On the government side the Duke of Norfolk (see Howard, Thomas, 3rd Duke), aware of the insufficiency of loyalist troops and armaments in the area, played for time by proposing a conference at Doncaster Bridge. At this meeting on 27 October the Duke promised to forward the insurgents' demands to the King. Henry, although furious, was also persuaded to temporize, in order that adequate forces could be assembled; he made a counter-proposal that the rebels should confer with Norfolk again in early December. Aske and his followers, in 'great council' at York on 21 November, agreed to this only on the guarantee of their safe conduct, and at a further meeting at Pontefract on 2 December they drew up their demands in writing. These articles went further than those of the Lincolnshire rebels for the cessation of the suppression of abbeys, no further taxation, and the dismissal of Cromwell and the heretical bishops: they required a return to papal obedience in certain matters and a reform of Parliament in which the influence of the King was to be considerably reduced.

On 6 December Aske, accompanied by thirty of his followers, met Norfolk and his council at Doncaster. The Duke agreed to remit the insurgents' articles to the King and made vague verbal promises of a full and free pardon. In return, on the naïve assumption that they had gained their objectives, Aske persuaded the insurgents to disband. Later, at the King's invitation the rebel leader travelled to London, where he was given (and believed) Henry's personal assurance that their grievances would be met. Following his return to the north, Aske and his friends put down a further rising at Scarborough and Hull, instigated by Sir Francis Bigod, in January 1537; other sporadic outbursts were swiftly quelled by government forces.

The King, however, had merely been biding his time. From February onwards arrests were made of the guilty parties, and altogether more than 200 men were executed in the various northern counties. A treasonable letter from Darcy to Aske was intercepted, and both men were arrested. Aske was taken to London for examination and, being sentenced to be hung, drawn, and quartered, was sent back to York, where he was hanged in chains from a church tower.

Although the Pilgrimage of Grace achieved nothing, it caused a grave crisis. Pope Paul III was dilatory in sending Cardinal Reginald Pole (q.v.) as legate to the Low Countries for the purpose of aiding the revolt; by the time he arrived it was over. The failure of the rising enabled Henry to proceed further to enforce the dissolution of the greater monasteries, hitherto spared.

Mary Bateson, 'The Pilgrimage of Grace and Aske's examination', *English Historical Review*, v (1890).
M. H. and R. Dodds, *The Pilgrimage of Grace 1536–7* (2 vols; Cambridge, 1915).

**Askew, Anne** (1521–1546), Protestant martyr.

Anne Askew was born in 1521, the second daughter of Sir William Askew of Stallingborough, near Grimsby, who came from an old Lincolnshire family. Intelligent and well educated, much of Anne's early life was spent in studying the Bible and arguing religious matters with the local clergy. On the death of her sister, who had been betrothed to Thomas Kyme of Kelsey, she was forced by her father to marry him herself; it was an unhappy marriage and Anne was later turned out of doors by her husband and went to London.

In 1545 she faced examination for heresy on account of her outspoken denial of transubstantiation. She was befriended by Edmund Bonner (q.v.), Bishop of London, and acquitted. Not long afterwards she was summoned again, this time before the Council at Greenwich. She refused to recant and was put to the rack in the hope that she might reveal the names of certain Protestant ladies at court who were believed to be encouraging her in her heretical activities; Thomas Wriothesley (q.v.), the Lord Chancellor, and Richard Rich (q.v.), the Solicitor General, attended her on the rack. Again refusing to recant, Anne was charged with heresy and, crippled from her torture, had to be carried to the stake at Smithfield, where, declining Wriothesley's last-minute offer of a pardon if she would recant, she was burned on 16 July 1546.

The examinations of Anne Askew are contained in John Bale, *Select Works* (ed. H. Christmas), published by the Parker Society (Cambridge, 1849).

**Aubigny, 6th Seigneur d'** (?1542–1583), see Stuart, Esmé.

**Audley, Sir Thomas** (1488–1544), Baron Audley of Walden, Lord Chancellor from 1533 to 1544.

Born at Earls Colne, Essex, Thomas Audley studied at Cambridge and subsequently at the Inner Temple, where he was autumn reader in 1526. Little is known of his early life, but he appears to have been town clerk of Colchester in 1516 and to have held several other local offices in the next few years. He may have been steward to the Duke of Suffolk and, if so, probably first came to the notice of Henry VIII (q.v.) while serving in this capacity. First returned to Parliament in 1523, he rose to become Speaker of the House of Commons in 1529, having in the previous six years held various appointments, including those of member of the Princess Mary's council (see Mary I), Groom of the Chamber, and attorney to the Duchy of Lancaster. He was also in the service of Cardinal Thomas Wolsey (q.v.), on whose fall from power he became Chancellor of the Duchy of Lancaster in succession to Sir Thomas More (q.v.). Appointed King's Serjeant in 1531, he was granted lands in Colchester and Mile End, Essex.

Having successfully obtained Parliament's acceptance of the King's anti-papal policies, Audley was rewarded by Henry in 1532 with the office of Lord Keeper of the Great Seal and, the following year, on the resignation of More, with the post of Lord Chancellor. From that moment he became completely subservient to the desires of his royal master, starting with the divorce from Catherine of Aragon (q.v.), the break with Rome, and the establishment of Henry as head of the Church of England.

As Chancellor, Audley presided at the trials of More and John Fisher (q.v.), both of whom were executed for their refusal to take the oath repudiating papal supremacy. In 1536 he conducted Anne Boleyn (q.v.) to the Tower and was named in the commission for her trial. He also played a prominent part in securing the attainder of Thomas Cromwell (q.v.) when he fell from favour in 1540, as well as that of Henry's fifth consort, Catherine Howard (q.v.), in 1542.

Audley was twice married, firstly to a lady from Suffolk, and secondly, in April 1538, to Elizabeth, daughter of Thomas Grey, Marquess of Dorset, by whom he had two daughters. In that same year he was created Baron Audley of Walden. Among the generous grants of lands from the dissolved monasteries given to him by the King was the former Benedictine abbey of Walden, the site on which Audley's grandson, Baron Howard de Walden (see Howard, Lord Thomas), would in 1603 commence the building of the great house called Audley End.

Towards the end of his life Audley interested himself in reconstituting the foundation of Buckingham College at Cambridge; this was accomplished in 1542, when the college was renamed by royal licence the 'College of St Mary Magdalene' (now Magdalene College). Increasing infirmity forced him in April 1544 to send the Great Seal to the King, begging him to accept his resignation. On the last day of that month Audley died in London. He was buried at Saffron Walden, in the magnificent tomb he had designed for himself.

*Portrait*: engraving, by P. W. Tomkins, after painting by Holbein: British Museum, London.

**Aylmer, John** (1521–1594), Bishop of London in the reign of Elizabeth I (q.v.).

Born at Tivetshall St Mary, Norfolk, in 1521, Aylmer was educated at Cambridge through the generosity of Henry Grey, Marquess of Dorset and later Duke of Suffolk. He obtained his

B.A. in 1541 and, having taken holy orders, was appointed as his patron's chaplain and tutor to his daughter, the Lady Jane Grey (q.v.). At some date that is not known he married a lady from Suffolk, Judith Bures, who was to bear him seven sons and three daughters.

In 1553 Aylmer was made archdeacon of Stow, but shortly afterwards, following the accession of Mary I (q.v.) and the restoration of Roman Catholicism in England, he lost this office on account of his opposition to the doctrine of transubstantiation, and fled to the Continent. He remained in exile until after the accession of Elizabeth, first in Strasbourg and then in Zurich, tutoring various young English exiles and assisting John Foxe (q.v.) in the preparation of the Latin edition of *Actes and Monuments,* later known as the *Book of Martyrs.* It was while he was in Strasbourg that Aylmer wrote and published *An Harborowe for Faithfull and Trewe Subjectes,* in reply to the *First Blast of the Trumpet against the Monstrous Regiment of Women* written by John Knox (q.v.). He returned to England later that year and was restored to the archdeaconry of Stow. In 1562 he was appointed Archdeacon of Lincoln. A member of the Convocation that revised the doctrine of the Church of England, he subscribed to the Thirty-Nine Articles and in March 1577 was consecrated as Bishop of London.

A man of quarrelsome disposition, Aylmer made himself unpopular from the start by a disagreement with his predecessor over revenues. He ruled his diocese with the utmost severity, rigorously enforcing the Act of Uniformity and taking action against all those who opposed the Church settlement, Puritans and Catholics alike. Not unnaturally he made many enemies, some of whom tried unsuccessfully to bring charges against him of misappropriating episcopal revenues. Towards the end of his life Aylmer requested a transfer to a quieter see, and it is believed that had it not been for his refusal to come to terms with the man proposed as his successor, Richard Bancroft (q.v.), a future Archbishop of Canterbury, the Queen would have given Aylmer the see of Worcester. In the event, he remained in London, where he died on 3 June 1594. He was buried in St Paul's Cathedral.

John Aylmer was one of the bishops against whom the satirical Martin Marprelate tracts of 1598 were directed; he is also said to have been the 'proude and ambitious pastour' given the name of Morrell by Edmund Spenser (q.v.) in his *Shepheard's Calendar.* His habit of playing bowls on Sundays gave particular offence to the Puritans.

John Strype, *Historical Collections of the Life and Acts of the Right Reverend Father in God, John Aylmer, Lord Bishop of London* (1701; rev. ed. Oxford, 1821).

# B

**Babington, Anthony** (1561–1586), conspirator.

Born in October 1561 at Dethick, Derbyshire, Babington came from an old-established and wealthy Catholic family; he was the eldest son of Sir Henry Babington by his second wife, Mary Darcy, granddaughter of Baron Darcy of Templehurst (see Darcy, Thomas), who had been executed for his part in the Pilgrimage of Grace. Anthony was brought up as a Catholic. His father died when he was ten years old, and for the next six years he lived with his mother at Dethick, his education being supervised by her second husband, Henry Foljambe. As a youth Anthony was for a short time a page in the household of the 6th Earl of Shrewsbury (see Talbot, George) while Mary, Queen of Scots (q.v.) was in the Earl's custody; it is not certain that he actually met Mary at this time, but his admiration for her dates from this period in his life. In 1579 he married a member of a prominent Catholic family, Margaret, daughter of Philip Draycot of Paynsley, Staffordshire.

In 1580 Babington left England for a six months' tour of France, where he was in touch with a number of recusant English exiles, including the young Chidiock Tichborne (q.v.). In Paris he made the acquaintance of Thomas Morgan, agent of the Queen of Scots, and through him met Mary's ambassador, James Beaton, Archbishop of Glasgow.

On his return Babington settled in London, enrolling as a student at Lincoln's Inn. Handsome, gay, and well-to-do, he had a large circle of friends, most of them dedicated to the Catholic cause. He joined the clandestine society formed to protect Jesuit missionaries in England and took an active part in helping Edmund Campion (q.v.) and Robert Parsons (q.v.) to move about the country. The English Catholics at this time had formulated their own plot for the rescue of the imprisoned Queen of Scots which was quite separate from the foreign conspiracy in which Morgan and Gilbert Gifford, John Savage, and the priest John Ballard were the prime movers. In May 1586, when Ballard returned to England and visited Babington, the two plots became fused. When Ballard explained that a rising of the English Catholics was to be supported by a foreign invasion, that Queen Elizabeth (q.v.) was to be assassinated and Mary put on the throne, Babington was at first sceptical; however, he allowed himself to be persuaded. After discussing the plans with his Catholic friends, it was decided that he himself should leave England, and he applied for a licence to travel to Italy. This was refused, for Sir Francis Walsingham (q.v.), having learned of the conspiracy from the treacherous Gifford, had intercepted and retained a letter from Morgan to the Queen of Scots, recommending Babington. Walsingham set one of his agents to trap the latter into divulging details of the plot. The agent reported that Babington had spoken of the lawfulness of murdering Elizabeth. Walsingham then forwarded Morgan's letter to Mary – and intercepted her reply, which was written on 25 June and received by Babington on 6 July.

Correspondence to and from the imprisoned Queen of Scots was passed in and out of Chartley in a cask of beer with the knowledge of her custodian, Sir Amias Paulet, so that she did not suspect that it was being intercepted. In fact the entire exchange of letters was known to the government. Babington's reply, received by Mary on 14 July, outlined the whole conspiracy, including her own deliverance, the foreign invasion, and the 'dispatch of the usurping Competitor [Queen Elizabeth]'. Her reply, dated 17 July, approving the plans, was in Walsingham's hands on the 19th and was transmitted to Babington on the 29th; with the help of Tichborne, he deciphered it the following day, and sent the Queen an acknowledgment on 3 August.

Walsingham now had all the incriminating detail he needed. Ballard was arrested the next day. According to William Camden (q.v.), Babington, having protested to Walsingham about Ballard's arrest, was lured to the Secretary of State's house on the promise of sanctuary there, only to find himself a prisoner; he managed to escape and fled to St John's Wood, where he lay low for several days with friends, but was seized on 14 August and taken to the Tower; the bells were rung to celebrate his capture.

Under interrogation Babington confessed every detail of the conspiracy, fully implicating the Queen of Scots; he even reconstructed for Walsingham the texts of Mary's letters which he had destroyed. At his trial on 13 and 14 September, he tried to put all the blame on Ballard. Sentenced, along with the other conspirators, to be hanged and quartered, he wrote to Elizabeth begging for mercy and offered a large reward to a friend if he could secure his release. It was

of no avail. He, Savage, and Tichborne were in the first batch of conspirators to be executed publicly at Tyburn on 20 September; they were put to death in the most brutal way, being disembowelled while still alive. The Queen, on hearing of their tortures, ordered that those who were to be executed the following day should not be cut down until they were dead.

Although not the originator of the plot which bears his name, Anthony Babington became its active agent. He was too much of a dreamer to be an effective leader, and at the end he lacked the strength to withstand the pain of torture for his convictions. The conspiracy is historically important in that Mary's approval of the plans – in particular that for the assassination of Elizabeth, as written in her letter to Babington of 17 July – finally brought the Queen of Scots to the scaffold. There has been much controversy concerning this letter and how much of it, if any, was forged by Walsingham; the consensus of opinion is that he forged the postscript asking for the names of the six men who were to be Elizabeth's assassins, but that the rest of the letter was written by Mary.

J. H. Pollen, 'Mary Queen of Scots and the Babington Plot', *Scottish History Society,* 3rd series, iii (Edinburgh, 1922).
Conyers Read, *Sir Francis Walsingham,* vol. iii (1925).
A. G. Smith, *The Babington Plot* (1936).

**Bacon, Anthony** (1558–1601), diplomatist.

The elder of two sons of Sir Nicholas Bacon (q.v.) and his second wife, Ann, daughter of Sir Anthony Cooke, Anthony Bacon was born, probably at Gorhambury, Hertfordshire, in 1558. He was a delicate child and all his life suffered from gout and arthritis.

In April 1573 he and his younger

brother Francis took up residence at Trinity College, Cambridge, under John Whitgift (q.v.), later Archbishop of Canterbury. Because of illness Anthony's studies were frequently interrupted, and for six months from August 1574 both brothers were kept away from Cambridge on account of an outbreak of plague. They left the university in March 1576 without taking degrees, and in June the same year were admitted as 'ancients' at Gray's Inn. Little definite is known of Anthony's movements for the next three years, while his brother entered the service of Sir Amias Paulet, English ambassador to France, but it seems likely that he too travelled abroad, probably with a view to a diplomatic career.

On the death of his father in February 1579 Anthony inherited the family estates in Hertfordshire and Middlesex, with the exception of Gorhambury, which was left to Lady Bacon for life and then to him. Nathaniel Bacon, one of the sons of Sir Nicholas's first marriage, disputed the bequests, but the matter was settled in Anthony's favour by Lord Burghley (see Cecil, William), whose second wife was Lady Bacon's sister.

At Burghley's suggestion, later that year Bacon set out on a prolonged tour of the Continent; his mission was to obtain political intelligence for the government. He spent some time in Paris, from where he sent back regular reports to Sir Francis Walsingham (q.v.) and where he became very friendly with one of the latter's secretaries, Nicholas Faunt. For the purpose of extracting intelligence he was also in contact with William Parry (q.v.), the English Catholic refugee who was to be executed for conspiracy in 1585.

In August 1580 Bacon moved on to Bourges and then to Geneva, where he was entertained by Theodore Beza. Granted permission in 1582 to remain abroad for another three years, he travelled extensively from one foreign court to another, but chiefly in France, spending some fifteen months in Bordeaux, where he tried to improve the position of the Protestants; he also made the acquaintance of Montaigne and visited Henri de Navarre at Béarn. From early 1585 onwards he stayed at Montauban, where for five years he was in close touch with Navarre's counsellors and the French Protestant leaders.

Anthony enjoyed Continental life, and probably the climate suited his frail health. But he was extravagant and was constantly borrowing money from his friends and family. His mother and younger brother took a poor view of his extended absence, and Lady Bacon tried unsuccessfully to obtain his recall as early as 1583. When Anthony returned to Bordeaux in 1590 and became friendly with Anthony Standen, an English Catholic (actually one of Walsingham's spies) who was then in prison, they were even more uneasy; in fact Bacon was reporting back regularly to Walsingham all the time he was abroad and he was able to use his influence to procure Standen's release. (Recent research in the French archives by Miss Du Maurier has revealed the reason for Bacon's extended stay at Montauban – his arrest there on a charge of sodomy – and the fact that he was saved from the death sentence only through the personal intervention of Henri de Navarre.)

At last in February 1592 Bacon returned to England. He was in poor health, his eyes were failing, and due to attacks of gout and stone he was unable to pay his respects to Queen Elizabeth (q.v.); he later believed that through this he lost his chances of preferment and he was bitter when Burghley failed to help either him or Francis, accusing his uncle of 'fair words, with no show of real kindness'. But he only further antagonized the Secretary of State when, early in 1593, having been returned to Parliament as member for Wallingford, he opposed the government bill imposing new penalties on recusants. It was a sore point with Anthony also that Burghley appeared to take all the credit for his foreign intelligence work of the past years.

In these circumstances it was not surprising that the Bacon brothers decided to ally themselves with the Earl of Essex (see Devereux, Robert), the Queen's favourite and a serious rival to the Cecil family. Anthony entered the Earl's service in 1593, undertaking to obtain for him, more rapidly than his other advisers, foreign intelligence which he could pass on to Elizabeth and so enhance himself in her favour. He was to remain Essex's faithful servant until the latter's downfall and death, maintaining an elaborate correspondence with agents in Scotland and on the Continent, as the Earl wished to advance the claim of James VI (q.v.) as successor to the English throne and also to remain on cordial terms with Henri IV of France. Bacon also played a prominent part in the investigation of Dr Roderigo Lopez, physician to the Queen, and in the uncovering of a plot for Elizabeth's murder in which Lopez was implicated. He supported his patron in the dispute which arose concerning the Cadiz expedition in June 1596; when Essex was forbidden by the Council to publish his *True Relation of the Action*, Bacon had the manuscript copied, translated, and distributed in Scotland, France, and the Low Countries.

Up to 1594 Anthony shared his brother's chambers at Gray's Inn. For a short time in 1594–5 he leased houses in Bishopsgate and in Chelsea, but in October 1595 his patron invited him to live at Essex House, off the Strand, an offer which Bacon, still short of money and borrowing heavily, was glad to accept. As one of Essex's recent biographers has said, the house, where Bacon worked with four secretaries, was a hive of activity, an 'embryo Foreign Office'. Some of Anthony's family, however, disapproved of his connection with Essex, and Lady Russell, his aunt, tried unsuccessfully to get him away; whereupon Bacon defended himself and sent Essex a long account of their interview.

Bacon's voluminous extant correspondence with Essex comes to an end in 1598; he is believed to have destroyed all later papers after the Earl's disgrace. From October 1599 Essex was confined at York House, but when in March 1600 the Queen ordered his removal back to Essex House, Bacon, together with other members of the Essex household, was ordered to leave. After the trial in June that year, and the Earl's release in August, a number of letters purporting to have passed between Essex and Anthony Bacon were drafted by Francis, in an attempt to regain the Queen's favour. They did not achieve the desired result. During the next few months, while Essex was busy making sinister plots against the Queen, Anthony, by this time severely crippled, was again living in Essex House; but for fear that he might be betrayed to Francis, who now sought patronage elsewhere, Essex kept Anthony in ignorance of the proposed rebellion. Unlike his brother, Anthony was to remain utterly loyal to Essex to the very end and even at the last, after the failure of the Earl's rebellion and his confinement in the Tower, he did his best to prove him innocent of the worst accusations.

The shock of the events leading up to Essex's execution in February 1601 undoubtedly hastened Anthony Bacon's own death, which occurred the following May, at the age of forty-three. He was buried in St Olave's Church, Hart Street, on 17 May 1601.

The papers of Anthony Bacon are at Lambeth Palace Library, London; a comprehensive index to them has recently been published by the Library (1975). Some transcripts and other papers are at the British Library and at the Public Record Office, London. A number of them have been printed in *Memoirs of the reign of Queen Elizabeth . . . from the original papers of Antony Bacon, esquire* (2 vols; 1754).

Daphne Du Maurier, *Golden Lads: A study of Anthony Bacon, Francis and their friends* (1975).
See also the titles listed under Robert Devereux, 2nd Earl of Essex, and Sir Francis Bacon.

*Portrait*: a bust at Gorhambury (Earl of Verulam) may be of either Anthony or Francis Bacon (Roy Strong favours its identification as Anthony). N.B. A portrait also in the Gorhambury Collection hitherto considered to be of Robert Devereux, 2nd Earl of Essex, and traditionally attributed by the owner to Nicholas Hilliard, is now believed to be of Anthony Bacon.

**Bacon, Sir Francis** (1561–1626), Baron Verulam and Viscount St Albans, lawyer, courtier, statesman, philosopher, and author.

Born on 22 January 1561 at York House, off the Strand, London, Francis Bacon was the younger of two sons of Sir Nicholas Bacon (q.v.) and his second wife, Ann, daughter of Sir Anthony Cooke. Through his mother's sister he was related by marriage to Lord Burghley (see Cecil, William).

In April 1573, together with his brother Anthony Bacon (q.v.), Francis was sent to study under John Whitgift (q.v.), later Archbishop of Canterbury, at Trinity College, Cambridge. Sharing rooms, the Bacons remained at the university until March 1576; their studies were broken by periods of ill-health and also by an enforced six months' absence from Cambridge due to an outbreak of plague from August 1574, and neither of them took a degree. Francis afterwards wrote that young men 'learn nothing there [at Cambridge] but to believe': in other words that they were taught never to question what they were told. It was also during his time at the university that he claimed he 'first fell into the dislike of the philosophy of Aristotle'.

Francis was a clever, precocious boy and soon attracted the attention of Queen Elizabeth (q.v.); she was in the habit of calling him her 'young lord keeper'. In the autumn of 1576, shortly after both brothers had been admitted as 'ancients' of Gray's Inn, he entered the service of Sir Amias Paulet, the ambassador to France, with whom he spent the next three years in Paris. Unlike his older brother, however, European life did not appeal to him and after his return to England in February 1579, on the death of his father, Francis never again crossed the Channel.

While Anthony was well provided for under Sir · Nicholas's Will, Francis inherited only a few modest properties. He took up residence at his father's old chambers in Gray's Inn, where he became a barrister in about 1582 and later would be reader, bencher and, eventually, Queen's Counsel Extraordinary. From the early days of his career, however, Bacon made it clear that the law was merely a stepping-stone towards politics and power.

Member of Parliament for Melcombe Regis, Dorset, in 1584, he now began to learn at first hand the problems of government; in later years he was to represent in turn Taunton, Liverpool, Middlesex, Southampton, St Albans, Ipswich, and Cambridge University. He demonstrated considerable promise in

the field of politics, having a gift for reconciliation and a fluent and busy pen. By 1585 he was pressing actively for patronage and preferment in a series of letters to Sir Francis Walsingham (q.v.) and to Burghley. To the latter Bacon mentioned his great interest in natural philosophy and his ambition to found a college or university where medicine, astronomy, and 'things of the earth', stones, plants, and animals would be studied. It met with no enthusiasm whatever from the Secretary of State, and, disillusioned with his kinsman, Francis decided to attach himself to the Queen's young favourite, rival to the Cecils, the Earl of Essex (see Devereux, Robert). When Anthony returned to England in 1592 and joined him at Gray's Inn, he introduced his brother to Essex; the following year, however, Francis's own political hopes were finally dashed when the Queen took offence at his opposition to the government's demand for subsidies to meet the expenses of the war against Spain and he found himself in disgrace. Essex tried on his behalf to placate Elizabeth and to obtain for Bacon the office of Attorney General when this fell vacant in 1594, but after months of expectation the post went instead to Sir Edward Coke (see *Lives of the Stuart Age*).

While his brother was content to act as Essex's loyal secretary, Francis regarded the Earl's patronage as a step to higher things. But he was not successful in his aims. Although both Essex and Burghley recommended him for the office of Solicitor General, again the Queen, having kept Bacon on a string for months, passed him over in October 1595. To atone for his disappointment Essex gave him some land at Twickenham; subsequently he recommended him for the office of Master of the Rolls, and later for that of Vice Chancellor of the Court of Chancery. By the time all these requests had been denied, Bacon was not unnaturally beginning to feel somewhat disenchanted with Essex's patronage. In October 1596 he put in writing a frank assessment of Essex's virtues and faults, coupled with advice on how to conduct himself with the Queen. Unfortunately the headstrong Earl was incapable of the subtleties advocated, and most of his friend's excellent counsel was ignored. Nevertheless, although he had advised against it, when Essex incurred Elizabeth's wrath over his abortive campaign in Ireland, Bacon generously pleaded for him with the Queen. It was at about this time that Bacon himself was taken back into royal favour, being given the nominal office of Queen's Counsel Extraordinary and the reversion of an office in the Star Chamber, worth £2,000 a year.

In June 1600 he was commanded to take part in Essex's trial at York House. It seems that Essex bore Bacon no grudge for his stated obligation to act firstly as a 'good citizen' and secondly as a 'good man', but Essex was incapable of taking good advice or following a steady course. He and Essex saw less of one another thereafter, and Bacon was kept in ignorance of the Earl's sinister plans for rebellion. At the ensuing trial at Westminster Hall, conducted by Attorney-General Coke, Bacon, who now saw Essex as a traitor, spoke against him; as a result he incurred not only a hysterical outburst from Essex at what he saw as his friend's betrayal, but also the subsequent cold shoulder from erstwhile allies and colleagues. The official report denouncing Essex, entitled *A Declaration of the Practices and Treasons attempted and committed by Robert, late Earle of Essex,* which appeared later in 1601, has been attributed to Bacon, who three years afterwards published his *Apologie in certaine imputations concerning the late Earle of Essex,* defending his (Bacon's) actions.

In the last two years of Elizabeth's reign Bacon spent most of his time at Twickenham where, denied the fulfilment of his ambitions in other fields, he turned increasingly to philosophy and literary pursuits. On the accession of James I in 1603, he lost no time in seeking preferment; through his cousin Sir Robert Cecil (q.v.), later 1st Earl of Salisbury, he asked for, and obtained, a knighthood, and in 1605 he published his *Advancement of Learning,* dedicated to the King. He also sought, but had to wait two years to obtain, the office of Solicitor General.

In May 1606, at the age of forty-five, Sir Francis married Alice Barnham, the fourteen-year-old daughter of a City alderman. She was a spirited young woman, like her mother, who was to prove exceedingly troublesome to Bacon. Alice bore her husband no children and at the end of his life he cut her out of his Will 'for just and great causes' (she married an usher of his household only three weeks after Bacon's death).

At last in June 1607 Bacon's efforts to persuade Parliament to approve the King's proposals for union with Scotland were rewarded with the office of Solicitor General. He remained dissatisfied, however, blaming his lack of political influence on the jealousy of Salisbury. It was not until after the latter's death in 1612 that he began to make the progress he so much desired; he achieved it by dint of persistent letter-writing recommending himself to the King, by his diligent service, and with the assistance of James's favourite the Duke of Buckingham (see Villiers, George, 1st Duke, in *Lives of the Stuart Age*). The intervening years were marked by intense rivalry with Coke, who, as Chief Justice of the Common Pleas, championed the common law and the independence of the judges and argued with Bacon over the royal prerogative. In 1613 the King was persuaded to transfer Coke to the King's Bench and that October Bacon was sworn in as Attorney General. In June 1616, following Coke's defiance of the King's order in the 'case of Commendams', charges were brought against him by the Privy Council at Bacon's instigation, and in November that year Coke was dismissed. Appointed Lord Keeper in March 1617, Bacon became Lord Chancellor in 1618 and that year he was raised to the barony as Baron Verulam. In January 1621 he was created Viscount St Albans.

By this time Bacon was achieving wide recognition as a scholar. From 1608 onwards he had worked on numerous drafts of his *Novum Organum* ('New Instrument'), published in 1620. He also developed the *Instauratio Magna* ('Great Instauration'), a scheme for the reorganization of the sciences, and wrote several philosophical works. His collection of ten *Essayes*, first published in 1597, was enlarged to include thirty-eight in 1612, and in 1609 he produced an interpretation of ancient myths, *De Sapientia Veterum* ('Wisdom of the Ancients').

As Lord Chancellor, Bacon was head of the legal profession and a leading figure in the government; according to a notebook he kept at this period of his life he busied himself with a variety of matters involving his own and the King's business. The King sometimes disregarded his advice, while Bacon sought at all times to uphold the royal prerogative. Among those on whom he was commissioned to sit in judgment were the Earl of Somerset (see Carr, Robert, in *Lives of the Stuart Age*) in 1615, Sir Walter Ralegh (q.v.) in 1618, and Thomas Howard, Earl of Suffolk, in 1619.

Not unnaturally Bacon had enemies who sought his downfall. In March 1621 charges of bribery were brought against him by a committee appointed to inquire into abuses in the Courts of Justices. He admitted having received certain gifts, but denied that they had affected his judgment in any way. Refused an audience with James, he was sentenced to be imprisoned in the Tower during the King's pleasure and to pay a fine of £40,000, and was barred from sitting in Parliament or holding any public office. In the event, he was held in the Tower for only three days; he then withdrew to Gorhambury, where he was to spend the next five years in scholarly pursuits. In the autumn of 1621 the fine was assigned to trustees for Bacon's own use, but until he agreed to sell York House to Buckingham, his pardon was delayed and it was not until January 1623 that he was allowed to kiss the King's hand. In 1622 he applied for, but was refused, the post of Provost of Eton.

Bacon's literary output during the last years of his life was prolific. He worked under great difficulties, for he was forbidden to go within twelve miles of London and so was deprived of access to the great library of Robert Bruce Cotton (q.v.); however the latter frequently sent manuscripts to him at Gorhambury. Bacon had promised the King not only a digest of the laws of England, but also a history of England, of which the *History of the Reign of Henry the Seventh*, completed by October 1621, was published the following year; he did not live to complete the series. In addition he planned a six-volume work on natural history, publishing *Historia Ventorum* ('History of the Winds') in 1622 and *Historia Vitae et Mortis* ('History of Life and Death') in 1623. A Latin translation of the *Advancement of Learning*, with numerous addenda, *De Augmentis Scientiarum*, also appeared in 1623, and two years later came a third and enlarged edition of the *Essayes*. His *New Atlantis*, a philosophical treatise written in the form of a fable, begun in 1610, was published in 1626, unfinished, after the author's death; likewise the *Sylva Sylvarum* ('Forest of Forests'), which appeared in 1627.

Gradually, in these years, Bacon appears to have drifted back to London, albeit without permission. Leaving his wife at Gorhambury, he probably spent his last few months at Gray's Inn. He went on experimenting and adding to his work on natural history. In March 1626, while driving near Highgate, to the north of the City, he was struck with the idea of finding out whether flesh could be preserved in snow; stopping his carriage, he purchased a hen, had it drawn, and then helped to stuff it with snow. He caught a severe chill, and was taken to the house of the Earl of Arundel near by, where, on the morning of 9 April, he died. He was buried in St Michael's Church, St Albans.

Sir Francis Bacon was a man who claimed all knowledge as his province. He broke new ground by urging his contemporaries to abandon the 'dark idols' of old books and old philosophies and to study instead the natural phenomena, methodically observing *things* as a means of gaining dominance over nature. All his life he worked for the fulfilment of his vision of a new age of learning in England, and so pointed the way towards the development of philosophy and science. The keystone of Baconian thought is the *Novum Organum*, in which the method is outlined whereby this renovation of knowledge, or new philosophy, was to be achieved, replacing that of Aristotle. Controversy concerning Bacon's character and his innocence or guilt arising from the events of 1621 began in his own lifetime and has continued ever since. In many respects he was more highly regarded, both as Lord Chancellor and in academic circles, in Europe than in England.

Although he wrote much of his important work in Latin, his English style was polished, varied, and distinguished, and his popularity through the centuries has rested largely on the worldly wisdom of his essays. Brilliant, sensuous, and enigmatic, Bacon's personality intrigued many of his contemporaries, among them Nicholas Hilliard (q.v.), the miniaturist, who once remarked, 'Oh, that I had a canvas to paint his *mind*.'

Bacon's writings may be divided into the philosophical, the literary, and the legal; of the last category, his two most important works were not published until long after his death: a collection of early writings on the *Elements of the Common Laws of England* (1630) and *The*

*Learned Reading of Sir Francis Bacon upon the Statute of Uses* (1642), based on lectures he had given at Gray's Inn at the turn of the century. The *Collected Works* (including *Life and Letters*) were edited by James Spedding (14 vols; 1857–74). See also R. W. Gibson, *Francis Bacon: A Bibliography of His Works and of Baconia to the Year 1750* (1950; supplement, 1959).

The theory that Bacon wrote the plays attributed to William Shakespeare (q.v.) was first voiced in the mid-eighteenth century and has attracted some support. It is not however supported by the recent research of American cryptologists W. S. and E. F. Friedman in *The Shakespearian Ciphers Examined* (1957). Space does not permit a discussion of the controversy here, but see, *inter alia*, Sir E. Durning-Lawrence, *Bacon is Shake-speare* (1910; reprinted 1971), and J. M. Robertson, *The Baconian Heresy* (1913; reprinted 1971).

E. Abbott, *Francis Bacon: An Account of His Life and Works* (1885).

F. H. Anderson, *Francis Bacon: His Career and His Thought* (1962).

Catherine Drinker Bowen, *Francis Bacon: The Temper of the Man* (1963).

J. Nichol, *Francis Bacon: His Life and Philosophy* (2 vols; 1888–9).

J. Spedding, *An Account of the Life and Times of Francis Bacon* (2 vols; 1878).

*Portraits:* miniature, by Nicholas Hilliard, 1578: Belvoir Castle (The Duke of Rutland); oil, attributed to William Larkin, *c.* 1610: Raveningham (Sir Edmund Bacon, Bt.); oil on panel, three-quarter length, attributed to Abraham Blyenberch, *c.* 1618: The Royal Society, London (full-length later versions, by unknown artists, at Gorhambury and at the National Portrait Gallery, London, and copies of Gorhambury portrait by John Vanderbank, 1731: N.P.G., Badminton House (The Duke of Beaufort), and elsewhere); tomb effigy: St Michael's Church, St Albans; bust, by Rysbrack: National Maritime Museum, Greenwich; bust, by Roubillac, 1751; Trinity College, Cambridge. N.B. A bust at Gorhambury of a son of Sir Nicholas Bacon, *c.* 1565, may be of Francis, but Roy Strong favours its identification as of his brother Anthony.

## Bacon, Sir Nicholas (1509–1579), Lord Keeper.

The second son of Robert Bacon of Drinkstone, Suffolk, and Isabella, daughter of John Cage of Pakenham, Nicholas Bacon was born in 1509 (the exact date is not known). He is believed to have attended the Abbey School at Bury St Edmunds before going on to Corpus Christi College, Cambridge, in 1523. He took his B.A. in 1527 and while at Cambridge formed intimate friendships with William Cecil (q.v.), later 1st Baron Burghley, and Matthew Parker (q.v.), the future Archbishop of Canterbury.

After leaving the university Bacon travelled on the Continent, staying for a short time in Paris. He then returned to London and entered Gray's Inn as a student of common law; he was called to the bar in 1533 and became an 'ancient' of the Inn in 1536, a bencher in 1550, and Treasurer in 1552. His first professional appointment appears to have been that of Solicitor of the Court of Augmentations in 1537; at about this time he was also a solicitor of Cambridge University, in which capacity he was in 1540 appointed as one of the commissioners to administer the dissolution of the collegiate church of Southwell. In 1545 he sat as Member of Parliament for Dartmouth, and the following year he became Attorney of the Court of Wards and Liveries, in which office he was continued in the reign of Edward VI (q.v.). In February 1548 he was one of the commissioners appointed to survey the suppressed colleges of Norfolk and Suffolk.

Bacon was among those members of the English gentry who waxed rich from the monastic properties confiscated by Henry VIII (q.v.). Originally he put forward a scheme for the foundation of a college for the training of young statesmen out of the revenues from the dissolved monasteries, but this did not meet with a favourable reception and most of the estates were distributed among the King's friends. By the early 1550s Nicholas Bacon had acquired lands formerly belonging to the monasteries of St Albans, Walsingham, and Thetford, as well as those of the executed Countess of Salisbury; other estates were added later, until eventually he owned land in six counties of England and employed a retinue of some seventy servants. On his estate of Gorhambury, near St Albans, Hertfordshire, which was celebrated for its gardens, he spent a large sum on building a new manor house. This was completed in 1568, and in later years he frequently entertained Queen Elizabeth (q.v.); he added a 128-foot-long wing and, in 1576, a gallery, in honour of his royal visitor.

In spite of his professed Protestantism, Bacon managed to evade persecution during the reign of Mary I (q.v.); he kept his post in the Court of Wards, but was prohibited from leaving England in case he should enter into dangerous relations with the Protestant exiles on the Continent. During these years he was occupied in raising a family, for his first wife, Jane, daughter of William Fernley of West Creting, Suffolk, bore him three sons and three daughters. After Jane's death and some time before 1558 Bacon married again; his second wife was Ann, daughter of Sir Anthony Cooke and sister of his friend William Cecil's second wife. She was to become the mother of Anthony Bacon (q.v.), born in 1558, and Francis Bacon (q.v.), born in 1561.

Shortly after the accession of Elizabeth, Bacon entered upon his political career, due largely to the influence of Cecil, now Secretary of State. In December 1558 he was appointed Lord Keeper of the Great Seal and shortly afterwards he received a knighthood and was made a member of the Privy Council. He was granted the official residence of York House, off the Strand. One of his first public duties of the reign was to arrange, together with Nicholas Heath (q.v.), Archbishop of York, and preside over the disputation held at Westminster in March 1559 between the Protestant and Catholic leaders; because of the stubbornness of the Catholics he dissolved the meeting at the beginning of April and committed two of the disputants to prison. A few days later the Queen issued letters patent authorizing Sir Nicholas to hear cases in chancery and to exercise the full jurisdiction of Lord Chancellor.

His qualities as a statesman were soon apparent. In December 1559 he made a powerful address in the Lords urging delay in Cecil's proposal to aid the Scottish Protestants against Mary, Queen of Scots (q.v.) and her Catholic supporters, and arguing against a breach of the peace, considering France as a potential and strong enemy, and doubting the wisdom of encouraging subjects to oppose a sovereign. He did not hesitate, however, in 1561 to advocate an alliance with the French Calvinists, when he saw a chance of success against the Catholics. He advised the Queen against her proposed meeting with Mary, Queen of Scots, in 1562, and in the Parliament of 1563 he spoke forcibly against the internal disorders of the country, against the laxity of religious observances and, with regard to Scotland, of the dangerous influence of the Guises. Increasingly he distrusted the Queen of Scots, believing that her influence would be used to injure Protestantism in England. Nevertheless, at the two conferences held in London in 1568 and 1570 to consider the fortunes of the Scottish Queen and English relations with Scotland, Bacon showed impartiality as a judge. In 1569 he opposed the plan to marry Mary to the Duke of Norfolk (see Howard, Thomas, 4th Duke), and when Elizabeth appeared to be considering Mary's restoration, he went so far as not only to advise against this course but to imply that her execution might be expedient in the interests of Protestantism.

Sir Nicholas frequently took an independent line in the Council, and he was never a mere spokesman to the Queen. On occasions he incurred Elizabeth's displeasure, as in 1564 when he was wrongfully suspected of being connected with the pamphlet on the succession by John Hales (q.v.) and was temporarily dismissed from court. In 1566 he had the duty of reading to the Queen an address urging her to marry or at least to make arrangements for the succession, and the following year he was ordered to dissolve Parliament and to express Elizabeth's displeasure when a deputation arrived to address her on the same subject.

Because of his strong Protestant views, Bacon became the butt of the Catholic libellers hidden in England or in exile abroad, especially after the St Bartholomew's Day Massacre in 1572, when he supported a bill for the expulsion of French denizens from England. In a royal proclamation against all such libels, issued in 1573, Bacon's services to the state and to the established religion were singled out for special commendation.

In the last years of his life Sir Nicholas suffered much from ill-health, principally from attacks of asthma, gout, and stone. He also grew exceedingly fat, to the extent that he had difficulty in mounting the judicial bench. He died at York House on 20 February 1579, and was buried at St Paul's Cathedral, London.

A gifted orator, and a politician whose opinions were tinged with honest conviction, Sir Nicholas Bacon enjoyed wide popularity during his lifetime. He took a keen interest in education, a field in which his ideas were ahead of his time; in a memorandum to Cecil dated 1561 he outlined a scheme for the reform of the Court of Wards and for the training of young men and women in literature and the arts, morals and athletics. He founded a grammar school at Redgrave and in his Will created six scholarships to enable poor scholars of that school to study at Cambridge; he also gave £200 towards a chapel at his old college, Corpus Christi.

J. P. Collier, 'On Sir Nicholas Bacon, Lord Keeper, with extracts from some of his unprinted papers and speeches', *Archaeologia*, xxxvi (1865), pp. 339–48.

*Portraits*: oil, by unknown artist, 1562: Corpus Christi College, Cambridge; oil, by unknown artist, 1579: National Portrait Gallery, London; bust, in terracotta, *c*. 1571: Gorhambury House (Earl of Verulam). N.B. The tomb effigy at St Paul's was destroyed in the Great Fire of London.

**Bainbridge, Christopher** (?1464–1514), Archbishop of York and cardinal.

Born at Hilton, near Appleby, Westmorland, in about 1464, Christopher Bainbridge studied at Queen's College, Oxford, where he received the degree of LL.D. He became a provost of that college before 1495, and among other preferments was made a prebendary of Salisbury, and later, of Lincoln; in 1497 he became Treasurer of St Paul's. Further promotion followed rapidly: Archdeacon of Surrey in 1501, prebendary and Dean of York in 1503,

Master of the Rolls in 1504 (an office which he held until 1507), and Dean of Windsor in 1505, Bainbridge was in 1507 elevated to the bishopric of Durham. In September 1508 he was translated to the archbishopric of York.

In 1509 Bainbridge was sent as ambassador to Rome by Henry VIII (q.v.). He was one of a batch of cardinals created by Pope Julius II in 1511 and was given command of an army against the French invaders of Italy. An enemy of France to the end of his life, he persuaded Pope Leo X to invest Henry with the title of Most Christian King forfeited by Louis XII, but this was forestalled by the conclusion of the peace between England and France in 1514. Bainbridge died in suspicious circumstances in Rome, probably poisoned at the instigation of a rival ambassador, on 14 July 1514, just before the negotiations for this peace had been completed. He was buried at the English hospital (later English College) in Rome.

David S. Chambers, *Cardinal Bainbridge in the Court of Rome, 1509–1514* (1965).

**Bancroft, Richard** (1544–1610), Bishop of London during the reign of Elizabeth I (q.v.) and later Archbishop of Canterbury; effective opponent of Puritanism.

Born in September 1544 at Farnworth, Lancashire, the son of John and Mary Bancroft, Richard Bancroft was related on his mother's side to the Bishop of Oxford, who took an interest in his education. After some schooling in his native town, he went to Christ's College, Cambridge, where he became a scholar and took his B.A. in 1566–7. When that college came under suspicion of Puritanism, Bancroft transferred to Jesus, as college tutor. Soon after 1572 he became chaplain to Richard Cox (q.v.), Bishop of Ely.

Collated by Cox to the rectory of Teversham, near Cambridge, in March 1576, later the same year Bancroft was one of twelve preachers licensed to preach by the university. A Doctor of Divinity at Cambridge in April 1585, he had already by this time taken a stand as a vigorous opponent of Puritanism. The following year he was appointed as Treasurer of St Paul's; in July 1587 he became a canon of Westminster, and three years later he was given a prebend at St Paul's; other benefices quickly followed.

Preaching at Paul's Cross in February 1588, Bancroft made an outspoken attack on the Puritans, asserting that episcopacy and heresy were in direct opposition to each other; this aroused indignant feelings, particularly among the Presbyterians of Scotland. He also spoke out against the Marprelate tracts, and it was as a result of his efforts that the printers of these tracts were subsequently discovered and brought before the Star Chamber.

In 1592 Bancroft was appointed as chaplain to John Whitgift (q.v.), Archbishop of Canterbury. He played a prominent part in the campaign against Henry Barrow (q.v.), Thomas Cartwright (q.v.) and other Puritan leaders, and by 1595 had so gained in royal favour that Elizabeth was prepared to appoint him as successor to John Aylmer (q.v.), Bishop of London, who wished to be transferred. However, Bancroft and Aylmer could not agree on terms, and it was not until April 1597 that Bancroft was elected to the bishopric; he was enthroned on 5 June the same year. By this date Whitgift was failing in health, and Bancroft, being completely in his confidence, was, in practice, according to Thomas Fuller (see *Lives of the Stuart Age*), virtually Primate of England. From this time onwards he appears to have taken part in political affairs,

negotiating with ambassadors from Denmark and, in 1601, raising a body of pikemen against the rebellious Earl of Essex (see Devereux, Robert).

Bancroft was present at the deathbed of Elizabeth in March 1603; he welcomed James VI of Scotland (q.v.) at Royston with an imposing retinue when he came south on his accession to the English throne, and subsequently entertained the new monarch at his palace at Fulham. His severity towards the Puritans, however, earned him a royal reprimand at the Hampton Court Conference of 1604. On Whitgift's death shortly afterwards, Bancroft was appointed to preside over the Convocation that assembled in March the same year. The coercive book of canons compiled under his direction aroused the opposition of Parliament and brought him into antagonism with the civil courts that was to last for the rest of his life.

In November 1604 Bancroft was appointed as Archbishop of Canterbury. He supported the King in regard to the Authorized Version of the Bible, and in return received the support of James for the 'Articles of Abuse', laid before the Privy Council by Bancroft in protest against the 'prohibitions' which the civil court judges were in the habit of issuing against proceedings in the ecclesiastical courts. For the next six years he campaigned unremittingly for the bishops against a growing Puritan movement; measures were enacted against Roman Catholic recusants, and even more severe steps taken against the Puritan clergy, several scores of whom were deprived of their benefices.

Appointed Chancellor of the University of Oxford in 1608, Bancroft conceived the project of a new college of divinity at Chelsea, but this did not come to fruition. He also failed to get through Parliament, in 1610, a scheme for the

*Portraits*: oil, by unknown artist, after 1604: National Portrait Gallery, London; oil, half-length, by unknown artist: Knole, Sevenoaks, Kent (The Lord Sackville); other versions at Cambridge (Jesus College, Trinity College, and the University Library), New College, Oxford, Lambeth Palace, and elsewhere.

## Barclay, Alexander (?1475–1552), poet, scholar, and divine.

Born probably in Scotland in about 1475, Alexander Barclay is believed to have studied at either Oxford or Cambridge, or possibly both, and to have spent some of his early life at Croydon, Surrey. He completed his studies on the Continent, travelling widely in France, Germany, the Netherlands, and Italy.

On his return to England, some time before 1508, Barclay was ordained and appointed as chaplain at the College of St Mary Ottery, Devon. It was almost certainly while in Devon that he wrote his most famous work, *The Shyp of Folys of the Worlde*, which was published in 1509. This poem was based on a popular German satire, *Das Narrenschiff*, by Sebastian Brant, and was in fact partly translation and partly imitation.

In about 1511 Barclay became a Benedictine monk at Ely. At the monastery there, during the years 1515–21, he wrote his *Eclogues*, the earliest known English eclogues; sometimes moral, sometimes satirical, they contain vivid and often entertaining vignettes of contemporary manners and rural life. Both in the *Shyp of Folys* and the *Eclogues* Barclay refers scathingly to a contemporary poet, John Skelton (q.v.). Among his other works at this period were translations of the life of St George from Baptist Mantuan and the *Bellum Jugurthinium* ('Jugurthine War') of the Roman historian Sallust. In 1520 his literary talents were called upon by Henry VIII (q.v.) on the occasion of his

betterment of conditions of the clergy. The Archbishop died in London, after a severe illness and much pain, on 2 November 1610; he was buried in Lambeth Church.

The sermon preached by Bancroft at Paul's Cross on 9 February 1588 has been printed in several editions, dated 1588, 1637, and 1709 respectively. His *Survay of the Pretended Holy Discipline, contayning the Beginnings, Successe, Parts, Proceedings, Authority, and Doctrine of It,* was published in 1593; and another work, *Daungerous Positions and Proceedings, published and practised within this Iland of Brytaine, under Pretence of Reformation and for the Presbiteriall Discipline,* in two editions, in 1593 and 1640. For his other writings, see A. Peel (ed.), *Tracts ascribed to Richard Bancroft* (Cambridge, 1953).

Stuart S. Babbage, *Puritanism and Richard Bancroft* (1962).

Owen Chadwick, 'Richard Bancroft's Submission', *Journal of Ecclesiastical History*, iii (1952), pp. 58–73.

R. G. Usher, *The Reconstruction of the English Church* (2 vols; New York, 1910).

meeting with the French King at the Field of the Cloth of Gold.

Some time before the dissolution of the monasteries, Barclay entered the Franciscan order and became a friar at Canterbury. He must have conformed, at least outwardly, to Protestantism, however, for in 1546 he was presented to the livings of Great Baddow, Essex, and Wokey, Somerset, both of which he retained throughout the reign of Edward VI (q.v.). In 1552 he was presented by the Dean and Chapter of Canterbury to the rectory of All Hallows, Lombard Street, in the City of London. A few weeks later Barclay died at Croydon, where he was buried in the parish church on 10 June.

Modern editions of Alexander Barclay's works include *Certain Eglogues*, published by the Spenser Society (Manchester, 1885); the *Eclogues*, edited by B. White (Early English Text Society, 1928); and T. H. Jamieson's edition of *The Ship of Fools* (1874); the latter includes a bibliography and a brief life.

**Barlow, William** (d. 1569), Bishop of Chichester.

The date of Barlow's birth is unknown, and there is little evidence on his early life except that he was one of four sons of John Barlow, who was implicated in the rebellion of Perkin Warbeck (q.v.). His sister was lady-in-waiting to Margaret Tudor (q.v.), wife of James IV of Scotland (q.v.). The biographical details of the brothers have often been confused.

It is not certain whether Barlow was educated at Oxford or Cambridge, or when he was ordained. He held a series of preferments, including that of Prior of Bromehill, Norfolk, from 1525. When this house was dissolved three years later, he appears to have been employed by Thomas Wolsey (q.v.), and was attached

to an embassy sent to Italy on the matter of the King's divorce. On his return he became Prior of Haverfordwest, thanks to the patronage of Anne Boleyn (q.v.). His views as a reformer were not well received by the Welsh, who threatened him with persecution. Barlow complained to Thomas Cromwell, who transferred him to Bisham and in 1535 sent him on a mission to the court of James IV. Probably as a reward for this service Barlow was appointed Bishop of St Asaph's and shortly afterwards Bishop of St David's.

At St David's Barlow again ran into trouble with his local clergy, but he held firm and showed his earnest desire to help the people by founding Christ's College, Brecon. In 1548 he attracted the attention of the Protector, Somerset (see Seymour, Edward), by preaching against images and was translated to the see of Bath and Wells. He resigned from this bishopric on the accession of Mary I (q.v.) and fled to Germany, but returned when Elizabeth I (q.v.) came to the throne. He assisted in the consecration of Matthew Parker (q.v.) as Archbishop of Canterbury, and in 1559 was made Bishop of Chichester and a prebend of Westminster. Barlow died in 1569 and was buried at Chichester.

Although a man of decided opinions, Barlow had, according to Cranmer (q.v.), a fondness for jests. His five daughters all married Anglican bishops.

E. G. Rupp, *The English Protestant Tradition* (1949).

**Barnes, Robert** (1495–1540), Protestant martyr.

Born at Lynn in Norfolk in 1495, Robert Barnes was educated at the universities of Cambridge and Louvain. Very early in life he became a member of the Austin Friars at Cambridge, and on his return from Louvain was made Prior. He took his doctorate of divinity in 1523.

Under Barnes the Austin house at Cambridge became a centre of classical learning, and Miles Coverdale (q.v.) was one of his pupils. Influenced by Thomas Bilney (q.v.), Hugh Latimer (q.v.), and others, Barnes embraced the new reformist doctrines and was one of the leading members of the White House tavern group who met regularly to discuss the Lutheran doctrine. He ruined his academic career by preaching on Christmas Eve 1525 against clerical litigiousness; he was summoned before the university authorities and his case was sent to Thomas Wolsey (q.v.) in London. He refused to recant, and after the trial was not allowed to return to Cambridge. He was put under house-arrest in London, but incurred danger by selling copies of the forbidden Tyndale New Testament and was more closely confined at Northampton. Friends there helped him to feign a suicide attempt, and he escaped to Antwerp and subsequently to Wittenberg, where he formed a close friendship with Martin Luther (q.v.). Under the pseudonym of Antonius Anglus he published several works, in English and German, including the *Articles of the Christian Church* and a *Supplication unto the most gracious prynce Henry VIII*, a copy of which was sent to the King.

Thomas Cromwell (q.v.) secured a safe conduct for Barnes to visit England in 1531, and he was employed on various diplomatic missions between England and Germany in connection with the new anti-Papal policy, and also in the negotiations for the marriage of Henry VIII (q.v.) with Anne of Cleves (q.v.). By dedicating his *History of the Popes* to the King, Barnes hoped to gain some preferment, but Cromwell was unable to secure anything more than a minor Welsh prebend for his protégé, who was never in the royal favour.

During Lent 1540 Barnes became involved in a controversy with Stephen Gardiner (q.v.), Bishop of Winchester. He signed a recantation and was pardoned, but soon afterwards preached again in Gardiner's presence in such a manner that he was sent to the Tower. In the meantime Cromwell had fallen and, lacking a protector, Barnes was condemned on a charge of heresy and burned at the stake on 30 July 1540, together with two other Lutheran 'heretics'.

M. L. Loane, *Pioneers of the Reformation in England* (1964).
E. G. Rupp, *Studies in the making of the English Protestant tradition* (1947).

**Barrow or Barrowe, Henry** (1550–1593), Separatist.

Born in about 1550 at Shipdham, Norfolk, Henry Barrow was the third son of Thomas Barrow and his wife, Mary Bures; his parents were gentlefolk, and Henry was distantly related to both Francis Bacon (q.v.) and William Cecil (q.v.). Nothing is known of his early life until November 1566, when he matriculated at Clare Hall, Cambridge. According to his own account, he led a dissolute life at the university. Nevertheless, he took his B.A. there in 1569–70, and in 1576 he became a member of Gray's Inn.

The chance hearing of a preacher's voice when walking through London one day in about 1580–1 changed Barrow's life, causing him to enter a church and subsequently to give up the law and his carefree, undisciplined existence in order to devote himself to religious studies. Soon afterwards he came under the influence of John Greenwood, and through him Barrow became acquainted with the writings of Robert Browne (q.v.), founder of the so-called 'Brownists', the forerunners of the modern Congregationalists, who favoured the foundation of churches separate from governmental control. When Greenwood was sent to prison and Barrow went to visit him in the Clink on 19 November 1586, he too was arrested on the orders of John Aylmer (q.v.), Bishop of London. Interrogated by a commission headed by Archbishop John Whitgift (q.v.), Barrow refused to recant and was taken to the Fleet prison, together with Greenwood. Altogether he was examined five times, once in the presence of William Cecil, then Baron Burghley.

Barrow's ideal was a church consisting of the faithful, separated from the unbelievers and sinners; there was to be no distinction between clergy and laity, and each congregation was to have autonomous sovereignty. While in prison he and Greenwood, together with a fellow prisoner, John Penry, who was alleged to be the author of the Martin Marprelate tracts, wrote a joint account of their treatment by the authorities; this, together with a number of other pamphlets and treatises defending their views, was smuggled out of the Fleet on small slips of paper for printing on the Continent. As a result of the publication of these works, on 11 March 1593 Barrow and Greenwood were charged with circulating seditious books. Convicted and sentenced to death on 23 March, they were both executed at Tyburn on 6 April.

As one of the leaders of the Separatist movement founded by Browne, Henry Barrow has come to be regarded as a founder of modern Nonconformity or Congregationalism. Among his published writings are *A True Description, out of the Word of God, of the Visible Church* (1589) and *A Brief Discovery of the False Church* (1590). There is no firm evidence that he wrote or contributed to the Martin Marprelate tracts.

F. J. Powicke, *Henry Barrow, Separatist, and the exiled Church of Amsterdam* (1900).

**Barton, Elizabeth** (?1506–1534), the 'Nun (or Maid) of Kent'.

According to local tradition, Elizabeth Barton was born at Aldington, Kent, where she was a domestic servant in the house of Thomas Cobb. In 1525 she fell ill with intestinal trouble and began to show symptoms of religious mania, including trances in which she cried out against sin and vice and uttered prophesies. (A modern theory is that she was suffering from a form of epilepsy combined with hysteria.)

Her first prophesy, of the death of her employer's child, came true almost instantly. The parish priest believed the girl to be inspired by the Holy Ghost, and Archbishop Warham (q.v.) appointed a commission consisting of Edward Bocking, William Hadleigh, and Friar Barnes, monks of Christ Church, Canterbury, to investigate. They pronounced themselves satisfied that Elizabeth was a good Christian, and at a thanksgiving mass to celebrate the outcome the girl underwent a miraculous cure. Bocking quickly saw the advantage of exploiting Elizabeth as propaganda for the Catholic Church and became her confessor and manager. He had her removed to the priory of St Sepulchre, Canterbury, where she became a source of income for the monks. Her fame as a holy woman quickly spread through the county and beyond: Thomas Wolsey (q.v.), John Fisher (q.v.) and even, for a time, Thomas More (q.v.), all believed her to be genuine. Her 'revelations' now took place almost weekly and increasingly she was 'told by the Holy Spirit of God' of the punishments in store for the world as a result of the 'sins of the princes and people'. She correctly foretold Warham's death, and that the King's daughter Mary (see Mary I) would become Queen of England.

The Nun's undoing was the dire series of prophesies with which she began to threaten Henry VIII (q.v.) if he divorced Catherine of Aragon (q.v.) and married Anne Boleyn (q.v.). The King at first ignored them, went ahead with the divorce and married Anne; he did not die within six months as Elizabeth had foretold. Then she announced that Henry was no longer King in the eyes of God. This was nothing short of high treason; Thomas Cromwell (q.v.) regarded it as incitement to rebellion, and Thomas Cranmer (q.v.), by this time Archbishop of Canterbury, intervened. Elizabeth, Bocking, and half a dozen others were arrested. Under close examination the Nun broke down and confessed to having feigned her trances, and the others also admitted the imposture. All were condemned under an act of attainder and were executed at Tyburn, London, on 20 April 1534.

Historians and jurists have since questioned her guilt on the grounds that, as a woman of poor intellect and little education, Elizabeth may have been tricked by complicated legal procedures into a false confession and that she was nothing more than a deluded and hysterical, but otherwise sincere, girl, a tool manipulated by others. Alan Neame, in his recent book, has traced the plot, said to have been inspired by the Nun, though it was not brought out into the open at the time, to depose the King and place Henry Courtenay, Marquess of Exeter, on the throne. Treason having been proved, a special act of attainder had to be established as a pretext for execution; the reason for this

drastic measure was not the Nun's prophesies but the fact that she was the apostle of a possible Catholic rebellion within the kingdom. Seen in this context, Elizabeth Barton takes on a new importance.

A. D. Cheney, 'The Holy Maid of Kent', *Transactions of the Royal Historical Society*, xviii (1904).
A. Neame, *The Holy Maid of Kent* (1971).

**Beaton or Bethune, David** (?1494–1546), statesman, cardinal, and Archbishop of St Andrews.

David Beaton was born in about 1494, the third son of John Beaton of Balfour and nephew of James Beaton, Archbishop of St Andrews. After studying at St Andrews and Glasgow, at the age of sixteen he was sent to Orleans to study civil and canon law. He later became the Scottish resident at the French court.

Beaton was presented by his uncle first to the rectory of Campsie and in 1523 to the abbacy of Arbroath; in 1537 he was consecrated Bishop of Mirepoix in Foix, France, and the following year Pope Paul III made him Cardinal of San Stefano. In 1539 the Cardinal succeeded his uncle as Archbishop of St Andrews.

His political career began in 1529, when he became Lord Privy Seal; between that date and taking up his appointment as Archbishop, Beaton was frequently employed on diplomatic missions, including the negotiations for the marriage of James V (q.v.) to the Princess Madeleine of France; he was subsequently one of the commissioners sent to bring the King's second bride, Marie de Guise (q.v.), to Scotland in 1538. A dedicated supporter of the 'Auld Alliance' of Scotland and France, he worked closely with Queen Marie to influence the King against the pro-Reformist policies of Henry VIII (q.v.).

After James's death in December 1542,

Beaton was involved in a power struggle with the Earl of Arran (see Hamilton, James, 2nd Earl) for the Regency; he is said to have forged the King's Will. He lost to Arran and was imprisoned for a few months. On his release Beaton raised a faction against the proposed treaty with England which provided for the marriage of the young Mary, Queen of Scots (q.v.) and Prince Edward (see Edward VI); in July 1543 he assembled some 7,000 supporters and marched to Linlithgow to take the Queen and her mother to Stirling. Arran then changed sides and joined the Cardinal's party, and in December that year Beaton became Chancellor (and virtual ruler) of Scotland, initiating a cruel régime of persecution against the Protestants. When the Earl of Hertford (see Seymour, Edward) invaded Scotland the following year, he had explicit instructions from the English King to seize Beaton and to raze the castle of St Andrews, his stronghold; Beaton, however, had prudently fled.

In March 1546 the Archbishop caused much bitterness by having the popular reformer, George Wishart (q.v.), burned at the stake. In retaliation Beaton himself was murdered, in his bedroom at St Andrews, on 29 May the same year, by John Leslie, a friend of Wishart's, and other Protestant lords.

David Beaton had the gift of influencing others; he succeeded, in turn, in gaining power over James V, Arran, and Marie de Guise. His persecution of the Protestants aroused the anger of many of the Scots and turned many of them against the Roman Catholic Church. A hard, implacable statesman, Beaton led an immoral private life, fathering at least eight illegitimate children. He was at one time accused by John Knox (q.v.) of having lascivious relations with Marie de Guise, but

historians do not now believe this to be the case.

J. Herkless and R. K. Hannay, *The Archbishops of St Andrews,* vol. 4 (5 vols; Edinburgh, 1907–15).

*Portrait:* oil, by unknown artist: private collection (anon.).

**Beaufort, Margaret** (1443–1509), Countess of Richmond and Derby, mother of Henry VII (q.v.), known as 'the Lady Margaret'.

A great-granddaughter of John of Gaunt (see *Lives Before the Tudors*) and daughter of John Beaufort, 1st Duke of Somerset, Margaret was born on 31 May 1443. In 1455 she was married to Edmund Tudor, Earl of Richmond, who died the following year before the birth of their son, the future Henry VII. During the Wars of the Roses the young widow and her son lived at Pembroke Castle. Her second husband, whom she married about 1459, was Sir Henry Stafford, a Lancastrian, and following the Yorkist triumph of 1461 she was detained 'in honourable confinement' at

the castle. On her release she went to court, the young Henry having for safety been dispatched to France. Some time after Stafford's death she married for the third time, probably about 1482, Thomas Stanley, later 1st Earl of Derby (see *Lives Before the Tudors*).

The Beaufort family had been deprived by Act of Parliament of all rights of succession, but the Lady Margaret, an intelligent, highly-educated and shrewd woman, had ambitious schemes for her son. She played a prominent part in planning his marriage to Elizabeth of York (q.v.) and was involved both in the abortive insurrection of 1483 and in that of 1485 which eventually won Henry the crown. A pious if somewhat formidable lady, and a strict disciplinarian, she is reputed to have ruled his court with a rod of iron; but conflicting accounts state that after 1486 she spent most of her days in retirement. In any event, she seems to have remained on good terms with Henry, who was generous to her in her last years.

The Countess was a patron of scholarship and especially of the printers William Caxton (q.v.) and his successor, Wynkyn de Worde. On the advice of her friend and confessor, John Fisher (q.v.), later Bishop of Rochester, she founded the Lady Margaret professorships of divinity at Oxford and Cambridge in 1502. Fisher also influenced her in the endowment of two colleges at Cambridge, Christ's College in 1505 and St John's, to which in her Will she left the bulk of her estates. She died on 29 June 1509, and was buried in Henry VII's Chapel, Westminster Abbey.

C. H. Cooper, *Memoir of Margaret, Countess of Richmond and Derby* (1874).
C. A. Halsted, *Life of Margaret Beaufort* (1839).
E. M. G. Routh, *Lady Margaret* (1924).

*Portraits:* oil, full length, possibly by Maynard: Christ's College, Cambridge; oil, full length at prayer, by Rowland Lockey, *c.* 1598: St. John's College, Cambridge; oil on panel, half length, by unknown artist, sixteenth century: National Portrait Gallery, London; oil, by unknown artist: Royal Collection, Windsor; electrotype, from bronze effigy on tomb in Westminster Abbey by Pietro Torrigiano, *c.* 1514: N.P.G.; oil, *called* Lady Margaret Beaufort, by unknown artist: N.P.G.; other versions at Old Schools, Cambridge, Bodleian Library, Brasenose College, and Lady Margaret Hall, Oxford, and elsewhere.

**Beaumont, Francis** (1584–1616), dramatist, see *Lives of the Stuart Age.*

**Bedford, 1st Earl of** (?1486–1555), see Russell, John.

**Berners, 2nd Baron** (?1467–1533), see Bourchier, John.

**Bertie, Peregrine** (1555–1601), Baron Willoughby de Eresby, military commander.

The son of Richard Bertie and his wife Catherine, Baroness Willoughby de Eresby in her own right, Peregrine Bertie was born at Lower Wesel, Cleves, on 12 October 1555, while his parents were fleeing from the Marian persecution in England; he was so named because he was born in *terra peregrina*. In August 1559, following the family's return to England, he was naturalized. Educated under the guidance of Sir William Cecil (q.v.), later 1st Baron Burghley, Bertie married Mary, daughter of John de Vere, 16th Earl of Oxford; a few years later, in 1580, on the death of his mother, he succeeded to her title as Lord Willoughby de Eresby. He was generally known as Lord Willoughby.

In 1582 Willoughby was sent to Denmark on a mission to discuss commercial relations between that country and England. He successfully accomplished this task, and in 1585 he was sent again to Denmark in an attempt to persuade the King to assist Henri de Navarre by supplying money or men, and also to help England in the Netherlands against Spain. Negotiations were protracted, but at the end of December Frederick II yielded in part to Willoughby's requests. Having obtained a promise from the Danish king that he would use his influence to induce Spain to withdraw from the Netherlands and would send 2,000 horse to swell the English forces there, Willoughby set out for Flanders. He was engaged to serve under Sir John Norris (q.v.) in the relief of Grave, and shortly afterwards he was made Governor of Bergen-op-Zoom. He took part in the attack on Axel at the end of May and in the fighting at Zutphen in September, in which his close friend, Sir Philip Sidney (q.v.), was mortally wounded.

In early 1587, following a series of disagreements between the English commanders, Leicester (see Dudley, Robert) and Norris, and also between the English government and the States General, Norris was recalled and Willoughby succeeded him as commander of the cavalry. In July that year he and Leicester failed to relieve Sluys. After several other futile engagements Leicester also was recalled, Willoughby replacing him as commander of the English forces in the Netherlands. Frustrated by the lack of supplies both from England and from the States General, he complained to Burghley that restrictions imposed on his authority prevented him from carrying on the war. In the summer of 1588, having been ordered to send 2,000 men to England to await the threatened Spanish invasion, he begged to be recalled. His request was not granted, and he had to content himself with keeping watch on the Duke of Parma's fleet in order to prevent them

sailing to aid the Armada. Later that year, when the Spanish took the offensive in the Netherlands, Willoughby successfully defended Bergen. His position became increasingly embarrassing, however, as the States General protested at their treatment by the English government, especially after Willoughby had in December that year been ordered to send part of his force to Portugal. At last, in March 1589, he was given permission to return home. By this time his health and his finances were ruined as a result of the continual worry and expense incurred in paying for supplies out of his own pocket.

In September 1589 Willoughby was given command of a force of 4,000 men sent to aid Henri de Navarre at Dieppe. He took part in the capture of Vendôme, Mons, Alençon, and Falaise, but when no money or supplies reached them from England, so many of his men succumbed to disease for want of food and proper clothing that in January 1590 Willoughby was given permission to return home with his depleted army.

Ill-health forced him to spend the next few years travelling on the Continent, mainly in Italy. In the autumn of 1596 he returned to England, and the following February he was appointed as Governor of Berwick and Warden of the East March, from where he sent regular reports to Sir Robert Cecil (q.v.) on the situation in Scotland. Willoughby died at Berwick on 25 June 1601. He was survived by his widow, five sons, and one daughter.

Willoughby's valiant exploits in the Netherlands, particularly in the defence of Bergen-op-Zoom, caught the public imagination and were commemorated in several sixteenth-century ballads.

Lady Georgina Bertie, *Five Generations of a Loyal House*, part i (1845).

*Portrait:* engraving, by unknown nineteenth century engraver after unknown artist: location not known.

**'Bess of Hardwick'** (1520–1608), see Hardwick, Elizabeth.

**Bethune, David** (?1494–1546), see Beaton, David.

**Bilney, Thomas** (?1495–1531), martyr.

Little is known of Bilney's early life, but he is thought to have been born in about 1495 at East Bilney, near Norwich. He was educated at Trinity. Hall, Cambridge, where he took his degree in law. He had every intention of pursuing a legal career, but while at Cambridge he underwent a spiritual crisis and, greatly influenced by reading the Latin New Testament of Erasmus (q.v.), abandoned the law for a religious vocation. He was ordained priest in 1519.

Known to his friends as 'little Bilney' on account of his small stature, he was a popular member of the circle of younger Cambridge dons who frequented the White Horse tavern to discuss the new learning and the new religious doctrines, and he soon became their accepted leader. Among his closest friends were Hugh Latimer (q.v.), Matthew Parker (q.v.), the future Archbishop of Canterbury, and Robert Barnes (q.v.). Unlike other members of the group, however, Bilney remained orthodox to the Catholic Church on several major points such as the power of the pope, the sacrifice of the Mass, and the doctrine of transubstantiation, while at the same time preaching against the invocation of the saints and the worship of images, which led to his being regarded, mistakenly, as a Lutheran.

Bilney's sermons were bold and provocative, and he soon ran into trouble. In 1526 he was examined informally by Thomas Wolsey (q.v.) and gave an undertaking that he did not subscribe to the Lutheran doctrine and would not preach on that subject; the following year, as a result of a series of sermons given in London in which he denounced the idolatry of the Church, he was brought before Cuthbert Tunstall (q.v.), Bishop of London, charged with being a relapsed heretic. Anxious to save him from the stake, Tunstall more than once suspended the trial to give him time to reconsider; then, on the seventh day, Bilney recanted. He was sentenced to do penance at St Paul's, to refrain from preaching and saying Mass in public, and to be imprisoned in the Tower for so long as Wolsey deemed fit.

After his release by Wolsey a year later Bilney returned to Cambridge, his spirit broken and tortured by the memory of his recantation; even his friends were unable to console him. Finally he resolved to find relief through defiance: he preached such a bold sermon at an open-air gathering near Norwich that the local bishop had no choice but to order his arrest. He was tried and condemned as a relapsed heretic, and was burned at the stake on 19 August 1531.

The influence of Bilney on his contemporaries was probably as great as that of any of the English reformers, even though because of his orthodoxy he cannot be termed a Protestant martyr in the strict sense of the word. The controversy that waged after his death as to whether or not he had made a full recantation at the eleventh hour has never been convincingly resolved.

John Foxe, *Acts and Monuments,* vol. iv (1877).
M. L. Loane, *Masters of the English Reformation* (1954).
E. G. Rupp, 'The Recantation of Thomas Bilney', *London Quarterly* (April 1942).

**Blackwell, George** (?1545–1613), archpriest.

Born in Middlesex in about 1545, George Blackwell was the son of a London pewterer. He studied at Trinity College, Oxford, graduating as B.A. in 1562, and becoming a perpetual fellow of the College in 1565 and M.A. two years later. He resigned his fellowship shortly afterwards because of his adherence to the Catholic rather than the reformed religion and retired for some time to Gloucester Hall. In 1574 he left the university for the English College at Douai, where he was ordained as priest in 1575 and took his degree as Bachelor of Divinity at the university that same year.

Blackwell returned to London in November 1576 as part of the English Catholic mission, but he lived in constant fear of arrest and in 1578 was imprisoned for a short time. He periodically visited the Continent and was well known to the church leaders in Rome. After the death of Cardinal William Allen (q.v.) in 1594, the English Catholic movement lacked leadership and discipline, and in March 1598 Blackwell was appointed by Pope Clement VIII as archpriest, with absolute authority over the secular clergy and instructions to follow the Jesuit lead. The appointment was highly unpopular among the secular priests, who refused to accept Blackwell's authority and made a series of appeals to Rome on the issue; the archpriest's autocratic manner and rigid fulfilment of his duties kept the conflict alive for the next six years, and it was brought to a head when, in spite of its having been twice condemned by the Pope, he advised his clergy to accept the oath of allegiance imposed on all Catholics by James I (see James VI of Scotland) in 1606. Blackwell himself, arrested and imprisoned in 1607, subscribed to the oath and was deprived of his office by the Pope in 1608. He died on 12 January 1613, having maintained to the last the lawfulness of the oath.

J. H. Pollen, *The Institution of the Archpriest Blackwell* (1916).

**Blount, Charles** (1563–1606), 8th Baron Mountjoy and later Earl of Devonshire, soldier and Lord Deputy of Ireland.

The second son of James Blount, 6th Baron Mountjoy, and his wife Catherine, daughter of Sir Thomas Leigh of St Oswald's, Yorkshire, Charles Blount was born in 1563. After studying at Oxford, he entered the Middle Temple in 1579. The family's fortunes being in a sorry state, the young Blount, on coming to London, determined to remedy the situation and with this in mind, in about 1583 he made his way to court. He was a strikingly handsome young man of twenty and soon attracted the attention of Queen Elizabeth (q.v.). A token sent to him by the Queen was noticed by the then favourite, Essex (see Devereux, Robert), and resulted in a duel between the two men, but they were afterwards

good friends. Another intimate friend was Sir Philip Sidney (q.v.).

Some years before coming to court Blount had had a liaison with Essex's sister Penelope, who had subsequently been forced by her father to marry Lord Rich. Sidney was also in love with her, immortalizing her as the 'Stella' of his sonnets, but after his death in 1586 Penelope openly became Blount's mistress; she bore him three sons and two daughters, the eldest born in about 1597. They were to be married only in December 1605, after her divorce from Lord Rich.

In 1586 Blount was in command of troops in the Low Countries under the Earl of Leicester (see Dudley, Robert); he was knighted for his services the following year. From that time until early 1594 he served almost continually on the Continent, both in the Low Countries and in Brittany. He returned to England in January 1594 to take up an appointment as Captain of Portsmouth, and later that year, on the death of his father, he succeeded to the barony.

Mountjoy sailed with Essex in the expedition to the Azores of 1597. Shortly after his return he was made a Knight of the Garter, and it seemed likely that he would be given command of the English forces in Ireland. The appointment, however, went to Essex, and only after the latter's dismal failure and eventual dismissal, and in spite of being implicated in his friend's conspiracies, was Mountjoy given the office of Lord Deputy in February 1600. He waged a highly successful campaign against the rebellious Earl of Tyrone (see O'Neill, Hugh) and in December 1601 he distinguished himself at Kinsale (where 4,000 Spanish troops had landed to support the Irish), routing the Ulster troops marched south by O'Neill and forcing the Spaniards to evacuate the fortress. His further successes in Ulster, combined with those of Sir George Carew in the south, resulted in Tyrone's submission to Mountjoy in Dublin on 30 March 1603. He brought Tyrone to England and was able to obtain lenient treatment for him from the new King, James I (see James VI of Scotland).

High in royal favour at the beginning of the new reign, created Earl of Devonshire, appointed Master of the Ordnance in 1603 and Keeper of Portsmouth Castle the following year, the last months of Mountjoy's life were marred by the scandal and displeasure of the King at his marriage to the divorced Lady Rich. He died on 3 April 1606 in London and was buried in Westminster Abbey.

Cyril Falls, *Mountjoy: Elizabethan General* (1955). F. M. Jones, *Mountjoy, 1563–1606* (1958).

*Portraits:* two miniatures, by Nicholas Hilliard: Sir John Carew Pole and The Earl of Beauchamp; oil, by unknown artist, *c.* 1597: National Gallery of Ireland, Dublin; engravings, by Cockson, Green, and another unknown engraver: British

Museum, London. N.B. The figure in the group portrait of the Somerset House Conference, 1604 (National Portrait Gallery, London; copy at National Maritime Museum, Greenwich) is considered to be a good likeness.

## Blount or Blunt, Edward (*fl.* 1588–1632), stationer and translator, publisher of the First Folio of plays by William Shakespeare (q.v.).

The son of Ralph Blount (or Blunt), a Merchant Taylor of London, Edward Blount was in 1578 apprenticed for ten years to a London stationer, William Ponsonby; on 25 June 1588 he was admitted as a freeman of the Stationers' Company. He claimed to be an intimate friend of Christopher Marlowe (q.v.), in whose memory he published the poet's *Hero and Leander* in 1598. He also published works by John Florio (q.v.): the Italian-English Dictionary, *A Worlde of Wordes*, in 1598, and a translation of the essays of Montaigne in 1603. The first English translation of *Don Quixote*, by Thomas Shelton, was issued by Blount in 1620.

In 1623 Blount joined with a fellow printer, Isaac Jaggard, to produce, under the direction of John Heminge and Henry Condell, the First Folio of Shakespeare's plays; his name appears on the title page and in the colophon.

In the early days of his career Blount had a shop in St Paul's Churchyard, 'at the sign of the Black Beare'. Some time before the end of 1623 he married the widow of a fellow stationer, Elizabeth Bankworth. Little is known of his later years, except that he was still in business in 1632, the date of his edition of the collected plays of John Lyly (q.v.).

Many of the books issued under his imprint contained a preface or dedication written by Blount himself; among these were translations from the Spanish and the Italian, some of them his own work.

## Blount, William (d. 1534), 4th Baron Mountjoy, statesman and patron of learning.

Born at Barton, Staffordshire, William Blount was the son and heir of John Blount, 3rd Baron, and grandson of Walter Blount, 1st Baron Mountjoy. The date of his birth is not known, but he was still a child in 1485 when he succeeded to the title on his father's death. He studied in Paris in 1496, at the time when Erasmus (q.v.) was lecturing at the university there; teacher and pupil became lifelong friends.

On his return to England Mountjoy married his first wife, Elizabeth, daughter of Sir William Saye of Bedwell, Hertfordshire. In September 1497 he held a command in the campaign against Perkin Warbeck (q.v.). Formally granted the possession of his estates in 1499, he became page to the young Prince Henry, the future Henry VIII (q.v.), to whom he appears also to have acted as a tutor of history. In that same year Mountjoy invited Erasmus to England, and on the occasion of this visit took the great man to the royal nursery to be presented to the Prince. After Henry's accession in 1509 he again invited Erasmus to England and agreed to pay him a handsome pension. Mountjoy's London house became a meeting place for the scholars of the day; his intimate circle included Roger Ascham, Sir Thomas More, William Grocyn, and John Colet (qq.v.), and he was also a patron of other scholars such as John Leland (q.v.), Richard Sampson, and Richard Whyteforde.

Appointed Lieutenant of the Marches of Calais at the end of 1509, from 1514 to 1517 Mountjoy was Bailiff of Tournai, where he was visited by Erasmus. Early in 1517 he was recalled at his own request, probably for family reasons. He became Chamberlain to Catherine of

Aragon (q.v.), serving the Queen in this capacity throughout the troubled period of the divorce, until in 1533 he begged to be relieved of his duties. For his services to the crown Mountjoy was made a Knight of the Garter.

His first wife died young, leaving him two daughters, and some time before 1517 Mountjoy married Alice, daughter of Sir Henry Kebel and widow of a Lord Mayor of London, who bore him a son and a daughter; following her death in 1521 he married again, but his third wife, Dorothy, daughter of the Marquess of Dorset, died before 1524, leaving him one son and two daughters. According to Erasmus, he at one time contemplated a fourth marriage.

In 1520 Mountjoy was present at the meeting between Henry VIII and François I at the Field of the Cloth of Gold; he also attended the King at his historic meeting with Charles V (q.v.) in 1522. The following year he took part in the unsuccessful invasion of France under the Duke of Suffolk (see Brandon, Charles), and soon after his recall he was appointed Master of the Mint. He signed the articles drawn up against Thomas Wolsey (q.v.) in 1530 and also the declaration sent in 1533 by Parliament to Clement VII, in which Henry threatened to renounce papal supremacy if the Pope refused to annul his marriage; as Chamberlain, he had the task of informing Catherine that the King was resolved to divorce her.

Mountjoy died on 8 November 1534 and was buried in Grey Friars' Church in the City.

**Blunt, Edward** (*fl.* 1588–1632), see Blount, Edward.

**Bocher, Boucher, or Butcher, Joan** (d. 1550), Anabaptist martyr, sometimes called 'Joan of Kent'.

Joan's birth and early life are obscure, but she was known to the ladies of Henry VIII's court in about 1540 through her efforts to distribute copies of the New Testament translated by William Tyndale (q.v.). She was a friend of Anne Askew (q.v.).

Joan's first brush with the authorities came in 1542, when she was examined by Thomas Cranmer (q.v.), Archbishop of Canterbury, but released. In 1549 the Kentish Justices reported her to the Council for being an Anabaptist and for spreading the view that Christ had not taken the flesh of the Virgin. Arrested and brought before the Commission, Joan defiantly refused to recant; she was subsequently excommunicated and condemned to be burned unless she recanted.

Meanwhile Henry VIII's heresy laws had been repealed, and the Protector, the Duke of Somerset (see Seymour, Edward), postponed Joan's execution for more than a year; during this time both Cranmer and Nicholas Ridley (q.v.), Bishop of London, tried at regular intervals to get her to recant, but met only with obstinacy and abuse. On 2 May 1550 Joan was burned at Smithfield; she went to her death uttering screams and curses.

G. Burnet, *History of the Reformation of the Church of England*, ed. N. Pocock, vol. 5 (1865).

**Bodley, Sir Thomas** (1545–1613), scholar, diplomat, and founder of the Bodleian Library, Oxford.

Bodley was born at Exeter on 2 March 1545, the eldest son of Protestant parents, who a few years later fled to Geneva to escape the Marian persecution. Thomas, together with his younger brothers, Josias and Laurence, therefore received his early education in Geneva. When the family returned to England after the accession of Elizabeth I (q.v.) in 1558, he entered Magdalen College, Oxford. He became a Fellow of Merton College in 1563 and took his M.A. three years later.

For some time Bodley lectured at the university in natural philosophy; he was elected university proctor in 1569 and also held office as deputy public orator. Probably as a result of his Geneva education he began to acquire a reputation as a linguist, and he now resolved to use his abilities in the service of the state. In order to gain experience, he left Oxford in 1576 and spent the next four years travelling on the Continent.

Returning to England, he entered Parliament in 1584 as Member for Portsmouth. The following year he was sent on a diplomatic mission to Denmark and Germany and in 1588 on a secret mission to France. Shortly afterwards he was appointed English representative in the United Provinces and took up residence at The Hague.

Bodley remained in The Hague until 1596, but he was not happy in his post, due largely to difficulties arising out of intrigues among the Queen's ministers in London, and he made several requests to be recalled. When he was eventually allowed to return, it was proposed that he should become Secretary of State, but he resisted several offers of this office and insisted on retiring from public life.

He had married in 1587 a wealthy widow; there were no children of the marriage. In retirement Bodley conceived the idea of refounding the university library at Oxford, which had been practically destroyed by the commissioners for university reform appointed by Edward VI (q.v.). To this great scheme he devoted the rest of his life and most of his fortune. He solicited help from rich friends in England and on the Continent, and on 8 November 1602 the library was opened. It then contained some 2,000 books representing all fields of learning. In 1609 Bodley endowed the library with lands in Berkshire as well as some London property, and the following year he negotiated with the Stationers' Company an agreement under which they undertook to present to the library one copy of every book printed in England and registered by the Company.

Bodley was knighted in 1604. He died in London on 28 January 1631 and was buried in the chapel of Merton College. In his Will he left most of his fortune to the library which bears his name and specifically made provision for its enlargement.

Sir Thomas's autobiography, which goes up to 1609, was published together with the draft statutes for the library and his letters to Thomas James, the librarian, in T. Hearne's *Reliquiae Bodleianae* (1703). More recently his *Letters . . . to Thomas James* and *Letters . . . to the University of Oxford* have been edited by G. W. Wheeler (1926 and 1927 respectively).

W. D. Macray, *Annals of the Bodleian Library* (2nd ed. 1890).
*Trecentale Bodleianum*, published for the Bodleian Library (1913).

*Portraits*: two oils, one three-quarter length, both by unknown artists, a miniature (school of Hilliard), and a marble bust: all at Bodleian Library, Oxford.

**Boleyn, Anne** (?1507–1536), see Anne Boleyn.

**Boleyn or Bullen, Sir Thomas** (1477–1539), Earl of Wiltshire and Ormonde, father of Anne Boleyn (q.v.).

Thomas Boleyn was born in 1477 (exact date unknown), the second son of Sir William Boleyn of Blickling, Norfolk, and his wife, Margaret, daughter and co-heiress of Thomas Butler, Earl of Ormonde. Little is known of his early life, but there is a record of his having held arms with his father against the Cornish rebels in 1497. Some time in the next few years he married and settled with his wife, Lady Elizabeth Howard, daughter of the Duke of Norfolk (see Howard, Thomas, 2nd Duke), at Hever Castle, near Edenbridge, Kent, which had been acquired by Sir Thomas's grandfather, Sir Geoffrey Boleyn, a wealthy merchant and Lord Mayor of London, in 1458. The three children of this marriage were all later to achieve notoriety: Mary, the elder daugher, as a mistress of Henry VIII (q.v.), Anne as the King's second wife, and George, later Viscount Rochford, when he was implicated in the trial of his younger sister, charged with high treason and incest, and beheaded.

During the first years of Henry VIII's reign Sir Thomas rose steadily, but not spectacularly, in favour as a courtier and minister. His first official post was that of Keeper of the Exchange at Calais and of the Foreign Exchange in England, to which he was appointed in 1509. Three years later, in 1512, he was made Joint Constable (with Sir Henry Wyatt) of Norwich Castle. Also in that year he accompanied Sir Edward Poynings (q.v.) on a mission to the Low Countries, and in April 1513 he and his colleagues concluded at Mechlin the treaty by which the King of England joined the Emperor Maximilian, Pope Julius II, and Ferdinand of Spain in an alliance for the invasion of France. When the invasion took place later that summer, Sir Thomas participated in it. As a reward for these services, he was given lands and various other marks of royal favour. In 1516 he was one of four courtiers chosen to hold a canopy over the baby Princess Mary (see Mary I) at her christening. The following year he was appointed Sheriff of Kent.

Early in 1519 Sir Thomas was sent to France to negotiate the preliminary arrangements for a meeting between Henry and François I. According to contemporary records, he was very much at home at the French court. The elder Boleyn girl, Mary, had been maid-of-honour to Mary Tudor (q.v.), wife of Louis XII, and, incidentally, mistress to the French King and several others; she had been sent back to England in disgrace. Her father now introduced the younger daughter, Anne, who entered the royal service as maid-of-honour to Queen Claude, wife of François. Sir Thomas remained in France until March 1520; he was not present at the meeting between Henry and François, known as the Field of the Cloth of Gold, in June that year, but he was in attendance at a meeting between Henry and the Emperor Charles V (q.v.) which took place the following month.

Back in England, his next duty was to serve on the special commission which indicted the Duke of Buckingham (see Stafford, Edward) for treason. Early in 1522 Sir Thomas was appointed Treasurer of the Royal Household. In May that year he attended Henry on the occasion of Charles V's arrival at Canterbury; shortly afterwards he was sent on an embassy to Spain, in order to promote war with France, but was recalled by the King in April 1523.

By this date the younger members of his family were becoming well known at the English court. Anne had returned from France the previous year and was in the service of Catherine of Aragon (q.v.). Her sister Mary, now married to William Carey, a member of the Royal Household, either had been or was about to become the King's mistress. George Boleyn was rapidly coming into favour and would be appointed a Gentleman of the Privy Chamber by 1525.

In May 1523 Sir Thomas was appointed to the Order of the Garter. There is little doubt that this and other honours heaped on him during the next few years had their origin in the King's growing fascination with the younger Boleyn daughter. An elevation to the peerage as Viscount Rochford in June 1525 was followed in December 1529 by his creation as Earl of Wiltshire and Ormonde. Then, on 24 January 1530, he was appointed Lord Privy Seal.

Throughout this period he was often employed on missions abroad, especially to France; he was one of a few English noblemen to whom François I granted pensions for their work in promoting understanding between the two countries. Inevitably also, Wiltshire was drawn into the negotiations for the King's divorce. After failing to impress Charles V with Henry's reasons for seeking a divorce in 1530, he went on to Paris in an attempt to get the doctors of the university there to give their opinion, but following his return home in August that year he remained generally resident at court, a helpless spectator of the drama involving his daughter Anne and the King, and often fearful of its consequences. One of his last recorded official duties was to accompany Sir William Paulet (q.v.) on a visit to the Princess Mary, in order to try to persuade her to renounce her title and acknowledge herself as illegitimate.

In May 1536 the Earl was spared the ordeal of sitting on the tribunal of peers which tried Anne Boleyn and her brother George, Viscount Rochford, for high treason and incest; but after their execution he was a broken man. Dismissed from his official posts at court and having lost his wife in April 1538, he retired to Hever, where he died on 13 March 1539. His altar tomb and effigy may still be seen in the village church.

After Wiltshire's death the King seized the Boleyn estates, and in the summer of 1540 he gave Hever to his discarded fourth wife, Anne of Cleves (q.v.).

See bibliography listed under Anne Boleyn.

*Portrait:* drawing, by Holbein: Royal Collection, Windsor.

## Bonner, Edmund (?1500–1569), Bishop of London.

The son of Edmund Bonner of Hanley, Worcestershire, Bonner was born probably in 1500. He studied at what is now Pembroke College, Oxford, where he took his degree in civil and canon law and was also ordained. An outstanding lawyer, he became a doctor of civil law in 1525. Wolsey (q.v.) appointed him as his chaplain in 1529.

After Wolsey's death Bonner served Henry VIII (q.v.) on a number of important diplomatic missions, principally in the matter of the King's divorce from Catherine of Aragon (q.v.). In return he was given a number of preferments and in 1538 was appointed ambassador to the French court and also Bishop of Hereford, both of which appointments greatly offended Stephen Gardiner (q.v.). The following year, before he could be consecrated to Hereford, he was made Bishop of London.

Throughout Henry's reign Bonner remained loyal to the crown and the ecclesiastical policy of the day, but with the accession of Edward VI (q.v.) he felt himself unable to accept the advancing Protestantism and in particular the view of the Protector, Somerset (see Seymour, Edward), that royal supremacy should be vested in the Privy Council during the King's minority. In 1547 he spent two months imprisoned in the Fleet for resisting the Visitation and Injunctions;

two years later he was reprimanded for not enforcing the new Prayer Book and, having omitted to preach on the royal supremacy when ordered to do so, was examined and committed to the Marshalsea prison, where he remained from 1549 to 1553.

On the accession of Mary I (q.v.) he was restored to his bishopric and devoted himself to the affairs of his diocese. Inevitably he became involved in the large-scale persecutions of the Protestants, since London was then the centre of the Puritan movement; but the fact that he was rebuked by the Queen for treating heretics too lightly demolishes the charge levelled against him by John Foxe (q.v.) and others that he enjoyed sending men and women to the fire.

After Bonner had again neglected to use the new Prayer Book at St Paul's and refused to take the oath of supremacy under Elizabeth I (q.v.), he was once more deprived of his bishopric and sent to the Marshalsea, where he spent the last ten years of his life. He died at the prison on 5 September 1569 and was buried in St George's, Southwark.

Bonner was one of the most unpopular conservative bishops of the English reformation. Although in his young days he had accepted the need for reform, he changed his views after the death of Henry VIII and came to regard the Reformation more as a revolution than a spiritual change. As a lawyer he tended to put the legal viewpoint far more often than the spiritual; he was accused by Thomas Cranmer (q.v.) of being 'too full' of his law. Bishop John Bale, in an attack written some years before the Marian persecutions for which Bonner was held largely responsible, coined the phrase 'bloody bishop Bonner'; this has since influenced many historians, and the image of a somewhat inhuman man has persisted through the centuries.

E. C. Messenger, 'Bishop Bonner and Anglican orders', *Dublin Review*, cxcviii (1936).
L. Baldwin Smith, *Tudor Prelates and Politics* (1953).

**Borough, Stephen** (1525–1584), navigator, the first European to reach the southernmost end of the Arctic archipelago, Novaya Zemlya.

Borough was born on 25 September 1525 in the parish of Northam, Devon. Virtually nothing is known of his parentage or early life, but there is little doubt that he first went to sea when quite young. In 1553 he sailed as master of the *Edward Bonaventure* in the expedition led by Richard Chancellor and Sir Hugh Willoughby to the Arctic, hoping to discover a North-East Passage that would open up an easy route to Asia. Willoughby and his crew succumbed to the icy conditions in Lapland, but Chancellor and Borough in the *Edward Bonaventure* passed the North Cape and reached Archangel, from where they made contact with the Tsar of Moscow. Of the three vessels that comprised the expedition, only the *Edward Bonaventure* navigated by Borough returned safely.

As a result of this voyage the Muscovy Company was set up in 1555 for the purpose of trading with Russia. Borough did not accompany Chancellor on his second and disastrous Russian expedition that year, but in 1556 he sailed as master of the *Searchthrift* on a voyage during which he discovered Novaya Zemlya and the entrance to the Kara Sea. He was, however, unsuccessful in his search for the three ships that had been lost on previous voyages, and eventually arrived back in England during the summer of 1557. He made one journey to the south, during the reign of Queen Mary I (q.v.), probably in 1558, when he was fêted by the Spanish at Seville; thereafter he made a number of annual visits to Russia on behalf of the Merchant Adventurers to Muscovy, sailing in the *Swallow*. In 1560 he brought back to England from St Nicholas Anthony Jenkinson, who had made a spectacular journey across the Caspian and Central Asia. The following May Borough set out on his last visit to Russia, taking Jenkinson back to St Nicholas on the first stage of his journey as English ambassador to Persia.

In January 1563 Borough entered the service of the crown as chief pilot and one of four masters of the Queen's ships in the Medway. He remained in the royal service for the rest of his life, making occasional sea voyages in the course of his official duties. He died on 12 July 1584 and was buried in Chatham Church.

Stephen Borough was the prime mover in getting the Merchant Adventurers to sponsor an English edition of a popular work on navigation written by the Spaniard Mario Cortes; translated by Richard Eden, it was first published in London in 1561 as *The Arte of Navigation* and ran into eight editions by 1616.

See Richard Hakluyt, *The Principall Navigations* (1589; ed. W. Raleigh, 12 vols, Glasgow, 1903–5).

## Borough, William (1536–1599), navigator and author.

Born at Northam, Devon, in 1536, William Borough was the younger brother of Stephen Borough (q.v.). In 1553, aged only sixteen, he served under his brother as an ordinary seaman on the first English expedition to Russia; he also sailed with Stephen on the voyage of 1556 which discovered Novaya Zemlya. Like his brother, he was subsequently employed by the Merchant Adventurers and sailed on the Muscovy Company's annual voyages to Russia; in 1574–5 he was employed as an agent, travelling overland between St Nicholas and Moscow. He made meticulous notes of all his observations, both at sea and on land, and in 1581 published *A Discourse of the Variation of the Compas, or Magneticall Needle*, in which he pointed out the uselessness of many charts of the period because of their cartographers' failure to observe variation, some places appearing twice on the same chart, several degrees apart.

At some date that is not known, but possibly before 1579, Borough followed his elder brother into the royal service. In 1582 he was appointed Clerk of the Ships. In the summer of 1586 he sailed with Sir John Hawkins (q.v.) to the Spanish coast, but having been delayed in the Channel for fear of a French invasion, they missed the treasure ships and returned home at the end of October with only a few prizes. Borough had earlier clashed with Hawkins over the so-called First Bargain relating to repairs to the Queen's ships, but on this voyage the two men worked harmoniously together, and thereafter Borough firmly supported Hawkins.

In 1587 he was appointed as second-in-command to Sir Francis Drake (q.v.) on the expedition that was to attack the Spanish fleet in Cadiz harbour and earn the popular name of 'singeing the King of Spain's beard'. Unfortunately the temperaments of the two commanders proved totally incompatible, and when Borough argued with his superior against a landing, Drake not only had him held prisoner in his own ship, the *Golden Lion*, but when the crew mutinied, he convened a court-martial and had Borough sentenced to death. On their return, Borough sent an account of his version of the episode to the Lord Admiral, Lord Howard of Effingham (see Howard, Charles), who considered the accusation unjust. The sentence was quashed, and Borough was restored both

47

to his seat on the Navy Board and, temporarily, to the command of his ship; but in order to avoid another clash with Drake, he was soon afterwards transferred from the *Golden Lion* to the *Galley Elenor* and given command of the supply ships in the Thames, where he remained throughout the Armada campaign.

Borough had far from excelled as a naval commander in the attack on Cadiz, and he was given no second chance to prove his worth. The last ten years of his life appear to have been spent in comparative obscurity. According to the article in *D.N.B.*, he had some part in the preparations for the voyage of Martin Frobisher (q.v.) to the Azores in 1589 and some connection with the expedition to Portugal under Drake and Sir John Norris (q.v.); this may have been with regard to supplies. In the same year he wrote of his intention to marry a certain Lady Wentworth. There was a threat to his life in 1590, which came to nothing. He died in 1599.

Some of William Borough's charts and manuscripts have been preserved and are at the British Museum, the Public Record Office, the National Maritime Museum, and elsewhere.

His short autobiography is printed in Richard Hakluyt, *The Principall Navigations* (1589; ed. W. Raleigh, 12 vols, Glasgow, 1903–5).

**Bothwell, 4th Earl of** (?1535–1578), see Hepburn, James.

**Bothwell, 5th Earl of** (d. 1624), see Hepburn, Francis Stewart.

**Boucher, Joan** (d. 1550), see Bocher, Joan.

**Bourchier, John** (?1467–1533), 2nd Baron Berners, statesman and writer, best known for his translation of Froissart's *Chronicles* (see Froissart, Jean, in *Lives Before the Tudors*).

Born in about 1467, John Bourchier was the son of Humphrey Bourchier, who was killed at the Battle of Barnet in 1471. He became the 2nd Baron Berners in 1474, on the death of his grandfather, William, the 1st Baron. He is believed to have studied at Oxford and at the age of fifteen to have taken part in an early, but unsuccessful, attempt to place Henry Tudor, Earl of Richmond, later Henry VII (q.v.), on the throne.

Berners's recorded military career began after the accession of Henry VII. In 1492 he signed a contract with the King, whereby he undertook to fight on his behalf overseas for the period of one year. In 1497 he helped to suppress the rebellion led by Perkin Warbeck (q.v.). Under Henry VIII (q.v.) he achieved more prominence and was on a number of occasions sent abroad on diplomatic missions. He travelled as a member of the King's retinue to Calais in 1513, and later the same year he was marshal of the Earl of Surrey's army in Scotland (see Howard, Thomas, 2nd Duke of Norfolk). Appointed Chancellor of the

Exchequer in 1516, two years later Berners was sent to Spain with John Kite, Archbishop of Armagh, for the purpose of negotiating an alliance between Henry and Charles V (q.v.). In 1520 he and his wife (Catherine, daughter of John Howard, 1st Duke of Norfolk) were in attendance at the meeting between the English and French monarchs at the Field of the Cloth of Gold.

In 1521 Berners became Lord Deputy of Calais. He was to hold this office, apart from a five-year break between 1526 and 1531, for the rest of his life. This appointment enabled him to pay off large debts which he had previously accumulated to the King. It also gave him ample leisure in which to pursue his literary inclinations, and in 1523 he published the first volume of his translation of Froissart's *Chronicles*, followed in 1525 by a second volume. Vividly written in a style that recaptured the glamour of medieval chivalry and manners, the work was dedicated to the King and apparently undertaken at his suggestion. Berners also translated into English the French romance, *The Boke Huon de Bordeux*, probably printed in 1534; Diego de San Pedro's *The Castell of Love*, printed in 1540; and, his most popular work, *The Golden Boke of Marcus Aurelius*, taken from the French version of Antonio de Guevara and published in 1534.

Berners died on 16 March 1533 and was buried at Calais, where, according to an inventory taken after his death, he had lived in sumptuous style.

*Portrait*: oil, by unknown artist of the Netherlands School: National Portrait Gallery, London.

**Boyle, Richard** (1566–1643), 1st Earl of Cork; Anglo-Irish adventurer, colonizer, landowner, capitalist, and politician, see *Lives of the Stuart Age*.

**Brackley, Viscount** (?1540–1617), see Egerton, Sir Thomas.

**Brandon, Charles** (?1484–1545), 1st Duke of Suffolk; soldier and statesman.

Charles Brandon was the son of William Brandon, standard-bearer to Henry VII, who was killed at Bosworth. He was born probably in 1484.

From an early age he was in the favour of Henry VIII (q.v.) and held a series of posts in the Royal Household, including those of Squire of the Royal Body, Chamberlain of the Principality of North Wales, Marshal of the King's Bench, and Ranger of the New Forest. His first marriage ended in divorce, and a second wife, Anne Browne, died in 1511. In May 1513 Brandon was created Viscount Lisle, having entered into a contract of marriage with his ward, Elizabeth Grey, Viscountess Lisle; she, however, on coming of age, refused to marry him.

Brandon fought with distinction in the French campaign of 1513, and the King, hoping that he would marry Margaret of Savoy, Regent of the Netherlands, created him Duke of Suffolk on 1 February 1514. Already, however, there was a bond of affection between Brandon and Henry's sister, Mary Tudor (q.v.), and when the French king, Louis XII, whom Mary was forced to marry for political reasons, died only a few months after the marriage and Brandon headed the mission sent by Henry to congratulate the new king, François I, that affection was cemented. There were difficulties: Suffolk already had a wife living, Margaret Mortimer, from whom he had obtained a divorce on grounds of consanguinity, and he also had many political enemies; furthermore Henry would not acquiesce in the marriage until he was sure of laying his hands upon the dowry which had been promised to his sister by Louis. Mary, fearing that she might be forced into another political marriage, persuaded Suffolk to marry her secretly in Paris at the end of February 1515.

They were spared the full force of Henry's anger by the intercession of Thomas Wolsey (q.v.), and eventually the King became reconciled to the marriage on the promise of £24,000 to be paid in annual instalments, plus the entire dowry Mary had received from Louis, as well as her plate and jewels. They were openly married at Greenwich on 13 May 1515, and the validity of their marriage was subsequently secured by a papal bull. It was a happy union, although unpopular in England, and most of their life was spent in retirement in the country. A son was born in 1516, but died young; of the two daughters of the marriage Frances, born 1517, was to marry the Marquess of Northampton and to become the mother of Lady Jane Grey (q.v.).

Suffolk accompanied the King to the Field of the Cloth of Gold in 1520, and in 1523 he commanded the unsuccessful invasion of northern France. Always high in Henry's favour, his influence and power increased when he supported the King's effort to obtain a divorce from Catherine of Aragon (q.v.), and especially after the fall of Wolsey. He was one of the noblemen sent to obtain the Great Seal from Wolsey, and one of those responsible for informing Catherine of the King's marriage with Anne Boleyn (q.v.); he acted as high steward at the coronation of the new Queen. In return for all these services he received a large share of the plunder after the suppression of the monasteries.

Following the death of his wife Mary in 1533, Suffolk remarried; his new bride was Katherine, Baroness Willoughby de Eresby, who had been his ward and the intended wife of his eldest son by Anne Browne. In 1540 he became Great Master of the King's Household, an office which he held for the rest of his life.

As commander of the English force which invaded France and captured Boulogne in 1544, Suffolk fulfilled his last military mission. He died at Guildford, Surrey, on 24 August 1545, and was buried at Windsor at the King's expense.

*Portraits:* oil, by unknown artist: National Portrait Gallery, London; oil, with Mary Tudor, by unknown artist: The Duke of Bedford Collection, Woburn Abbey; oil, by unknown artist, possibly Holbein, formerly in Norbert Fischman Collection, destroyed during World War II; other versions at Woburn Abbey, Longleat, and elsewhere.

**Bray, Sir Reginald** (d. 1503), statesman and architect.

Born in the parish of St John Bedwardine, near Worcester, Reginald Bray was the second son of Sir Richard Bray, a Privy Councillor and possibly physician to Henry VI (see *Lives Before the Tudors*).

In early life Bray held the post of receiver-general in the household of Sir Henry Stafford, second husband of the Countess of Richmond and Derby (see Beaufort, Margaret), in whose service he continued when she later married Thomas Stanley, 1st Earl of Derby. In 1478 he represented Newcastle, Staffordshire, in Parliament. He played a prominent part in bringing about the marriage of the young Earl of Richmond, later Henry VII (q.v.), to Elizabeth of York (q.v.). High in favour with Henry, he was created a Knight of the Bath at the King's coronation. Other honours soon followed: a Knight of the Garter and Privy Councillor, Bray was made joint chief justice of the forests south of the Trent, as well as under-treasurer of England and Chancellor of the Duchy of Lancaster. In 1492 he served as paymaster of the forces

sent to Brittany and in 1494 as high steward of the universities of Oxford and Cambridge. He was present in June 1497 at the Battle of Blackheath, in which Lord Audley led the Cornish rebels. Created a knight banneret for his part in quelling the uprising, Bray was subsequently granted the estates of the attainted Lord Audley in Surrey.

A skilled architect and a generous benefactor to churches, monasteries, and colleges in various parts of the realm, Sir Reginald Bray was commissioned by the King to carry out improvements to St George's Chapel at Windsor, where, at his own expense, he also built a chapel in the south aisle. He is said to have designed the Henry VII Chapel at Westminster, but this he did not live to see completed. He laid the foundation stone in January 1503 and died some six months later, on 5 August. He was buried in the Bray Chapel which he had founded at Windsor.

*Portrait:* engraving, by unknown artist, after a window in Great Malvern Church, Worcestershire: location not known.

**Breton, Nicholas** (?1545–1626), poet.

Descended from an old-established Essex family, Nicholas Breton was the son of William Breton (pronounced 'Britton') and his wife Elizabeth, daughter of John Bacon; his father, having settled in London, had amassed a considerable fortune in trade. Nicholas's birthdate is not known, but as it is on record that he was a boy at the time of his father's death in 1559, he was probably born not earlier than 1545 and not later than 1553.

The elder Breton left Nicholas the manor of Burgh-in-Marsh, near Wainfleet, Lincolnshire, as well as a considerable sum of money and other goods. He also left his wife a large estate, on condition that she did not remarry; but some time before October 1568 she married the poet George Gascoigne (q.v.), who thus became Nicholas's stepfather. Gascoigne was an extravagant spender, and a case was brought by the Lord Mayor against him and his wife for misuse of the property of the Breton children.

Nicholas is said to have studied at Oriel College, Oxford, but there is no documentary evidence to support this statement. By 1577 he was living in lodgings in Holborn, and although in his later work he attacked the dishonest practices of town life, he seems to have spent most of his time in London. He was a prolific writer, and from 1577 onwards published a constant stream of prose and poetical works. His chief patron was Mary, Countess of Pembroke, with whom he is believed to have had a relationship in the early days of his literary career; he dedicated other works to various patrons, including James I (see James VI of Scotland).

Breton married Ann Sutton at St Giles's Church, Cripplegate, on 14 January 1593. She bore him two sons and two daughters, one of whom died in 1603 and the other in 1625. The poet himself is believed to have died in about 1626, as his last published work bears that date.

A versatile writer, Nicholas Breton was at his best in pastoral lyrics such as *The Passionate Shepheard* (1604), and in the short verses which appeared in the miscellany *England's Helicon* (1600). Considered to be one of the best lyric poets of the day, his satires and essays were less successful. He wrote several character books: *Fantasticks*, an anthology of observations of people and things arranged according to seasons, days, and hours, and later *The Good and the Badde* and *Characters upon Essaies*. A full list of his work will be found in the *D.N.B.* entry. N.B. A Captain Nicholas Breton who served under the Earl of Leicester in the Low Countries in 1586 has sometimes been confused with the poet.

**Briggs, Henry** (1556–1630), mathematician, see *Lives of the Stuart Age*.

**Brinkelow, Henry** (d. 1546), satirist.

The son of Robert Brinkelow, a farmer of Kintbury, Berkshire, Henry Brinkelow was in his early years a friar of the Franciscan order. At a date that is not known he left the order, married, and became a citizen and mercer of London. He adopted the views of the reformers and began to write satirical pieces on religious and social subjects, using the pseudonym 'Roderigo Mors'. According to his own statement, Brinkelow was at one period banished from England by the bishops. He probably spent some time in Geneva, for his best known work, *The Complaynt of Roderyck Mors, sometyme a gray fryre, unto the Parlement house of Ingland, his natural cuntry*, was first published there in about 1545; a

second edition was dated Geneva, 1550, and a third published in Turin. His Will, proved in 1546 by his widow Margery, shows that Brinkelow was a man of means.

*The Complaynt* has been edited by J. M. Cowper for the Early English Text Society (1874), together with another of Brinkelow's writings, *The Lamentacion of a Christian against the Citie of London made by Roderigo Mors . . . Prynted at Jericho in the Land of Promes by Thome Trauth*, first published in 1542. Two *Supplications*, attributed by Cowper to Brinkelow, have been printed in the E.E.T.S. volume containing Simon Fish's *Supplication for the Beggars* (1871).

**Bromley, Sir Thomas** (1530–1587), lawyer, Lord Chancellor from 1579.

Thomas Bromley was born in 1530, a son of Sir George Bromley, who was reader at the Inner Temple; the family was an old-established one in Staffordshire and Shropshire. He was educated at Oxford, where he took the degree of B.C.L. in 1560.

Bromley represented Bridgnorth in the Parliament of 1558, Wigan in 1559, and Guildford in 1562. On taking up residence in London, where at one time he had a house near the Old Bailey, he entered the Inner Temple, becoming autumn reader there in 1566. He was appointed Recorder of London the same year and held that office until March 1569, when he was made Solicitor General. In 1572 Bromley acted as counsel for the crown at the trial of the Duke of Norfolk (see Howard, Thomas, 4th Duke), his first notable case. In 1574 he became Treasurer of the Inner Temple.

Reputed to be an honourable member of the legal profession, scrupulous in undertaking cases only when convinced of their justice, Bromley was patronized by Lord Burghley (see Cecil, William), Lord Hunsdon, and other eminent courtiers. He was increasingly consulted by Burghley on state matters, and in the spring of 1579, following the death of the Lord Keeper, Sir Nicholas Bacon (q.v.), he was rewarded with the office of Lord Chancellor. He took his seat in the House of Lords in January 1582, and in 1586 presided over the trial of Mary, Queen of Scots (q.v.). After sentence had been passed and Queen Elizabeth (q.v.) had in February 1587 been persuaded to sign the death warrant, Bromley affixed the Great Seal to it, acting with Burghley and other members of the Privy Council to effect its immediate execution. The strain of the trial and its aftermath seriously affected his health, however, and he died on 12 April the same year. He was buried in Westminster Abbey.

As Chancellor, Sir Thomas Bromley acquitted himself to the general satisfaction of the legal profession of the day, proving himself to be a good equity judge but wise enough to avoid conflict with the common-law judges. He was married, having by his wife, Elizabeth, daughter of Sir Adrian Fortescue, K.B., four sons and four daughters.

**Brooke, 1st Baron** (1554–1628), see Greville, Sir Fulke.

**Brooke, George** (1568–1603), conspirator.

The fourth and youngest son of William Brooke, 10th Baron Cobham, and his second wife, Frances, daughter of Sir John Newton, George Brooke was born at Cobham, Kent, on 17 April 1568. He was educated at King's College, Cambridge, where he matriculated in 1580 and took his M.A. in 1586. He obtained a prebend at York and was promised by Queen Elizabeth (q.v.) the post of Master of the Hospital of St

Cross, near Winchester. When shortly after her death James I (see James VI of Scotland) gave this post to one of his own candidates, the disappointed Brooke became associated with Sir Griffin Markham, Lord Grey of Wilton, and some Jesuit priests in a plot to seize the King's person, and to compel him to change the members of his Council and to tolerate Roman Catholicism. Generally known as the 'Bye' plot, it was also called the 'treason of the priests' and the 'Surprise' plot. Had it succeeded, Brooke was to have become Lord Treasurer.

Word of the conspiracy reached Sir Robert Cecil (q.v.), and Brooke and his fellow plotters were arrested in early July 1603 and taken to the Tower. In his confession Brooke divulged details not only of the 'Bye' plot, but also of the 'Main' plot in which his eldest brother, Baron Cobham (see Brooke, Henry), and Sir Walter Ralegh (q.v.) were involved; they too were arrested. Although he pleaded not guilty and appears to have counted on a pardon from Cecil, who had some years earlier married his sister Elizabeth, George Brooke was executed at Winchester on 5 December 1603. He left a wife, Elizabeth, daughter of Thomas, Lord Borough, one son, and two daughters.

**Brooke, Henry** (1564–1619), 11th Baron Cobham, conspirator. (N.B. In the *D.N.B.* and other works Brooke is frequently mentioned as the 8th Baron Cobham. *Burke's Peerage*, however, clearly demonstrates that he was the 11th Baron.)

Born on 22 November 1564, Henry Brooke was the eldest son of William Brooke, 10th Baron Cobham, and his second wife, Frances, daughter of Sir John Newton. Little is known of his early life, which was probably spent at the family seat of Cobham Hall in Kent. His father, Lord Chamberlain of the Household and Constable of the Tower, was also Lord Warden of the Cinque Ports and Lord Lieutenant of Kent, and as he grew up Henry too acquired considerable influence locally, being in 1588–9 returned as Member of Parliament for Kent. In 1593 he sat as Member for Hendon.

Brooke succeeded to the barony on the death of his father in April 1597, and some time afterwards he married Frances, daughter of the Earl of Nottingham (see Howard, Charles), and widow of the Earl of Kildare. His sister Elizabeth, who had died in 1596, had been married to Sir Robert Cecil (q.v.), and as an intimate of his brother-in-law, Cobham was hostile to Essex (see Devereux, Robert). He defeated the latter in a contest for the vacant office of Lord Warden of the Cinque Ports in 1597, and in 1599 was made a Knight of the Garter. In February 1601 he was among those who rallied to the support of the Lord Admiral against the Essex rebellion, one of the objectives of which was to remove Cobham from court.

In the summer of 1603 Sir Robert Cecil, investigating the conspiracy against James I (see James VI of Scotland) known as the 'Bye' plot, in which Cobham's youngest brother George Brooke (q.v.) was implicated, became suspicious of Cobham and Sir Walter Ralegh (q.v.); they were both arrested in early July and taken to the Tower. Brooke's confession laid bare the details not only of the 'Bye' conspiracy but also of a second treason known as the 'Main' plot which aimed to place Arabella Stuart (q.v.) on the throne; it was discovered that to this end Cobham had been in communication with the Spanish ambassador. Cobham declared that he had done so at the instigation of Ralegh, and at the latter's trial written evidence from Cobham convinced the judges of Ralegh's guilt. At his own trial on 18 November Cobham put up a cowardly defence and was condemned to death. After a last-minute reprieve on the scaffold in December, he was taken back to the Tower and remained there until 1617, when he was permitted, on health grounds, to pay a visit to Bath. He was on his way back to London when he suffered a stroke and, after remaining in a semi-conscious paralysed state for over a year, he died on 24 January 1619. His wife had deserted him in his disgrace, and Cobham was said to have died more of hunger than disease, being almost destitute; however, other sources show that the King paid him an annual allowance.

See titles listed under Sir Walter Ralegh and Arabella Stuart.

**Browne, Robert** (?1550–1633), the earliest Separatist from the Church of England, regarded as the founder of modern Congregationalism.

The third son of Anthony Browne and his wife Dorothy Boteler, Robert Browne was born in about 1550 at the family seat of Tolethorpe Hall, near Stamford, Rutland. His family had connections with a number of wealthy and influential people, including William Cecil (q.v.), later 1st Baron Burghley. Nothing is known of his early life until 1570, when he went to Cambridge, taking his B.A. at Corpus Christi College two years later. While at the university Browne came under the influence of Thomas Cartwright (q.v.), whose views on Church government were then attracting much attention. He may have been ordained in about 1573.

On leaving Cambridge, Browne spent three years as a schoolmaster in London, preaching on Sundays in Islington, but without a licence; he may also have held a post for a while in Northamptonshire. In 1578, on the outbreak of plague in London, he was ordered home by his father and soon afterwards returned to Cambridge, where he began preaching in the town and the surrounding villages, first against ordination and the prevailing parochial system, and later expounding his views on the separation of Church and State. Again he had no licence, and when his brother obtained one for him from the Bishop of Ely, Browne destroyed it.

In 1580 he went to Norwich, where he and his friend Robert Harrison established the first separate, or 'independent', church; its members became known as 'Brownists'. The following year Browne was arrested at Bury St Edmunds, charged with seditious preaching, and imprisoned. He obtained his release through the good offices of Burghley and shortly afterwards emigrated to Middelburg, in Zeeland, accompanied by his congregation. From there he was to issue a number of pamphlets, the most important of which were *A Booke which sheweth the Life and Manners of all True Christians* and *A Treatise of Reformation without Tarrying for Anie*, both printed in Middelburg in 1582.

The next two years were, however, fraught with dissension among the group, due largely to Browne's complex and difficult character, which made him intolerant and aggressive; the unhappy episode had its culmination in a violent quarrel with Harrison, who turned the rest against their leader. Browne then left Holland for Scotland, taking with him a few supporters.

After a cool reception in both Scotland and England, and another spell of imprisonment, from which he was once more rescued by Burghley, Browne again began preaching to Separatist congregations in Northampton. Excommunicated for ignoring his bishop's citation, and by this time sadly disillusioned, he eventually submitted to the Anglican doctrine and took up his former career of schoolmastering. In 1591, having previously been ordained as a deacon and priest in the Anglican Church, he was presented by Burghley with the living of Achurch in Northamptonshire. Browne was to spend the next forty years as rector of that country parish. This last period of his life was marred by marital troubles and by an incident in 1630 when, in a fit of temper, he struck a constable and was sent to jail. He died in Northampton in October 1633. His first wife, Alice Alden, of Yorkshire, who had borne him four sons and three daughters, had died in 1610, and although he had married again, Browne had separated from his second wife.

A somewhat unstable, eccentric character and a man who was not altogether consistent in his views, Robert Browne nevertheless had his followers, the 'Brownists' or 'Separatists' as they were known at the time, and it is from the movement which he founded that the present-day Congregationalist Church is derived.

Champlin Burrage, *The True Story of Robert Browne, Father of Congregationalism* (1906).

F. J. Powicke, *Robert Browne, Pioneer of Modern Congregationalism* (1910).

D. C. Smith, 'Robert Browne, Independent', *Church History*, vi (1937), pp. 289–349.

**Bruno, Giordano** (1548–1600), Italian philosopher, astronomer, and mathematician.

Born at Nola, near Naples, in 1548, Giordano Bruno was the son of a professional soldier. After studying at Naples, in 1565 he entered the Dominican convent in that city and in

1572 was ordained as a priest. Continuing his theological studies, he was threatened with excommunication because of his reading of Erasmus (q.v.) and his free discussion of the Arian heresy denying the divinity of Christ; he fled to Rome in 1576 and from there to northern Italy, in order to avoid a further excommunication process. Then he abandoned the Dominican order altogether and in 1578 settled in Geneva, where he earned his living as a proofreader and became a Calvinist. Within a few years, having crossed swords with the Calvinist leaders, he went to France, first to Toulouse and then, in 1581, to Paris, where he received the protection of the French King, Henri III.

In the spring of 1583 Bruno travelled to England, bearing a letter of introduction from Henri to the French ambassador in London. He soon made the acquaintance of influential men at court such as the Earl of Leicester (see Dudley, Robert) and Sir Philip Sidney (q.v.). It was at Sidney's suggestion that he gave a series of lectures at Oxford on the Copernican theory of the movement of the earth; but these aroused such a hostile reaction that Bruno soon returned to London. The following February, on the invitation of Sir Fulke Greville (q.v.), he entered into a discussion of the same theory with some Oxonian professors, which resulted in a quarrel. He spent the next eighteen months writing his six *Italian Dialogues*, in three of which he attacked contemporary Christian ethics and in the other three elaborated on his theory of the universe.

In October 1585 Bruno returned to Paris, but was obliged to flee that city after attacking the Aristotelians in his *120 Articles*. During the next few years he wandered from one German university to another, expounding his somewhat obscure philosophical doctrines. His *160 Articles*, attacking contemporary mathematicians and philosophers, was published in 1588, but other works on natural and mathematical magic, written at this time, did not appear until after his death. Formally excommunicated by the Lutheran Church at Helmstadt in January 1589, Bruno went on to Frankfurt, where he took up residence in a Carmelite convent and began lecturing to Protestant doctors; there he published three Latin poems, *De minimo, De monade,* and *De innumerabilibus sive de immenso*, reiterating the theories he had expressed in the *Dialogues* and putting forward an entirely new concept of the atomic basis of matter.

In August 1591 Bruno accepted an invitation to return to Italy. He failed to obtain the chair of mathematics at the University of Padua and on returning to Venice was denounced to the Inquisition in May 1592 for his heretical theories, arrested and tried. Extradited to Rome in January 1593, he tried to argue that his theories were not incompatible with Christian belief; when pressed by his inquisitors, however, he refused to make a retraction and was burned as a heretic at the Campo dei Fiori, Rome, on 17 February 1600.

One of the most important figures in the history of Western philosophy and thought, Giordano Bruno was years ahead of his time in anticipating modern science. Although he has been criticized for his adherence to the magical and the occult, his theories on a number of widely differing subjects have greatly influenced philosophers and scientists from the seventeenth century to the present day.

The standard edition of Bruno's six dialogues is that by Giovanni Gentile, *Dialoghi Italiani* (3rd ed. by Giovanni Aquilecchia, 1958). Not all of his writings have been translated into

English, but a comprehensive and up-to-date bibliography will be found in the appendix to Aquilecchia's biography listed below.

G. Aquilecchia, *Giordano Bruno* (Rome, 1971).

Dorothea Waley Singer, *Giordano Bruno: His Life and Thought* (1950).

Frances A. Yates, *Giordano Bruno and the Hermetic Tradition* (1964).

Frances A. Yates, *The Art of Memory* (1966).

**Bucer or Butzer, Martin** (1491–1551), German Protestant reformer.

Bucer was born at Schettstadt, Alsace, on 11 November 1491, and studied at Heidelberg, where he was influenced by the works of Erasmus (q.v.) and Martin Luther (q.v.). He entered the Dominican order in 1506, but in 1521 he withdrew from it and subsequently married a former nun. Following excommunication, he sought the protection offered by his parents' citizenship of Strasbourg and settled there.

As leader of the reformed church in Strasbourg from 1523 onwards, he worked ceaselessly for a reconciliation between Luther and Ulrich Zwingli (q.v.), the Swiss reformer, both of whose strongholds bordered on Strasbourg. He was not successful in this aim, but under his leadership there were in Strasbourg far fewer persecutions of Anabaptists and other minority groups than elsewhere. He tried all his life to heal the Protestant–Catholic rift, and put forward a series of compromise solutions as well as his own programme of reform. Bucer had accepted Erasmus's ideals of Christian humanism and he sought a rebirth, or conversion, of man and all aspects of society through the preaching of the true Gospel. In 1549 he was strongly opposed to the acceptance by Strasbourg of the Augsburg Interim of Charles V (q.v.), but was overruled and discharged.

Archbishop Cranmer (q.v.) invited him to England, where in December 1549 he was appointed Regius Professor of Divinity at Cambridge. He spent the last years of his life supporting and defending the moderate reform programme of Cranmer and Nicholas Ridley (q.v.) against the more radical one of John Hooper (q.v.) and John Knox (q.v.), and had some influence on the Second Prayer Book which was published in 1552.

Bucer died at Cambridge on 28 February 1551. In the reign of Mary I (q.v.) his body was exhumed and burned at the stake together with those of other so-called 'heretics'.

Hastings Eells, *Martin Bucer* (1931).

Constantin Hopf, *Martin Bucer and the English reformation* (1946).

*Portrait:* oil, by unknown artist: Edinburgh University.

**Buchanan, George** (1506–1582), Scottish humanist, historian, and poet.

Buchanan was born in February 1506 in the parish of Killearn, Stirlingshire, in humble circumstances, although his father claimed descent from the house of Lennox. Educated initially at local schools, he was sent by an uncle to study at the University of Paris, but returned penniless to Scotland on the latter's death, and took part in the expedition of the Duke of Albany (see Stewart, John) against England in 1523.

After resuming his studies and taking his B.A. at St Andrews, he decided to go back to Paris, where he took a post as Bursar to the Scots College and lived in near-poverty, graduating as an M.A. of the university in 1528. He joined the staff of the Collège de Ste Barbe, where he rejected the old methods and began to earn a reputation as a teacher of Latin

according to the new grammar book of Thomas Linacre (q.v.).

In about 1532 Buchanan became tutor to the young Earl of Cassillis, with whom he returned to Scotland two or three years later. There James V (q.v.) appointed him tutor to the eldest of his natural sons, the future Earl of Moray (see Stewart, Lord James). His stay in Scotland was shortlived, however; some satirical verses written against the Franciscans led to his being attacked as a heretic in 1539, and he escaped through the window of his prison in St Andrews and fled to London.

During the next twenty years he held teaching posts at Bordeaux (where Montaigne was one of his pupils), at the University of Coimbra in Portugal (where he was imprisoned by the Inquisition), and at the Collège de Boncourt in Paris; from 1554 to 1559 he was tutor to the son of the Comte de Brissac, one of the marshals of France. In this last post he began to write *De Sphaera*, a long poem in Latin defending the old Ptolemaic system against that

advocated by Copernicus (q.v.), and other poems.

On his return to Scotland, in about 1561, Buchanan was hailed as one of the foremost poets of his generation. He professed himself a Protestant and sat in the General Assembly; in 1566 he was appointed Principal of St Leonard's College, St Andrews. He also acted as court poet and taught Livy to Mary, Queen of Scots (q.v.), but after the murder of Darnley (see Stewart, Henry) in 1567 he became one of her most bitter enemies. He helped the Regent Moray to prepare the case against her presented to Queen Elizabeth I (q.v.), and vouched that the 'casket letters' were in Mary's own handwriting; subsequently he published his own vivid and hostile account of the Queen's conduct.

Under the Regent Lennox, Buchanan was made tutor to the young King, James VI (q.v.), and appointed Keeper of the Privy Seal, a post which he resigned in 1578. Thereafter his influence declined, possibly on account of ill-health or because of disagreements with the later Regent, Morton (see Douglas, James). The most important of his political writings, *De Jure Regni*, which asserted that kings exist only by the will and for the good of the people and that subjects may resist misgovernment, was published in 1579; it proved tremendously popular and played a considerable part in shaping the democratic inclinations of the Scots. The *Rerum Scoticarum Historia*, which Buchanan was finishing at the time of his death, also greatly influenced contemporary thought and remained a standard work for many years.

An eloquent, unconventional personality, and regarded as the finest Latin poet in Renaissance Europe, Buchanan was a man of great erudition; he excelled in virtually every field of literature, and by his example did much to encourage higher education in Scotland. Labelled as a turncoat by the followers of Mary, he was nevertheless revered by most Scots as a humanist and hero of the Reformation. He died on 29 September 1582 and was buried in Greyfriars churchyard, Edinburgh.

P. Hume Brown, *George Buchanan, Humanist and Reformer* (1890).

*Portraits:* two oils, both by unknown artists, probably early seventeenth century and late seventeenth or early eighteenth century, respectively: Edinburgh University; oil, by unknown artist: Bodleian Library, Oxford; oil on panel, by unknown artist: Scottish National Portrait Gallery, Edinburgh; oil, by unknown artist, after A. van Brounckhorst, 1580: National Portrait Gallery, London.

**Buckhurst, 1st Baron** (1536–1608), see Sackville, Thomas.

**Buckingham, 3rd Duke of** (1478–1521), see Stafford, Edward, 3rd Duke of Buckingham.

**Bull, John** (?1562–1628), organist and composer.

John Bull's parentage and birth are obscure, but he is believed to have come from a Somerset family and to have been born in about 1562. Educated as a choir boy in the Chapel Royal under William Blitheman (possibly also under William Byrd, q.v.), he was appointed organist of Hereford Cathedral in December 1582. He held this post until January 1585, when he returned to the Chapel Royal. On Blitheman's death in 1591 he succeeded his old master as organist. He had taken his B.Mus. at Oxford in July 1586 and was to obtain his doctorate of music at both Cambridge and Oxford (the latter in 1592).

In 1596 the Queen appointed Bull as the first Professor of Music at the newly-founded Gresham College (see Gresham, Sir Thomas). This post was tenable only by an unmarried man, and in 1607 Bull resigned from it prior to his marriage.

Several years previously, in 1601, he had made an extensive tour on the Continent, where he was greatly admired for his virtuosity on the keyboard. What finally decided him to leave England is not known; it seems that although he retained his post at the Chapel Royal after the death of Elizabeth I (q.v.), there must have been some later trouble at court which led to his departure from the country, without permission, in 1613. He went first to Brussels, where the British ambassador declared him to be a fugitive from punishment for various misdeeds; this was not proved, and Bull was nevertheless warmly welcomed by the Archduke Albert and entered the royal service. In 1617 he settled at Antwerp, where he was appointed organist at the cathedral. He died there on 12 or 13 March 1628.

Bull has been called the 'Liszt of his age'. He played an important part in the development of harpsichord music and ranks as one of the founders of keyboard repertory. Through his close friendship with the contemporary Amsterdam organist, J. P. Sweelinck, he undoubtedly had an influence on the Dutch and North German school of organ playing as well as on Scheidt and other German musicians, including, much later, Bach.

Hardly any of Bull's vocal music has survived; his reputation therefore rests largely on compositions for the virginal and organ, of which there are about 150 pieces extant. In 1611 Bull collaborated with William Byrd and Orlando Gibbons (see *Lives of the Stuart Age*) in *Parthenia*, the first collection of virginal music to be printed in England.

59

M. H. Glyn, *About Elizabethan virginal music and its composers* (1934).

L. Henry, *Dr John Bull, 1562–1628* (1937).

W. Mellers, 'John Bull and English keyboard music', *Musical Quarterly*, 40 (July-Oct. 1954).

*Portrait:* oil, by unknown artist, 1589: Music School, Oxford University.

**Bullen, Sir Thomas** (1477–1539), see Boleyn, Sir Thomas.

**Burbage, James** (*c.* 1530–1597), actor, and builder of the first theatre in England.

The exact date of James Burbage's birth is not known. It has been claimed that he came from Stratford-on-Avon, but according to his son Cuthbert's application for a coat of arms in 1634, the Burbages belonged to a Hertfordshire family.

Originally a joiner by trade, James Burbage is first mentioned in the records in May 1574, when he heads the list of players in the Earl of Leicester's company. He had probably joined that company several years earlier and almost certainly took a prominent part in the entertainment provided by the Earl of Leicester (see Dudley, Robert) at Kenilworth on the occasion of the Queen's visit there in 1575. Burbage had by this time married the daughter of a fellow actor, Ellen (or Helen) Braine (or Brayne) of London. She was to bear him three daughters and two sons, Richard (q.v.), who became the greatest actor of his day, and Cuthbert.

In April 1576 Burbage took his first step towards a venture that had probably been in his mind for some time, arising out of opposition from the Lord Mayor of London to performances in the courtyards of inns within the City boundary: the building of his own theatre. With financial help from his father-in-law, he obtained from a Mr Giles Allen a twenty-one-year lease of houses and land situated between Finsbury Fields and the Bishopsgate–Shoreditch road. There, on a site reached by a path across the Fields, he set up an enclosed wooden structure, the first purpose-built playhouse in England.

'The Theatre', as it came to be known, opened in the summer of 1577 and was an immediate success with the public, making large profits for its owner. Its popularity seems to have been hardly affected by the opening of a rival theatre, the Curtain, in the same neighbourhood soon afterwards. At 'The Theatre' dramatic performances were interspersed with occasional fencing displays; Burbage himself is not thought to have been a great actor, but he personally selected and trained the players, who included his father-in-law and his young son, Richard. Among those who made their reputation at Shoreditch was Richard Tarleton (q.v.), the best comic actor of the Elizabethan period.

Although for the next twenty years the Puritans clamoured for the 'plucking down' of all playhouses, Burbage, encouraged by his success, in 1596 acquired part of a former Dominican monastery, situated in the City between Ludgate Hill and the river Thames. Amid angry protests from neighbouring tenants, he proceeded to convert the building (which before the dissolution of the monasteries had belonged to the Black Friars) into another playhouse. Because of opposition, however, he was forced to lease it to a private children's company, and the 'Blackfriars Theatre' as such was not in fact opened until shortly after Burbage's death in 1597.

At the time of his death, James Burbage was engaged in a lawsuit with Giles Allen over the renewal of his Shoreditch lease. The dispute was carried on by his sons Richard and Cuthbert, who inherited their father's property. Ultimately Richard Burbage, who continued to live at the family home in Holywell Street, Shoreditch, had 'The Theatre' removed to Bankside, where it was re-named the 'Globe' (see under Burbage, Richard).

J. O. Halliwell-Phillips, *Outlines of the Life of Shakespeare* (1885).

Charlotte Carmichael Stopes, *Burbage, and Shakespeare's Stage* (1913).

**Burbage, Richard** (?1567–1619), actor.

Richard Burbage was probably born in London in about 1567. As the son of James Burbage (q.v.) and Ellen (or Helen) Braine (or Brayne), he was associated with the theatre from early childhood. Trained by his father, he made his début as a young boy at the latter's Shoreditch theatre and by the age of twenty had become very popular.

He joined the Earl of Leicester's players in about 1587 and was to act with this company through its various changes of name – Earl of Derby's, Lord Chamberlain's – until in 1603, on the accession of James I (see James VI of Scotland), it became the King's Men. One member of that company from about 1594 onwards was William Shakespeare (q.v.), with whom Burbage was to be associated for many years and whose leading characters he interpreted so brilliantly. At Christmas 1594, Shakespeare and another actor, William Kempe, were summoned to court to play before the Queen at Greenwich; this was the first of many court performances.

When James Burbage died in 1597, Richard and his brother Cuthbert inherited the theatres at Shoreditch and Blackfriars. They also inherited the dispute started by their father with Giles Allen concerning the renewal of the Shoreditch lease. This theatre had been closed in 1597, and when it appeared that Allen might pull it down, the Burbage brothers decided to demolish it themselves and rebuild it at Southwark. With the help of a carpenter, Peter Street, some time towards the end of 1598 or early 1599 they dismantled the original theatre and had the timbers carried to the new site. The project was a costly one, and they had to borrow heavily in order to carry it through; Shakespeare was among those who put up money. The new theatre, named the Globe, was completed in the autumn of 1599.

Richard Burbage made his name at the Globe. Although originally he had intended that Southwark should be used as a summer playhouse, and Blackfriars in the winter months, in practice he himself acted much less frequently at Blackfriars. Between 1595 and 1619 Burbage was in demand by all the leading dramatists, as well as Shakespeare, for whom he was the first player to create Richard III, Hamlet, Macbeth, Othello, Lear, and Romeo. Being the major shareholder in the Globe, he also accumulated considerable wealth. This enabled him, in 1609, to buy out the lessees of the Blackfriars theatre and to install in it the company to which he still belonged, the King's Men. As at the Globe, the players were to a greater or lesser extent 'sharers' in the theatre, while the bulk of the profits were reserved to Burbage.

On 29 June 1613 the Globe was burned down during a performance, and Burbage was lucky to escape with his life; immediately he set to work to rebuild the theatre, which reopened the following year. There were still several years of acting in front of him.

In appearance Burbage was short and stout. He had married in about 1601 and up to the time of his death lived with his wife, Winifred, and their several children, in the house formerly occupied by his father in Holywell Street, Shoreditch. When he died, at some date between 9 and 13 March 1619, he was buried at St Leonard's in that parish.

Richard Burbage was the greatest actor of the Elizabethan stage. He excelled at tragedy and was perhaps most popular for his portrayal of Richard III. Another talent was painting: at Dulwich College today there is a portrait of a woman which is believed to be by Burbage; at one time the Chandos portrait of Shakespeare was attributed to him.

J. P Collier, *Lives of the Actors in Shakespeare's Plays* (1846) (N.B. To be used with caution, as some of the documents quoted are not authentic).
J. O. Halliwell-Phillips, *Outlines of the Life of Shakespeare* (1885).
Charlotte Carmichael Stopes, *Burbage, and Shakespeare's Stage* (1913).

*Portrait*: oil, by unknown artist (? himself), *c.* 1615: Dulwich College Picture Gallery.

**Burghley, 1st Baron** (1520–1598), see Cecil, William.

**Burgundy, Duchess of** (1446–1503), see Margaret, Duchess of Burgundy.

**Butcher, Joan** (d. 1550), see Bocher, Joan.

**Butler, Thomas** (1532–1614), 10th Earl of Ormonde, called 'The Black Earl'.

The son and heir of James Butler, 9th Earl of Ormonde, and Lady Joan Fitzgerald, heiress of the 11th Earl of Desmond, Thomas Butler was born in 1532. He was brought up in England at the court of Henry VIII (q.v.), where he absorbed pro-English sympathies and became a Protestant. His father was poisoned in October 1546, and Thomas, at the age of fourteen, succeeded to the earldom. He became known as 'The Black Earl' on account of his dark hair and swarthy complexion.

In 1554 Ormonde went to Ireland to put down a revolt of the peasantry on his estates. Appointed a Privy Councillor and Lord Treasurer of Ireland, he tried by peaceful means to reconcile the Irish and English, and in 1561 he managed to persuade the rebellious Shane O'Neill (q.v.) to submit to Queen Elizabeth (q.v.). However, the continued aggression of the Earl of Desmond, whose family had traditionally maintained a feud with the Ormondes, finally drove him to retaliate, with the result that in 1565 both Earls were summoned to court by the Queen and made to enter recognizances to keep the peace.

Elizabeth was noticeably attracted by Ormonde, granting him favours and keeping him at court for nearly five years. In the meanwhile Desmond took advantage of his rival's absence to ravage the Earl's lands in Munster, for which he was committed to the Tower by the Lord Deputy, Sir Henry Sidney (q.v.). Ormonde returned to Ireland in 1569, to find that his brothers had allied themselves with James Fitzmaurice Fitzgerald in resisting the proposed 'plantation' of Munster. Although at one time suspected by Sidney of disloyalty, Ormonde continued to fight for England against his own countrymen, putting down the Earl of Thomond's rebellion early in 1570 and, with the help of Humphrey Gilbert (q.v.), the Munster risings of 1571. Following the release and return of Desmond to Ireland in 1573, he campaigned fiercely against his old adversary, finally crushing him in Kerry in 1583.

In 1588 Ormonde helped to massacre the Spaniards who had been wrecked on the Irish coast after the Armada; for his services the Queen made him a Knight of the Garter. Appointed Lieutenant-General of the Army in Ireland in October 1597, he made strenuous efforts to put down the rebellion of Tyrone (see O'Neill, Hugh) in 1598–9, in spite of difficulties arising from an uneasy relationship with Essex (see Devereux, Robert), each man entertaining suspicions as to the loyalty of the other. In 1602 the Queen granted Ormonde the much-confiscated lands in Munster, and in 1612 he became Vice-Admiral of Ireland. He died on 22 November 1614, aged eighty-two.

Of all the Irish lords of the Elizabethan age, Thomas Butler, 10th Earl of Ormonde, was the most consistently loyal to the crown.

Richard Bagwell, *England under the Tudors* (3 vols; 1885–90).
Cyril Falls, *Elizabeth's Irish Wars* (1950).

**Butzer, Martin** (1491–1551), see Bucer, Martin.

**Byrd, William** (?1543–1623), organist and composer.

Nothing definite is known of Byrd's early life, but he was probably born in Lincolnshire in about 1543. He was a pupil and protégé of Thomas Tallis (q.v.) and may therefore have been related to the Thomas Byrd who was a member of the Chapel Royal with Tallis in the reigns of Edward VI (q.v.) and Mary I (q.v.).

The earliest authenticated fact about Byrd is his appointment as organist at Lincoln Cathedral in February 1563. He spent nearly ten years at Lincoln, during which time he married his first wife, Juliana Birley; the marriage took place on 14 September 1568 at St Margaret's-in-the-Close, where their two eldest children, Christopher and Elizabeth, were later baptized.

At the end of 1572 Byrd and his family moved to London. He had been appointed a Gentleman of the Chapel Royal in February 1570, but it was not until nearly three years later that he actually took up this appointment, sharing the duties of organist at the Chapel Royal with Tallis.

The close personal and professional association of Byrd and Tallis lasted until the latter's death in 1585 and was of great

consequence in the musical world. In January 1575 Queen Elizabeth (q.v.) granted the two men a licence for the printing, publishing, and sale of music, as well as for the printing of music paper – a monopoly that was to last for twenty-one years. That same year they produced the first work to be published under this imprint: an important collection of *Cantiones Sacrae*, dedicated to the Queen and containing sixteen motets by Tallis and eighteen by Byrd. This was a manifesto of what the new school of Elizabethan composers, of which they were the leaders, could achieve.

In 1577 Byrd went to live at Harlington, Middlesex. About 1580 he became reconciled to the new and aggressive counter-Reformation Catholicism of the Jesuits; this ardent faith is magnificently expressed in his work. It is remarkable that in spite of his openly professed Catholicism (some of his published work was dedicated to prominent Catholics, and he and his family were listed as recusants from 1592 onwards), Byrd continued to hold down his position at the Chapel Royal. Certainly his loyalty to the government was never questioned; he was quite unpolitical, thoroughly English and never went abroad. He dedicated other work to the Queen and members of the court, and he also composed music for the Anglican Church.

After the death of Tallis in 1585, Byrd published several collections of his own music: *Psalms, Sonets and Songs of Sadnes and pietie*, for five voices (1588); *Songs of sundrie natures* (1589); and two further volumes of *Cantiones Sacrae*, for five voices (1589 and 1591). In 1591 he also prepared a manuscript volume of keyboard music for 'my ladye Nevell' (now in the possession of the Marquess of Abergavenny, at Eridge Park, near Tunbridge Wells, Kent, transcribed and

published in 1926). Some of his keyboard music was copied and included in the *Fitzwilliam Virginal Book* (now at Cambridge).

The date of his second marriage is not clear, but in 1592 Byrd with his wife Ellen, two sons and three daughters, moved to Stondon Massey, near Ongar in Essex. Here the composer unfortunately became involved in lengthy litigation concerning the lease and ownership of Stondon Place, which had been sequestrated to the crown in 1583 following the attainder of its owner, William Shelley. Only after the death of Mrs Shelley in 1610 was Byrd able to purchase the property. He was to live there until his death on 4 July 1623.

In the last years of his life Byrd issued more of his work: two sets of *Gradualia* (1605 and 1607); a collection of three Masses composed in the 1590s; and in 1611 his last published work, *Psalms, Songs and Sonnets*. That same year there appeared the first collection of virginal music to be printed in England: *Parthenia*, to which Byrd, in collaboration with John Bull (q.v.) and Orlando Gibbons (see *Lives of the Stuart Age*), contributed eight pieces.

William Byrd has been called the father of keyboard music and one of the founders of the English madrigal school. He was a pioneer in the composition of works for the virginal and string instruments and the most prolific English composer of his time. His output was enormous: more than 140 pieces for the keyboard and some sixty anthems. In his songwriting he showed both originality and versatility and he was one of the first to write songs for solo voice with instrumental accompaniment. He was keen that everyone should be taught to sing properly; in a preface to one of his collections he listed eight reasons for people to sing well, one of which was that 'there is no music of instruments whatsoever which is as good as that which is made by the voice of Man'. Byrd was greatly esteemed by his contemporaries, both as a composer and performer; his work paved the way for the later achievements of musicians such as Giles Farnaby (q.v.), John Bull, Orlando Gibbons, and Thomas Tomkins, who was one of Byrd's pupils. When all is said, Byrd was probably the greatest of English composers.

Byrd's *Collected Works* have been edited by E. H. Fellowes (1937–50); see also *Tudor Church Music*, edited by P. C. Buck and others (10 vols; 1923–30), and the *Fitzwilliam Virginal Book*, edited by J. A. Fuller-Maitland and W. Barclay Squire (1899). Byrd's madrigals have been published in volumes 14 to 16 of *The English Madrigal School*, edited by E. H. Fellowes (1913–24).

E. H. Fellowes, *William Byrd* (rev. ed. 1948).

M. H. Glyn, *About Elizabethan virginal music and its composers* (2nd ed. 1934).

G. Murray, 'William Byrd', *Downside Review*, lv (1937).

J. A. Westrup, 'William Byrd (1543–1623)', *Music and Letters*, xxiv (1943).

*Portrait*: engraving, by M. van der Gucht, after V. Haym, 1730: British Museum, London.

**Cabot, John** (*c.* 1450–*c.* 1499), navigator and explorer.

There are few known facts about John Cabot's life and these, as well as details of his voyages, have been much disputed by historians and cartographers.

It is believed that John Cabot (Giovanni Caboto in Italian) was Genoese by birth but that in about 1461 he moved to Venice, where he became a naturalized citizen in 1476. His work for a Venetian mercantile firm trading in spices from beyond the Levant probably involved him in voyages to the eastern Mediterranean, and he may even have travelled as far as Mecca; while acquiring navigational skills he seems to have developed the idea (quite independently of Columbus (q.v.)) that the spices might be obtained by sailing westwards to the east coast of Asia. Between the years 1484 and 1494 his movements are uncertain, and it is possible that having been denied support for such a voyage of exploration in Venice, Cabot sought the patronage of Spain and Portugal. When he was unsuccessful, he determined to try England, and at some time in the years 1490–5 he arrived, with his wife and three sons, in Bristol.

News of Columbus's success spurred the wealthy Bristol merchants, anxious themselves to profit from the spice trade, to support the Italian with men and ships. Cabot did not believe Columbus's claim to have discovered the mainland, holding the view that he had not gone far enough. He managed to convince Henry VII (q.v.), who, remembering that he had once been offered but had turned down Columbus's enterprise, on 5 March 1496 issued letters patent granting Cabot and his heirs a monopoly of any trade they might establish in the lands they discovered and giving the port of Bristol the sole right to operate such trade.

Cabot's first voyage took place in 1496, when he sailed from Bristol with one ship, but was forced to return on account of stormy weather, lack of provisions, and mutiny among his crew. On 20 May 1497 he set out again in a 50-ton vessel, the *Matthew*, with a crew of about eighteen men; she was the first English ship to cross the Atlantic. They sailed around Ireland and then took first a northerly and then a westerly course, sighting land on 24 June. A small landing party went ashore and took possession in the name of Henry VII; Cabot unfurled the English and the Venetian flags. They met no natives, although they saw signs of occupation, and since the weather was hot, Cabot believed that he had discovered the north-east coast of Asia (in fact his true landing place has never been established, but it was on what is now either the Maine, the Novia Scotia, or the Newfoundland coast). He spent the next three weeks exploring the coastline, but did not go ashore again. Taking advantage of good weather, he made the return crossing from what is now southern Newfoundland to Brittany in fifteen days and was back in Bristol on 6 August.

He received an enthusiastic welcome and soon became a well-known and popular figure in the streets of Bristol and at court; Henry VII gave him a gratuity of £10 and a pension of £20 for having added a 'new isle' to his realm. On 3 February 1498 Cabot was granted letters patent for a new expedition, which was to be much better equipped than the previous one. The plan was to return to the original landing place and continue from there to the tropics and Cipango (Japan) in order to promote trade in spices and precious stones.

Cabot sailed from Bristol on his third voyage early in May 1498. There are next to no records of this expedition, but it is known that one ship was badly damaged early on and put into an Irish port; there were probably four other vessels which sailed on westwards. No further trace of them exists, although there has been much speculation as to whether or not Cabot reached North America again, or, as some have suggested, explored the tropics and even the Caribbean. The fact that his pension was still being paid out of the royal exchequer in 1499 is not conclusive proof that Cabot returned safely to England, since it may have been paid to his wife; one contemporary source definitely states that the expedition was lost at sea.

John Cabot's reputation has suffered because of the lack of adequate records, yet his early exploration of the North American continent was the start of a much later British claim to Canada. The idea which he conceived of sailing westwards was not an imitation of Columbus, but an original plan of his own based on his understanding of Marco Polo's writings and a thorough study of the maps and globes then available. His second son, Sebastian Cabot (q.v.), became one of the most brilliant cartographers of the age.

J. A. Williamson, *The Cabot Voyages and Bristol Discovery under Henry VII* (Hakluyt Society, 1962).
G. P. Winship, *Cabot Bibliography* [with introductory essay on the careers of the Cabots] (New York, 1900).

**Cabot, Sebastian** (*c.* 1480–1557), navigator, cosmographer, and cartographer.

Sebastian Cabot was the second son of John Cabot (q.v.) and was born probably in Venice some time before 1484; he was brought to England by his parents in about 1490–5, when the family settled in Bristol. Very little is known of his early life, and there is no evidence that Sebastian accompanied his father on his voyages. He was apparently far removed from the likeable personality of John Cabot, being, in the words of one historian, 'a vain egoist, fond of giving vent to mysterious utterances containing a maximum of self-praise and a minimum of hard fact', and apt to take for himself the glory that should have been his father's by suppressing the truth about the latter's voyages.

It is not known when he entered the royal service, but by 1512 he was employed as cartographer to Henry VIII (q.v.). Before that date he had probably drawn up charts and maps for the voyages made by various Bristol merchants in 1501 and 1502; it also seems fairly certain that Sebastian himself took an expedition, partly financed by the King, to the New World in 1508 or 1509 in an attempt to find what we know as the North-West Passage. He discovered the coast of Labrador or 'New Found Land' (then thought to be China) and the Hudson Strait; he may even have penetrated as far north as the Foxe Channel before his crew mutinied in the face of floating ice and he turned for home.

In 1512 Cabot accompanied the force sent to France under the command of the

Marquess of Dorset to aid Ferdinand of Aragon against the French. Shortly afterwards he transferred his services to Spain and for the next few years lived in Seville. At some time during this period he was commissioned as a captain in the Spanish navy, but a voyage he was to have made in 1516 was cancelled as a result of the death of the Spanish King. Cabot may have returned briefly to England at about this time; he was certainly back in Spain in 1518, when the Emperor Charles V (q.v.) appointed him as pilot major and examiner of pilots, and he was also made a member of the Spanish Council of the New Indies.

In 1521 Cabot probably went to England to discuss a voyage to the west planned by Henry VIII, but this came to nothing due to lack of subscriptions, and in 1525 he took command of a Spanish expedition whose purpose was to develop trade with the Orient. Lured by reports of the riches to be found in the Rio de la Plata region of South America, however, he disregarded his orders and spent nearly three years on abortive exploration there; on returning to Spain he was held responsible for the expedition's failure and was banished to Africa for two years, but two years later he was pardoned and reappointed as pilot major.

On the accession of Edward VI (q.v.) to the English throne, Cabot was invited to return to England, which he did in 1548; he was granted a pension the following year. Although Charles V tried hard to get him to return to Spain, Cabot remained in the service of England for the rest of his life. In 1551 he was appointed governor of the newly-formed Merchant Adventurers of England, for whom he helped to organize three voyages, including that of 1553 under Hugh Willoughby and Richard Chancellor which set out to find a North-East Passage to China. He died in London in 1557.

Sebastian Cabot was one of the most experienced cartographers of his day; a draft of his celebrated 'mappe-monde' has been preserved at the Bibliothèque Nationale in Paris. He was immensely interested in the shape of the world and held some original ideas concerning the geography of the polar regions. The first to look for the North-West Passage, towards the end of his life Cabot also promoted a search for a North-East Passage to China which, although equally unsuccessful, led directly to the development of trade between England and Russia. In England from 1548 onwards he was a chief influence on the next generation of seamen, stimulating them to new voyages of discovery.

R. Biddle, *Memoir of Sebastian Cabot* (1915).
E. G. R. Taylor, *Tudor Geography* (1930).
J. A. Williamson, *The Cabot Voyages and Bristol Discovery under Henry VII* (Hakluyt Society, 1962).
G. P. Winship, *Cabot Bibliography* [with introductory essay on the careers of the Cabots] (New York, 1900).

*Portraits*: copies of an original portrait destroyed by fire in 1845: New York Historical Society and Massachusetts Historical Society, U.S.A.

**Calvin, John** (1509–1564), French theologian and reformer.

John Calvin was born on 10 July 1509 at Noyon, in Picardy, where his father, Gérard Cauvin (the name 'Calvin' comes from *Calvinus*, the Latinized form of Cauvin), had risen from humble birth to become secretary to the bishop. He was from an early age destined for an ecclesiastical career.

Calvin was brought up in the household of the Hangest family in Noyon, and later went to Paris to study theology, and then to Orleans to study law. In Paris he had his first contact with the spirit of humanism, and he returned there in 1531 to learn Greek and Hebrew. By 1533 the French court was favourable to the humanists, but when Calvin's friend Nicholas Cop, newly elected rector of the university, dared to quote some passages from Luther (q.v.) in his address, both he and Calvin were forced to flee the city. At Angoulême, in the home of Louis du Tillet, where he found refuge, Calvin spent the next few months in reading and reflection.

The date of his conversion to Protestantism is not clear, but it is considered to have been some time between 1528 and 1533. By the following year, 1534, he was already regarded as the intellectual leader of those who advocated reform in France. His statement of the French Protestant faith, originally written in Latin, but published in French under the title *L'Institution de la réligion chrétienne* ('Institutes of the Christian Religion') in Basle in 1536, was immediately recognized as an important statement of the reformed theology. In it he not only put forward his anti-Roman opinions, but expounded his views on original sin, predestination, and election.

Calvin intended to settle in either Basle or Strasbourg, but on his way there he was stopped in Geneva on account of the war between François I and Charles V (q.v.). The reformer Farel enlisted his aid; Calvin began to lecture in the city and was later received as a pastor. The Farel-Calvin influence became increasingly strong, but they were both expelled by the city council at Easter 1538 following a row over the authority of ministers. After a happy three-year interlude in Strasbourg, where Calvin established relations with Martin Bucer (q.v.) and produced a number of new treatises, as well as a revised edition of his *Institutes*, he finally complied with an official request to return to Geneva.

By this time the city was threatened by religious chaos, and he determined to put into effect his original scheme of reform. His 'Ecclesiastical Ordinances' provided for pastors, teachers, elders, and deacons, and also a consistory body (composed of pastors and elders) to control church affairs. Calvin became virtually a dictator, not only in religious matters, but also in questions of trade, law, economy and diplomacy. Inevitably there were controversies, the most sordid of these being the dispute with Michael Servetus over the Trinity, which resulted in the latter being burned at the stake in 1553. Meanwhile a stream of works poured from Calvin's busy pen.

In 1559 he founded an academy in Geneva which was to become the intellectual centre of Calvinism for many years to come; the curriculum brought together classical studies on humanist lines and reformed theology.

Throughout his life Calvin suffered from ill-health; he drove himself incessantly, eating frugally and sleeping very little. He preached his last sermon on 16 February 1564 and died on 27 May the same year. His wife, whom he had married in 1540, had died in 1549.

The influence of Calvinism on the Puritans in England was long-lasting. It was at its most extreme in the years after 1568, when, under the leadership of Thomas Cartwright (q.v.), Walter Travers (q.v.), and others, a Presbyterian movement gathered strength with the aim of abolishing the bishops and replacing them with the Genevan system of ministers and elected elders. With Cartwright and Travers driven from England in 1573, the movement became more moderate. In Scotland Calvin is considered as the spiritual father of John Knox (q.v.) and the founder of Scottish Presbyterianism.

Lord Acton, essay on Calvin in *Lectures on Modern History* (1906).
J. T. McNeill, *The History and Character of Calvinism* (1954).
Williston Walker, *John Calvin, Organizer of Reformed Protestantism* (1906).

*Portrait*: engraving, by R. Houston, after unknown artist, *c.* 1560: location not known.

**Camden, William** (1551–1623), antiquary and historian, author of *Britannia*, the earliest topographical survey of the British Isles.

The son of Samson Camden, a painter, and his wife Elizabeth Curwen, William Camden was born in London on 2 May 1551. He received his early education at Christ's Hospital, then from 1564 at St Paul's School; in 1566 he went up to Oxford. Camden studied first at Magdalen College, from where he migrated first to Broadgates Hall (later Pembroke College) and then to Christ Church. After being denied an All Souls fellowship because of his involvement in a religious controversy, Camden left Oxford in 1571 for London.

With the encouragement of Gabriel Goodman, Dean of Westminster, Camden devoted the next few years to antiquarian studies, travelling throughout the country studying its topography and collecting archaeological material. On the recommendation of Goodman, in 1575 he was appointed as Second Master of Westminster School, where Ben Jonson and other distinguished pupils profited from his teaching. He continued his researches and, with the encouragement of the Flemish cartographer and antiquary, Abraham Ortelius, who visited England in 1577, he began seriously to prepare for publication the survey which he entitled *Britannia*. The completion of this work involved Camden in extensive travelling over some ten years. It was published, with a dedication to William Cecil (q.v.), 1st Baron Burghley, on 2 May 1586, Camden's thirty-fifth birthday, and achieved great success, running into four editions by 1594; a sixth and greatly enlarged edition was published in 1607. *Britannia*, written in Latin, was first translated into English by Philemon Holland in 1610.

In March 1593 Camden succeeded Dr Edward Grant as Headmaster of Westminster School, and in 1597 he published a Greek grammar for the use of pupils at the school. In October that year, on the recommendation of Sir Fulke Greville (q.v.), he was appointed Clarenceux King-at-Arms; this aroused the antagonism of Ralph Brooke, York Herald, who proceeded to launch an attack on Camden for errors in *Britannia*, to which the author replied in his fifth edition (1600), justifying his use of Leland's *Itinerary* (see Leland, John) as a source and defending his text as a work of history and topography rather than as one of genealogy or heraldry.

In 1600 Camden published a list of

epitaphs in Westminster Abbey. A collection of the chronicles of early English historians, *Anglica, Normanica, Hibernica, a veteribus scripta*, which had been part of his preparatory work for *Britannia*, appeared in 1603; it contained the famous interpolated passage in the text of Asser concerning the foundation of Oxford University by King Alfred (see *Lives Before the Tudors*). At about this time Camden conceived the idea of writing a general history of England, but he soon abandoned it on realizing the extent of such a scheme and concentrated instead on smaller projects, such as the publication in 1605 of *Remains*, which he himself called 'the rude rubble and outcast rubbish of a greater and more serious work' (i.e. *Britannia*), issued under the initials 'M.N.' and dedicated to his friend Sir Robert Bruce Cotton (q.v.). Following the discovery of the Gunpowder Plot of November 1605 (see Fawkes, Guy, in *Lives of the Stuart Age*), Camden undertook his first official commission, an account (in Latin) of the trials of the conspirators, published in 1607.

Early in 1608, following a severe injury caused by a fall from his horse the previous autumn which laid him up for nearly nine months, Camden turned to a project that had been in his mind for some years, a history of the reign of Queen Elizabeth (q.v.). This had originally been encouraged by Burghley, but had been set aside after the latter's death. After another interruption as a result of illness, and his subsequent removal from London to Chislehurst, in Kent, Camden completed the work up to the end of 1588, and it was published as *Annales rerum Anglicarum et Hibernicarum, regnante Elizabetha . . . ad annum 1589* in 1615, with English translations in 1625, 1628, and 1635. The second part of the *Annales*, completed by Camden in 1617,

was not, on his instructions, published until after his death; it appeared first in Leyden in 1625, and in London in 1627. There is no proof that, as has been alleged, he watered down his account of Scottish affairs to please the King.

In about 1618 Camden retired to his house in Chislehurst on account of his health. During this last period of his life he wrote a skeleton history of the reign of James I (see James VI of Scotland), which was not in fact printed until 1691, and, his earlier scheme to found a college of learning in Chelsea having been abandoned in 1610 for lack of funds, in March 1622 he put into effect another plan that had been his intention for some time, the endowment of a professorship of history at Oxford. Little over a year later he was struck down with paralysis, and died at Chislehurst on 9 November 1623; he was buried in Westminster Abbey. In his Will Camden bequeathed his manuscripts and books to his friend Cotton, but in fact the printed books were placed in the library of Westminster Abbey.

William Camden was a pioneer of historical and genealogical research, as well as a vigorous defender of the achievements of Queen Elizabeth. He was the central figure in a society of antiquaries meeting at the end of Elizabeth's reign, by all of whom he was regarded as the master. His impulse was largely responsible for the series of county surveys by Richard Carew, William Lambarde (q.v.), Sampson Erdeswicke and others, thus initiating county topography. Camden's *Annales*, the best translation of which is that of 1688, is generally regarded as the outstanding contemporary account of the reign. *Britannia*, the first comprehensive survey of its kind, has been used as a valuable source by successive generations of local historians; in addition to the first English edition by Holland of 1610, it has been translated in three volumes by Richard Gough (1789). Camden's correspondence, together with a short life and various other pieces, including the historian's autobiographical *Memorabilia*, was published by Dr Thomas Smith in 1691.

The Camden Society, founded in his honour in 1838, is devoted to the publication of documents relating to the early history and literature of Britain.

Richard Gough, Memoir in his edition of *Britannia* (3 vols; 1789).
A. L. Rowse, *The England of Elizabeth* (1950).
E. G. R. Taylor, 'Leland's England and Camden's England', in H. C. Darby (ed.), *The Historical Geography of England before 1800* (Cambridge, 1936).
Thomas Smith, *Camdeni Vita* (1691).
Anthony à Wood, *Athenae Oxonienses*, edited by Philip Bliss, vol. ii (4 vols; 1813–20).

*Portraits:* oil, by Marcus Gheeraerts the Younger, ?1609: Bodleian Library, Oxford; oil, by or after Marcus Gheeraerts the Younger, 1609: National Portrait Gallery, London; oil, by unknown artist: Worcester College, Oxford; engraving, by R. Gaywood, in Morgan's *Sphere of Gentry*, 1661.

**Campion, Edmund** (1540–1581), Jesuit martyr.

Edmund Campion was born on 25 January 1540, the son of a London bookseller. Helped financially by the Grocers' Company, he was educated first at a London grammar school and then at Christ's Hospital, before going on to the newly-founded St John's College at Oxford. He became a junior fellow of the college in 1557 and took his M.A. in 1564.

A precocious boy, Campion soon acquired a reputation as an orator. As early as 1553, when only thirteen years old, he was chosen to make a speech to Queen Mary I (q.v.) on her triumphal entry into London, and in 1566 an oration he made on the occasion of the visit of Queen Elizabeth I (q.v.) to Oxford University won him royal praise and the patronage of the Earl of Leicester (see Dudley, Robert). It was probably at this time that he first made the acquaintance of Philip Sidney (q.v.). For several years Campion taught at Oxford, and in 1568 he was ordained a deacon in the Anglican Church. Not long afterwards he underwent a spiritual crisis from which he emerged with the realization that his true sympathies lay with Roman Catholicism. Forced to leave the university because of his religious views in 1570, he was given sanctuary in Ireland by Sir Henry Sidney (q.v.), father of Philip and then Lord Deputy, and while there wrote a metrical *History of Ireland* which he dedicated to Leicester. The following year, when he came under suspicion from the English government and was in danger of arrest, a warning from Sir Henry enabled him to flee to the Continent in disguise.

Campion made his way to the seminary at Douai, in northern France, founded by the Lancashire priest William Allen (q.v.). There he was received into the Roman Catholic Church and took his degree as Bachelor of Divinity. He then travelled on foot to Rome, where he joined the Society of Jesus. His novitiate was spent at Brünn, in Bohemia (now Czechoslovakia), and in September 1574 he was appointed to the Jesuit College in Prague as Professor of Rhetoric. Philip Sidney visited him there in 1577.

In 1580 he was chosen by Allen, leader of the English Catholics in Rome, to accompany Robert Parsons (q.v.) on the first Jesuit mission to England. Parsons went on ahead, and Campion, together with a lay brother, Ralph Emerson, crossed from Calais to Dover on 24 June. Although the authorities were on the watch for him, Campion managed to evade arrest. He was taken to a house in Chancery Lane, London, where he waited ten days for Parsons to join him. In the interval he preached at Smithfield and at several secret meetings, but London was full of government agents, some of whom were posing as Catholics in order to trap them, and it was agreed that they should leave the city and go their separate ways. Riding out of London together, Parsons and Campion were overtaken by a Catholic named Thomas Pounde, who urged them to put in writing the reasons for their mission to England, which might be published in the event of their arrest. Campion therefore wrote a letter to the Privy Council and, trusting Pounde, gave it to him unsealed, with instructions to use it only if they were arrested. Unfortunately, Pounde proved totally incapable of keeping a secret; news of the letter spread from one friend to another; then copies were circulated. One reached the Bishop of Winchester, who passed it on to the government. Efforts to capture the two Jesuits were redoubled, for this was a time of crisis, on the threshold of war

with Spain, and the Jesuits were regarded as traitors.

Meanwhile, with Parsons claiming that some 50,000 people no longer conformed to the Anglican Church, the very success of the mission alarmed the government. The two Jesuits were moving from one Catholic house to another, preaching, hearing confession, celebrating Mass, giving Communion, and reconciling lapsed Catholics. Campion's itinerary took him through Berkshire, Oxfordshire, Northamptonshire, and Lancashire, while Parsons remained nearer London. On 27 June 1581 alarm was caused by the distribution before a service at St Mary's, Oxford, of 400 copies of a pamphlet denouncing Anglicanism; entitled *Decem Rationes* ('Ten Reasons'), it had been written by Campion and secretly printed.

Campion's chances of evading arrest were now slighter than ever. Believing that he would be safer farther away from London, Parsons ordered him to Norfolk but first sent him, with Emerson, to collect his books and papers in Lancashire. They stopped overnight at Lyford Grange, in Berkshire, the home of a Mr Yate, and the following morning went on their way; they were intercepted near Oxford by a deputation of Catholics who persuaded Campion to return to Lyford. This he did, and was arrested there on 17 July; the local magistrate had been tipped off by a scoundrel named Eliot, who had gained access to Campion's Mass in the house through his friendship with the cook.

Forced to ride through the London streets wearing a paper stuck in his hat on which was written, 'Campion the seditious Jesuit', he was taken to the Tower, where he was offered a pardon if he would conform. This he refused to do. He was then put to the torture in an attempt to make him recant his religious beliefs, but only when racked for the third time did he divulge the names of a few of those Catholics in whose houses he had stayed. Debates were set up in which he had to face unprepared the Deans of Windsor and St Paul's and other theologians. At the trial held in Westminster Hall on 14 November Campion was so weak from the rack that he was unable to raise his own hand to plead 'Not guilty'. He was convicted of treason and on 1 December was tied to a hurdle and dragged through jeering London mobs to Tyburn, where a huge crowd witnessed his execution.

Edmund Campion is the best known of the English Jesuits martyred by the government of Elizabeth's reign. He had a faith which never wavered; unlike Parsons, he had no political motives, but had affirmed his loyalty to the Queen. This made his execution unpopular. Campion Hall at Oxford has been named after him, and he was beatified in 1886.

Campion's *History of Ireland* has been edited by James Ware and published in *Ancient Irish Histories* (2 vols; Dublin, 1908; reprinted New York, 1940). The pamphlet *Decem Rationes* was printed in translation by the Manresa Press (1914).

C. Hollis, 'Edmund Campion, S.J.', in K. Garvin (ed.), *The Great Tudors* (1935).
R. Simpson, *Edmund Campion* (1867).
E. Waugh, *Edmund Campion* (1935).

*Portraits*: engraving, by J. M. Lerch, Campion in 1581: location not known; other engravings, by unknown artists: British Museum, London.

## Cartwright, Thomas (1535–1603), Puritan divine.

Cartwright was born in Hertfordshire of yeoman stock in 1535, and educated at Cambridge, where he matriculated at Clare Hall and then in 1550 went as a scholar to St John's. He became a convinced Protestant while at Cambridge. During the reign of Mary I (q.v.) he left the university and took up law. He went back to Cambridge on the accession of Elizabeth I (q.v.) as a fellow of St John's and later became a fellow of Trinity; in 1569 he returned to his old college as Lady Margaret Professor of Divinity, but was deprived of his professorship a year later on account of his criticisms of the Church of England. His sermons at the university drew enormous crowds, but his view that the rule of church government had been laid down in the scriptures and that the episcopal system set up by Elizabeth was contrary to that rule involved him in a lengthy conflict with the Vice-Chancellor, John Whitgift (q.v.), later Archbishop of Canterbury. Cartwright, like John Calvin (q.v.), held that ministers must be chosen by the people.

In 1570 he went into exile in Geneva, but returned briefly to England two years later to support the demands of Walter Travers (q.v.), John Field, and Thomas Wilcox for the introduction in

England of the Genevan system of church government. Cartwright was probably the author of the *First Admonition to Parliament* (June 1572), but not of the *Second Admonition*. Once again he was forced to leave England. He spent the next few years on the Continent and was for some time minister to the English congregation at Antwerp. He was joined by Travers, and together they conducted a protracted pamphlet warfare against the episcopacy and in defence of Presbyterianism. In 1574 Travers's *Ecclesiasticae disciplinae* (often confused with the later *Book of discipline*) was published, together with a translation by Cartwright under the title, *A full and plain declaration of ecclesiastical discipline*.

In 1585 Cartwright was allowed to return to England, where he was appointed Master of a hospital (almshouse) founded by the Earl of Leicester (see Dudley, Robert) in Warwick. The post was not subject to episcopal jurisdiction, but Cartwright's ceaseless activities as leader of the Puritan movement, as well as his erudite attacks on Richard Hooker (q.v.), led eventually to his arrest. Imprisoned from 1590 to 1592, but released for lack of conclusive evidence, he went to the Channel Islands and helped to found the Puritan movement there. He died at Warwick on 27 December 1603.

Thomas Cartwright is generally regarded as the most learned and cultured Puritan of the Elizabethan age.

A. F. S. Pearson, *Thomas Cartwright and Elizabethan Puritanism* (1925).

**Catherine de' Medici** (1519–1589), Queen consort of Henri II of France, and Regent of France 1560–1574.

Born in Florence on 13 April 1519, the daughter of Lorenzo de' Medici, Duke of Urbino, and Madeleine de la Tour

d'Auvergne, a Bourbon princess, Catherine was related to many of the French nobility through her mother. Orphaned when a few days old, she was brought up and educated by nuns in Florence and Rome.

In 1533 she was married by her uncle, Pope Clement VII, to Henri, Duc d'Orléans, son of François I of France, whom he was to succeed in April 1547. Although Henri was deeply attached to his mistress Diane de Poitiers, and for the first ten years Catherine produced no children (for which reason it was strongly rumoured in 1538 that she would be discarded and sent back to Italy), the marriage was not unhappy. In April 1543 Catherine at last became pregnant. Her first child, François de Valois, was born the following January, and in subsequent years she was to bear her husband ten children, of whom four sons and three daughters survived. Despised by many at the French court for her lack of royal blood, Catherine's vivacious, artistic, and extrovert personality nevertheless won her much admiration; however, as yet she took little part in state affairs, being totally involved with the supervision of the royal nursery (enlarged in the autumn of 1548 by the addition of the young Mary, Queen of Scots (q.v.), who was to marry the Dauphin, François, ten years later) and with the education of the infant princes and princesses. Her first state duty was to act as Regent during her husband's absence at the siege of Metz in 1552.

Henri's death from a wound received in a tournament at the wedding celebrations of their daughter, Elizabeth de Valois, and Philip II of Spain (q.v.) in July 1559 caused Catherine intense grief, from which it is believed she never fully recovered. During the brief reign of her son, François II, and Mary, the crown was dominated by the Duc de Guise and his brother, the Cardinal de Lorraine; from this period stems Catherine de' Medici's lifelong struggle against the powerful Guise family, who had the support of Spain and the papacy.

On the death of François in December 1560, Catherine succeeded in obtaining the regency on behalf of her second son, the eleven-year-old Charles IX; the Guisard domination was thus temporarily broken. For the next ten years Catherine played an important but exceedingly complex role in French politics; as the power behind the throne, she intrigued with and played off against each other in turn the Guises, the Bourbon princes Antoine de Navarre and Louis de Condé, and the Montmorency family. One of her first acts was to make clear to her widowed daughter-in-law that there would be no further place for her in French state affairs; fearing for her own daughter Elizabeth's position, Catherine also vetoed Mary's proposed marriage to Don Carlos of Spain, leaving

the Queen of Scots little choice but to accept the invitation of the Scottish Parliament to return to her own kingdom.

At the time of the Huguenot conspiracy at Amboise earlier in 1560, when an attempt had been made to rescue François from the Guisard faction, Catherine de' Medici had demonstrated her firm belief in moderation so far as religion was concerned; now, with the support of the French chancellor, Michel de l'Hôpital, she pursued a determined policy of religious reconciliation. Her Edict of January 1562 proved unacceptable to the Catholic extremists, however, and brought about the first French war of religion; towards the end of this conflict the Duc de Guise was assassinated by a Protestant fanatic, and peace was concluded in March 1563. During the next four years, however, Catherine found it increasingly difficult to withstand the Guises, now headed by the Cardinal de Lorraine, and war was renewed in September 1567. After an uneasy and short-lived peace arranged in March 1568, the third war of religion broke out and was not brought to an end until August 1570, when, under the Treaty of St Germain-en-Laye, the Huguenots gained far-reaching concessions and their leader, Admiral Gaspard de Coligny, became a member of Charles IX's Council.

Catherine now turned her attention to marriage alliances as a means of reconciliation. In November 1570 her daughter, Marguerite de Valois, was betrothed to the young Protestant leader Henri de Navarre (later Henri IV of France). Negotiations were also started, through Sir Francis Walsingham (q.v.), for the marriage of her second surviving (and favourite) son, Henri, Duc d'Anjou (later Henri III), to Queen Elizabeth (q.v.). When this suit was abandoned in

1572, Catherine's youngest son, François, Duc d'Alençon (q.v.), began a long-drawn-out courtship of the English Queen.

Although Charles IX had been declared of age by his mother in 1563 and had been taken by her on a prestige tour of the kingdom in the interval between the first and second civil wars, 1564–6, he had been up to this time still very much under Catherine's domination. Now he came under the influence not only of Coligny, but of Louis of Nassau and other young Protestant Flemish exiles, who urged him to take action against the Spanish in the Netherlands. Catherine did her best to dissuade him from this course, but in July 1572 preparations were made to send French troops under the command of Coligny to assist the revolt of William of Orange (q.v.) against the Duke of Alva.

Alarmed at her son's new policy, Catherine initiated an abortive attempt on the life of Coligny. The resultant fury of the Huguenots, who threatened to wipe out the entire French court, coupled with a danger of war with Spain, finally induced Charles to yield to pressure from his mother and to order the massacre of the Huguenot leaders who were assembled in Paris for the wedding of Marguerite de Valois and Henri de Navarre. On the night of 23–4 August, the eve of the feast of St Bartholomew, no less than 3,000 Huguenots were killed in Paris alone; in the next few days the massacre spread to the provinces, and many thousands more lost their lives. This ugly deed caused an outcry and revulsion throughout continental Europe and the start of yet another war of religion in France.

On the death of Charles IX in May 1574, Catherine once more assumed the regency until the return to France of Henri, Duc d'Anjou, now Henri III, who had been elected King of Poland in May the previous year. She did not dominate Henri as she had done her other sons, but contented herself with trying to make up for his shortcomings and, above all, to avoid war with Spain. On her advice Henri attempted to nullify the Catholic Holy League, but in 1584 it was revived under the leadership of Henri, Duc de Guise, following the death of François, Duc d'Alençon, which left Henri de Navarre as heir presumptive to the throne.

Although her health was already failing, Catherine strove gallantly to avert an open breach between the crown and the Guises; in so doing she committed Henri under the Treaty of Nemours (July 1585) to revoking his former toleration to the Huguenots. This engendered a new conflict, the so-called 'war of the three Henrys', which was dynastic. In December 1586 Catherine met Navarre at Cognac and tried unsuccessfully to come to terms with him. She lived to see the King driven from Paris by a revolutionary mob in May 1588, but not his reconciliation with Navarre in April the following year, forced on him by increased hostility on the part of the League as a result of the murder of Guise and his brother. Catherine died at Blois on 5 January 1589, just eight months before her son Henri was stabbed to death at Saint-Cloud and Henri de Navarre became the first Bourbon King of France.

The most prominent figure in France in the last thirty years of her life, and a powerful influence throughout Europe, Catherine de' Medici remains a controversial personality. Traditionally she has been blamed for the St Bartholomew's Day Massacre; however, it is not established that she did more than authorize the death of Coligny and his chief-followers. In all her intrigues she worked consistently for the preservation of royal authority, for religious moderation in the face of the Reformation, and against war between France and Spain. Much has been written concerning her relations with, and influence on, Mary, Queen of Scots; it seems that Mary almost certainly learned the art and value of intrigue from her mother-in-law, and that the latter showed her jealousy only after the death of François, when Mary had ceased to be useful to her.

The *Lettres de Catherine de Médicis* have been edited, with valuable introductions, by H. de la Ferrière-Percy and the Comte Baguenault de Puchesse (10 vols; Paris, 1880–1909).

P. A. Cheruel, *Marie Stuart et Catherine de Médicis* (Paris, 1858).

Irene Mahoney, *Madame Catherine, The Life of Catherine de Medici* (1976).

L. Romier, *Le Royaume de Catherine de Médicis* (2 vols; 2nd ed., Paris, 1922).

N. M. Sutherland, *The Massacre of St Bartholomew and the European Conflict 1559–1572* (1972).

P. van Dyke, *Catherine de Médicis* (2 vols; 1922).

*Portraits*: oil, by G. Vasari, 1553: Palazzo Vecchio, Florence; oil, by unknown artist, 1561: Bibliothèque Nationale, Paris; drawing, by F. Clouet, *c.* 1570: B.N.; oil, by unknown artist, *c.* 1580: Musée du Louvre, Paris; miniature, by Clouet: Victoria and Albert Museum, London; tapestry, with her sons Henri and François: Uffizi Gallery, Florence.

## Catherine Howard (d. 1542), fifth Queen consort of Henry VIII (q.v.).

The exact date of Catherine's birth is unknown, but she was one of ten children of Lord Edmund Howard, younger son of the Duke of Norfolk (see Howard, Thomas, 2nd Duke) who fought at Flodden.

Catherine's upbringing was somewhat neglected, partly on account of her father's poverty and partly through the laxity of her grandmother, Agnes, the widowed Duchess of Norfolk, with whom she went to live after the death of her own mother. She was a strong-willed, irresponsible girl who, lacking adequate supervision, drifted into a series of indiscreet attachments. The first of these was with her music teacher, Henry Mannock (or Manox), in about 1536. Catherine subsequently became secretly engaged to one of her grandmother's retainers, Francis Dereham, who called her his wife but disappeared to Ireland when she was introduced at court. There was also some question of her later engagement to a cousin, Thomas Culpepper, which Catherine denied to Dereham on his return from Ireland.

She was probably about seventeen years old in 1540, when she was introduced to court under the auspices of her uncle, the 3rd Duke of Norfolk (see Howard, Thomas, 3rd Duke), and Bishop Stephen Gardiner (q.v.). The King was immediately attracted to her, and his desire was encouraged by Gardiner, who saw in Catherine a possible Catholic replacement for Anne of Cleves (q.v.).

Thomas Cromwell (q.v.) fell from grace in June 1540, and early in July the marriage between the King and Anne was annulled. Henry and Catherine were married privately at Oatlands on 28 July, and on 8 August the King acknowledged her in public as his Queen. In September–October Catherine accompanied the King on his midland progress, and the following summer the couple made a royal progress in Yorkshire. Henry, for his part, appeared still to be enamoured of his latest wife, but Catherine, with the connivance of her cousin, Jane, Viscountess Rochford, foolishly embarked on a series of clandestine meetings at Pontefract with her former lovers Dereham and Culpepper, and appointed the former as her secretary.

On their return to Hampton Court in November 1541, Archbishop Cranmer (q.v.) revealed to Henry details, obtained from maidservants, of Catherine's indiscretions before her marriage and also of her recent meetings with Culpepper and Dereham. At the ensuing investigation Dereham confessed to having often lain with Catherine before her marriage to the King, although she herself denied all the charges. Torture was used to wring further confessions from Dereham and Culpepper, but the Queen's adultery after marriage was never proved; in accordance with the contemporary custom, however, legally she had committed adultery by marrying the King when engaged to Dereham.

In November Catherine was given by the King a promise that her life would be spared, and she was sent to Sion House. Meanwhile the proceedings dragged on and evidence of her adultery continued to be sought. Culpepper and Dereham were executed in December, and several of Catherine's relatives and accomplices, including Lady Rochford, were arrested. Early in February 1542 Parliament passed a bill of attainder against Catherine and Lady Rochford (who by this time had gone out of her mind), declaring it treasonable for an unchaste woman to have married the King. A new confession was wrung at this point from Catherine, who continued to deny all charges of adultery after her marriage. She was taken to the Tower on 10 February, where, together with Lady Rochford, she was beheaded three days later. The King was said to have been deeply distressed.

L. Baldwin Smith, *A Tudor Tragedy: the life and times of Catherine Howard* (1961).

*Portraits*: oil, *called* Catherine Howard, by Holbein: Toledo Museum of Fine Arts, Ohio, U.S.A. (copy at National Portrait Gallery, London, and another in private hands); miniature, by unknown artist, traditionally known as Catherine Howard: Buccleuch Collection, Drumlanrig Castle, Dumfries (copy in Royal Collection, Windsor).

**Catherine of Aragon** (1485–1536), the first Queen consort of Henry VIII (q.v.).

The youngest daughter of Ferdinand II of Aragon and Isabella of Castile, Catherine was born on 16 December 1485 at Alcala de Henares, north-east of Madrid. She was christened Catalina after her English great-grandmother on the maternal side, Catherine of Lancaster.

Catherine's childhood was spent at the turbulent Spanish court, where the royal household was perpetually on the move. She was betrothed to Arthur, Prince of Wales (q.v.), under the treaty of Medina del Campo of 1489, when only three years old. Negotiations for the contract were not satisfactorily concluded until 1500, however, and she did not meet her future husband until her arrival in England in October 1501. Catherine was then nearly sixteen, Arthur fourteen. The marriage took place at St Paul's, London, on 14 November that year, and the young Prince and Princess of Wales set up their court at Ludlow. They were considered too young to cohabit, and when Arthur died on 2 April 1502, the marriage had not been consummated.

Having worked so hard to achieve the marriage alliance with the Spanish royal family, Henry VII (q.v.) was reluctant to allow the young Princess to return to Spain, and more than reluctant to give up the half of her handsome dowry (100,000 crowns) which had already been paid. Negotiations were therefore begun almost immediately for her betrothal to the King's second son, Henry. (At one stage, soon after the death of his own wife, Elizabeth of York (q.v.), the King considered marrying her himself, but this suggestion met with a prompt and downright refusal from Isabella.) The question was raised whether Catherine was in fact married in the eyes of God, since the marriage to Arthur had not been consummated. Eventually, at the end of June 1503 the new marriage treaty was signed; a papal dispensation was obtained, and it was agreed that the wedding of Catherine and Prince Henry should take place in 1505, when the bridegroom would have reached the age of fourteen.

Catherine's mother died in 1504, and the ensuing struggle for Castile between Ferdinand and Philip of Burgundy, which drove the former into an alliance with France and Henry VII to side with Burgundy and the Hapsburgs, at one time looked like delaying the marriage plans indefinitely. During these unsettled years Catherine was used as a pawn in the delicate relationship that existed between England and Spain. She led a miserable existence first at Durham House, off the Strand, and later in whatever lodgings the King saw fit to grant her at court, pawning her jewellery and plate and falling deeper and deeper into debt because Henry would allow her little or no money and Ferdinand would not send his daughter any. She was seldom permitted even to see her future husband. A young woman of considerable intelligence and intellectual ability, Catherine behaved throughout with the utmost diplomacy and a shrewdness equal to that of any of the official ambassadors.

The death of Henry VII in April 1509 brought a change of policy and the removal of all obstacles to the marriage. Immediately after his father's funeral, the new King took Catherine to Greenwich, where, six weeks later, they were quietly married. They were crowned at Westminster on Midsummer's Day. The English people immediately took the Queen to their hearts.

The new reign opened in an atmosphere of festivity, in strong contrast to the old, and for the next fifteen years Henry and Catherine led a reasonably happy married life. In addition to the many interests they shared – the new learning, music and dancing, sport – the King had much confidence in his wife's proven judgment in the fields of foreign relations and diplomacy. At the beginning of the reign she succeeded in reviving his interest in a Spanish alliance. It was a mark of his esteem that he made her Regent while he campaigned in France in 1513, and Catherine was largely responsible for the organization of the English forces that won a decisive victory against the Scots at Flodden in September that year.

The Queen wisely closed her eyes to Henry's temporary infidelities, while he for his part treated her with affection and the utmost courtesy. Dutifully she bore him six children in the years 1510–18, but only one, a daughter (the future Queen Mary I (q.v.), born in 1516), survived. The King's disappointment at his failure to beget a healthy male heir (one boy, born in January 1511 and christened Henry, had lived for only fifty-two days, and another had been stillborn), coupled with a distinct lessening of his desire for an alliance with the treacherous Ferdinand of Spain, gradually eroded their relationship. Although they were still seen together in public and remained on friendly terms for the next five years, they were now beginning to go their separate ways, Henry to find consolation in continual revelling, Catherine in charitable and devotional pursuits. For a short time the King's anxiety about the succession was allayed by Catherine's cleverness in procuring a promise from her nephew, the young Emperor Charles V (q.v.), that he would marry the Princess Mary, but in 1525 Charles went back on his word, jilting Mary in favour of a Portuguese princess. Then Henry became infatuated with Anne Boleyn (q.v.) and started seriously to contemplate divorce.

In May 1527 Henry initiated a secret suit before Thomas Wolsey (q.v.) and Archbishop Warham (q.v.) with the purpose of getting the marriage to his brother's widow declared invalid. It failed, for Catherine, having decided to fight her case to the last ditch, had already alerted the Pope, insisting that she was the King's lawful wife and demanding that her case should be heard in Rome. In her stand she was supported by the mass of the English people, but the power-seeking Cardinal Wolsey was her bitterest enemy. Even her nephew Charles V would not come to her assistance, and Pope Clement VII put off giving a verdict until it was too late. Almost the only person she could trust was Eustace Chapuys, the Imperial ambassador.

These were wretched years for Catherine. From the day in July 1531 when the King had left Windsor, riding gaily away with a hunting party that included Anne Boleyn, without saying good-bye to her, the Queen found herself humiliated at every turn. Courageously she resisted all pressures to abandon the title of Queen or to acknowledge that the marriage had been illegal from the start. Constantly in fear of poison, moved from one house to another, denied access to her daughter, deprived of jewels, income, servants, even at the last of household furnishings, Catherine nevertheless retained her dignity and her faith in God. For five years she persistently warned the Pope that if he did not pronounce that she was Henry's lawful wife, England would break from Rome. When at last the Pope spoke out, on 23 March 1534, it was too late; Henry had married Anne the previous year and Parliament by Act of Succession had declared Catherine's marriage null and Anne to be his lawful wife and Queen. The Princess Mary was pronounced a bastard and Anne's baby daughter, Elizabeth (see Elizabeth I), born in September 1533, was now the lawful heir to the throne.

Steadfastly Catherine refused to accept the Act of Succession and the royal supremacy. She had been under great strain, and with many of her supporters executed and increasingly isolated from advisers and friends, as well as from her daughter, it was not surprising that her health now gave way. She died at Kimbolton, Huntingdonshire, on 7 January 1536. To the very last she insisted that she was Henry's lawful and loving wife; in her final letter to him, dictated on the morning of the day of her death, she said that she desired above all things to see him again. The letter was said by Polydore Vergil (q.v.) to have brought tears to the King's eyes; but Chapuys wrote a hostile report that Henry appeared at a ball at Greenwich dressed in a gay yellow costume and carrying the Princess Elizabeth in his arms, saying 'God be praised, the old harridan is dead'.

By royal command, Catherine was buried in the choir aisle of Peterborough Abbey. It was said that when the embalmer opened up her body he saw that all her organs were healthy except for the heart, which had turned black and had a grotesque black growth attached to it. From this it has been deduced that Catherine died of cancer of the heart, but at the time stories were in circulation that she had been poisoned.

Catherine of Aragon was much loved by the ordinary English people. Her faithful adviser and friend, Chapuys, summed her up as 'the most virtuous woman [he had] ever known and the highest hearted, but too quick to trust that others were like herself, and too slow to do a little ill that much good might come of it.'

G. Mattingley, *Catherine of Aragon* (1942).

*Portraits:* oil on panel, by unknown artist, probably *c.* 1530: National Portrait Gallery, London (identical copy at Museum of Fine Arts, Boston; other versions in Royal Collection, Windsor, at Merton College, Oxford, and elsewhere); oil, by unknown artist: Petworth House, Sussex (Lord Egremont); rectangular miniature, by unknown artist, probably contemporary: Duke of Buccleuch and Queensberry Collection; watercolour, *called* Catherine of Aragon, by Wilfred Drake, 1921 (copy of head in east window at St Margaret's, Westminster): N.P.G.; oil, three-quarter length, by unknown artist, probably posthumous: John Guinness Collection. N.B. there is no definite proof that the portrait by Sittoz in the Kunsthistorisches Museum, Vienna, is of Catherine.

**Catherine Parr** (1512–1548), see Katherine Parr.

**Cavendish, Thomas** (1560–1592), seaman, the second Englishman to circumnavigate the world.

Born at Trimley St Martin, Suffolk, in 1560, Thomas Cavendish (the name is sometimes spelled Candish) squandered his inherited fortune by extravagant living at court as a young man and turned to piracy as a source of income. In 1585 he contributed a ship to the expedition mounted by Sir Walter Ralegh (q.v.) under the command of Sir Richard Grenville (q.v.) to found a colony in North America. He returned with Grenville to England and began immediately to plan an expedition of his own modelled on that of Sir Francis Drake (q.v.) of eight years earlier.

Sailing from Plymouth on 21 July 1586 in his flagship *Desire* (140 tons), and accompanied only by two other ships, the *Content* (60 tons) and the *Hugh Gallant* (40 tons), with a total crew of 123, Cavendish made his first landfall at Sierra Leone in August. He called at the Cape Verde Islands and then sailed on to Brazil. In mid-December he reached a harbour on the Patagonian coast of South America and named it Port Desire (now Puerto Deseado, Argentina). Early in January 1587 the ships reached the Straits of Magellan; it took them forty-nine days to negotiate the Straits, and on 24 February they entered the Pacific.

Cavendish next sailed up what is now the coast of Chile towards Costa Rica, determined to plunder as much as possible on the way. He attacked Spanish settlements and shipping, but met with fierce opposition and, having lost about thirty of his men, was forced to abandon the *Hugh Gallant*. Nevertheless he took some prizes, the most valuable of which was the galleon *Santa Anna*, laden with gold and other precious cargo, seized off California early in November.

On 19 November the two remaining ships set sail for England, but the *Content*, whose crew had come near to mutiny over their share of the treasure, veered off independently and was never seen again. Cavendish, in the *Desire,* reached the Philippines in the middle of January and, after touching the Moluccas and Java, rounded the Cape of Good Hope. In June he called at the Portuguese-occupied island of St Helena, where he revictualled. He arrived at Plymouth on 9 September 1588, having, at the age of twenty-eight, circumnavigated the globe.

Cavendish now became a popular figure. Warmly received by the Queen at Greenwich, his exploits were commemorated in a number of ballads. Financially he had done well out of the voyage, and he was eager to embark on a second venture. In 1591 he persuaded John Davys (q.v.) to join in an expedition to China and the South Sea, promising the older man the chance to look for his long-sought-after North-West Passage from the Pacific side.

Leaving Plymouth in August that year, Cavendish sailed in the *Galleon,* with Davys in command of the *Desire*; *Dainty, Roebuck,* and *Black Pinnace* made up the total fleet. Reaching the Brazilian coast on 29 November, they took the town of Santos, but delayed setting out again until the end of January 1592, when they encountered severe storms and Cavendish became separated from the others. His qualities of leadership appear to have deserted him in this crisis; he quarrelled with his own officers to such an extent that when the *Galleon* again linked up with the *Desire,* Cavendish abruptly left his own ship and joined Davys in the *Desire.*

Half way through the Straits of Magellan they were forced to take refuge from further bad storms, and by the middle of May all their ships and men were in a poor state. Davys, ever anxious to find the North-West Passage, was in favour of going on, but Cavendish wanted to turn back and attempt to reach the East Indies via the Cape of Good Hope; the men, hoping for plunder, favoured Davys's scheme to continue. Cavendish was apparently persuaded to go on, but on regaining his own ship, he suddenly altered course on the night of 20 May and made for the Brazilian coast. He lost 25 men in an attack by the Portuguese and, unable to land, persuaded the survivors to make for St Helena where they could be refitted and revictualled. Contrary winds, however, drove the *Galleon* away when only two leagues from that island, and things went from bad to worse when Cavendish missed Ascension Island and set course for the Cape Verde Islands; he died at sea a few days later. In a letter written to his executor just before his death he made a bitter accusation against Davys of having deserted him and ruined the whole venture. (Davys, having failed to find the North-West Passage after three attempts, and not finding Cavendish at Port Desire as he expected, eventually sailed home alone.)

Richard Hakluyt, *The Principall Navigations* (1589; ed. by W. Raleigh, 12 vols, Glasgow, 1903–5).

E. J. Payne, *Voyages of the Elizabethan Seamen to America* (2 vols; Oxford, 1893–1900).

*Portrait:* engraving, by unknown artist: Mansell Collection, London.

**Caxton, William** (?1422–1491), the first English printer.

William Caxton was born in Kent, and apprenticed in 1438 to a rich London merchant. Following his master's death he moved in 1441 to Bruges, then the centre of the European wool trade, where he lived and prospered for thirty years. As Governor of the English merchants in the Low Countries, an influential post which he held from 1465 to 1469, Caxton successfully negotiated commercial treaties with the Dukes of Burgundy, and this led a few years later to his entering the service of Margaret, Duchess of Burgundy (q.v.).

Already his interests were turning from commerce towards literature. In March 1469 he had begun to translate *The Recuyell of the Historyes of Troye*, but had lost confidence in himself and abandoned it. Stimulated by his patron the Duchess, Caxton now continued his work, but did not finish it until 1471, by which time he was living in Cologne.

Caxton lived in Cologne for about eighteen months in 1471–2, and it was there that he learned the art of printing. He may have worked for a printing house in the town. In his epilogue to Book III of the *Recuyell* he has recorded that, tiring of the labour of copying with a pen, he 'practised and learnt' to print. Returning to Bruges, he perfected his art under the guidance of Colard Mansion, a printer of that town, and with his help and that of Jan Veldener of Louvain set up his own press. In 1475 he published the *Recuyell*, the first book to be printed in English, and presented a copy of it to his patron, Margaret, Duchess of Burgundy. *The Game and Playe of the Chesse*, translated by Caxton from the French, appeared the following year.

Caxton left Bruges towards the end of 1476, after publishing two or three books in French, and returned to England, where he set up his press at Westminster. The first known piece of printing he did there is an *Indulgence* of Abbot Sant dated 13 December 1476, and his first dated book, a translation by Earl Rivers of *The Dictes and Sayenges of the Phylosophers*, appeared in 1477. Altogether Caxton printed nearly a hundred books, which included virtually all the English literature available to him (Chaucer, Malory, etc.), as well as his own translations. He used eight founts of type

and although not considered to be a particularly original typographer, he strove continually for greater accuracy and clarity and pioneered the way for his successors. He started to use woodcuts in about 1480, and *Myrrour of the World*, printed by him in 1481, was the first illustrated English book.

Much of Caxton's work was commissioned by wealthy patrons, but the numerous devotional and service books that came from his press fulfilled the needs of the general literate public of his day, since the Continental presses were then concentrating mainly on Latin and Greek texts.

When he died in 1491 Caxton was survived by a daughter, Elizabeth, but no heir. The printing establishment was taken over by one of his apprentices, Wynkyn de Worde of Alsace, who a few years later became a naturalized Englishman.

Caxton's importance as the first English printer has tended to eclipse his achievements as a translator, which were considerable; his work in this field contributed much to the formation of a contemporary prose style in English.

William Blades, *The biography and typography of William Caxton* (2 vols; rev. ed. 1897).

N. F. Blake, *Caxton: England's First Publisher* (1976).

W. J. B. Crotch, *The Prologues and Epilogues of William Caxton* (Early English Text Society, 1928).

E. G. Duff, *William Caxton* (1905).

**Cecil, Robert** (1563–1612), 1st Earl of Salisbury, statesman.

Robert Cecil was born on 1 June 1563 in London, the only surviving son of William Cecil (q.v.), later 1st Baron Burghley, and his second wife, Mildred, daughter of Sir Anthony Cooke. It is believed that he was dropped by a nurse when a baby, for he grew up deformed – almost dwarflike, with a crooked back and an awkward gait.

Robert received his formal education at home, in the company of his father's wards and other young noblemen. From an early age he was groomed by his father in every aspect of the art of statesmanship, and in the atmosphere of the family home the precocious, sensitive boy had, and made the most of, the opportunity to reflect on the political issues of the day and to observe and talk with politicians and other prominent men in the government and at court. He was as ambitious and industrious as his father, and public affairs dominated his life.

In 1580 Robert was admitted to Gray's Inn, where he followed in his father's footsteps by studying law. He subsequently spent a short time at St John's College, Cambridge. At the age of eighteen his father arranged for him to become a Member of Parliament; this was planned by William Cecil as part of his son's education. A period of travel on the Continent followed, in order to acquaint him with foreign languages and institutions. By the age of twenty he was fully equipped to launch on a political career and was already adept at dealing diplomatically with those who sought his help in their relations with Burghley.

At about this time Robert Cecil attracted the attention of Queen Elizabeth I (q.v.), who nicknamed him first her 'Pygmy' (which he did not much care for) and later her 'Elf'. In the autumn of 1586 she commissioned him to write a pamphlet for her on her reasons for not wishing to execute Mary, Queen of Scots (q.v.). Two years later, in 1588, he was sent on his first diplomatic mission abroad, acting as an unofficial observer to the team headed by Lord Derby which went to the Netherlands to discuss peace terms with the Duke of Parma, commander of the Spanish forces there.

On his return to England Cecil fell in love with Elizabeth Brooke, daughter of Lord Cobham. They were betrothed in April 1589 and were married quietly on 31 August, the wedding having been delayed by the death of Lady Burghley. It was a happy marriage, but a short-lived one, for Elizabeth Cecil died on 24 January 1596, leaving a son, William, and two daughters, Frances and Catherine. Robert was deeply grieved; his hair turned grey and friends feared that he would lapse into melancholy. He never remarried, although his name was linked in later years with several married ladies at Court and he was said by his enemies to be unchaste.

It was not long before professional ambition and dedication to political work eclipsed private sorrow. Since the death of Sir Francis Walsingham (q.v.) in April 1590, Cecil had acted as unofficial Chief Secretary to the Queen (Cecil at that date being considered too inexperienced for the post, Burghley had succeeded in persuading Elizabeth to let him take it over temporarily, which meant in practice that he delegated much of the work to his son). Neither father nor son made any secret of their ambition that Robert should in due course be made Secretary, and when the Queen was sumptuously entertained at Burghley's country residence, Theobalds, in May 1591, the theatricals performed in her honour contained certain sly jokes about 'Mr Secretary Cecil'. At the end of her visit Elizabeth knighted Robert and three months later appointed him a member of the Privy Council; he was not, however, officially appointed as Secretary of State until July 1596.

In the meanwhile, as his father's health began to fail, Sir Robert gradually took over more of the duties of Secretary. He also busied himself increasingly with parliamentary work: he had sat as M.P. for Westminster in 1584 and 1588, and for Hertfordshire in 1588, and he represented the latter constituency again in 1592, 1597, and 1601, being especially active in securing measures for the relief of the poor and the suffering. In 1598 he was sent to France on an abortive mission to discover whether Henri IV intended to make peace with Spain and to attempt to secure repayment of a debt owed by the French King to Elizabeth.

Burghley died in the summer of 1598, shortly after Cecil's return. In his dying words to his son he urged him to avoid engaging the country in war, to seek peace with Elizabeth's enemies, and to work to put the lawful successor (James) on the throne after the Queen's death. To these ends Sir Robert, now more than ever a sad and melancholy man, devoted all his energies.

For a number of years he had to use all his skill and ingenuity to combat rivalry for the Queen's favour, firstly on the part of Sir Walter Ralegh (q.v.) and the Earl of Essex (see Devereux, Robert), and later from his cousins, Anthony Bacon (q.v.) and Francis Bacon (q.v.). The appeal of men like Ralegh and Essex lay in their heroic, warlike, and romantic image, representative of the mood of the new generation who failed to see the merit of seeking peace with Spain, as advocated by the cautious Cecil. After Ralegh's disgrace, Essex, the Queen's favourite, was chief contender for the coveted office of Secretary of State, and great was his disappointment when Elizabeth wisely put personal considerations aside and appointed Sir Robert to the post in 1596. Nevertheless, Cecil did not feel really secure until after Essex's execution for rebellion against the Queen in 1601. Always sensitive on account of his physical appearance, he was well aware of his unpopularity both at court and among the general public.

During Essex's trial Cecil was able to disprove the allegation, which had come to the knowledge of James VI of Scotland (q.v.), that he considered that only the Spanish Infanta had a rightful claim to the English throne after Elizabeth; this opened the way to secret negotiations which Cecil now conducted with James in order to achieve his recognition by the Queen as her rightful successor. The Secretary of State's advice that James should cultivate the Queen's goodwill rather than pester her for formal recognition paid off, in that in the event not only did James succeed unopposed, but Cecil himself retained the post of Secretary in the new reign.

Cecil, now nicknamed the 'Great Little Secretary', was for the first eight years of the reign of James I the most powerful man in England. Yet he was never at ease with his new sovereign. The long record of close relationship between the Cecils and their monarch was past, and although Sir Robert flattered the King outrageously, and James referred to the minister as his 'little beagle', the

King's totally different political outlook and the new corrupt atmosphere at court created a gulf between them. Worry and overwork showed itself in Cecil's appearance: grey-haired and haggard, at forty he looked like an old man.

Before he could turn his attention to ending the war with Spain, Cecil had to deal with two plots against the government aimed at ousting him from power, kidnapping the King, and forcing England into an alliance with France. Known as the Bye Plot and the Main Plot respectively, they were inspired by Cecil's two brothers-in-law, George Brooke (q.v.) and Baron Cobham (see Brooke, Henry), together with his old rival, Ralegh. All the conspirators were attainted, tried for treason, and sentenced to death, but Cecil used his influence to get Ralegh's sentence reprieved to imprisonment in the Tower.

In 1604 Cecil, who had been created Lord Cecil of Essendon in May the previous year, successfully negotiated a peace treaty with Spain; as a reward for his services the King raised him higher in the peerage, as Viscount Cranborne, in August 1604, and the Spanish government granted him a pension of £1,000 a year. Greater honours followed: in May 1605 James created him Earl of Salisbury, and a year later he was made a Knight of the Garter.

During the next two years Salisbury devoted most of his attention to the maintenance of order and unity at home. Pursuing a moderately anti-Roman Catholic, anti-Puritan policy, he made it clear to both religious groups that there must be one national church in England to which all should conform. The Counter-Reformation was at this time sweeping the Continent, and Salisbury greatly feared the power of the English Catholics.

His fears were not unfounded. On the night of 4–5 November 1605 Guy Fawkes (see *Lives of the Stuart Age*) was discovered in the cellars of the Houses of Parliament with barrels of gunpowder. A plot to blow up Parliament was revealed and the conspirators were quickly rounded up; all were tried and sentenced to be executed (hung, drawn, and quartered), Salisbury taking an active part in the examination of the prisoners. It has been suggested that he was aware of the plot and had let it get so far in order to be in a position to crush the plotters the more thoroughly. Certainly the Gunpowder Plot enabled him to get the King to agree to sterner measures against the Catholics, but there is no firm evidence to support the theory that Salisbury used his own agents to start the plot in order to enhance his personal position.

A comparatively calm period followed, and in the next couple of years Salisbury was able to indulge a personal interest and pastime which he had inherited from his father: building houses. Like his father, he enjoyed living on a grand scale and entertained sumptuously. Unable to participate in active sports because of his deformity, he was fond of partridge-netting and hawking. He spent money lavishly, even recklessly, which was in direct contrast with his prudence in public life. He already had a house in Chelsea, built in the last years of Elizabeth's reign. A far more splendid London residence, Salisbury House, south of the Strand, had been started in 1602, and at the same time he was adding to and embellishing Theobalds, which had come to him on his father's death. Other projects included a commercial property in the Strand district, known as Briton's Burse, and the transformation of a medieval hunting lodge at Cranborne, in Dorset, into a country house. In 1607 the King offered Salisbury a number of properties, including the old palace at Hatfield, in exchange for Theobalds, which James coveted as a royal hunting lodge. Salisbury accepted and enthusiastically began to design a new palatial residence near to the old one, which he mostly pulled down. Hatfield House took five years to build and cost over £38,000. It has remained the home of the Cecil family for more than three and a half centuries.

By this time Salisbury's health was failing, due largely to the extra burden of work which had fallen on his shoulders when in April 1607 James had appointed him Lord Treasurer in addition to his post as Secretary of State. He was burdened by the King's extravagance and indebtedness, while his worries were increased by the fact that James had fallen in love with a young Scottish nobleman, Robert Carr (see *Lives of the Stuart Age*), on whom he persisted in lavishing land, money and jewels. The gulf between the King and his chief minister became wider.

In an attempt to solve the financial position, Salisbury initiated numerous economies, collected old debts, and sold crown properties; he also devised a scheme, which later became known as the Great Contract, under which the crown was to relinquish certain feudal rights and dues in return for an annual grant from Parliament. He was unsuccessful in steering the scheme through Parliament, where it was debated at length in 1610, and ultimately the King also rejected it.

By this time a twelve-year truce had been agreed between the Netherlands and Spain, and Salisbury, sympathetic to the Dutch, aligned England with France to guarantee against any infringement of the truce by Spain.

At home his position became even more precarious, as Carr rapidly gained influence and supporters at Court. The view was widely held that Salisbury was on the way out, and many people felt that he was clinging to office out of obstinacy.

He was not to have the opportunity to oust Carr as he had done Essex and other earlier rivals. In February 1612 he was taken ill with a tumour in the abdomen. Doctors advised him to travel to Bath to take the waters, which he did, but he became worse and on the return journey he died at Marlborough on 24 May. At his own wish, he was buried privately at Hatfield.

After Salisbury's death, a torrent of abuse was unleashed which showed how unpopular he had been with the English people, Protestants and Catholics alike. He had served his country well, for under his ministry England had been well governed; like his father, Robert Cecil had pursued middle-of-the-road policies with national security and unity as his greatest aim. Thanks to his statesmanship, continuity was achieved during the transition from Tudor to Stuart rule, and also peace with Spain on favourable terms in 1604.

There are two printed volumes of Salisbury's correspondence with James VI (I): that edited by John Bruce for the Camden Society (vol. lxxviii) in 1861 and *The Secret Correspondence of Sir Robert Cecil with James I*, edited by Lord Hailes (Edinburgh, 1766). His letters to Sir George Carew on the Irish question were edited by John Maclean for the Camden Society (vol. lxxxviii) and published in 1864. A discourse by Cecil on 'The state and dignity of a secretary of state's place' is printed in *Harleian Miscellany*, volume v (edited by T. Park, 10 vols, 1808–13).

Salisbury's papers are preserved at Hatfield House, and microfilms of the

Hatfield MSS are at the British Museum and at the Folger Library, Washington. For printed sources see *Calendar of State Papers: Elizabeth* (Foreign and Domestic series) and *James I* (Domestic); and *Calendar of the Manuscripts of the Marquess of Salisbury . . . preserved at Hatfield House, Hertfordshire* (Historical Manuscripts Commission, 18 vols; 1883–1940).

A. Cecil, *A Life of Robert Cecil* (1915).
David Cecil, *The Cecils of Hatfield House* (1973).
P. M. Handover, *The Second Cecil* (1959).
J. Hurstfield, 'Robert Cecil, Earl of Salisbury: Minister of Elizabeth and James I', *History Today*, 7 (May 1957).

*Portraits*: oil, by John de Critz the Elder, 1599: Ingatestone Hall, Essex (Lord Petre); oil on panel, by same de Critz, 1602: National Portrait Gallery, London; oil, by same de Critz, after 1606: Hatfield House (Marquess of Salisbury); oil, by or after de Critz: Old Schools, Cambridge; oil, after de Critz, probably early nineteenth century: N.P.G.; miniature, by Isaac Oliver: Burghley House (Marquess of Exeter); illumination, Salisbury in funeral procession of Queen Elizabeth I: British Museum Additional MS 35324; tomb effigy, by Maximilian Colt: Salisbury Chapel, Hatfield Church; other versions by or after de Critz at Welbeck Abbey, Knole, New College, Oxford, and in other collections.

**Cecil, William** (1520–1598), 1st Baron Burghley, statesman, chief minister of Elizabeth I (q.v.).

William Cecil was born on 13 September 1520 at Bourne, Lincolnshire, the elder son of Richard Cecil and his first wife, Jane Heckington. The Cecils were of Welsh descent. William's grandfather, David Cecil, had fought for Henry VII (q.v.) at Bosworth Field and had become, in return for his services, a Yeoman of the Guard and later a Groom of the Privy Chamber to Henry VIII (q.v.); he laid the foundation of the family fortunes, on which Richard Cecil, who held several minor appointments at court, continued to build.

William, after a short spell as a court page, received his early education at the grammar schools of Grantham and Stamford. In 1533 he went up to St John's College, Cambridge, where he spent the next six years. He proved himself to be a first-class classical scholar and associated with the go-ahead intellectual circle that included men like John Cheke (q.v.) and Roger Ascham (q.v.). A Protestant of firm though moderate views, like his father, Cecil had however no inclination to go into the Church; from the first, politics was his chosen career.

While still an undergraduate Cecil became engaged to Mary, sister of John Cheke; he married her in August 1541, shortly after leaving Cambridge. The match was frowned on by his father, for the bride's mother kept an ale-house in the town, and Mary had no dowry. She died two years later, leaving one son, Thomas, later 1st Earl of Exeter, who never got on with his father and proved to be a disappointment to him, in spite of a life devoted to public service.

From Cambridge Cecil went to Gray's Inn, where he studied law. Through his father's influence he became a Member of Parliament in 1543 and a J.P. In 1545 he married again. He chose his second wife well: Mildred, daughter of Sir Anthony Cooke, tutor to the young Prince Edward (see Edward VI), was a Greek scholar and favourite pupil of Ascham, and was said to be one of the most learned women of the day; she also had the right connections to further Cecil's career. The Cooke family were to be a considerable influence in his life; Sir Anthony was a pioneer of Protestantism in England, and Mildred's sister Ann was later to marry Nicholas Bacon (q.v.), Lord Keeper under Elizabeth, and to become the mother of Anthony and Francis Bacon (qq.v.).

At about this time Cecil attracted the attention of Henry VIII, who took him into the royal service. He quickly made a name for himself at court, especially among the Protestants. After the King's death in January 1547, Edward Seymour (q.v.), when he became Duke of Somerset and Protector of the young King Edward, took Cecil on to his staff as Master of Requests. That September Cecil accompanied Somerset on his Scottish campaign and was nearly killed by a stray bullet at the Battle of Pinkie Cleugh; on their return Somerset appointed him as his private secretary. By this date Cecil was again sitting in Parliament, as Member for Stamford; he served on a commission to inquire into Anabaptism and on another dealing with religious books printed in England. He also held, from 1547 to 1561, the lucrative office of *custos brevium* in the Court of Common Pleas.

When Somerset was driven from power in 1549, Cecil followed him to the Tower. Both were released after a brief imprisonment, and for a few months Cecil contrived to work with both the Duke of Northumberland (see Dudley, John) and his old master. It was an uneasy period, and eventually Cecil threw in his lot with the former, who made him his principal secretary in September 1550. He was knighted the following year. By that time he had also been appointed by the Princess Elizabeth as surveyor, or manager, of her real estate.

Cecil was not in sympathy with Northumberland's religious policies nor with his scheme to put Lady Jane Grey (q.v.) on the throne, and he showed considerable adroitness in thwarting the Duke's plans while not openly antagonizing him. Although he continued to act as principal secretary during the nine-day reign, he secretly conspired with those who brought about Northumberland's downfall and was one of the first to receive a pardon from Mary I (q.v.) on her accession.

He had already shown himself to be a professional politician, shrewd and pliant and willing to work with whoever was in power, even under the Catholic rule of Mary. He did not, however, continue in office, although the Queen employed him on two important missions abroad – once to escort Cardinal Reginald Pole (q.v.) back to England, and on another occasion to negotiate (unsuccessfully as it turned out) between Charles V (q.v.) and the King of France. It was during the period of comparative inactivity that Cecil began to build himself two great residences, one in London and the other at Burghley, near Stamford, on the Northamptonshire-Lincolnshire border. In 1555 he sat in Parliament as Member for the latter county.

When Elizabeth came to the throne she immediately made him her Principal Secretary of State, an appointment which began a remarkable forty-year partnership between the Queen and her chief minister. During this time Cecil was to hold three important offices of state: from 1558 to 1572 he was Principal Secretary of State; from 1561 to 1598, Master of the Court of Wards; and from 1572 to 1598, Lord Treasurer. Another office which he held from 1559 was that of Chancellor of Cambridge University, in which capacity he attended the Queen on her state visit there in 1564.

It was a stormy period, fraught with intrigue both in foreign affairs and at home, and relations between sovereign and loyal servant were not always smooth: Cecil, financially shrewd and worldly wise, had sometimes to restrain the Queen's impulsiveness, and she was often difficult to please, always mistress of the situation and insistent on having the final say. In the long run they subordinated their differences in the common aim of a united, secure, and economically strong England: except in two major instances Cecil, having stated his views, usually yielded to Elizabeth in the end. The first occasion on which he forced his policy upon the Queen was in expelling the French from Scotland; the Treaty of Edinburgh (1561) was a personal triumph. The second occasion was in the matter of the execution of Mary, Queen of Scots (q.v.). As the years went on, Elizabeth's opinion of her chief minister did not waver, and he for his part never once betrayed her trust.

As Principal Secretary of State, for fourteen years Cecil was virtually the administrative head of the government. In foreign policy at this time, being fully aware of the importance of the Netherlands, he favoured Spain rather than France. Aware of the dangers that faced England and the Queen, he set up an elaborate secret service under Sir Francis Walsingham (q.v.), whose agents were spread all over the Continent. At home he concentrated on a programme of economic reform which restored a sound, silver-based currency, cut public expenditure, and made the country less dependent on foreign sources for ammunition and stores. He disliked the idea of war, but realized that the army and navy must be prepared. In religious matters he curbed his own Puritan leanings to conform to Elizabeth's avowed 'middle way' and protected the re-established Anglican Church from both Puritan and Catholic attacks. Inevitably, he had enemies among the nobility and the Catholic faction in England, and he greatly feared the power of Mary, Queen of Scots, and her supporters. For this reason he tried more than once to persuade Elizabeth to marry and so perpetuate the Tudor line of succession; he was, however, strongly opposed to the Queen's favourite, the Earl of Leicester (see Dudley, Robert). The latter's attempt to oust him from office in 1568, and also an uprising in the north the following year, aimed at overthrowing the Protestant government, ended in failure, but Cecil's position was not fully secure until after he had successfully unravelled the Ridolfi Plot (see Ridolfi, Roberto di) of 1571 and dealt firmly with the conspirators.

In 1571 he was raised to the peerage as Baron Burghley, and the following year he was made a Knight of the Garter. His appointment as Lord Treasurer in 1572 relieved him of day-to-day duties, while giving him final control of the administration. Burghley remained for the rest of his life the Queen's closest councillor and adviser. He was still wary of the Catholics and determined that Mary, Queen of Scots, should never sit on the English throne; his action in forcing the Queen to sign Mary's death warrant in 1587 and then acting on it when she shirked the final responsibility led to the one serious quarrel between him and Elizabeth, following which he was relegated from her presence for several months.

The religious issue had split the Privy Council in 1573 into a Puritan group led by Walsingham and Leicester, and a more moderate central group led by Burghley. The Puritans wanted the Queen to head a Protestant league and to support the Dutch rebels against Spain and the Huguenots in France, which meant war; Burghley and Elizabeth were in favour of peace. By 1585 it was clear that England's future depended on the survival of the Netherlands and, all diplomatic interventions having failed, the Queen and Burghley reluctantly came to accept that a war of national unity, rather than one fought on religious grounds, was inevitable. Thus for the remainder of Elizabeth's reign (and Burghley's lifetime) England was at war with Spain; it was ironic that from 1590 onwards, with both the warmongers Leicester and Walsingham dead, responsibility for the conduct of that war should rest with Burghley, who had not wanted it in the first place. He was then seventy years of age.

From his offices and grants Burghley amassed a considerable fortune. This enabled him to adopt a grand living style and to build a magnificent house in London, as well as two palatial country residences, Theobalds in Hertfordshire and Burghley House in Northampton-shire. Of these, only Burghley House now stands. Theobalds, where William Cecil entertained the Queen on no less than twelve occasions, was inherited by his son Robert (q.v.), who exchanged it for the Palace of Hatfield and built the Hatfield House which exists today.

Although he lived in style, Burghley himself ate and drank little. At heart he was a family man, a devoted husband and

at his happiest with his children, grandchildren, and entire household around him. He was intensely ambitious for his family and took tremendous care over their education; his house was filled with men of learning and often as many as twenty 'pupils', some of whom were his legal wards, others young noblemen sent to him to be educated by their parents. Of the three surviving children of his second marriage, Anne, Elizabeth, and Robert, both daughters were to cause him much sorrow: Elizabeth by her early death less than two years after her marriage to Lord Wentworth, and his beloved 'Tannakin' (Anne) through her unhappy marriage to the Earl of Oxford (see Vere, Edward de). Robert was groomed to follow his father as chief minister. 'Serve God by serving of the Queen, for all other service indeed is bondage to the devil,' Burghley once advised his son.

Deeply saddened by his wife's death in 1589, and suffering increasingly from attacks of gout which forced him to ride round on a mule, Burghley withdrew from social life. Although deaf, he retained his mental faculties to the last; in spite of being so weak that he had to be carried everywhere, he continued to sit with the Privy Council until the seventy-eighth (and last) year of his life. In 1596 he was proud to see his son Robert take over the reins of government as Secretary of State.

When Burghley lay dying in his London home in the summer of 1598, the Queen visited his bedside and fed him with her own hand. He died on 4 August. For a long time afterwards tears came into Elizabeth's eyes whenever his name was mentioned.

William Cecil was one of the greatest statesmen of the sixteenth century; he is also one of the most constructive English statesmen of all time. Under his guidance

England virtually completed her transition from a medieval to a modern nation. She had a sound, strong government; the transformation of religion was effected without recourse to civil war; and the long-threatened Spanish invasion was defeated, partly by adverse weather conditions but also by the diplomatic and military preparations that had been made. Cunning and decisive whenever these qualities were in the interests of Queen and country, or the Cecil dynasty, Burghley succeeded in effectively governing and shaping the destiny of England during the most glorious reign of her history. He also provided well for both branches of his family.

A mass of Cecil's official papers has survived. These are preserved at the Public Record Office, the British Museum (Lansdowne MSS), and Hatfield House. Microfilms of the Hatfield MSS are at the British Museum and at the Folger Library, Washington, D.C. For printed sources, see *Calendar of State Papers: Elizabeth* (Foreign and Domestic series); *Collection of State Papers . . . left by William Cecil, Lord Burghley*, edited by S. Haynes and W. Murdin (2 vols; 1740–59); and *Calendar of the Manuscripts of the Marquess of Salisbury . . . preserved at Hatfield House, Hertfordshire* (Historical Manuscripts Commission, 18 vols; 1883–1940).

B. W. Beckingsale, *Burghley, Tudor Statesman, 1520–1598* (1967).
David Cecil, *The Cecils of Hatfield House* (1973).
J. Hurstfield, *The Queen's Wards* (1958).
Conyers Read, *Mr Secretary Cecil and Queen Elizabeth* (1955).
Conyers Read, *Lord Burghley and Queen Elizabeth* (1960).

*Portraits:* oil, by unknown artist, possibly Hans Eworth, *c.* 1558: Hatfield House (Marquess of Salisbury); oil on panel, by or after van Brouckhorst, *c.* 1560–70: National Portrait Gallery, London (numerous other versions at Hatfield, Burghley House, Knole, St John's College and Old Schools, Cambridge, and in the Earl Beauchamp and other private collections); oil, full length, riding a mule, by unknown artist: Bodleian Library, Oxford; several oils, in Garter robes, by unknown artists, *c.* 1585: N.P.G., Hatfield, Burghley, Merton College, Oxford, and elsewhere; oil, probably by Marcus Gheeraerts the Younger after 1585: N.P.G.; oil, full length, seated, by unknown artist, *c.* 1596–7: Hatfield; miniature, by Hilliard: formerly in the Sotheby Collection (sold 1955); bust: Hatfield; tomb effigy: St Martin's Church, Stamford.

**Chapman, George** (?1559–1634), poet, dramatist, translator of Homer.

Born probably in or near Hitchin, Hertfordshire, in about 1559, George Chapman studied at Oxford, but left the university without taking a degree; he may subsequently have studied at Cambridge. He published his first work, *The Shadow of Night . . . Two Poeticall Hymnes*, in 1594, followed in 1595 by *Ovids Banquet of Sence*. By that date he was in the employment of Sir Ralph Sadler (q.v.) in London. His poem in praise of Sir Walter Ralegh (q.v.) was prefixed to Lawrence Keymis's *Second Voyage to Guiana*, published in 1596.

In 1598 Chapman published a continuation to the unfinished poem by Christopher Marlowe (q.v.), *Hero and Leander*. Also published that year were his first known play, a comedy written in 1596, *The Blind Beggar of Alexandria*, and the first part of his translation of Homer's *Iliad*. The complete text of Chapman's fourteen-syllable rhyming version of the *Iliad* was published in 1611, followed by a rhyming ten-syllable translation of the *Odyssey* in 1616.

In 1605 Chapman collaborated with Ben Jonson and John Marston (for both, see *Lives of the Stuart Age*) in writing the play, *Eastward Ho!* Because of its satirical allusion to the Scots, at which the King (see James VI of Scotland) took offence, all three dramatists suffered a short term of imprisonment. Chapman wrote a number of original plays, of which about a dozen, mostly tragedies, have survived; these include *Bussy D'Ambois* (1607), *The Conspiracie and Tragedie of Charles, Duke of Byron* (1608), *The revenge of Bussy D'Ambois* (1613), *Caesar and Pompey* (1631) and, in collaboration with James Shirley (see *Lives of the Stuart Age*), *The Tragedie of Chabot* (1639). Among his comedies were *An Humorous Day's Mirth* (1599), *All Fools* (1605), *The Gentleman Usher* and *Monsieur D'Olive* (1606), *May-Day* (1611), and *The Widdowe's Teares* (1612). Chapman's non-dramatic work includes a major poem, *Euthymiae Raptus, or the Teares of Peace* (1609), translations from Petrarch, Musaeus, and Hesiod, and a satire of Juvenal (1629). A prolific writer, he also composed verses for his friends' books, a court masque (1614), and sundry other poems. He may have been the 'rival poet' referred to by William Shakespeare (q.v.) in his sonnets.

George Chapman died in London on 12 May 1634. He was buried in St Giles's churchyard, where a monument by Inigo Jones (see *Lives of the Stuart Age*) was erected.

While much of Chapman's dramatic output belongs to the Jacobean period, his translation of Homer was regarded as one of the chief literary achievements of the Elizabethan age. It directly inspired the sonnet by John Keats beginning 'Much have I travelled in the realms of gold'. All Chapman's work is of a serious and intellectual nature, with no easy fluency, but of considerable originality and power.

His *Collected Works* have been edited by R. H. Shepherd in three volumes, 1873–5, together with a biographical essay by Swinburne. See also the *Plays*, edited by G. C. Parrott (2 vols; 1910–14), and the *Poems*, edited by Phyllis Brooks-Bartlett (1941).

F. S. Boas, *Introduction to Stuart Drama* (1946).
H. Ellis, *George Chapman* (1934).
J. M. Robertson, *Shakespeare and Chapman* (1917).

**Charles V** (1500–1558), King of Spain and Holy Roman Emperor from 1519 to 1556.

The son of Philip the Handsome, King of Castile, and Joan the Mad, and grandson of the Emperor Maximilian I, Charles was born at Ghent on 24 February 1500. Following the death of his father in 1506, he was brought up by his aunt, Margaret of Austria, then Regent of the Netherlands. He assumed rule over the Netherlands at the age of fifteen, and in 1516, on the death of his grandfather, Ferdinand II, he was proclaimed as Charles I, King of Spain. In 1519 he was elected as King of Germany, and at the same time he assumed the title of Holy Roman Emperor-elect. Betrothed for a short period to the six-year-old Princess Mary of England (see Mary I), daughter of his great-aunt Catherine of Aragon (q.v.) and Henry VIII (q.v.), he subsequently jilted her and in 1526 married Isabella, daughter of King Manuel I of Portugal.

In the spring of 1521, by rejecting the doctrines of Martin Luther (q.v.) at the Diet of Worms, Charles declared war on Protestantism. He spent the next thirty years trying to keep his empire intact in the face of this and other external pressures, chiefly from France and Turkey. His greatest rival was François I, but in 1526 the Pope joined France, Milan, and Venice in establishing the League of Cognac against Charles. After the Emperor's troops had sacked Rome in 1527, a compromise was reached which led to the Peace of Cambrai of 1529, and at Bologna in February the following year Charles was crowned by the Pope as Holy Roman Emperor. He won a decisive victory over the German

Protestants at Muhlberg in April 1547, and at the Diet of Augsburg he presented an 'Interim' formula which gave certain concessions to the Protestants but retained the basic Roman Catholic ritual, hoping thereby to get the Protestants to return to the Catholic church; it was rejected out of hand, and four years later the German princes entered into an alliance with France.

His aim of a politically and religiously united empire virtually in ruins, Charles now turned his attention to a marriage alliance for his son, Philip (see Philip II of Spain), with Mary I of England. The marriage took place in July 1554, but failed to realize Charles's purpose, for Mary proved childless and the English Parliament stubbornly refused to crown Philip as King. Disheartened by the failure of yet another campaign against France, in 1555 and 1556 Charles abdicated all his powers, handing over the Netherlands and Spain to Philip and the imperial crown to his brother Ferdinand. He retired to the monastery of Yuste, in Spain, from where he was active in procuring funds to enable Philip to continue the struggle against France, and where he died on 21 September 1558.

The last of the medieval rulers, Charles V clung fiercely to the old idea of a universal Christian empire. A moral and upright man with a deep Catholic faith, he enjoyed power but had the wisdom to retire from affairs of state once he realized the impossibility of achieving the peace and unification he sought.

M. F. Alvarez, *Charles V, Elected Emperor and Hereditary Ruler* (1976).
E. Armstrong, *The Emperor Charles V* (2 vols; 1902, 1913).
K. Brandi, *Kaiser Karl V* (2 vols; Munich, 1937; 3rd ed. 1941); English translation, *The Emperor Charles V: The Growth and Destiny of a Man and of a World Empire* (1939).
R. Tyler, *The Emperor Charles the Fifth* (1956).

*Portraits*: oil, attributed to L. Cranach the Elder, 1533: Thyssen Collection, Lugano; oil, by Titian, *c.* 1534: Prado Museum, Madrid; oil, by Titian, 1548: Bayerische Staatsgemaldesammlungen, Munich.

**Châtelherault, Duke of** (d. 1575), see Hamilton, James, 2nd Earl of Arran.

**Cheke, Sir John** (1514–1557), Greek scholar and humanist.

Born on 16 June 1514, John Cheke was the son of Peter Cheke, an esquire-bedel (beadle) at the University of Cambridge, and his wife Agnes Dufford. Educated at St John's College, Cambridge, where he soon embraced the Protestant doctrines of the Reformation and achieved a reputation as a classical scholar, Cheke took his M.A. in 1533. Within a few years he came to be regarded as the leader of Greek studies; in 1540 Henry VIII (q.v.) made him the first Regius Professor of Greek at the University.

Under Cheke's teaching Cambridge became the centre of the 'new learning'. With his friend Sir Thomas Smith (q.v.), he discovered the correct pronunciation

of ancient Greek, but this involved him in a heated dispute with Stephen Gardiner (q.v.), which resulted in his having publicly to conform to the latter's view, while privately maintaining his own. Among the brilliant young men whom he influenced at Cambridge was William Cecil (q.v.), later 1st Baron Burghley, who was to marry Cheke's sister Mary.

In 1544 Cheke was appointed tutor to the young Prince Edward (see Edward VI). He was also made a canon of King Henry VIII's College, Oxford (later Christ Church). When the King changed the college into a cathedral he gave Cheke a pension to compensate for the loss of this office. For the next few years he devoted himself to educating Edward in the classics; a strong bond of affection is said to have existed between them. He also taught the Princess Elizabeth (see Elizabeth I).

On Edward's accession in 1547 Cheke was granted a number of royal favours – lands; the post of Provost of King's College, Cambridge, in 1548; and a knighthood in 1552. He sat as M.P. for Bletchingly in 1547 and again in 1553, and as an ardent Protestant and Clerk of the Council he played an important role in effecting the religious changes of the new reign. On Edward's death he accepted Lady Jane Grey (q.v.) as Queen and acted briefly as a Secretary of State.

When Mary I (q.v.) came to the throne Cheke lost all his official positions and in July 1553 was committed to the Tower. He was released in September the following year and went into exile on the Continent. He travelled first to Basle and then to Italy; later he taught Greek at Strasbourg. While he was abroad he published some important letters on Greek pronunciation.

In 1556 two English emissaries employed by Philip II (q.v.) lured him to Brussels, where he was taken prisoner, conveyed back to England, and again imprisoned in the Tower. Fear of being burned at the stake made him publicly recant his Protestantism, but immediately afterwards he became so ashamed of his recantation that he fell gravely ill. He died in London on 13 September 1557.

John Cheke was one of the most erudite men of the age. John Milton (see *Lives of the Stuart Age*) later wrote of him that he had 'taught Cambridge and King Edward Greek'. Although a prolific writer and translator, his English works are not of any great significance. Cheke was an exponent of the reformed phonetic spelling, and an English language which, in the words of his celebrated letter to Sir Thomas Hoby, the diplomat and translator, 'shold be written cleane and pure, unmixt and unmangeled with borrowing of other tunges, wherin if we take not heed by tijm, ever borrowing and never payeng, she shall be fain to keep her house as bankrupt.'

C. H. Garrett, *The Marian Exiles* (1938).
John Strype, *Life of the Learned Sir John Cheke* (1705).

*Portraits:* oil, by unknown artist, *c.* 1545–50: The Lord Sandys; medal, *c.* 1555: British Museum, London; oil, by unknown artist, *c.* 1550–5: The Duke of Manchester; engraving, by W. van de Passe: B.M.; engraving, by S. Passe, 1620: location not known.

**Chettle, Henry** (d. ?1607), dramatist and pamphleteer.

The son of Robert Chettle, a dyer of London, little is known of Henry Chettle's early life except that in 1577 he was apprenticed to a stationer, Thomas East, for eight years. In 1591 he became a partner in a printing business which failed, whereupon he took to writing plays, both on his own account and in collaboration with others.

Chettle first achieved prominence on the literary scene in 1592, when he edited the *Groatsworth of Witte*, written by Robert Greene (q.v.) and published soon after his death. Both he and Thomas Nashe (q.v.) were at the time believed to have had a hand in the posthumous tract. A few years later Chettle took Nashe's part in his fierce dispute with Gabriel Harvey. His first satirical pamphlet, *Kind-Hart's Dream*, was written in 1592 and published probably early in 1593, and in 1595 he issued his *Pierce Plainnes Prentiship*.

It is not known exactly when Chettle began to write for the stage, but in the course of his career as a dramatist he is believed to have been the sole author of thirteen plays and part-author of some thirty-five others produced in the period 1598–1603. Only one play attributed to his sole authorship is extant: *The Tragedy of Hoffman* (1602; first printed in 1631 and reprinted 1851). Among the best-known plays to which he contributed are *The Blind Beggar of Bethnal Green*, *Robin Hood*, and *Patient Grisel*. (A full list will be found in the *D.N.B.*)

All his life Chettle was in financial difficulties, and in 1599 he spent some months in the Marshalsea Prison for debt. Philip Henslowe (q.v.), for whom he wrote plays, constantly came to his aid. In 1603, shortly after the death of Queen Elizabeth (q.v.), Chettle published an elegy entitled *Englande's Mourning Garment*; this was well received and ran into two editions the same year, as well as one pirated edition. According to Thomas Dekker (see *Lives of the Stuart Age*), with whom he collaborated, Chettle died not later than 1607; his death is referred to in Dekker's *Knight's Conjuring*, published that year. He was married and is believed to have had one daughter, Mary, who died in 1595.

Harold Jenkins, *The Life and Work of Henry Chettle* (1934).

**Cobham, 11th Baron** (1564–1619), see Brooke, Henry.

**Cokayne, Sir William** (d. 1626), Lord Mayor of London, see *Lives of the Stuart Age*.

**Coke, Sir Edward** (1552–1634), judge, M.P., and writer on English law, see *Lives of the Stuart Age*.

**Colet, John** (?1466–1519), theologian and founder of St Paul's School.

John Colet was born in London in either 1466 or 1467, and came from a distinguished and wealthy family: his father, Sir Henry Colet, had been twice Lord Mayor of London, and on his mother's side he was related to the de Ruthyn and Stafford families. The eldest and only one of a large family of sons and daughters to survive infancy, John spent his early years at the family home in Stepney. He attended the school of St Anthony in Threadneedle Street, in the City, and later studied at Magdalen College, Oxford, where he took his M.A. in 1490. He spent the next three years travelling and studying on the Continent, mainly in Italy. By the time he returned to England, in 1496, he had decided to take holy orders, and after being ordained he was given several lucrative benefices, in accordance with the custom of the age.

Colet now settled at Oxford and began to earn a high reputation for the originality of his lectures there on the Pauline Epistles, which drew large audiences. Among his intimate friends were Thomas More (q.v.), Thomas

Linacre (q.v.), and William Grocyn (q.v.), whose view that the so-called writings of Dionysius were not his own work Colet eventually accepted. When Erasmus (q.v.) visited Oxford, the two men formed a lifelong friendship.

In 1505 Colet was appointed Dean of St Paul's, London, a post which he held for the rest of his life. He preached often in the cathedral, sometimes in English, and inveighed against the abuses in the Church with such frequency and unorthodoxy that Richard FitzJames, then Bishop of London, in 1510 charged him with heresy. The charge was dismissed by Archbishop Warham (q.v.), but FitzJames continued to attack Colet to such an extent that the Dean began to weary of the fight and to contemplate retirement. Nevertheless in 1513 he spoke forcibly in Convocation against the corruption of the Church, and on another occasion the same year, when the King was on the point of going to war with France, he preached before Henry VIII (q.v.) against war. Colet's plans to spend his last years among the Carthusians at Sheen, Surrey, were overtaken by ill-health, and he died at Sheen on 16 September 1519.

He had inherited a considerable fortune from his father in 1505, and not long afterwards had formulated the plan to found a new school at St Paul's. The statutes for the school were drawn up in 1518, and in these Colet also demonstrated his unorthodoxy, stipulating that the school was to be managed not by the clergy, but by the Mercers' Company; he also insisted that the classics be taught, expressing in this way his devotion to the 'new learning' which he and his fellow Oxford humanists had so enthusiastically embraced. He also made arrangements to pay an annuity to Erasmus (q.v.). Most of his works remained unpublished until the nineteenth century, when they were edited by his biographer, Lupton. The statutes for St Paul's school and a Latin grammar written by Colet especially for the school are included in the life by Lupton (see below).

Although Colet continually spoke out against the corruption and abuse he found in the Church, it is thought unlikely that he would ever have gone so far as to sanction a breach with Rome.

E. W. Hunt, *Dean Colet and his theology* (1956).
J. H. Lupton, *A life of John Colet* (1887).
J. A. R. Marriot, *The life of John Colet* (1933).

*Portraits*: miniature on vellum, by unknown artist, 1509: University Library, Cambridge; oil, by unknown artist, after Holbein: Magdalen College, Oxford; drawing, by Holbein (probably from monument by Torrigiano, destroyed in Great Fire of London): Royal Collection, Windsor; oil, by unknown artist, seventeenth or early eighteenth century: Old Schools, Cambridge.

**Columbus, Christopher** (1451–1506), seaman, colonizer, and discoverer of the New World.

There has been much speculation about Columbus's origin, but he is believed to have been born in the autumn of 1451 in Genoa, the son of a master weaver, Domenico Colombo, and his wife Susanna. Christened Juan, He later changed his name to Cristóforo. The family were probably of Spanish–Jewish extraction, although there is some support for the theory that Columbus was a native of the island of Majorca. Among his younger brothers and sisters, Bartholomew and Diego were both to play an important part in his life.

Little is known of Christopher's early years. He probably had a very rudimentary education and was trained in his father's business. Some time before 1470 the family moved to Savona, an Italian port to the east of Genoa, where as a boy he must have had many opportunities to sail between ports along the Italian coast and to learn the art of seamanship. At some date between 1470 and 1473 he was in the service of René of Anjou, who was chartering Genoese ships to support a rebellion against Juan II of Aragon. He later made several trips to the island of Chios in the Aegean. In the summer of 1476 he sailed with a convoy of Genoese ships laden with mastic from Chios for Portugal, England, and Flanders, but off Cape St Vincent the convoy was attacked by the French and in the ensuing battle Columbus's ship was sunk. He managed to reach the Portuguese coast with the aid of an oar and made his way to Lisbon, where his brother Bartholomew was working as a cartographer.

Lisbon at this time was an exciting city, the meeting-place of seafaring men who sailed regularly to Africa and Madeira and spoke of more daring voyages of exploration into the unknown; it was also a centre of the arts, cosmography, and astronomy. For the next eight years Columbus sailed under the Portuguese flag, working during the winter months in partnership with his brother as a map-maker and bookseller and losing no opportunity to learn Portuguese and elementary Latin. On a voyage to Iceland during this period he is believed to have heard stories of the unknown land that lay to the west, which excited his imagination. He soon became obsessed with the idea of opening up a direct route to the Indies by sailing westwards.

In 1478 or 1479 Columbus married Felipa Perestrello, a member of a prominent Portuguese family. Shortly afterwards he and his wife settled on the island of Porto Santa, off Madeira, where their only son, Diego, was born in 1479 or 1480. They later moved to Funchal,

the capital of Madeira, from where Columbus gained experience of sailing the south Atlantic; he may even have sailed as far as the Portuguese trading post of Mina, on the Gold Coast. His appetite for further exploration was whetted by the tales he heard from sea captains who put in to Madeira, and also by objects washed up on the shores that convinced him that land existed beyond the western horizon, and he formulated the idea of sailing due west from the Canary Islands on latitude 28°N, which he believed would lead him to Japan.

Returning to Lisbon in 1484, he determined to find a patron. He was granted an audience of King John, but made such high-flown demands that the King mistrusted him and rejected the project. Columbus then suffered another major setback to his fortunes in the death of his wife. In the summer of 1485, dejected and in debt, he left Portugal for Spain, taking with him his five-year-old son.

At the Franciscan friary of La Rábida, near Huelva, where he placed the young

Diego, Columbus made the acquaintance of the astronomer-friar Antonio de Marchena, and through him of the Count of Medina Celi, a grandee of Spain and owner of a large merchant fleet. For several months Medina Celi housed the poverty-stricken sailor while he considered his great scheme; finally he decided that such an immense project ought to have the backing of the crown and he sent Columbus to the court of Ferdinand and Isabella.

For the next five years Columbus was obliged to follow the court as it moved from town to town, waiting for a decision. After his first audience with the King and Queen at Cordova in the spring of 1486, a commission was set up to investigate the proposal; four years later, in 1490, it reported unfavourably. It was during this period of waiting that Columbus fell in love with a girl of humble family, Beatriz de Enriques, who bore him a son, Fernando. In about 1489 Bartholomew Columbus is said to have visited England in an abortive attempt to interest Henry VII (q.v.) in his brother's proposed enterprise. By this time both brothers had hispanicized their names, Columbus signing himself as Cristóbal Colón.

Bartholomew now settled in France, where Columbus, believing that Ferdinand and Isabella would have nothing more to do with his scheme, intended to join him and to offer his services to the French king. Meanwhile influential friends were arguing his case at court, and unexpectedly, on the point of departure, he was summoned back to court at Santa Fé, near Granada, this time to name his terms. There were more delays, owing to his audacious demands – among them a knighthood, the hereditary title of Admiral of the Ocean Sea, and one-tenth of all revenues arising from the voyage – but in April 1492 a contract was signed between him and the Spanish sovereigns. Immediately Columbus made for the port of Palos where, with the help of the prosperous shipowning Pinzón family, he spent three months recruiting and equipping the three ships with which he was to sail – the caravels Niña and Pinta, provided by the citizens of Palos under royal orders, and the third and largest vessel, chartered by the Admiral himself, the Santa Maria.

This small fleet sailed from Palos in the early morning of 3 August 1492, with Columbus in command of the Santa Maria and the two caravels captained by the Pinzón brothers, Martin and Vicente. The Admiral had with him a letter of introduction from Ferdinand and Isabella addressed to the 'Great Khan' (the supposed emperor of China); confident that he would make landfall in the Orient, he had tremendous faith in God and in his mission as 'Christ-bearer' (a translation of his first name, Cristóforo) to bring Christianity to the East; also he felt sure he would find gold. The riches he brought back would finance his long-cherished dream of liberating Jerusalem from the Moors.

They reached the Canary Islands on 12 August and remained there for three weeks doing necessary repairs and stocking up with provisions. On 6 September they sailed westwards. Early in October, after several false sightings of land and trouble from a potentially mutinous crew, the Admiral took Martin Pinzón's advice and altered course to the south-west. At 2 a.m. on 12 October land was sighted, and later that day Columbus and the Pinzón brothers went ashore and took possession in the name of Ferdinand and Isabella. They had reached the most westerly of the group of islands now known as the Bahamas; Columbus named it San Salvador.

Convinced that he was in the Orient,

the Admiral spent the next two weeks wandering among the islands in search of gold. He did not find any, but discovered natives who smoked tobacco and slept in hammocks. He learned from them of the existence of a large island to the south-west, which he believed must be Cipango (Japan); but when he reached Cuba on 28 October, Columbus felt sure he was on the mainland of Cathay. A landing party failed either to find gold or the kingdom of the 'Great Khan' and, disappointed, Columbus now turned eastwards while Pinzón, in defiance of the Admiral's instructions, went off in the opposite direction.

In early December Columbus reached an island which he named La Isla Española (Hispaniola), where he found the natives wearing huge ornaments made from gold dust panned from the river beds. He took possession in the name of the Spanish sovereigns, and when the *Santa Maria* ran aground on a reef at midnight on Christmas Day and became a total loss, he decided to set up a trading post with thirty-eight men and sufficient stores for a year; he named the settlement 'Villa de la Navidad' and on 4 January 1493 set sail for Spain in his one remaining vessel, the *Niña*.

Two days later, when he was joined by the *Pinta*, there was a stormy quarrel between the Admiral and Pinzón. Finally the two ships set out together on 16 January, Columbus deliberately setting a more northerly course for the homeward voyage. In mid-February they ran into gales and were separated; tormented by the thought that he might be drowned and his discovery never known, Columbus wrote an account of his voyage, put it into a cask and threw it overboard. Then on 15 February land was sighted, and three days later he anchored at Santa Maria, the southern-most island of the Azores. Worse storms

developed on the next lap of the voyage, forcing Columbus to seek refuge in the Tagus river. He was received with full honours by the Portuguese king, but he declined the latter's suggestion that he should take an overland route to Spain. After dispatching his celebrated 'First Letter' to Ferdinand and Isabella recounting his achievement, Columbus set sail again and made a triumphant entry into the port of Palos on 15 March 1493, 224 days after his departure. Pinzón returned a few days later; exhausted by the strain of the voyage, he died on 20 March.

Much acclaimed as he travelled in triumph from Seville to Barcelona, Columbus was received at court amid great splendour at the beginning of April. Wealth and honours were heaped on him, and in addition to the agreed titles, Ferdinand and Isabella appointed him 'Viceroy and Governor of the Islands which have been discovered in the Indies' and gave him the right to bear royal symbols on his coat of arms. In case Portugal should beat Spain to it, preparations were hastily made for a second voyage, the main object of which was to bring Christianity to the new territories and to develop them as a Spanish colony.

Columbus was impatient to be away, but unfortunately his high-handed manner upset the state officials responsible for the preparations and caused unpleasant rows and, inevitably, delays. Among those who assisted in the fitting out of this second voyage was Amerigo Vespucci, an Italian working in Seville in the shipchandlery business, who would later make his own voyages of discovery, and after whom the New World would be named. At last, on 25 September 1493, a fleet of seventeen vessels and over 1,000 participants sailed from Cadiz; in view of the quest for gold there was no lack of volunteers, and among the gentlemen who sailed with Columbus on his second voyage were his youngest brother Diego and Juan Ponce de Leon, the future discoverer of Florida.

After the usual stop in the Canaries, they set out to cross the Atlantic on 13 October, taking a more southerly course than the previous year. The weather was good, and on 3 November they reached the archipelago known today as the Leeward Islands; Columbus named them in turn Dominica, Maria Galante, Guadalupe, and Montserrat. To the north-east he came to another group and named them the Virgin Islands; then, taking a westerly direction, he reached an island which he called San Juan (now Puerto Rico), and from there set course for Hispaniola.

On arrival at the end of November, they saw that the entire Spanish settlement had been wiped out by the natives; the bodies of their compatriots had been left decomposing on the beach. Columbus immediately began to search for a safer site; eventually he chose a position on the northern coast of the island, where in January 1494 he founded the first European city of the New World and named it Isabella in honour of the Spanish Queen. Twelve ships were sent back to Spain with Antonio de Torres, bearing a message to the court, where news of the disaster was received with dismay and doubts began to be voiced as to whether Columbus was going to prove worth the expense.

Meanwhile, on 12 March, leaving his brother Diego in command of Isabella, Columbus set out to explore the central region of the island, where the natives had led him to believe 'gold was born'. Sending an advance party further into the interior to investigate the rumoured gold-mine, Columbus established a fortified settlement, which he called San Tomás; he left fifty-six men there and returned to Isabella, where he found the settlers in a mutinous frame of mind. Some had died, their dwindling provisions were going bad in the hot climate, confidence in the Admiral was evaporating, and many of the Spaniards, seeing there was no gold near at hand, were anxious to get home. Columbus had the ringleaders executed and as a result came into conflict with the friar appointed by the Queen to look after the spiritual needs of the men. News then arrived from San Tomás that a native chieftain was preparing to attack, and Columbus sent an expeditionary force to relieve the fort and explore further into the interior. He imposed a gold-tax on the native population and threatened those who would not work for the colonizers with either death or shipment to Europe as slaves.

On 24 April, having set up a council under the chairmanship of Diego to administer Isabella in his absence, Columbus set sail aboard the *Niña*, together with two other caravels, towards Cuba, which, being still convinced he was in 'the Indies', he was anxious to explore. He cruised along the southern coast, reaching the south-westerly point (Columbus called it Cabo de Cruz) on 3 May; there he learned through a native interpreter of an island that lay to the south where sizeable nuggets of gold were to be found and, lured as always by his desire for gold, the Admiral altered course to a southerly direction, reaching two days later an island which he named Santiago (now Jamaica). Impressed by its beauty but again disappointed at the lack of gold, he determined to return to Cuba, which he still believed to be the mainland. For a while they followed the Cuban coastline westwards, but after navigating between the reefs and through the shallows the caravels were in such bad condition that Columbus reluctantly decided to return to Isabella; he also realized that he would have to convince his royal patrons that the next expedition would be successful, and with this in mind he forced all the crew to swear an oath that they were in no doubt that they had seen the mainland. (It is ironic that if in fact he had continued westwards Columbus would have reached Mexico.)

On 13 June he set an easterly course, then dropped south to call at an island that lay to the south, which Columbus named Evangelista (now the Island of Pines), and to pass round the southern coast of Jamaica, before turning eastwards again towards Hispaniola. At this point Columbus fell ill and was near death for several days. When they reached Isabella on 29 September, they found that Bartholomew Colón had arrived from Europe. He was made Governor of Hispaniola, an appointment which aggravated the growing resentment against the Colón administration; several of the colonists had already departed for Spain, where they intended to lodge formal complaints at court.

For nearly five months Columbus was ill, due partly to the strains and deprivations of the previous months and the onset of arthritis, and partly to a nervous breakdown brought on by a sense of frustration and failure. Meanwhile de Torres returned from Spain with a letter from the King and Queen commending the Admiral's enterprise and requesting that he or someone in authority should return to the court as soon as possible to discuss the situation. Declining to go himself, Columbus sent instead his brother Diego, together with 500 native slaves.

In June 1495 a hurricane struck Hispaniola and sank three of the vessels anchored off Isabella, leaving Columbus with only the *Niña*. A relief force arrived from Spain in October under the command of Juan de Aguado, who had authority from the Spanish sovereigns to investigate and report on the colony. Aguado was determined to humiliate Columbus; friction inevitably followed, and Columbus soon realized that he would have to return to Spain in person if he were to win back credibility and trust. Leaving the colony in charge of Bartholomew, with instructions to build a new capital on a safer site, Columbus sailed for Spain on board the *Niña*, accompanied by one other caravel, on 10 March 1496. Overcrowded and badly provisioned, both vessels were in poor shape when they reached Cadiz on 11 June.

Expecting a hostile reception, Columbus donned a petitential robe before making his way via Seville to Burgos, but Ferdinand and Isabella gave him a warmer welcome than he had dared to hope for, and with his personal magnetism the Admiral soon won over his adversaries at court. He was reunited with his two sons, Diego and Fernando, now pages to the Infante Don Juan; all his privileges were confirmed, and permission was granted to mount a third expedition.

For financial and other reasons the preparations for the third voyage were considerably delayed, and it was not until 30 May 1498 that Columbus sailed from Sanlúcar with a fleet of six ships. He called first at Madeira and then at the Canaries, where he sent three ships on the direct route to Hispaniola, himself taking a south-westerly course with the other three. He made a brief stop at the Cape Verde Islands, then took first a southerly and then a westerly course; sighting land with three summits on 31 July, he named it Trinidad. (Had he kept on for a few more days in a southerly direction he would have discovered the Amazon.) Next, Columbus sailed along the southern coast of Trinidad and into the gulf of Paria, and on 5 August actually set foot on the mainland (now Venezuela) but, believing it to be yet another island or land mass tailing off from the Malay Peninsula, and anxious to get back to Hispaniola, he did not linger except to marvel at the pearls worn by the natives and at the volume of fresh water emptying into the gulf, which convinced him that he had discovered not the Indies, but an 'otro mundo' (Other World).

At Hispaniola Columbus found that construction of the new capital, Santo Domingo, had been started but that a rebellion had broken out against the Colón administration. He spent the next few months bargaining with the rebel leader and finally capitulated, dividing the land among the Spaniards and allowing them to have slaves and concubines. Further trouble arose when a surprise fleet arrived from Spain under the command of Alonso de Ojeda, whom Columbus regarded as a poacher on 'his' territory.

Meanwhile disquieting reports were reaching the Spanish court of the Colón régime; it was even rumoured that the brothers were engaged in treasonable dealings with Genoese agents. Reluctantly the Spanish sovereigns came to the conclusion that their beloved Admiral was useless as an administrator, and in the spring of 1499 they decided to dispatch a member of the royal household, Francisco de Bobadilla, to deal with the situation; his departure was, however, delayed for more than a year, possibly while information was sought concerning the alleged dealings with the Genoese. Bobadilla, appointed Governor of the colony over Columbus's head, arrived in Santo Dom-

ingo in August 1500; he carried a letter from Ferdinand and Isabella not only commanding the Viceroy to surrender all royal property to him but giving the new Governor authority to send back to Spain anyone he thought fit to arrest, regardless of rank. When Bobadilla found that the Colón brothers were sending rebellious Spaniards to the gallows and that they refused to accept his authority, he had all three put in irons and transported back to Spain.

The Admiral's humiliating homecoming at Cadiz at the end of October caused much public indignation, and a month later, by order of the King and Queen, the brothers were released. On 17 December the dejected Columbus, summoned at last to court, fell to his knees before his royal patrons and begged their forgiveness. He and his brothers were pardoned, but never again appointed to positions of administrative responsibility; in September 1501 a new Governor, Nicholas de Ovando, was appointed to succeed Bobadilla under terms that made him, in effect, Viceroy.

Bitterness mounted in Columbus as he learned of seamen of other nationalities now sailing 'his' seas, while he was kept waiting for permission to make another voyage. Ferdinand and Isabella, preoccupied with negotiations for the marriage of their daughter, Catherine of Aragon (q.v.) to Prince Arthur of England (q.v.), were in no hurry to commit themselves to a costly fourth expedition. The Admiral tried to fill in the tedious waiting period by compiling a *Book of Prophecies* from biblical sources to substantiate his theory that Jerusalem would one day be liberated by Spain.

At last, in March 1502, permission was granted for Columbus to sail; he was, however, expressly forbidden to put in to Santo Domingo. He left Cadiz early in May with a fleet of four caravels and accompanied by his youngest son, Fernando, and his brother Bartholomew. After the usual stop in the Canary Islands, they began the Atlantic crossing on 25 May. Three weeks later Columbus reached an island which he called Matininó (Martinique) and from there, in defiance of royal orders, he made straight for Santo Domingo. Refused permission to land by Ovando, he was forced to shelter from a hurricane further along the coast, and on 14 July he sailed for Jamaica. Then, taking a south-westerly course, he reached what we now know as the coast of Honduras, which Columbus believed to be the Malay peninsula. Next, hoping to find the strait that would lead to the 'Spice Islands', he turned south-east. His men were mutinous, the weather was terrible, and when they safely rounded a cape on 14 September, he named it Gracias a Dios, in gratitude to God. Dogged by more storms and mutiny among the crew, persistently Columbus sailed on until the beginning of December, when he turned westward again and on 6 January 1503 dropped anchor off a river which he called Belén (Bethlehem). His intention was to establish a trading post there, under the command of Bartholomew, but the project had to be abandoned because of hostility from the native population. By the middle of May they were heading back to Hispaniola via Cuba.

More gales followed, and with two of his original caravels having been abandoned and the remaining two in bad repair, Columbus decided to seek refuge in Jamaica, where he dropped anchor on 23 June. There he was to be marooned for a whole year, while a message was sent by canoe to Ovando asking for help. During this time Columbus's health again deteriorated, and he had to cope with yet another mutiny among his men.

Eventually two caravels arrived to take him off, and on 28 June 1504 he sailed for Santo Domingo, and from there, on 12 September, on his last homeward voyage.

On arrival at Sanlúcar on 7 November, Columbus was so crippled with arthritis that he had to be conveyed to Seville. The usual summons to court did not come; on 26 November the death of Queen Isabella put paid to any last hope Columbus might have entertained of being reinstated as Viceroy of 'his' Indies. Although the gold he had brought home and his tenth share of the revenue from Hispaniola, to which he was entitled under his original agreement with Ferdinand and Isabella, had made him rich, he was a sick and disappointed man. He wrote a series of memoirs to the King on the Indies and their gold, but when at last he was able to make the journey to court in May 1505, although he was received sympathetically by Ferdinand, he was still denied the reappointment he sought. Despondent and believing himself to have been a failure, Columbus died at Valladolid on 20 May 1506. He was buried in Seville, but in 1542 his remains and those of his son Diego were exhumed and reinterred in the cathedral at Santo Domingo, where more recently the Columbus Memorial Lighthouse has been designed as their final resting-place.

Christopher Columbus was one of the greatest seamen of all time. His four voyages opened the way for European exploration and colonization of the New World and so changed the course of world history. His failure was one of temperament, which showed itself in excessive self-confidence and arrogance and made him a poor administrator; his tragedy was that he discovered a new continent, but never knew it. Columbus's estimate of the size of the globe was smaller than that of many of his contemporaries, but no one at that time even suspected the existence of a vast continent like America to bar the sea route to the Indies.

The *Select Letters of Christopher Columbus*, edited by R. H. Major, have been published by the Hakluyt Society (2nd ed., 1870).

Ernle Bradford, *Christopher Columbus* (1973).
F. Fernández-Armesto, *Columbus and the Conquest of the Impossible* (1974).
S. de Madariaga, *Christopher Columbus* (1939; rev. ed. 1949).
S. E. Morison, *Admiral of the Ocean Sea, A Life of Christopher Columbus* (2 vols; 1942).
S. E. Morison, *Christopher Columbus, Mariner* (1955).

*Portraits*: oil, by Sebastiano del Piombo: Biblioteca Nacional, Madrid; oil, attributed to del Piombo, 1519: Metropolitan Museum of Art, New York; oil, attributed to Ghirlandaio: Museo Navale, Pegli-Genoa; oil, by Lorenzo Lotto: Museo Naval, Madrid.

**Copernicus, Nicolaus** (1473–1543), Polish astronomer, whose heliocentric theory revolutionized planetary astronomy.

Born on 19 February 1473 in Torún, Copernicus was the son of a prosperous copper merchant. He studied at the University of Cracow under the leading astronomers of the day, Glogoviensis and Brudzevius. His uncle and guardian, the Bishop of Warmia, sent him to Bologna to study law, but he neglected his legal studies in favour of his main interest and came under the influence of the astronomer Domenico Novara. He then spent several years at the University of Padua studying medicine and Greek as well as pursuing his astronomical work, before returning to Frombork in Poland, where he acted as secretary and physician to his uncle until the latter's death in 1512. Thereafter Copernicus remained at Frombork, continuing his work as physician to the poor and representative of the cathedral chapter, while at the same time carrying on his astronomical observations.

Increasingly he came to question the Ptolemaic system which said that the earth was the centre of the universe and that the sun, planets, and stars revolved round it. He turned to the Greek philosophers and, reading them in the original, discovered that the theory of a moving earth had been suggested; but only after years of study was he himself really convinced of its truth. By this time his fame had spread and friends were urging him to publish his great work, *De revolutionibus*, which he had begun to write in about 1515. Fearing the uproar this would provoke, Copernicus continued to revise the work and to resist publication, but was finally persuaded by his friend, the German astronomer and mathematician Rheticus. The book appeared in the spring of 1543 and a copy is said to have been brought to the author as he lay unconscious on his deathbed. Copernicus died at Frombork on 24 May 1543.

The controversy arising out of the publication of *De revolutionibus* was both fierce and prolonged. Martin Luther (q.v.) and the theologians in particular were hostile to the Copernican theory, but the work of Galileo (1564–1642) and Kepler (1571–1630) helped it to gain gradual acceptance during the seventeenth century. In England Robert Recorde (q.v.) was the first to publish a discussion of the teaching of Copernicus, and Thomas Digges (q.v.), whose own research marked a turning point in the study of astronomy, was its earliest and greatest protagonist.

H. Świderska and S. Tyacke, *Copernicus and the New Astronomy* (Trustees of the British Museum, 1973).

F. Hoyle, *Nicolaus Copernicus* (1973).

*Portrait*: head, by unknown artist: part of frieze in Upper Reading Room, Bodleian Library, Oxford; engraving, by J. Falck, *c.* 1500, after unknown sixteenth-century artist: location not known.

**Cork, 1st Earl of** (1566–1643), Anglo-Irish adventurer, colonizer, landowner, capitalist, and politician, see Boyle, Richard, in *Lives of the Stuart Age*.

**Cotton, Sir Robert Bruce** (1571–1631), antiquary and founder of the Cottonian Library.

Born on 22 January 1571 at Denton, Huntingdonshire, Robert Bruce Cotton was the eldest son of Thomas Cotton of Conington and his first wife, Elizabeth, daughter of Francis Shirley of Staunton-Harold, Leicestershire. The family was an old-established one which traced its descent back to the Saxon and Norman royal line and to the Bruces of Scotland. Robert's father was a wealthy country gentleman who in 1557 had represented Huntingdonshire in Parliament. His mother died while he, his brother Thomas and his three sisters were still

quite young, and Thomas Cotton senior married again, to have six more children by his second wife, Dorothy, daughter of John Tamworth.

Robert was sent at an early age to Westminster School, where he came under the influence of William Camden (q.v.), then Second Master at the school, with whom he was later to be closely associated. He subsequently studied at Cambridge, matriculating at Jesus College in 1581 and taking his B.A. in 1585. At the age of eighteen he determined to devote his life to antiquarian studies, and shortly after leaving university he moved to London. He married, probably in about 1592, a young woman of fortune, Elizabeth, daughter of William Brocas of Thedingworth, Leicestershire; their only son, Thomas, was born in 1594. Robert's father died in October 1593, leaving generous bequests to his second wife and her children which seriously eroded his own inheritance as eldest son; in a letter written not long afterwards to William Cecil (q.v.), later 1st Baron Burghley, he begged to be excused from the office of Sheriff of Cambridgeshire and Huntingdonshire on the grounds that he could not afford to live on his estate at Conington.

In the last decade of the century the Cottons settled in a house in London near Old Palace Yard, Westminster. There Cotton began to indulge his passion for collecting manuscripts, coins, and other antiquities, many of them rescued from the dissolved monasteries. He had joined the Antiquarian Society in 1590 and renewed his acquaintance with Camden and met all the contemporary men of learning. He read a number of papers to the Society in the ensuing years, and many others who read papers generously acknowledged help from Cotton's library of manuscripts. Over the years

Cotton House became a meeting-place for scholars from all over England and the Continent.

In 1600 he accompanied Camden on an antiquarian tour to Carlisle; he was at the time helping his friend and former tutor with the fifth edition of *Britannia*. It is possible that before this Cotton made a trip to Europe, since he refers in some of the papers he read before the Antiquarian Society to a visit to Italy.

On the accession of James I (see James VI of Scotland) Cotton was taken into royal favour. He was knighted in May 1603 and, because the King playfully called him 'cousin' on account of his descent from the Bruces, thereafter he always signed himself as 'Robert Bruce Cotton'. The new King's tastes accorded very much with his own, and Cotton drew up a pedigree for James and wrote a number of treatises at his request; his advice was also sought on other matters, including abuses in the navy administration and the thorny question of increasing the royal revenues. Among those with whom he was intimate at

court were Lord and Lady Hunsdon and later (with disastrous consequences) the royal favourite, Robert Carr, Earl of Somerset (see *Lives of the Stuart Age*). It was undoubtedly through Lord Hunsdon that Cotton was first returned to Parliament in 1601 as Member for Newtown, Isle of Wight. Three years later he became Member for Huntingdonshire.

Meanwhile Cotton was devoting much of his time and energy to assisting his friends John Speed (q.v.) and Camden with their historical writings. He supplied some valuable material and corrected the proofs for the former's *History of England*; his share in Camden's *Annales* of the reign of Elizabeth seems however to have been the subject of controversy, and may have been exaggerated by Cotton's contemporaries. Among other scholars to whom Cotton loaned manuscripts from his collection were John Selden and Ben Jonson (for whom see *Lives of the Stuart Age*), Sir Walter Ralegh (q.v.), busy at work in the Tower on his *History of the World,* and Francis Bacon (q.v.), for his *History of the Reign of Henry VII*; after the latter's disgrace and denial of access to London, Cotton sometimes had papers specially sent to him at Gorhambury. In 1610 he made a substantial gift of manuscripts to Sir Thomas Bodley (q.v.) for the new university library at Oxford. The following year he was raised to the new rank of baronet.

By this time anxiety was growing in some quarters, fanned by the jealousy of Sir Robert's contemporaries, that the vast collection of private and official documents which he was amassing might become a danger to the state; it was not so much this, however, as his intimacy with the fallen favourite, Somerset, which was to effect Cotton's own eclipse at court. In October 1615 he was arrested and imprisoned for having tampered with some incriminating letters of Somerset's in order to prove his patron's innocence, the latter being then in the Tower on the charge of murdering Sir Thomas Overbury (see *Lives of the Stuart Age*). Under examination Cotton also confessed to having, at Somerset's request, assured the Spanish ambassador of the favourite's support for an alliance with Spain. It was not surprising, therefore, that after his release and pardon eight months later, his friendship with the new ambassador from Spain, Gondomar, should be viewed with suspicion. There were in fact no sinister implications, for the learned Spaniard was only one of the many scholarly foreigners entertained at Cotton House, and Sir Robert's interest in politics was purely domestic – principally in the argument then current over the respective powers of King and Parliament, in which he allied himself with Sir John Eliot, John Pym (for whom see *Lives of the Stuart Age*) and others. Member for Old Sarum in 1624 and for Thetford in 1625, Cotton represented Castle Rising in the Parliament of 1628–9.

In 1629 he was arrested on account of an anti-Royalist pamphlet alleged to have been found in his library. The case was referred to the Star Chamber, but nothing was proved and at the end of May 1630 Cotton was released; his library, however, was ordered to remain closed while a commission was appointed to search it for papers and other records that rightfully belonged to the King and to make a catalogue. Deprived of access to all that most interested him in life, Cotton became ill. Twice he petitioned the King for a pardon and the restitution of his books, but in vain. He died on 6 May 1631 and was buried at Conington.

Sir Robert Bruce Cotton's great memorial is the Library which he founded. From his own pen there have survived only two short works which are an inadequate record of his great learning – *The Reigne of Henry III*, published in 1627, and *The Dangers wherein the Kingdom standeth*, 1628; many of his pamphlets were circulated in manuscript form, but some of these were printed during the early years of the Civil War. The *Cotton Posthuma*, edited by James Howell, contains several of his studies on the relations of King and Parliament (1657, 1672, and 1679).

Cotton continued to add to his library right up to the date of his arrest. In 1614 a valuable private collection had been bequeathed by Arthur Agard, Keeper of the Public Records, and in 1623 Camden also left his papers to his old friend. Eventually, after Cotton's death, his son Thomas was allowed to take possession of the library again; the family made a splendid effort to maintain the founder's tradition of giving all scholars free access to it, in spite of acute financial difficulties. In 1700 Sir John Cotton, grandson of Sir Robert, announced his intention to bequeath the collection to the nation. After various removals and other vicissitudes, including partial destruction by fire in 1731, the library found a permanent home in the British Museum in 1753. Catalogues were published in 1696, 1732, and 1802. Many of the MSS are available on microfilm in the United States of America.

Hope Mirrlees, *A Fly in Amber; being an extravagant Biography of the Romantic Antiquary, Sir Robert Bruce Cotton* (1962).

Thomas Smith, *Vita Cottoni* [memoir of Cotton, in Latin, attached to catalogue compiled by the same author] (1696).

*Portraits*: oil, by unknown artist, holding the *Genesis* (one of his greatest treasures), 1626: private collection; oil, by Cornelius Johnson, 1629: British Museum, London; oil, by unknown artist after Johnson: National Portrait Gallery, London; engravings by G. Vertue, T. Cross, and R. White: location not known; posthumous bust, by Roubillac: Trinity College, Cambridge. N.B. The portrait *called* Sir Robert Bruce Cotton, by an unknown artist, in the N.P.G. is not, in Roy Strong's opinion, that of Cotton.

**Courtenay, Sir William** (d. 1512), courtier to Henry VII (q.v.); possible claimant to the English throne.

The son of Edward Courtenay, created Earl of Devonshire by Henry VII in 1485, Sir William Courtenay married the Princess Catherine, youngest daughter of Edward IV (see *Lives Before the Tudors*) and sister of Elizabeth of York (q.v.). So long as Elizabeth was alive, Courtenay was secure in royal favour. In 1487 he was made a Knight of the Bath. Together with his father he helped to repel the advance of Perkin Warbeck (q.v.) at Exeter in 1497. Nevertheless, after the Queen's death in 1503, Henry, seeing in Courtenay's close relationship a possible threat to his throne, should he be tempted into conspiracy, had him committed to the Tower on the charge of having corresponded with the Earl of Suffolk (see Pole, Edmund de la), then the last remaining leader of the Yorkist faction.

Attainted as a claimant to the crown, Courtenay was held a prisoner for the rest of Henry VII's reign. He was released by Henry VIII (q.v.) on his accession, and although in 1511 he was allowed to succeed to his father's earldom, the formalities of restoration in blood had not been completed by the date of his death, 9 June 1512. Buried at Blackfriars Church, Courtenay was survived by his wife, the Princess Catherine, who died at Tiverton on 15 November 1527. Their son Henry succeeded to the title.

**Coverdale, Miles** (?1488–1568), translator of the first printed Bible in English.

Little is known of Coverdale's early life except that he was born in Yorkshire, probably in 1488, and studied theology at Cambridge. He was ordained priest at Norwich in 1514 and entered the convent of the Austin Friars at Cambridge. There, through the influence of the Prior, Robert Barnes (q.v.), he became familiar with the teachings of Erasmus (q.v.) and Martin Luther (q.v.) and probably also made the acquaintance of William Tyndale (q.v.) at the White Horse tavern, where the theologians of Lutheran sympathies used to forgather.

When Barnes was summoned to London to stand trial on a charge of heresy in 1526, Coverdale accompanied him to help in his defence. In London he formed a friendship with Thomas Cromwell (q.v.), who helped him to buy books to continue his biblical studies at Cambridge. In 1528, however, Coverdale left the convent to become a secular priest, preaching against the worship of images and the Mass.

The following year he was invited by Tyndale to Hamburg, where he spent several months helping with the translation of the Pentateuch; by 1529 he had settled at Antwerp and was employed by Jacob von Meteren, a well-known Protestant printer, to translate the entire Bible and Apocrypha into English. Coverdale was no Greek or Hebrew scholar; therefore he did not use original sources, but worked from five different versions, mainly Latin and German, including the Luther translation and also the Tyndale Bible. When the work was completed it was too dangerous to have it printed in Antwerp, and the Coverdale Bible is thought to have been produced in Zurich by Froschouer (other sources say it was printed by Cervicorn and Soter of Cologne); what seems certain is that it was introduced into England in 1535, with a dedication to the King, by James Nicholson of Southwark, and was reprinted in a modified version by him in 1537.

Coverdale now returned to England and devoted himself to the cause of reform, translating tracts by Luther and others and, on Cromwell's commission, editing the Great Bible which Henry VIII (q.v.) had commanded was to be installed in every church. In 1540, when Cromwell was beheaded and Barnes burned at the stake, Coverdale fled to the Continent with his wife, whom he had married in defiance of the Six Articles, and settled first at Strasbourg and then at Tübingen, taking his doctorate of divinity at the university there; he later moved to Bergzabern, near Strasbourg, where he was for four years schoolmaster and assistant pastor. His writings were denounced in England and his books publicly burned.

On the death of Henry VIII Coverdale returned to England and for a short time was almoner to the Queen Dowager, Katherine Parr (q.v.). He was also a royal chaplain and a popular preacher. He continued his translation work, producing among other writings the paraphrases of Erasmus and translations of German hymns. In 1549, accompanying John Russell (q.v.) in his campaign against the Devonshire rebels, he preached on the battlefield at Exeter and pacified the diocese afterwards, and for this service he was consecrated Bishop of Exeter in 1551.

He lost his bishopric under Mary I (q.v.) and was saved from the stake by the intercession of the King of Denmark, who invited him to that country. After a short time there, Coverdale returned to Bergzabern and in the autumn of 1558 moved to Geneva, together with his wife

and two children, where he is said to have advised on the translation of the Geneva Bible of 1560.

Following the accession of Elizabeth I (q.v.), Coverdale returned once more to England and was for some time preacher and tutor in the household of the Duchess of Suffolk. His years abroad had strengthened his Protestantism, and he adamantly refused to resume his bishopric; in December 1559 he took part in the consecration of Matthew Parker (q.v.) as Archbishop of Canterbury but wore a black gown instead of the customary vestments. He refused all other preferments except that of St Magnus, near London Bridge, which he held from 1564 to 1566 but eventually resigned rather than conform to the Act of Uniformity. His last book, *Letters of Saintes*, was published in 1564.

In his last years Coverdale continued to preach and always drew large crowds. However, following an attack of the plague in 1563 and the death of his wife in 1565, his health began to fail. He married for the second time in 1566, but died two years later, in February 1568, at the age of eighty-one. He was buried in the church of St Bartholomew, in the City, but when that church was demolished in the nineteenth century his remains were transferred to St Magnus.

Coverdale was not as fine a linguist as Tyndale, but his style is generally considered to be the more musical. His Psalter, while not the most accurate translation of the Psalms, is indisputably the best so far as singing is concerned; his translation of the Bible into English was the direct forerunner of the Authorized Version which appeared in 1611.

H. Guppy, 'Miles Coverdale and the English Bible, 1488–1568', *Bulletin of the John Rylands Library*, 19 (July 1935).
J. F. Mozley, *Coverdale and his Bibles* (1953).

## Cox, Richard (?1500–1581), Bishop of Ely.

Cox was born at Whaddon, Buckinghamshire, probably in 1500, and was educated at Eton and at King's College, Cambridge. In 1524 he joined the new college at Oxford founded by Thomas Wolsey (q.v.) and took his M.A. there in 1526. He became Schoolmaster (headmaster) of Eton, and from 1544 to 1550 was tutor to Prince Edward (see Edward VI). Cox was a favourite of Archbishop Cranmer (q.v.), from whom he received a number of preferments, including that of Dean of Westminster in 1549. Two years previously he had been made Chancellor of Oxford University, an office which he held from 1547 to 1552, during which time he had all the 'popish' books, pictures, and statues of the university destroyed; he also encouraged the continental reformers such as Peter Martyr. He played a prominent part in drawing up both the 1549 and the 1552 Prayer Book.

On the accession of Mary I (q.v.), Cox was sent to prison, but he was released shortly afterwards and escaped to Frankfurt in June 1554. There he became involved in a fierce dispute with the supporters of John Knox (q.v.) and William Whittingham (q.v.) over the use of the Prayer Book, which culminated in Knox being expelled from the city.

In 1559 Cox returned to England. He was a member of the commission appointed to visit Oxford University in that year, and he also took part in the disputation with the Roman Catholics at Westminster. He became Bishop of Norwich also in 1559, and shortly afterwards Bishop of Ely.

During his lifetime Cox seems to have been unpopular with many of his contemporaries. He was intolerant of anyone who held opinions different from his own, whether Roman Catholic or Puritan; and he refused to give in to those courtiers who sought to acquire episcopal property and lands. Queen Elizabeth (q.v.) herself intervened on behalf of her favourite, Christopher Hatton (q.v.), in the matter of the palace at Holborn, which Cox had to relinquish. He resigned his see in 1580 and died on 22 July 1581.

E. Arber (ed.), *A Brief Discourse of the Troubles at Frankfurt 1554–1558* (1908).
C. H. Garrett, *The Marian Exiles* (1938).

## Cranmer, Thomas (1489–1556), Archbishop of Canterbury, martyr.

Thomas Cranmer was born at Aslacton, Nottinghamshire, on 2 July 1489. His father, Thomas Cranmer, was a member of the gentry but had insufficient property to endow all his three sons; Thomas, the second son, and his younger brother were therefore destined for the church.

In later life Cranmer recalled that he had been educated under 'a marvellous severe and cruel schoolmaster'. He then went to Cambridge, where in 1515 he was elected a fellow of Jesus College. He was shortly afterwards forced to vacate his fellowship on account of his marriage, but when his wife died in childbirth a year later, it was restored to him. (The fact that Cranmer's wife Joan was a relative of the landlord of the Dolphin inn and that they took up residence there when they had to leave Jesus College has given rise to the erroneous story that he was once an ostler.)

Cranmer now entered the church and devoted himself to theological studies. From about 1520 onwards he was a leading member of the 'Little Germany' group who gathered at the White Horse tavern to discuss Lutheranism and the new learning, where his friends included

William Tyndale (q.v.), Robert Barnes (q.v.), John Frith (q.v.) and Thomas Bilney (q.v.).

A chance meeting with Stephen Gardiner (q.v.) and Edward Fox, two of the King's advisers, and both Cambridge men, at which Cranmer is said to have suggested that Henry VIII (q.v.) might benefit from consulting the divines at European universities in the matter of his divorce, led to his being summoned to an interview with the King. He was given a commission to write a treatise on this subject and found himself thrust into the royal service. In the next few years he was employed on a variety of diplomatic missions, which included accompanying the Earl of Wiltshire (see Boleyn, Thomas, q.v.), father of Anne Boleyn to Germany as ambassador to Charles V (q.v.). Here Cranmer made contact with the Lutheran princes. In defiance of his priest's order, he married a German lady, the niece of Andreas Osiander the theologian; as a result of her influence, his views veered even further in the direction of Continental thinking. It was not until 1548, however, that he was able to acknowledge his marriage publicly.

In 1533 the King chose Cranmer as Archbishop of Canterbury in succession to William Warham (q.v.). It was an office which Cranmer was at first reluctant to accept, and from this time onwards his life became fraught with difficulties. To please the King he had to enforce the royal supremacy; he declared the marriage of Henry VIII with Catherine of Aragon (q.v.) to be null and void and that with Anne Boleyn (q.v.) to be legal; in 1536 he invalidated the Boleyn marriage (but tried to save the Queen's life); in 1540 he married the King to Anne of Cleves (q.v.), and six months later freed him from that union. In religious matters Cranmer found himself drifting more and more towards Protestantism, and in the wave of Tudor reaction towards orthodoxy he made many enemies.

He co-operated with Thomas Cromwell (q.v.) in issuing the Great Bible of 1539 to all churches, and to further the replacement of Latin by English in church services he composed the Litany, which was authorized by Henry in 1544 and which is still in use. He fought vigorously but unsuccessfully against the passing of the Act of the Six Articles, particularly the clause relating to the marriage of clergy, which forced him to send his wife back to Germany. At least three times Cranmer's enemies tried to get him condemned for heresy, but the King would hear nothing of it; for others, such as Anne Boleyn, Thomas More (q.v.), John Fisher (q.v.), Cromwell, and many more who incurred the royal displeasure, the Archbishop pleaded courageously but in vain that their lives should be spared.

Nominated by Henry a member of the Council of Regency, Cranmer came into his own with the accession of Edward VI (q.v.) and the move towards Protestantism. He deserted the falling Somerset (see Seymour, Edward) and gradually moved towards a more radical Protestantism, although at the same time he stoutly withstood Northumberland's (see Dudley, John) attempts to despoil the Church; he also made overtures to Melanchthon concerning a union of the reformed churches. Cranmer's *Book of Homilies* was produced in 1547, and in 1549 came the first, but only moderately Protestant, Prayer Book and the first Act of Uniformity, for which he was largely responsible. These were followed in 1552 by a second Prayer Book and a second Act of Uniformity which came much closer to the principles of Strasbourg and Zurich and reflected the influence of the continental reformers Martin Bucer (q.v.), John à Lasco (q.v.), and others.

Although Cranmer's influence on affairs of state amounted to very little at this time, within the Church his authority was enforced. His monumental Forty-Two Articles, acceptance of which was required of all clergy, were issued in 1553. An attempt at revision of the canon law, however, failed. So did his efforts to get the Princess Mary (see Mary I) to recognize the new Prayer Book. He wrote against transubstantiation and successfully withstood the attempts of John Hooper (q.v.) towards the adoption of Zwinglianism (see Zwingli, Ulrich) in England.

With the death of Edward VI, Cranmer against his will became inextricably involved in politics. As the King lay on his deathbed the Archbishop had been persuaded to sign the document transferring the succession from the Princess Mary to Lady Jane Grey (q.v.). Consequently, when Mary came to the throne, he could expect little mercy, nor did he receive any. Arrested on a charge of treason, he was condemned but kept in

the Tower until the revival of the heresy laws; the Queen was not going to send him to his death merely for his support of Jane, but unless he publicly recanted she intended to have him burned for his Protestantism.

In March 1554 Cranmer was removed, together with Nicholas Ridley (q.v.) and Hugh Latimer (q.v.), to Oxford, where they faced a public disputation. There Cranmer refused to recant and was returned to prison; in October that year he was made to witness the martyrdom of Ridley and Latimer. He was now an old man, lonely and utterly broken in health and in spirit. Various pressures were employed to get him to recant, and he did in the end make six recantations; they did not however save him from the vengeance of the Queen and Cardinal Reginald Pole (q.v.), and on 21 March 1556 Cranmer was led to the stake outside Balliol College. At St Mary's church, where he was required to recant publicly all his heresies before the burning, Cranmer astonished everyone present by disavowing his recantations, rejecting the Pope, and reasserting his disbelief in transubstantiation. He proclaimed that his right hand, which had offended by signing the false declarations, should burn first, and when he was tied to the stake and the flames shot up, he immediately thrust his hand into them, holding it there until it was consumed, as was his whole body soon afterwards.

Cranmer's courageous denial and his dignified manner at the stake struck a major blow at Mary's propaganda and gave heart to the reformers. He has since been unfairly maligned by historians as timid and inconsistent; it has to be remembered that he was at heart a scholar, a very human person who did not seek high office and did not enjoy it. He worked hard for the union of all the

Protestant churches and gave to the Anglican Protestant Church, of which he was virtually a founding father, a liturgy which is still considered a masterpiece today. His *Works* have been edited by J. E. Cox for the Parker Society, Cambridge (2 vols; 1844–6).

G. W. Bromiley, *Thomas Cranmer: Archbishop and Martyr* (1955).

G. W. Bromiley, *Thomas Cranmer, Theologian* (1956).

F. E. Hutchinson, *Cranmer and the English Reformation* (1951).

J. G. Ridley, *Thomas Cranmer* (1962).

C. H. Smyth, *Cranmer and the Reformation under Edward VI* (1926).

*Portraits:* oil on panel, by Gerlach Flicke, 1545/6: National Portrait Gallery, London; oil, by unknown artist: Trinity College, Cambridge; other related portraits at Lambeth Palace, London, Jesus College, Cambridge, Helmingham Hall (Lord Tollemache Collection), and Knole; engravings in *Icones*, 1581, and *Herwologia*, 1620.

**Crichton, James** (1560–1582), scholar and orator, known as 'The Admirable Crichton'.

Born at Eliock House, Dumfriesshire, Scotland, in August 1560, James Crichton was the son of Robert Crichton, a member of the Scottish judiciary, and his first wife, Elizabeth Stewart; through his mother, a Stewart of Beith, he claimed royal descent.

James received his early education at either Edinburgh or Perth. In 1570, at the age of ten, he entered the University of St Andrews, where he came under the influence of George Buchanan (q.v.), tutor to the young King James VI (q.v.). Crichton took his B.A. in 1573–4 and, exceptionally, his M.A. one year later; he was a brilliant linguist and debater and had the reputation of being able to repeat accurately anything that he had heard or read only once. He was also skilled in horsemanship and athletics.

On leaving the university Crichton travelled to Paris, where he distinguished himself at the Collège de Navarre by disputing some scientific questions in no less than twelve languages and at the Louvre in a tilting match. He then served in the French army for nearly two years, retiring in 1579 in order to go to Italy. In July that year he gave an oration in the ducal palace at Genoa. Proceeding to Venice, he introduced himself to the printer Aldus Manutius, who was probably the originator of a handbill dated 1580 proclaiming Crichton's extraordinary intellectual and athletic abilities. Through Manutius Crichton met the Italian humanists, who were greatly impressed by him; a series of private and public debates was arranged, and Crichton was also given the honour of pronouncing an oration before the Doge and Senate.

In 1581 he left Venice for Padua, where, challenged as a charlatan, he responded by offering to dispute the academic interpretation of Aristotle, a challenge which was accepted and from which Crichton emerged with his reputation more enhanced than ever. Manutius paid tribute to his success in the preface to Cicero's *Paradoxa*, which he published in June that year.

Some time in 1582 Crichton entered the service of the Duke of Mantua. The Duke, impressed by his skilled swordsmanship, invited him to become tutor to his son. Shortly afterwards he was slain in a brawl, if not actually at the hand of the young prince, whose jealousy had been aroused, certainly at his instigation. (The later date of 1585, sometimes quoted as that of Crichton's death, is incorrect, confusion having arisen on account of another James Crichton who was in Italy in 1584–5.)

Crichton's extant works consist of odes and orations to Italian nobles and senators. The epithet 'admirable' was first applied to him by John Johnston, author of *Heroes Scotici* (1603); it was taken up and much exaggerated by Sir Thomas Urquhart (see *Lives of the Stuart Age*) in his *Eskubalauron*, better known as *The Discovery of a Most Exquisite Jewel* (1652). The name has come to denote a person of all-round talent.

P. F. Tytler, *The Life of the Admirable Crichton* (1819).

*Portrait*: oil, by unknown artist: Royal Collection, Holyrood House, Edinburgh.

**Cromwell, Thomas** (?1485–1540), 1st Earl of Essex, statesman, principal minister to Henry VIII (q.v.) from 1532 to 1540.

All that is known of the early life of Thomas Cromwell is that he was born probably in about 1485, the son of a Putney blacksmith, brewer, and cloth merchant, Walter Cromwell. Thomas had no formal schooling and at an early age quarrelled with his father, left home, and went to the Continent. He is believed to have served as a soldier in Italy before settling in Florence to work for a merchant, and subsequently to trade himself. In spite of his lack of education, he was an avid reader and lover of books; he taught himself the rudiments of Latin and Greek, French and Italian, and also acquired some legal knowledge. While in Italy he may have met or become familiar with work of Machiavelli (q.v.), but this is by no means certain.

Some time before 1512 Cromwell left Italy for the Low Countries, where he became clerk to an English merchant adventurer in Antwerp, and also became involved in commercial enterprises on his own account. By 1513 he had returned to England, married a widow of some means, Elizabeth Wykys, and set up his own legal practice in London. His

linguistic abilities and first-hand knowledge of continental affairs, coupled with his contacts abroad, attracted business, and he is known to have made at least two trips to Rome in the years between 1514 and 1520. It was during this time that he began to undertake legal and administrative work on behalf of Cardinal Thomas Wolsey (q.v.). In 1523 he entered Parliament, and the following year he became a member of Gray's Inn.

In 1525 he was employed by Wolsey in the destruction of certain monasteries, in order to raise funds for the endowment of colleges at Oxford and Ipswich; the zeal and ruthlessness with which he accomplished this task won him the Cardinal's approbation, and secured for him the position of his most powerful legal adviser and confidential servant.

Cromwell's wife died in 1527, leaving him with a young son and two daughters; he did not remarry, and his house in Austin Friars in the City of London became the meeting place of an intellectual circle who earnestly discussed the issues of the day, principally the doctrine of the Church and the need for reform.

On Wolsey's fall in 1529 Cromwell remained loyal to his master and spoke out forcibly for him, and against the bill of attainder, in Parliament. His outstanding performance and qualities attracted the attention of the King, and early in 1530 he entered the royal service. Over the next two years he steadily won Henry's confidence, much to the chagrin of Norfolk (see Howard, Thomas, 3rd Duke), Sir Thomas More (q.v.), Bishop Stephen Gardiner (q.v.), and others close to the throne. Although from 1531 he was a Privy Councillor and was rapidly gaining ascendancy in Parliament at this time, Cromwell was not given a royal appointment until April 1532, when he was made Master of the King's Jewels. Two further minor appointments followed: he became Clerk of the Hanaper three months later, and Chancellor of the Exchequer in April 1533. From September 1532 he acted as Secretary of State during Stephen Gardiner's absence abroad and he succeeded, in April 1534, in ousting the latter from that post; in October the same year Cromwell was appointed Master of the Rolls. By July 1536, when he was made Lord Privy Seal, taking the title of Lord Cromwell of Wimbledon, he had become the most powerful of the King's ministers.

Cromwell's rise to power was not the result of his legal and administrative skills, but rather of his ability to win the confidence of his monarch. After the failure to get his divorce in 1529, Henry had adopted a somewhat inconsistent policy that his chief minister soon realized would get him nowhere; thus when in 1532 Cromwell put forward his own carefully worked out plan for the establishment of the royal supremacy in England, it was eagerly seized on by Henry as the solution that would enable him both to marry Anne Boleyn (q.v.) and to swell his own coffers. The idea of a royal supremacy had originally been the King's, but it was Cromwell who made it feasible. He tackled the task speedily and with vigour, drafting and steering through Parliament early in 1533 the Act in Restraint of Appeals, which ended the system of appeals to Rome in matrimonial and testamentary cases. In January that year the King secretly married Anne, who was pregnant, and on 23 May Archbishop Thomas Cranmer (q.v.) made his historic pronouncement that Henry's marriage to Catherine had been invalid from the outset and that he was lawfully married to Anne. More legislation followed, culminating in the passage through Parliament of the Act of Supremacy and its ratification in the last months of 1534.

Next Cromwell launched a vicious attack on the monasteries. Appointed Vicar General in January 1535, with powers to visit and reform all monastic institutions in the country, he initiated the *Valor Ecclesiasticus*, a survey of the wealth of the Church throughout the kingdom; the men and the methods he employed in order to obtain the information required were often harsh. In March 1536 a bill was introduced into Parliament for the suppression of the smaller monastic houses, a measure regarded both by the King and by Cromwell, who was now Vice-Regent and deputy head of the Church, as a preliminary to dissolving the rest; a further visitation took place in 1538, and by 1540 all monastic property had been surrendered to the crown. A Court of Augmentations was set up to supervise the making of grants and leases arising from the dissolution of the monasteries, and although practically everyone in the royal favour at this time benefited materially from the transfer of this enormous wealth from the Church to the crown, Cromwell's own pickings were modest by comparison with those of others, and he did make some effort to see that funds were wisely administered.

Involvement in the King's matrimonial affairs, which had won Cromwell his power in the first instance, was eventually to bring about his fall from grace. When Henry tired of Anne, it was Cromwell who had the unpleasant task of bringing her to trial for adultery and alleged incest. Soon after the King's marriage to Jane Seymour (q.v.) the minister cleverly brought about a marriage between his son Gregory and the Queen's sister, Elizabeth Seymour; but this move to consolidate his position was rendered useless by the Queen's death the following year. In 1538 Cromwell made his fatal mistake by urging on the King, for diplomatic reasons, a marriage to Anne of Cleves (q.v.).

At this date there was a danger of an alliance between France and Spain against England, and Cromwell, who unlike his monarch had no particular religious convictions, strongly advocated an alliance with the German Lutheran states. To this Henry, a staunch Catholic, would not agree. There followed a long and bitter struggle between Cromwell and his rival councillors, Norfolk and Gardiner, who represented the more conservative, Catholic view; first one side, and then the other, appeared to have ascendancy. In 1539 Henry reluctantly gave permission for the marriage negotiations to be opened; but when, on Anne's arrival in England for the wedding, he took an instant dislike to his bride and complained that he had been misled as to her looks, Cromwell's fate was virtually sealed. Norfolk lost no time

in introducing his niece Catherine Howard (q.v.) as a rival attraction, and Cromwell, soon required by the King to devise some means of release from his hated fourth marriage, was placed in the dilemma (not unlike Wolsey's before him) that compliance with Henry's demand meant furthering the ambitions of his enemies.

At the opening of Parliament in April 1540 Cromwell pleased the King by his confiscation of the properties belonging to the Knights of the Order of St John; on the 17th of that month he was created Earl of Essex, and the following day Lord Great Chamberlain. But by the beginning of June those who sought his downfall had succeeded in persuading Henry that his chief minister was a heretic. Cromwell was given no prior warning; at a Council meeting on 10 June he was denounced by Norfolk for high treason, arrested, and taken to the Tower. A bill of attainder was brought in Parliament the following week and was passed on 29 June; he was executed at Tyburn on 28 July.

Historians have long argued the question of whether it was the King who dominated Cromwell, or vice versa. Certainly Henry had cause to regret having sacrificed 'the best servant he ever had', for no other minister of the age could equal Cromwell's exceptional talent for administration. He revolutionized the system of government, taking it out of the hands of the royal household and establishing a national administration which was the forerunner of the modern bureaucratic system. Of permanent value to historians has been his directive for the compulsory maintenance of parish registers.

Thomas Cromwell played the leading role in the establishment of the Reformation in England. Ruthless in the methods he employed to dissolve the monasteries, he was unpopular among his contemporaries but was, in his time, utterly loyal to two successive masters, Wolsey and Henry VIII.

A. G. Dickens, *Thomas Cromwell and the English Reformation* (1959).

G. R. Elton, *Policy and Police: the Enforcement of the Reformation in the Age of Thomas Cromwell* (1972).

G. R. Elton, *Reform and Renewal: Thomas Cromwell and the Common Weal* (1973).

G. R. Elton, *The Tudor Revolution in Government* (1953).

R. B. Merriman, *The Life and Letters of Thomas Cromwell* (2 vols; 1902).

N. Williams, *The Cardinal and the Secretary* (1975).

W. G. Zeeveld, *Foundations of Tudor Policy* (Cambridge, Mass., 1948).

*Portraits:* oil, by Hans Holbein the Younger: Frick Collection, New York; oil, by unknown artist after Holbein, *c.* 1533–4: National Portrait Gallery, London.

# D

**Darcy, Thomas** (?1467–1537), Baron Darcy of Templehurst, statesman and rebel.

A descendant of the prominent Darcy de Knayth family, Thomas Darcy was born in about 1467, probably at the family seat of Templehurst, the son of Sir William Darcy and his wife Euphemia, daughter of Sir John Langton. Little is known of his upbringing or personal life. He was married twice, his first wife being Dowsabella, daughter of Sir Richard Tempest, who bore him four sons; through his second marriage, to Edith, widow of Lord Neville and mother of the young Earl of Westmorland, Darcy greatly strengthened his power and prestige in the north of England.

In 1588 he succeeded to his father's estates in Lincolnshire and Yorkshire. A number of official appointments followed, including those of Captain of Berwick and Warden of the East Marches. Steward to the Earl of Westmorland in 1505, he was raised to the peerage the same year, and in 1509 summoned to Parliament as Lord Darcy de Darcy; he also became a Knight of the Garter and later Baron Darcy of Templehurst. His position in the north of England was second only to the Earl of Northumberland.

In 1511 Darcy was given command of troops sent to Spain to assist Ferdinand and Isabella against the Moors. He later served in the French campaign of 1513, when he took part in the Battle of Thérouanne. On his return home, he was principally employed in governing the borders. At first he sided with Henry VIII

(q.v.) on the matter of the King's divorce, but in 1529 Darcy turned against his former friend, Cardinal Thomas Wolsey (q.v.), and in 1532 asserted that in his view the papacy alone should have jurisdiction over matrimonial cases; for this bold statement he was held in London for nearly three years. It was during this period of enforced unemployment that Darcy's hatred of Thomas Cromwell (q.v.) and his policies took root. Together with Lord Hussey he began to intrigue with the imperial ambassador, Eustace Chapuys, concerning a possible invasion of England by the Catholic powers led by the Emperor Charles V (q.v.).

Some time in 1535 Darcy was allowed to return to Templehurst. When the rising known as the Pilgrimage of Grace broke out in October 1536, at first he held Pomfret Castle (Pontefract) for the King, but then showed his sympathy for the rebel cause by surrendering it on 21 October to Robert Aske (q.v.), leader of the rising, and by taking the Pilgrims' oath. When the rebellion was over, Darcy pleaded that during his absence in London the stronghold had fallen into disrepair and was inadequately supplied; he received a pardon from the King and in January 1537 supported Aske in putting down a rising at Hull and Scarborough instigated by Sir Francis Bigod. Nevertheless Henry continued to view Darcy with suspicion and, a treasonable letter from the latter to Aske having been intercepted, he was arrested soon afterwards and taken to London to stand trial. Found guilty of high treason,

his peerage was forfeited, he was beheaded on Tower Hill on 30 June 1537,
and his head was exhibited on London
Bridge.

M. H. and R. Dodds, *The Pilgrimage of Grace* (2
vols; 1915).

**Darnley, Lord** (1545–1567), see Stewart, Henry.

**Davys or Davis, John** (*c.* 1550–1605),
navigator and explorer.

John Davys was born at Sandridge,
near Dartmouth, Devon, in about 1550.
Nothing is known of his ancestry or
parentage, but he was brought up with
the neighbouring Gilbert and Ralegh
families and undoubtedly went to sea
when quite young. He first put forward
his plan to look for a North-West
Passage to Sir Francis Walsingham (q.v.)
in 1583.

In 1585 Davys was given command of
an expedition organized by Adrian
Gilbert and financed by London and
West Country merchants. He reached
the east coast of Greenland, where he
headed south and sailed round Cape
Farewell and then northwards along the
west coast of Greenland, but after going
some way up the Cumberland Sound he
turned back.

In May 1586 he sailed from Dartmouth on his second expedition, taking
with him the *Mermaid* and the *Moonshine*
and having sent the *Sunshine* on ahead
to explore the east coast of Greenland.
He sailed in the same direction as the
previous year, up the strait named after
him and then westwards to Labrador.
On this trip he made contact with many
friendly Eskimos and also caught and
salted a load of cod, which he took home
to England, arriving back in October.

Davys's third attempt to find the
North-West Passage was made the following summer (May to September

1587). This time he sailed in the *Ellen*, a
small pinnace of only about 20 tons,
accompanied by the *Elizabeth* and the
*Sunshine*. His idea was to explore in
the *Ellen*, while the two other vessels
headed for the fishing grounds. The
vessels duly separated, and Davys sailed
northwards along the western coast of
Greenland, through the Davis Strait and
into what is now Baffin Bay, as far
as Disko Island, almost 73°N, before
turning south again. The *Elizabeth* and
the *Sunshine*, however, had not waited
for him, and he had to return home
alone.

In the fight against the Spanish
Armada of 1588 Davys was in command
of the *Black Dog*. He served in the Azores
the following year, and in 1591 sailed
with Thomas Cavendish (q.v.) on his last
voyage to the South Sea. Cavendish had
promised Davys the opportunity to look
for the North-West Passage from the
Pacific, but this was not achieved as the
two men were separated by bad weather
and when Davys, in the *Desire*, after
three times attempting to find a way
through the Straits of Magellan to the
Pacific, made for the expected rendezvous, Cavendish was not there and
once more he sailed home alone. On this
voyage Davys discovered the Falkland
Islands, which Sir Richard Hawkins
(q.v.) was later to claim to have found in
1594.

Davys sailed with Sir Walter Ralegh
(q.v.) on the Cadiz expedition of 1596
and also on the 'Islands Voyage' of 1597.
The following year he joined a Dutch
expedition to the East Indies as chief
pilot. In 1601 he took part in the first
expedition sent out by the East India
Company, sailing in the *Red Dragon* as
pilot major. On the second venture
financed by the company, which sailed in
December 1604, Davys served under Sir
Edward Michelbourne in the *Tiger*.

They were attacked by Japanese pirates near what is now Bintan, off Singapore, and Davys was brutally murdered on 29 or 30 December 1605.

John Davys was all his life obsessed with the ambition to find a North-West Passage through the Arctic to the Pacific. Although he failed to find it, the voyages he made were daring feats of seamanship. Davys was a scientific navigator, and his treatise on navigation, the first practical work on the subject, entitled *Seaman's Secrets*, was published in 1594. He also wrote *The World's Hydrographical Description* (1595), an attempt to answer his critics and prove the existence of the North-West Passage. His account of the disastrous voyage to the East Indies in 1598 was included by Samuel Purchas (see *Lives of the Stuart Age*) in his *Pilgrimes* (1625). Davys invented the backstaff, a type of quadrant that was in use until the end of the eighteenth century.

A. H. Markham, *The Voyages and Works of John Davis* (Hakluyt Society, lix, Pt. i, 1880).
C. R. Markham, *A Life of John Davis, the navigator, 1550–1605* (1889).
G. M. Thomson, *The North-West Passage* (1975).

**Day, John** (1522–1584), printer.

Born probably at Dunwich, Suffolk, in 1522, and apprenticed to a printer, John Day set up his own press in the parish of St Sepulchre's, London, in about 1546. Three years later he moved to premises in Aldersgate. A zealous reformer, in 1552 he was licensed to print the English version of Bishop John Ponet's *Catechism*, which was ordered to be published by Edward VI (q.v.), the Latin version being issued by an established printer of Latin books, Raynold Wolf.

Day was imprisoned briefly in the Tower under Mary I (q.v.). He managed to escape for a while to the Continent and there used his time to advantage by studying the work of European printers;

it is doubtful, however, whether he actually did any printing himself while in exile. He returned to England before the end of the reign and was one of the freemen mentioned in the charter granted to the Stationers' Company in 1557. In 1559 he produced his most elegant piece of typography, the title page to John Betts's *The Cosmographical Glass,* for which he used a new italic type.

Day imported most of his type from the Continent, introducing into England not only a new italic, but also new Greek, Roman, and Anglo-Saxon types. He found an enthusiastic patron for the new Anglo-Saxon type in Archbishop Matthew Parker (q.v.), whose translation of the Psalms he printed in 1560. In that same year he issued the first English church service book with musical notation. A complete version of the Psalms, set to music by Thomas Tallis (q.v.) and others, was printed by Day in 1563, as was the first edition of his most famous book, Foxe's *Actes and Monuments*, better known as the *Book of Martyrs* (see Foxe, John). He used the new Anglo-Saxon type for a translation of Ælfric's *Homily*, by Parker, printed in 1567. At the instigation of Dr John Dee (q.v.), Day printed a series of mathematical books, in which he introduced into England several mathematical signs. Of more than 200 works printed during the course of his prosperous career, the most popular and financially successful were the *ABC with the Catechism* and the *Psalms in Metre*.

In 1572 Day took the lease of a shop in St Paul's Churchyard to accommodate his growing stock of books. A few years later, following a complaint made to the Queen by other printers and stationers concerning the privileges granted to certain individuals, a printer named Roger Ward printed ten thousand copies of the *ABC with Catechism* for which

Day and his son Richard held the licence. A case was brought in the Star Chamber, as a result of which several printers, among whom the most generous was Day himself, in 1584 surrendered copyrights for the benefit of the poor of the Company.

John Day died on 23 July 1584, on a journey to Suffolk; he was buried at the church of Bradley Parva in that county. Twice married, he had twenty-six children, the last years of his life being marred by the unhappiness of a quarrel with his son Richard, who was his partner in the printing business.

C. L. Oastler, *John Day, the Elizabethan Printer* (Oxford, 1976).

**Dee, John** (1527–1608), astrologer, mathematician, geographer, and diarist.

According to Dee's own account, he came from a Welsh family with a long genealogy. He was the son of Roland and Joanna Dee, born in London on 13 July 1527. His father may have been in the service of Henry VII (q.v.).

Dee was educated at Chelmsford grammar school and later at St John's College, Cambridge, where he took his B.A. in 1544 and became a fellow the next year. In 1546 he was appointed by Henry VIII (q.v.) as one of the original fellows of the newly-founded Trinity College, in which capacity he was responsible for the staging of several classical plays. The effect he achieved in one production of Aristophanes' *Peace* with an actor being raised aloft to Jupiter's palace caused such astonishment that Dee was described by many as a magician, a reputation which was to stick for the rest of his life.

In November 1547 he went to the Low Countries to confer with other men of learning. He brought back to England the first astronomical instruments ever seen there: an astronomer's staff and ring of brass designed by Gemma Frisius, and two globes constructed by Mercator. Not long afterwards, having taken his M.A., he presented these instruments to Trinity College before leaving Cambridge for Louvain. For the next two years he studied at Louvain University, where he was taught by, and formed lifelong friendships with, all the leading Continental geographers. (Although during his lifetime he was frequently referred to as 'Dr' Dee, there is no record that he ever took a higher degree than the M.A. at Cambridge.)

Leaving Louvain in July 1550, he went to Paris, where audiences flocked to hear his series of lectures on Euclid, the first on that subject to be given in public. On his return to England, however, he declined an invitation to lecture at Oxford on the mathematical sciences. Ambitious for preferment, he got Sir John Cheke (q.v.) to give him an introduction to William Cecil (q.v.), and through Cecil he obtained an introduction to Edward VI (q.v.). The King gave him an annuity of £100, which Dee later exchanged for the living of Upton upon Severn.

England was on the verge of her great maritime expansion. Dee threw himself into that movement with all his energies and geographical expertise; for the next thirty years he was an influence behind the scenes, directing the navigators first to seek out the North-East Passage and then the mythical 'Terra Australis Incognita', or southern continent, that he so earnestly believed in. Many great seamen of the day – men like Francis Drake (q.v.), Martin Frobisher (q.v.), Stephen and William Borough (qq.v.), Walter Ralegh (q.v.) – came to him for advice and technical instruction.

In 1553 he was accused of a plot to dispose of Queen Mary I (q.v.) and was sent to prison. Acquitted of treason, he

123

was put under the surveillance of Bishop Edmund Bonner (q.v.) as a possible heretic. The Queen eventually gave him a full pardon, but three years later, when Dee petitioned her to create a royal library for the preservation of historical manuscripts, she turned the idea down.

After the accession of Elizabeth I (q.v.) Dee came into royal favour. Having by means of astrological calculation named a propitious day for the new Queen's coronation, thereafter he was consulted by her on various matters, both at the court and at his own house. She is said once to have listened to his explanation of a new comet during three sessions.

For many years Dee lived at Mortlake, where his extensive library and instruments were always at the disposal of students and fellow scientists. In 1565 he married Katherine Constable, the widow of a London grocer. She died in 1574, and three years later he took a second wife, Jean Fromond, who bore him eleven children.

In this middle period of his life Dee travelled extensively, visiting among other places Antwerp, Venice, and even Hungary, where he met the Emperor Maximilian II. Hoping for preferment at home, he wrote from Antwerp in 1562 to Cecil telling him of a treatise on ciphers, *Steganographia* by John Trithemius, a copy of which had come into his possession. Although he was later employed by the government on investigations concerning the possible adoption of the Gregorian calendar by England, none of the posts of which he had hopes – such as that of Dean of Gloucester or Provost of Eton – ever came his way. Only in 1595 was he appointed Warden of Manchester College. By that time, however, his reputation, finances, and physical health had been tarnished through his association with the medium Edward Kelley.

Dee's experiments in crystal-gazing and raising spirits were probably begun in earnest about 1580. He also headed a group of alchemists who were searching for the 'philosophers' stone' which would convert baser metals into gold. Kelley, a fellow astrologer, alchemist, and necromancer, became indispensable to Dee as a medium. In 1583 the two men set out on a trip to Poland and Bohemia, where the Emperor Rudolph and the King of Poland were anxious for their services, but soon saw through their impostures. When after their return home Kelley announced at a séance that the spirits had directed that they should share their wives in common, Dee reluctantly agreed. Later, following a violent quarrel, they parted company.

While he was abroad, a mob broke into Dee's house at Mortlake and, believing him to be a magician, destroyed many of his books and instruments. The stigma of sorcery was laid against him publicly, and he was unable to rid himself of it; his petition to James I (see James VI of Scotland) in 1604 that he might be tried and cleared of the charge was not allowed.

Broken in health, Dee resigned from the post of Warden of Manchester College in 1604. He spent the last few years of his life in some poverty, being forced to sell off books from time to time in order to make ends meet. He died at Mortlake in December 1608.

Few of Dee's prolific writings have been printed (about seventy-nine are listed in the *D.N.B.*). His preface to the first English translation of Euclid, by Billingsley, which appeared in 1570, was influential in suggesting a programme of future work. His Diary is informative, the most interesting of his writings to us today – see *The Private Diary of Dr John Dee*, edited by J. O. Halliwell (Camden Society, xix, 1842).

Like many of his contemporaries, John Dee combined genuine science with intellectual explorations of a more dubious nature. Nevertheless his work as a geographer was outstanding, and he was unquestionably the finest mathematician of his time, although inferior to the later Thomas Harriot (q.v.). The expression 'the British empire' is reputed to have been coined by Dee, who also introduced the word 'unit' into the English language.

P. J. French, *John Dee* (1972).
A. L. Rowse, *The Cultural Achievement* (vol. ii of *The Elizabethan Renaissance*, 1972), chapter VII, 'Science and Society'.
C. F. Smith, *John Dee* (1909).
E. G. R. Taylor, *The mathematical practitioners of Tudor and Stuart England* (1954).

*Portrait*: oil, by unknown artist: Ashmolean Museum, Oxford.

**Dekker, Thomas** (?1570–1641), dramatist, see *Lives of the Stuart Age.*

**Devereux, Robert** (1567–1601), 2nd Earl of Essex, courtier, favourite of Queen Elizabeth I (q.v.).

Born at Netherwood, in Hertfordshire, on 10 November 1567, Robert Devereux was the eldest son of Walter Devereux, Viscount Hereford, and his wife Lettice, daughter of Sir Francis Knollys (q.v.) and Mary, sister of Anne Boleyn (q.v.), and thus, on his mother's side, a distant cousin of the Queen. He inherited the earldom at the age of nine, when his father, who had been created Earl of Essex in 1572 and appointed Earl Marshal of Ireland in 1575, died in Dublin in September 1576, leaving the family heavily in debt. Two years later the beautiful and flirtatious Lady Essex married the Queen's favourite, the Earl of Leicester (see Dudley, Robert).

The young Essex became a ward of Burghley (see Cecil, William), but most of his boyhood was spent with his two sisters at the Devereux family home of Chartley, in Staffordshire, under the tutorship of Richard Broughton. At the beginning of 1577 Robert lived for a few months in London at the house of his guardian, where he met for the first time his future rival, Burghley's hunchback son, Robert Cecil (q.v.), and captivated everyone who met him by his charm and outstanding good looks. Later that spring Essex went up to Cambridge, and for the next four years he studied under John Whitgift (q.v.) at Trinity College, taking his M.A. there in July 1581. In 1584, at the age of seventeen, he presented himself at court under the aegis of his stepfather, the Earl of Leicester, determined to enhance the dwindling family fortunes. In introducing his handsome young stepson to the royal circle, Leicester may have had an ulterior motive, for his position as the Queen's favourite was being increasingly threatened by a rival courtier, Sir Walter Ralegh (q.v.), and by interesting Elizabeth in Essex he hoped to safeguard his own place in her affections.

Essex took part in his stepfather's military campaign in the Netherlands in 1586 and was awarded the title of Knight Banneret for his valour at the Battle of Zutphen; he returned home bearing the sword left to him by his cousin Sir Philip Sidney (q.v.), who had died as a result of wounds received at the same battle.

From the spring of 1587 onwards he attracted the attention of the Queen and was increasingly in her company. In June that year he was appointed Master of the Horse; the following summer he paraded before his sovereign at Tilbury a company of some sixty harquebusiers and 200 light cavalry wearing the Devereux colours of tangerine and white. Leicester died early in September, and not long afterwards the twenty-year-old Essex, the Queen's new favourite, received the Order of the Garter.

Their relationship was stormy from the outset, for the young courtier had inherited an impetuous, sometimes violent, temperament from his Celtic forbears; he took great risks and went further than anyone had ever dared to go with Elizabeth, yet always in those early years she forgave him. A woman who hated the certain knowledge that she was growing old, she desperately needed the reassurance and compliment of youthful attentions, and he knew it.

Denied the chance of action against the Spanish Armada of 1588, and after quarrelling with Ralegh, having challenged him to a duel which the Privy Council forbade him to fight, in April the following year Essex deliberately went against the Queen's wishes by running away from court to join the expedition against Lisbon commanded by Sir Francis Drake (q.v.) and Sir John Norris (q.v.). He did not return until June, and then only at Elizabeth's furious demand. But when they met she was so pleased to have her 'Robin' back that she immediately forgave him, and as a result of the escapade Essex found himself the darling of the populace. Then he risked his position even further the following year by a secret marriage to Frances Walsingham, widow of Sir Philip Sidney; but again Elizabeth, when she learned of it, although furious for a time, soon wanted him back at her side. She found it difficult to refuse him anything he asked. Already she had lent him £3,000, but when the extravagant young courtier still pleaded financial hardship, she granted him the so-called 'Farm of Sweet Wines' – the right to levy duty on imported sweet wines – that had previously been Leicester's principal source of income.

Essex's next demand was less readily granted. He longed for action and begged to be allowed to lead the second force Elizabeth had promised to send to the assistance of Henri IV in his campaign against the French Catholics. The Queen was unwilling to let him out of her sight, but in June 1591 she yielded to his entreaties and gave him the coveted command. He landed in France in August with a force of 4,000 men, and after acquitting himself tolerably well under difficult conditions, captured Gourlay, but then deliberately went against the Queen's known wishes by taking it upon himself to knight some two dozen of his officers. Summoned back to England, he suffered her icy reception and indulged in a fit of sulks before being sent back to the Continent with instructions to behave 'like a general'. A few weeks later, following the fruitless siege of Rouen, Essex was again recalled temporarily to court, this time for no better reason than that the Queen felt it was beneath his dignity (and hers) that he should skirmish in the French provinces – privately, she wanted him back at court. Early in the New Year 1592, Essex reluctantly gave up his command and returned to her side, but was unable to resist making one last flamboyant gesture in the shape of a personal challenge to the Governor of Rouen (which was declined).

This homecoming marked a turning-point in his life: the realization that if he were to secure his position he would have to become a trusted councillor rather than rely on the uncertain fortunes of being the favourite of a capricious Queen. Already by virtue of his relations with Elizabeth he constituted a serious threat to the power of Burghley, who was grooming his son Robert to succeed him as first minister; now Essex deliberately set his sights on challenging that power by endeavouring to become a statesman himself. Backed by the two Bacon brothers, Francis (q.v.) and Anthony (q.v.), and other diplomats such as Thomas Bodley (q.v.), all of whom resented the monopoly of the Cecils, Essex devoted the next four years to the study of foreign affairs and statecraft, in order to enhance his political reputation in the eyes of the Queen. Essex House became the centre of a network of intelligence set up by Anthony Bacon through his contacts on the Continent, which enabled his patron to rival Burghley's own service. Essex was sworn a Privy Councillor in February 1593, but in the Parliament of that year he and Francis Bacon clashed with Robert Cecil on the question of a subsidy for the Queen; this so displeased Elizabeth that she repeatedly refused Essex's requests to make Bacon Attorney-General first, and later Solicitor-General. Tempers were lost, and to make up for Francis's disappointment, Essex generously gave him the estate of Twickenham Park.

Early in 1594 Anthony Bacon passed on to Essex his suspicions concerning the Queen's physician, Dr Roderigo Lopez, a man of Portuguese Jewish extraction; but when Essex had the doctor summarily searched, Elizabeth showed her anger. Humiliated and furious, Essex ordered the elderly doctor to be put to the rack on trumped-up charges of a plot to poison Her Majesty, and eventually, when Lopez had 'confessed', he was largely responsible for bringing the Jew to execution. Although by this action Essex increased his popularity with the public, it won him further enmity on the part of the Cecils and continued coolness from Elizabeth. And when a few months later one of his closest followers, the young Earl of Southampton (see Wriothesley, Henry), became involved in a

sordid scandal which Essex did his best to hush up, he too lost face. The arrival in England of a tract entitled *A Conference on the Next Succession to the Crown of England*, dedicated to Essex and suggesting that he would have a major part to play in the decision of 'this great affair', infuriated Elizabeth more than ever.

In 1596 Essex was appointed to command one of the five squadrons which sailed from England in June that year to reopen the offensive against Spain. This expedition, under the overall command of the Lord Admiral, Lord Howard of Effingham (see Howard, Charles), proved very successful. Essex, as restless and impetuous as ever, and longing for action, did not wait for the sea battle off Cadiz to be over before giving orders for his force of 1,000 men to land; triumphantly he captured and sacked Cadiz on 22 June. Little plunder was obtained, however, for the Spaniards promptly scuttled their fleet in the Bay, and when the English subsequently moved on to Faro and Essex landed a force there, all that he obtained was the contents of the library of the Bishop of Algarve. Essex then proposed that they should proceed to the Azores to attack the Spanish treasure fleet, or at least enter the Tagus river and lie in wait to intercept the Spaniards when they reached Lisbon, but he was overruled by the Lord Admiral. The fleet arrived back in Plymouth at the beginning of August, Essex himself to a hero's welcome from the populace but to a cool reception from the Queen and the news that in his absence his old enemy Robert Cecil had been appointed Secretary of State.

Elizabeth took a stern view of the manner in which her favourite had yet again taken it upon himself to distribute knighthoods among his officers, and she was disappointed in the small profits of the expedition. Prior to Essex's home-coming she had also learned of the document that he had sent ahead by the incompetent and untrustworthy Sir Anthony Ashley, *A true relation of the action at Cadiz the 21st June*, and had issued an order prohibiting it to be printed. Nevertheless the loyal Anthony Bacon arranged for handwritten copies to be distributed among his patron's friends at home, as well as in Scotland and France. By the time news reached the court at the beginning of September that the Spanish treasure ships had in fact entered the Tagus just two days after the departure of the Lord Admiral's fleet, Essex's popularity in the country had become so great that Elizabeth was in no mood to vindicate him.

In October the same year Francis Bacon, disenchanted with his patron's inability to secure for him the promotion he wanted, set down in writing a frank account of Essex's faults, coupled with advice on how to improve his relationship with the Queen; he warned the Earl of the dangers of arousing Elizabeth's jealousy through his own popularity. The advice was not heeded, and Essex's relationship with his sovereign continued to blow hot and cold; by early 1597 Francis Bacon was making overtures to the aged Burghley.

In March 1597 Essex was appointed Master of the Ordnance; he spent the next two months preparing for a large naval and military expedition of which the Queen had agreed to give him the command. The aim was to sail first to Ferrol, where intelligence reports indicated that Philip II (q.v.) was preparing another armada to avenge Cadiz, and then on to the Islands to intercept and destroy the Spanish treasure fleet on its way back from South America.

From the outset the expedition proved a dismal failure. Within a few days of sailing from Plymouth on 10 July, severe storms forced the fleet back to port, and they did not sail again until the middle of August. Then further gales decided them to abandon the attack on Ferrol and instead to sail straight for the Azores; but the objective of their voyage was jeopardized chiefly by the inept command exercised by Essex and by quarrels between Essex and Ralegh, which culminated in their missing the treasure ships altogether. In October Essex returned home to find England in a state of alarm due to reports of another Spanish armada heading for the Cornish coast, and also to find that he was yet again out of favour with the Queen.

A week later, bitterly resenting the earldom granted to the Lord Admiral, Charles Howard of Effingham, who was also made Lord Steward of the new Parliament, which gave him precedence over Essex, the Earl pleaded illness and retired from court. A recent biographer, Robert Lacey, endorses the contemporary gossip that Essex was suffering from syphilis, which would account for his erratic behaviour; other historians have put it down to a fit of the sulks. Elizabeth was concerned, and the more so when she heard from Sir Francis Vere (q.v.), who had been with Essex in the Azores, a somewhat different version of the latter's conduct from what she had been told by Ralegh. As a result, the relationship was patched up yet again, and in December Essex became Earl Marshal of England.

The improved relationship was however shortlived, and after Essex had connived with the Earl of Southampton in his secret marriage to one of the Queen's maids-of-honour there were many angry exchanges. Harsh words were spoken on the question of who should command the expedition to Ireland to crush the rebellious Earl of Tyrone (see O'Neill, Hugh); Essex is said to have told Elizabeth that her conditions were 'as crooked as her carcase', whereupon she boxed his ears and he flounced out of the court in temper, brandishing his sword.

After a further reconciliation, in November 1598 Essex was made Lord Lieutenant of the largest and best-equipped force yet sent against the rebellious Irish. He arrived in Dublin in April 1599, but instead of plunging directly into the attack on Ulster, he first engaged in a trivial campaign in Munster and then embarked on another in Athlone to the west of Dublin; nothing was achieved except considerable losses in men and horses. When eventually Essex marched into Ulster in August, it was almost hesitantly and with a sadly depleted army; disregarding instructions from Elizabeth, he arranged a meeting with Tyrone and negotiated a truce with him. (Many historians have believed that Essex was at this time gambling on the succession to the throne, in the knowledge that Elizabeth would not live much longer. He is known to have been at this time in correspondence with James VI of Scotland (q.v.), and it may have suited his purposes to have a friendly Tyrone at the head of an army in Ireland.)

A series of furious communications now reached Essex from the Queen, accusing him of perilous and contemptible behaviour. He brooded on them, indulged in more bouts of melancholy, and then, at the end of September, maintaining that Elizabeth was listening to his detractors, he suddenly deserted his command and made post-haste for England in a bid to justify his actions to her in person. Finding that the Queen was at Nonsuch, he staked all on a surprise confrontation and without knocking entered her bedroom in the early morning. She received him kindly at first, and listened to all he had to say, but later the same day he was subjected to her icy cross-examination and finally dismissed. They were not to meet again.

After examination by the Privy Council on six charges of offence against the Queen, Essex was put in the custody of the Lord Keeper, Sir Thomas Egerton (q.v.), at York House. In March 1600 he was allowed back to Essex House, but still in confinement, pending a full inquiry and hearing of his case. The proceedings took place before a specially appointed Commission at York House in June, which recommended that Essex should remain a prisoner during Her Majesty's pleasure; among the lawyers for the crown was his old associate, Francis Bacon. At the end of August Essex was given his liberty, but the Queen directed that he was never again to come to court.

Politically ruined and in debt, and only just recovering from a serious illness brought on by his confinement, Essex now resorted to desperate measures. Francis Bacon had sought to make amends for his treachery by concocting some correspondence that purported to have been exchanged between his brother Anthony and Essex, in which the former wrote that the Queen did not intend to destroy him altogether and Essex replied that so long as he was denied access to her, he could not hope to make the amends he so earnestly wished to make; unfortunately Francis overdid the praise and aroused Elizabeth's suspicions, with the result that in October she refused to renew the grant to Essex of the Farm of Sweet Wines, which provided the bulk of his income. Thereafter he and Francis Bacon saw little of one another, and for fear of betrayal to Francis, Essex also kept his brother Anthony in ignorance of the sinister plans he and his friends now began to formulate.

The young men of action who now rallied to Essex's side – the Earl of Southampton, Sir Christopher Blount, the Earl of Rutland, Lord Mounteagle, Sir Charles Danvers, and Henry Cuffe, among others – were thirsting for a continuation of the war with Spain and bitter at their exclusion from office by Cecil and his government. The point of open revolt of this Essex faction had not yet been reached, but passions were rising and secret overtures had been made to James VI in Scotland. During the first week of February 1601 plans were discussed for the overthrow of the Cecil government.

The constant comings and goings at Essex House did not go unnoticed; and on the evening of 7 February at the instigation of some of the Earl's followers, in order to stir the public to rebellion, there was a special performance at the Globe Playhouse of Shakespeare's *Richard II*, which included the controversial deposition scene. That same night, a messenger from the Privy Council arrived at Essex House demanding the Earl's immediate presence. Essex cleverly played for time, and when the messenger had departed he and his advisers held a council-of-war. It was decided to act the next day.

On the morning of 8 February, when a deputation of Privy Councillors presented themselves at Essex House, Essex had them put under lock and key. Meanwhile he himself rode confidently towards the City at the head of his followers, loudly proclaiming a plot against his life on the part of Cecil, Ralegh, and others, and shouting, 'For the Queen! For the Queen!' In an atmosphere of turmoil and utter confusion, in which supporters either vanished into thin air or failed to materialize in their promised numbers, while the court sent troops to barricade the streets, it soon became clear that the Earl had little choice but to slink home down the river. In the short time left to him before arrest he managed to burn some of his more incriminating papers. Late that night he and the Earls of Southampton and Rutland, together with other conspirators, surrendered to the Lord Admiral and were taken to the Tower.

At the trial held in Westminster Hall on 19 February, the prosecution was conducted by Sir Edward Coke (see *Lives of the Stuart Age*). Francis Bacon was among those who gave evidence against his former patron. At one point the outcome rested on the allegation that Robert Cecil had said that the Spanish Infanta was the rightful heir to the English throne after Elizabeth, but Essex's case collapsed on the evidence of Sir William Knollys to the effect that Cecil had at the time been discussing the tract on the next succession published under the pseudonym of Doleman. Both he and Southampton were found guilty and condemned to death.

In the six days he spent in the Tower between his trial and execution, the hysterical Essex made a full confession, incriminating all those who had joined in the conspiracy but had not yet been brought to trial. (The story that the Queen had given him a ring in an earlier stage of their relationship with a promise to pardon him if in a moment of danger he sent it back to her, and that Lady Nottingham, to whom he now en- trusted it, deliberately omitted to deliver the jewel to Elizabeth, is of doubtful authenticity.) The execution took place in the courtyard of the Tower on the morning of 25 February 1601; among the dignitaries of Church and state present was the Earl's old enemy, Sir Walter Ralegh. It took three blows of the axe to sever the head from the body.

Handsome, charming, courageous, and impulsive, Robert Devereux cap- tivated not only the public imagination of his day, but also the heart of his ageing monarch. Yet their relationship was demonstrably far shallower than in the many romantic stories since written round it: in the words of biographer Robert Lacey, it was on his side 'in the first instance, a calculated exercise in financial survival and later an instrument of political ambition', and on hers 'a calculated, wilful infatuation whose main constituent was fear of old age'. The real root of Essex's tragedy lay in his lack of discipline and failure to realize that the personal attraction which he exercised over Elizabeth would not be allowed to influence her political judgment or her determination to allow no one to influence her choice of a successor. Francis Bacon compared him to Icarus, his powers of flight destroyed by the heat of the sun.

Essex's letters have been printed in *Lives and Letters of the Devereux, Earls of Essex ... 1540–1646*, edited by W. B. Devereux (2 vols; 1853); some of the originals are preserved in the British Museum (Add. MSS 46188–9).

G. B. Harrison, *The Life and Death of Robert Devereux, Earl of Essex* (1937).
R. Lacey, *Robert, Earl of Essex: An Elizabethan Icarus* (1971).
A. L. Rowse, 'Robert Devereux, Earl of Essex', in K. Garvin (ed.), *The Great Tudors* (1935).
Lytton Strachey, *Elizabeth and Essex* (1928).

*Portraits:* oil, by William Segar, 1590: National Gallery of Ireland; miniature, full length, by Nicholas Hilliard, *c.* 1595: The Lady Lucas; oil, by Marcus Gheeraerts the Younger, *c.* 1596: Woburn Abbey (The Duke of Bedford); oil, by unknown artist after Gheeraerts: National Portrait Gallery, London; engraving, by R. Boissard, 1602: Victoria and Albert Museum, London; numerous other versions and some portraits of doubtful authenticity elsewhere. (N.B. The portrait in the Gorhambury Collection attributed to Nicholas Hilliard, and hitherto believed to be of Essex, is now considered to be of Anthony Bacon.)

**Devonshire, Earl of** (1563–1606), see Blount, Charles.

**Digges, Thomas** (d. 1595), mathema- tician and astronomer.

A member of a distinguished Kentish family, Thomas Digges was the son of Leonard Digges, the well-known mathematician, who is believed to have anticipated the invention of the telescope. The exact date of his birth is not known, but it probably took place at the family residence in Wotton, Kent.

In a home environment where mathematical observations and military matters were freely discussed, the young Digges received an early education in the liberal sciences. These he pursued at Cambridge, where he was a pensioner at Queen's College in May 1546 and subsequently took his B.A. (1550–1) and

M.A. (1557). It may have been at Cambridge that he met and formed a close friendship with the mathematician and astrologer John Dee (q.v.).

Nothing is known of the next fifteen years of Digges's life. Presumably he continued his mathematical and astronomical research, working closely with his father, for after the latter's death, in about 1571, Thomas devoted considerable time to editing and publishing the elder Digges's works. The first of these to appear was a three-volume work entitled *A Geometricall Practice, named Pantrometria*, which Thomas first published in 1571 (he was to bring out a revised edition in 1591).

In 1572 Digges sat in Parliament as Member for Wallingford. This was the year in which the new star, or super-Nova as it was called, made its appearance in the constellation of Cassiopeia. It shone for some seventeen months and upset many people, who looked upon it as a portent of disaster. In 1573 Digges published a treatise, *Alae seu scalae mathematiciae*, based on his observation of this star. (He wrote it in Latin in order that it should be read on the Continent.) Because the super-Nova had appeared in a region above the Moon where Aristotle had believed no changes could occur, Digges set aside the Greek philosopher's doctrine of the changeless heavens in favour of the new heliocentric theory of Nicolaus Copernicus (q.v.). His study won the praise of the great Danish astronomer, Tycho Brahe.

Hitherto, Robert Recorde (q.v.) had been the only English scientist to acclaim the Copernican theory, and was the first to publish a discussion of it in English. Digges now went further. In a supplement to another of his father's works, *A Prognostication everlasting*, which he brought out in a revised edition in 1576, he published the first authoritative exposition in English of the heliocentric theory. Called *A perfit description of the caelestiall orbes*, it stated Digges's firm belief in the infinity of the heliocentric universe. This was supported by diagrams and by a translation (by Digges) of sections of Copernicus's *De revolutionibus*. The work became instantly popular and ran into as many as seven editions before 1605.

Alongside his astronomical and mathematical research, Digges still found time to continue his interest in military engineering. In 1579 he completed and reshaped yet another of his father's works, *An Arithmetical Militare Treatise, named Stratioticos*. Thomas Digges's own studies in this field did not go unrewarded: in 1582 he was appointed by the Queen as a member of the commission for the repair of Dover harbour; he was to serve in this capacity for several years.

By this time Digges had married Agnes, daughter of William St Leger; two of their sons were later to achieve renown: Dudley, as a diplomatist and judge, and Leonard, as a poet and translator.

In 1585 Digges again sat in Parliament, this time as Member for Southampton. Other public appointments were to follow in the last years of his life, including that of Muster-Master-General of the English forces in the Netherlands, a post which he held from 1590 to 1594 in spite of constantly complaining that he was inadequately paid for his services. To a revised edition of his father's *Militare Treatise*, which he issued in 1590, Digges added an account of his own in which he defended the efforts of the Earl of Leicester (see Dudley, Robert) to relieve Sluys in 1587. He later served on a commission appointed to equip a fleet for the exploration of Cathay and the Antarctic. This was probably the last of

Digges's official duties, for he died in London on 24 August 1595. He was buried in the church of St Mary Aldermanbury.

Thomas Digges ranks among the first English mathematicians of the sixteenth century. His observations on the super-Nova of 1572–3 marked a turning-point in the history of astronomy in England.

F. R. Johnson, 'The influence of Thomas Digges on the progress of modern astronomy in 16th century England', *Osiris*, i (1936).

F. R. Johnson and S. V. Larkey, 'Thomas Digges, the Copernican system and the idea of the universe in 1575', *Huntingdon Library Bulletin*, v (1934).

**Donne, John** (1572–1631), poet and ecclesiastic, see *Lives of the Stuart Age*.

**Dorset, 1st Earl of** (1536–1608), see Sackville, Thomas.

**Douglas, Archibald** (?1489–1557), 6th Earl of Angus.

A member of the 'Red' Douglas branch of the family and the son of George Douglas, Master of Angus, who was killed at Flodden in 1513, Archibald was born in about 1489 and succeeded to the title on the death of his grandfather, the 'Great Earl' nicknamed 'Bell the Cat', in 1514.

He antagonized the Scottish nobility by his marriage in 1514 to Margaret Tudor (q.v.), who was then deprived of the regency and guardianship of her son, the infant James V (q.v.), and fled to England. During her absence Angus formed a liaison with a daughter of the Laird of Traquair, and when Margaret returned to Scotland the following year she quarrelled with her husband over his infidelity and over money matters and began to press for a divorce. She subsequently allied herself with the Duke of Albany (see Stewart, John), in whose absence abroad Angus engaged in a power struggle with the Earl of Arran (see Hamilton, James, 1st Earl). He defeated Arran in a spectacular battle in the streets of Edinburgh in April 1520, but the victory was shortlived. The war between the rival factions of the Hamilton and Douglas clans continued unabated, and in 1522, following Albany's return, Angus was sent into exile in France.

Two years later, with the support of Henry VIII (q.v.), he returned to Scotland, where in July 1524 the young James V was 'erected' as sovereign (i.e. declared fit to govern with the advice of his mother and a council). Albany's governorship was at an end, and now Margaret was gradually edged out of power by her estranged husband. James was to have been held by each of the four principal earls in turn, but in 1526 Angus refused to relinquish the King and held him in captivity in Edinburgh Castle. By this time Angus had become the dominant influence in the realm, and the Royal Household a Douglas stronghold in which more and more posts were filled by kinsmen appointed by Angus, who had himself replaced Archbishop David Beaton (q.v.) as Chancellor. In 1527 Margaret obtained her divorce from Angus.

Several attempts to rescue James failed, but in 1528 he was able to communicate with his mother and escaped to Stirling Castle, where enthusiastic and influential followers rallied to the King's side against Angus. The bitter hatred James bore for his stepfather and all the Douglases showed itself in an act of forfeiture against Angus and revenge on his family which included the burning at the stake of his sister, Janet Douglas, Lady Glamis. Angus himself took refuge in England.

After the death of James in 1542, the

act of forfeiture was annulled and Angus returned to Scotland. With him went a number of Scottish lords who had been captured by the English at Solway Moss; they had been freed by Henry VIII on the promise of securing an alliance and the marriage of his son Edward (see Edward VI) with the infant Mary, Queen of Scots (q.v.). Angus and his party lost no time in furthering the English cause. They swiftly won domination over the irresolute Earl of Arran (see Hamilton, James, 2nd Earl), who had been declared Governor of the Realm. Arran's rival contender for the regency, Archbishop Beaton, was imprisoned, and under the Treaty of Greenwich, ratified in August 1543, peace between England and Scotland was assured for the duration of the reigns of Henry and Mary, as well as the betrothal of the Scottish Queen to Prince Edward.

Within a week, under the influence of Beaton's supporters, Arran changed his mind; in December the treaty was annulled by the Scottish Parliament. Henry was furious, and in the following May launched an attack on Scotland. Marauding English troops under the command of the Earl of Hertford (see Seymour, Edward) landed at Leith and stormed into Edinburgh, Stirling, and St Andrews and beyond, with orders to meet resistance by killing all, including women and children, and to burn and ransack all that lay in their path.

Outraged and shocked by this act, Angus immediately switched his loyalty to the Scottish side. He was appointed Lieutenant of southern Scotland, and in February 1545 he defeated the English at the Battle of Ancrum Moor. In September 1547 he led the van at Pinkie, where the Scots suffered a humiliating defeat.

Angus died at Tantallon Castle, East Lothian, in January 1557, and was suc-

ceeded by his nephew. His only surviving legitimate child, Lady Margaret Douglas (q.v.), daughter of Margaret Tudor, married the 4th Earl of Lennox (see Stewart, Matthew) and was the mother of Lord Darnley (see Stewart, Henry), the future husband of Mary, Queen of Scots.

Sir William Fraser, *The Douglas Book* (4 vols; 1885).

**Douglas, Archibald** (1555–1588), 8th Earl of Angus.

Born in 1555, the son of David Douglas, 7th Earl of Angus, Archibald was the nephew of James Douglas, 4th Earl of Morton (q.v.). He succeeded to the title on his father's death in 1557 and to the earldom of Morton in 1586.

Douglas supported the marriage of Mary, Queen of Scots (q.v.) to Lord Darnley (see Stewart, Henry). He studied at the University of St Andrews, and during the regency of his uncle, Morton, rose rapidly to power. In 1573 he became a Privy Councillor and Sheriff of Berwick, and the following year Lieutenant-General of southern Scotland; the offices of Warden of the West Marches and Steward of Fife were subsequently conferred on him and in 1578, in return for his loyalty to Morton when the latter was removed from the regency, he was appointed Lieutenant-General of the realm on his uncle's restoration to power.

When Morton finally fell in 1581 Douglas fled to England, where he allied himself with the Protestant faction. One of the conspirators of the Ruthven Raid of 1582 (see Ruthven, William), he was among the banished lords who returned to Scotland in 1584 to overthrow the Earl of Arran (see Stewart, James, Earl of Arran). In the last years of his life he held office as Warden of the Marches and Lieutenant-General on the border, but

James VI (q.v.) distrusted his support of Presbyterianism and he was never high in the favour of the King.

Douglas died of consumption at Smeaton, near Dalkeith, on 4 August 1588. He had married three times, but left no surviving male issue. His first wife, Mary, daughter of the Regent, the Earl of Mar (see Erskine, John), had died in 1575; Douglas had divorced the second, Margaret, daughter of the Earl of Rothes; and in 1587 he had taken as his third wife Jean, daughter of the 8th Earl of Glamis, by whom he had one daughter.

Sir William Fraser, *The Douglas Book* (4 vols; 1885).

**Douglas, James** (?1516–1581), 4th Earl of Morton, Regent of Scotland (1572–8) during part of the minority of James VI (q.v.).

James Douglas was born in about 1516, the younger son of Sir George Douglas of Pittendriech by his wife Elizabeth, daughter of David Douglas of Pittendriech; his father was the younger brother of the 6th Earl of Angus (see Douglas, Archibald, 6th Earl) and Master of the Household during the time that Angus held James V (q.v.) in captivity. Up to 1528, when the act of forfeiture passed by the King on the Douglases forced his father to flee to England, James's education was supervised by Sir George. He was probably influenced towards the Reformation from an early age, for his father later supported George Wishart (q.v.), the popular reformer.

During his father's absence James lived first with some relatives under a false name and then, fearing discovery, he spent some time in the northern part of Scotland as an overseer of lands and rents. In 1543 he married Elizabeth Douglas, daughter of James Douglas, 3rd Earl of Morton, through whom in 1553 he inherited the earldom; she later became insane, and died in September 1574. After serving in the campaign against the English invasion of 1545, Douglas was taken prisoner on the capture of Dalkeith Castle in 1548 and is believed to have been held captive until about 1550.

Little is known of his activities during the next ten years. Although he was a Protestant, he does not seem to have played a prominent part in the conflict between Marie de Guise (q.v.) and the rebel lords. When Mary, Queen of Scots (q.v.), arrived in Scotland to assume personal rule in 1561, Morton was made a member of her Privy Council. In 1563 Mary appointed him as Chancellor. He supported the Queen's marriage to Lord Darnley (see Stewart, Henry) and helped to suppress the rebellion led by the Earl of Moray (see Stewart, Lord James) which arose in opposition to it; but in so doing he incurred the suspicion of the Queen because of his former friendship with Moray.

Resentment at the growing influence of Mary's French secretary, David Riccio (q.v.), brought Morton and Moray together in a conspiracy to murder. Together with Patrick Ruthven, 3rd Baron Ruthven, and a number of other Protestant lords, they cleverly secured Darnley's services as an accomplice. Riccio was killed at Holyroodhouse on the evening of 9 March 1566, and while Moray and his associates returned to Edinburgh from England where they had been exiled, Morton and the other conspirators fled across the Border.

Pardoned by Mary in December that year, Morton returned to Scotland but refused to join the Earl of Bothwell (see Hepburn, James) in his plot to murder Darnley, although he went so far as to conceal his knowledge of the conspiracy. On the night of Darnley's murder, 9

February 1567, he prudently absented himself from Edinburgh. When Bothwell subsequently compromised the Queen by carrying her off to Dunbar, however, Morton broke with him. At Carberry Hill on 15 June he commanded the force which confronted Mary and her husband and refused to accept Bothwell's offer to decide the issue by single combat; after the latter's flight and the Queen's surrender he accompanied Mary, as a prisoner, to Edinburgh; it was at his suggestion that she was sent to Lochleven rather than executed. He attended the coronation of James VI (q.v.) following Mary's abdication, and took the oath under the regency of Moray, being appointed one of the Regency Council pending the latter's arrival back in Scotland from France. During Moray's short term of office Morton was his chief adviser and most able ally; when the Queen escaped from Lochleven in May 1568, he played a prominent part in her final defeat at Langside. In September 1568 he handed over to Moray a silver casket containing the controversial letters and other papers said to have been written by Mary and implicating her in Darnley's murder, which had come into Morton's possession the previous summer.

During the civil war that broke out in Scotland following Moray's assassination in January 1570, Morton campaigned unremittingly on behalf of the young King; he was the *éminence grise* behind the two ensuing Regents, the Earl of Lennox (see Stewart, Matthew) and the Earl of Mar (see Erskine, John). Under the latter's regency he held office as Lord General of the kingdom. In October 1572 he was present, with Mar, at the conference with Sir Henry Killigrew, emissary of Queen Elizabeth I (q.v.), held at Dalkeith to discuss the project to deliver Mary, Queen of Scots, to her enemies. Negotiations were suspended when Mar died shortly afterwards, and on 24 November (the day of John Knox's death) Morton was elected as Regent.

For the next six years Morton's supremacy was unchallenged. A ruthless and resolute administrator with a total disregard for personal danger, he succeeded, with English assistance, in capturing Edinburgh Castle from the rebels in 1573 and in restoring the rule of law. His pursuance of the English alliance, however, antagonized the Catholic lords, while his attempt to introduce a reformed episcopacy and to tax the benefices of the clergy led to friction with the Kirk. Morton's failure to establish a good personal relationship with the young King also eventually turned James against him, by which time he had lost the favour of the tradespeople through his debasement of the coinage rather than risk the unpopular measure of higher taxation.

Morton made many enemies, among them the Earls of Atholl and Argyll, whom he disciplined for feuding in March 1578; they promptly banded together and applied to the King for arbitration. Morton protested and threatened to resign, but the King, barely twelve years old, was flattered and needed little urging to accept the Regent's resignation. Morton staged a counter-coup and regained power, but not the regency; a coalition was established, in which he became First Lord of the Council and the Earl of Atholl his second-in-command. When Atholl died suddenly in the spring of 1579, it was rumoured that he had been poisoned by Morton.

In the autumn of 1579 the Seigneur d'Aubigny (see Stuart, Esmé) arrived at the Scottish court and proceeded to worm his way into the favour and affection of the young King. It did not take him long to see that Morton was the one obstacle to his acquiring supreme power, and on 31 December 1580 he got James Stewart (q.v.), later Earl of Arran, to accuse the former Regent before the Privy Council of having been 'art and part' of the murder of Darnley fourteen years earlier. There were many lords willing to see his downfall, and upon accusation Morton was imprisoned first in Edinburgh and later in Dumbarton. At his trial, where the sole witness against him, Sir James Balfour, could prove nothing more than that the ex-Regent had been aware of the proposed murder, Morton confessed his foreknowledge and concealment and was sentenced to death for high treason. The execution took place publicly the following day, 2 June 1581, in Edinburgh; the ex-Regent's severed head was fixed on the highest gable of the Tolbooth and left there for six months. His earldom and lands were forfeited and his two natural sons banished; it is not known what happened to the three surviving daughters of his marriage.

An analysis of the Earl of Morton's papers will be found in the 2nd Report of the Historic Manuscripts Commission (1871).

M. Lee, 'The fall of the Regent Morton: a problem in satellite diplomacy', *Journal of Modern History*, xxviii (Chicago, 1956), pp. 111–29.
T. Thomson, *Registrum Honoris de Morton* (2 vols; Bannatyne Club, No. 94, Edinburgh, 1853).
See also the titles listed under Mary, Queen of Scots, and James VI.

*Portraits*: oil, by unknown artist, 1577: Scottish National Portrait Gallery, Edinburgh; oil on panel, by unknown artist: S.N.P.G.

## Douglas, Lady Margaret (1515–1578), Countess of Lennox, intriguer for succession to the throne.

Margaret Douglas was the daughter of Margaret Tudor (q.v.) by her second husband, the 6th Earl of Angus (see Douglas, Archibald, 6th Earl); grand-daughter of Henry VII (q.v.); mother of Lord Darnley (see Stewart, Henry); and grandmother of James VI of Scotland (q.v.), later James I of England.

Margaret had a most unsettled childhood. Born at Harbottle Castle, Northumberland, on 8 October 1515, she was taken by her mother to London the following May and lodged at Greenwich. In 1517 she accompanied Margaret Tudor back to Scotland, but on the separation of her parents was taken by her father to Tantallon Castle; it is possible that she went with Angus to France during his brief exile there in 1522. When he was driven from Scotland in 1528, Margaret was housed first at Norham Castle and then at Berwick, before Henry VIII (q.v.) took pity on her and placed her in his daughter's establishment at Beaulieu, where she formed an intimate friendship with the Princess Mary (see Mary I).

She was in favour with Anne Boleyn (q.v.), and on the birth of Elizabeth (see Elizabeth I) was made the Princess's first

lady-in-waiting. Following the act passed after Anne's execution which declared both Mary and Elizabeth to be illegitimate, Margaret's status was that of lady of the highest rank in England, and her right to the throne was considered by some to be more valid than that of James V of Scotland (q.v.), as she had been born in England.

In June 1536 she incurred the King's displeasure by her secret betrothal to Lord Thomas Howard, uncle of Anne Boleyn, and was sent to the Tower; she was subsequently removed to Syon Abbey, near Isleworth, where she was held until 29 October 1537. Restored to favour after the birth of Prince Edward (see Edward VI) and made first lady-in-waiting to Anne of Cleves (q.v.) while she was Queen, and later to Queen Catherine Howard (q.v.), she was again in disgrace in 1541 for her courtship with Sir Charles Howard, Catherine's brother, and was confined at Syon and later at Kenninghall.

The renewal of Angus's influence in Scotland restored Margaret once more to the favour of Henry VIII; her marriage to the Earl of Lennox (see Stewart, Matthew), which took place on 6 July 1544, was arranged by the King. The Catholic leanings which she began to demonstrate in the next few years much offended Henry, however, and in his last Will she was excluded from the right to succession. During the reign of Edward VI she lived mostly at Temple Newsam, Yorkshire, where her son, Henry Stewart, Lord Darnley, was born on 7 December 1545. Under Mary, the Countess of Lennox was again prominent at court, where she was accorded precedence over the Princess Elizabeth, but the latter, after her accession, became suspicious of the Catholic intrigues that so obviously had their centre at Temple Newsam; however, spies sent to try to find out what was afoot could discover nothing punishable.

At about this time the Countess, realizing that her own chances of succession to the thrones of Scotland and England were exceedingly remote, began to concentrate her ambitions on the marriage of her eldest son to Mary, Queen of Scots (q.v.), who was next in line to Elizabeth. When this scheme was revealed prematurely to the Queen in 1562, Lennox was sent to the Tower and his wife and Darnley were confined at the home of Sir Richard Sackville at Sheen; but as a result of a flattering letter written to the Queen by the Countess, all three were released and again received at court. In 1565 Lennox was permitted to go to Scotland and Darnley to join him there. However, once intelligence reached London in June that year that Darnley was about to marry Mary, Elizabeth sent the Countess of Lennox to the Tower, and she was not freed until after her son's murder in February 1567.

While Lennox tried to get the Earl of Bothwell (see Hepburn, James) convicted of Darnley's murder, the Countess denounced the Queen of Scots for the crime. She remained hostile to Mary throughout her husband's difficult period as Regent to James VI after the death of the previous Regent, the Earl of Moray (see Stewart, Lord James), in 1570, but after Lennox's death in September 1571 she was reconciled with her.

In October 1574 she set out for the north, ostensibly to return to Scotland, accompanied by her second son, Charles, now Earl of Lennox. When news reached the Queen that en route Lennox had been married to Elizabeth Cavendish, daughter of 'Bess of Hardwick', Countess of Shrewsbury (see Hardwick, Elizabeth), she summoned his mother back to London; at the end of December both

Margaret, Countess of Lennox and the Countess of Shrewsbury were committed to the Tower. The Lady Margaret was released in the spring of 1577, but died about a year later, on 7 March 1578, so poor that she had to be buried at the royal expense. Four sons and four daughters all pre-deceased her, but she was survived by two grandchildren, James VI, son of Lord Darnley, and Arabella Stuart (q.v.), daughter of her second son, Charles.

Although the Lady Margaret Douglas failed to achieve her great aim in life, her family aspirations were to be fulfilled after her death by the accession of her grandson, James VI, to the throne of England.

William Fraser, *The Lennox* (2 vols; 1874).

*Portraits*: oil, full length, by unknown artist, 1572: Royal Collection, Holyroodhouse; oil on panel, *called* Margaret Douglas, Countess of Lennox, by unknown artist: National Portrait Gallery, London; tomb effigy, by unknown artist: Westminster Abbey; electrotype from tomb effigy: N.P.G.

**Dowland, John** (?1563–1626), lutenist and composer.

Little is known of Dowland's origins or early life, but there is a slight possibility that he was born in Dublin. Before the age of twenty he is known to have been in the service of Sir Henry Cobham, whom he accompanied to Paris on his appointment as ambassador there in 1579. In Paris he fell in with a group of exiled Catholics, who persuaded him to change his religion. When Cobham was recalled in 1583, Dowland remained for a short time in Paris in the service of the next ambassador, Sir Edward Stafford (q.v.). In 1584 or shortly afterwards he returned to England, where he married.

In July 1588 Dowland received the degree of B.Mus. at Oxford. In 1594,

disappointed at his failure to obtain a post as one of the royal musicians, and feeling that he had been passed over because of his religion, he set out for a long tour of the Continent. He went first to Germany, to the court of the Duke of Brunswick and then on to the Landgrave of Hesse; from there to Italy, where he visited Venice, Rome, and Florence. Everywhere he met with musical success through his virtuosity on the lute, and he soon won the friendship of leading continental musicians. In Florence Dowland became involved with the English Catholics there; then, on the point of going to study under Marenzio in Rome, he suddenly took fright at his association with exiles known to be treasonable to the Queen. On the pretext of being homesick for his family and children, he turned northwards again. From Nuremburg he wrote to Robert Cecil (q.v.), giving him information concerning the English Catholics in Italy and professing that he had abandoned them and their religion. This letter paved the way for his return to England.

In 1596 some of Dowland's lute pieces appeared in Barley's *New Book of Tableture*. The following year his *First Booke of Songs or Ayres of Foure Partes with Tableture for the Lute* was published by Peter Short. These songs were harmonized tunes rather than madrigals, a new departure in English music. They were an immediate success on account of their melodic quality and the book ran into five editions by 1613. In 1598 he contributed some verses to the volume of *Canzonets* issued by Giles Farnaby (q.v.), and the following year a sonnet by Dowland was included in Richard Alison's *Psalms*. The *Second Book of Songs or Ayres* appeared in 1600 and the *Third and Last Book* in 1603. *Lachrymae, or Seven Tears*, a collection of 'seven passionate pavans' for viols and lute, his most famous composition, was published in 1605. By this time Dowland was again living abroad.

In November 1598 Dowland had been appointed lutenist to Christian IV of Denmark, at a good salary. This did not prevent his falling into debt, which, added to his habit of overstaying leaves of absence in England, finally exasperated the Danes. He was dismissed from the royal service in February 1606 and returned to London, where he took up residence in Fetter Lane, off the Strand.

During his absence abroad a new school of lutenists had emerged in England, and Dowland now found himself regarded as old-fashioned by the younger generation. He occupied himself by translating the *Micrologus*, a lengthy treatise on music by Ornithoparcus. In 1610 he contributed several songs to his son Robert's *A Musicall Banquet*, as well as a short treatise on lute playing to the latter's *Varietie of Lute Lessons* which appeared the same year.

The long-awaited recognition from the English court came in 1612, the year in which Dowland published his last and finest work, *A Pilgrim's Solace*. That October he was appointed one of the King's musicians for the lutes. In 1613 he and Robert were among the musicians who performed in one of Chapman's masques at Whitehall. During 1622-3 he spent some months abroad in the service of the Duke of Wolgast, in Pomerania. He died probably on 20 or 21 January 1626, in London.

Dowland was unsurpassed throughout Europe both as a performer on the lute and as a songwriter. He was the forerunner of the English school of lutenists that came to the fore at the beginning of the seventeenth century, none of whom however equalled the melancholic intensity of his more personal, serious compositions. Melodies such as 'Lachrymae' were among the most celebrated of their time. Most of Dowland's compositions were in four parts or to be sung as solos with lute accompaniment. Some seventy to eighty pieces of his solo lute music have survived, many of them in manuscript in English and German libraries. The songs are printed in *The English School of Lutenist Song Writers*, edited by E. H. Fellowes (1920-32).

E. H. Fellowes, 'The Songs of John Dowland', *Proceedings of the Musical Association*, lvi (1929).
Rosemary J. Manning, 'Lachrymae: a study of John Dowland', *Music and Letters*, xxv (1944).
Diana Poulton, *John Dowland* (1972).
P. Warlock, *The English Ayre* (1926).

**Drake, Sir Francis** (?1542-1596), the first Englishman to circumnavigate the world and indisputably the greatest seaman of the Tudor age.

Drake was born at Crowndale, near Tavistock, Devon, at the home of his grandparents, John and Margery Drake, who were tenant farmers on Lord Bedford's estate; the exact date of his birth is uncertain, but Francis Russell, later 2nd Earl of Bedford, was the boy's godfather. His father, Edmund Drake, was an ardent and outspoken Protestant; he sought refuge in Plymouth Castle at the time of the rising of the West Country peasants against the Prayer Book of Edward VI (q.v.) in 1549, and later took his family to live on a hulk in the river Medway near Chatham Dockyard, where during the reign of Mary I (q.v.) he found employment as a 'reader of prayers to the Navy'. Drake's mother bore her husband twelve sons, of whom at least three, including Francis, became sailors.

In 1560 Edmund Drake was ordained and appointed to the living of Upchurch, Kent. At the age of about ten or twelve

Francis was apprenticed to an elderly skipper trading between the Thames and the Channel ports. From this master mariner Drake learned much of the sailor's craft and the coasting trade, and eventually inherited his boat. For a short time afterwards he traded on his own account, but already his imagination was fired by the exploits of his distant kinsman, John Hawkins (q.v.), in the Indies. In 1563 Drake joined a Hawkins expedition to the Guinea Coast, sailing as third officer. Three years later, in 1566, he participated in another Hawkins-sponsored voyage, a slaving expedition to the Cape Verde Islands and the Spanish Main under the command of Captain John Lovell. On his return Hawkins invited Drake to join the new, but ill-fated, expedition which sailed from Plymouth in October 1567. He sailed in one of the Queen's ships, the *Jesus of Lubeck*, to Tenerife and Sierra Leone, but was later given his first command, that of the *Judith*, and only narrowly escaped from a disastrous battle with the Spanish fleet in the port of San Juan de Ulua. He arrived back in England in January 1569.

In July that year Drake married a Saltash girl, Mary Newman. He may have served at this time in Irish waters; certainly he was one of the most successful corsairs raiding the Spanish Main. In the next three years he was also planning future voyages to harass the Spaniards, with whom the English were now in open conflict although not officially at war. Drake made voyages to the West Indies in 1570 and 1571, and in May 1572 he sailed from Plymouth on his most daring exploit to date: an attack on Nombre de Dios, Panama, where the gold and silver from Peru were stored until they could be conveyed to Spain.

The squadron consisted of the *Pasche* (or *Pasco*), 70 tons, belonging to the

Hawkins brothers, the *Swan*, 25 tons, owned by Drake himself, and three pinnaces, with a total crew of seventy-one, which included two of Drake's brothers, John, the second-in-command, and Joseph, both of whom were to lose their lives on the voyage. Drake was wounded in the leg during fighting at Nombre de Dios; just when his men were on the point of breaking into the treasure house he fainted and was carried protesting back to his ship, the gold left untouched. The expedition nevertheless went on to other remarkable achievements: the capture of several Spanish vessels, the sacking of Venta Cruces, a successful raid on a mule-train laden with gold and silver. When the expedition returned triumphant to Plymouth in August 1573, bringing with it thirty survivors of the original crew and some £20,000 worth of plunder, the foundation of Drake's fortune was laid. News of his exploits had spread from the Caribbean to Europe, causing much alarm in Spain, and a directive came from London that he should lie low for a while. He bought three ships and a house in Plymouth, and in between short bouts of employment, which included a spell under Walter Devereux, 1st Earl of Essex, ferrying soldiers to and from Ireland, Drake began to plan his next adventure, the fulfilment of his vow to sail an English fleet on the Pacific, the 'Great South Sea' that he had glimpsed for the first time from Panama.

The fleet which left Plymouth on 13 December 1577 with Drake in command of the 120-ton *Pelican* (later to be renamed the *Golden Hind*) and four smaller vessels, the *Elizabeth*, the *Marigold*, the *Swan*, and the *Christopher*, with a complement of about 164 men, boys, and 'gentlemen adventurers', had more than one objective. The official venture, backed by Sir Francis Walsingham (q.v.), Sir Christopher Hatton (q.v.), and others, with Drake himself contributing £1,000, was for a reconnaissance of the conjectured 'terra australis' or southern continent and the discovery of trading bases there and in the Moluccas. Privately the Queen had commissioned Drake to take revenge on the King of Spain by raiding the west coast of South America. It is not certain whether he meant to search for the western exit of the North-West Passage which would turn the flank of Spanish America and provide a northern route to the East.

The expedition's first major success was the capture off Cape Verde of a Portuguese cargo ship, whose pilot Drake took with him as far as Guatulco. But the voyage down the east coast of South America to Magellan's Straits was beset with difficulties, not least of which were suspicions and quarrels between the crew and the 'gentlemen'; these culminated in the trial and execution of Thomas Doughty. After wintering at San Julian for two months, they sailed south and at the entrance to the Straits Drake changed the name of his flagship to the *Golden Hind*. By this time his squadron had been reduced to three ships. They negotiated the tricky passage without incident and emerged into the Pacific on 6 September 1578. A few days later a ferocious storm blew up in which the *Marigold* went down with all hands and the only two surviving ships, Drake's *Golden Hind* and the *Elizabeth* under Captain John Wynter, nephew of Sir William, became separated. Wynter waited for three weeks at a rendezvous just inside the Straits, but when the *Golden Hind* failed to show up, he set sail for England. Meanwhile Drake, who had been driven south to 57° by the storm, probably guessed that the Straits did not, as Magellan (q.v.) thought, separate America from a vast new continent which he called the *Tierra del Fuego*, but lay between America and a group of islands, beyond which the two great oceans met.

Now the *Golden Hind* sailed on alone up the coasts of Chile and Peru, plundering shipping as she went. She made a rich haul, one of her most valuable prizes being a treasure ship, *Nuestra Señora*, popularly known to sailors as the *Cacafuego* ('Spitfire'). Then on up the coast of California to a point farther north than any European ship had ventured before. Accounts vary as to the exact position, but Drake himself believed it to be 48°. If he was searching for the western exit of the North-West Passage, he did not find it, for cold weather forced him south again and he is thought to have anchored in the lagoon now called Drake's Bay, to the north of San Francisco on the Californian coast. While the *Golden Hind* was being refitted there, Drake annexed the country for the Queen, naming it 'New Albion'.

After a three-month voyage across the

Pacific to the Moluccas, where six tons of cloves were taken aboard, he set course for home. The *Golden Hind* hit a reef in the east Indian archipelago. First Drake urged his men to pray; then reluctantly he gave the order to lighten the ship. Some cannon and provisions were cast overboard, and half the cloves, when suddenly the wind eased, and the ship righted herself and slid into deeper water. Eight months later, having rounded the Cape of Good Hope and called *en route* at Sierra Leone, on 26 September they put into Plymouth Sound.

Drake was summoned to court to tell the Queen personally of his adventures. The total value of the treasure he brought back on this occasion was reported to be £450,000. In April 1581 the Queen knighted Drake on board the *Golden Hind* at Deptford.

With his share of the profits (£10,000) Drake purchased Buckland Abbey in South Devon. In 1582 he became Mayor of Plymouth, and in 1584 Member of Parliament for Bossiney. The following year he married Elizabeth, daughter of Sir George Sydenham, his first wife having died in 1582; there were no children of either marriage.

In 1584–5 Drake was given the command of the first act of open war against Spain: an attack in force on Spanish possessions in the Caribbean. The fleet of twenty-one ships and eight pinnaces, Drake in the flagship *Elizabeth Bonaventure* and his vice-admiral, Martin Frobisher (q.v.), in the *Primrose*, sailed in September 1585. Sacking Vigo on the way, they went on to attack Santo Domingo, Cartagena, and San Augustin in Florida; then proceeding to Virginia they brought home Ralph Lane (q.v.) and his fellow colonists left there by Sir Richard Grenville (q.v.), reaching Portsmouth in July 1586.

Drake's next brilliant exploit was to attack, in Cadiz harbour in the spring of 1587, the fleet which Philip II of Spain (q.v.) was preparing for an invasion of England. More than twenty-four ships were taken or burned, and on the way home he not only captured Sagres Castle at Cape St Vincent, with all its supplies and armaments, but seized a most valuable prize, the Portuguese carrack *San Felipe*, worth about £114,000. This daring feat became popularly known as 'singeing the King of Spain's beard'. It was marred only by a clash of temperament between Drake and his second-in-command, William Borough (q.v.), against whom Drake brought a case in Council on his return.

In 1588 Drake was appointed to command the third section of the combined fleet under the Lord High Admiral, Lord Howard of Effingham (see Howard, Charles) at Plymouth. His plans to attack the Armada before it left Spain were sanctioned too late to be effective. On 19 July the Spanish fleet was sighted off the Lizard. The authenticity of Drake's alleged comment on the bowling green at Plymouth Hoe, when the news was told him – 'We have time to finish the game and beat the Spaniards afterwards' – has been challenged, but the tradition is an early one.

The English fleet put to sea to chase the Spaniards up-Channel, and on the first night out Drake in the *Revenge* broke line to seize a valuable prize, the galleon *Rosario*, commanded by Don Pedro de Valdes. Rejoining Howard, he fought on the seaward wing of the fleet. At a council-of-war on 28 July, when both fleets lay off the Calais Roads, he was one of the protagonists for the use of the fireships which ultimately caused so much havoc to the Armada; at the ensuing decisive Battle of Gravelines he engaged in a brilliant action in close combat with the Spanish commander, the Duke of Medina Sidonia, in the *San Martin*.

The defeat of the Spanish Armada was not the close of Drake's naval career, although he never again achieved such glory. In the following year, 1589, he commanded the naval force in a joint sea and land attack on Lisbon, together with Sir John Norris (q.v.). That it failed was due largely to delays, bad provisioning, and disagreements between the two leaders, and Drake was not commissioned again for five years. He devoted much of the intervening time to his affairs in the West Country and to promoting a scheme for the supply of water to the town of Plymouth.

In 1595 a new expedition to the Caribbean was mounted under the command of Drake and Hawkins, in the hope of repeating earlier successes. It proved disastrous: the Spanish defences were too strong; Hawkins, sixty-three years old, died off Puerto Rico; then Drake succumbed to the sickness that swept through the fleet and died off Portobello, on the night of 27 January 1596. He was buried at sea.

The most spectacular of all the Tudor privateering captains, a folk-hero in his own time and a legendary figure ever since, Drake was a great navigator and a brilliant leader of men: quick-witted and brave, a strict disciplinarian, God-fearing, restless and ruthless, yet humane, as his Spanish prisoners testified. His Protestant upbringing undoubtedly added impetus to the struggle against England's Catholic adversary, and *el Draque* was much feared in Spain. In fact Drake so injured Spanish prestige as to justify considering him as an individual element in Spain's eventual defeat. His voyage to the Moluccas was the precursor of the East India Company and the expansion of England's trade with the East.

K. R. Andrews, *Drake's Voyages* (1967).
J. Barrow, *Life, Voyages and Exploits of Sir Francis Drake* (1843).
J. S. Corbett, *Drake and the Tudor Navy* (2 vols; 1898–9).
T. W. E. Roche, *The Golden Hind* (1974).
G. M. Thomson, *Sir Francis Drake* (1972).
N. Williams, *Francis Drake* (1974).
J. A. Williamson, *The Age of Drake* (1938; revised 1946, 1952).
J. A. Williamson, *Sir Francis Drake* (1951).

*Portraits:* two miniatures by Nicholas Hilliard, 1581: The Earl of Derby (on loan to Manchester City Art Gallery) and Kunsthistorisches Museum, Vienna; oil, full-length, by unknown artist, *c.* 1580–5: National Portrait Gallery, London; oil, head and shoulders, by unknown artist, *c.* 1583: N.P.G.; engraving, attributed to Jodocus Hondius, *c.* 1583, finished by G. Vertue: N.P.G.; oil by Marcus Gheeraerts the younger, 1594: Lt-Col Sir George Tapps-Gervis-Meyrick (copies at National Maritime Museum, Greenwich; Plymouth Corporation; Knole; Ashmolean).

## Drayton, Michael (1563–1631), poet.

Born at Hartshill, near Atherstone, Warwickshire, in 1563, Michael Drayton spent his early years in the service of Sir Henry Goodere of Powlesworth, Warwickshire, who educated him and became his first patron.

His earliest work *The Harmonie of the Church*, a metrical rendering of songs and prayers from the Old Testament and Apocrypha, published in 1591, gave offence to the authorities and was ordered to be destroyed. In 1593 Drayton followed in the tradition of Edmund Spenser (q.v.) by publishing a volume of eclogues entitled *Idea, the Shepheards Garland*; these were later much revised for inclusion in *Poems Lyrick and Pastoral* (c. 1605) and re-published as *Pastorals* (1619). In 1593 Drayton also wrote his first historical poem, *Piers Gaveston*. The following year he published *Ideas Mirrour*, a series of sonnets inspired by the French and written probably to Anne Goodere, daughter of his patron; among these is the exquisite 'Since there's no help, come let us kiss and part'. *Endimion and Phoebe*, as pastoral, was written in about 1595, and his two historical poems, *Robert, Duke of Normandy* and *Mortimeriados*, the following year. The latter, Drayton's first important work, was rewritten in 1603 as *The Barrons Wars*.

In 1597 Drayton published *Englands Heroicall Epistles*, a series of imaginary letters in verse exchanged between historical personages. By this date he was living mainly in London, where, according to the diary of the theatrical manager Philip Henslowe (q.v.), he collaborated with Henry Chettle (q.v.), Thomas Dekker, and later, John Webster (for the last two, see *Lives of the Stuart Age*) in writing for the stage. On the accession of James I (see James VI of Scotland), Drayton, in company with his fellow poets, duly acclaimed the new King in verse; but he found no favour with James and was increasingly neglected. This he came much to resent.

Work continued to flow from Drayton's pen. A satire, 'The Owle', appeared in 1604; *Poems Lyrick and Pastoral*, which included the splendid 'Ballad of Agincourt' ('Fair stood the wind for France') and introduced into English poetry the 'ode', modelled on Horace, appeared in about 1605. In 1613 a volume containing the first eighteen 'songs' of *Poly-Olbion*, the poet's most ambitious work to date, was published with annotations by John Selden. In *Polyolbion*, as it was spelt in later editions, Drayton's idea was to put on record the beauties of Elizabethan England, interspersing topographical description with fragments of history and legend written in the form of thirty 'songs'. He completed the work, which owed much to Camden's *Britannia* (see Camden, William) in 1622.

In 1619 Drayton published a collection of all the poems, excluding *Polyolbion*, that he wished to preserve. A further volume of miscellaneous poems, issued in 1627, contained the delightful fairy poem 'Nymphidia', much influenced by his fellow Warwickshireman's *A Midsummer Night's Dream* (see Shakespeare, William). His last work was 'The Muses Elysium', published in 1630.

Michael Drayton died in 1631 and was buried in Westminster Abbey. He was above all an immensely patriotic poet who drew his inspiration from English history and the countryside he loved, especially Warwickshire. He was the first to write odes in the English language after the style of Horace. Drayton's *Works* have been edited by J. W. Hebel (5 vols; 1931–41).

John Buxton, *Elizabethan Taste* (1963).
O. Elton, *Michael Drayton, A Critical Study* (1905).
B. H. Newdigate, *Michael Drayton and his Circle* (1941).

*Portrait*: oil, by unknown artist, 1628: Dulwich College Picture Gallery, London.

**Dudley, Lady Jane** (1537–1554), see Jane Grey, Lady.

**Dudley, John** (?1504–1553), Earl of Warwick and 1st Duke of Northumberland, lawyer, soldier, sailor, and statesman, virtual ruler of England, 1549–53, during part of the minority of Edward VI (q.v.).

John Dudley was born in about 1504, the eldest son of Edmund Dudley by his second wife, Elizabeth Grey, daughter of Viscount Lisle. His father was a lawyer and Privy Councillor to Henry VII (q.v.) who accumulated much wealth; he was executed for treason by Henry VIII (q.v.) in August 1510, when John was about six years old, but the attainder was repealed two years later and his son restored in blood. After Elizabeth Dudley's re-marriage, John was probably brought up at the home of Sir Edward Guildford, who was his guardian. He subsequently married Guildford's daughter Jane.

Like his father, John Dudley became a lawyer. In his early career he was involved in legal actions designed to recover his father's forfeited estates and to add to his own sources of wealth. Introduced to court probably by his guardian, in 1523 Dudley received his first appointment as a lieutenant to serve in France under the command of the Duke of Suffolk (see Brandon, Charles); he received a knighthood for his part in that campaign. A series of minor official appointments followed: the posts of Joint Constable of Warwick Castle, Master of the Armoury at the Tower, and Master of the Horse to Anne of Cleves (q.v.).

By 1537 Dudley had not only become an established figure at court; he was also acquiring a reputation for military and naval ability. In 1536 he had taken part in the pacification of the Pilgrimage of Grace under the Duke of Norfolk (see Howard, Thomas, 3rd Duke); the following year he was Vice-Admiral of a fleet which successfully cleared the Channel of French pirates; in 1538 he became Deputy Governor of the English-controlled port of Calais. Elevated to the peerage as Viscount Lisle in 1542, towards the end of that year he was sent to the Border to replace the Earl of Hertford (see Seymour, Edward) as Lord Warden, but a few weeks later he was appointed Lord High Admiral and recalled to London. After serving under Hertford in the invasion of Scotland in 1544, in September the same year he captured Boulogne, of which he was made Governor. He and Lord Paget (see Paget, William) were among those who negotiated with the French for the Treaty of Camp, signed in June 1546, which allowed England to retain Boulogne for eight years. For his military and diplomatic achievements Henry VIII rewarded Lisle generously with lands; in 1546 he created him Earl of Warwick.

When Henry died in January 1547, Warwick was one of the executors of the King's Will and a member of the Regency Council set up to govern during the minority of Edward VI (q.v.). He readily agreed to Hertford's assumption of power as Protector and Duke of Somerset, and initially the two men worked well together. Warwick resigned the office of Lord High Admiral and in September 1547 acted as Lord Lieutenant of the army that defeated the Scots at Pinkie Cleugh, a victory which was due largely to his military strategy. In August 1549 he crushed the Norfolk rebellion led by Robert Ket (q.v.).

At about this time, along with other members of the Council, he began to lose confidence in Somerset. Fame and high office had made Warwick greedy for power on his own account, and taking advantage of his popularity as a military commander and of the widespread unrest caused by the Protector's policies, he joined with those Councillors who sought to overthrow their leader. Following Somerset's arrest and imprisonment in the Tower in October 1549, Warwick took control, with the majority of the Council behind him; for the next four years he was virtually ruler of England. Great Master of the Household in 1550, and Earl Marshal the following April, in October 1551 he made himself Duke of Northumberland. Ostensibly there had been a brief reconciliation between him and Somerset the previous year, when the latter had been reinstated to the Council, but the new leader never ceased to scheme for his rival's downfall; finally, towards the end of 1551, he had Somerset arrested on trumped-up charges of treason, tried, condemned, and executed the following January.

Under Northumberland's rule England moved further forward into Protestantism; a number of episcopal estates were annexed to the crown, and Catholic bishops imprisoned; peasants who resisted enclosure were suppressed, and law and order enforced in the countryside. In foreign affairs England pulled out of involvement in Scotland, and Boulogne was returned to France.

Having acquired a dominating influence over the young King, whose health had begun to deteriorate markedly by the beginning of 1553, Northumberland readily fell in with Edward's own plans for the succession, which involved cutting out his two sisters from the succession – Mary because of her fanatical Catholicism, Elizabeth on account of her dubious legitimacy. Instead, the King was determined to make a Will leaving the crown to Lady Jane Grey (q.v.) and her male heirs. In May that year Northumberland brought about the marriage of his fourth son, Lord Guildford Dudley, to the Lady Jane.

Edward died on 6 July 1553, but in order to give the Council time to capture the Princess Mary, the King's death was kept secret for three days. Mary evaded her pursuers and rallied supporters in Norfolk, while on 10 July Northumberland proclaimed the Lady Jane Grey as Queen. When London and the rest of the country appeared to be rising on behalf of Mary, Northumberland knew that he was defeated, and having marched from London to Cambridge to fight, on 20 July he declared for Mary without entering into battle. Arrested and taken to the Tower three days later, he was tried for high treason on 18 August and condemned to death. In a speech on the scaffold on 22 August he confessed his fault, asked forgiveness of the Queen, and asserted that he was a 'true Catholic Christian'.

Lady Jane Grey and Lord Guildford Dudley were executed in February 1554, following the rebellion of the younger Sir Thomas Wyatt (q.v.). The Duchess of Northumberland died in January 1555, her three eldest sons, John, Earl of Warwick, Ambrose, and Robert, later Earl of Leicester (see Dudley, Robert), having been released from the Tower the previous October.

John Dudley, Duke of Northumberland, although an able soldier and sailor, was a ruthless schemer, set on gain and self-aggrandizement. A political gambler, he was caught out by the early death of Edward VI. The French ambassador said that there were only two men capable of governing the country in this perilous time, Somerset and Northumberland. Both perished at the job.

B. L. Beer, *Northumberland, The Political Career of John Dudley, Earl of Warwick and Duke of Northumberland* (Kent, Ohio, 1973).

P. Lindsay, *The Queenmaker: A Portrait of John Dudley* (1951).

C. Sturge, 'The Life and Times of John Dudley, Viscount Lisle, Earl of Warwick, and Duke of Northumberland', University of London Ph.D. thesis (1927).

*Portraits:* According to Roy Strong, in *Tudor and Jacobean Portraits* (1969), neither the portrait at Knole nor that at Penshurst can be substantiated as being Northumberland; the only possible likeness is that in the group painting *Edward VI and the Pope*, by an unknown artist: National Portrait Gallery, London.

**Dudley, Robert** (?1532–1588), Earl of Leicester, courtier, favourite of Queen Elizabeth I (q.v.).

Robert Dudley was the fifth son of John Dudley (q.v.), later Earl of

Warwick and 1st Duke of Northumberland, and his wife Jane, daughter of Sir Edward Guildford. The precise date of his birth has never been established, but traditionally it is said to have taken place on 24 June in either 1532 or 1533, probably in London, where his father was at the time Master of the Armoury at the Tower.

Throughout Robert's childhood his father, rapidly advancing in royal favour, saw to it not only that his children were given the best education but also that they learned the social graces through attendance at court. Thus Robert was tutored by Roger Ascham (q.v.), who also taught the Princess Elizabeth, and from an early age he was a playmate of the Princess, and later of her brother, the future Edward VI (q.v.).

During Edward's reign (1547–53) and especially after the fall of the Protector Somerset (see Seymour, Edward), the arrogant, scheming Northumberland increased his power over the young King until he became virtual ruler of England. He endeavoured to cement his position by arranging suitable marriages for his children, and in June 1550, at the age of seventeen, Robert was married to Amy, daughter and heiress of Sir John Robsart, a wealthy Norfolk landowner; the wedding took place at the royal palace at Sheen, in the presence of the King. The young couple settled in Norfolk, and for the next three years Robert lived partly the life of a wealthy country squire and partly that of a courtier. The marriage, described later by Sir William Cecil (q.v.) as having 'begun in passion, ended in mourning', seems to have been a love match at the outset but was to prove childless, and after the first few years husband and wife lived increasingly separate lives. In 1551 Northumberland secured for his son an appointment as a Gentleman of the Privy Chamber, but there is no record of Lady Robert Dudley's accompanying him on his frequent attendances at court, even in January 1552 when he took part in two tournaments. At home in Norfolk Robert Dudley also held several minor official appointments, and in 1553 he was returned as Member of Parliament for the county.

He supported Northumberland in his plan to place the Lady Jane Grey (q.v.) on the throne when Edward died in early July 1553, and at their father's command he and his elder brother, the Earl of Warwick, rode in pursuit of the Princess Mary (see Mary I) when she fled to Norfolk in order to rally her supporters. Robert eventually gave up the chase at King's Lynn, surrendered to the royal followers, and was taken to join the rest of the Dudley family in the Tower. His father went to the scaffold at the end of August, and his brother Guildford and sister-in-law the Lady Jane Grey early in February 1554 after the rebellion of the younger Sir Thomas Wyatt (q.v.). While the Duchess of Northumberland and her youngest son, Henry, were released, the three remaining brothers, Warwick, Ambrose, and Robert, all of whom had been condemned to death, were kept in confinement. For a short period the Princess Elizabeth was also imprisoned in the Tower; contrary to the romantic tradition, however, it is unlikely that there was any communication between the prisoners. In October 1554 the Duchess at last won a free pardon for her sons, but their release was clouded by the death a few days later of the Earl of Warwick, leaving only Ambrose, Robert, and Henry to inherit the few family possessions that had not been confiscated when she herself died the following January.

Little is known of Robert Dudley's life during the next two and half years.

All his property had been seized by the crown, and although his rich father-in-law was able to provide, Robert, used to the glamour of court life, did not take kindly to his reduced life-style or to the quiet domestic existence in the Norfolk countryside with a dull and sterile wife to whom he had by this time become largely indifferent. He yearned to be on active service, but while England was at peace there was no opportunity, and he had not been trained for any profession but that of courtier. Once at least he risked the journey to London, for he was present at some secret gathering in St Paul's and was subsequently given a stern warning to remain in the country.

In the summer of 1557 England's declaration of war against France, as an ally of Spain, gave the Dudleys their long-awaited chance. Robert failed to raise a company to fight under his command but he obtained an appointment as Master of the Ordnance to the Earl of Pembroke, leader of the expeditionary force. All three Dudley brothers distinguished themselves at the Battle of St Quentin on 10 August; after the action Robert was given the honour of bearing dispatches to Mary at Greenwich, and in March the following year, as a reward for his gallantry, Parliament restored him in blood, lifting the attainder that had been passed on his father's execution for high treason.

He was to achieve no more during Mary's reign. But already English nobles with an eye on the future were seeking the favour of the Princess Elizabeth, next in succession; Lord Robert Dudley was among those who sent her the proceeds from the sale of lands in case she should need to fight for her throne. Immediately it became known that Mary had died on the morning of 17 November 1558, he rode to Hatfield to pay homage to the new Queen.

His fortunes now took a spectacularly upward turn. Elizabeth appointed the handsome and ambitious Dudley as Master of the Horse, a post for which his skilled horsemanship well suited him, and he threw himself into it with zest and enthusiasm. In April the following year he was created a Knight of the Garter. Much jealousy was aroused by Dudley's rapid advance in the royal favour, and it was soon obvious that the Queen had become infatuated with the charming courtier, whom she fondly nicknamed her 'eyes'. Rumours circulated that but for his wife, Dudley would marry Elizabeth, and when Lady Robert Dudley was found dead at the foot of the stairs of the house in which she was then living near Abingdon, Berkshire, in September 1560, malicious tongues hinted at murder. (Modern research has established that Amy Dudley died from a fall brought on by cancer of the breast.) A jury returned a verdict of accidental death, but Dudley was traduced by popular hatred on account of his closeness to the Queen. Their relations became even closer after Amy's death and when greater honours were bestowed upon him. These included the post of High Steward of Cambridge University in 1562, the post of Chancellor of Oxford University in 1564, and membership of the Privy Council, with a promise extracted from her ministers by the Queen when she lay ill with smallpox that in the event of her death he would be made Protector of the Realm. In 1563 Elizabeth gave him the most lavish of all her gifts, and the most cherished by Dudley for the rest of his life – the castle and parklands of Kenilworth in Warwickshire.

The Queen, however, would not make up her mind to marry. At one moment she encouraged his courtship, the next she chided him for his presumption. She made the astonishing suggestion, which he did not much care for, that he should marry Mary, Queen of Scots (q.v.), and it may have been to further this plan that she raised him to the peerage as Baron Denbigh and created him Earl of Leicester in September 1564. When the Scottish Queen's marriage to Lord Darnley (see Stewart, Henry) put an end to the protracted negotiations in 1565, Leicester consulted his old friend Sir Nicholas Throckmorton (q.v.) on how to find out whether or not Elizabeth really intended to marry him; Throckmorton's advice was that he should pay attentions to another lady and observe the Queen's reactions. But Leicester's subsequent flirtation with Lettice Knollys, Viscountess Hereford, won him only the Queen's recriminations and temporary disfavour. A more serious indiscretion was his liaison with Douglass Sheffield, widow of Lord Sheffield, which may have started as early as 1568. Although this lady later tried to prove that Leicester had secretly married her, he never did so. The son,

christened Robert, to whom Lady Sheffield gave birth in 1574 was however openly acknowledged as his, and Leicester made himself responsible for the boy's upbringing.

Meanwhile, restored to royal favour, in May 1574 he was granted a patent for a company of players to be known as 'Lord Leicester's Men', of whom the chief actor was James Burbage (q.v.). Much of Leicester's time was now devoted to embellishing his town residence, Leicester House, off the Strand, which he had leased from the Paget family in 1569, and in making preparations for his entertainment of the Queen at Kenilworth the following summer. There, from 9 to 27 July 1575, he staged the most magnificent social event of the reign, with masques and pageants and fireworks and sumptuous food and drink. Among the probable spectators was young William Shakespeare (q.v.) of Stratford, then a boy of eleven, who would in later years draw upon this memory when writing his *A Midsummer Night's Dream*.

Although still ambitious and thirsty for power, by 1578 Leicester had abandoned for good all hope of marriage to the Queen. His old love affair with Lettice Knollys, whose husband was now Earl Marshal of Ireland and Earl of Essex, had been revived in about 1575. Inevitably, when Essex died suddenly in Dublin in the autumn of 1576, there was gossip that Leicester had had him poisoned, but an inquest attributed the death to natural causes. Two years later, on 21 September 1578, Leicester and Lady Essex, who was then in an advanced state of pregnancy, were married at Wanstead (an earlier, clandestine, ceremony is believed to have been performed at Kenilworth). This was a love-match to a beautiful woman of strong character, marred only by the death in infancy in 1584 of their one child, Robert – the son whom Leicester hoped to marry to Arabella Stuart (q.v.) – and some later indiscretions on the part of Lady Leicester. For eleven months the secret was kept from Elizabeth. When she learned of the marriage, she was furious, threatening to send her former suitor to the Tower. Afterwards she forgave him, but although outwardly their relationship seemed undamaged the Queen never ceased to detest 'that she-wolf', as she persisted in calling his wife, even long after Leicester's death when she had come to dote on his stepson, the 2nd Earl of Essex (see Devereux, Robert), Lettice's son by her first husband.

As the leading Protestant in the country, Leicester had long been urging action against the Spaniards on the Continent as well as action against the growing Catholic menace at home. It was probably he who originated the Bond of Association, whose signatories pledged themselves to protect the Queen's life and to pursue to the death any person who should murder her. His unpopularity among the English Catholics was such that when a scurrilous attack, printed in Antwerp, reviving all the old scandals relating to the deaths of Lady Robert Dudley, Essex, and so on, and containing a cruel, and lying, exposé of Leicester's character, began surreptitiously to circulate in England in September 1584, it caused an instant sensation which even the Queen's Order-in-Council was powerless to stem; originally entitled *Copie of a leter retten by a Master of Arte of Cambridge*, in later editions it was called *Leycester's Commonwealth*. Wrongly attributed at the time to Robert Parsons (q.v.), it may have been written by Charles Arundell. In reply Sir Philip Sidney (q.v.) wrote a spirited *Defence* of his uncle, but this was not published during his lifetime.

By the late summer of 1584 Leicester had directed his last remaining ambitions towards service in the Netherlands, where William of Orange (q.v.) had been assassinated and the Dutch had appealed to the English Queen to accept sovereignty over them. This she refused, but reluctantly agreed to send an expeditionary force, under the command of Leicester, to aid their struggle for independence.

Leicester landed at Flushing on 10 December 1585 to an ecstatic welcome which turned his head. Three weeks later, contrary to the express instruction he had been given by the Queen, he accepted the States General's offer of the post of Supreme Governor of the United Provinces. Cashiered by the Queen, his authority was undermined. Nor was he suited to the impossible task. His lack of experience in military matters, together with a total inability to combine the Dutch factions, resulted in the dismal failure of the campaign, and he was finally recalled in November 1587.

Preparations were then being made to withstand the anticipated Spanish invasion of England, and Elizabeth gave him a warm welcome. Overlooking his shortcomings, she appointed him as Lieutenant General of her armies, and in this capacity he organized the Queen's brilliant review of the army at Tilbury at the beginning of August 1588. A month later, when the danger from the Armada had passed, he stopped at his house at Cornbury, near Oxford, on his way to take the waters at Buxton, and died there on the morning of 4 September after a 'continual burning fever' (probably malaria). He was buried in the Beauchamp Chapel of St Mary's, Warwick, where his wife erected a magnificent monument at a cost of some £4,000.

Of Leicester's enduring devotion to the Queen, albeit motivated by personal ambition, there is little doubt. That Elizabeth loved him is borne out by her actions during their long and sometimes turbulent relationship, but she determinedly put the unity of England, which she felt depended upon her remaining unmarried, above emotional considerations, and was never his mistress. Robert Dudley's failure as a political and military leader was one of character, but he should also be remembered for his encouragement of the drama and for his patronage of, among others, the poet Edmund Spenser (q.v.). In 1572 he endowed an almshouse for twelve poor men at Warwick. The historian William Camden (q.v.) wrote that 'The Earl of Leicester . . . saw farther into the mind of Queen Elizabeth than any man.'

There is no scholarly life of Leicester. Some of his correspondence has been published in *Queen Elizabeth and Her Times* by T. Wright (2 vols; 1838); in *The Compleat Ambassador* by Sir Dudley Digges (1655); and in *Letters of Thomas Wood, Puritan, 1566–77*, edited by P. Collinson (1960). The *Correspondance inédite de Robert Dudley* [and others], edited by P. J. Blok (Haarlem, 1911) and *Correspondentie van Robert Dudley . . . 1585–8*, edited by H. Brugmans (3 vols; 1931), cover the period of his governorship of the United Provinces. The Dudley papers are in the collection of the Marquess of Bath at Longleat, Wiltshire.

F. J. Burgoyne (ed.), *Leycester's Commonwealth* (1904).
E. Jenkins, *Elizabeth and Leicester* (1961).
M. Waldman, *Elizabeth and Leicester* (1944).

*Portraits:* oil, half-length, attributed to Steven van der Muelen, *c.* 1560–5: Wallace Collection, London; miniature, by unknown artist, *c.* 1565: Belvoir Castle (Duke of Rutland); oil, by S. van der Muelen: private collection, several other versions elsewhere; oil, by unknown artist, *c.* 1570: National Portrait Gallery, London; drawing, full-length, by F. Zuccaro: British Museum, London; miniature, by N. Hilliard, 1576: N.P.G.; oil, by unknown artist, *c.* 1575: N.P.G., duplicate at Hatfield House; oil, full-length, by unknown artist, *c.* 1585–6: Parham Park Collection, Sussex; oil, attributed to W. Segar, *c.* 1587: Hatfield (The Marquess of Salisbury), other versions elsewhere; miniature, full-length, by N. Hilliard, *c.* 1585–8: Penshurst Place (The Viscount De L'Isle); tomb effigy by Hollemans: Beauchamp Chapel, St Mary's, Warwick.

**Dungannon, 3rd Baron of** (*c.* 1540–1616), see O'Neill, Hugh.

# E

**Edward VI** (1537–1553), King of England and Ireland from 1547.

Edward VI was the only legitimate son of Henry VIII (q.v.). His mother, Jane Seymour (q.v.), died twelve days after his birth at Hampton Court on 12 October 1537. Historians have previously considered that Edward was from the outset a sickly child, but in the view of more recent authorities he was a robust, even athletic, boy; this is borne out by references in Edward's own journal to hunting and tilting at the ring.

As a baby the Prince was cared for by the women of the Royal Household until, at the age of six, he was handed over to tutors. He was given a strenuous education under Roger Ascham (q.v.), Sir John Cheke (q.v.), Richard Cox (q.v.), the future Bishop of Ely, Sir Anthony Cooke, and others. An intellectual, precocious child, he was proficient in French, Latin, and Greek by the age of thirteen.

When Henry VIII died on 28 January 1547, Edward became, at nine years old, King of England and Ireland. His father had decreed that the kingdom was to be governed during Edward's minority by a Regency Council, but the boy's uncle, the Duke of Somerset (see Seymour, Edward) took control as Protector of the Realm. Factions soon developed round the young King, however, Somerset's brother, the Lord High Admiral (see Seymour, Thomas) and the Earl of Warwick (see Dudley, John; later the 1st Duke of Northumberland) being the chief contenders for guardianship of the King's person.

Edward was crowned at Westminster on 25 February 1547. He behaved with dignity during the long public appearances imposed on him and won popularity with the people. It was soon evident, however, that he had inherited all the qualities of the house of Tudor. In personal relationships he could be cold; among the few people for whom he showed genuine affection were his tutor, Sir John Cheke, and Barnaby Fitzpatrick, son of Lord Ossory, who shared his education and with whom he kept up a correspondence to the end of his short life, and Sir Nicholas Throckmorton (q.v.).

During Somerset's absence in Scotland, where he had gone in an attempt to force the Scots into fulfilling their agreement that Edward should marry Mary, Queen of Scots (q.v.), Edward's uncle, Thomas Seymour, and the Earl of Warwick took the opportunity to influence the King's mind against the Protector and to gain influence over him for their own purposes. When the Protector was overthrown and executed, the King calmly recorded in his journal, 'The Duke of Somerset had his head cut off upon Tower Hill between eight and nine a clock in the morning.'

Edward had a definite religious point of view. A Protestant of precocious firm conviction, he supported fully the Protector's plan to transform the Church of England into a Protestant church, and later the more extreme brand of religious reform forwarded by Northumberland and Thomas Cranmer (q.v.), Archbishop of Canterbury.

Once it became clear that the marriage of Edward and Mary, Queen of Scots was not going to take place, new plans were made for his betrothal. In July 1551 a treaty was signed at Angers, whereby the King resigned his claim to the hand of Mary and betrothed himself to Elizabeth, daughter of Henri II of France; the marriage never took place, however, for in 1552 the young King's health took a turn for the worse. Much weakened by attacks of measles and smallpox, in January 1553 he showed the first signs of consumption. In May he contracted a chill which worsened his condition, and it was obvious that he would not live.

The unscrupulous Northumberland, who, having ousted Somerset, now held the reins of government, supported the King's own 'Device' for the succession, excluding his sisters Mary (see Mary I) and Elizabeth (see Elizabeth I) as 'but of the half-blood' – since Henry VIII had declared each illegitimate. There was no doubt about the legitimacy of his cousin, the Lady Jane Grey (q.v.). Showing an already fully developed Tudor will,

Edward insisted on his Councillors agreeing to his 'Device'; Northumberland was only too ready to support him, having recently married his son to Lady Jane.

Edward VI died at Greenwich on 6 July 1553 and was buried in Westminster Abbey two days later. He had made little impact on events during his short reign, on account of his youth, although he showed a potential talent for administration. The general consensus of scholarly opinion is that, had he lived, his radical Protestantism, combined with Tudor obstinacy, might have divided England far more than did his premature death, which brought his fanatically Catholic sister Mary to the throne.

Edward's journal and other writings have been edited by J. G. Nichols under the title *Literary Remains of King Edward VI* (2 vols; 1857). A more recent work is W. K. Jordan's *The Chronicle and Political Writings of King Edward VI* (1966).

Hester W. Chapman, *The Last Tudor King: a Study of Edward VI* (1958).
W. K. Jordan, *Edward VI: The Young King* (1968).
W. K. Jordan, *Edward VI: The Threshold of Power* (1970).
C. Morris, *The Tudors* (1955).

*Portraits:* drawing by Holbein, 1539: Royal Collection, Windsor; oil, by Holbein, 1539: Andrew Mellon Collection, National Gallery of Art, Washington; oil, by unknown artist, after Holbein, *c.* 1542: National Portrait Gallery, London; oil on panel, by William Scrots, *c.* 1546: N.P.G.; oil, three-quarter length, by unknown artist, 1549: Loseley Park (J. R. More-Molyneux, Esq.); oil on panel, by William Scrots, 1546: N.P.G.; oil, three-quarter length, by unknown artist: Royal Collection, Windsor; oil, full length, by William Scrots: Musée du Louvre, Paris (an identical one is in Los Angeles County Museum); oil, full length, by William Scrots: Royal Collection, Hampton Court; miniature, after Hilliard: Royal Collection, Windsor; numerous other versions elsewhere.

**Egerton, Sir Thomas** (?1540–1617), Baron Ellesmere and Viscount Brackley,

Lord Chancellor in the reign of James I.

Born in about 1540, Thomas Egerton was the natural son of Sir Richard Egerton of Ridley, Cheshire. He is believed to have been educated at Brasenose College, Oxford. In 1559 he entered Lincoln's Inn, where in 1572 he was called to the bar and soon acquired a large practice. Egerton became Governor of the Inn in 1580 and Treasurer in 1587.

In 1581 Queen Elizabeth (q.v.), said to have been impressed by his pleading in a case against the crown, appointed Egerton as Solicitor-General. Thereafter promotion followed rapidly: he became Attorney-General in 1592, Master of the Rolls in 1594, Lord Keeper of the Great Seal in 1596. He took part in the trial of Mary, Queen of Scots (q.v.), in 1586. Knighted in 1597, he enjoyed Elizabeth's confidence and was increasingly consulted by her on matters of home and foreign policy. At court he became a close friend of both Francis Bacon (q.v.) and Essex (see Devereux, Robert). He counselled the latter to show more prudence in his actions and to apologize to the Queen; he was among the officers of state detained at Essex House on the day of the Earl's rebellion and subsequently took a prominent part in his trial.

On the accession of James I (see James VI of Scotland) in 1603, Egerton was reappointed Lord Keeper. In July the same year he was created Baron Ellesmere and Lord Chancellor, an office which he was to hold for twenty-one years. He helped to draft the Act of Union between England and Scotland (1606–7) and was a loyal supporter of James's royal prerogative and ecclesiastical policy. He came into conflict with Sir Edward Coke (see Lives of the Stuart Age), Chief Justice of the King's Bench, over the jurisdiction of the common-law courts, and in 1616 was successful in obtaining the King's decision in favour of equity, thus establishing the unquestioned jurisdiction of his own Court of Chancery. When later that year James created him Viscount Brackley, Coke and his friends corrupted the new title to 'Breaklaw'.

By this time Brackley's health was failing rapidly, and he begged the King to allow him to retire. This he was not allowed to do until the beginning of March 1617, when he officially resigned the office of Lord Chancellor. Twelve days later, on 15 March, he died at his London home. He was buried at Dodleston, Cheshire.

Highly esteemed by his contemporaries, Sit Thomas Egerton was responsible for securing the independence of the Court of Chancery from the common-law courts. He published nothing during his lifetime, but left a number of manuscript legal and judicial treatises. Three times married, he and his second wife, Elizabeth, widow of Sir John Wolley, were early patrons of the poet John Donne (see Lives of the Stuart Age), who in 1598 became secretary to Sir Thomas.

The Ellesmere MSS are now in the Huntington Library, California, U.S.A.

F. H. Egerton, Life of Thomas Egerton (first published in Kippis's Biographia Britannica, 1793; enlarged ed., 1798; best ed., 1816).

Portraits: oil, by unknown artist, c. 1596: National Portrait Gallery, London; oil, by unknown artist, c. 1603: The Lord Leigh; other versions at the Bodleian Library and Brasenose College, Oxford, and elsewhere.

**Elizabeth I** (1533–1603), Queen of England from 1558 to 1603.

Born at Greenwich Palace on 7 September 1533, Elizabeth was the daughter of Henry VIII (q.v.) by his second wife, Anne Boleyn (q.v.). In May

1536, when she was less than three years old, her mother was executed; at the same time Elizabeth and her elder half-sister Mary, the future Mary I (q.v.), were declared illegitimate and deprived of their rank as princesses of the realm. Henry immediately married Jane Seymour, who died in October 1537, shortly after giving birth to a son, the future Edward VI (q.v.), with whom Elizabeth was later to share the greater part of her education.

During most of her childhood and her father's subsequent marriages to Anne of Cleves (q.v.) and Catherine Howard (q.v.), Elizabeth was brought up at Hatfield in Hertfordshire. Only after Henry had married his sixth and last wife, Katherine Parr (q.v.), in 1543 was much paternal kindness shown to her. Katherine persuaded Henry to restore both his daughters to their former status as princesses, and she arranged for Elizabeth to share with the young Prince Edward the tutorship of first-class scholars such as Roger Ascham (q.v.), John Cheke (q.v.), and William Grindal, all men of the 'new learning'. Under their tuition the Princess soon showed her intellectual abilities and became proficient in Latin, Greek, French, and Italian; she was also much influenced by the Reformation doctrines.

After the King's death in 1547, Elizabeth was allowed to reside at her stepmother's house. Already wise beyond her years as a result of her childhood experiences, she prudently refused a proposal of marriage from Thomas Seymour (q.v.), brother of the Protector, whereupon the Lord Admiral lost no time in marrying her stepmother. The Princess then went to live with the Seymours at Sudeley Castle in Gloucestershire until, in the early summer of 1548, Katherine sent her away under a cloud on account of the questionable advances being made by her husband to the innocent young girl. Katherine died a few months later, and the Lord Admiral resumed his ambitious plans in regard to her and his factious opposition to his brother, the Protector, for which he lost his head on a charge of high treason. The Princess's reputation was somewhat touched by the scandal of these proceedings.

Elizabeth was on good terms with her half-brother Edward, but he may have been influenced by these considerations to put her out of the succession, along with the uncompromisingly Catholic Mary, in favour of Lady Jane Grey (q.v.), who was indubitably legitimate and Protestant. Northumberland (see Dudley, John) naturally fell in with Edward's design. The country, however, preferred Henry VIII's daughters to his niece. Therefore, when Mary made her triumphant entry into the City in July 1553, Elizabeth, always popular with the London people, rode at the new Queen's side. However, Mary and her advisers soon became suspicious of the Princess's known identification with the Protestant cause. After the failure of the Wyatt rebellion (see Wyatt, Thomas, 'the younger') against the Queen's proposed marriage with Philip II of Spain (q.v.) in 1554, Elizabeth was taken to the Tower and examined by the Council as to her involvement in the uprising. Wyatt exonerated her on the scaffold, and Elizabeth herself, although very frightened, was astute enough to supply no evidence that could justify her being sentenced to death; she had learned early in life how to give the 'answer answerless' that was later on to be her characteristic way of dealing with a tricky situation. Transferred to Woodstock, she was held in custody until April 1555. Soon after that the Princess was allowed a visit to Hampton Court, where she made a favourable impression on Philip but was taxed by Mary with plotting against the throne. For the next two years Elizabeth lived mainly at Hatfield, quietly biding her time. When Mary died on 17 November 1558, she entered on her own long and eventful reign, to the acclamations of the English people in general, and of the Protestants in particular, who were overjoyed to feel that religious persecution was at an end. London gave her a rapturous welcome, which pushed her into a more Protestant settlement of religion than she wished.

Twenty-five years old, the new Queen was vivacious, attractive, and dominating. Like her father she loved music and dancing, fine clothes and, above all, jewellery. She enjoyed the company of men who admired her, but was reluctant to marry. Not that offers of marriage were lacking; but in the first years of her reign, Elizabeth turned them all down. Aware of the need for cautious statesmanship in order to handle the complex situation of a nation divided in religion, fraught with inflation and rising prices, at war with France and supported only by a dubious alliance with Spain, one of her first acts was to appoint Sir William Cecil (q.v.) as her principal Secretary of State. Their partnership of sovereign and chief minister was to be the longest, and probably the most successful, in all English history.

In the first twelve years of her reign, Elizabeth consolidated her position at home to the general acceptance of both the Protestant and the Catholic elements. Under her moderate Acts of Supremacy and Uniformity, passed in 1559, the Protestant religion was enforced, the celebration of Mass was made illegal, and Catholics were fined for abstention from church attendance. In 1570, however, this ambiguous situation was disrupted when Pope Pius V issued a bull of

excommunication against 'Elizabeth, the Pretended Queen of England' which released her Catholic subjects from allegiance to her. This bull had been intended by the Pope to coincide with a rising of the northern Catholic earls in support of a plan to marry the Duke of Norfolk (see Howard, Thomas, 4th Duke) to Mary, Queen of Scots (q.v.), and, eventually, to depose Elizabeth. It misfired altogether, for by the time it was issued the uprising (1569) had already taken place and had been put down.

The situation with regard to Scotland was extremely delicate for Elizabeth since Mary, Queen of Scots, then married to François de Valois, heir to the throne of France, was by her descent from Margaret Tudor (q.v.), Henry VIII's sister, heir presumptive to the English throne. In fact, those who took the view that Henry's marriage to Anne Boleyn had not been lawful already considered Mary to be the rightful Queen. At the beginning of the reign Scotland, under the regency of Marie de Guise (q.v.), had been dominated by the French

Catholics; that régime, however, had proved unpopular and was soon challenged by the Protestant Lords of the Congregation. Elizabeth had in the meanwhile made peace with France under the Treaty of Câteau Cambrésis, signed in April 1559. Nevertheless, in 1560 she felt bound to support the Scottish Protestants. Troops were sent to Leith, the French being then expelled from Scotland altogether and Protestant rule, favourable to England, established. From the moment Mary returned to her kingdom in 1561, after the death of her French husband, it was clear that her one objective was to have her claim to the English succession recognized. When Mary's opponents eventually drove her to seek sanctuary across the Border in 1568, Elizabeth shrank from the course advocated by some of her ministers, that of ordering her cousin's execution. Since the Scots would not have her back at any price, and to have sent Mary abroad would have risked an invasion on her behalf by France or Spain, Elizabeth decided to keep her in confinement as the safest course.

While in custody Mary managed to become involved in three major conspiracies: the Ridolfi Plot of 1571 (see Ridolfi, Roberto di), the invasion planned by the Duc de Guise in 1582, and the Babington Plot of 1586 (see Babington, Anthony). As each plot in turn was uncovered, with their threats to Elizabeth's life and their plans for a Spanish invasion of England, pressure was put on the Queen to order Mary's execution. Increasingly, too, sterner measures were taken against English Catholics. As a result of the Babington Plot, Mary was brought to trial and condemned, but even then Elizabeth hesitated for nearly three months before signing the death warrant; once she had done so the Privy Council acted speedily

and carried out the Queen of Scots' execution at Fotheringay on 8 February 1587. The prolonged strain brought Elizabeth to the point of a nervous breakdown. She had been forced to take action by Parliament and public opinion, and the nation rejoiced at it.

All England wanted the Queen to marry, so as to secure the succession; Parliament several times pressed her on the subject. But Elizabeth held back and kept her own counsel. In the first years of the reign she had refused offers from Philip of Spain, several foreign princes, and the Earl of Arran (see Hamilton, James, 3rd Earl), already aware that remaining unmarried was the best trump card she possessed in diplomatic affairs; also, she had no intention of repeating the mistake her half-sister had made in marrying a foreigner. There was another reason. By 1560 Elizabeth had been attracted by the one man whom she might have made her husband, had it been politically possible: Lord Robert Dudley (q.v.), whom she created Earl of Leicester in 1564.

Elizabeth's ambiguous love for Leicester was to last until the Earl's death in 1588, surviving the gossip that followed the accidental death of his first wife in 1560, and his later secret marriage, in 1578, to the Queen's cousin, Lettice Knollys. The relationship was probably at its closest in 1575, when Leicester staged a magnificent entertainment for Elizabeth at Kenilworth Castle, which she had given him in 1563. But still she would not make up her mind. A marriage to Leicester would have affronted half the country; he himself admitted that for twenty years the Queen had told him that she would never marry. There were the dangers attendant upon childbirth, the warnings from the experiences of her sister Mary and her cousin, Mary, Queen of Scots.

Moreover, Elizabeth always intended to remain her own master. Not unnaturally malicious tongues began to wag, but it is evident that nothing disturbed her self-control, and she succeeded in turning her virginity to political advantage in the end. (There is some reason to believe that the traumatic experiences of Elizabeth's childhood – principally the executions of her mother and her stepmother, Catherine Howard – had left some deep psychological scar that never quite healed.)

In the early 1570s, when France was looking to England for an alliance to counterbalance the power of Spain, there had been tentative negotiations for Elizabeth to marry, in turn, each of the three surviving sons of Catherine de' Medici (q.v.) – Charles IX, Henri, Duc d'Anjou (later Henri III), and François, Duc d'Alençon (q.v.; later also Duc d'Anjou). These proposals petered out, but in 1579 Alençon, who had been asked by the Dutch Protestants to support them in a revolt against their Spanish oppressors (a cause to which Elizabeth had herself been lending moderate support), was persuaded by his determined mother to renew his suit with the English Queen. For political reasons Elizabeth agreed to enter into negotiations. She was to keep her 'frog', as she nicknamed her French suitor, on the end of a string for the next four years, much to the amusement of the courts of Europe. It paid political dividends.

Other favourites whom the Queen honoured were Sir Christopher Hatton (q.v.), Sir Walter Ralegh (q.v.) and, in the last years of her reign, the popular but unstable Robert Devereux (q.v.), Earl of Essex, stepson of Leicester. After Leicester's death in 1588, the ageing Queen welcomed in Essex a renewal of her youth. Essex, however, badly miscalculated both her judgment and the

influence he exerted over her, with tragic consequences for himself. He took liberties and opposed her will. In Ireland he not only failed but made a disloyal truce with the rebel Tyrone (see O'Neill, Hugh); he returned to enter upon conspiracy and an open rebellion. But Elizabeth was a true daughter of Henry VIII and Queen of England; she would not countenance treason. Essex therefore was executed in February 1601.

Except perhaps in the case of the romantic, adventurous Essex, who had talents and whom she spoiled as a substitute for a son and lover, Elizabeth was a shrewd judge of character and a good picker of men. When Cecil became Lord High Treasurer, she appointed as Secretary of State the loyal and extremely able Sir Francis Walsingham (q.v.). But the Queen was to outlive nearly all her closest advisers and friends. Leicester died in 1588, Walsingham in 1590, Hatton in 1591, Burghley in 1598; all had served her well, not least in the crisis period of the threatened Spanish 'enterprise' of 1588.

For many years Elizabeth lived with the threat of foreign invasion. She was however, unlike her father, always careful not to waste the nation's resources on adventures abroad. She maintained the Navy in a high degree of efficiency, so that it was ready to challenge the Spanish Armada. Sir Francis Drake (q.v.) had her support in his campaigns against the Spaniards. It was Drake's daring attack on Cadiz harbour in the spring of 1587, coupled with the English intervention in the Netherlands and finally the execution of the Queen of Scots, that finally determined Philip to launch an Armada against England. This he did, after several delays, in July 1588.

In August Elizabeth reviewed her troops assembled at Tilbury Camp to meet the invading forces. In an eloquent address, one of the greatest speeches of her reign, she said:

> My loving people, we have been persuaded by some that are careful of our safety to take heed how we commit ourselves to armed multitudes for fear of treachery. Let tyrants fear. I have always so behaved myself that, under God, I have placed my chiefest strength and safeguard in the loyal hearts and goodwill of my subjects. And therefore I am come amongst you, as you see at this time, not for my recreation and disport, but being resolved, in the heat and midst of the battle, to live and die amongst you all; to lay down for my God and for my kingdom and for my people my honour and my blood, even in the dust. I know I have the body of a weak and feeble woman, but I have the heart and stomach of a king, and a king of England too; and think foul scorn that Parma or Spain, or any prince of Europe, should dare invade the borders of my realm. . . .

The land battle was never fought. Even as the Queen spoke the Armada had been decisively defeated by a fortunate combination of English naval skill and bad weather. The news, when it came through, was greeted with relief and with rejoicing. Not for a long time had English men and women felt so much pride in their nationhood.

Elizabeth was now at the height of her popularity. She had another fifteen years to live, but inevitably those last years of her reign were to prove an anticlimax. The long and expensive struggle with Ireland, the continued wars in the Netherlands and France, all were a drain on the national finances; the Queen herself was forced to sell crown lands and jewellery. There were other troubles: feuds between the different religious factions, feuds between the crown and Parliament, feuds at court, where impatient young men like Essex fretted for lack of opportunity and demanded new policies.

The last fifteen years of Elizabeth's reign were marked by a great upsurge of patriotism in England, reflected largely in contemporary literature. Edmund Spenser (q.v.) was chief among the many poets and playwrights who drew their inspiration from the extraordinary woman who had ruled the nation so well and for so long. To them she was not merely the 'Virgin Queen' or 'good Queen Bess', but 'Gloriana' and 'The Faerie Queen'. At the close of the reign William Shakespeare (q.v.), Francis Bacon (q.v.) and Ben Jonson (see *Lives of the Stuart Age*) were coming to the forefront. Not only drama, but architecture, music, and portrait painting were flourishing; overseas trade was increasing, and so was overseas expansion – although the Queen had always been cautious in this respect, being unwilling to waste resources by investing in the expeditions of her great seamen unless she could see a handsome profit in it for the crown.

Visibly affected by Essex's death, Elizabeth carried on, apparently in good health until towards the end of 1602. In the previous year she held her last Parliament of the reign, meeting the Members' discontent over monopolies with which she had rewarded her servants by cancelling some of them. Early in 1603 the Queen fell ill; her vitality ebbed, and she began to refuse food. She would not go to bed. Speechless at the very last, but still in possession of her mental faculties, she was asked to give a sign if she acknowledged James VI of Scotland (q.v.) as her successor. This she did, thereby ensuring a peaceful succession. Attended by her physician, Dr William Gilbert (q.v.), and the Archbishop of Canterbury, Dr John Whitgift (q.v.), Elizabeth died early the next morning, 24 March 1603, at the royal palace of Richmond. Her funeral took place at Westminster Abbey on 28 April.

The forty-five-year-long reign of Elizabeth I may be summed up in her own words to the deputation from Parliament that had waited on her in 1601, in order to thank her for abolishing certain monopolies: 'Though God hath raised me high, yet I count this the glory of my crown, that I have reigned with your loves.'

The survival of England as an independent power was Elizabeth's greatest achievement, and directly attributable to her personal qualities and political acumen. She knew very well that a marriage alliance with either France or Spain would not work. Compromise on religious matters, leaving aside her own personal leanings (albeit not very strong ones) towards Protestantism, helped to achieve national unity. Her tight hand on the country's purse strings, though unpopular, built up the nation's resources and put England on a sound economic footing. Mercurial in temperament, disingenuous and insincere when necessary, a gifted linguist and speaker, she was a natural politician and grew to be a statesman, cautious in judgment, but with a sound instinct for her people. Hence the English people as a whole loved her. She had captured their hearts as a young Princess with the striking red-gold hair and aquiline nose inherited from her Tudor forbears; she retained their admiration as a wrinkled old woman, her teeth black with decay, a maiden lady who tried to disguise her years by elaborate dressing, fine jewels and an auburn wig. Among other things, the Queen was a great actress; she always played to the gallery. She would never accept the disadvantage of being a woman in a man's world; her inclinations were distinctly feminist. By the end of her reign, Elizabeth had become a legend throughout Europe. She remains one of the greatest of all women rulers in history.

There is a vast bibliography on Elizabeth I. Authoritative modern studies include:

J. B. Black, *The Reign of Queen Elizabeth, 1558–1603* (2nd ed., 1959).

Mandell Creighton, *Queen Elizabeth* (1896; 1899; reprinted New York, 1966).

Joel Hurstfield, *Elizabeth I and the Unity of England* (1960).

Elizabeth Jenkins, *Elizabeth the Great* (1958).

Paul Johnson, *Elizabeth I: A Study in Power and Intellect* (1974).

W. T. MacCaffrey, *The Shaping of the Elizabethan Regime* (Princeton, 1968).

Sir J. E. Neale, *Queen Elizabeth I* (1934; reprinted 1960).

Sir J. E. Neale, *Elizabeth I and her Parliaments* (2 vols; 1953–7).

A. L. Rowse, *The Elizabethan Renaissance* (2 vols, 1971, 1972).

A. L. Rowse, *The England of Elizabeth* (1950).

A. L. Rowse, *The Expansion of Elizabethan England* (1955).

Neville Williams, *Elizabeth, Queen of England* (1967).

See also *The Letters of Queen Elizabeth*, edited by G. B. Harrison (1935); *The Public Speaking of Queen Elizabeth*, edited by G. P. Rice (1951); as well as titles listed under Cecil, William, 1st Baron Burghley; Devereux, Robert, 2nd Earl of Essex; Dudley, Robert, Earl of Leicester.

*Portraits:* the iconography of Elizabeth I is extremely complicated, and space does not permit a full listing here. For further information, see Roy Strong, *Portraits of Queen Elizabeth I* (Oxford, 1963).

The major portraits are as follows: oil, by unknown artist, *c.* 1546: Royal Collection, Windsor; oil, by unknown artist (Coronation portrait), ?1559: Warwick Castle (The Earl of Warwick); oil, by unknown artist, *c.* 1558 (the 'Northwick Park' pattern): versions at National Portrait Gallery, London, National Gallery of Ireland, Dublin, and elsewhere; oil, by unknown artist, *c.* 1563 (the 'Barrington Park' pattern): versions at Barrington Park, Burford, Oxon. (Col. C. T. Wingfield), the Duke of Beaufort Collection, Kunsthistorisches Museum, Vienna, and elsewhere; oil, by the monogrammist 'H.E.', 1569, *Queen Elizabeth and the Three Goddesses*: Royal Collection, Hampton Court; miniatures, by Nicholas Hilliard, various dates from 1572: N.P.G., Berkeley Castle, Glos., Royal Collection, The Earl Beauchamp, Mauritshuis, The Hague, Victoria and Albert Museum, London; drawing, by Federico Zuccaro, 1575: British Museum, London; oil, attributed to Nicholas Hilliard (the 'Pelican-Phoenix' pattern), c. 1575–80: versions at N.P.G. and Walker Art Gallery, Liverpool; oil, by unknown artist (the 'Darnley' pattern), c. 1575: N.P.G. and many other versions elsewhere (the so-called 'Cambridge', 'Raveningham', 'Penshurst', 'Kitchener', 'Sieve', 'Hampton Court', 'Arbury', 'Weavers' Company', and 'Brocket' portraits); oil, attributed to William Segar (the 'Ermine' portrait), 1585: Hatfield House (The Marquess of Salisbury); oil, small full length, attributed to Marcus Gheeraerts the Elder, c. 1585: Welbeck Abbey (The Duke of Portland); oil, attributed to George Gower (the 'Armada' pattern), c. 1588 onwards: Woburn Abbey (The Duke of Bedford), and other versions in F. Tyrwhitt-Drake Collection and at Christ Church, Oxford, N.P.G., Toledo Museum of Art, Ohio, U.S.A., and elsewhere; oil, by Marcus Gheeraerts the Younger, c. 1592 onwards (the 'Ditchley' pattern): N.P.G., and other versions at Blickling Hall, Aylsham, Norfolk (National Trust), Burghley House, Stamford, Northants., and elsewhere; two oils, by unknown artists (the 'Buccleuch' pattern), c. 1594–5: The Duke of Buccleuch and Queensberry Collection and the Deanery, Westminster; oil, by unknown artist: St John's College, Cambridge; miniature, by Isaac Oliver: V. & A.; oil, attributed to Marcus Gheeraerts the Younger (the 'Rainbow' portrait), c. 1600: Hatfield (The Marquess of Salisbury); oil, the Queen in procession, attributed to Robert Peake, c. 1600: Sherborne Castle (S. Wingfield Digby, Esq.).

**Elizabeth of York** (1465–1503), Queen consort of Henry VII (q.v.).

Elizabeth was the daughter of Edward IV and Elizabeth Woodville (for both see *Lives Before the Tudors*), and was born at Westminster on 11 February 1465. From a very early age her father made marriage plans for Elizabeth, but they did not proceed smoothly. When five years old her betrothal to George Neville, son of the Earl of Northumberland (see Neville, John, in *Lives Before the Tudors*), had to be cancelled when Northumberland sided with the Lancastrians against the King;

next, Edward made her marriage with the French Dauphin a condition of peace between him and Louis XI, but broke off the engagement when it became clear that Louis did not intend to keep his side of the bargain. It is believed that he then offered Elizabeth to Henry, then Earl of Richmond (whom she eventually married), but that Henry declined, suspecting a plot to put him in the King's power.

After the death of Edward IV, a plan was conceived by the Duke of Buckingham (see Stafford, Henry, 2nd Duke, in *Lives Before the Tudors*) and approved by Henry's mother, the Lady Margaret Beaufort (q.v.), to marry Elizabeth to Henry of Richmond, who was then in France. At about this time Elizabeth figured in the popular 'Song of the Lady Bessy' as having persuaded Lord Stanley to join Richmond in France. Henry swore an oath in Vannes cathedral on Christmas Day 1483 that he would marry her once he had secured the throne. There were temporary frustrations concerned with the protection promised to Elizabeth's mother, and it

was rumoured that Elizabeth had received a proposal of marriage from Richard III, but on 18 January 1486 Henry honoured his word and took her as his wife; she was crowned at Westminster Abbey on 25 November 1487.

The marriage is thought to have been a happy one. Elizabeth was gay, fond of hunting, dancing, and music; her great weakness was that she tended to overspend. When her husband broke the news of the death of their son, Prince Arthur (q.v.), to her, she is reported to have reacted 'with comfortable words', reminding him that they had still one other prince and two princesses, and adding, 'God is where he was and we are both young enough.' They were brave words, for it is generally accepted that Elizabeth's death on 11 February 1503 (her thirty-eighth birthday) was a result of her intense grief over the loss of her eldest son. Sir Thomas More (q.v.) wrote an elegy upon her.

Nancy L. Harvey, *Elizabeth of York, Tudor Queen* (1973).
N. H. Nicolas, *Privy Purse Expenses of Elizabeth of York* [with a memoir] (1830).

*Portraits:* oil, by unknown artist, probably late sixteenth century: National Portrait Gallery, London; oil, by unknown artist: Royal Collection, Windsor; oil, on panel, by unknown artist: Royal Collection, St James's Palace; oil, by unknown artist: Christ Church, Oxford; funeral effigy by Laurence: Westminster Abbey; bronze tomb effigy by Torrigiano: Westminster Abbey; electroplate, detail of Torrigiano bronze: N.P.G.; oil, by van Leemput, after Holbein (copy of group painting of Henry VII, Elizabeth of York, Henry VIII, and Jane Seymour, originally in Privy Chamber at Whitehall, burnt 1698): Royal Collection, Hampton Court.

**Ellesmere, Baron** (?1540–1617), see Egerton, Sir Thomas.

**Elyot, Sir Thomas** (*c.* 1490–1546), diplomatist and writer.

Born probably in Wiltshire in about 1490, Thomas Elyot was the only son of the judge Sir Richard Elyot and his first wife Alice. Details of his early life are obscure. He may have been educated at home; he is known to have studied Latin and Greek and to have been much influenced by the works of Galen and other medical writers.

Elyot accompanied his father on the western circuit, being employed as clerk of assize from 1511 to 1528. In 1522 he was made a Justice of the Peace for Oxfordshire. At about this date he attracted the notice of Cardinal Thomas Wolsey (q.v.), who appointed him as clerk to the Privy Council. After the fall of his patron in 1530, Elyot was deprived of his post and rewarded only with a knighthood. Because of his friendship with Sir Thomas More (q.v.), he was suspected of opposition to the plan of Henry VIII (q.v.) to divorce Catherine of Aragon (q.v.), and consequently gained no further advancement.

In 1531 Elyot published *The Boke named the Governour*, a treatise on education and politics, which he dedicated to the King. Its immediate result was his appointment as ambassador to Charles V (q.v.), with instructions to obtain the Emperor's assent to the King's divorce. He visited Germany and the Low Countries in the autumn of that year, with orders also to procure the arrest of William Tyndale (q.v.), who had taken refuge in Antwerp. Unsuccessful, Elyot returned to England a few months later and thereafter devoted himself almost exclusively to literary work. Following More's execution he came under suspicion of being a Catholic, but was able to justify himself in correspondence with Thomas Cromwell (q.v.).

Elyot's *Doctrine of Princes*, a translation from the Greek of Isocrates, was published in 1534. In 1536-7, with the encouragement of Henry VIII, he began work on a Latin-English *Dictionary*. Published in 1538, it was the first work in English to be called a 'dictionary'. Elyot's later works included translations of Platonic dialogues; *The Image of Governance*, translated from the Greek of Eucolpius; *The Castel of Helth*, a medical treatise with prescriptions for various ailments; and a number of other treatises, all of which bear witness to the influence of Erasmus (q.v.) and the Italian humanists.

Elyot was elected M.P. for Cambridge in 1542 and sheriff of Cambridgeshire and Huntingdonshire in 1544. He died at Carleton, Cambridgeshire, on 20 March 1546, leaving a widow, Margaret, but no children.

Thomas Elyot was not only the author of the first English treatise on moral philosophy (*The Boke*); through his translations he made available for the first time to the English reading public the classics and the work of Italian authors. A champion of the use of English, he added many new words to the language. The best modern edition of *The Boke named the Governour*, which ran into eight editions before 1581, is by H. H. S. Croft (2 vols; 1883). Of the thirteen sixteenth-century editions of *The Castel of Helth*, which was immensely popular, the earliest extant edition is that of 1539.

S. E. Lehmberg, *Sir Thomas Elyot* (1960).

*Portrait*: drawing, by Hans Holbein the Younger: Royal Collection, Windsor.

## Erasmus, Desiderius (1469-1536), humanist, and the greatest figure in Renaissance Europe.

The illegitimate son of a monk, Roger Gerard, and a physician's daughter, Erasmus was born in Rotterdam on the night of 27-8 October 1469 and christened Erasmus, the Greek form of Gerard, meaning 'desired'. Many years later he himself added Desiderius, the Latin form of Erasmus, and in 1506 used for the first time the full name, Desiderius Erasmus Rotterdamus.

He first attended school at Gouda and then the Latin school of St Lebuinus at Deventer, where he came under the influence of the new humanist ideas through the teaching of Hegius and Synthen. After the death of his father and mother in 1484, Erasmus was sent by his guardians to a school in 's-Hertogenbosch and later, against his will, to the monastery of Steyn, near Delft. He found the monastic discipline irksome and, having been ordained in 1492, seized the chance to escape from it two years later by accepting the post of secretary to the Bishop of Cambrai. In 1495 he obtained permission to study theology at the university of Paris, and there came into contact with the humanists, with whose views he found himself much in sympathy. He began to build up a reputation as a man of letters and earned a livelihood by taking pupils.

Erasmus paid his first visit to England in 1499, at the invitation of one of these pupils, Lord Mountjoy (see Blount, William). He made the acquaintance of Thomas More (q.v.), who took him to visit the royal nursery, where he saw the young Prince Henry (the future Henry VIII, q.v.), and at Oxford he met John Colet (q.v.) and other English humanists. Colet influenced him to pursue his theological studies, and Erasmus became convinced that he would have to learn Greek. The visit was marred on his departure, when all his money was confiscated by the customs at Dover, under laws relating to the export of currency; in order to earn more money

Erasmus published *Adagia*, a collection of Latin and Greek proverbs with his own witty commentary; this was one of the first works of the 'new learning'.

For the next few years he became a wandering scholar, devoting much of his time to the mastery of Greek. In 1505, on a second visit to England, he secured the patronage of Archbishop Warham (q.v.) and renewed his friendships with Colet and More. His English friends now included John Fisher (q.v.), Bishop of Rochester, Richard Foxe (q.v.), Bishop of Winchester, William Grocyn (q.v.), Thomas Linacre (q.v.), and the classical scholar William Latimer. Henry VII (q.v.) made a vague promise to give him a benefice in the Church, but when this appeared not to be forthcoming, Erasmus left for Italy.

In 1509 he returned to England again on a visit of longer duration. It was while staying with More that he wrote the satire on contemporary society which won him such popularity, *Encomium Moriae* ('The Praise of Folly'); directed against theologians and church dignitaries, it was translated from the original Latin into most European languages and ran into many editions. Erasmus then went on to Cambridge where, at Fisher's invitation, he lectured on Greek and theology. Archbishop Warham gave him a benefice in Kent, which he later exchanged for a pension of £20 a year. By 1514, however, Erasmus had tired of Cambridge and, complaining of kidney trouble which he said was caused by bad English beer, he returned to the Continent.

In Basle he was hailed as a great scholar, and his works appeared under the imprint of the publishing house of Johann Froben. Here also he met the painter Hans Holbein the younger (q.v.). In June 1514 Erasmus was recalled to monastic life, but made an eloquent appeal for freedom to pursue his vocation of letters, and in January 1517 Pope Leo X granted him dispensations allowing him to live in the world, freeing him from the obligation to wear monastic dress, and removing the impediments which had barred him from ecclesiastical promotion due to his illegitimacy. He received these dispensations from Ammonius Andreas, the Papal Legate in London, while on one of several short visits to England.

The *Novum Instrumentum*, a new Latin version of the New Testament and his most important work, appeared in 1516 and attracted much attention from contemporary scholars. This was followed two years later by the first edition of the *Colloquia* ('Dialogues'), which became his most widely-read work.

After a short stay at Louvain, Erasmus settled finally at Basle in 1521. In the last fifteen years of his life he issued a stream of works, translations of the classics and of the early fathers of the Church, and conducted an immense correspondence with scholars and fellow humanists throughout Europe. Sympathetic initially to the Reformation, for which his writings had largely prepared the way, Erasmus refused to take a stand either for or against Martin Luther (q.v.) at the Diet of Worms, urging moderation on both sides. Gradually however he became more and more alienated from the Reformers, and in 1524 was persuaded to publish an attack on Luther in *De Libero Arbitrio* ('On Free Will'). After the triumph of the Reformation in 1529 he lived for some years in Fribourg, but returned to Basle in 1535 and died there on the night of 11–12 July 1536.

Undoubtedly the greatest scholar and theologian of his time, Erasmus did more than anyone else towards the revival of Latin and Greek learning. A restless, sometimes querulous, unhappy man of high intellect, sincere and enduring of purpose, he had a genuine capacity for friendship and a sense of humour which was his saving grace. He believed in liberty of thought and in the use of reason and moderation in all things. His friends included staunch supporters of the old Catholic faith as well as leaders of the Reformation. At a time when the printed word was reaching an ever-increasing audience in western Europe he knew the importance of spreading the humanist doctrine as rapidly and as widely as possible. His influence was many-sided and far-reaching, in England as much as on the Continent. In his own words, he was truly a 'citizen of the whole world'.

The collected works of Erasmus are being translated and published by the University of Toronto Press. Volume I, *Correspondence 1484–1500*, came out in 1974. The hitherto standard edition of the letters of Erasmus is that edited by P. S. and H. M. Allen and others, published in 11 volumes (1906–7).

J. Huizinga, *Erasmus of Rotterdam* (1952).

*Portraits*: oil, by Matsys, 1517: Galleria Nazionale, Rome; oil, by Holbein, 1523: Earl of Radnor Collection, Longford Castle, Wilts (copy at All Souls, Oxford); medallion, by Holbein, *c.* 1532: Museum of Art, Basle; tempera, by Holbein, Musée du Louvre, Paris; oil, after Holbein: Royal Collection, Hampton Court (other versions at Bodleian Library, Oxford, and elsewhere); engravings and woodcuts by Cranach, Dürer, Holbein, and others: locations too numerous to list here.

**Erskine, John** (d. 1572), 6th Baron Erskine and 1st (18th) Earl of Mar, Regent of Scotland 1571–2 during part of the minority of James VI (q.v.).

John Erskine was the third and eldest surviving son of John Erskine, 5th Baron Erskine, and his wife, the Lady Margaret Campbell, daughter of Archibald Campbell, 2nd Earl of Argyll. His father, Keeper of Edinburgh Castle and guardian of both James V (q.v.) and Mary, Queen of Scots (q.v.) during their minorities, was *de jure* 17th Earl of Mar, the earldom having been seized by the crown in 1457.

Erskine was educated to enter the Church, but after the death of his two elder brothers he became the prospective heir. He succeeded his father in 1555 and was given the custody of Edinburgh Castle. Later he supported the Reformation and signed the letter requesting John Knox (q.v.) to return to Scotland. He was, however, never more than a moderate Protestant and strove during the next few years to achieve a peaceful settlement between the Protestant faction and the Catholic Regent, Marie de Guise (q.v.); he refused to subscribe to the *First Book of Discipline*.

On the return of Mary, Queen of Scots, to take over personal rule in 1561, Erskine was made a Privy Councillor. He married Annabella, daughter of Sir William Murray of Tullibardine, reputed to be a formidable lady and a close friend of the Queen; it may have been due to her influence that Mary was persuaded to restore the Erskines to the earldom of Mar in June 1565; another reason probably was that Erskine supported the Queen's marriage to Lord Darnley (see Stewart, Henry). In August that year Mar helped to suppress the rebellion of the Earl of Moray (see Stewart, Lord James) against the Queen's authority.

On the birth of Mary's son, the future James VI, in December 1566, Mar was given the guardianship of the young Prince. In April 1567 he was confirmed in the post of Captain of Stirling Castle. He absolutely refused to give James up to the Queen's third husband, the Earl of Bothwell (see Hepburn, James), and from 1567 onwards devoted himself exclusively to the interests of his young charge. He was one of the leaders among the nobles who confronted Mary and Bothwell at Carberry Hill in June that year and who forced the Queen to abdicate in favour of James; he also signed the order committing the Queen to imprisonment on Lochleven after her defeat at Langside.

The assassination of the Regent Moray in January 1570 plunged Scotland into bitter civil war, and it was not until September 1571 that Parliament met at Stirling to choose a new Regent. Of the three candidates – Mar, the Earl of Morton (see Douglas, James), and Archibald Campbell, 5th Earl of Argyll – Mar, known to be a man of integrity and desirous of peace, was elected. In practice, however, he turned out to be the tool of Morton, and since the bitter fighting continued in Edinburgh throughout the winter and spring of 1572, he had no opportunity to prove his qualities as a peacemaker.

In October 1572 Mar was present with Morton at the conference at Dalkeith with Sir Henry Killigrew, the emissary of Elizabeth I (q.v.), concerning the latter's proposals that Mary should be delivered to her enemies. He was taken ill shortly afterwards and died at Stirling on 29 October, when he was succeeded as Regent by Morton and in the earldom by his son John; the latter was to exercise considerable influence in Scottish affairs under James VI.

John Erskine, 1st Earl of Mar, succeeded in the difficult task of winning the respect of both sides as keeper of the young King. His major importance, however, lies in the role he played in deposing Mary, Queen of Scots.

See the titles listed under Mary, Queen of Scots, and James VI.

*Portrait:* oil, by unknown artist: Scottish National Portrait Gallery, Edinburgh.

**Essex, 1st Earl of (fourth creation)** (1485–1540), see Cromwell, Thomas.

**Essex, 2nd Earl of (sixth creation)** (1567–1601), see Devereux, Robert.

**Eworth, Hans** (?1520–?1574), portrait painter.

Very little is known of Eworth's life, except that he was born in Antwerp (where his brother was a jeweller) and that he was established in England by about 1546; he is believed to be identical with the Jan Eeuworts who was a freeman of the Antwerp Guild of St Luke in 1540. His name appears in the records as Haunce Eworth, Nycholas Ewotes, John Ewout, John Euwouts, Maister Hanse, John Ewottes, Hans Eywooddes, Jan Evertz, Hans Heward, Haunce Evance, Hewe Hawarde and Haunce painter (for full list see Dr Roy Strong). It is only since 1913 that the monogram 'HE' has been attributed to Eworth, it having previously been considered to be that of the Flemish artist Lucas De Heere, who did not arrive in England until 1566.

The earliest documentary evidence of Eworth in England is in 1549, when he is recorded as living in the parish of St Thomas's Hospital; his first known painting (signed with the HE mono-gram), *A Turk on Horseback*, is also dated that year. By 29 October 1550, when he was granted letters of denization as 'John Euwots', he was resident in the parish of St Saviour's, Southwark, and it was in that same year that he executed his allegorical painting of Sir John Luttrell, probably in connection with the Treaty of Boulogne, which ended the war with France.

In 1554 Eworth was commissioned to paint Mary I (q.v.); from this single sitting he was to paint five known (signed or attributed) portraits, and also one miniature, of the Queen. How he came to receive royal patronage can only be conjectured, but Dr Roy Strong has suggested that Eworth may have had some connection with Catholicism and the Catholic revival in England on Mary's accession; he bases this on the fact that nearly all Eworth's identifiable sitters were members of prominent Catholic families and points out that Eworth did not receive the favour of Elizabeth I (q.v.) when she came to the throne. Among his sitters were Lord Darnley (see Stewart, Henry) in 1555; Frances Brandon, Duchess of Suffolk, and Adrian Stokes, 1559; the Earl of Moray (see Stewart, Lord James) and his bride, Agnes Keith, 1561; several members of the aristocratic Norfolk and Dacre families, and a number of gentry; in addition, there are some Eworth portraits of unknown sitters. (For a list of signed and attributed works, see the cata-logue of the National Portrait Gallery exhibition, 1965, and Roy Strong, *The English Icon*, pp. 83–106.)

In 1560–1 Eworth must have visited Scotland in order to paint the Earl of Moray and his bride. He may have been 'Haunce the drawer' paid by Katherine, Duchess of Suffolk, 'for drawing the storie of David and Sall' in 1562. During these years the painter was still resident in Southwark, as 'Hans Eywoddes' in 1559, and as 'Hans Heward' in the parish of St Mary Overies, Southwark, described as 'born in Antwerpe, and goeth to the Dutch Church', in 1568; other records include mention of a 'Jan Evertz' living in the parish of Bridge Without in 1567, and (a more certain reference) in 1571, of 'Haunce Evance, pictorer, a denizen, borne in Anwarpe, came into the realm about xxviij yeres past, Douch j.' in the parish of Faringdon Without, St Brides.

In the late spring of 1572 Eworth was called in by the Office of the Revels to assist in the design of costumes and décor for the festivities ordered by Queen Elizabeth to welcome the French treaty commissioners in June that year. He was subsequently employed as a designer of masques to be performed at Hampton Court, but after 1573 there are no references to him in the records of the Office of the Revels, and it is presumed that he died in about 1574.

Hans Eworth is considered to be the most important large-scale portrait painter working in England in the twenty-five years following the death of Hans Holbein the Younger (q.v.). His technique owes much initially to the influence of the Dutch painter, Jan van Scorel, and later to that of Holbein and his successor as court painter, William Scrots; all the Eworth sitters are por-trayed in the pale, luminous manner of Scorel. As Dr Strong has written, Eworth was painting at a period of crisis in England, yet the members of society he portrayed appear self-confident and assured, as they would wish to be seen by posterity.

Eworth's works are in the Royal

Collection, National Portrait Gallery, Tate Gallery, and various private collections in the United Kingdom, the National Gallery of Canada, Ottawa, and elsewhere. The controversial portrait of Mary I, 1554, on which the monogram has been altered from HE to HF (it is believed in order to pass it as a Holbein), is at the Society of Antiquaries of London. The allegorical painting of Sir John Luttrell, 1550, is at the Courtauld Institute of Art, London; the allegory of the Wise and Foolish Virgins, dated 1570, is at the Royal Museum of Fine Arts, Copenhagen. A painting of Henry VIII, based on the Holbein wall painting in the Privy Council Chamber and painted by Eworth in 1567, is at Trinity College, Cambridge. The miniature of Mary I (c. 1555) is in the Duke of Buccleuch and Queensberry Collection. (N.B. The painting of Queen Elizabeth and the Three Goddesses, once thought to be by Eworth, is now believed to be by an unknown Flemish artist who used a different HE monogram.)

E. Auerbach, 'Holbein's Followers in England', *Burlington Magazine*, xciii (1951), pp. 44–51.
R. Strong, *Hans Eworth: A Tudor Artist and his Circle* (Leicester, 1965); 'Hans Eworth Reconsidered', *Burlington Magazine*, cviii (1966), pp. 225–33; both are reproduced in the same author's *The English Icon* (1969).

*Portraits*: no self-portraits are known.

# F

**Fabyan, Robert** (d. 1513), chronicler, see *Lives Before the Tudors*.

**Farnaby, Giles** (?1560–1640), composer.

Little is known of the life of Giles Farnaby except that he was born in about 1560 in Truro, where his father at one time taught at the local grammar school. After studying for twelve years at Oxford, Farnaby took his degree as bachelor of music in July 1592. In the same year he harmonized nine tunes for the *Book of Psalms*, which was published by Thomas East. In London, both Giles and his father were members of the Joiners' Company and a cousin, Nicholas, was a virginal maker.

More than fifty of Farnaby's compositions for the virginal are contained in the *Fitzwilliam Virginal Book* at Cambridge. Of these the most individual are 'His Rest' and 'His Dream', and his piece for two virginals is the earliest known work for two keyboard instruments. He was also well known for his madrigals, but his only published work was the *Canzonets to Foure Voyces, with a Song of eight parts*, which appeared in 1598.

Farnaby died in London in 1640. Some of his manuscripts have survived and are in Philadelphia, U.S.A. The *Fitzwilliam Virginal Book* (edited by J. A. Fuller-Maitland and W. Barclay Squire, 1899) also contains four compositions by his son Richard. Farnaby's madrigals have been published in volume 20 of *The English Madrigal School*, edited by E. H. Fellowes (1913–24).

M. H. Glyn, *About Elizabethan virginal music and its composers* (2nd ed. 1934).

**Ferrar, Robert** (d. 1555), Protestant martyr, Bishop of St David's.

According to tradition Robert Ferrar was born at Ewood, near Halifax, Yorkshire, probably around 1502–4. Educated at both Cambridge and Oxford, where he became an Augustinian canon and monk at St Mary's Priory, Ferrar was subsequently converted to Lutheranism; when involved in a charge of heresy in 1528, however, he was forced to recant. He accompanied William Barlow (q.v.) on his mission to Scotland in 1535 and on his return was appointed Prior of St Oswald's, Nostell.

Shortly after the accession of Edward VI (q.v.) Ferrar was made chaplain to the Protector, Somerset (see Seymour, Edward), and through him nominated as Bishop of St David's. This appointment was by letters-patent, with election by the Chapter, and Ferrar soon encountered animosity in his Welsh diocese. His enemies in the Chapter brought a long series of trivial charges against him, and following Somerset's fall from power he had no protection. A commission was set up to examine the charges, and Ferrar was kept in prison. When Mary I (q.v.) came to the throne he was deprived of his bishopric as a married priest and cited to answer charges of denial of Roman Catholic doctrine on the Eucharist. Stephen Gardiner (q.v.) sent him to be tried at Carmarthen by his successor as Bishop of St David's. Refusing to accept a list of

articles subscribed, Ferrar was condemned as a heretic and burned at the
stake at Carmarthen on 30 March 1555.

R. Bretton, 'Bishop Robert Ferrar', *Halifax
Antiquarian Society Transactions 1934* (1935).

**Fisher, John** (1469–1535), Bishop of
Rochester, cardinal, and martyr. He was
canonized in 1935.

Fisher was born at Beverley, Yorkshire, the son of a wealthy mercer, and
educated at Michaelhouse, Cambridge.
According to a contemporary source he
was a man of upright bearing, six foot
tall, with dark eyes and hair, 'his skinne
somewhat tawnie mixed with manie
blew vaines'. He pursued a distinguished
career as a scholar, was ordained in 1491,
and at the age of twenty-eight was
elected master of his college. Vice-
Chancellor in 1501, he held office as
Chancellor of the University from 1504
onwards. Throughout his life he was
devoted to Cambridge, where much of
his work was aimed at the training of
scholarly priests. In 1511 he persuaded
Erasmus (q.v.) to lecture at the university
on Greek, a language which Fisher set
himself to master at the age of fifty. He
also took up the study of Hebrew in later
life.

His learning brought him to the notice
of the Lady Margaret Beaufort (q.v.),
who appointed him as one of her
chaplains and subsequently as her
confessor. They became close friends,
and Fisher influenced her to endow
professorships of divinity at Oxford and
Cambridge and to build two new
colleges, Christ's and St John's, at
Cambridge. He himself contributed
£500 to St John's, as well as the lands
given to him by his benefactress.

In 1504 he was appointed to the
bishopric of Rochester where, in contrast
to other bishops of the period, he seems
to have devoted an unusual amount of
attention to diocesan matters.

Strongly opposed to Lutheranism,
Fisher's work as a controversialist and his
reputation in Europe as a theologian
stemmed from the lengthy replies he
wrote (in Latin) to books published by
Martin Luther (q.v.): his *Confutatio*
(1523), a reply to Luther's *Assertio*, was
some 200,000 words long. He made
forthright attacks upon the vices within
the Church and against the heresies of the
day. His sermons, delivered in the
vernacular, were popular if long-
winded: at the public burning of
heretical books ordered by Thomas
Wolsey (q.v.) at Paul's Cross in 1520
he is said to have preached for two hours.
Fisher held the view that Church reform
must come from within the Church, and
frequently spoke in the House of Lords
and in Convocation against the interference of the state in Church affairs.
A man of integrity and moral courage,
he offended Wolsey by preaching on the
need to set an example by leading a
devout and simple life, and in 1523 he
opposed the latter's financial policies.

He incurred the displeasure of Henry
VIII (q.v.) by defending Catherine of
Aragon (q.v.) in the matter of the King's
divorce, and this was accentuated by his
refusal to agree to the royal supremacy.
The King then launched an attack on the
Bishop on the grounds that he had
concealed from him the prophesies made
by the Nun of Kent, Elizabeth Barton
(q.v.); Fisher was found guilty of
misprision of treason under an act of
attainder (March 1534) and, in lieu of
imprisonment, deprived for one year of
all revenue from his diocese. The
following month both he and Sir
Thomas More (q.v.), having refused to
take the oath of supremacy required
under the new Act of Succession, were
sent to the Tower. Several attempts were

made to persuade Fisher to change his mind but, although prepared to accept the succession, he remained adamant in his view of the Pope's supremacy. The King, further incensed by the Pope's conferring a cardinalship on Fisher, had him brought to trial, and on 17 June 1535 he was condemned to death for high treason. He was executed at Tower Hill on 22 June, and More a fortnight later. It was a triumph of the new order over the old, and Europe was outraged. Erasmus spoke of them as 'the wisest and most saintly men England had'.

Fisher's English works were published by the Early English Text Society in 1876.

T. E. Bridgett, *Life of the Blessed John Fisher* (1888).
John Lewis, *The Life of Dr John Fisher* (2 vols; 1855).
E. E. Reynolds, *Saint John Fisher* (1955).
E. Surtz, *The Works and Days of John Fisher, 1469–1535* (Cambridge, Mass., 1967).

*Portraits*: drawing, by Holbein, *c.* 1528: Royal Collection, Windsor; oil, silhouetted, after Holbein: National Portrait Gallery, London; oil, by unknown artist after Holbein, *c.* 1528: St John's College, Cambridge; others at Old Schools, Trinity and Christ's Colleges, and Divinity School, Cambridge, and elsewhere.

**Fisher, John** (1569–1641), Jesuit priest, see *Lives of the Stuart Age*.

**Fitch, Ralph** (d. 1616), merchant and traveller.

There is virtually no material available concerning Ralph Fitch's personal life, but he must have been born some time about 1555–60. By 1583 he was a well-known merchant in London.

At this date the City merchants were beginning to explore the possibilities of trade with the Levant and beyond. In 1581 Elizabeth I (q.v.) had granted letters patent to the newly-formed Company of Merchants of the Levant, founded by Sir Edward Osborne, Richard Staper, Thomas Smythe (Smith), and William Garret, to trade with Turkey for a period of seven years. Among the pioneers were John Eldred, who had lived in Baghdad for two years, and John Newbery, who had reached Ormuz, the gateway to India, in his search for spices in 1582.

On Newbery's return to England, Osborne and Staper decided to finance a new voyage. For this purpose they drew other merchants, including Fitch, into the scheme and equipped the *Tyger* for the outward voyage to Aleppo. On 12 February 1583 this vessel left the Pool of London, with Fitch, Newbery, Eldred, William Leedes, James Story, and two other merchants aboard.

They reached Syria in late April, and from Aleppo travelled overland to the river Euphrates and thence to Baghdad; next, they sailed down the river Tigris to Basra, where they arrived in July. Eldred left the party there but Fitch and the others took a boat down the Persian Gulf. On reaching Ormuz some Venetian merchants had them arrested and transported to the Portuguese island of Goa, where they were imprisoned, but they were subsequently released on a bond provided by two Jesuits. Story decided to remain in Goa, and in the following April (1584) Fitch, Newbery, and Leedes made their escape from the island and set out on the overland journey across India. At Fatehpur Sikri, near Agra, they visited the court of the Mogul Emperor Akbar, where Leedes accepted the post of court jeweller. Newbery also now parted from Fitch; in July 1584 he set out on his return journey to England but died on the way home, probably while still in India.

Fitch decided to go on alone and to make a leisurely journey across India to Bengal. He sailed down the Jumna and Ganges rivers, visiting en route Vārānasi (Benares) and Patna. He then proceeded overland to Kuch Behar at the foot of the Himalayas and through east Bengal. In November 1586 he embarked for Burma, where he sailed up the Irrawaddy river to Pegu and into the Shan State of Siam. By early 1588 he was in the Malay Peninsula and visiting Malacca, the first Englishman to penetrate so far into Asia.

Fitch left Malacca on 29 March 1588 on the long journey back to England. Revisiting Pegu and the Bay of Bengal, he stopped at Colombo and then at Cochin, on the south-western tip of India. There he found a Portuguese ship sailing for Basra and Baghdad. From Baghdad he journeyed via Aleppo to Tripoli, where he embarked on an English boat bound for London. Fitch arrived home in April 1591; he had been away for eight years.

Throughout his wanderings he had kept a travelogue and, more important, notes of everything that he had learned about trading in the areas he had visited. This was of immense value to the City merchants, who were anxiously awaiting a renewal of the charter for the Levant Company. The account was to be published in 1599 by Richard Hakluyt (q.v.) in his *Principall Navigations, Voiages and Discoveries of the English Nation*, but before that date a copy was sent to Lord Burghley (see Cecil, William); undoubtedly it helped to influence him in granting a new charter (this time to run for twelve years) to the Governor and Company of Merchants of the Levant, from 7 January 1592. Sir Edward Osborne became the first Governor of the Company, and Fitch was one of its members. This new charter not only covered the Turkish areas of the previous one, but extended to the dominions of the Venetian Republic and 'by land through the countries of the Sultan of Turkey and into and from the East Indies

lately discovered' by Fitch and his companions.

It is known that Fitch paid at least one return visit to the Levant, for in 1596 he was elected Consul at Aleppo by the English merchants established there. By 1599, however, he was again living in London. Preparations were being made at this time for a voyage to the East Indies, and although Fitch did not subscribe to it, his advice was sought. His eye-witness reports were considered of immense value by the founders of the East India Company, which was granted a charter by Parliament at the end of 1600.

The exact date of Fitch's death has not been established, but Michael Edwardes, a recent biographer, basing his information on a mention of him in the Company's Court Minutes of 1606 and a Will proved in London in 1616, puts it as between 3 and 15 October 1616.

When Ralph Fitch set out on his remarkable journey he himself regarded it as a purely commercial venture. But it must have captured the imagination of the Elizabethans, for Shakespeare (q.v.) has his witches refer to it in *Macbeth*. Fitch was the first Englishman to reach the heart of India and to penetrate to the threshold of South-East Asia, an achievement which was to have far-reaching effects on English trade through the foundation of the East India Company. He was not only immensely courageous, but also a keen observer who had a writer's gift and the diligence to put his observations on paper.

M. Edwardes, *Ralph Fitch: Elizabethan in the Indies* (1972).

**Fitzalan, Henry** (?1511–1580), 12th Earl of Arundel.

Born in about 1511, Henry Fitzalan was the only son of William Fitzalan,

11th Earl of Arundel, and his second wife, Lady Anne Percy, daughter of Henry Percy, 4th Earl of Northumberland. His godfather was Henry VIII (q.v.), whose service he entered at the age of fifteen. He accompanied the King to France in 1532 and was in 1540 appointed Lord Deputy of Calais.

Recalled home by the death of his father in January 1544, the new Earl of Arundel was shortly afterwards created a Knight of the Garter. In July the same year, together with the Duke of Suffolk (see Brandon, Charles), he took an invading force to France and successfully stormed Boulogne; as a reward for his services he was made Lord Chamberlain. He retained this office on the accession of Edward VI (q.v.) and was appointed a member of the Privy Council. Arundel joined the Earl of Warwick (see Dudley, John; later Duke of Northumberland) in seeking the overthrow of the Protector Somerset (see Seymour, Edward), but was himself ousted from the Council when Warwick grew jealous of his influence. Arundel then re-allied himself with his former enemy, but in 1551, when Somerset was committed to the Tower for the second time, he too was implicated in the charge of treason. Imprisoned for nearly a year and severely fined, Arundel was freed and restored to his place in the Council only because Northumberland found it expedient to conciliate the nobility in view of the King's failing health. He protested against the instrument of succession forced on the young King, and after Edward's death on 6 July 1553, while appearing at first to support Northumberland's plan to put the Lady Jane Grey (q.v.) on the throne, he secretly sent a letter to Mary (see Mary I), informing her of her brother's death and urging her to retire to a place of safety. He continued to attend Council meetings

and took part in the preparations for Jane's coronation, but as soon as Northumberland had been persuaded to leave London to take command of the force raised against Mary, Arundel called a meeting of his fellow Councillors and, with the help of the Earl of Pembroke (see Herbert, William), had Mary proclaimed as Queen in the City. He then rode to Cambridge, where he seized Northumberland, who was taken to the Tower to await trial.

As a reward for his loyalty, Arundel was appointed by Mary to the office of Lord Steward, with a seat in the Privy Council. One of the commissioners chosen to mediate between Charles V (q.v.) and the French crown in 1555, he was appointed by the Queen as Lieutenant-General and Captain of the forces for the defence of the realm in July 1557. He retained his office of Lord Steward and seat in the Council under Elizabeth, whom he entertained on several occasions at Nonsuch Palace, near Cheam, in Surrey, the home of his son-in-law, Lord Lumley, where he lived after the death of his second wife. (He had married, firstly, Katherine, second daughter of Thomas Grey, Marquis of Dorset, by whom he had one son and two daughters, and secondly, Mary, daughter of Sir John Arundell, of Lanherne, Cornwall, who died in October 1557.) As a widower, Arundel was among those named as a possible suitor for the Queen's hand; this led to a violent quarrel with the Earl of Leicester (see Dudley, Robert) in 1561.

Arundel resigned the office of Lord Steward in 1564, at a time when he was out of favour with the Queen over a meeting held to consider the matter of the succession. In 1566 he went to Italy on the pretext of seeking a cure for his gout, and although partially restored to favour on his return the following year, as leader of the 'old' nobility he was resolved to work for the marriage of Mary, Queen of Scots (q.v.), and the Duke of Norfolk (see Howard, Thomas, 4th Duke) and the restoration of Catholicism. In 1569, on discovery of the marriage plot, Arundel was placed under house arrest, first at Arundel House in the Strand, and later at Nonsuch. He was recalled to Council on the recommendation of Leicester the following year and made clear his opposition to the marriage of the Queen and the Duc d'Alençon (q.v.). As soon as his part in the Ridolfi conspiracy (see Ridolfi, Roberto di) had been disclosed in September 1571, he was again placed under guard and was kept at Arundel House until December 1572. He spent the last few years of his life largely in seclusion at his London home, where he died on 24 February 1580.

The Life of Henrye Fitzallen, supposedly written by his chaplain, preserved in the King's MSS, British Museum, London; printed in Gentleman's Magazine, ciii (1833).

Portrait: oil on panel, by unknown artist: National Portrait Gallery, London.

**Fitzherbert, Sir Anthony** (1470–1538), judge.

Born in 1470, the sixth son of Ralph Fitzherbert of Norbury, Derbyshire, and his wife, Elizabeth, daughter of John Marshall of Upton, Leicestershire, Anthony Fitzherbert is believed to have been educated at Oxford. He was a member of Gray's Inn. After being called to the bar he was in March 1509 appointed Recorder of Coventry. A serjeant-at-law in 1510 and King's Serjeant in 1516, he was raised to the bench as a justice of the Court of Common Pleas and knighted in about 1521–2.

In 1524 Fitzherbert was one of the commissioners selected to negotiate peace in Ireland between the Earls of Ormonde and Kildare, a mission that was successfully accomplished. Little is known of his activities for the next few years, until in 1529 he signed articles of impeachment against Cardinal Thomas Wolsey (q.v.). In 1535 he was a member of the commission that tried the Carthusians Robert Feron, John Hale, and others, and a few months later he took part in the trials of Bishop John Fisher (q.v.) and Sir Thomas More (q.v.).

Sir Anthony Fitzherbert died on 27 May 1538. He was buried in the parish of Norbury. He had been twice married and had several children by his second wife, Matilda, daughter of Richard Cotton of Hamsell Ridware, Staffordshire. Although he did not attain the office of Chief Justice, Fitzherbert was one of the most prominent lawyers of his day and author of a number of legal works, of which La Graunde Abridgement, published in 1516, was the first notable attempt to systematize English law.

**Fitzroy, Henry** (1519–1536), Duke of Richmond, natural son of Henry VIII (q.v.).

The son of Henry VIII and Elizabeth Blount, a lady-in-waiting to Catherine of Aragon (q.v.), Henry Fitzroy was born in 1519. In June 1525, at the age of six, he was made a Knight of the Garter and a few days later created Earl of Nottingham and Duke of Richmond and Somerset, with precedence over all other dukes except the King's lawful issue. At the same time several important offices were bestowed on him, ensuring a substantial income, mostly in Scotland, Ireland, and the north of England, where he received also the grant of extensive lands. In July that year he was made Lord High Admiral.

Richmond's education was entrusted

to Richard Croke, one of the pioneers of Greek scholarship in England; it was shared at Windsor by the young Henry Howard (q.v.), Earl of Surrey, whose father, the Duke of Norfolk (see Howard, Thomas, 3rd Duke), was his godfather. The two became close friends. Together they accompanied the King and Anne Boleyn (q.v.) to France in the autumn of 1532, and shortly after their return Richmond married his friend's sister, the Lady Mary Howard. There was some speculation that the King intended to make him King of Ireland, but instead Richmond remained at court, possibly on account of fragile health. He was present at the execution of Anne Boleyn in May 1536.

On 22 July the same year Richmond himself died at the royal palace in St James's, when suspicion became rife that he had been poisoned by the late Queen and her brother, Lord Rochford. Buried at Thetford, his remains were removed at the dissolution to St Michael's Church, Framlingham, Suffolk.

**Fletcher, John** (1579–1625), dramatist, see *Lives of the Stuart Age*.

**Florio, John** (?1553–?1625), lexicographer and translator.

The son of Michael Angelo Florio, a Protestant refugee of Tuscan origin, John Florio was born in London in about 1553. His father, a teacher of Italian, preacher at the Italian church in London and author of a biography of Lady Jane Grey (q.v.), fled with his family to the Continent on the accession of Queen Mary I (q.v.), so that John received his early education abroad. He subsequently studied at Oxford, matriculating at Magdalen College in 1581.

Florio was for some years a tutor at Oxford. He produced a grammar and series of dialogues in Italian and English,

entitled *Florio His Firste Fruites*, in 1578, dedicated to his patron, the Earl of Leicester (see Dudley, Robert). This was followed in 1580 by a translation from the Italian of Giovanni Battista Ramusio's account of the voyages of Jacques Cartier, published in English as *Navigations and Discoveries*, and in 1591 by *Second Fruites* and also a collection of proverbs, *Giardino di Ricreatione*.

Towards the end of the century Florio moved to London, where he became intimate with the literary circle and acquired several new patrons, including the Earl of Pembroke, the Earl of Southampton (see Wriothesley, Henry), and the Earl and Countess of Rutland. His Italian-English dictionary, *A Worlde of Wordes*, was published in 1598; in it he relied heavily on the works of the contemporary Italian philosopher Giordano Bruno (q.v.). Florio was at this time also engaged on his greatest work, the translation into English of the *Essais* of Montaigne, which he first published in 1603. That same year Florio was appointed reader in Italian to Anne of Denmark (see *Lives of the Stuart Age*); in 1604 he became a Groom of the Privy Chamber, a post which he held until 1619. The much enlarged edition of his dictionary, issued in 1611, bore the new title, *Queen Anna's New World of Words*. A revised edition of Montaigne's essays appeared in 1613.

By 1620 Florio had retired from court and was living with his wife, Rose, in Fulham. He died there some time in late 1625 or early 1626 (his will, dated 20 July 1625, was proved the following May).

*Portrait:* engraving, by W. Hole: British Museum, London (in 1611 edition of Florio's Italian-English dictionary, see above).

**Forman, Simon** (1552–1611), astrologer, alchemist, 'doctor', and diarist.

Forman was born at Quidhampton, Wiltshire, on 30 December 1552, the fourth son and one of eight children of William and Mary Forman. The family came from good yeoman stock: Simon's father was one of the free tenants of Quidhampton, a village lying between Salisbury and Wilton; his grandfather had been steward to William Herbert, Earl of Pembroke, at Wilton Park.

Forman's home life was not happy; unpopular with his mother but much loved by his father, as a child he would have dreams and visions that he later interpreted as signifying the troubles he was to meet in adult life.

His education was intermittent. After early schooling at the local free school he went on to the grammar school at Salisbury. Here, in two years, Simon acquired a basic knowledge of Latin, but his desire for an academic training was frustrated by the death of his father in January 1564. At this date he began to keep the diary which, together with the later case books, is the main source of information concerning his life.

In February 1567 Simon apprenticed himself to a mercer and grocer in Salisbury, from whom he learned the hosiery trade, as well as the buying and selling of cloth, apothecary drugs, and groceries, and with whom he stayed for over five years. He then returned to teach at Quidhampton and Wilton, with a brief interlude at Oxford, where he acted as servant to two cousins (B.A.s and sporting clerics who spent their time hunting, dancing, and chasing young women), and picked up what learning he could in his free hours.

During his teaching period at Wilton Forman made the acquaintance of a 'Mr Cox', probably Francis Cox, a gentleman who dabbled in astrology, magic, and necromancy. Forman was Cox's pupil in these arts until their association ended in a quarrel a year later and he returned to schoolmastering.

For the next few years Forman drifted from one tutoring or teaching post to another, until in January 1579 he resolved to set up on his own as a practitioner of physic and magic. He rented the parsonage of Fisherton Anger, on the outskirts of Salisbury, and swiftly built up a reputation. In his own words, 'This year I did prophesy the truth of many things which afterwards came to pass.' This practice, however, was shortlived; in June the same year the authorities caught up with him, deprived him of his goods and books, and sent him to prison. He was not released until over a year later in July 1580, after an appeal to the Council.

The day after his release, Forman set out for London. He had little money and no friends in the City, and in order to live took work as a carpenter in Greenwich. He began once more to practice his 'physic', treating one Henry Johnson for consumption at this time and travelling with his patient to the Low Countries that summer. By the autumn Forman was back at Quidhampton, sometimes doing manual work for a living, sometimes curing the sick and often himself suffering bouts of ill-health. In October 1581 he took another house in Salisbury, where he set up a practice in physic and surgery. The following year he became tutor to the Penruddocks, a well-known Wiltshire family, while keeping up his practice in his spare time; but not long afterwards he gave up tutoring altogether. His reputation was growing, and the practice frequently took him to London and further afield. In Salisbury, in spite of frequent changes of address, the inevitable prosecutions and imprisonments followed. By this time, however, Forman had friends to intercede for him, and on several

occasions he was discharged from the assizes. In 1588 he began to practise necromancy; the following year, he decided to settle permanently in London, where the opportunities, both for astrology and medicine, were greater than in the provinces.

In London, in spite of initial hardships, Forman began to widen and increase his practice; he also wrote a number of tracts and pamphlets on medical, astrological, magical, and related subjects (only one of which, a tract entitled *The Grounds of the Longitude*, was ever printed).

In 1592 came the turning point in his life. The plague was raging in London, and in July Forman and his household fell victims to the disease. Although he was ill for five months, Forman succeeded in curing himself by lancing the sores and drinking 'strong water' which he had distilled. He also treated many others, and by the time the plague waned, towards the end of 1593, his reputation and financial success were assured. The following year he was summoned to appear before 'the Doctors' (the Royal College of Physicians, all of whom had fled from London when faced by the plague), forbidden to practise and fined £5. In the next three years he was called before the same body on two further occasions, fined, and committed to prison. Friends in high places obtained his release, and he took up temporary residence in Lambeth, outside the jurisdiction of the College.

Women from all walks of life came to consult Forman, often medically but even more frequently concerning affairs of the heart. With many of his clients he entered into physical relationships, as he did with servant girls and numerous other women; these sexual activities are frankly recorded in his diary and case books. The astrologer had a passionate but tempestuous affair with Avis Allen, wife of William Allen, who was his mistress from 1593 until her death in 1597.

Forman was anxious to marry and frequently cast horoscopes to discover whether or not a particular relationship would be auspicious. Finally, at the age of forty-seven, he took as his wife a young Kentish girl of gentle birth, Anne Baker, who had recently joined his household; the ceremony took place at Lambeth on 22 July 1599. Marriage made little difference to his way of life, except that in 1601 he left the chambers in Billingsgate he had occupied from 1593 to 1599 and settled for good in a house at Lambeth. A son, Clement, was born in 1606.

In 1603 Forman finally won his battle with 'the Doctors', being granted a licence to practise by Cambridge University. Although his practice was predominantly medical, over the years horoscope-casting played an increasingly important part in his work; he was also sometimes consulted as to the whereabouts of hidden treasure or stolen goods. The Forman papers (now in the Ashmole MSS at the Bodleian Library, Oxford) are a hitherto unknown gold-mine of information on the sexual and social life of the period, for the clients of 'the doctor' were drawn from a cross-section of Elizabethan society: court ladies and public officials, naval com-manders and sailors' wives, city mer-chants and church dignitaries, members of the gentry, actors and actresses, even whores. (Only the medical profession remained aloof.) Famous names appear alongside the unknown, and through his recent study of the case books Dr A. L. Rowse has unravelled the identity of the 'Dark Lady' of Shakespeare's sonnets as that of Emilia Lanier, the discarded mistress of Lord Chamberlain Hunsdon, the patron of the company to which Shakespeare belonged. Among other important clients was Frances Howard, who was to become Countess of Hertford and later Duchess of Richmond and Lennox. Another Frances Howard (her cousin), the young Countess of Essex, who consulted Forman towards the end of his life, was to blacken the astrologer's name posthumously – and falsely – through her poisoning of Sir Thomas Overbury (see *Lives of the Stuart Age*), a murder which was committed some two years after Forman's own death.

After a full and active life, Simon Forman died on 8 September 1611, having accurately predicted his death to his wife a few days previously. He never lost his interest in the female sex; only a few weeks before he died he had cast to know how matters stood between him and a certain lady. He left a fortune of £1,200. His papers, bequeathed to a Dr Napier, Rector of Great Lindford, Buckinghamshire, eventually found their way into the Ashmole collection

and thus to the Bodleian Library, Oxford. In addition to the case books, which contain notes on the astrologer's dream life as well as his consultations, there is his diary, a fragment of autobiography and family history, and an account of four plays of Shakespeare (q.v.) which Forman saw performed at the Globe Theatre in April 1611.

Forman is mentioned by name several times in the works of the dramatist Ben Jonson (see *Lives of the Stuart Age*); he was obviously also the inspiration behind the latter's play, *The Alchemist*.

A. L. Rowse, *Simon Forman* (1974).

*Portrait*: engraving, by R. Godfrey, 1776, from portrait by unknown artist, *c*. 1600, once in Lord Mountstuart Collection: private (anon.) col-lection, London.

**Foxe, John** (1516–1587), martyrologist, author of *The Book of Martyrs*.

Born into a middle-class family at Boston, Lincolnshire, in 1516, Foxe lost his father while still young; his mother married again soon afterwards and through his stepfather, Richard Melton of Coningsby, also in Lincolnshire, John, a promising scholar, came to the notice of John Hawarden, a fellow (and later Prin-cipal) of Brasenose College, Oxford. The latter persuaded Melton to send his step-son to Brasenose in 1534. Foxe took his B.A. at the college in 1537 and was made a fellow two years later, an appointment which he held for the next seven years. He studied theology, Greek, Latin, and Hebrew, and took his M.A. in 1543. Normally he would then have been ordained, but having come under the influence of the Reformation and being unable to accept the doctrine of celibacy of the clergy, he refused ordination and thus came under suspicion from the university authorities of harbouring extreme Protestant views. Foxe was not expelled, but in July 1545, together with five of his colleagues, he resigned his fellowship.

He spent the next year as tutor to the family of William Lucy at Charlecote Park, Warwickshire. In 1547 Foxe married Agnes Randall of Coventry and moved to London, where he was appointed as tutor to the grandchildren of the imprisoned Duke of Norfolk (see Howard, Thomas, 3rd Duke). He formed a close friendship with the eleven-year-old son of the executed Earl of Surrey (see Howard, Henry), himself a future Duke of Norfolk (see Howard, Thomas, 4th Duke). Among his pupils was another member of the Howard family, Charles, later Lord Admiral of England (see Howard, Charles, 2nd Baron Howard of Effingham).

In 1550 Foxe was ordained as a deacon. In addition to his tutorial duties in the Norfolk household, he found time to write a number of tracts on behalf of the Reformation movement; he was also outspoken in pleading for the lives of Joan Bocher (q.v.) and other martyrs.

On the accession of Mary I (q.v.), Norfolk was released from the Tower and regained the guardianship of his grandchildren; shortly afterwards Foxe fled to the Continent, taking with him the manuscript of his partly-completed *Commentarii rerum in ecclesia gestarum* ('Commentaries on affairs within the Church'), an early draft of his later work; he published it in Strasbourg the following year. Moving from Strasbourg to Frankfurt, and then to Basle, he was in contact with the English Protestant exiles but acted as a moderating influence on the Calvinists under John Knox (q.v.). While in Basle, employed as a reader of the press by the printer Herbst, Foxe worked on manuscripts sent out to him from England, bringing his account of the English

Protestant martyrs up to 1556; he also addressed an appeal, *Christus triumphans* (1557), to the English nobility to restrain the Queen from persecuting the Protestants. When Mary died in 1558, Foxe remained abroad long enough to oversee the publication (in Latin) of his work before returning to England, penniless, in 1559. He was taken in by his former pupil and patron, now Duke of Norfolk, in whose household he resided for the next few years. He was ordained as an Anglican priest by Edmund Grindal (q.v.) in 1560.

Foxe's chief concern at this time was to bring up to date and to complete his account of the English martyrs from the fourteenth century, and although he preached frequently he did not accept any office in the Church; the bulk of his time was spent working on his text in close association with his printer John Day. The English translation first appeared in 1563 under the title *Actes and Monuments of These Latter and Perilous Days*; dedicated to the Queen, it won instant acclaim, and by royal command a copy was placed in every parish church. The work soon acquired the popular title *The Book of Martyrs*; a greatly improved second edition was published in 1570, and during Foxe's lifetime there would be a third (1576) and a fourth (1583) edition.

In 1563 Foxe ministered to the victims of the plague in London. The following year, after the death of the Duchess of Norfolk, he moved with his family to Waltham; two of his five children were baptized there. By 1570 he was back in London, living in Grub Street, which was to be his home for the rest of his life. He had little money, apart from a small pension from the Duke of Norfolk, and is said to have worn very shabby clothes. In 1563 Foxe had been appointed a canon of Salisbury Cathedral and had been

given the lease of the vicarage of
Shipton; but he refused to conform,
objecting to the use of the surplice and to
contributing towards the repair of the
cathedral, and in 1568 he was absent from
the Bishop's visitation and was declared
contumacious. In 1570 he preached his
famous sermon 'On Christ Crucified' at
Paul's Cross, and the following year
published his *Reformatio Legum*.

A kind-hearted, unworldly man who
cared little for personal wealth or success and who hated suffering and cruelty,
Foxe was nevertheless a man of great
courage. In 1569 he sent a courteous
letter to his patron, the Duke of Norfolk,
warning him against the proposed
marriage with Mary, Queen of Scots
(q.v.). When Norfolk was imprisoned in
the Tower, Foxe visited him there and
subsequently attended him at his
execution; the Duke left him an annuity
of £20. In 1575 Foxe courted danger by
pleading eloquently for the lives of the
Anabaptists in a personal letter to Queen
Elizabeth (q.v.), and in 1581 he took up
the cause of the condemned Jesuits. The
last years of his life were devoted largely
to the preparation of the third and fourth
editions of *The Book of Martyrs*. By 1586
his health was failing; he died on 18 April
1587 and was buried at St Giles's,
Cripplegate.

John Foxe's *Book of Martyrs* was, in its
day and for at least a hundred years, the
most widely read book next to the Bible;
in many of the poorer English Puritan
households it was probably the only
book apart from the Bible. Although
much criticized by modern historians as
carelessly edited and in parts (principally
the pre-Marian section) inaccurate, it
remains a valuable, unique, and informative source on the English Reformation. The book made a tremendous
impact on the age, stirring up and
fanning the already inflamed anti-

Catholic and anti-Spanish feelings of the
Protestants by its account of the
Inquisition.

Foxe's papers form part of the
Harleian MSS in the British Museum; a
few will be found among the Lansdowne
MSS.

W. Haller, *Foxe's Book of Martyrs and the Elect
Nation* (1963).
J. F. Mozley, *John Foxe and his Book* (1940).
E. G. Rupp, *Six Makers of the English Reformation,
1500–1700* (1957).
W. Winters, 'John Foxe, the martyrologist and his
family', *Transactions of the Royal Historical
Society*, v (1877), pp. 28–82.
N.B. The memoir of his father by Simeon Foxe,
printed in the 1641 edition of *Actes and
Monuments*, is considered to be of doubtful
authenticity. For a hostile view of Foxe, see S. R.
Maitland, *Essays on Subjects connected with the
Reformation* (1849).

*Portraits*: oil, by unknown artist, 1587: National
Portrait Gallery, London; oil, by unknown
artist: private collection, U.S.A.; engravings by
W. and M. van de Passe in *Herwologia*, 1620, and
by R. Glover in the 1641 edition of *Actes and
Monuments*.

**Foxe or Fox, Richard** (?1448–1528), bishop, statesman, and founder of Corpus Christi College, Oxford.

Richard Foxe was born at Ropesley, near Grantham, Lincolnshire, and is believed to have studied at Magdalen College, Oxford. In 1484 he was in the service of Henry Tudor, Earl of Richmond (later Henry VII, q.v.) in Paris, and following Henry's victory at Bosworth he became Secretary of State and Lord Privy Seal.

Foxe was an able diplomatist and negotiator; he acted as chief English envoy in the conclusion of the treaty of Étaples (1492) and in the *Intercursus Magnus* with the Netherlands in 1496. In 1497 he defended Norham Castle against a Scottish raid in support of the Pretender Perkin Warbeck (q.v.), and later the same year negotiated Warbeck's retirement from the Scottish court. He was also responsible for concluding the treaties which led to the marriages of Henry's daughter, Margaret Tudor (q.v.), to James IV of Scotland (q.v.), and of Prince Arthur (q.v.) to Catherine of Aragon (q.v.). During his lifetime he held a succession of bishoprics: Exeter (1487–92), Bath and Wells (1492–4), Durham (1494–1501), and Winchester (1501–28).

His prominent role in the shaping of Henry's financial policies led to unpopularity in some quarters. Foxe was one of the King's executors, and although very much in favour at the start of the reign of Henry VIII (q.v.), he was soon undermined by Thomas Wolsey (q.v.). Disagreeing with the involvement of England in foreign wars, he resigned the Privy Seal in 1516 and devoted the remainder of his days to the administration of his diocese at Winchester. In the last years of his life he was almost totally blind. He died at Winchester on 5 October 1528.

A great patron of scholarship, Foxe edited the Sarum *Processional* in 1508 and had it printed at Rouen; in 1517 he translated the *Rule of St Benedict for Women*. He was Chancellor of the University of Cambridge for the year 1500, and Master of Pembroke College there in 1507–9. As one of the executors of the Lady Margaret Beaufort (q.v.) he took a chief part in her endowment of St John's College at that university. He himself built and endowed schools at Taunton and Grantham, and made generous gifts to Magdalen College, Oxford, and Pembroke College, Cambridge. The peak of his achievement however was reached in 1515–16 with the foundation of Corpus Christi College, Oxford, where Foxe's insistence on provision for teaching Greek won him the praise of Erasmus of Rotterdam (q.v.).

P. S. and H. M. Allen, *Letters of Richard Foxe* (1928).

E. C. Batten, *The Register of Richard Fox* [with short life] (1889).

*Portraits*: oil, by Johannes Corvus, undated: Corpus Christi College, Oxford (also copy by W. Sonmans, 1670); oil, by unknown artist after Corvus, late sixteenth century: National Portrait Gallery, London; several other versions at Corpus Christi, Sudeley Castle, Gloucestershire, and elsewhere.

**Frith, John** (1505–1533), Protestant martyr.

John Frith was born in 1505, the son of an innkeeper of Westerham, Kent. He was educated at Eton and at King's College, Cambridge, where he was a pupil of Stephen Gardiner (q.v.).

It is not established whether he actually met William Tyndale (q.v.) at the university, but as a personable young man of wit and scholarship, Frith almost certainly frequented the White House tavern meetings at which the young

Cambridge theologians discussed the new doctrines. He took his degree in 1525 and was transferred the following year to Wolsey's college at Oxford. Shortly afterwards he was arrested and imprisoned for heresy, but was released by Thomas Wolsey (q.v.) and forbidden to move outside a radius of ten miles from Oxford. He disobeyed, and in 1528 fled to Antwerp, where he was in contact with Tyndale and possibly assisted him with some of his later translations.

Efforts were made to persuade Frith to return to England and renounce his heretical opinions, but he refused. He was, however, in England in 1530 and again in 1532, when he was arrested and imprisoned in the Tower. The charge against him is not known, but it may have been on account of his *Disputacion of Purgatorye* in which he attacked Thomas More (q.v.) and John Fisher (q.v.). While in prison, against Tyndale's advice, Frith wrote down his views on the sacrament, which were considered extremely heretical. He was brought before a commission of bishops presided over by Thomas Cranmer (q.v.) who, together with Gardiner, made every effort to save him, but Frith obstinately refused to recant. He was condemned and burned at Smithfield on 4 July 1533.

Frith was the first Protestant to formulate written views on the sacrament; years later his doctrine was adopted in the Book of Common Prayer.

M. L. Loane, *Pioneers of the Reformation in England* (1964).

**Frobisher, Sir Martin** (1539–1594), navigator and explorer.

Born in 1539 in the West Riding of Yorkshire, Frobisher was the son of Bernard Frobisher and his wife, daughter of Sir John York, Master of the Mint and a Merchant Adventurer. The family was one of the most important in Yorkshire, but was of Welsh origin.

Martin's father died in 1542, and the boy went to live with his grandfather in London. Sir John soon realized that he was no scholar, and Martin was sent to sea in 1553 as a member of the expedition to the coast of Guinea commanded by Thomas Wyndham. In the following year he went on a second expedition to Guinea led by John Lok; on this occasion he was left as a hostage in the hands of a native chief, but was later captured and imprisoned by the Portuguese. Eventually released, he was back in England by 1559, when he is known to have taken part in a voyage to the Barbary coast. In May that year he married Isabel, widow of Thomas Rickard of Snaith.

For the next fifteen years Frobisher was employed as a pirate. He was several times imprisoned, but never brought to trial; he may have been too useful to the government. In 1572 he was involved in a plan to rescue Gerald Fitzgerald, 15th Earl of Desmond, from imprisonment in London, but this was revealed beforehand to the Council. Frobisher was approached by an emissary of Philip II (q.v.) and may have toyed with the idea of collaborating with Spain, but there is no evidence that he actually did so. Two years later he had some connection with the adventurer Sir Thomas Stukeley (q.v.), but on this occasion appears to have been dissuaded from his plans by his wife, and thereafter to have turned his attention wholly to searching for the North-West Passage, a project which had intrigued him for some time. He had already discussed it at length with men like Sir Humphrey Gilbert (q.v.), Richard Hakluyt (q.v.) and John Dee (q.v.), and at last in 1575 he obtained the necessary licence and financial backing.

Frobisher left England on 7 June 1576 with a fleet of three ships, the *Gabriel*, the

183

*Michael*, and a small pinnace, and a crew of thirty-five. He reached the southernmost tip of Greenland, but then lost contact with both the *Michael*, which returned home, and the pinnace. Alone in the *Gabriel*, with only eighteen men, Frobisher pressed on courageously through fog and ice until on 11 August he entered what he believed to be the North-West Passage and named it 'Frobisher's Strait'; he was in fact at Baffin Island. Gifts were exchanged with the native Eskimos, one of whom Frobisher brought home to England, but five of the men whom he put ashore were never seen again.

Frobisher arrived back at Harwich on 2 October 1576. He was excited about the prospect of gold mines in the area explored, but London goldsmiths who examined a piece of black ore the men had brought home with them declared that it had no gold in it. An Italian assayer being more optimistic, a second voyage was immediately planned under the auspices of the newly-formed Cathay Company, of which Michael Lok (q.v.)

was Governor. Subscriptions flowed in from courtiers and City merchants eager to make profits out of the gold; Queen Elizabeth (q.v.) subscribed £500 and lent a ship, the *Aid*, of 200 tons.

This second expedition sailed on 27 May 1577 and returned on 23 September with a load of 200 tons of ore and three native Eskimos, who died soon after arrival. There was much wrangling about the value of the ore, and when a German expert forecast a good yield from it, people rushed to invest in a third expedition which it was planned would establish a colony in the Arctic region.

Frobisher sailed on his third attempt to find the North-West Passage on 31 May 1578. The voyage was to prove a great disappointment to all concerned, for although Frobisher formally annexed the territory and penetrated what is now Hudson Strait (he named it the 'Mistaken Strait' when he realized it was not the one he was seeking), he returned home in October without having found the Passage; in the meanwhile, exhaustive tests on the ore he had brought back on the previous expedition pronounced it to be of little worth. A number of people, including the Queen, suffered severe financial loss as a result; Lok, who had been the prime mover behind the three expeditions, was virtually ruined. Frobisher himself, also in financial difficulties, was no longer a popular hero: public opinion turned against him when the new load of ore was found to be even less valuable than the earlier consignment. Not surprisingly, after a brief period of service under Sir William Wynter (q.v.) in Ireland, Frobisher took up his old – and far more profitable – pursuit of piracy. By 1582 he had so far improved his position as to be able to subscribe £300 towards the expedition sponsored by the Earl of Leicester (see Dudley, Robert) to the East Indies and Cathay; he had himself intended to sail as joint commander with Edward Fenton, but subsequently withdrew from this commitment.

In September 1585 Frobisher sailed in the *Primrose* as second-in-command under Sir Francis Drake (q.v.) in the attack on the Spanish West Indies. In 1587 he was given command of the Channel Fleet which was to guard against a Spanish invasion. He fought a brilliant campaign against the Armada of 1588, commanding the *Triumph* in several engagements as the enemy proceeded up-Channel. Knighted for his services by the Lord Admiral, Frobisher was then given command of one of the four squadrons into which Howard (see Howard, Charles, 2nd Baron Howard of Effingham) then divided the English fleet.

After the defeat of the Armada Frobisher was an outspoken supporter of the theory advanced by Sir John Hawkins (q.v.) that England's best weapon against the Spain lay in cutting off her treasure supply from the Indies. He served as second-in-command to Hawkins in the expedition to the Azores of 1590, and subsequently made two other voyages to the islands in attempts to intercept the Spanish treasure fleet. It was during the expedition of 1592, headed by Frobisher and Sir John Burrows, that the valuable Spanish carrack *Madre de Dios*, worth about £150,000, was captured.

In September 1594 Frobisher was in command of a squadron sent to the aid of the French Huguenots in Brittany. He was wounded in the hip during bitter fighting against the Spanish at Crozon, near Brest, and died on 22 November, soon after being brought back to Plymouth. Three years previously, in 1591, he had married his second wife, Dorothy, daughter of Lord Wentworth.

Martin Frobisher failed to find the North-West Passage, but in searching for it he added considerably to the geographical knowledge of his age. Physically very strong, he was one of the steadiest and bravest of the Tudor seamen. He lacked the polish of men like Ralegh and Drake, but was respected by his men and popular at court.

R. Collinson, *The Three Voyages of Martin Frobisher* (Hakluyt Society, xxxvii, 1867).

R. Hakluyt, *The Principall Navigations* (1589; ed. by W. Raleigh, 12 vols, Glasgow, 1903–5).

F. Jones, *The Life of Sir Martin Frobisher* (1878).

W. McFee, *Sir Martin Frobisher* (1928).

G. M. Thomson, *The North-West Passage* (1975).

*Portraits*: oil, full length, by Cornelius Ketel, 1577: Bodleian Library, Oxford; engraving by C. van de Passe, 1620: National Maritime Museum, Greenwich.

# G

**Gardiner, Stephen** (?1483–1555), Bishop of Winchester and Lord Chancellor.

The youngest son of a clothmaker of Bury St Edmunds, Suffolk, Stephen Gardiner was born in about 1483 and from an early age was destined for a career in the Church. He was a brilliant Greek scholar at Trinity Hall, Cambridge, and later distinguished himself in canon and civil law, taking his doctorate in both in 1520–1; he was elected Master of his college in 1525, an office which he held throughout his public career, except when deprived of it for a short time during the reign of Edward VI (q.v.).

Through an early appointment as tutor to the son of the Duke of Norfolk (see Howard, Thomas, 3rd Duke), Gardiner attracted the attention of Thomas Wolsey (q.v.), and in 1525 he became the latter's secretary. When the matter of the King's divorce was raised, he found himself pressed into the royal service on account of his legal qualifications, and in 1529 he became secretary to Henry VIII (q.v.). For the next few years he was kept busy on the divorce and on diplomatic missions abroad. He enjoyed the King's confidence during this time, and as a reward for his services was given the wealthiest see in England, the bishopric of Winchester, in 1531.

At about this time the reformers in the House of Commons were launching a campaign against clerical privileges and the Church courts, and Gardiner, whose conservative religious views were totally opposed to this 'Supplication against the Ordinaries', defended the established ways vigorously in the House. In so doing he fell out with Henry's new adviser, Thomas Cromwell (q.v.), and gradually lost the confidence of the King himself, with the result that he was passed over for the vacant see of Canterbury in 1532, which was given instead to Thomas Cranmer (q.v.). Two years later Cranmer ousted Gardiner from his royal secretaryship.

The Bishop's animosity towards Cranmer and Cromwell now increased, both on personal grounds and on account of their reformist policies. He regained some favour at court in 1534 by signing a declaration repudiating Roman jurisdiction in England, following this a year later with *De Vera Obedientia*, a forceful attack on the papacy which was regarded as the best treatise written in support of the royal supremacy.

For the next few years Cromwell deliberately kept Gardiner out of the way on diplomatic business in France. In 1539, however, the Bishop returned to England to lead the reaction towards orthodoxy and to pilot the King towards the passing of the Act of the Six Articles, said to be mainly the work of Gardiner. On Cromwell's downfall in 1540, Gardiner was elected his successor as Chancellor of the University of Cambridge; he was greatly disturbed by the increasing Protestant influence he found there. He never quite regained the King's confidence or won the high office which he sought at the time, for although he was useful in many ways to the King, his persistent attacks on Cranmer, whom he tried repeatedly to destroy on charges of heresy, were not countenanced by Henry.

Gardiner was not a member of the Council of Regency after Henry's death in 1547, and so was powerless against the Protector, Somerset (see Seymour, Edward), and Cranmer and their policies. He was imprisoned first in the Fleet and later in the Tower, and in 1551, after Northumberland (see Dudley, John) had come to power, he was deprived of his bishopric; he remained in the Tower throughout the young King Edward's reign.

On the accession of Mary I (q.v.) Gardiner was thrust immediately into high office: he was restored to his bishopric and in August 1553 was appointed Lord Chancellor. He found his new position of power far from easy: the Queen was set on a restoration of full obedience to Rome, which he had earlier repudiated; he was loath to accept the Queen's proposed marriage to Philip II of Spain (q.v.), and was against the return of Cardinal Reginal Pole (q.v.) to England. For political and patriotic reasons he acquiesced in all these, but he was never wholly in tune with the Spanish-dominated court of Mary's reign. At the same time it was he who revived the old heresy laws and sent many Protestants to be burned at the stake; Gardiner's responsibility in the Marian persecution may have been exaggerated, however, since he certainly tried to save Cranmer and others from the fire by persuading them to recant.

The strain soon began to affect his health, and he died in office in November 1555.

Ambitious, often overbearing and arrogant in his manner, Stephen Gardiner never quite succeeded in obtaining the power and influence he sought. Nevertheless, he has probably been over-maligned by historians for his incon-

sistency and his ruthlessness in the persecution of Protestants. He was thwarted first by Cranmer, and then by Pole, from becoming Archbishop of Canterbury. As the leading exponent of conservatism in the English Reformation of his day, he lacked the ability to accept the force of change and in consequence his thirty years of public life made little lasting impact.

A collection of some 200 letters of Stephen Gardiner has been edited by J. A. Muller (Cambridge, 1933).

J. Gairdner, in *Typical English Churchmen*, ed. W. E. Collins (2 vols; 1902).
J. A. Muller, *Stephen Gardiner and the Tudor Reaction* (1926).
L. Baldwin Smith, *Tudor Prelates and Politics* (1953).

*Portraits:* oil on panel, by unknown artist: Trinity College, Cambridge; oil, by unknown artist: Bodleian Library, Oxford; oil, by unknown artist: Corpus Christi, Oxford; engraving, by P. Germst, after A. van der Werff, after contemporary portrait: location not known.

**Gascoigne, George** (?1525–1577), poet.

Born in about 1525, George Gascoigne was the elder son of Sir John Gascoigne of Cardington, Bedfordshire, and his wife Margaret, daughter of Sir Robert Scargill of Scargill, Yorkshire.

Little is known of his early life, but it is believed that he was brought up in Westmorland. He studied at Trinity College, Cambridge, but left the university without a degree. In 1555 he entered Gray's Inn, London, where he was called as an 'Ancient' of the Inn on 24 May 1557. He served as Member of Parliament for Bedford in 1557–9.

A disappointment in love interrupted his career, and he spent the next few years travelling through England and France. Gascoigne lived extravagantly and ran up debts to such an extent that he was disinherited by his father. It was during this period of his life that he began to write poetry; *The Complainte of Phylomene* was commenced while riding from Chelmsford to London in 1562, but not finished until fourteen years later. At Gray's Inn in 1566 Gascoigne produced *The Supposes*, an adaptation of Ariosto's comedy *I Suppositi* and the first prose comedy translated from Italian into English; his *Jocasta*, also performed that year, and derived from Euripides' *Phoenissae*, was the first Greek tragedy to be presented on the English stage.

At some date prior to October 1568 he married Elizabeth Breton, a wealthy widow and the mother of five children, including Nicholas Breton (q.v.), the future poet, and took up residence with her at a house in Walthamstow that had been part of her first husband's estate. In October 1568 a case was brought by the Lord Mayor of London on behalf of the Breton children to inquire into the misuse of their property by Gascoigne and their mother. Evidently Gascoigne's

extravagant and disorderly mode of life continued, for on his election as M.P. for Midhurst, a band of creditors presented a petition against his taking his seat, and he fled the country.

He spent the next three years in military service in the Low Countries, initially as a captain under William of Orange (q.v.) and later with the English force under Sir Humphrey Gilbert (q.v.). After distinguishing himself at the siege of Middelburg, he was captured at Leyden and spent four months as a prisoner-of-war before being repatriated. Gascoigne wrote two accounts of his experiences, *The Fruites of Warre, written uppon this Theame Dulce Bellum inexpertis* and *Gascoigne's Voyage into Hollande, An. 1572.*

On his return to England, Gascoigne discovered that an anonymous volume of his work, *A Hundreth sundrie Flowres*, had been published without his authority in 1573; it contained *Supposes, Jocasta,* the *Adventures of Master F.J.* (translated from Bandello, one of the earliest known Italian tales in English prose), the semi-autobiographical *Delectable History of Dan Bartholomew of Bathe,* and several shorter poems, which caused something of an outcry as they were suspected of attacking well-known personalities under fictitious names. He issued a revised edition in 1575, under the title *The Posies of George Gascoigne,* which also contained 'Certayne Notes of Instruction concerning the making of Verse', the first English critical essay.

Gascoigne now devoted himself entirely to literary work. He was commissioned to write verses for the entertainment of Queen Elizabeth (q.v.) at Kenilworth in the summer of 1575; the same year he published his only original play, a 'tragicall comedie' on the Prodigal Son theme, entitled *The Glasse of Government.* 1576 was even more productive: the earlier *Complainte of Phylomene* was completed, and also a satire in blank verse, *The Steele Glas* (on which his young friend Walter Ralegh (q.v.) wrote some commendatory stanzas), and two prose works, *The Droome of Doomesday*, translated from the Italian of Lottario Conti, and *A delicate Diet for daintie-mouthde Droonkardes*. As a result of a visit to Sir Humphrey Gilbert in April that year, the poet was inspired to prepare for publication the latter's *Discourse* on the discovery of a North-West Passage.

Gascoigne earned much praise for his work from his contemporaries, and among his close friends were the leading poets of the day, Edmund Spenser (q.v.), George Whetstone, and George Turberville. But in spite of literary success, he was still leading a somewhat disorderly life and was always short of money. It may have been for this reason that he entered the royal service in the autumn of 1576 and went to Holland as an agent of the government. He was present at the sacking of Antwerp by the Spaniards that November and wrote a prose tract on the subject, *The Spoyle of Antwerp*.

By mid-1577 his health was beginning to fail, and on 7 October that year, while visiting his friend George Whetstone at Barnack, near Stamford, Lincolnshire, he was taken ill and died. He left one son, William. Gascoigne's *Tales of Hemetes* was published posthumously, and a collection of moral elegies, *The Grief of Joye*, dedicated to the Queen, of which the manuscript is at the British Museum, not until the nineteenth century.

George Gascoigne was a notable pioneer in several branches of literature and one of the most talented writers of the age. His use of the verse narrative form was followed by William Shakespeare (q.v.) in *Venus and Adonis* and *Lucrece*, and the dramatist also drew on Gascoigne's *Supposes* as a sub-plot for *The Taming of the Shrew*.

The works of George Gascoigne have been edited, with a memoir, by W. C. Hazlitt, in the Roxburghe Library edition, (2 vols; 1868–9), and by Professor J. W. Cunliffe, in Cambridge English Classics (2 vols; 1907–8).

C. T. Prouty, *George Gascoigne, Elizabethan courtier, soldier, and poet* (New York, 1942).

G. Whetstone, *Remembraunce of the wel imployed and godly end of George Gascoigne, Esquire* (1577).

*Portrait*: woodcut, by unknown artist: *The Steele Glas*, 1576.

**Gibbons, Orlando** (1583–1625), composer, see *Lives of the Stuart Age*.

**Gilbert, Sir Humphrey** (?1539–1583), soldier, navigator, colonizer, and explorer.

Humphrey Gilbert came from a West Country seafaring family and is believed to have been born in 1539, the second of three sons of Otho Gilbert of Greenway, on the river Dart, and his wife, Katherine, daughter of Sir Philip Champernowne. After the death of his father in 1547, Katherine Gilbert married Walter Ralegh of Fardell; through this marriage Humphrey became half-brother to Sir Walter Ralegh (q.v.).

Brought up as a Protestant, he first received a classical education at Eton, and then went to Oxford. He subsequently enrolled in the Inns of Chancery, London, and was for a short time a page in the household of the Princess Elizabeth (see Elizabeth I) at Hatfield. He then entered military service under Ambrose Dudley, Earl of Warwick, being wounded at the siege of Le Havre in France in June 1563. In 1566 he served in Ireland under the Lord Deputy, Sir Henry Sidney (q.v.), in his campaign to put down the rebellious Shane O'Neill (q.v.).

Like others before him, Gilbert was convinced of the existence of the North-West Passage, which would provide a short cut to the East and so enable England to seize the lucrative trade in spices and silks. While in Ireland he wrote the influential *Discourse of a Discoverie for a New Passage to Cathaia,* addressed to the Queen, and when Sidney sent him to London with dispatches to the Council in November 1566, he seized the opportunity to present his treatise at court. Failing to interest Elizabeth in this project, he was ordered back to Ireland but managed to secure her permission for an enterprise there, in which he and a number of his West Country relations were involved – the plantation (colonization) of Ulster. This enterprise was eventually transferred to Munster, where in the next three years Gilbert rose to be a Colonel and pursued a ruthless and vigorous policy of suppression against James Fitzgerald (Fitzmaurice). He was knighted for his services in 1570, and two years later wrote a *Discourse on Ireland,* setting out the benefits to be derived from colonization by England.

On his return from Ireland later that year, Gilbert married a suitable heiress, Anne Ager of Ottenden, Kent, by whom he was to have six sons and one daughter. In 1571 he was returned, with Sir John Hawkins (q.v.), as Member of Parliament for Plymouth; he soon became an unpopular figure in the House of Commons, because of his defence of the royal prerogative in the matter of licences. This provoked a quarrel with Peter Wentworth (q.v.), in which the latter called Gilbert 'a flatterer, a liar and a naughtie man'; but the Queen rewarded him with an appointment as Surveyor of Artillery.

In 1572 Gilbert was given command of 1,500 English volunteers sent to the Netherlands to assist the Dutch revolt against the Spanish. He made valiant but unsuccessful attempts to take Sluys and Goes, and returned to England having achieved virtually nothing.

From now on Gilbert became increasingly involved in projects for the colonization of North America. He influenced Martin Frobisher (q.v.) to look for the North-West Passage; he revised and polished his earlier *Discourse,* which his friend, the poet George Gascoigne (q.v.), who had served with him in the Netherlands, published in 1576; the following year, he put forward schemes for seizing the fishing fleets of Spain, France, and Portugal in Newfoundland, intercepting the Spanish silver fleet, and taking Santo Domingo and Cuba for the English crown. At last, in June 1578, the Queen granted him letters patent, valid for six years, to 'inhabit and possess at his choice all remote and heathen lands' not in the actual possession of any Christian prince. That year, mortgaging virtually all his own resources and with financial help from a number of others, including his half-brother, Walter Ralegh, Gilbert managed to mount an expedition of eleven ships, one of which, the *Falcon,* was supplied by the Queen. There were difficulties from the outset: delays in the vessels from London reaching Devon; winds which drove them back into port after their initial sailing; the desertion of Henry Knollys, Gilbert's second-in-command, with four ships. When finally they set out on 19 November, the fleet numbered only seven vessels, with Gilbert in command of the flagship *Anne Ager.* Although their exact destination is not known, they probably intended to cross the Atlantic via the West Indies and then to proceed up the coast of North

America. It was to be a voyage of reconnaissance prior to one of colonization; they were heavily armed against possible attack from the Spaniards. Of the seven ships only Ralegh, aboard the *Falcon*, got as far as the Cape Verde Islands, the others having long since dispersed and returned home or gone over to piracy as a result of bad weather conditions, lack of supplies, and poor discipline. Gilbert himself returned to port on 26 February.

After helping to suppress his old enemy, Fitzmaurice, in Munster in the summer of 1579, Gilbert's thoughts again turned to the colonization of North America. A small reconnaissance expedition was dispatched in 1580, and for the next three years, his patent having only a few years to run, Gilbert attempted, by every means he could devise, to raise money for a new expedition; he sold to investors large tracts of land not yet discovered, and some Catholics were persuaded to part with money on the promise of the foundation of a Catholic state in which they might continue both to serve the Queen and practise their own religion; in return for financial help the merchants of Southampton were promised a monopoly of trade with the new colony. Even so, the expedition was delayed for several months for lack of funds.

In February 1583 the Queen suddenly forbade both Gilbert and Ralegh to accompany the expedition. Then she relented, so far as Gilbert alone was concerned, and on 11 June a fleet of five small ships and about 260 men sailed from Plymouth. Gilbert was in command of the *Delight* (120 tons); the other vessels were the *Bark Ralegh* (200 tons), the *Golden Hind* (40 tons), the *Swallow* (40 tons) and the *Squirrel* (about 10 tons). Of these, the *Bark Ralegh* returned home two days later, for lack of supplies, and

the *Swallow* and the *Squirrel* became separated in fog, to be reunited with the others only on arrival off Newfoundland on 3 August. There Gilbert went ashore and took possession of St John's in the name of the Queen, together with '200 leagues in every way'. Many of the crew succumbed to sickness, however, and a number of them died; others deserted and took to piracy. Gilbert decided that he would establish a colony at St John's, but first he wanted to explore the coastline. He sent all the sick men back to England in the *Swallow* and with the remaining three vessels set sail southwards. When the *Delight* ran aground on a shoal on 29 August and went down with a hundred men, due to Gilbert's obstinate refusal to take advice from his navigator, discontent verging on mutiny broke out among the crew. Gilbert was forced to agree to set course for home, determining to return to Newfoundland the following spring. In spite of tempestuous weather conditions, he refused to transfer from the *Squirrel* to the larger *Golden Hind*, and

191

on 9 September, when a sudden storm blew up after they had passed the Azores, Gilbert was last seen on the deck of the *Squirrel*, a book in his hand; just before she was engulfed by the waves, he was heard to shout across to the *Golden Hind*, 'We are as near to Heaven by sea as by land.'

Sir Humphrey Gilbert was an idealist, a man of intellect and imagination, ahead of his contemporaries in his ideas on colonial expansion. Not only was he responsible for the revival of interest in a North-West Passage; he was the first Englishman to devise ambitious projects of overseas colonization. He succeeded in annexing Newfoundland, but failed to establish a colony in North America, due largely to the very great difficulties he encountered, but also in part to his own inadequate leadership, his obstinacy and temperament, which cost him the support of his men. Among Gilbert's other interests was a project for the establishment of an academy in London for the all-round training of young gentlemen for the service of the state; his treatise on this subject, *Queen Elizabethes Achademy . . . for education of Her Majesty's Wardes*, has been published by the Early English Text Society in *Early English Treatises and Poems on Education, Precedence and Manners in Olden Time*, edited by F. J. Furnivall and others (London, 1869). The *Discourse of a Discoverie for a New Passage to Cathaia*, originally published in 1576, has been reprinted in Hakluyt's *Principall Navigations* (see Hakluyt, Richard).

M. Foss, 'Sir Humphrey Gilbert', in *Tudor Portraits* (1973).

W. G. Gosling, *The Life of Sir Humphrey Gilbert, England's First Empire Builder* (1911).

E. Hayes,* *A Report of the Voyage . . . by Sir Humphrey Gilbert*, printed in Hakluyt, *op. cit.*, and in E. J. Payne, *Voyages of the Elizabethan Seamen to America* (2 vols; London, 1880; Oxford, 1893–1900).

D. B. Quinn, *The Voyages and Colonizing Enterprises of Sir Humphrey Gilbert* (2 vols; 1940).

A. L. Rowse, *The Elizabethans and America* (1959).

*Hayes was owner and captain of the *Golden Hind*.

*Portraits:* oil, by unknown artist: Commander W. R. Gilbert, Compton Castle, Devon; engraving, by unknown engraver, after C. van de Passe: Holland's *Herwologia*, 1620.

**Gilbert, William** (1540–1603), physician and scientist.

Born at Colchester, Essex, on 24 May 1540, William Gilbert was educated at St John's College, Cambridge, where he became a fellow in 1561, M.A. in 1564, and M.D. and Senior Fellow in 1569. Although medicine was his chosen profession, he became deeply interested in scientific research at an early date, making his first meteorological observations while still at Cambridge.

After leaving the university Gilbert travelled on the Continent for a time, settling in about 1573 in London, in a house at St Peter's Hill, near Upper Thames Street, where he soon acquired a large practice. He joined the Royal College of Physicians and was elected as its President in 1599. Appointed as personal physician to Elizabeth I (q.v.) in 1601, Gilbert attended the Queen during her last illness. He was afterwards appointed as physician to James I (see James VI of Scotland), but died a few months later, at Colchester, on 10 December 1603.

Parallel with his medical career, Gilbert devoted much of his life to scientific investigation. He was in fact not only the most eminent physician in London, but also the most distinguished man of science of the age, and recognized as such by the great European intellectuals with whom he corresponded. A pioneer of research into magnetism, he dismissed all earlier work on the subject as speculation and was especially critical of the Aristotelian theories. Gilbert was the first to use the terms 'electricity', 'electric attraction', 'electric force', and 'magnetic pole' in English and thus laid the foundations for all future electrical studies. His great work, *De Magnete*, published in 1600, was based on more than 300 experiments on magnetic bodies and electrical attractions.

Gilbert's other work, published posthumously in 1651, was *De Mundo*, edited from two manuscripts containing his views on the structure of the universe. In this he agreed with Nicolaus Copernicus (q.v.) that the earth rotated on its axis and put forward his conclusion that the planets were held in their orbits by a form of magnetism.

The instruments and papers left by Dr William Gilbert to the Royal College of Physicians perished in the Great Fire of London in 1666. His other surviving works have been edited by S. P. Thompson (1902).

A. L. Rowse, *The Cultural Achievement* (vol. ii of *The Elizabethan Renaissance*, 1972), chapter vii, 'Science and Society', pp. 233–8.
Silvanus P. Thompson, *Gilbert of Colchester* (1891).

*Portrait*: engraving, by Clamp, 1796, of portrait by unknown artist (now destroyed but formerly in Bodleian Library, Oxford), 1591: Royal College of Physicians, London.

## Gower, George (d. 1596), Serjeant-Painter to Queen Elizabeth (q.v.).

A gentleman of Yorkshire origins who, by his own admission, spent an unprofitable youth and took up painting only in middle life, George Gower had become a successful and fashionable portrait painter by the early 1570s. He lived in London in the parish of St Clement Danes.

In 1581 Gower succeeded William Herne as Serjeant-Painter to the Queen. He and Nicholas Hilliard (q.v.) together tried to obtain a monopoly for the production of royal portraits in 1584. In 1593 he became painter to the Navy.

George Gower died in August 1596. His three certain works are the portraits of Sir Thomas Kytson and his wife Elizabeth, both dated 1573, now in the Tate Gallery, and a self-portrait, 1579. Attributed portraits include those of several other members of the Kytson family of Hengrave, and about twenty of the aristocracy, all painted between the years 1570 and 1586, as well as a portrait of Queen Elizabeth of *c*. 1588, now in the Duke of Bedford Collection at Woburn. Gower's fine portraiture is characterized by its precision of outline and, in the words of Dr Roy Strong, 'the outturned, bulbous staring eyes which serve almost as a signature'.

J. W. Goodison, 'George Gower, Serjeant-Painter to Queen Elizabeth', *Burlington Magazine*, xc (1948), pp. 261–5.
Roy Strong, *The English Icon* (1969), pp. 167–84.

*Self-portrait*: oil on panel, 1579: The Earl Fitzwilliam Collection.

## Gowrie, 1st Earl of (?1541–1584), see Ruthven, William.

## Grafton, Richard (*c*. 1513–*c*. 1573), printer and chronicler.

Little is known of Richard Grafton's parentage or early life. He was a grocer by trade and a member of the Grocers' Company of London. A zealous Protestant, in 1537 he joined with a fellow merchant, Edward Whitchurch, in arranging for the printing in Antwerp of the 'Matthew Bible', so called as the translation was attributed to 'Thomas Matthew', probably a pseudonym of John Rogers (q.v.), who had worked with William Tyndale (q.v.); the text was drawn from the work of Tyndale and Miles Coverdale (q.v.).

In May 1538 Grafton and Whitchurch

went to Paris, where in November that year they saw through the press a revised version of Coverdale's English Bible, which they dedicated to Thomas Cromwell (q.v.). A licence was granted by Henry VIII (q.v.) for the preparation of a further revision by Coverdale, based on 'Matthew's Bible', and with the assistance of Edmund Bonner (q.v.), later Bishop of London but at that time ambassador in Paris, and Coverdale, Grafton began work on the preparation of the edition later to be known as the 'Great Bible', or 'Cromwell's Bible'. When the French government stopped the printing on a charge of heresy, Grafton fled to England with as many of the sheets as he could salvage, and the Bible was eventually published there in 1539. It ran into seven editions, the second of which (1540) contained a prologue by Thomas Cranmer (q.v.) and became known as 'Cranmer's Bible'; all parish churches were required to possess a copy.

In London Grafton began a new career by printing The Chronicle of John Hardynge; he himself brought the work up to date from the beginning of the reign of Edward IV (see Lives Before the Tudors) to the year of publication, 1543. In 1547 he published an edition of Hall's Chronicle, continuing it up to the end of the reign of Henry VIII. In April that year he was appointed as the King's official printer, in which capacity he was responsible for the first Book of Common Prayer (1549), the Actes of Parliament (1552–3), and a number of other works printed at his office within the precincts of Christ's Hospital, of which he was said by the diarist Henry Machyn (q.v.) to be 'chief master'.

Because he printed the proclamation on the accession of the Lady Jane Grey (q.v.), Grafton was deprived of office by Queen Mary I (q.v.). After a brief term of imprisonment, he made his peace with the authorities but appears to have retired from the printing business at about this time. He represented London in Parliament in 1553–5 and 1556–7 and Coventry in 1562–3, and was Warden of the Grocers' Company in 1555 and 1556; among other duties he acted as Master of Bridewell Hospital and was one of the overseers for the repair of St Paul's Cathedral.

In 1562 Grafton published the first of three original works, An Abridgement of the Chronicles of England, which ran into five editions before 1572. In 1565 he issued his Manuell of the Chronicles of England, in the preface of which he stated that he had been 'impudently plagiarized' by the rival chronicler, John Stow (q.v.). This was followed in 1568 by A Chronicle at large and meere History of the Affayres of England . . . to the first yeere . . . of Queen Elizabeth, in two volumes. The dispute with Stow continued, Stow attacking Grafton for garbling the work of Hall and Hardynge, and Grafton making valiant attempts at vindication; of the two historians, there is little doubt that Richard Grafton, for all his efforts, lacked Stow's dedication to original research. He is believed to have died in about 1572.

J. A. Kingdon, Richard Grafton, Citizen and Grocer of London (1901).

**Gray, Patrick** (d. 1612), 6th Baron Gray, usually known as the Master of Gray.

Gray was the eldest son of Patrick Gray, 5th Lord Gray, by his wife Barbara, fourth daughter of William Ruthven (q.v.), 4th Baron Ruthven and 1st Earl of Gowrie. The date of his birth is not known.

Educated at St Andrews, Gray married soon after leaving the university

Elizabeth, the second daughter of Lord Glamis, but within a year had separated from his wife and settled in France, where he became an intimate of the circle of Mary, Queen of Scots (q.v.) and the Guise family. He is believed to have returned to Scotland briefly either with the Seigneur d'Aubigny (later 1st Duke of Lennox, see Stuart, Esmé) in 1579, or after the fall of the Earl of Morton (see Douglas, James) in 1581, but to have gone back to France rather than subscribe to the Kirk's articles denouncing Catholicism.

After the escape of James VI (q.v.) from the Ruthven raiders in June 1583, Gray appeared again at the Scottish court, where he obtained the confidence of the Earl of Arran (see Stewart, James, Earl of Arran); in November that year he was sent to France to bring Lennox's son to Scotland. Commissioned by Mary to represent her interests, Gray dis-honourably betrayed her to James in an attempt to curry favour with the King; being a handsome, witty, and accomplished young man, he did not find this difficult.

In October 1584 James sent him to England to propose a defensive league between the two countries and to negotiate for the return of the banished Scottish lords. Gray was not slow to seize the opportunity of double dealing, both in betraying Mary's secrets to Elizabeth I (q.v.) and in suggesting to the English Queen that the banished lords might be returned to Scotland for the purpose of overthrowing Arran. He then went back to Scotland to put the conspiracy into operation, while giving the impression to James that his true mission had been successful. The King appointed him as Master of the Wardrobe in 1585, and in the same year Gray married his second wife, the Lady Mary Stewart, elder daughter of Robert Stewart, Earl of

Orkney, by whom he was to have two sons and six daughters.

In spite of a general awareness of the plot against Arran, especially after the murder of Francis Russell, 2nd Earl of Bedford, and the discovery of Arran's counter-plot for the murder of Gray, the latter continued to be trusted by the King. In November 1586 he was commissioned, together with Sir Robert Melville, to go to London to protest about the death sentence passed on Mary, Queen of Scots. After the Queen's execution it was widely believed in Scotland that Gray had advocated her death to Elizabeth; nevertheless, he still retained James's favour, although he no longer had much influence in political matters.

On his return to Scotland in the spring of 1587, Gray was charged with having conspired with Spain and the Pope 'to the injury of the Protestant religion in Scotland', with having plotted to assassinate John Maitland (q.v.; later 1st Baron Maitland of Thirlestane), who was then Vice-Chancellor, with having tried to prevent the King's marriage to Anne of Denmark (see *Lives of the Stuart Age*), and with having consented to Mary's death in return for rewards in England. After making a voluntary confession of sedition, he was declared a traitor; his life was spared by the King on condition that he left the country within a month. At the beginning of June he went to Paris, and then on to Italy.

In May 1589 Gray was permitted to return to Scotland; six months later he was restored to the office of Master of the Wardrobe and took his seat on the Privy Council. His return to favour did not prevent him from joining with the 'Wizard' Earl of Bothwell (see Hepburn, Francis Stewart) in his attempt on the King's person at Falkland in 1592; in fact during the next few years he continued to act in a lawless manner and on several occasions was summoned to answer for his behaviour.

The Master of Gray succeeded his father in 1609 and died three years later, in 1612.

The *Letters and Papers relating to Patrick, Master of Gray* have been published by the Bannatyne Club (Edinburgh, 1835).

See the titles listed under Mary, Queen of Scots, and James VI.

**Greene, Robert** (1558–1592), poet, pamphleteer, and playwright.

Robert Greene was born in Norwich, probably in July 1558. His parents were not rich, but they gave him a good schooling, and in November 1575 Greene went to St John's College, Cambridge, as a 'sizar', a student who waited at table in return for his tuition. He graduated from St John's in 1578 and afterwards travelled in Spain and Italy with friends he had made at the university. Unable to keep up with the spendthrift habits of his more wealthy companions, the impoverished student drifted into a Bohemian and (by his own admission) villainous mode of life. Nevertheless, he returned to Cambridge and took his M.A. at Clare Hall in 1583; five years later he was granted an M.A. at Oxford.

He had no taste for the academic life, but was drawn rather to the pleasures of the town and the company of idle wits. After an unsatisfactory period in which he drifted aimlessly between Cambridge and Norwich, failing to settle in either place in spite of having married a gentleman's daughter from Lincolnshire, who bore him a child, and having deceived his trusting parents over money, in about 1585 Greene abandoned his family and went to seek his fortune as a hack writer in London.

Within three years he achieved success. Initially a writer of romantic stories (he called them 'Love Pamphlets'), in which he was much influenced by the *Euphues* of John Lyly (q.v.), Greene was clever enough to turn his versatile pen to whatever was in public demand. Among his successful romances was *Menaphon*, first published in 1589 and reprinted as *Greene's Arcadia* in 1599; his pastoral, *Pandosto* (1588), in which the prose passages were interspersed with some of his finest lyrics, was to provide William Shakespeare (q.v.) with the plot for *The Winter's Tale*. Greene also experimented in romantic comedy, and one of his early plays, *The Comicall Historie of Alphonsus King of Aragon*, probably written in 1588, was in imitation of his friend and fellow dramatist, Christopher Marlowe (q.v.). He is believed to have collaborated in the original *Henry VI* plays, which were later re-written by Shakespeare, and there is little doubt that Greene's use of fairy characters in *The Scottish Historie of James the Fourth, slaine at Flodden*, written in about 1590, was copied by Shakespeare in *A Midsummer Night's Dream*. None of his dramatic work was published during his lifetime; his most successful comedy, *The Honorable Historie of Friar Bacon and Friar Bungay*, in prose and verse, was written in about 1591 and first acted in 1594.

While the romances, poems, and plays he wrote secured him rich patrons, including the Earl of Arundel and the Earl of Essex (see Devereux, Robert), Greene led such a dissolute life that all the money he obtained was invariably squandered. His regular drinking companions were the writers Thomas Nashe (q.v.) and Thomas Lodge (q.v.), and the dramatists Thomas Kyd (q.v.) and Christopher Marlowe.

In about 1590 Greene started to write

some serious stories, all on the prodigal son theme and drawing on his own experiences. *Greene's Mourning Garment* and *Never Too Late* both appeared in 1590, *Farewell to Folly* in 1591, and *A Quip for an Upstart Courtier* in 1592. At about the same time he began a series of pamphlets aimed at exposing the seamier side of London life, in which he made use of his own intimate knowledge of the underworld, the City brothels and taverns, the pickpockets and rogues who lived by cheating at cards and dice; *A Notable Discovery of Coosnage* was published in 1591, and four tracts on 'Conny-catching' the following year.

Continual riotous living made Greene not only notorious, but also the object of disapproval in many quarters. He had seduced the sister of a well-known City rogue and had an illegitimate son by her; he moved from lodging to lodging and left debts behind him everywhere; inevitably his health was affected. In 1592, seized with repentance for his evil ways, he began an autobiographical work, *A Groatsworth of Witte, bought with a Million of Repentance*, which was to be published posthumously later that year. In this book he attacked Shakespeare as an 'upstart crow', presumably because the young actor-playwright had copied and, in some cases, re-written Greene's own work.

On 3 September 1592, after what his enemy Gabriel Harvey later described as a 'fatal banquet of pickle herring', washed down with a large quantity of Rhenish wine, Greene died in the most miserable and squalid conditions, deserted by all his literary friends and attended only by his mistress and his landlady. He was buried in the New Churchyard, near Bedlam.

Attacked the same year by Harvey in his *Foure Letters* as 'the Ape of Euphues', but defended by his friend Nashe in *Strange Newes* (1593), Robert Greene was in his day one of the most popular prose writers. He was the first to depict ordinary life in English fiction, and historians have since relied on his work for details of the lower end of society in the late sixteenth century. Of striking appearance, with a long, pointed red beard, Greene had a ready wit, marred by a weakness for the bottle and a liking for the company of rogues. He produced thirty-eight publications, among which are five plays. His *Complete Works* were edited by A. B. Grosart in 1881–6. A recent bibliographical catalogue of early editions is A. F. Allison's *Robert Greene, 1558–1592* (1976).

M. Foss, 'Robert Greene', in *Tudor Portraits* (1973). J. C. Jordan, *Robert Greene* (1915).

**Gregory XIII** (1502–1585), Pope from 1572 to 1585.

Born on 7 January 1502 at Bologna, his real name was Ugo Buoncompagni. He studied jurisprudence at the university of Bologna, graduating as a doctor of civil and canon law. From 1531 to 1539 he lectured at the same university on jurisprudence, and then resigned his chair and went to Rome, where his skill as a jurist and diplomat soon won him a succession of offices in the Curia under Paul III and Pius IV.

In 1558 he was ordained and made Bishop of Viesti. Under Pius IV he was sent to the Council of Trent, where he remained until 1563. In 1565 he was made a cardinal and was also appointed as the Pope's emissary to Spain, but in the following January, after the election of Pope Pius V, Buoncompagni was given the office of Secretary of Papal Briefs and returned to Rome. When Pius V died on 1 May 1572, the Cardinal was elected to succeed him. He took office as Gregory XIII on 14 May.

Already in his seventy-first year, the new Pope was nevertheless a fit and energetic man. He lost no time in implementing the decrees of the Council of Trent for chuch reform and initiating a vigorous campaign to stem the tide of Protestantism. In the belief that the best way of achieving a restoration of Catholicism in those countries which, like England, had abandoned the old faith, was to send missionaries to go among the people, he founded a number of seminaries and colleges where the Jesuits could train priests for this task. He also set up committees to examine abuses in the ecclesiastical profession and to establish a list of prohibited books, the *Index Librorum Prohibitorum*. From the outset he demonstrated his zeal for the extirpation of heresy; in August 1572, on hearing the news of the St Bartholomew's Day Massacre in France, he ordered a *Te Deum* to be sung in Rome in celebration and a commemorative medal to be struck.

Gregory backed the policy of Philip II of Spain (q.v.) in the Netherlands and encouraged the Irish rebels to resist the anti-Catholic moves of Elizabeth I (q.v.) in Ireland. He gave his enthusiastic support to the Jesuit campaign in England led by Edmund Campion (q.v.) and Robert Parsons (q.v.); to this end he endowed among others the English College in Rome and the Gregorian University, both of which became centres of Jesuit education and training. In 1580 he issued a revised edition of canon law, on which he had worked as a cardinal.

A worldly man, fond of display, Gregory is said to have led a not entirely blameless youth, having fathered a son by an unmarried woman. His great building programme, which included the splendid Quirinal Palace in Rome, coupled with his political and anti-Protestant policies, virtually drained the papal treasury. When he tried to refill the coffers by confiscating the estates of the aristocracy, much hatred was engendered and a group of *banditti* (young men of noble families, who were protected both by the barons and by the peasantry) began to wage a campaign of terror against the papal government; they were not suppressed until the time of Gregory's successor, Pope Sixtus V.

Gregory is chiefly remembered for his revision of the calendar. Helped by the Neapolitan astronomer and physician, Luigi Lilio Ghiraldi, and a German Jesuit mathematician, Christopher Clavius, he corrected the errors of the Julian calendar (created by Julius Caesar in 46 B.C.); within a few years the new Gregorian calendar was adopted by most Catholic countries, but not by England until 1752.

In January 1584 the Pope issued a definitive edition of Roman martyrology, *Martyrologium Romanum Gregorii XIII jussu editum*, ordering all previous editions to be suppressed.

Gregory XIII died in Rome on 10 April 1585. He had succeeded in partially restoring the Catholic religion in Europe, but only to a small extent in England. Undoubtedly his policies, and in particular his reaction to the St Bartholomew's Day Massacre, hardened Elizabeth in her anti-Catholic attitude. The only defence of Gregory in this can be that he rejoiced not at the actual bloodshed, but at the successful suppression of a religious rebellion.

See the entry in the *Catholic Encyclopedia*, and also L. von Pastor, *History of the Popes*, vol. 20 (1930).

*Portraits*: monument, by Pier Paolo Olivieri, sixteenth century: Sta Maria in Arcoeli, Rome; engraving, by F. Hulsius: location not known.

**Grenville, Sir Richard** (1542–1591), soldier and naval commander.

Born on or about 15 June 1542, he was the son of Roger Grenville, Marshal of Calais; the Grenvilles were an old-established West Country family, with estates in Cornwall and Devon. Young Richard's father died on 19 July 1545, when his ship, the *Mary Rose,* capsized in Portsmouth harbour.

On the death of his grandfather in March 1550, Grenville, now heir to the family estates, became a ward of Sir Hugh Paulet, but since the latter was frequently abroad he had little influence on the boy, who grew up somewhat wilful and wayward. There is no record of his schooling; he probably had a private tutor. The proximity of Plymouth and Bideford, and the seafaring traditions of his family, must have influenced him as a youth. In 1559, at the age of seventeen, he entered the Inner Temple as a student, and for the next few years lived in London. There, in November 1562, he became involved in a street affray near the Strand in which a certain Robert Bannester was killed by Grenville; as a minor he received a pardon not long afterwards and, in January 1563, was probably the same Richard Grenville who was returned as Member of Parliament for Dunheved (Launceston).

At the end of June that year Grenville obtained a licence to enter on his estates, and not long afterwards he married Mary St Leger, daughter of Sir John St Leger of Annery, near Bideford. A son and heir, Bernard, was born in 1567, and later another son, John, who was to show some of the same spirit of adventure as his father; there were also four daughters of the marriage.

Family responsibilities did not keep Grenville at home, although he was not yet to embark on his naval career. In 1566 he fought in Hungary against the Turks. In 1568-9 he took his wife and children

to Ireland, with the intention, with Sir Warham St Leger, of settling lands in Munster, but the enterprise failed on account of the Fitzmaurice rebellion, and after helping to suppress the uprising, Grenville returned to England. In 1571 he represented Cornwall in Parliament, and the following year was returned as M.P. for Launceston; he served on several committees during both sessions. His most important undertaking at this time was a project for a voyage of discovery in the South Seas, hoping to find Terra Australis, a continent conjectured to occupy the Southern Pacific, and a North-West Passage which would open up a direct route between England and Cathay.

Grenville's plan was to make the first English voyage through the Straits of Magellan and so break the monopoly hitherto enjoyed by the Spaniards; approved by the Queen in 1574, it was subsequently cancelled because of a temporary policy of appeasement towards Spain. Three years later, in 1577, Francis Drake (q.v.) was to use

Grenville's plans as the basis for his voyage of circumnavigation. In the meanwhile Grenville, as Sheriff of Cornwall in 1576–7, devoted himself to local matters, vigorously pursuing the government's anti-Catholic policy and earning himself a knighthood for his services. He also made extensive alterations to the family home at Buckland Abbey at this time.

In 1585 when the Queen forbade his kinsman Sir Walter Ralegh (q.v.) to sail to the New World, Grenville was given command of the fleet that took 100 men to plant a colony at Roanoke (now in North Carolina); he sailed from Plymouth on 9 April aboard the flagship *Tiger*, accompanied by six other vessels. Among the gentlemen who sailed with him was one of the Queen's equerries, Ralph Lane (q.v.), who was appointed to take charge of the new colony; he quarrelled with Grenville and later laid accusations against him of intolerable behaviour. On the homeward voyage Grenville captured a valuable Spanish prize, the *Santa Maria*, laden with sugar. The colonization was not a success, and when Grenville returned to Roanoke the following year bearing supplies for the men, he found them gone; unbeknown to him, they had left for home with Drake. Grenville, disappointed and foiled, sailed home via the Azores, where he captured some more Spanish prizes. A project to mount a third expedition to Roanoke was cancelled by the threat of the Spanish Armada; throughout 1587 Grenville was occupied with the defences of the West Country. Before the approach of the Armada, he was ordered to take the ships he was preparing for another voyage to Virginia to serve under Drake at Plymouth. He and Ralegh were subsequently ordered to maintain a watch on the sea approaches to Ireland, in case the Spaniards returned,

and in 1589–90 Grenville returned to his old plan of establishing a plantation in Munster.

In 1591 he was summoned back to England to become second-in-command, under Lord Thomas Howard (q.v.), of a squadron whose purpose was to sail to the Azores and intercept the Spanish treasure ships on their way back to Spain. The fleet consisted of about fifteen vessels, with Howard in the *Defiance* and Grenville, as Vice-Admiral, in the *Revenge*. Caught unawares at Flores by the main Spanish fleet of some fifty-five ships under the command of Don Alonzo de Bazan at the end of August, the English squadron retreated, but Grenville, with a large number of his men sick ashore, was delayed and trapped. For fifteen hours from the afternoon of 9 September until the following morning he held off the attacks, damaging some fifteen Spanish galleons in the process; but defeat was inevitable and the crew of the *Revenge*, defying Grenville's order to blow up the ship, surrendered. A few days later the wounded Sir Richard died on board his flagship, and not long afterwards the *Revenge* went down in a cyclone that destroyed a large number of the Spanish ships. (The terrified population of the Azores thought that Grenville was a devil; among the legends that circulated about him – mostly nonsensical, but believed at the time – was one of his having crunched his glass while at dinner until blood ran out of his mouth.)

Sir Richard Grenville was one of the most colourful seamen of his age. His great fight against overwhelming odds was vividly described by Ralegh, and also inspired a poem by Tennyson.

Sir Walter Ralegh, *A Report of the Truth of the Fight about the Isles of Azores* (1591; reprinted 1871).

A. L. Rowse, *Sir Richard Grenville of the Revenge* (1937).

A. L. Rowse, 'Sir Richard Grenville's Place in English History', Ralegh Lecture, *Proceedings of the British Academy*, xliii (1957).
A. L. Rowse, *The Elizabethans and America* (1959).

*Portraits*: oil, by unknown artist, 1571: National Portrait Gallery, London; engraving, Holland's *Herwologia*, 1620.

## Gresham, Sir Thomas (1519–1579), merchant and financier, founder of the Royal Exchange.

The second son of Sir Richard Gresham, a wealthy City merchant who lent money to Henry VIII (q.v.) and members of the court, and his first wife, Audrey, daughter of William Lynn of Southwick, Northamptonshire, Thomas Gresham was born in London in 1519. The legend that he was a foundling saved by the chirping of a grasshopper may be discounted: the family name, meaning 'grass-farm', came originally from the village of Gresham in Norfolk, and the famous grasshopper crest had been used by an ancestor, one James Gresham, as early as the fifteenth century.

Thomas was educated first at school and later at Gonville and Caius College, Cambridge. On leaving the university in about 1535 he was apprenticed for eight years to his uncle, Sir John Gresham, a mercer, with whom his father was in partnership. Both Sir Richard and Sir John were Lord Mayors of London, in 1537 and 1547 respectively.

Elected a Freeman of the Mercers' Company in 1543, Gresham was soon taking an active part in the family business, including certain financial dealings with the crown. In 1544 he married Anne Read, the widow of a fellow Mercer, who was related by marriage to the Bacon family; their only son, Richard, was baptized at St Lawrence Jewry on 6 September that year. Following the death of Sir Richard in 1549, Thomas and his family moved from the elder Gresham's house in Milk Street to Lombard Street.

The chief market for English cloth being in the Netherlands, Gresham made frequent visits to the Continent at this period. In 1552 his friend the Duke of Northumberland (see Dudley, John) secured for him the appointment of Royal Agent, or King's Merchant, at Antwerp, which was then the centre of the international money market. The crown was in serious financial difficulties, due to debasement of the coinage, inflation, and the debts left by Henry VIII; the interest on these debts alone amounted to some £40,000. Gresham immediately set to work with vigour and not a little cunning to remedy the position. He took up residence at Antwerp, and within two years he had succeeded in raising the rate of exchange from 16 to 22 Flemish shillings to the pound sterling, and was paying off the crown's debts at that figure. Because of his staunch Protestantism he was withdrawn from office on the accession of Mary I (q.v.), but was soon reinstated when finances got out of hand again, whereupon he returned to Antwerp and busied himself arranging for currency to be smuggled into England in containers that ranged from sacks of pepper to diplomatic bags. In 1554 he was successful in raising a loan from Spain and in obtaining a licence from Charles V (q.v.) for the export of bullion from that country.

Under Elizabeth I (q.v.) Gresham continued for almost another decade to serve as Royal Agent. Knighted in 1559, he was for three years ambassador to the Regent of the Netherlands in Brussels, and during this period he kept up a secret correspondence with the Secretary of State, Sir William Cecil (q.v.), in which he passed on much valuable political intelligence. In particular he warned

Cecil of the danger to England from what he foresaw as the imminent revolt of the Netherlands against Spain, and cleverly he arranged to ship ammunition to England under the guise of 'velvets'. In all these dealings Gresham was astute in lining his own pockets and, although no more unscrupulous than other financiers of his day, he invariably saw to it that all his transactions, whether trading, negotiating loans, or money-lending on his own account, showed a handsome profit.

In 1560 the reform of the English currency, long urged by Gresham, was at last effected. That same year, on one of his numerous journeys between the Netherlands and England, he fell from his horse and broke his leg; he was to be lame for the rest of his life. In 1568 he returned to England, but continued to act as the Queen's agent until about 1574, when he retired from business altogether. In these last years of his professional activity he constantly advocated the raising of loans from London merchants rather than from foreigners. As a Mercer

and Merchant Adventurer, he was involved personally in many complex business and financial dealings, and often in the lending of money to the aristocracy, which brought him a rich return. The fortune he amassed thereby was lavished on his fine town residence, Gresham House in Bishopsgate, and other houses at Osterley in Middlesex, Mayfield in Sussex, and several more in Suffolk.

After losing his only son in 1564, Gresham decided to use his wealth to bring to fruition a scheme originally proposed by his father some thirty years earlier: the building of a bourse, or Exchange, in the City. Work was started in 1566, and two years later the Exchange opened for business; when the Queen visited it in January 1571 she ordered it to be called the 'Royal Exchange'.

In 1575 Gresham made a will bequeathing Gresham House to his wife during her lifetime, and afterwards for the founding of a college in London, to be called Gresham College, where free lectures were to be available for all who wished to attend them. Unfortunately the scheme aroused the hostility of the university authorities at Cambridge and, in spite of Gresham's generosity, it was never very successful.

In the last years of his life Gresham acted as gaoler to Lady Mary Keys, sister of Lady Jane Grey (q.v.), who had incurred the Queen's extreme displeasure on account of her imprudent marriage. He found it an unhappy task and from 1569 continually begged Cecil to relieve him of it; he seems to have succeeded in 1573.

Gresham died suddenly on 21 November 1579. He was buried in St Helen's, Bishopsgate.

A man of great foresight and business acumen, with a special gift for negotiating loans, Sir Thomas Gresham made himself the richest merchant and financier of the age. The observation widely known as 'Gresham's Law', that bad money drives out good, was however wrongly attributed to him in the nineteenth century; it was stated first by Copernicus (q.v.). There may be some truth in the story referred to in a play by Thomas Heywood (see *Lives of the Stuart Age*) that on the occasion of the Queen's visit to the Exchange, Gresham drank her health in a cup of wine in which a precious stone worth £15,000 had been crushed.

J. W. Burgon, *The Life and Times of Sir Thomas Gresham* (2 vols; 1839).
Michael Foss, 'Sir Thomas Gresham', in *Tudor Portraits* (1973).
F. R. Salter, *Sir Thomas Gresham* (1925).

*Portraits:* oil, full length, by unknown artist, 1544: Mercers' Hall, London; oil on panel, by unknown Flemish artist, *c.* 1565: National Portrait Gallery, London.

## Greville, Sir Fulke (1554–1628), 1st Baron Brooke, poet and statesman.

The only son of Sir Fulke Greville and his wife Ann, daughter of Ralph Neville, Earl of Westmorland, he was born in 1554 at the family seat of Beauchamp Court, Warwickshire. In October 1564 he was sent to Shrewsbury School, where he formed an intimate friendship with a fellow-pupil, Philip Sidney (q.v.). He continued his studies at Jesus College, Cambridge, matriculating at the university in 1568; although Sidney went to Oxford, they kept in close touch, and it was through Philip's father, Sir Henry Sidney (q.v.) that Greville was in 1576 given a post in the Court of the Welsh Marches. He resigned from this office the following year, however, in order to join Philip Sidney at court.

Greville quickly became a favourite with Queen Elizabeth I (q.v.), who was reluctant to allow him to travel abroad;

nevertheless, he went on several diplomatic missions to the Low Countries, Ireland, and France. When the Duc d'Anjou (see Alençon, François, Duc d') came to woo the Queen in 1581, Greville was chosen to entertain and attend him. He shared fully in the literary tastes of his friend Sidney and was a member of the 'Areopagus' group led by Gabriel Harvey for the purpose of introducing classical metres into English verse. In 1583 Greville acted as host to the Italian philosopher Giordano Bruno (q.v.) when he visited London.

In the summer of 1585 Greville and Sidney, both thirsting for adventure and frustrated at being kept at court, made an arrangement with Sir Francis Drake (q.v.) to join his proposed expedition to attack the Spanish in the West Indies. They got as far as Plymouth but were forbidden to sail by the Queen and forced to return to London. Greville was subsequently refused permission to serve with Leicester (see Dudley, Robert) in the Low Countries, but Sidney was allowed to take part in the expedition;

wounded at Zutphen, he died on 17 October 1586, bequeathing his books to Greville and Dyer. The grief-stricken Greville was one of the pall-bearers at Sidney's funeral at St Paul's the following February. He wrote a poem lamenting his friend's death and later a biography, which was not published until 1652.

Denied the Queen's permission to join the expedition of Essex (see Devereux, Robert) to the Azores in 1597, Greville had to content himself with employment at home. He had been made Secretary for the Principality of Wales in 1583, a post in which he was later confirmed for life, and other minor offices followed. He sat as Member of Parliament for Southampton in 1580, and for Heydon, Yorkshire, in 1584; and in several subsequent Parliaments as Member for Warwickshire, up to 1621. In 1598 Greville was appointed Treasurer of the Navy. He retained this office on the accession of James I (see James VI of Scotland), when he was created a Knight of the Bath, but the hostility of Sir Robert Cecil (q.v.) prevented his gaining higher office until 1614, when he was made Chancellor of the Exchequer.

Greville's services to the crown were generously rewarded by James, who granted him Knowle Park and also the ruin of Warwick Castle, which he restored. In January 1621, on resigning from the post of Chancellor, he was created Baron Brooke. He died on 30 September 1628 from a stab wound inflicted by a manservant who believed himself to have been omitted from his master's will, and was buried at St Mary's Church, Warwick, beneath a monument bearing an epitaph composed by himself: 'Fulke Greville. Servant to Queen Elizabeth, Councellor to King James, Frend to Sir Philip Sidney, Trophaeum Peccati.' He had never married, but in his later years was a patron of literary men such as John Speed (q.v.), William Camden (q.v.), and William Davenant (see *Lives of the Stuart Age*); to Francis Bacon (q.v.) he gave his loyal friendship to the end.

With the exception of the tragedy *Mustapha*, probably piratically printed in 1609, and one or two poems, none of Greville's writings were published during his lifetime. The philosophical plays and poems are his most important works. *Caelica*, a collection of sonnets and love poems, and *Certain Learned and Elegant Workes*, some of his youthful writings, were published in 1633; his *Life of the Renowned Sir Philip Sidney*, remarkable not only for the biography of his friend but also for its vivid portraits of Queen Elizabeth and William of Orange (q.v.) and its commentary on the contemporary political scene, although written in about 1612, did not appear until 1652; *Remains, Poems of Monarchy and Religion* appeared in 1670. The *Complete Works* were reprinted by Grosart in 1870. Greville's correspondence with Sir John Coke, who was his secretary from 1597 and later Secretary of State, is calendared in the eleventh and twelfth reports of the Historical Manuscripts Commission.

A. B. Grosart, introduction to *Complete Works of Sir Fulke Greville, 1st Baron Brooke* (4 vols; 1870).
R. A. Rebholz, *The Life of Fulke Greville* (1971).
Joan Rees, *Fulke Greville, Lord Brooke* (1971).

*Portraits:* engraving, by Robert Cooper, from drawing by William Hilton: British Museum, London; engraving, by unknown engraver after unknown artist, 1586: location not known.

**Grey, Lady Jane** (1537–1554), see Jane Grey, Lady.

**Grey, Lady Katherine** (1540–1568), Countess of Hertford.

Katherine Grey was born in August 1540, at Bradgate, Leicestershire, the second daughter of Henry Grey, 3rd Marquess of Dorset (later Duke of Suffolk), and his wife, Frances, daughter of the 1st Duke of Suffolk (see Brandon, Charles) and Mary Tudor (q.v.). Her eldest sister was Lady Jane Grey (q.v.), Queen of England for nine days in 1553. Under the will of Henry VIII (q.v.) the Grey sisters, Jane, Katherine, and Mary, were granted the right of succession to the English throne after the King's own children.

Katherine was brought up in the harsh atmosphere of the Dorset family home and shared her elder sister Jane's tutors, of whom the most influential was John Aylmer (q.v.), future Bishop of London. She was prettier than Jane, but less intellectual, and had a quieter, more retiring nature.

On 21 May 1553, in a series of family alliances arranged by the Duke of Northumberland (see Dudley, John) to strengthen his own position, Katherine was married to Henry Herbert, Lord Herbert, heir to the Earl of Pembroke (see Herbert, William). She spent the next seven weeks with her husband at her father-in-law's house, Baynard's Castle, near Temple Gardens, but the marriage was not consummated.

Edward VI (q.v.) died on 6 July, and four days later Katherine was at the Tower to greet her sister Jane, now publicly proclaimed as Queen. She remained in the Tower, together with Lord Herbert and the Earl of Pembroke, until 19 July, when Northumberland was arrested and Mary I (q.v.) was proclaimed in London as the rightful Queen. Almost immediately Pembroke declared his allegiance to the new sovereign and was allowed to return home, together with his son and daughter-in-law. He then announced that his son's marriage was to be dissolved and turned Katherine out of his house. She went to Sheen,

where her parents joined her two weeks later; Jane was kept in the Tower and Katherine never saw her sister again.

Meanwhile the Queen acted with kindness towards the Suffolk family, receiving them at court and appointing the thirteen-year-old Katherine as a Lady of the Privy Chamber. At Mary's coronation on 30 November 1553 Katherine, by virtue of her royal blood, was given precedence over the other ladies of the court, and rode immediately behind the Queen and the Princess Elizabeth (see Elizabeth I). After the execution of her father and sister the following February, and her mother's remarriage a month later, she and her younger sister Mary were placed in the care of the Duchess of Somerset, one of the Queen's closest friends. It was at the latter's home, Hanworth Place, where she spent most of the summer of 1554, that Katherine met again and fell in love with Edward Seymour, Earl of Hertford (son of Edward Seymour, 1st Duke of Somerset, q.v.), who had once been betrothed to the Lady Jane Grey.

The love affair had to be kept secret, for throughout Mary's reign, and more especially towards the end of it when it became clear that the Queen would not bear a child, Katherine was at the centre of Spanish intrigue over the succession. Cleverly, while managing to give the impression that she conformed to the new religion, she resisted all attempts of the Spanish envoys and others to convert her to Catholicism.

Relegated to lower rank at court after the accession of Elizabeth, Katherine next became the victim of a new plot hatched by the Spaniards, in which she was to be kidnapped, married to Don Carlos, the son of Philip II (q.v.), and proclaimed heiress-presumptive to the English throne. There was also a counter-plot to marry her to the Earl of

Arran (see Hamilton, James, 3rd Earl). A letter from the Duchess of Suffolk to the Privy Council seeking the Queen's consent to the marriage of her daughter and Hertford was never sent, on account of the ill-health and subsequent death of the Duchess, and the lovers continued to meet clandestinely. At one stage Katherine almost jeopardized her position by an arrogant outburst in the Queen's presence; but Elizabeth, whose watchfulness and suspicion of her Grey cousin had developed into intense dislike, adopted the unexpected tactic of restoring Katherine to her former status, so leading her to the false hope that her marriage might be favourably received. Encouraged by Lady Jane Seymour, Hertford's sister, the lovers were secretly betrothed, and in early December 1560 (the exact date is not recorded), taking advantage of the Queen's departure for Eltham, they were married at Hertford's house in Cannon Row.

During the next few months Katherine and her husband met only at secret rendezvous, with the connivance of Lady Jane Seymour; after the latter's death in March 1561 their meetings not only became more difficult to arrange, but were marred by Katherine's anxiety about a possible pregnancy and Hertford's orders to proceed to France. He left in April, and by the following July Katherine realized that she could no longer keep secret the fact that she was pregnant. Ordered to accompany the Queen on a royal progress to Suffolk at the end of that month, she lost her nerve and when the party stopped overnight at Ipswich she blurted out the whole story to Lord Robert Dudley (q.v.; later Earl of Leicester) and begged him to intercede for her with the Queen.

Elizabeth took no action until her return to London, when she committed Katherine to the Tower, ordered Hertford to return from France, and set in motion an official examination by the Privy Council of all those who had known of the match. Sir William Cecil (q.v.; later 1st Baron Burghley) gave instructions that the marriage was to be proved invalid; in this way he insured that Katherine's unborn child would be declared illegitimate and that she would be discredited and eliminated from the succession.

On 24 September Katherine gave birth to a son, who was christened Edward Seymour and given the title of Viscount Beauchamp. Public sympathy for the young couple was aroused, and the Council, uncertain of the Queen's views with regard to the other claimants plotting against her – Mary, Queen of Scots (q.v.) and Margaret, Countess of Lennox (see Douglas, Margaret) – and fearing her possible marriage with Lord Robert Dudley, withheld its verdict for four months. In February 1562 Matthew Parker (q.v.), Archbishop of Canterbury, was instructed by Elizabeth to re-examine the prisoners, and on 12 May the Hertford marriage was pronounced to be illegal; Katherine and her husband were sentenced to life imprisonment. They remained in the Tower, but were allowed by their lenient gaolers to meet and occasionally to spend a night together, with the result that Katherine again became pregnant. Early in February 1563 a second son, christened Thomas Seymour, was born; Hertford was summoned to appear before the Star Chamber, severely fined, and thereafter denied any further opportunity of seeing Katherine. In August the same year when an outbreak of plague necessitated their removal from the Tower, Katherine and her younger son were placed in the charge of her uncle, Lord John Grey, at Pirgo in Essex, while Hertford and the elder boy were sent to the Duchess of

Somerset at Hanworth. They never saw one another again.

Meanwhile the matter of the succession continued to occupy the Council. In the autumn of 1562, when the Queen had fallen ill with smallpox, the situation had looked critical, with ministers divided in their support of the Lady Katherine and another Protestant candidate, the Earl of Huntingdon. They had just decided in favour of Katherine when the news broke of the birth of her second child. Once more, the problem seemed insoluble.

Katherine's cause was next championed by Francis Newdigate, the Duchess of Somerset's second husband, and John Hales, Clerk of the Hanaper to the Queen. Hales's pamphlet, *Declaration of the Succession*, caused an uproar in Parliament when it appeared in the spring of 1564, and this had barely died down when disclosure of the secret marriage of Katherine's sister, the Lady Mary Grey, to Thomas Keys, the Queen's Serjeant-Porter, further aroused Elizabeth's fury against the Grey family and put paid to any hope of better treatment for Katherine, who was reported to be pining away and likely to die of consumption.

Following the death of Lord John Grey in the autumn of 1564, Katherine was removed first to the care of Sir William Petre at Ingatestone, Essex, subsequently to that of Sir John Wentworth at Halstead and, on the latter's death, to the custody of Sir Owen Hopton at Cockfield Hall, Yoxford, where she died on 22 January 1568. She was given a splendid funeral by order of the Queen. Some sixty years later, in the reign of Charles I, when the Hertford family had been restored to respectability, her remains were taken from Yoxford churchyard and placed beside those of her husband in the Hertford memorial in Salisbury Cathedral. Hertford himself died in 1621; after a long battle to establish his sons' legitimacy, which he achieved in 1604, he lived to see his grandson, William Seymour, son of Viscount Beauchamp, re-enact the family drama by a secret marriage and attempted elopement with the Lady Arabella Stuart (q.v.).

A helpless pawn in the intrigue concerning the English succession, the tragedy of Lady Katherine Grey was that she failed to grasp the political significance of her Tudor descent. She was condemned by her contemporaries, and brought much misery on herself, not so much by falling in love, but by behaving in what was then considered to be an immoral manner in marrying the man of her choice rather than waiting for a husband to be picked for her, as was customary for those of royal blood. Yet, as her recent biographer points out, the two warring factions had only semi-degenerate husbands to offer her; also death on the scaffold was an accepted risk in Tudor times, which probably accounts for Katherine's apparent disregard for the possibility that she might share the fate of her elder sister.

Hester W. Chapman, *Two Tudor Portraits* (1960).

*Portraits*: oil, attributed to M. Gheeraerts: private collection (sold at Christie's); oil, with her son, Viscount Beauchamp, attributed to H. Eworth: versions at Petworth, Audley End, and Syon House; memorial: Salisbury Cathedral.

**Grindal, Edmund** (1519–1583), Archbishop of Canterbury.

Born in 1519 in the parish of St Bees, Cumberland, where his father, William Grindal, was a well-to-do farmer, Edmund Grindal was educated at Cambridge, initially at Magdalene College, then as a scholar at Christ's, and later at Pembroke Hall, from where he graduated as B.A. in 1538. He was elected a fellow of Pembroke the same year.

At Cambridge Grindal came under the influence of Nicholas Ridley (q.v.), who was almost certainly responsible for turning him towards Protestantism. An M.A. in 1541, he was ordained as deacon in 1544 and in 1549 was chosen by Ridley to argue the case for Protestantism in front of the commissioners sent by Edward VI (q.v.) to inspect the university. That year also he was appointed Lady Margaret Preacher and Vice-Master of Pembroke, and two years later, when Ridley became Bishop of London, Grindal was chosen to be one of his chaplains. In December 1551 he was made one of the royal chaplains, and the following summer he was installed as a prebendary of Westminster. It was strongly rumoured that, but for the death of the King in July 1553, he would have become a bishop.

On the accession of Mary I (q.v.) Grindal fled to the Continent, settling first in Strasbourg and then in Frankfurt, where, along with other Protestant exiles, he found himself in sympathy with the Calvinist doctrines emanating from Geneva. He returned to England in January 1559 and six months later was elected as Master of Pembroke. When Archbishop Matthew Parker (q.v.) chose him as the new Bishop of London, Grindal at first hesitated on account of his Puritan dislike of vestments and ceremonial, but after sounding out Peter Martyr and other friends abroad, he accepted the office and was duly consecrated and enthroned at St Paul's on 23 December 1559.

As Bishop of London, Grindal, being far too lenient with the Puritans and too harsh with the Roman Catholics, was to prove a great disappointment to Mat-

thew Parker. In 1570 Parker therefore recommended his appointment as Archbishop of York, on the grounds that Grindal was 'not resolute and severe enough for the government of London' but might find more congenial the task of rooting out the greater proportion of Romanists in York. This work he resolutely executed for the next five years until, on Parker's death in 1575, William Cecil (q.v.) persuaded the Queen (see Elizabeth I) to appoint Grindal as his successor. Within a short time of his translation to Canterbury the move was seen to be a mistake, for Grindal's Puritan sympathies soon brought him into serious conflict with the Queen and the court. When the Archbishop categorically refused to suppress all 'prophesyings' (private meetings of the clergy to discuss the scriptures), in June 1577 Elizabeth suspended him from his office; he was, however, permitted to continue his spiritual functions. This sequestration continued for five years, during which time Grindal became increasingly blind, but stubbornly would not resign. Towards the end of 1582 his health began to fail more rapidly, and preparations were being made for his resignation when he died at Croydon, Surrey, on 6 July 1583; at his own request, he was buried in the parish church there.

Edmund Grindal was a man of high principles who failed to fulfil his early expectations or to make a mark in high ecclesiastical office largely because of his refusal to conform to the official line. A man of considerable learning and much loved by his friends, he was immensely interested in improving the standard of the clergy and was a generous benefactor to the universities of Oxford and Cambridge, as well as to other charitable causes. His few writings have been edited, with a short biography, by W. Nicholson for the Parker Society (1843).

W. Nicholson, *The Remains of Edmund Grindal* (Parker Society, 1843).

John Strype, *The History of the Life and Acts of the Most Reverend Father in God, Edmund Grindal* (1710; reprinted Oxford, 1821).

F. O. White, *Lives of the Elizabethan Bishops of the Anglican Church* (1898).

*Portrait:* oil, by unknown artist: Pembroke College, Cambridge.

**Grocyn, William** (?1446–1519), English humanist and scholar.

The exact date of William Grocyn's birth is not known, but it probably took place in 1446 at Colerne, near Bath, where his father was a copyholder. He was educated at Winchester and at New College, Oxford, of which in 1467 he became a fellow. In 1481 he resigned his fellowship on being appointed to the living of Newton Longueville in Buckinghamshire, and the same year was appointed Divinity Reader at Magdalen College, Oxford, a post which he held until 1488.

Grocyn now left Oxford and travelled to Italy in order to perfect his knowledge of Greek under Polizano and Chalcondyles at Florence. It is believed that he had already learned the rudiments of the language while at Oxford from Vitelli, then Praelector of New College, or from one of the Greek scribes working there.

In 1491 he returned to Oxford, rented rooms at Exeter College, and began to give public lectures in Greek. Two years later he resigned his living at Newton Longueville in order to devote his entire time to teaching, and his reputation in this field grew rapidly. He was intimate with Thomas More (q.v.), John Colet (q.v.), and Thomas Linacre (q.v.), and

was held in great esteem by Erasmus (q.v.), whom he met on the latter's first visit to England in 1499.

At some date which has not been established Grocyn left Oxford again. In accordance with the custom of the age, he was a pluralist, holding several benefices of which he was non-resident but which brought him in a considerable income; many of these were given to him by Archbishop Warham (q.v.), whom he had tutored at New College. However, after his friend Colet became Dean of St Paul's in 1505, Grocyn seems to have settled in London, where he had been given the living of St Lawrence, Jewry, in 1496, and where he often preached, at Colet's invitation, in St Paul's. In London, too, he taught Greek to Thomas More. In 1506 Grocyn became Warden of All Hallows College, Maidstone, and died there, having been stricken with paralysis, in 1519. He left his entire fortune to Linacre 'for the weal of my soul . . . and all Christian souls'.

Grocyn's fame rests largely on his being the first Englishman to teach Greek. In company with Colet and Linacre, he was very much in sympathy with the 'new learning' and did much to prepare the way for the growth of humanism in England. After much study he came to question the authorship of the supposed writings of Dionysius; his views were eventually accepted by Colet, who had earlier believed in the authenticity of the writings.

M. Burrows, in *Oxford Historical Society Collectanea*, vol. ii (1890).

**Guise, Marie de** (1515–1560), see Marie de Guise.

# H

**Hakluyt, Richard** (?1552–1616), geographer, propagandist of overseas expansion and translator, best remembered as editor of *The Principall Navigations, Voiages and Discoveries of the English Nation*.

Born in London in about 1552, Richard Hakluyt came from a family probably Dutch in origin which had settled in the Welsh Marches. Following his father's death in 1557, he was entrusted to the care of a cousin, another Richard Hakluyt, a lawyer and a man of standing in the City whose friends included the prominent statesmen, geographers and explorers of the age. The young Richard's interest in geography was aroused when, on a visit to his guardian in the Middle Temple, he saw a map of the world lying on a table and the elder Hakluyt explained to him the exciting discoveries then taking place.

Richard was educated at Westminster School, from where he won a scholarship to Christ Church, Oxford. Entering the university in 1570, he took his B.A. in 1574 and his M.A. in 1577; at a later date he took holy orders. Hakluyt's all-absorbing interest was travel and geography, and he read widely on the subject, both in English and in foreign languages; he sought the company of seafaring men such as Humphrey Gilbert (q.v.), Francis Drake (q.v.), and Martin Frobisher (q.v.), and through his guardian became acquainted with the mathematician 'Dr' John Dee (q.v.) and the cosmographers Abraham Ortelius and Gerardus Mercator. Not long after taking his degree he gave a series of public lectures at Oxford, where he is regarded as the first to teach geography at the university.

Hakluyt was determined to lose no opportunity to promote the expansion of England overseas. In *A Discourse on the Strait of Magellan*, written in 1579–80, but not printed, he urged that an expedition be sent to look for a North-West Passage that would open up the market for English wool and provide a short route to the Spice Islands; he also advocated the foundation of a self-supporting colony there. Next, he persuaded his Oxford friend John Florio (q.v.) to translate into English an Italian account of Jacques Cartier's voyages to Canada, and in the preface which he wrote to this edition (published in 1580) Hakluyt expounded his policy of the establishment of England's claim to the discovery of North America based on the explorations of John and Sebastian Cabot (qq.v.), and again urged the setting up of a 'plantation' to foster trade.

In 1582 Hakluyt's first publication, *Divers Voyages to America*, a collection of documents relating to all the voyages to that continent made to date, brought him wide recognition as a cosmographer. The following year he was offered the post of chaplain to Sir Edward Stafford (q.v.), then English ambassador in Paris, and he eagerly seized this opportunity to make the acquaintance of the Continental geographers and seafaring men. From them he was ashamed to learn that the English were known for their 'sluggish security'. Hakluyt was to spend six years in Paris, where in addition to his duties as chaplain and tutor to the Stafford household, he acted as an agent gathering intelligence for Sir Francis Walsingham (q.v.), and also prepared a new edition of Peter Martyr Anglerius's *De Orbe Novo*, originally published in 1516 and later translated into English by Michael Lok (q.v.).

In 1584 Hakluyt wrote his *Discourse on Western Planting*, in support of the proposed colonization of Virginia by Sir Walter Ralegh (q.v.); this was a secret document, shown only to the Queen and her close advisers. In it the author put forward every possible argument in favour of 'planting' colonies and breaking the Spanish monopoly, stressing the economic and political benefits that would result. Queen Elizabeth (q.v.) was not entirely convinced, but she rewarded Hakluyt with a prebend at Bristol Cathedral.

The war with Spain put a stop to further exploration for the time being, but it fired Hakluyt with patriotism and gave him the incentive to begin work on a collection of documents covering all the exploits of English seamen to date. He returned to England in 1588, the year of the Armada, and the first edition of *The Principall Navigations, Voiages and Discoveries of the English Nation* appeared in 1589, with a dedication to Walsingham. The following year Hakluyt was appointed as Rector of Wetheringsett in Suffolk; he married at about this time a relative of the circumnavigator Thomas Cavendish (q.v.), but she died in 1597. It was while living at Wetheringsett that Hakluyt worked on a much enlarged version of *The Principall Navigations*, going back for his material to Geoffrey Chaucer (see *Lives Before the Tudors*), consulting contemporary historians such as William Camden (q.v.), and drawing also on foreign sources. The new edition, dedicated to the Lord Admiral, Lord Howard of Effingham (see Howard, Charles), was issued in three volumes in the years 1598–1600.

Hakluyt was granted a prebend at Westminster in 1602, and the following year he was appointed Archdeacon. Chaplain of the Savoy in 1604, he married for the second time that year. Meanwhile his enthusiasm for overseas exploration continued unabated: he was consulted by, and produced maps for, the newly established East India Company; instrumental in organizing a petition to James I (see James VI of Scotland) for patents to colonize Virginia in 1606, he was a member of the Virginia Company of London; in 1612 he became a charter member of the North-West Passage Company.

In the last years of his life Hakluyt probably made the acquaintance of a fellow-clergyman who was interested in contemporary exploration and discovery, Samuel Purchas (see *Lives of the Stuart Age*). Purchas published his *Pilgrimage* in 1613, and after Hakluyt's death he was to acquire some of his manuscripts (said to be sufficient for a fourth volume of the *Voyages*) and to use them in a continuation of the geographer's work entitled *Hakluytus Posthumas, or Purchas his Pilgrimes*, published in 1625.

Richard Hakluyt died on 23 November 1616 and was buried in Westminster Abbey three days later. His great collection, known popularly as *Hakluyt's Voyages*, inspired by the work of Ramusio, surpassed all previous geographical collections; it set down for contemporary readers and for posterity vivid and meticulously researched accounts of the adventures and achievements of the early explorers, and gave to the Elizabethan seamen, politicians, merchants and traders concerned with the maintenance of English naval power and overseas expansion in the late sixteenth and early seventeenth centuries a tremendous impetus and inspiration. The book is still widely read today.

The best modern edition of *The Principall Navigations* is that edited by Professor Walter Raleigh for the Hakluyt Society in 12 volumes (Glasgow, 1903–5); there is also a useful Everyman's Library edition in 8 volumes. *Divers Voyages* was edited by the Hakluyt Society in 1850, and the Society (founded 1846) has republished many of the narratives and translations; see E. G. R. Taylor, *The Original Writings and Correspondence of the Two Richard Hakluyts* (2 vols, Hakluyt Society, 2nd series, lxxvi–lxxvii, 1935), and also *The Hakluyt Handbook*, edited by D. B. Quinn, of which the Society has to date (1975) published volumes 1 and 2. Hakluyt's translations include Antonio Galvano's *Discoveries of the World* (1601) and Hernando de Soto's *Virginia richly valued by the description of . . . Florida* (1609).

G. B. Parks, *Richard Hakluyt and the English Voyages* (1961).
D. B. Quinn, 'Richard Hakluyt, Editor', issued with facsimile edition of *Divers Voyages* (Hakluyt Society, 1967).
A. L. Rowse, *The Elizabethans and America* (1959).
A. L. Rowse, *The Expansion of Elizabethan England* (1956).
J. A. Williamson, 'Richard Hakluyt', in *Richard Hakluyt and his Successors* (Hakluyt Society, 2nd series, xciii, 1946).

**Hales or Hayles, John** (d. 1571), author and Clerk of the Hanaper.

There is no record of the date or place of John Hales's birth, but he was the son of Thomas Hales of Hales Place in Halden, Kent. From his nickname 'Clubfoot Hales' he would seen to have had some disability, and it may have been for this reason that he was educated privately and not at university. Nevertheless he is said to have known Greek, Latin, French, and German.

Education appears to have been one of his early interests, for having acquired substantial grants of land in Coventry after the Dissolution of the Monasteries, in 1548 he turned the St John's Hospital there into a free school, the first of its kind to be established in the reign of Edward VI (q.v.). Hales's Latin grammar, *Introductiones ad grammaticam*, written partly in Latin and partly in English, was prepared for the use of pupils at this school. A few years earlier he had translated Plutarch's *Precepts for the Preservation of Health* and had also published a work entitled *Highway to Nobility* (1543).

In 1548 Hales, who is believed to have been appointed Clerk of the Hanaper before the end of the reign of Henry VIII (q.v.), was elected to Parliament as Member for Preston, Lancashire. A well-known opponent of enclosures, the Protector, Somerset (see Seymour, Edward), chose him as a member of the commission to enquire into their progress, and he was soon established as Somerset's closest ally in the anti-enclosures campaign. As a Protestant and spokesman of the group of reformers who called themselves the Commonwealth Party (from their concern with the 'common weal'), he was very active in Parliament. Three of the bills he introduced, aimed at helping the poor, did not succeed, but Somerset and the House accepted his plan for a tax on sheep and cloth to replace the unpopular purveyance system. When the Protector fell from power, however, Hales soon crossed swords with the ruthless Duke of Northumberland (see Dudley, John).

During the reign of Mary I (q.v.) Hales went to Strasbourg and Frankfurt;

as a result of his activities among the English exiles there, his property at home was confiscated. He returned to England on the accession of Elizabeth I (q.v.) but incurred the Queen's displeasure in 1564 on account of a pamphlet he had written supporting the marriage of the young Earl of Hertford and Lady Katherine Grey (q.v.) and the claim of the Suffolk line to the succession should Elizabeth die without producing an heir. He was imprisoned in the Fleet, but released shortly afterwards through the good offices of Lord Burghley (see Cecil, William). He died on 28 December 1571.

John Hales was almost certainly the author of *A Discourse of the Common Weal of this Realm of England*, written in 1549 but not published until 1581. In this work he set out the policy of the Commonwealth and for the first time asserted the necessity for the State to recognize and encourage private enterprise as an important source of revenue. The pamphlet *A Declaration of the Succession of the Crowne Imperiale of England*, first published in 1563, was reprinted in G. Harbin, *Hereditary Right of the Crown of England Asserted*, 1713. (N.B. Some writers have attributed the *Discourse* to Sir Thomas Smith, and the *Succession* pamphlet was at one time thought to have been written by Sir Anthony Browne or by Hales's nephew, also John.)

See the definitive edition of *The Common Weal of this Realm of England*, edited by Elizabeth Lamond (Cambridge, 1893; reprinted 1929).

**Hall, Arthur** (*c.* 1540–1604), politician and translator of Homer.

Born at Grantham, Lincolnshire, in about 1540, Arthur Hall was the son of Francis Hall, surveyor of Calais. His father died when he was young and he became a ward of Sir William Cecil (q.v.). He was educated in the Cecil household and at St John's College, Cambridge, where he was greatly encouraged in his classical studies by Roger Ascham (q.v.). As early as 1563 he began a translation from Homer, but temporarily abandoned it in order to travel in Italy and south-east Europe.

On his return to England from Constantinople in January 1569, Hall appears to have taken up residence in London, where he soon acquired a reputation for outspokenness and quarrelsome behaviour. He entered Parliament in April 1571 as Member for Grantham; re-elected the following May, he represented that constituency until 1581, and was elected for a third time in 1585. Within a few days of his second election Hall was reprimanded by the Speaker for making 'lewd speeches' in the House. On that occasion he was discharged, but in 1581 he was expelled and sent to the Tower for having produced an offensive pamphlet impugning the action of the Speaker in a case against one of his servants, Edward Smalley, who was alleged to have assaulted a certain Melchisdech Mallory whom Hall had accused of cheating at cards. He was released in 1583, but in the ensuing years was frequently in trouble with the authorities. In 1588 he was for a short time imprisoned in the Fleet. Little else is known of his life except that he corresponded with, and offered political advice to, both Cecil (now Lord Burghley) and James I (see James VI of Scotland) in the years 1591–1604. In 1597 Burghley interceded on Hall's behalf concerning a debt he owed to the crown.

Hall's *Ten Books of Homer's Iliades, translated out of the French*, printed by Ralph Newbery in 1581, was the first attempt to render Homer in the English language.

**Hall, Edward** (d. 1547), historian.

Born probably in about 1498 or 1499, Edward Hall was the son of John and Catherine Hall of Northall, Shropshire. Both his parents were prominent in the extreme reform movement and are known to have suffered a spell of imprisonment for their views; Edward himself was in later life wise enough not to go beyond the wishes of Henry VIII (q.v.), of whom he became a staunch supporter.

Hall was educated at Eton and King's College, Cambridge, where he was a fellow in 1517–18. On leaving the university he took up residence in London and was entered at Gray's Inn. Appointed common serjeant in 1532, he was the following year autumn reader at the Inn, and in 1540 Lent reader. In 1541 he was appointed as one of the commissioners authorized to investigate transgressions of the Six Articles. He sat in Parliament as Member for Bridgnorth in 1542.

Edward Hall died in 1547, The following year saw publication of his chronicle entitled *The Union of the Noble and Illustre Famelies of Lancastre and York*. A second and enlarged edition was issued in 1550 by Richard Grafton, who, using notes left by the author, brought the account up to date from 1532, where Hall had ended. In 1555 the work was prohibited by Queen Mary I (q.v.) and was not reprinted until 1809; a modern edition is that by Charles Whibley (2 vols; 1904).

The greatest value of Hall's chronicle lies in its account, albeit eulogistic, of the reign of Henry VIII, and in particular its vivid description of Henry's court and of his meeting with François I at the Field of the Cloth of Gold in 1520. Hall relied heavily on Polydore Vergil (q.v.) for the earlier part of his chronicle, and William Shakespeare (q.v.) in his turn is known to have drawn on Hall as source material for several of his historical plays, as did John Speed (q.v.) and other historians of the age in their work.

**Hall, Joseph** (1574–1656), bishop, controversialist, poet, moralist, and satirist, see *Lives of the Stuart Age*.

**Hamilton, James** (?1477–1529), 2nd Baron Hamilton and 1st Earl of Arran.

James Hamilton was the only son of James Hamilton, 1st Baron Hamilton, and his second wife, the Princess Mary Stewart, daughter of James II of Scotland (see *Lives Before the Stuarts*). Born in about 1477, he was still an infant when he succeeded to the title and estates on his father's death in 1479.

Hamilton was made a Privy Councillor by James IV (q.v.), and in 1503 he was one of the Scottish noblemen sent to England to negotiate for the King's marriage to the Princess Margaret Tudor (q.v.). He excelled at the courtly accomplishments of the day and was the chief performer at the celebrated tournaments at the Scottish court; his skill earned him the title of Earl of Arran in 1503. The following year, as Lieutenant-General of Scotland, he was sent to quell the Western Isles, and subsequently to the assistance of the King of Denmark. In 1507 Arran undertook a mission to France which aroused the jealousy and suspicion of Henry VII (q.v.), with the result that he was arrested on his return via England and was probably detained there until after the accession of Henry VIII (q.v.), when the friendship alliance between England and Scotland was revived.

In June 1513, after James, in the face of mounting tension with the English King, had renewed the 'Auld Alliance' with France and Henry had responded by

214

invading that country, Arran, aboard the *Great Michael*, was sent to the assistance of the French. Due to a combination of bad seamanship and appalling weather conditions he failed to arrive at his destination, and the final outcome of the expedition is not known. By the time he got back to Scotland his countrymen had been defeated by the English at Flodden, and James IV had been slain.

The old rivalry between the Hamiltons and the Douglases was re-kindled when the Queen Dowager married the Earl of Angus (see Douglas, Archibald, 6th Earl), and throughout the minority of James V (q.v.) Arran fiercely opposed Angus; after the marriage he joined with Albany and other nobles in depriving Margaret of her regency and guardianship. He supported the regency of the Duke of Albany (see Stewart, John), however, only in order to hold Angus in check, while secretly plotting against him. In 1517, when Albany went to France, Arran was appointed a member (and later President) of the Council of Regency.

In the spring of 1520 the feud between Arran and Angus led to fighting in the streets of Edinburgh, which ended in a victory for Angus. Arran and his son (see Hamilton, James, 2nd Earl of Arran) escaped, but their party suffered great losses. The Queen Dowager, having returned to Scotland, complicated the issue by pressing for a divorce from Angus and by continually shifting her support from one side to another. During Albany's further absence in France in 1522, Arran was again President of the Council of Regency; he now came to an understanding with the Queen Dowager and combined with her in ousting Albany from the regency. Following the latter's final departure from Scotland to France in the spring of 1524, Arran and the Queen Dowager regained control of the King and had him 'erected' (declared fit to govern) at Stirling.

In November 1525 Angus staged a *coup d'état* and seized the King, whom he held prisoner for the next two and a half years. During this time Arran and the Queen Dowager together made one unsuccessful attempt to rescue James; then, after Margaret's divorce and a third marriage (to Henry Stewart, later Lord Methven), Arran came to terms with Angus and supported him against John Stewart, 3rd Earl of Lennox, when the latter marched on Edinburgh to fight for possession of the King. Following Lennox's murder by one of the Hamiltons after the Battle of Linlithgow in 1526, Arran was granted some of the rebels' forfeited lands. Later, however, he again withdrew his support from Angus. After the King's escape from the Douglas régime in May 1528, Arran was among those who sat on the forfeiture of Angus and who benefited from the latter's forfeited estates.

Little is known of Arran's personal life, except that he was married three times: firstly, to Beatrix, daughter of John Drummond, Lord Drummond; secondly, to Elizabeth, daughter of Alexander Home, Lord Home, from whom he was divorced; and thirdly, to Janet, daughter of Sir David Bethune and widow of Sir Thomas Livingstone of East Wemyss, by whom he had two sons and four daughters. The exact date of his death in 1529 is not known, but it probably occurred in July of that year. He was succeeded by his eldest son James.

J. Bain, (ed.), *Hamilton Papers* (2 vols; Edinburgh, 1890–2).
W. Croft Dickinson, *Scotland from the Earliest Times to 1603* (Edinburgh, 1961).
G. Donaldson, *Scotland: James V to James VI* (Edinburgh, 1965).
J. D. Mackie, *History of Scotland* (1964).

**Hamilton, James** (d. 1575), 2nd Earl of Arran and Duke of Châtelherault, Regent of Scotland 1542–54 during part of the minority of Mary, Queen of Scots (q.v.).

Hamilton was the eldest son of the 2nd Baron Hamilton and 1st Earl of Arran (see Hamilton, James, 1st Earl) by his third wife, Janet, daughter of Sir David Bethune and widow of Sir Thomas Livingstone of East Wemyss. Because of the doubt cast on the validity of his father's divorce from his second wife, there was controversy as to his legitimacy or otherwise; as grandson of James III's sister Mary, he was the Queen's nearest adult male relative. If he were illegitimate, the other branch of his family, the Lennox Stewarts, could rightly claim to be the true heirs to the throne of Scotland.

The exact date of his birth is unknown. He is said to have been brought up under the guardianship of his kinsman, Sir James Hamilton of Finnart; this may have been during the period when his father was serving abroad or when he was detained by Henry VII (q.v.) in England. He married Lady Margaret Douglas, elder daughter of James Douglas, 3rd Earl of Morton, probably in about 1529, the date he inherited the earldom of Arran on the death of his father.

In 1536 Arran accompanied James V (q.v.) on his matrimonial excursion to France. Little else is known of his activities prior to 1542. Following the King's death in December that year, he was appointed Governor (Regent) of Scotland in the minority of the infant Queen. He achieved this on the plea of being 'the second person in the realm' and in the face of strong opposition from Cardinal David Beaton (q.v.).

Soon after his installation it was seen that Arran, although a wealthy, genial, and tolerant man, was both weak-minded and vacillating in state affairs. He was susceptible both to the influence of Henry VIII (q.v.), who was anxious to achieve domination of Scotland through a marriage between Prince Edward (see Edward VI) and the young Queen of Scots, and at the same time to the forceful arguments of Beaton and his followers. In 1543, having confirmed the alliance with England in the Treaties of Greenwich, he promptly repudiated them, which led Henry, out of frustration and disappointment, to invade Scotland. Revulsion against this so-called 'Rough Wooing' drastically reduced the pro-English party in Scotland, and Arran was forced to co-operate increasingly with Beaton and the Queen Dowager Marie de Guise (q.v.). The defeat of the Scots at Pinkie Cleugh in September 1547 lowered the Regent's prestige even further; reluctantly he now agreed to abandon his scheme to marry Mary, Queen of Scots to his eldest son, and he allowed her to be sent to France; as a reward for compliance with Marie de Guise in this scheme, he was given the French title of Duke of Châtelherault. Although Arran still retained the regency at this stage, the Queen Dowager's influence with the nobles was increasing rapidly, and in April 1554, deserted by virtually all his previous supporters, Châtelherault was persuaded to resign his powers in her favour. He retired first to England, where an intrigue aimed at undermining his credit at the court seriously affected his health, and then to France.

When the Lords of the Congregation rose in rebellion against Marie de Guise in 1559, Châtelherault returned to Scotland and became their leader; in November that year, the Queen Dowager's regency having been declared to be at an end, he was appointed as head of the Protestant council which was to rule in her stead. After the death of Mary's husband, François II of France, and the Queen's return to Scotland to assume personal rule, he again broached the subject of her marriage to his eldest son, now 3rd Earl of Arran (see Hamilton, James, 3rd Earl). This was refused. To his father's distress, the young man was already showing signs of mental disturbance; following a wild accusation that he had been advised by the Earl of Bothwell (see Hepburn, James) to abduct the Queen and force her to marry him, Châtelherault was obliged to keep him in confinement at Dumbarton Castle. When Arran later managed to escape and was brought before the Council for a second time, his father had to pay for his negligence by giving up Dumbarton.

In 1565 Châtelherault joined with the Earl of Moray (see Stewart, Lord James) and other Protestant lords in a rebellion against the Queen's marriage to Lord Darnley (see Stewart, Henry); he particularly resented Mary's choice of a Lennox Stewart, which effectively put paid to the ambitions he still held regarding the Hamiltons' rights to the throne. After the rebels' sound defeat at the hands of the Queen and her supporters, he received a pardon on condition that he lived in exile for five years.

Châtelherault returned to Scotland in 1569, but failed to regain his former influence. He felt bitter about Moray's appointment as Regent, which position he regarded as rightfully his own; now an old man, however, he no longer played an active role in political intrigues, leaving such action to his half-brother and two younger sons. In the civil war that followed Moray's assassination in January 1570 by a Hamilton kinsman (for whom he arranged an

escape to France), Châtelherault supported the Queen's party. Together with Sir William Kirkaldy of Grange, William Maitland of Lethington, and Lord Claud Hamilton, he made a resolute stand at Edinburgh Castle before finally coming to terms with the new Regent, the Earl of Morton (see Douglas, James), in 1573.

After the Pacification of Perth of 1573, Châtelherault retired altogether from public life. He died at Hamilton on 22 January 1575, when his title and estates were inherited nominally by his eldest son, but Arran being then insane, the estates were administered by his second son, Lord John Hamilton.

J. Bain (ed.), *Hamilton Papers* (2 vols; Edinburgh, 1890–2).
Caroline Bingham, *The Stewart Kingdom of Scotland 1371–1603* (1974).
W. Croft Dickinson, *Scotland from the Earliest Times to 1603* (Edinburgh, 1961).
G. Donaldson, *Scotland: James V to James VII* (Edinburgh, 1965).

*Portrait*: oil on panel, by Cornelius Ketel, 1578: Scottish National Portrait Gallery, Edinburgh.

## Hamilton, James (?1530–1609), 3rd Earl of Arran.

The eldest son of the 2nd Earl of Arran and Duke of Châtelherault (see Hamilton, James, 2nd Earl), and Lady Margaret Douglas, elder daughter of James Douglas, 3rd Earl of Morton, Hamilton was born in about 1530. At the time of negotiations for an alliance between Scotland and England in 1543, he was proposed by Henry VIII (q.v.) as a future husband for the Princess Elizabeth (see Elizabeth I), but his father subsequently repudiated the Treaties. Later there was some support for his marriage to the young Mary, Queen of Scots (q.v.), but this was also abandoned. In 1546 Hamilton was held as a hostage in the castle of St Andrews by the murderers of Cardinal David Beaton (q.v.), and an act was passed by the Scottish Parliament barring him from the right of succession to his family estates or the crown so long as he remained in captivity. After 1553, when his father became Duke of Châtelherault, he was styled as the Earl of Arran.

In about 1550 he went to France, where he served in the Scots Guards, distinguishing himself at St Quentin in 1557. While in France Arran was converted to Protestantism; in order to escape arrest he went to Geneva, but on the advice of John Knox (q.v.), Lord Burghley (see Cecil, William) sent for him to be brought to England to confer with the government. He was secretly dispatched to Scotland the following year, where he signed the letter depriving Marie de Guise (q.v.) of her regency and afterwards supported Châtelherault's Protestant policies. At the time of the Treaty of Berwick (1560) his name was again mentioned as a husband for Elizabeth, but a reply was sent from the English court to the effect that the Queen was 'indisposed to marry at present'.

Following the death of François II of France, Knox advised Arran to renew his suit to the widowed Mary, Queen of Scots. This also was refused, although Arran did become one of Mary's Privy Councillors. The next few years were marked by his bitter feud with the Earl of Bothwell (see Hepburn, James). Arran, who was by this time showing signs of mental disturbance and appeared to have a fixation about the young Queen, accused Bothwell of having advised him to carry Mary off to Dumbarton and force her to marry him; following this abduction, according to Arran, he and Bothwell were to have ruled Scotland jointly. Châtelherault, greatly distressed, clapped his son into confinement, but Arran cleverly escaped from a window

of the castle and made his way to Stirling, where he gave way to fits of madness. He was taken to St Andrews and brought before the Queen and the Privy Council. Having refused to withdraw his accusations, Arran was sent to Edinburgh Castle and placed under the charge of Lord James Stewart (q.v.).

Now almost totally insane and without the power of speech, he was kept at Edinburgh until 1566; after his release he lived in seclusion with his mother at Craignethan Castle. Arran came into the nominal possession of his father's estates on Châtelherault's death in 1575, but these were administered by his younger brother, Lord John Hamilton. In 1579 proceedings were brought against Lord John and his two brothers for wrongfully detaining Arran, and Craignethan Castle was beseiged. James VI (q.v.) subsequently had him confined at Linlithgow, where he died in March 1609.

For his part in the overthrow of the Regent, the Earl of Morton (see Douglas, James), in 1580–1, Lord John Stewart was created Earl of Arran by the King, in spite of the fact that the hereditary Arran, although insane, was then still alive.

J. Bain (ed.), *Hamilton Papers* (2 vols; Edinburgh, 1890–2).

Caroline Bingham, *The Stewart Kingdom of Scotland 1371–1603* (1974).

W. Croft Dickinson, *Scotland from the Earliest Times to 1603* (Edinburgh, 1961).

G. Donaldson, *Scotland: James V to James VII* (Edinburgh, 1965).

**Hardwick, Elizabeth** (1520–1608), Countess of Shrewsbury, known as 'Bess of Hardwick'.

The exact date of Elizabeth Hardwick's birth is not known, but it was probably in 1520. She was the daughter and co-heiress of John Hardwick of Hardwick, Derbyshire, a woman of remarkable personality and financial acumen.

Four times married, she derived considerable wealth from each of her husbands in turn. At the age of twelve she was married to Robert Barlow, who died a year later. In August 1549 she married Sir William Cavendish, by whom she had six children, and after his death in 1557 she carried on with the building of Chatsworth House which she had started four years earlier. (The Elizabethan mansion was later pulled down and the present classical style building erected at the end of the seventeenth century.)

Elizabeth's third husband was the wealthy Sir William St Loe of Tormarton, Gloucestershire, whom she married in 1559. After his death she was considered to be the richest woman in England.

In February 1567 she married one of the wealthiest and most powerful peers of the realm, the Earl of Shrewsbury (see Talbot, George), who two years later was entrusted with the custody of Mary, Queen of Scots (q.v.). By this time Bess was already scheming for the advancement of her children by the Cavendish marriage. In this she was over-ambitious and angered the Queen, who committed her to the Tower for a short period after Bess had arranged a match between her daughter Elizabeth and Charles Stuart, Earl of Lennox. Imprisonment failed to dampen the spirit of the Countess, however, and from 1578 onwards she campaigned vigorously (but unsuccessfully) for the recognition of the child of this marriage, the unfortunate Arabella Stuart (q.v.), as rightful claimant to the Lennox inheritance and to the throne of England in succession to Elizabeth I (q.v.).

Relations with her fourth husband deteriorated rapidly during this period,

and at one time a divorce was mooted. Bess took her revenge by accusing Shewsbury of intrigue with Mary, Queen of Scots, a charge which she was subsequently forced to retract, and by repeating scandal to Mary and Elizabeth in turn. For some time she lived apart from her husband, but Queen Elizabeth later brought about a formal reconciliation.

After Shrewsbury's death in 1590, Bess went to live at Hardwick, where she used her immense wealth to build the fine mansion which still stands today. Legend has it that she believed that if she once stopped building, she would die; in fact at the time of her death on 13 February 1608, building operations had been suspended because of frosty weather.

Bess of Hardwick was described by one contemporary as 'beautiful and discreet' and by another, Thomas Lodge (q.v.), as 'a woman of masculine understanding and conduct; proud, furious, selfish and unfeeling', who was at the same time builder, buyer and seller of estates, moneylender, farmer, and many others things besides. One of the most remarkable women of her day, she lived to the unusually old age (for Tudor days) of eighty-seven, and was buried at All Saints, Derby, under a splendid monument which she herself had put up and inscribed.

M. S. Rawson, *Bess of Hardwick and her circle* (1910). E. Carleton Williams, *Bess of Hardwick* (1959).

*Portraits:* three, at Hardwick Hall (National Trust), all by unknown artists: one called 'Queen Mary', considered to be of Bess, *c.* 1550–5; one, half-length, *c.* 1580; one, three-quarter length, *c.* 1590; oil, by unknown artist, probably seventeenth century: National Portrait Gallery, London.

**Harington, Sir John** (1561–1612), courtier, translator, wit, and inventor of the water-closet.

Harington was born at Kelston, near Bath, Somerset, in 1561, the son of John Harington and his second wife, Isabella Markham, one of Princess Elizabeth's attendants. Through his father's first wife, Etheldreda, perhaps a natural daughter of Henry VIII (q.v.), the family had inherited monastic properties in Somerset at the Dissolution. The elder Harington and Isabella had been imprisoned in the Tower with the Princess Elizabeth (see Elizabeth I), who later stood as godmother to their son, John.

Harington was educated at Eton and Christ's College, Cambridge; he also studied law at Lincoln's Inn. Brilliant and exceptionally witty, as a young man he was high in the affection of his godmother the Queen and was frequently at court. He married Mary Rogers in 1583, and when not in London (there were short periods when he was dismissed from court because of various escapades) he indulged his flair for mechanical inventions at Kelston, including a water fountain and the first known water-

closet, or, in modern terms, flush lavatory.

One of Harington's earliest escapades was to circulate among the Queen's maids-of-honour his translation of a rather improper tale from Ariosto's *Orlando Furioso*; as a punishment Elizabeth banished him from court until he had translated the whole epic poem. It was published in 1591, with a frontispiece of his own portrait engraved on copper-plate by Thomas Cockson, probably one of the first books thus illustrated in England. The following year, when Harington entertained the Queen at Kelston in his capacity as High Sheriff of Somerset, he presented to her a beautifully bound copy of his work.

In 1596, under the pseudonym Misacmos, he published a very different kind of book – *A New Discourse upon a Stale Subject*, a satire with the sub-title *The Metamorphosis of Ajax*. ('Ajax' was a pun on 'a jakes', meaning, in Elizabethan days, a privy.) In addition to describing his new invention in a somewhat Rabelaisian manner, his work contained some decidedly unsavoury details and veiled allusions to certain well-known personalities at court, including the Queen's favourite, the Earl of Leicester (see Dudley, Robert). Elizabeth was much displeased, but too fond of Harington to send him before the Star Chamber; instead it was ordered that the 'saucey poet' should leave the court 'till he be grown sober'. As always, however, she had a soft spot for her godson; by 1598 he was back in favour and had been commanded to install one of his water-closets at Richmond for the Queen's own use.

In 1599 Harington was sent to Ireland with the Earl of Essex (see Devereux, Robert); he had explicit instructions from Elizabeth to keep a full journal of the expedition. He was knighted by

Essex on this trip and, when the exercise proved a dismal failure and it was necessary to appease the Queen's wrath, went with him to plead his case; typically, Elizabeth in her fury at first ordered Sir John to leave for Kelston, but before he left, sent for him again and forgave him.

In 1602 Harington wrote a tract, *On the Succession to the Crown*, supporting the claim of James VI of Scotland (q.v.) to the English throne. He later produced some translations and original work for the use of James's son, the Prince Henry Frederick (see *Lives of the Stuart Age*), but much of his other epigrammatic writing gave offence and blocked his path to advancement. Nevertheless James treated him well, granting him a number of properties and making him a Knight of the Bath. In the last years of his life, however, Harington became involved in several lawsuits over properties which he attempted to claim by force; he was also deeply in debt. He died at Kelston on 20 November 1612.

Sir John Harington's collected letters and miscellaneous writings were edited by his son, the Rev. Henry Harington, and published under the title *Nugae Antiquae* (2 vols; 1769); and in another edition, edited by Thomas Park (2 vols; 1804). The letters contain some remarkably vivid descriptive sketches of Queen Elizabeth and of James I and his court. His tract, *On the Succession to the Crown*, was edited by C. R. Markham and published for the first time in 1880.

Ian Grimble, *The Harington Family* (1958).
N. E. McClure, *The Letters and Epigrams of Sir John Harington* (Philadelphia, 1930).
T. Rich, *Harington and Ariosto* (1940).

*Portraits*: oil, by Hieronimo Custodis: Nina, Lady Deramore (on loan to Ampleforth College, York); oil on panel, attributed to Custodis, *c.* 1590–5: National Portrait Gallery, London; oil, with his wife: J. B. Gold Collection; engraving by Thomas Cockson, frontispiece to Harington's translation of *Orlando Furioso*, 1591.

**Harriot or Hariot, Thomas** (1560–1621), mathematician and scientist.

Born at Oxford in 1560, Thomas Harriot was educated at St Mary Hall, Oxford, graduating as a B.A. there in 1580. On leaving the university he was employed by Sir Walter Ralegh (q.v.) as mathematical instructor. In this capacity he devoted himself initially to the problems of navigation and cartography, drawing up for his employer a whole series of tables showing the angles of sunrises and sunsets, corrections for every tenth degree of latitude, and much else besides. He also designed several backstaffs for observing the sun and avoiding glare.

Harriot worked closely with Ralegh on his plans for the colonization of Virginia and also for the later voyage to Guiana. He accompanied the expedition of 1585–6, which Ralegh envisaged would plant a colony at Roanoke in North America. It was on his return from this venture that Harriot wrote his *Brief and True Report of the new found land of Virginia*, a closely observed and detailed study not only of the flora and fauna, vegetation and other natural resources found in North America, but also a description of the natives, their customs and way of life – in fact the earliest anthropological study to be written in English. Harriot's book was included by Richard Hakluyt (q.v.) in the third edition of *Divers Voyages*, published in 1600 and later translated into several languages. It became the leading authority on the flora, fauna, and climate of North America for almost a century.

Through Ralegh, Harriot acquired the patronage of Henry Percy, 9th Earl of Northumberland, known as the 'Wizard Earl' because of his interest in scientific experiments. Northumberland granted him a pension and a residence at Syon House, Isleworth. During his long confinement in the Tower, the Earl frequently entertained Harriot and his mathematical friends to dinner there. At the time of the Gunpowder Plot in 1605 (see Fawkes, Guy, in *Lives of the Stuart Age*) Harriot came under suspicion through his association with Ralegh and Northumberland; he too suffered a spell of imprisonment when it was discovered that he had cast the King's horoscope for the Earl.

During the last fifteen years of his life Harriot developed his expertise in astrology and algebra. Simultaneously with Galileo, he was at the turn of the century employing the telescope to observe the comets and sunspots. He corresponded both with the German astrologer, Johannes Kepler, and with Galileo, agreeing with the latter on the Copernican theory (see Copernicus, Nicolaus), but not daring to publish his own discoveries of the elliptical orbit of the planets or the period of the sun's axial rotation, for fear of trouble with the English authorities. At Isleworth Harriot secretly continued his studies and observations until disease (cancer of the face) finally made this impossible. One of his last observations was that of the comet of 1618. He died on 2 July 1621.

A. L. Rowse has called Thomas Harriot 'the most original scientific intellect among Elizabethans'. That his contemporaries regarded him with suspicion stemmed largely from Harriot's fondness for ciphers and secret scripts, the characters being regarded as devils. Most of his work was never published, probably for this reason, but in 1631 his literary executor, the Rev. Nathaniel Torporley, issued Harriot's writings on algebra under the title *Artis Analyticae Praxis*. Collections of Thomas Harriot's papers are at the British Museum and Syon House (now in Greater London).

A. L. Rowse, *The Cultural Achievement* (vol. ii of *The Elizabethan Renaissance*, 1972), chapter VII, 'Science and Society', pp. 226–32.

Muriel Rukeyser, *The Traces of Thomas Hariot* (1972).

John W. Shirley (ed.), *Thomas Harriot, Renaissance Scientist* (1974).

H. Stevens, *Thomas Hariot* (1900).

**Hatton, Sir Christopher** (1540–1591), courtier, favourite of Queen Elizabeth (q.v.), and Lord Chancellor from 1587 to 1591.

The second son of William Hatton of Holdenby, Northamptonshire, and his wife Alice, daughter of Lawrence Saunders, Christopher Hatton was born at Holdenby in 1540. He was entered at St Mary Hall, Oxford, as a gentleman-commoner in about 1555, but left the university without taking a degree. In November 1559 he was admitted to the Inner Temple, where, however, he does not appear to have taken his legal studies very seriously. He played a prominent part in the masque performed at the Inner Temple at Christmas 1561.

A tall, handsome, and accomplished young man, Hatton was renowned for his graceful dancing. His performance at a court masque attracted the notice of Queen Elizabeth, who in 1564 appointed him as one of her gentlemen-pensioners. He rose rapidly in her favour and was soon on intimate terms with her, receiving in return a series of court appointments, grants of land and an annuity. Hatton became a Gentleman of the Privy Chamber and, in 1572, captain of the royal bodyguard. In 1576 the Bishop of Ely was ordered by the Queen to surrender the fee-simple of Ely Place for his benefit. Knighted at Windsor in 1577, Hatton was appointed as Vice-Chamberlain of the Royal Household, with a seat on the Privy Council, in November the following year.

By this date Hatton had become recognized as the Queen's mouthpiece in the House of Commons. He had first entered Parliament in 1571 as Member for Higham Ferrers, subsequently representing Northamptonshire in the Parliaments of 1572, 1584, and 1586. In 1581 he voiced opposition to the Queen's proposed marriage with the Duc d'Alençon (q.v.) and was later that year temporarily out of favour at court following an exhibition of jealousy against Elizabeth's rising favourite, Sir Walter Ralegh (q.v.). He was a member of the commissions that tried Anthony Babington (q.v.) and Mary, Queen of Scots (q.v.), in 1586, and spoke vehemently against Mary in Parliament. In 1587 he advised the hesitant William Davison, Elizabeth's secretary, to dispatch the warrant which the Queen had reluctantly signed for Mary's execution. Opposed to extreme measures against either the Catholics or the Protestants, he nevertheless supported Archbishop John Whitgift (q.v.) in his campaign against the Puritans. In foreign affairs he was sympathetic to those who favoured aggressive action against Spain. A middle-of-the-road man, with good judgment, he supported the Anglican establishment and was a reliable servant of the Crown. He was patron of Sir Francis Drake (q.v.), who named the *Golden Hind* after Hatton's crest.

In April 1587 Hatton was appointed Lord Chancellor. Despite his lack of legal qualifications he seems, with the aid of his friend Sir Richard Swale and four masters in chancery as assessors, to have carried out the duties required of him with competence. Created a Knight of the Garter in April 1588, Hatton was later that year, following the death of the Earl of Leicester (see Dudley, Robert),

appointed as Chancellor of Oxford University and also High Steward of Cambridge. He died in London on 20 November 1591 and was buried with great pomp and ceremony in St Paul's Cathedral. He was unmarried and left no will. A patron of the arts, he built a magnificent mansion, Holdenby House in Northamptonshire, subsequently purchased by James I (q.v.).

Sir Christopher Hatton was a friend and patron of men of letters such as Edmund Spenser (q.v.) and Thomas Churchyard. He himself wrote the fourth act of *Tancred and Gismund*, a tragedy performed before the Queen at the Inner Temple in 1568. His correspondence has been published in the biographical memoir by N. H. Nicolas (see bibliography below) and in Thomas Wright's *Queen Elizabeth and her Times* (2 vols; 1838).

E. St. John Brooks, *Sir Christopher Hatton, Queen Elizabeth's Favourite* (1946).
N. H. Nicolas, *Memoirs of the Life and Times of Christopher Hatton, K.G.* (1847).

*Portraits:* oil, by unknown artist, *c.* 1580: City of Northampton Central Museum and Art Gallery; oil on panel, by unknown seventeenth-century artist after unknown artist: Col. J. C. Wynne-Finch; two miniatures by Nicholas Hilliard, *c.* 1588–91: Victoria and Albert Museum, London; oil on panel, half length, by unknown artist, *c.* 1588–91: National Portrait Gallery, London; watercolour, attributed to S. Harding after N. Hilliard, 1848: N.P.G.; other versions elsewhere.

**Hawkins, Sir John** (1532–1595), naval commander and administrator, merchant, ship-designer and builder.

Born at Plymouth in 1532, Hawkins was the second son of a prominent merchant and seaman of the town, William Hawkins, and his wife Joan Trelawny; in the year of John's birth his father was Mayor of Plymouth. The brothers William and John received a good education and probably went to sea at an early age. The only record that has survived of Hawkins's youth is that when he was about twenty years old he killed a local barber, but was found not guilty by the coroner on the ground of having struck the man 'because he could not avoid him'; eventually he received a royal pardon. Following the death of their father about a year later (shortly before February 1554), John joined his elder brother in a business partnership, trading from Plymouth. During this period, until the business was wound up in 1560, John Hawkins made several voyages to the Canary Islands; while on his travels he became enthusiastic about the possibilities of trading slaves between Guinea, in West Africa, and the Spanish-occupied West Indies.

In about 1559 or 1560 Hawkins left Plymouth for London. He was already a wealthy man, his share of the family business having amounted to £10,000. The move probably took place at the time of his marriage to Katherine Gon-

son, daughter of Benjamin Gonson, Treasurer of the Navy. Their only child, Richard Hawkins (q.v.), was born the following year.

Hawkins sailed on his first slave-trading voyage in 1562. The expedition was financed by a syndicate which included Hawkins, his father-in-law, and Sir William Wynter (q.v.). Consisting of the *Salomon*, the *Swallow*, and the *Jonas*, with possibly one other vessel, it sailed from Plymouth in October. In setting out to trade with the Spanish West Indies without the necessary licences and taking goods that had not been declared at Seville, Hawkins was flagrantly breaking the law and inviting the wrath of the Spanish authorities; evidently he expected to get away with it on account of some special service he had earlier rendered to Philip II (q.v.), probably at the time of the latter's marriage to Queen Mary I (q.v.), when he may have served as part of the royal convoy that brought the Spanish monarch in stormy weather to England.

The expedition proved highly successful. After securing about 400 African negroes, some taken aboard Portuguese vessels laden with valuable commodities such as ivory, Hawkins headed for the Indies, where he had little difficulty in disposing of the slaves and his English cargo, since the Spanish colonists needed the trade. He took with him a Portuguese slave-ship which he had captured. This vessel was subsequently dispatched to Seville, but her captain disobeyed orders and sailed to Lisbon, where the cargo was impounded. Another vessel chartered by Hawkins in the Indies to carry his spoils to Seville had its valuable cargo seized there by the Spanish. Nevertheless, when Hawkins arrived back at Plymouth in August 1563, he brought with him sufficient spoils to show a handsome profit on the venture and to interest several Privy Councillors, and the Queen herself, in promoting a subsequent voyage.

On 18 October 1534 Hawkins sailed from Plymouth on his second slave-trading voyage; this time his fleet consisted of the *Jesus of Lubeck*, chartered to the syndicate by Queen Elizabeth (q.v.), and three vessels of his own – the *Salomon*, the *Tiger* and the *Swallow*. As before, he picked up slaves in Sierra Leone and traded them successfully for gold, silver, and other precious metals in the Indies; in Curaçao he obtained a large number of hides worth about £2,000. Stopping at Florida on the way home, Hawkins offered to assist the French settlement under Laudonnière by giving them a passage home; this was refused, but he sold them the *Tiger*, in return for a bill which he never discharged. He arrived back at Padstow on 20 September 1565, and in return for his services was granted a coat-of-arms by the Queen. The dividends on the expedition were reported to be 60 per cent.

Hawkins's third voyage was, by contrast, a disaster; it was also to have important political repercussions. By far the largest expedition yet mounted, it consisted of two ships contributed by the Queen – the *Jesus of Lubeck* and the *Minion* – and four belonging to the Hawkins brothers – the *William and John*, the *Swallow*, the *Judith*, and the *Angel* – a total tonnage of some 1,333. Over 400 men sailed with Hawkins, including among the officers Francis Drake (q.v.). Sailing from Plymouth on 2 October 1567, Hawkins obtained 500 negroes in Sierra Leone; as on the previous occasions, he traded these in the Indies. In July 1568 he set out on the homeward voyage; the royal ship *Jesus* being in poor condition, he wanted to get her out of the Caribbean as quickly as possible. He ran into stormy weather but loyalty to the

Queen would not allow him to let the ailing *Jesus* sink; in the hope of getting her repaired Hawkins put in to the Mexican port of San Juan de Ulua, where the governor at first mistook him for the anticipated Spanish plate fleet. When the Viceroy of Mexico arrived with his fleet the next morning an amicable arrangement was at first made with him, and hostages were exchanged; but the Viceroy broke the agreement by pouncing on Hawkins's ships. In the ensuing battle in the harbour on 21 September, only the two vessels commanded by Hawkins and Drake, the *Minion* and the *Judith*, managed to escape, Hawkins having first transferred the treasure aboard the *Jesus* to the *Minion*; he reached England at the end of January.

This episode marked the beginning of the long-drawn-out quarrel between England and Spain; the treachery of the Spanish at San Juan and their ill-treatment of the crews who had been taken prisoner also determined Hawkins to seek revenge, backing young Drake's ventures in the West Indies and Panama. With the full knowledge of the Secretary of State, William Cecil (q.v.), Hawkins took advantage of interviews with the Spanish ambassador, Don Guerau de Spes, ostensibly to plead for the release of the prisoners, to pretend that he was an ardent Catholic and so gained information concerning the conspiracy now known as the Ridolfi Plot (see Ridolfi, Roberto di) aimed at deposing Elizabeth and placing Mary, Queen of Scots (q.v.) on the English throne. Hawkins passed details of the plot on to Cecil, with the result that the conspirators were arrested and de Spes expelled.

In 1571 and 1572 Hawkins sat as a Member of Parliament for Plymouth. During the next decade he was to divide

his time between London and Plymouth, where both he and his brother William had civic and commercial responsibilities. As well as shipbuilding and normal trading pursuits, the brothers were involved in the equipping of, and investment in, other seamen's ventures in the West Indies. In October 1573 John Hawkins was severely wounded when, mistaken for Sir Christopher Hatton (q.v.) as he rode down the Strand, he was stabbed by a fanatic; but he made a full recovery. He invested £500 in Drake's proposed voyage to the Pacific in 1577.

Towards the end of 1577 Hawkins succeeded his father-in-law, Benjamin Gonson, as Treasurer of the Navy. His appointment antagonized Sir William Wynter, who had hoped to get the post himself, and during the next few years quarrels arose in which each accused the other of robbing the Queen by making her pay for repairs to her ships, but using worse and cheaper materials than were charged. Hawkins made a report on the corruption he discovered in the Navy on taking up his post and, as a result of it,

entered into what was called the First Bargain in 1579; this consisted of two agreements, one between the Queen and Hawkins, the other between the Queen and the master-shipwrights, whereby the ships would be repaired for a fixed annual payment and the work subject to supervision. His purpose was both to save the Queen money that had previously gone into the pockets of dishonest contractors and to rebuild and refit the Navy for the threatened war with Spain. Not unnaturally Hawkins was himself accused of corruption by those who lost most under this new system, in particular Wynter and William Borough (q.v.), but in 1583 an official inquiry completely exonerated him. Under the Second Bargain, entered into in 1585, Hawkins became virtually responsible for the upkeep of the whole Navy, excluding armaments; it was thanks to his insistence on rebuilding the older type of galleon and designing new vessels that were less heavily manned, faster moving, and yet more heavily armed, that the English fleet was able to out-manoeuvre the Spanish Armada of 1588 without the loss of a single ship.

In 1586 Hawkins was given command of a squadron whose mission is not clear, since the original instructions have not been preserved; it may have had a greater purpose than to operate a blockade along the Spanish coast. Sailing in the flagship *Nonpariel* (the former *Philip and Mary*), with William Borough as his second-in-command in the *Golden Lion*, he was delayed in the Channel until the end of September because of a sudden fear of invasion from France, and in consequence reached the Spanish coast too late to intercept the treasure ships. By the end of October he was home, having captured only a few prizes. The two commanders had worked well together and the old animosity had been buried.

During the fight against the Armada, Hawkins, sailing in the *Victory*, was second-in-command, next to Lord Howard of Effingham (see Howard, Charles), with Drake third. He took part in the several engagements as the Armada proceeded up-Channel and subsequently took command of one of the four squadrons into which Howard then organized the English fleet. He was knighted by the Lord Admiral aboard the *Ark Royal* on 26 July.

After the Armada campaign Hawkins was granted a year's leave for the purpose of putting the naval accounts in good order. Realizing how financially dependent Philip II of Spain was on treasure brought home from the New World, he saw that England's best protection lay in reliance on naval rather than military power, and he urged the setting up of a blockade to intercept the homeward-bound Spanish plate fleet in the Azores. Hawkins was supported in this view by Sir Martin Frobisher (q.v.), with whom he organized an expedition in 1590; while Frobisher sailed for the Azores with provisions for four months, Hawkins, accompanied by his son Richard, took a squadron to the Spanish coast. Philip, however, was informed of their movements and cancelled the sailings of his fleet from the West Indies; the few prizes taken by the English seamen were insufficient to cover the expense of the venture.

In 1589 William Hawkins died, and in 1591 Hawkins suffered a further personal loss in the death of his wife; not long afterwards he took a second wife, Margaret Vaughan. During these years he was active in helping sick and aged mariners. In 1590 he and Drake together established the Chest at Chatham for this purpose, and two years later he alone founded an almshouse in the same town, known as Sir John Hawkins's Hospital.

In 1595 Hawkins made his last voyage, sailing from Plymouth on 28 August with a fleet under the shared command of himself and Drake, and financed by a joint-stock company in which the Queen was a shareholder. Its objective had at first been to land a force at Nombre de Dios and capture Panama, but this plan was dropped when intelligence reached the commanders that the Spanish plate fleet had been damaged in a gale and had taken refuge in San Juan de Puerto Rico; the Queen gladly endorsed their new plan to sail direct to Puerto Rico to capture the treasure.

The enterprise was a disaster. From the beginning there were differences between the two commanders, both of whom were ageing sick men. The chief Spanish ports were more strongly fortified than they had been in earlier years. Hawkins fell ill at the end of October and died in the afternoon of 12 November, the day before an unsuccessful attack was to be made on Puerto Rico. He was buried at sea.

John Hawkins was one of the outstanding seamen of the sixteenth century, an able and totally uncorrupt administrator, and all his life a loyal and devoted servant of the Queen. Steadier than Drake, whose genius he could not equal, Hawkins, in his way, chiefly by reconstructing the English fleet, contributed as much towards the defeat of Spain as did his illustrious compatriot. He was ahead of his time in considering the welfare and hygiene of men at sea. In Plymouth for three generations the Hawkins family played a leading role in politics and in establishing that town as the principal port for trade with the New World.

E. Arber, *The Third Voyage of Sir John Hawkins, 1567–8* (1895).
Richard Hakluyt, *The Principall Navigations* (1589; ed. W. Raleigh, 12 vols, Glasgow, 1903–5).

C. R. Markham, *The Hawkins Voyages during the reigns of Henry VIII, Queen Elizabeth and James I* (Hakluyt Society, lvii, 1878).

J. A. Williamson, *Hawkins of Plymouth* (1949; 2nd ed. 1969).

J. A. Williamson, *Sir John Hawkins, The Times and the Man* (1927; rev. ed. 1949).

*Portraits*: oil, by unknown artist, 1581: National Maritime Museum, Greenwich; oil, by unknown artist, 1591: City Art Gallery, Plymouth; engraving, by R. Boissard, in *Bazileiwologia*, 1618: Bodleian Library, Oxford; engraving: *Herwologia*, 1620. N.B. For a discussion of the authenticity of the so-called Hope and Chatham Portraits (both at National Maritime Museum, Greenwich), see Williamson, *Hawkins of Plymouth*, pp. vii–viii.

## Hawkins, Sir Richard (1560–1622), seaman, merchant, and adventurer.

The only child of Sir John Hawkins (q.v.) and his first wife, Katherine Gonson, Richard was born in 1560. There are no records of his early life, but as a member of the prominent Hawkins family of Plymouth he grew up in an environment of shipping and commerce; he probably went to sea when quite young.

In 1582–3 he had command of a ship in a voyage undertaken by his uncle, William Hawkins, to Brazil and Puerto Rico. He later held command under Sir Francis Drake (q.v.) in the expedition to the West Indies of 1585–6. In the fight against the Spanish Armada of 1588 Hawkins commanded the Queen's ship, *Swallow*; he also provided two merchantmen, which were brought into use at Calais as fireships.

Immediately after the Armada Hawkins began to build a galleon of 350 tons, in which he planned to sail on an adventure of his own. His idea was to sail through the Straits of Magellan and on to Peru, where he hoped to obtain sufficient treasure to pay for his expedition; then across the Pacific to eastern Asia, where he would make a detailed survey of colonial and trading possibilities. In the meanwhile he accompanied his father on his voyage to the Spanish coast in 1590; he would have taken part in the projected expedition to Panama of 1592, had this materialized. At about this time he married a Plymouth girl, Judith Heale.

Hawkins's ship, christened the *Repentance* by his mother before her death in 1591, was renamed the *Dainty* at the insistence of the Queen. In April 1593 Hawkins sailed her from the Thames to Plymouth; delayed there by a gale, he was unable to leave until 12 June. He was to be away for ten years.

Having crossed the Atlantic and sailed through the Straits of Magellan, Hawkins was persuaded against his will by a mutinous crew to attack Valparaiso instead of first sailing farther north, as he had intended. Some treasure was taken, and the *Dainty* was lucky to escape from her first encounter with the Spanish; she had no chance when attacked a second time by six faster-moving vessels and 2,000 men against her own seventy-five. Severely wounded in the ensuing three-day battle in the Bay of Atacames, Hawkins surrendered on 22 June 1594, on condition that the survivors of his crew were sent back to England. He himself was detained for three years as a prisoner in Peru, before being transferred to Spain. There he made an attempt to escape. He was imprisoned in Madrid but promised release on payment of £3,000 in ransom. However, while he had been away Sir John Hawkins had died at sea off Puerto Rico, and his widow, Richard's stepmother, refused to pay the ransom. Eventually, through the good offices of Sir Robert Cecil (q.v.), the money was paid, and towards the end of 1602 Hawkins was free to return home to his wife and family in Plymouth.

Now head of the family and still a

wealthy man, Hawkins immersed himself in his former trading activities and in civic duties. He was knighted by James I (see James VI of Scotland) on his accession to the English throne in 1603 and appointed Vice-Admiral of Devon; in 1603–4 he was Mayor of Plymouth and also sat as a Member of Parliament for that town.

In 1620–1 Hawkins was second-in-command of an abortive and badly organized expedition against the Barbary pirates. He died suddenly very soon after his return, on 17 April 1622, leaving a widow, two sons, and four daughters.

Richard Hawkins's *Observations on his Voyage into the South Sea, A.D. 1593*, written in 1602–3 and actually being printed at the time of his death, was first published in 1622. It has been reprinted by the Hakluyt Society (1847) and edited by J. A. Williamson (1933), and is generally regarded as the best contemporary account of life at sea in the Elizabethan age.

J. A. Williamson, *The Observations of Sir Richard Hawkins* (1933).
See also titles listed under Hawkins, Sir John.


**Hayles, John** (d. 1571), see Hales, John.


**Heath, Nicholas** (?1501–1578), Archbishop of York, Lord Chancellor from 1555 to 1559.

Born in London in about 1501, Nicholas Heath was educated at St Anthony's School, London, at Corpus Christi College, Oxford, and at Christ's College, Cambridge. Elected a fellow of Christ's College in 1521, he took his M.A. there in 1522, and in 1524 was elected a fellow of Clare Hall, Cambridge. He became Vicar of Hever, in the deanery of Shoreham, in 1532, Archdeacon of Stafford in 1534, and a Doctor of Divinity in 1535.

In 1535 Heath accompanied Edward Fox, Bishop of Hereford, on a mission to Germany to negotiate with the princes of the Smacaldic League. On his return, in 1537, he was made almoner to the King (see Henry VIII). Bishop of Rochester in 1539, he was in December 1543 appointed to the see of Worcester, which had been vacant for some time following the resignation of Hugh Latimer (q.v.).

While Heath's sympathies were clearly conservative, he went along with Henrican policy. At Henry's command, he supervised the edition of the English translation of the Bible, known as the 'Great Bible', printed in 1541. However, Heath's refusal to accept the form of ordination prescribed by Cranmer in 1550 led to his being twice summoned before the Council; he was imprisoned and later deprived of his see, being then allowed to live in the house of Nicholas Ridley (q.v.), Bishop of London.

Restored to his bishopric on the accession of Mary I (q.v.), Heath was in 1555 elected Archbishop of York. During his period of office, which lasted for four years, he successfully used his influence with the Queen to obtain the restitution of Ripon, Southwell, and other manors to the see. He also built York House in the Strand at this time. In 1556 he was appointed as Lord Chancellor. He was continued in this office for a short while under Elizabeth I (q.v.) and, after relinquishing the Great Seal in 1559, retained his seat on the Council. Heath was responsible for the preliminary arrangements of the disputation of the reformed and unreformed divines at Westminster that took place in the first year of the new reign. He spoke out boldly against the oath required under the Act of Supremacy; on refusing to take the oath he was, together with other bishops, deprived of his see and committed to the Tower, but obtained his liberty soon afterwards on an undertaking that he would not meddle in public affairs. He kept his word and was widely respected for his moderate attitude, which was of considerable influence on the English Roman Catholics.

Heath spent the last years of his life in retirement on his estate at Chobham, Surrey, where the Queen visited him more than once and where he died towards the end of 1578.

*Portrait:* oil, by Hans Eworth, 1566: National Portrait Gallery, London.

**Henry VII** (1457–1509), King of England from 1485.

The son of Edmund Tudor, Earl of Richmond, and Margaret Beaufort (q.v.), Henry was born at Pembroke Castle on 28 January 1457, almost three months after his father's death, and was therefore Earl of Richmond from the time of his birth. On his father's side he was descended from a Welsh squire, Owen Tudor (see *Lives Before the Tudors*), and Catherine de Valois (see *Lives Before the Tudors*), widow of Henry V; his mother, who married again soon after his birth, was a great-grand-daughter of John of Gaunt (see *Lives Before the Tudors*).

Henry was entrusted to the care of his uncle, the Earl of Pembroke (see Tudor, Jasper, in *Lives Before the Tudors*), with whom he spent his early years in Wales. After the Yorkist victory at the Battle of Tewkesbury in May 1471 and the recovery of the throne by Edward IV (see *Lives Before the Tudors*), he was taken by his uncle to Brittany, where, as the last surviving male of the House of Lancaster, it was thought not only that he would be safer, but that he would probably have to remain in exile for the rest of his life. After the death of Edward

IV in April 1483 and the murder of the young Princes, Edward V and Richard, Duke of York (for both see *Lives Before the Tudors*), in the Tower, however, Henry Tudor emerged as the one leader with a solid claim against the usurper, Richard III (see *Lives Before the Tudors*), whose activities were already beginning to split the Yorkist party.

Plans were made for Henry to join the rebellion being organized by the Duke of Buckingham (see Stafford, Henry, in *Lives Before the Tudors*), and John Morton (q.v.), then Bishop of Ely. Prevented by severe storms from landing in England in October 1483, however, he and his fleet were forced back to Brittany, and when Richard III subsequently demanded that Henry should be handed over, he made his escape to the French court. There he was joined by many supporters, and a plan was formulated for the invasion of England; as part of a policy to unite the Yorkists and the Lancastrians, Henry swore on oath, on Christmas Day 1483, that he would marry Elizabeth of York (q.v.) once he had secured the crown.

Early in August Henry landed at Milford Haven in Wales, at the head of 2,000 men; he advanced towards London, rallying more supporters as he went. Even so, when battle was joined at Bosworth Field, near Leicester, on 22 August, his force numbered only about 5,000 to Richard's 10,000. At the last moment the Stanleys (Sir William Stanley and his brother Thomas Stanley, 2nd Baron Stanley, later 1st Earl of Derby, who by his marriage to Margaret Beaufort had become Henry's step-father: for both see *Lives Before the Tudors*) came over to Henry's side, and their support, combined with the defection of Henry Percy, 4th Earl of Northumberland, from Richard's cause, won the day for him; Richard was killed in the fighting. There is however no contemporary corroboration for the traditional story that after the battle Lord Stanley, finding the crown of England on a thorn-bush, placed it on Henry's head.

Henry VII was crowned in London on 30 October, and on 18 January 1486 he honoured his promise to marry Elizabeth of York. She was to bear him three sons, Arthur, Prince of Wales (q.v.), born in 1486, who died at the age of fifteen, Henry, born in 1491, later Henry VIII (q.v.), and Edmund, who died in infancy in 1500; and three daughters, Margaret (see Margaret Tudor), born in 1489, who married James IV of Scotland (q.v.), Elizabeth (born 1492, died 1495) and Mary (see Mary Tudor), born probably in 1496, who was to marry, Louis XII of France and then the Duke of Suffolk (see Brandon, Charles).

From the outset Henry's crown was far from secure. His claim to the throne was legally a weak one, an Act of Parliament having banned all members of the Beaufort family from the succession. Furthermore, he had no financial resources and no army or navy to back him. On the other hand, the discontented Yorkists who had been dispossessed or thrown out of office by the change of régime had a powerful champion in Margaret, Duchess of Burgundy (q.v.), Edward IV's sister, who was bent on making trouble. The first Yorkist plot, the rising of Lord Lovell (see Lovell, Francis, in *Lives Before the Tudors*) in 1486, was put down without too much difficulty; but in the following year the revolt of Lambert Simnel (q.v.), masterminded by the Duchess, and the later invasion of Perkin Warbeck (q.v.) in 1491, proved more difficult to combat. In the case of Simnel, Henry recognized that the young man had been merely a dupe and gave him

employment in the royal kitchens; but Warbeck and the unfortunate Earl of Warwick whom he had impersonated were both executed, probably at the insistence of Ferdinand and Isabella of Spain, who wanted all possible claimants to the throne removed before they would agree to their daughter, Catherine of Aragon (q.v.), marrying the Prince of Wales. There was a further threat from Edmund de la Pole (q.v.), Earl of Suffolk, who had fled to the Netherlands and had the support of the Emperor Maximilian; and not until 1506, after Suffolk had been seized and sent to the Tower, did the King feel really safe.

Henry's two other major preoccupations concerned the accumulation of wealth and the strengthening of the dynasty by suitable marriage alliances for his children, both of which he achieved with some success. At home he pursued a policy of economic caution, combined with the expansion of English trade abroad and the ruthless seeking out of all possible revenues due to the crown. When taxation proved unpopular and likely to incite revolt, as in the case of the Cornish uprising of 1497, Henry's financial advisers set up a system of extorting fines and dues that made them – chiefly Morton, Richard Foxe (q.v.), Sir Richard Empson, and Edmund Dudley – the most hated men in the land. The King himself was able to add to his coffers as a result of some shrewd diplomatic moves, and it was partly on account of her large dowry that Henry was so anxious that the widowed Catherine of Aragon should marry his surviving son, Henry.

That Spain agreed to the marriage alliance was evidence of the growing status of England in the eyes of the Continental powers at the turn of the century; a few years later, Henry was in a position to negotiate for the betrothal of his daughter Mary to the Prince of Castile, the future Emperor Charles V (q.v.), and when he died in 1509 the kingdom was not only soundly administered at home and respected abroad, but also solvent to the extent of about £1½ million.

Henry's foreign policy also was formulated with one eye on the exchequer and another on the dynasty. The war with France into which he had been drawn in the early years of his reign was turned to financial advantage under the peace of 1492; the quarrel with James IV of Scotland over his support for Perkin Warbeck was eventually patched up with a treaty for the Scottish King's marriage to Henry's daughter Margaret in 1502; while the Netherlands and Maximilian, who had also backed Warbeck, were persuaded into the *Intercursus Magnus* of 1496 and a later treaty, known as the *Intercursus Malus*, in 1506, both of which gave England important trading advantages.

Essentially a medievalist, orthodox in religion and conservative in the government of his realm, Henry nevertheless showed great foresight in his patronage of the Cabot family (see Cabot, John, and Cabot, Sebastian), whose voyages of discovery were aimed at opening up new trade routes in the New World. He broke new ground by choosing his advisers and Councillors from the lesser ranks of the nobility and the rising middle class. He showed some interest in scholarship and the arts and seems to have been not entirely the gloomy, sour, avaricious man described by Bacon. Music was in his Welsh blood, and it is on record that he sometimes spent money on entertainment; he also enjoyed hunting and hawking. His extreme wariness and the desire to hoard money undoubtedly stemmed from the circumstances of his early life.

A devoted family man as well as an able King, he was deeply grieved by the deaths of his sons Edmund and Arthur, and after the loss of his consort, Elizabeth, in 1503, Henry reacted strangely. On the one hand he became more miserly than ever; on the other he formulated some extraordinary proposals for his remarriage – in turn to the young Catherine of Aragon, to Juana of Castile, and to the Queen of Naples – none of which came to anything. His health began to fail, and on 21 April 1509 he died at Richmond. He was buried a few days later in the chapel at Westminster Abbey (now known as the Henry VII Chapel) which he had begun to build in 1503 and for which he had commissioned Pietro Torrigiano to design a magnificent tomb. The chapel was completed by his son, who succeeded him as Henry VIII.

F. Bacon, *Historie of the Reigne of Henry the Seventh* (1622; ed. J. R. Lumby, 1885).
S. B. Chrimes, *Henry VII* (1972).
J. Gairdner, *Henry the Seventh* (1889).
J. D. Mackie, *The Earlier Tudors, 1485–1558* (1952).

C. Morris, *The Tudors* (1955).

A. F. Pollard, *The Reign of Henry VII from Contemporary Sources* (3 vols; 1913–14).

R. L. Storey, *The Reign of Henry VII* (1968).

*Portraits:* oil, by unknown artist: Society of Antiquaries, London; drawing, by Jacques Leboucq, in *Recueil d'Arras*: Bibliothèque d'Arras, France; oil, by Master Michiel (Michel Sittow), 1505: National Portrait Gallery, London; polychrome bust, by P. Torrigiano, *c.* 1505–9: Victoria and Albert Museum, London; wax head, by unknown artist, for funeral effigy: Westminster Abbey; tomb effigy, by P. Torrigiano, 1512–19: Westminster Abbey.

## Henry VIII

**Henry VIII** (1491–1547), King of England from 1509 to 1547.

Born at Greenwich on 28 June 1491, Henry was the second son of Henry VII (q.v.) and Elizabeth of York (q.v.). He became heir to the throne in 1502, on the death of his elder brother, Arthur, Prince of Wales (q.v.). In order to prepare him for his future role, Henry's education was entrusted to the best available tutors. Latin, theology, and foreign languages were subjects in which he soon proved his ability; while outside the schoolroom he excelled in all the athletic pursuits of court life – jousting, archery, hunting, and tennis. An accomplished musician, the Prince spent hours practising on the lute and the virginals. He was a superb dancer. Six feet tall and strikingly handsome, with an extravagant taste in dress, his quick-wittedness, affability, and youthful exuberance were in such contrast to the atmosphere prevailing at his father's court that people tended not to observe Henry's less attractive traits – the tiny, suspicious eyes, the capricious temper, the exceptional egotism and obstinacy. Henry took after his Yorkist grandfather, Edward IV (see *Lives Before the Tudors*) in both physical appearance and character. Hopes ran high in England and on the Continent that the Prince would make a great monarch, and his accession in April 1509 was hailed by such eminent scholars as Erasmus (q.v.) and Thomas More (q.v.).

Having thus mounted the throne on a wave of popularity, Henry swept away some of his late father's most hated institutions, and with them most of the officials who had so harshly extorted revenues from the general public to swell the royal coffers. Yet within a few weeks he had plunged the court into a series of costly entertainments in celebration of his marriage to Catherine of Aragon (q.v.), his brother Arthur's widow. A special dispensation had been obtained from the Pope for the marriage, since canon law, based on Leviticus 20:21, expressly prohibited a man from marrying his brother's wife, prophesying that any such union would be childless. Henry, a virile young man of eighteen, would scarcely have paid any attention to this forecast at the time, but it was a phrase that began increasingly to prey upon his mind as Catherine, miscarrying or giving birth to babies that were either stillborn or failed to survive, in one pregnancy after another, proved unable to produce the healthy male heir on whom the continuance of the dynasty depended. (At that date no one even considered the possibility of a female succession; Henry's reaction to the survival of a daughter, born in 1516 and christened Mary – she was in fact the future Mary I (q.v.) – was one of renewed optimism concerning his ability to beget a son and heir.)

At the outset of their marriage (which was by no means an unhappy union, at any rate for the first ten years) Catherine influenced Henry, against the advice of his Councillors, to enter the power struggle in Europe by joining with her father, Ferdinand of Aragon, and the Pope against France. Military adventure appealed to Henry. He invaded France in

1512 and, rather more by luck than by soldierly skill, won the so-called 'Battle of the Spurs', later capturing Thérouanne and Tournai. On returning to England the King learned of the complete victory won over the Scots in his absence by the Earl of Surrey (see Howard, Thomas, 3rd Duke of Norfolk) at Flodden.

The French campaign had been organized by the man who was to be Henry's closest confidant and chief minister for the next sixteen years, Thomas Wolsey (q.v.). Formerly a royal chaplain and almoner, Wolsey next negotiated the peace treaty, with a separate treaty of marriage between the King's sister, Mary Tudor (q.v.), and Louis XII. In 1514 Henry rewarded him with the bishopric of Lincoln. By 1515 the King had not only made Wolsey Archbishop of York and Lord Chancellor of England, but had been instrumental in obtaining for him a cardinal's hat. In the next few years he was to lend his support to Wolsey's unsuccessful ambition to become Pope.

During the period of Wolsey's high office, 1515 to 1527, Henry was only too happy to leave the active conduct of state affairs in his Chancellor's hands, while making it clear that he held absolute authority as King. In foreign policy he and Wolsey worked together to maintain the role of England as 'arbiter of Europe' between the rival powers of France and Spain. Up to 1525 their allegiance lay firmly with France. In 1519, however, the balance of power had been upset by the death of the Emperor Maximilian and the succession of Charles V (q.v.), who represented the united crowns of Spain, Burgundy, the Netherlands, and Austria. The French King (now in an inferior position) and the new Emperor both did their best to woo Henry's support. In June 1520 Henry met François I in an atmosphere of splendour and lavish entertainment at the Field of the Cloth of Gold, near Calais. A few weeks later he met Charles at Gravelines and agreed with him to make no further alliance with France for two years. But when François was defeated by the Emperor at Pavia in 1525, Wolsey made a last-ditch attempt to switch sides yet again, pledging England to help France. Already by this time the image of England's 'greatness' in Europe, as portrayed by the King and Wolsey, was beginning to be seen at home in its true colours. The imposition of heavy taxes, coupled with the effect of reprisals taken by the Emperor against the English cloth trade in the Netherlands, now made Wolsey the most hated man in the country. Not a little of this unpopularity rubbed off on the King, with the result that he himself began to ponder on the continued usefulness of his right-hand man.

By this date Henry had begun to feel not merely disappointed, but extremely worried, and then angry, at his failure to secure the dynasty. Suspicious of all those who might possibly have a claim to the throne, he had already eliminated men like Sir William Courtenay (q.v.) and Edmund de la Pole (q.v.), Earl of Suffolk. In 1521 he had the Duke of Buckingham (see Stafford, Edward, Duke of Buckingham) executed on trumped-up charges of treason connected with the succession. He blamed Catherine for her inability to produce a healthy male child; the fault, he maintained, could not be his, since one of his mistresses, Elizabeth Blount, a lady-in-waiting to the Queen, had in 1519 borne him a son. (Later the King was to be so desperate that he was tempted to name this boy, Henry Fitzroy (q.v.), Duke of Richmond, as his heir. Catherine, six years older than Henry, her health and looks affected by the series of unhappy pregnancies, no longer attracted him.

Some time before 1527 – possibly even as early as 1525 – Henry became infatuated with another of his wife's ladies at court, the vivacious, dark-haired Anne Boleyn (q.v.). That the King was genuinely in love with Anne may be deduced from the letters he addressed to her in his own hand. She, however, refused to become his mistress without the guarantee of a higher status. Thus Henry began to turn over in his mind ways in which he might legitimately rid himself of Catherine. In this, 'the King's great matter' as it came to be known, he turned first for help to Wolsey, hopeful that the Cardinal's influence with the Pope would obtain him a divorce.

Henry's decision to seek a divorce marked the turning-point of his reign. It put Wolsey in a dilemma, since he well knew not only the improbability of getting Clement VII to declare as illegal a marriage that had been specifically licensed by a previous Pope, but also that his own survival in power depended upon a successful outcome. Yet if he were successful on the King's behalf, the chances were that he would be playing into the hands of the anti-clerical Boleyns, who would almost certainly engineer his downfall within a short time. The position of the Pope was equally delicate, for by the time Henry sought annulment of his marriage Clement had become virtually a prisoner of Charles V (who was Catherine's nephew) and was unwilling to risk flouting the Emperor's wishes.

Haunted increasingly by the words of Leviticus, the King soon convinced himself that by marrying Catherine in the first place he had infringed the law of God; after living in mortal sin all these years, his conscience told him that the only way back to grace lay in an annulment. In May 1527 he persuaded Wolsey to act, and was duly summoned before the Cardinal to 'explain' why he had married his brother's widow. A few days later Henry informed Catherine that they must live apart.

For the next two years the divorce hung in the balance, while the power struggle in Europe continued to shift, first in favour of the Emperor, and then in favour of the French. In 1528 the Pope sent Cardinal Campeggio to England to try the case, together with Wolsey, and to pronounce on the validity of the King's marriage. However, within weeks of the Cardinals opening their court, in the early summer of the following year, the political situation again changed and Clement, under pressure from Charles, suddenly revoked the case to Rome. Soon afterwards Henry stripped Wolsey of his high office and appointed Sir Thomas More as Chancellor in his stead.

Persuasion having failed, Henry now sought to win the divorce on which he had determined by putting pressure on

Rome. He summoned a Parliament in November 1529 with the purpose of obtaining its support and, hopefully, in order to force the Pope's hand. He sent ambassadors to the universities of Europe to ascertain their views. But at home there was much conflict of opinion between the anti-clerical House of Commons and the new Chancellor, More; John Fisher (q.v.), Bishop of Rochester, also spoke out against the divorce. Amid the confusion and inaction that followed, the King hesitated between hope that Rome would still allow the trial of his marriage to Catherine to take place in England and implementation of his threat to break with the papacy altogether. Thomas Cranmer (q.v.), a leading Cambridge scholar, came forward with a justification for nullifying Henry's unfortunate marriage. Thomas Cromwell (q.v.) followed with a plan that would establish the royal supremacy over the Church in England. These proposals were seized on by Henry as the solution that would enable him to marry Anne and swell the depleted royal exchequer at the same time. Thus the Reformation in England got under way. It gathered momentum as Cromwell, its vigorous and ruthless architect, gained the King's confidence and won promotion from Privy Councillor to Secretary of State and, by 1536, to the office of Lord Privy Seal.

Early in 1533 Cromwell steered through Parliament the Act in Restraint of Appeals, which ended the system of appeals to Rome in matrimonial and testamentary cases. In January that year the King was secretly married to Anne, who was pregnant; it was essential that if she gave birth to a boy, he should be legitimate. In May the newly-appointed Archbishop Thomas Cranmer (q.v.) formally pronounced Henry's first marriage to be annulled and the succession to be vested in his issue by Anne. Crowned in June, the new Queen gave birth to a daughter, the future Elizabeth I (q.v.), in September. Too late, in the spring of the following year, the Pope declared in favour of Catherine; on discovering that he had been outmanoeuvred by Henry, he issued a sentence of excommunication. To this the King, secure in his new position as supreme head of the Church of England, paid no attention.

Henry, who had been brought up as a loyal Catholic, was to give much thought to religious matters over the next decade. He had been deeply interested in theological studies in his youth, and in 1521 had staunchly defended the papacy against Martin Luther (q.v.) in his book on the sacraments, *Assertio septum sacramentorum*, for which Pope Leo X had rewarded him with the title of *Fidei Defensor* ('Defender of the Faith'). Now, although he had separated the Church of England from the Church of Rome, and had gone to great lengths to defy the Pope, Henry still clung to the old faith, especially in regard to the doctrines of transubstantiation and clerical celibacy. He had no intention, as Cromwell and Cranmer had, of furthering the Protestant Reformation in England, let alone Lutheranism. His quarrel was to be seen as a quarrel with the Pope and not with the fundamental teachings of the Catholic Church. Supporters of Luther would be severely dealt with, as would those who, like More and Fisher, refused to take the oath acknowledging the King's supremacy and ultimately paid for their courage with their lives.

In 1535 Cromwell began to enforce the transfer of all monastic property to the crown. As a preliminary to complete dissolution, a bill was introduced into Parliament suppressing all monasteries

236

with a revenue of less than £200 a year. Unpopular in the North, it sparked off a formidable insurrection in the northern counties in October that year, known as the Pilgrimage of Grace. By 1540 all the monastic houses in the country had been dissolved. A Court of Augmentations was set up to handle the redistribution of grants and leases to the King's friends and those who had served him well; this ultimately greatly reinforced the property basis of the gentry and middle classes.

The Pilgrimage of Grace, led by Robert Aske (q.v.), was directed mainly against the dissolution of the smaller monasteries; but it was also in part a revolt against agrarian policy, principally the enclosure of land. Its failure and suppression enabled Henry to proceed with the dissolution of the larger and richer monasteries. In 1537 he sanctioned the publication of *The Institution of a Christian Man*, also known as *The Bishops' Book*, which was orthodox in all respects except that of the supremacy of the Pope. In 1538 the King ordered a copy of the English Bible to be placed in every parish church throughout the realm; to this end he licensed the publication of the so-called 'Great Bible' (also known as 'Cranmer's Bible'), which was printed the following year. Then in 1539 Henry took a further step towards securing uniformity with the conservative Statute of the Six Articles, sometimes called the 'whip with six strings' or the 'Bloody Bill'; this laid down harsh penalties for infringement, including the death sentence for anyone who spoke against transubstantiation. It was followed in 1543 by restrictions on the use of the English Bible and an even more orthodox definition entitled *The Necessary Doctrine and Erudition of Any Christian Man,* popularly known as *The King's Book* on account of the influence

Henry had brought to bear on the bishops who prepared the work.

Meanwhile the King still had no male heir. Disappointed at the birth of the Princess Elizabeth, as early as 1534 he had begun visibly to tire of Anne and was casting his eyes in the direction of one of her ladies-in-waiting, Jane Seymour (q.v.). When Anne gave birth to a stillborn child in January 1536, shortly after the death of his first wife, Catherine of Aragon, Henry lost no time in employing Cromwell to get rid of her, in order that he could be free to marry Jane, an indubitable marriage which could not be questioned. Trumped-up charges of treasonable adultery were accordingly brought against Anne and five so-called 'lovers', all of whom were executed in May that year. Henry then married Jane Seymour, to whom he appears to have been genuinely attached. She bore him the son he so earnestly desired, the future Edward VI (q.v.), but herself died a few days later, in October 1537.

There followed a three-year search throughout Europe for another suitable bride for the English King. At last Henry agreed to a lady chosen by Cromwell for political reasons (to further an alliance with the German Lutheran states, so as to counter the threatened alliance of France and Spain) – Anne of Cleves (q.v.). Unfortunately for Cromwell, who fell from power as a result, Henry took an instant dislike to his fourth bride on sight. Anne wisely kept her head by complacently agreeing to a divorce six months later, in return for a generous financial settlement. Her place was taken briefly by the young Catherine Howard (q.v.), a niece of the Duke of Norfolk (see Howard, Thomas, 3rd Duke); her promiscuous adventures behind the King's back brought her to the block eighteen months later.

In the last years of his life, Henry found

a modicum of domestic happiness with Katherine Parr (q.v.), his sixth wife, whom he married in July 1543. Through her beneficial influence he was persuaded to restore to his two daughters the rank of princess which he had taken from them on the grounds of their bastardy. By this date, however, he was no longer the debonair, pleasure-loving monarch of earlier years, but a sick man, constantly complaining that his misfortunes and ill-health were totally undeserved, unpredictable in his moods and given to outbursts of violent temper. An ulcer on his leg had for some time prevented him from taking the strenuous exercise to which he had been accustomed in his youth, with the result that he had grown excessively fat; often melancholic and bitter, he looked older than his fifty years. By 1547 the King was in constant pain and so swollen in body that his legs would not carry his weight and he had to be helped to move about. Yet he remained in as full control of government as ever; foreign observers paid tribute to his ability.

After Cromwell's fall, which later he regretted, Henry acted as his own chief minister and policy maker. When hostilities were resumed between Charles V and France, both sides once again wooing the English King for support, he allied himself with the Emperor. In his third French war the Scots were allies of the French, and Henry aimed at forcing English supremacy upon Scotland. In October 1542 he sent an army across the Border under the command of Norfolk. This invasion was a fiasco, but when James V (q.v.) counter-attacked the following month, the English successfully routed the Scots at the Battle of Solway Moss. However, Henry failed to achieve the alliance he sought by means of the betrothal of his son Edward to the infant Mary, Queen of Scots (q.v.).

France and Spain came to terms in 1544. The Emperor left Henry in the lurch, for England now had to face France, much bigger and stronger, alone. Irrespective of the ruinous drain on his finances, Henry held on to Boulogne, which had been captured, and stubbornly refused to make peace for another two years. He had created a strong navy and now fortified the Channel coast against attack by superior French forces. He tried to meet the enormous cost of the war first by taxation and borrowing, then by selling off some of the former monastic lands, and finally by debasing the coinage. Weak in body, but mentally alert as ever, and so hot-tempered that no one dared to let him know that he was dying, the King kept his hand on the helm until the very end. In his determination to control the succession of his son to the throne, he had several years before got rid of the last possible surviving Plantagenet claimants; now, on his deathbed, one of Henry's last acts was to order the execution of the Duke of Norfolk and his son, Henry Howard (q.v.), Earl of Surrey, for treasonable plotting connected with the succession.

Henry died at Westminster on 28 January 1547, the day before the sentence on Norfolk was to have been carried out, but he had determined the arrangements for the minority rule of his nine-year-old son. He left Edward under the control of his uncle, the Earl of Hertford (see Seymour, Edward), with the majority of the Councillors named to rule for him ready to continue to further the Reformation. The kingdom he left his son was, however, divided in religion and beggared by a pointless war. Henry was not to know that because of Edward's frail health, the problem that had dominated the best part of his own life – that of the succession – was in no way solved.

A controversial figure in his own day

and since, Henry VIII represented to his subjects an outsize embodiment of monarchy. A faux-bonhomme, capricious and cruel, he was always popular and – in many respects – a successful ruler. No one less strong could have piloted the country through a religious revolution. Henry, domineering and arrogant, determined to get his own way in all things, and continually seeking to improve his kingdom's status in the eyes of the rest of the world, gave his people a new feeling of pride in their nation. He also gave them an English Bible, union with Wales, and the foundation of the Tudor navy. He understood the importance of a good relationship between crown and Parliament, and had the political sense to drive through Parliament the subjection of the Church and the religious changes representing the will of the nation. He was not, in relation to the morals of the age, grossly immoral. His sexual adventures have been much exaggerated. Henry's tremendous personal charm won a place in the hearts of the ordinary people that endured, unaffected by the series of matrimonial mishaps that turned him into a laughing-stock throughout Europe in the last decade of the reign.

The King's divorce was not the cause of the Reformation in England, but it provided the occasion for it. Although he presided over the early stages of that Reformation, Henry himself did not challenge religious doctrine, but rather lent his authority and influence to restrain the reformers and, so far as was in his power, upheld the orthodoxy of Catholic doctrine in England.

Frustration over his failure to beget a legitimate male heir dominated Henry's middle years and, with the opposition he encountered from both Catherine and her daughter, and also from Anne, was largely responsible for the hardening in his personality: the transformation from

a debonair, affable Prince when young to the capricious, almost megalomaniacal, tyrant of the last years. In spite of ill-health, and often agonizing pain, he retained his ability and will-power, and his grip on government, to the last.

L. Baldwin Smith, *Henry VIII: The Mask of Royalty* (1971).
A. F. Pollard, *Henry VIII* (1902; reprinted 1966).
J. J. Scarisbrick, *Henry VIII* (1968).

*Portraits:* oil, by unknown artist, *c.* 1520: location unknown (sold at Christie's, 7 July 1967); miniature, by Lucas Hornebolte, *c.* 1526–7: Fitzwilliam Museum, Cambridge; oil, by unknown artist, *c.* 1527: location unknown (sold at Christie's, 23 March 1956); oil, attributed to Joos van Cleve, *c.* 1535: Royal Collection, Hampton Court; oil, by Hans Holbein the Younger, *c.* 1536: Thyssen-Bornemicza Collection, Lugano, Switzerland; oil, by unknown artist after Holbein, *c.* 1536: National Portrait Gallery, London; ink and watercolour, by Holbein (cartoon for wall painting), 1536–7: N.P.G.; oil, attributed to Hans Eworth, 1537: Walker Art Gallery, Liverpool; two oils, by unknown artists of a late non-Holbein pattern, *c.* 1535–47: N.P.G.; oil, attributed to Holbein, *c.* 1542: Castle Howard (George Howard Esq); oil, by unknown artist, probably early seventeenth century copy of Castle Howard portrait: N.P.G.; miniature (posthumous), by Nicholas Hilliard, after Holbein: Royal Collection, Windsor. See also two groups: copies by R. van Leemput, mid-seventeenth century, after wall painting by Holbein of Henry VII, Elizabeth of York, Henry VIII, and Jane Seymour: Royal Collection, Windsor, and Petworth House, Sussex; cartoon by Holbein for painting of Henry VIII and the Barber-Surgeons: Royal College of Surgeons of England, London; also the series of historical pictures, *The Meeting of Henry VIII and Maximilian I, The Battle of the Spurs, The Embarkation of Henry VIII for Boulogne,* and *The Field of the Cloth of Gold,* all in the Royal Collection. For details of numerous other copies and engravings, see the iconography in Roy Strong, *Tudor and Jacobean Portraits* (1969), vol. 1, pp. 157–61.

## Henslowe, Philip (?1550–1616), theatrical manager.

The fourth son of Edmund Henslowe and his wife, Margaret Ridge of Lindfield, Sussex, Philip Henslowe was born probably in about 1550, and was first employed as a servant to a man called Woodward, a dyer and bailiff to Viscount Montagu, who owned Battle Abbey, Cowdray Park, and Montagu House, Southwark. Some time before 1577 Henslowe's duties required him to settle in Southwark, where eventually he married his employer's widow, wealthy Agnes Woodward; through her he became the owner of considerable property in that locality.

Henslowe was a shrewd businessman with diverse interests – dyeing, starch-making, moneylending, and theatrical management. He bought and sold property in Sussex and Southwark, and in the latter district owned a number of inns and lodging houses. Over the years his influence in the parish, of which he was a churchwarden, became quite considerable.

The first of Henslowe's theatrical ventures began in March 1585, when he purchased land in Southwark on which there already stood, on Bankside, near Southwark Bridge, a playhouse called the Little Rose. He rebuilt the theatre, and opened it in 1592 under his own management, letting it to Lord Strange's and other companies of players continually until 1603. He also had an interest in the theatre at Newington Butts in 1594; later he was involved in the Swan Theatre at the Paris Garden, Bankside.

In 1592 Henslowe's step-daughter, Joan Woodward, married the actor Edward Alleyn (q.v.), and from that time onwards Alleyn was closely concerned with his father-in-law's many theatrical enterprises. One of the most profitable of these was the Paris Garden on Bankside, of which they acquired the lease in 1594 and where they were licensed to present bear- and bull-baiting. In 1604 Henslowe and Alleyn jointly became Master of the Royal Game of Bears, Bulls and Mastiff Dogs. Alleyn later sold his interest to Henslowe, who with a new partner, Jacob Meade, demolished the old buildings and erected on the same site a new playhouse, the Hope, designed for both players and bear-baiting, and also an inn called the Dancing Bears.

The Fortune theatre, in Golden Lane, Cripplegate, built by Henslowe and Alleyn for the Admiral's Men (the rival company to the Lord Chamberlain's, for which William Shakespeare (q.v.) wrote exclusively, and which played at the Globe under the management of James Burbage (q.v.)), was opened in November 1600; it was the largest playhouse of the day, and Henslowe remained actively interested in it for the rest of his life.

As owner-manager of the Rose, Hope, and Fortune playhouses, Henslowe was on intimate terms with all the leading Elizabethan dramatists. His practice was to buy plays outright from their authors and to hire them out, together with the necessary theatrical properties, to the various companies. He kept a tight control over policy and over his actors, who were under contract to him personally and with whom in consequence relations were not always the most cordial; he himself once stated that if ever his players ceased to be in his debt, he would have no rule over them. In the last years of Henslowe's life a charge was brought against him by some of his actors, but its outcome is not known.

The most important theatrical manager of the Elizabethan age, Philip Henslowe died on 6 January 1616 and was buried at St Saviour's, Southwark. The diary in which he had kept details of playhouse accounts, expenses on costumes, payments to playwrights and actors, and so on, is the best documentary source for theatrical history of the period. The original diary is in Dulwich College Library; it has been edited by W. W. Greg in two volumes (1904–8). The same author has also published *Henslowe papers* (1907).

E. K. Chambers, *The Elizabethan Stage*, vol. ii (Oxford, 1923).

**Hepburn, Francis Stewart** (d. 1624), 5th Earl of Bothwell, sometimes called the 'Wizard Earl'.

Francis Stewart Hepburn was the eldest son of John Stewart, Prior of Coldingham, one of the natural children of James V (q.v.), and nephew of the Earl of Moray (see Stewart, Lord James). His mother was the Lady Jane Hepburn, only daughter of the 3rd Earl of Bothwell and sister of the 4th Earl (see Hepburn, James). The date of his birth is not known, nor are there any details of his early life.

On 29 July 1576, it being presumed that the 4th Earl was already dead (in fact he was still held in captivity in Denmark), Stewart was created Earl of Bothwell and also appointed to a number of his uncle's offices. He attended Parliament as a supporter of the Regent, the Earl of Morton (see Douglas, James) in July 1578, and the following month was married to the Lady Margaret Douglas, elder daughter of David Douglas, 7th Earl of Angus, a kinsman of Morton.

Following the Regent's fall from power in 1580, Bothwell fled to the Continent. He returned after Morton's execution to pose as an ardent champion of the Protestant cause at court. He won the favour of James VI (q.v.), which lasted until the King's discovery that Bothwell had been implicated (albeit not actively) in the Ruthven Raid of 1582 (see Ruthven, William). In 1585 he joined the conspiracy of the Master of Gray (see Gray, Patrick) for the over-throw of the Earl of Arran (see Stewart, James, Earl of Arran); when the latter had fled the country Bothwell was restored nominally to favour, but his influence was curtailed by the rise to power of John Maitland (q.v.; later 1st Baron Maitland of Thirlestane). Bothwell constantly changed sides; he tried unsuccessfully to persuade James to take advantage of the proposed Spanish Armada of 1588 to invade England from the north; the following year he supported the rebellion of George Gordon, 6th Earl of Huntly, and the northern lords, for which he was imprisoned briefly at Tantallon; a few months after his release the unstable Earl took up with Maitland against Huntly.

In 1590–1 the scandal of the North Berwick witchcraft trials disclosed not only that Bothwell had instigated black magic rituals to raise storms at sea during James's marriage journey to Denmark, but also that he had caused waxen images to be made and had indulged in other sinister practices aimed at the King's destruction. Arrested and imprisoned in Edinburgh Castle in the spring of 1591, he escaped the following June and was declared an outlaw.

Bothwell now embarked on a campaign of terrorism against James, hoping to frighten the King into restoring him to favour. On the night of 27 December 1591 at Holyroodhouse he carried out the first of a series of raids against the King and Maitland, but managed to escape before he could be arrested. Secretly some of the nobles sympathized with him on account of their mutual jealousy of Maitland, with the result that when James offered a reward to anyone who would kill the Earl, there was no response. On 20 June 1592, shortly after he had been forfeited by Parliament, Bothwell attacked Falkland Palace. This time the King had been warned by his watch, and the local population came to his assistance; again, however, the Earl escaped. His forfeiture was confirmed by Parliament in July 1583, and on the 24th of that month he entered Holyroodhouse and got as far as the King's bedchamber, where he laid his sword at James's feet. An understanding was reached that the Earl would stand trial for the outstanding charge of witchcraft, from which he would be acquitted and then retire from court.

In April 1594, however, Bothwell launched a fourth (and last) futile attack against the King. Afterwards he joined up with Huntly and the Catholic lords; the Kirk, who had until now supported him as a 'sanctified scourge' in the hope that he might cause the King to desist from his policy of favouring the Catholic lords, finally turned against him. James mustered his forces and in the autumn of 1594, together with Andrew Melville (q.v.), marched against Bothwell and Huntly. Faced with the threat of having his castle blown up if he did not hand the Earl over, Huntly allowed Bothwell to escape before surrendering.

Excommunicated by the Kirk at the King's request in February 1595, Bothwell fled to France, and then to Spain and Italy; he was to spend the rest of his life as a wandering exile. He died in extreme poverty in Naples in 1624.

See the titles listed under James VI.

**Hepburn, James** (?1535–1578), 4th Earl of Bothwell, third husband of Mary, Queen of Scots (q.v.).

James Hepburn was born probably in 1535, the son of Patrick Hepburn, 3rd Earl of Bothwell (known as the 'Fair Earl'), whom he succeeded in 1556 as 4th Earl, Warden of the Scottish Marches, and Lord High Admiral of Scotland.

James was brought up by a relative, the Bishop of Moray, and received an excellent education. Although a Protestant, he supported the policy of Marie de Guise (q.v.), who was Regent for the young Mary, Queen of Scots; she trusted him absolutely and just before her death was about to send him on a mission to France to raise troops and money. He travelled instead to Denmark, where he seduced a young Norwegian woman, Anna Throndsen, whom he later abandoned in poverty, and then on to France, where his first meeting with the Queen of Scots took place. On the death of Mary's husband, François II, Bothwell was sent by the Queen to Scotland as one of her commissioners; the following year he became a member of her Privy Council.

Bothwell was constantly in trouble because of his feud with the powerful Earl of Arran (see Stewart, James, Earl of Arran); when the latter accused him of trying to kidnap the Queen in 1562, he was for a short time imprisoned in Edinburgh Castle. He managed to escape, and was on his way by ship to France when a storm forced him to put in to Holy Island; for the next few months he was detained in England, eventually reaching France in September 1564.

In 1565 Mary recalled him to help suppress the rebellion led by her half-brother, the Earl of Moray (see Stewart, Lord James) in opposition to her marriage to Lord Darnley (see Stewart, Henry). In February of that year Bothwell married the Lady Jean Gordon, sister of the Earl of Huntly. Both he and Huntly were at Holyroodhouse on the night of the murder of David Riccio (q.v.), 9 March 1566, but they had no part in it. Bothwell's resolute action in getting the Queen and Darnley to the safety of Dunbar Castle, where he later joined them, won the Earl Mary's gratitude and affection; by the end of the year she had made him one of her most powerful courtiers. When precisely he became determined to marry the Queen, and when Mary, disillusioned with Darnley, accepted Bothwell as her lover, is not clear (the authenticity of the Casket Letters is a matter of controversy); it seems fairly certain, however, that by early 1567 the Queen knew that she was pregnant by Bothwell, and also that it had been agreed between him and the other lords that Darnley must be eliminated, either by divorce or other means.

After Darnley's murder at Kirk o' Field in February 1567, public opinion accused Bothwell of the deed and the Queen of foreknowledge of it. But when Darnley's father, the Earl of Lennox (see Stewart, Matthew), brought an action against him, Bothwell was formally acquitted in what was blatantly an 'arranged' trial; far from losing his influence at court, his position was enhanced by the grant of more lands. In April he intercepted the Queen on her way from Stirling to Edinburgh, with her collusion, and carried her off to Dunbar Castle. Early in May Bothwell was granted a divorce from his wife; on the 15th of the same month, Mary having the previous day created him Duke of Orkney and Shetland, they were married in the chapel at Holyroodhouse.

Immediately the Catholic and Protestant lords, regarding Bothwell as a usurper, joined together in revolt. Warned that an attempt would be made to seize them, Mary and Bothwell fled to Borthwick Castle, and from there to Dunbar. On 15 June they faced the rebels at Carberry Hill, near Musselburgh. There Mary's supporters dwindled away, and she surrendered without a fight, on condition that Bothwell was allowed to escape. While she was taken

in captivity to Edinburgh, he rode to Dunbar. They never met again.

Visiting first his old friend, the Bishop of Moray, at Spynie, and then the islands of Orkney and Shetland, where he was hotly pursued by Sir William Kirkaldy of Grange (who had sworn to bring his corpse to Edinburgh or die in the attempt), Bothwell next landed on the coast of Norway. There he had the misfortune to come into contact with some old creditors and also relatives of Anna Throndsen, the former mistress whom he had abandoned; they combined to have him captured and taken, first to Bergen, and then to Copenhagen. Frederick II of Denmark held him initially as a pawn against Elizabeth I (q.v.), but once he had ceased to be useful in this respect the rigours of his imprisonment were hardened. Bothwell spent his last years incarcerated in the fortress of Dragsholm, where he was driven insane by the terrible conditions and died on 4 April 1578.

R. F. Gore-Brown, *Lord Bothwell* (1937).

H. Cockburn and T. Maitland (eds.), *Les Affaires du Conte de Boduel, 1568* (Bannatyne Club, Edinburgh, 1829).

J. Stuart, *A Lost Chapter in the History of Mary, Queen of Scots, recovered* (Edinburgh, 1874).

F. Schiern, *James Hepburn, Earl of Bothwell,* translated from the Danish by the Rev. D. Berry (Edinburgh, 1880).

*Portrait:* miniature, by unknown artist, 1566: Scottish National Portrait Gallery, Edinburgh.

## Herbert, Sir William (?1501–1570), 1st Earl of Pembroke (of the second creation).

The eldest son of Sir Richard Herbert, illegitimate son of William Herbert, Earl of Pembroke (of the first creation) and his wife Margaret, William Herbert was born in about 1501. Entering the service of his kinsman, the Earl of Worcester, at an early age, he soon attracted attention at court and in 1526 became an Esquire of the Body of Henry VIII (q.v.). He was known as a fighter, and after involvement in an affray at Bristol in which a man was killed, in 1527, he fled to the Continent and served for a time in the French army.

On returning to England Herbert married Anne, daughter of Sir Thomas Parr and sister of Katherine Parr (q.v.), who in July 1543 became the sixth wife of Henry VIII; following the marriage of his sister-in-law to the King, Herbert's fortunes took a dramatic upward turn. Knighted in 1543, he was the following January appointed Captain of the town and castle of Aberystwyth; in 1546 he became a Gentleman of the Privy Chamber, Steward of crown properties in the west of England, and Keeper of Barnard's Castle on the banks of the Thames, which he used as his London residence. Among royal favours were the grants of Cardiff Castle and the dissolved Abbey of Wilton, near Salisbury, where Herbert began to build himself a fine mansion in keeping with his influential position.

Herbert was an executor of Henry VIII's will and a member of the Council of the new sovereign, Edward VI (q.v.). He supported the assumption of the role of Protector by the Earl of Hertford (see Seymour, Edward), and was himself created a Knight of the Garter and made Master of the Horse by the young King. In 1549 he raised 2,000 men from his Welsh estates to put down disturbances in the west of England. Both Somerset and his rival for power, the Earl of Warwick (see Dudley, John; later Duke of Northumberland), had for some time been seeking his support, but by this date Herbert had lost his former confidence in Somerset and had joined Warwick in seeking the Protector's overthrow. Appointed President of Wales in 1550, Herbert took part in Somerset's trial at the end of 1551 and was generously rewarded for his services by Northumberland, being created Earl of Pembroke and granted the deposed Protector's Wiltshire estates. He worked closely with Northumberland in the conspiracy to put the Lady Jane Grey (q.v.) on the throne in succession to Edward; but in the event, on realizing the extent of the support for Mary (see Mary I) throughout the country, he swiftly changed sides and declared for the new Queen.

On her accession Mary and her advisers not unnaturally regarded Pembroke with some suspicion, for his Protestant sympathies were well known. He greatly feared losing his estates and managed to convince the Queen of his loyalty, first by his part in suppressing the Wyatt rebellion of 1554 (see Wyatt, Thomas, the younger) and then by winning the confidence of Mary's consort, Philip II of Spain (q.v.). In 1555 he was one of the envoys sent to France in an attempt to arbitrate between that country and the Holy Roman Empire; the negotiations failed, and on his return Pembroke retired to Wilton. The following year he accompanied Philip to Brussels and was appointed as Governor of Calais. When Philip returned to

England in the spring of 1557, in order to organize aid for the Spanish forces in Flanders, Pembroke was given command of the English force that was sent to St Quentin and successfully stormed that town.

Under Elizabeth I (q.v.) Pembroke zealously supported Sir William Cecil (q.v.) and the return to Protestantism. A severe illness prevented him from taking a major part in political affairs for some time, but in 1568 he was appointed Lord Steward of the Royal Household. The following year, however, he made clear his sympathy for the scheme to marry the Duke of Norfolk (see Howard, Thomas, 4th Duke) to Mary, Queen of Scots (q.v.), and he was arrested on a charge of disloyalty to the Queen. He managed to clear himself of the charge and, on pleading to be allowed to prove his loyalty, he was restored to favour.

Pembroke died at Hampton Court on 17 March 1570. He was buried in St Paul's Cathedral.

John Aubrey, *Brief Lives* (1898).
J. E. Nightingale, *Some Notices of William Herbert, 1st Earl of Pembroke* (1878).

*Portraits*: oil, by unknown artist: Wilton House; engraving: Holland's *Herwologia*, 1620. (N.B. The portrait by Hans Eworth, acquired by the National Gallery, London, as that of Pembroke, has now been established as a portrait of Anthony Browne, 1st Viscount Montague.)

**Hertford, Countess of** (1540–1568), see Grey, Lady Katherine.

**Hertford, 1st Earl of** (?1500–1552), see Seymour, Edward.

**Heywood, John** (?1497–?1580), singer and player on the virginals, epigrammist, playwright, and actor.

Born either in London or in North Mimms, Hertfordshire, in about 1497, John Heywood is believed to have started his career as one of the Children of the Chapel Royal. From 1519 onwards he was on the payroll of Henry VIII (q.v.), with whom he was a favourite singer and player on the virginals; he was probably introduced at court by Sir Thomas More (q.v.) following his marriage to Elizabeth Rastell, More's niece. The grants made to him out of the privy purse indicate that, despite his devout Catholic beliefs (he had been made to recant publicly his denial of the King's supremacy in 1544), Heywood continued in favour throughout the reign of Edward VI (q.v.). He was even more highly regarded by the Princess Mary, later Mary I (q.v.), to whom he was at one time a teacher of music, his fortunes being at their peak during her reign.

Pageant-maker, actor, and playwright, Heywood turned his hand to a variety of theatrical tasks and was equally at home in rustic farce or court masque. His own plays, or interludes, were all written in his middle years. The four interludes definitely ascribed to him are *The Four P's*, first printed probably in 1545, *The Play of the Wether* and *A Dialogue concerning Wytty and Wytless* (both 1533), and *A Play of Love* (1534). Among other plays believed to have been written by Heywood are the anticlerical satire *The Pardoner and the Frere* and the domestic comedy *Johan Johan*. His collection of English proverbs appeared in 1549 and a collection of epigrams, issued as *John Heywoodes Woorkes*, in 1562. He was also the author of several ballads and a long allegorical poem contrasting Catholicism and Protestantism, *The Spider and the Flie*, published in 1556.

On the accession of Elizabeth I (q.v.) Heywood, as a Catholic, deemed it prudent to go abroad. Leaving his property in the care of John Donne (father of the poet), he settled in Belgium, initially at Malines, but later at Antwerp and Louvain. He died in exile in about 1579–80, aged over eighty.

John Heywood was the first of the Tudor dramatists to use characters drawn from everyday life rather than from the Bible, thus pointing the way to the development of later Elizabethan comedy. He differed from his predecessors, the writers of the morality plays, also in that he set out as much to entertain as to instruct.

R. W. Bolwell, *The Life and Works of John Heywood* (1921).
J. De la Bère, *John Heywood, Entertainer* (1937).

**Heywood, Thomas** (*c.* 1574–1641), dramatist, see *Lives of the Stuart Age.*

**Hilliard, Nicholas** (?1547–1619), miniature painter.

Born probably in 1547, Nicholas Hilliard was the son of an Exeter goldsmith, Richard Hilliard, who in 1560 held office as High Sheriff of Devon. At an early age he was appren-

ticed to a London goldsmith, whose daughter he later married.

While training to be a jeweller and goldsmith, from about 1560 onwards Hilliard began to experiment in 'limning', as miniature painting was known in the sixteenth century. He seems to have been a precocious youth: at the age of thirteen he painted a self-portrait in miniature, and at eighteen a portrait of Mary, Queen of Scots (q.v.). As he himself later acknowledged, he was much influenced by studying the works of Hans Holbein the younger (q.v.).

In about 1572 Hilliard was appointed as limner and goldsmith to Queen Elizabeth I (q.v.), of whom he was to paint a number of portraits. He had the good fortune to portray the Queen as she wished to be portrayed, and at some time in the 1580s was accorded the monopoly of painting the sovereign in miniature. He seems also to have painted most of the Queen's courtiers, although not all his work has survived; among his special friends at court were Sir Philip Sidney (q.v.) and Sir Christopher Hatton (q.v.).

After his marriage, at the age of twenty-nine, Hilliard was allowed to spend a short time in France in the service of the Duc d'Alençon (q.v.); he became a favourite among the French courtiers and stayed abroad for about two years, returning to London early in 1578.

Hilliard never painted on ivory, but on card, vellum, or chicken-skin; sometimes he used the backs of playing-cards. Parallel with his career as a painter, he carried on the trade of goldsmith and jeweller, and in 1584, at the Queen's request, he redesigned the Great Seal of England. His miniatures were designed as jewels, to be worn in the pendants and lockets which he made for them. Much of this intricate work was carried out under Hilliard's surveillance by apprentices, including his son Laurence, who was born in about 1582, Rowland Lockey, and the most brilliant of all the painter's pupils, Isaac Oliver (q.v.).

By the turn of the century Oliver had become a serious rival; on the accession of James VI of Scotland (q.v.) as James I of England in 1603, when the royal patronage was continued, Hilliard was appointed as limner to the King and Oliver as limner to Queen Anne (see Anne of Denmark in *Lives of the Stuart Age*). In spite of the fact that he was still earning considerable fees for his work, Hilliard appears to have been in serious financial difficulties at this time, due largely to his own extravagance, but also because he adhered to his linear technique without shadowing, which some considered as old-fashioned. For a short time in 1617 he was imprisoned in Ludgate; however, this may have been as surety for someone else.

In about 1600 Hilliard began to write a *Treatise on the Arte of Limning*, in which he described his technique and, among other sidelines, recorded his conversations with the Queen. The manuscript was unfinished at the time of the painter's death in the parish of St Martins-in-the-Fields, Westminster, on 7 January 1619, at the age of seventy-two.

Nicholas Hilliard was the greatest English-born painter of the Elizabethan period. His work raised the standard of miniature painting to its highest level and considerably influenced English portraiture of the sixteenth and seventeenth centuries. The poet John Donne (see *Lives of the Stuart Age*) wrote

A hand or eye
By Hilliard drawn is worth an history
By a worse painter made.

Equally gifted in portraying men and women, youth and middle age, Hilliard also painted a series of more sentimental, emblematic portraits, including *An Un-known Youth leaning against a Tree Among Roses* and *An Unknown Man against a Background of Flames*. He accomplished a vast amount of work in his long life; it is known that he executed some large-scale pictures, but apart from his miniatures much of his work is unidentifiable. There are no known oils that can be attributed to him with any certainty.

Many of Hilliard's paintings are in the Royal Collection; the National Portrait Gallery and Victoria and Albert Museum, London; the National Maritime Museum, Greenwich; the Bodleian Library, Oxford; the Fitzwilliam Museum, Cambridge; and the Metropolitan Museum, New York. His treatise *The Arte of Limning* was published in 1912.

Erna Auerbach, *Nicholas Hilliard* (1961).
N. Blakiston, 'Nicolas Hilliard at court', *Burlington Magazine*, xcvi (1954), pp. 17–18.
G. Reynolds, *Nicholas Hilliard and Isaac Oliver* (Victoria and Albert Museum Handbook, 1947).

Portrait: self-portrait, at the age of thirty, 1577: Victoria and Albert Museum, London.

**Hobson, Thomas** (?1544–1631), Cambridge carrier.

Hobson was born in about 1544, probably at Buntingford, Hertfordshire, the son of Thomas Hobson, a carrier by trade, who settled in Cambridge in 1561 and at the time of his death was one of the treasurers of the corporation. On his father's death in 1568 Thomas inherited copyhold lands at Granchester and the team of cart and eight horses. He continued the business and conducted it so successfully that he amassed a considerable fortune. His terminus in London was the Black Bull at Bishopsgate.

The statement that he was the first to let out horses for hire in England is doubtful; Hobson's fame rests on his stubbornness in refusing to let any horse be taken from his stables out of turn, telling his customers that they could have 'this one or none'. From this grew the saying 'Hobson's choice'.

Hobson looked after his horses with extreme care and used to tell Cambridge scholars that they would reach London soon enough 'if they did not ride too fast'. His reputation as a carrier extended far beyond the university town, and he continued his regular journeys to London until 1630, when they had to be suspended by order of the authorities on account of plague. During this enforced cessation of trade Hobson died, in his beloved Cambridge, on 7 January 1631. The poet John Milton (see *Lives of the Stuart Age*) wrote two epitaphs on him.

He was a benefactor to Cambridge, where a street is named after him. He gave to the town and university lands on which the Spinning House, known as 'Hobson's Workhouse', was built, and also provided in his will for the perpetual maintenance of the conduit in the market place.

*Portraits*: oil, equestrian portrait, by unknown artist, 1620: Cambridge Guildhall; oil, by unknown artist, probably late seventeenth or early eighteenth century: National Portrait Gallery, London; other versions at University Registry and Queens' College, Cambridge.

**Holbein, Hans** (?1497–1543), known as Hans Holbein the Younger, painter, miniaturist, book illustrator, designer of stained glass and jewellery; the greatest portrait painter of his age and possibly of all time.

The second son of Hans Holbein the Elder, a leading master of the Late Gothic School of Augsburg, Germany, Holbein was born during the winter of 1497–8. Both his father and his uncle Sigmund were well-known artists in their native country, and from an early age Hans and his elder brother Ambrosius received a sound training in the family workshop, where they learned the traditional techniques and were also in contact with a younger generation of artists who were beginning to be influenced by Italian art.

In 1514 Ambrosius went to Constance, Switzerland, to work independently, and the following year Hans travelled to Basle, where his brother later joined him. By 1516 both brothers were apprenticed to Hans Herbster, a well known Basle painter. Hans soon began to make a name for himself as an illustrator working for the great Swiss publishers Johann Froben and Johann Amerbach. In order to improve his education, he became an evening pupil of a local schoolteacher, Oswald Myconius, who introduced him to the work of Erasmus (q.v.), and it was during his first months in Basle that Holbein began to do the marginal drawings for the latter's *Encomium Moriae* ('In Praise of Folly'). Myconius was so impressed that he sent copies to Erasmus and to Froben.

In 1517 Holbein travelled to Lucerne, and from there to northern Italy. He returned to Basle in 1519 and, like his brother before him, became a free master; when Ambrosius died later that year, Hans took over his brother's workshop in the city. The following year he married Elizabeth Schmid, the widow of a master tanner, and became a citizen of Basle. One of his first major commissions was the mural decoration for the council chamber of the Town Hall, which he began in 1521; he also received commissions for altar pieces, portraits, designs for glass painting, and decorations on the façades of buildings, but the bulk of his time was still devoted to designs for woodcuts for the title pages and illustrations of books, the best known of which are those he did for the Old Testament and the *Dance of Death* series, probably executed in about 1523–6. Through his contacts with the Basle publishers Holbein became acquainted with the humanist circle; the most fruitful meeting of his career undoubtedly took place in 1521, when Erasmus settled in Basle. Holbein painted three portraits of the Dutch humanist in 1523, all of them showing a strong influence of the Netherlands painter, Quentin Matsys.

The rapid growth of Protestantism in Basle from 1522 onwards brought an unfavourable climate to the arts, and in 1524 Holbein journeyed to France, hoping to win the patronage of the French King; although unsuccessful, he visited Lyons and Avignon and greatly increased his knowledge of French Renaissance art. In 1526, encouraged by Erasmus and armed with introductions from him to Sir Thomas More (q.v.), Archbishop Warham (q.v.), and John Fisher (q.v.), he set out for England, travelling via Antwerp, where he made the acquaintance of Matsys.

Holbein remained in England for eighteen months. His fame spread rapidly, and he was able to support himself wholly by portraiture. During part of his visit he was invited to stay at More's house in Chelsea, where he painted one of his greatest works, the group portrait of the More family; nothing of this kind had previously been seen in England, and it created a sensation. (The original has not survived, but the painting is known from its copy by Rowland Lockey in the National Portrait Gallery, London; there is a drawing by Holbein for the portrait at Basle, and drawings for seven of the heads are in the Royal Collection at Windsor.)

Returning to Basle in 1528, Holbein took up again the abandoned mural for the Town Hall; he also painted a portrait of his wife and two sons, which is now at the Kunstmuseum, Basle. More commissions flowed in from the town council and publishers, but not enough to satisfy the artist; he turned down the offer of a pension from the authorities and in 1532 once more abandoned his family to work in England, where he was sure of a more remunerative income from portraiture.

For the next nine years Holbein was at the height of his professional career. Finding that his friend More was out of favour, he accepted commissions from the Hanseatic merchants of the Steelyard, for whom he painted a remarkable series of half-length portraits; the most famous of these is *The Ambassadors*, painted in 1533 and now in the National Gallery, London. That same year he painted Thomas Cromwell (q.v.), soon to become Secretary of State, through whom Holbein probably entered the royal service. It is generally accepted that he first painted Henry VIII (q.v.) in about 1536 (the Thyssen portrait); he was also commissioned that year to paint Jane Seymour (q.v.). From 1537 onwards he received a salary as official court painter and was given a workshop in the tower of Whitehall Palace.

In 1537 Holbein was commissioned to paint his major work for the King, a fresco on the wall of the Privy Chamber portraying Henry with his Queen, Jane Seymour, Henry VII and Elizabeth of York; destroyed in the fire of 1698, part of the cartoon for this painting is at the National Portrait Gallery, London. The figure of Henry was used as a model for many later versions of the King.

Holbein's duties were many and varied. His royal master not only required him to paint portraits of himself and his family and members of the nobility; he also expected him to execute extensive wall and ceiling paintings for the royal palaces, and to design jewellery, table silver, weapons, book-bindings, and the King's state robes. After the death of Jane Seymour in 1537, Holbein was on several occasions sent abroad to accompany the delegations whose mission was to inspect prospective brides for the King; he was required to paint true-to-life portraits of these women, who included the Duchess of Milan, Louise de Guise and, in 1539, Anne of Cleves (q.v.).

In 1538 he took the opportunity of one of these missions to revisit Basle. The authorities staged a banquet in the artist's honour and offered generous financial inducements if he would return permanently, but he turned them down. It is possible, however, that Holbein may have envisaged returning to Basle one day, since he retained his citizenship there and never applied to become an English citizen.

As a New Year gift for the King in 1539, he painted a portrait of the baby Prince Edward (see Edward VI). In addition to royal commissions, Holbein was much in demand by Henry's courtiers, and during this second stay in England, from 1532, he is believed to have painted almost 150 portraits, large and small. In his later period he adopted the practice of painting from drawings rather than from the sitter, with the result that his work became rather more linear in style.

Early in October 1543 Holbein fell a victim to the plague. He made his will on 7 October and must have died soon afterwards, as there is a record dated 21 November of the will being administered. He was buried in the parish of St Anthony Undershaft, where he had been living.

Holbein left unfinished his great group portrait of Henry VIII and the Barber Surgeons (the cartoon for which is at the Royal College of Surgeons, London). He also left considerable debts in England, and two illegitimate children. The two sons of his legal family, Phillip and Jakob, were both apprenticed to goldsmiths, in Paris and Basle respectively; a daughter, Katharina, was with her mother in Basle.

Hans Holbein was one of the few artists of the sixteenth century whose work did not reflect involvement in the religious strife of the age. This spiritual detachment enabled him to evolve his own life style, while profiting from the influence of other foreign painters. His portraits, both life size and miniature, are honest and without exaggeration, but, masterpieces as they are, they reveal little of the inner characters of the sitters. For all that, Holbein, a prolific painter and designer, left to posterity a truly remarkable realistic record of a King and his court, unsurpassed by that of any other artist in history.

The largest collections of Holbein's works are at Basle and in the Royal Collection at Windsor, where there are eighty-five drawings for portraits.

A. B. Chamberlain, *Hans Holbein the Younger* (2 vols; 1913).
P. Ganz, *The Paintings of Hans Holbein the Younger* (1950).
K. T. Parker, *The Drawings of Hans Holbein in the Collection of His Majesty the King at Windsor Castle* (1945).
R. C. Strong, *Holbein and Henry VIII* (1967).

*Portraits*: drawing, so-called self-portrait, *c.* 1523–6: Öffentliche Kunstsammlung, Basle; drawing, by Hans Holbein the Elder, of his two sons, Ambrosius and Hans Holbein the Younger: Print Room, Berlin; oil, self-portrait, 1542: private collection, U.S.A.; drawing, self-portrait, 1542–3: Uffizi Gallery, Florence; three miniatures, watercolour on vellum (playing cards), self-portraits in front of his easel, 1543: Wallace Collection, London, Drumlanrig Castle, Scotland (The Duke of Buccleuch), and Mayer van der Bergh Museum, Antwerp; engraving, by unknown engraver, of 1523–6 self-portrait: location not known.

**Holinshed, Raphael** (d. *c.* 1580), chronicler.

Raphael Holinshed is believed to have belonged to a Warwickshire family, where he was born. He was probably the Holinshed who studied at Christ's College, Cambridge, in 1544–5; according to Anthony à Wood (see *Lives of the Stuart Age*), he took holy orders and was at one time 'a minister of God's word'. He came to London early in the reign of Elizabeth I (q.v.) and by 1560 was employed as a translator in the printing office of Reginald Wolfe, who was then working on a voluminous universal history, based largely on the manuscripts of John Leland (q.v.), to which he had access.

After Wolfe's death in 1573, Holinshed continued to work on an abridged version of the history, which he planned as *The Chronicles of England, Scotland and Ireland*, now popularly known as *Holinshed's Chronicles*. He himself compiled the greater part of the first edition, principally 'The Historie of England', for which he relied to a considerable extent on the work of John Stow (q.v.), while William Harrison, Richard Stanyhurst, and Edward Campion contributed various other sections. Published in two volumes in 1577 by John Harrison and George Bishop, the *Chronicles* enjoyed instant popularity and were extensively drawn on as source material by the Elizabethan dramatists, especially William Shakespeare (q.v.), for their legendary and historical plays. Certain passages dealing with Ireland offended the Queen, however, and were ordered to be deleted.

Holinshed did not live to see the second edition of his work. By October 1578, when he made his will, he was employed as steward to a certain Thomas Burdet, of Bramcote, Warwickshire. The will was proved in 1582, but, according to Wood, Holinshed died at Bramcote towards the end of 1580.

A second edition of the *Chronicles*, published in three volumes in 1587 under the editorship of John Hooker and containing contributions by John Stow and others, taking the narrative up to the year 1586, again gave offence and some passages were ordered by the Privy Council to be taken out; these deletions, chiefly about the Babington Plot (see Babington, Anthony) and the Earl of Leicester's expedition to the Netherlands (see Dudley, Robert), were published separately in 1725 and are included in the edition edited by Henry Ellis in six volumes (1807–8).

A. and J. Nicoll, *Holinshed's Chronicle as used in Shakespeare's Plays* (1927).
Boswell Stone, *Shakespeare's Holinshed* (1896).

**Hooker, Richard** (?1554–1600), theologian, known as 'judicious Hooker'.

Richard Hooker was born at Heavitree, near Exeter, of middle-class parentage, probably in March 1554. The family was not wealthy, and Richard was educated at Exeter School through the generosity of an uncle, who also secured for him the patronage of John Jewel (q.v.), Bishop of Salisbury.

He was a promising scholar, and Jewel was so impressed with him that he provided the money to send the boy to Corpus Christi College, Oxford, in 1568. After Jewel's death three years later, Hooker was elected to a scholarship and so remained at Oxford, taking his M.A. in 1577; two years later he became Reader in Hebrew to the university. He was ordained in 1581, and later that year preached at Paul's Cross. He resigned his fellowship in 1584, the year in which he was given the living of Drayton Beauchamp, but it is not thought that he took up residence there.

Hooker's next appointment, a deliberate move by the Anglican leaders to counter the Puritans' attack on the established Church, was that of Master of the Temple in 1585. He went to live at the home of the Churchman family in Watling Street, which for the next few years became an anti-Puritan campaign headquarters, and there Hooker began to write his classic work, *The Laws of Ecclesiastical Polity*; he subsequently married the daughter of the family, Joan Churchman.

At the Temple the new Master found himself in conflict with the Calvinist Walter Travers (q.v.), who lectured there in the afternoons. Thomas Fuller, the historian (see *Lives of the Stuart Age*), in a much-quoted phrase, has recorded that on Sundays 'the pulpit spake pure Canterbury in the morning and Geneva in the afternoon'.

In 1591 he gratefully seized the chance to leave London when offered the living of Boscombe, near Salisbury. There he finished the first four books of his *Laws of Ecclesiastical Polity*, which were published in 1593, and worked on the later volumes, only one of which however appeared in the author's lifetime.

As a reward for his distinguished work, which was of tremendous importance both theologically and politically, the Queen gave Hooker the living of Bishopsbourne, near Canterbury, in 1595. He died there on 2 November 1600, leaving the last three volumes of his *magnum opus* virtually ready for the printer (volume 5 had been published in 1597). In the event they did not appear until after 1648; allegations were made concerning their suppression and that the texts had been tampered with, and inevitably the long delay aroused doubts as to the authenticity of Hooker's authorship, but it now seems certain that he did complete the manuscripts before his death. The standard edition of the work is in three volumes, edited by J. Keble, revised by W. Church and F. Paget (1888).

Hooker's brilliant defence of the Elizabethan Church and State against both the Roman Catholic and Puritan doctrines, together with his patient and logical explanation of the Anglican teaching, in temperate, persuasive language, was considered to be a masterpiece of contemporary literature. 'Judicious' was the inscription placed on his monument at Bishopsbourne; his work provided a philosophic exposition of the central position of the national established Church which held good for the ensuing centuries.

R. H. Murray, *Richard Hooker and his teaching* (1934).

Christopher Morris, *Political Thought in England: Tyndale to Hooker* (1954).

A. L. Rowse, *The England of Elizabeth* (1951).

C. J. Sisson, *The Judicious Marriage of Mr Hooker* (1940).

Izaak Walton, *Life of Richard Hooker* (1665; many later editions).

*Portraits*: oil on panel, unknown man *called* Richard Hooker, by unknown artist: National Portrait Gallery, London; sculpture, by unknown artist, on tomb: church of St Mary Virgin, Bishopsbourne, Kent.

**Hooper, John** (d. 1555), martyr, Bishop of Gloucester and Worcester.

John Hooper's family origins are unknown, but he is believed to have been born in Somerset towards the end of the fifteenth century. He took his B.A. at Oxford in late 1518 and joined the Cistercian order as a monk at Cleeve, Somerset. After the Dissolution of the Monasteries he was employed in the household of Sir Thomas Arundel in London, where he read and was influenced by the work of the reformers Ulrich Zwingli (q.v.) and Henry Bullinger. Stephen Gardiner (q.v.), Bishop of Winchester, at Arundel's request made an abortive attempt to dissuade him from his Protestant views, and following the passing of the Act of the Six Articles Hooper fled to the Continent.

He lived abroad for nearly ten years, first in Paris and then in Switzerland, where he married in Basle and later moved to Zurich. During this period he was in contact with the leading Continental reformers, including Bullinger, Martin Bucer (q.v.) and John à Lasco (q.v.).

Hooper returned to England in 1549 to participate in the Protestant reformation there and was made chaplain to the Protector Somerset (see Seymour, Edward). He soon acquired a reputation for preaching the more extreme views of Protestantism, and always drew large audiences. He survived Somerset's fall from power and became chaplain to his rival, Northumberland (see Dudley, John), failing to see through the latter's feigned sincerity.

In 1550 he was involved in a controversy over vestments. He had been offered the see of Gloucester but declined to be consecrated according to the ordinal. Both Thomas Cranmer (q.v.) and Nicholas Ridley (q.v.) argued with him at length, but Hooper maintained his stubborn refusal and was sent to the Fleet prison. After a few weeks he was persuaded that he could be more useful to the Protestant cause as an active bishop than as a dissenter confined in prison, and he was consecrated bishop on 8 March 1551; the following year when the sees of Gloucester and Worcester were amalgamated he became Bishop of both.

Hooper was notoriously active in his diocese. Not only did he preach several times a day; he also sat regularly in his consistory court, made a thorough visitation of his see, and tried to organize and discipline the diocese on Zwinglian lines. For this reason he was one of the first Protestant bishops to be attacked when Mary I (q.v.) came to the throne. He was arrested on 1 September 1553, deprived of his bishopric, and again imprisoned in the Fleet. Excommunicated for his refusal to recant, Hooper was held in the Fleet until the heresy laws had been revived; he was finally condemned on 29 January and burned at the stake at Gloucester on 9 February 1555.

By all accounts a stern, uncompromising man, but one who merits much respect for his martyrdom, Hooper exerted through his writings (chiefly *A Godly Confession* and *Protestation of the Christian Faith*) a considerable influence on the later Puritans. His works have been published by the Parker Society of Cambridge: *Early writings*, edited by Samuel Carr (2 vols; 1843); *Later writings*, edited by Charles Nevinson (2 vols; 1852).

F. D. Price, 'Gloucester diocese under Bishop Hooper, 1551–3', *Bristol and Gloucestershire Archaeological Society Transactions 1938*, lx (1939).
L. Baldwin Smith, *Tudor Prelates and Politics* (1953).

Portraits: oil, by unknown artist: Balliol College, Oxford; engraving, by unknown engraver, after R. White: location not known.

**Howard, Catherine** (d. 1542), see Catherine Howard.

**Howard, Charles** (1536–1624), 2nd Baron Howard of Effingham and later 1st Earl of Nottingham, Lord High Admiral, commander of the English fleet against the Spanish Armada of 1588.

Born in 1536, Charles was the eldest son of Lord William Howard (q.v.), 1st Baron Howard of Effingham, and his wife Margaret, daughter of Sir Thomas Gamage of Coity, Glamorganshire. He was educated in the household of his uncle, the Duke of Norfolk (see Howard, Thomas, 3rd Duke), and for a short time in France. He joined his father in Calais in 1552–3 and served under him at sea in 1554–7, when Lord William was Lord High Admiral. He also accompanied his father to the peace conference of Cateau-Cambrésis in 1559. Later that year he was given his first independent embassy to France, ostensibly to carry a message from Queen Elizabeth (q.v.) to the wounded and dying Henri II, but possibly also secretly to take money to the Continent for the purpose of smuggling the Earl of Arran (see Hamilton, James, 3rd Earl) back to Scotland.

In company with the other young noblemen of the day, Howard spent the next few years at court hoping to attract some special mark of favour from the Queen or at least for the chance to perform a service. In the meanwhile he was returned as a Member of Parliament for Surrey in 1562, and again in 1566 and 1572; he entered Gray's Inn in 1564 and took an M.A. at Cambridge in 1571. In July 1563 he married Katherine Carey, eldest daughter of Lord Hunsdon and cousin of the Queen's Lord Chamberlain.

The rebellion of the northern earls in November 1569 brought Howard an appointment as general of the horse under the Earl of Warwick, but, because the uprising was put down before he had got any further north than Yorkshire, he was denied the long-sought-after opportunity of action. The following summer, however, he was given the honour, together with William Wynter (q.v.), of escorting the Spanish fleet taking the new bride of Philip II (q.v.), Anne of Austria, through the Channel to Spain. He is believed to have been knighted for his services.

In January 1573 Lord William Howard died, and Charles succeeded to the title as the 2nd Baron Howard of Effingham; he inherited his father's manors of Blechingley and Effingham, together with others in Surrey and elsewhere, but since these were insufficient to make him a wealthy landowner he was to remain dependent to a large extent upon the rewards bestowed by the crown in return for services rendered. He was not immediately appointed to high office, but in view of the poor health of the new Lord Chamberlain, Howard was commissioned to act as Sussex's deputy in 1574; in this capacity he attended the Queen on her progress of that summer and continued in office during most of the following year. In April 1575, as a mark of royal esteem, he was elected to companionship of the Order of the Garter. For the next eight years Howard led a comparatively inconspicuous life at court, fulfilling the occasional minor role such as that of escorting the Queen's French suitor, the Duc d'Alençon (q.v.), back to the Continent in 1581, and devoting much of his time to local affairs in Surrey. At last, on 1 January 1584, he was appointed as Lord Chamberlain. He was to hold this office for only eighteen months, however, for in May 1585 he became Lord High Admiral in succession to Lord Clinton, who had died in January. He was the fifth member of his family to hold the office, which brought with it not only the prestige and influence Howard so badly wanted but also a substantial income from its perquisites.

In 1586 the Lord Admiral was named as a member of the commission for the trial of Mary, Queen of Scots (q.v.). Although he did not take part in the proceedings at Westminster, Howard was responsible for persuading Elizabeth to sign Mary's death warrant and was among those Councillors who authorized the execution before the Queen could change her mind.

Throughout 1587 the threat of a Spanish invasion gathered momentum. In December Howard was given the

supreme command of naval and military preparations for war with Spain; Sir John Hawkins (q.v.) and Sir Francis Drake (q.v.) served under him in command of the second and third squadrons of the fleet at Plymouth. In May 1588 Howard, on board his flagship *Ark Royal*, led the main English fleet to join Drake off the south-west coast. He had been campaigning for months for adequate supplies, while Drake had pleaded to be allowed to take the initiative against the Spaniards. The Lord Admiral had himself eventually been won over to Drake's plan, but permission from the Queen was too late in coming, and on 19 July the Armada was sighted off the Lizard. The news was brought to Plymouth, where Howard and Drake are traditionally believed to have been enjoying a game of bowls.

With Hawkins and Drake as second- and third-in-command respectively, Howard proceeded cautiously to harass the Spanish fleet with long-range cannon as it sailed up-Channel. He then divided the English fleet into four squadrons, to

255

be led by himself, Hawkins, Drake, and Martin Frobisher (q.v.). At a council-of-war of 28 July, when both fleets lay off the Calais Roads, he sanctioned the sending in of fireships proposed by Sir William Wynter. Howard was later much criticized for his action the following day, during the decisive battle off Gravelines, when, lured by the prospect of a rich prize, he stopped to capture the crippled Spanish galleass *San Lorenso*.

Although after the defeat of the 1588 Armada the immediate danger had been averted, there was still a constant threat of invasion, and during the next few years the Lord Admiral was kept busy by a series of alarms and the necessity of maintaining the fleet and military fortifications in a state of readiness. He continued to make a good income from the perquisites of office and from privateering, and he also invested in the voyages of his cousin, Lord Thomas Howard (q.v.), and Sir Walter Ralegh (q.v.). But the plans for Howard himself to take command of an expedition failed for the time being to materialize, and he had to be content with new responsibilities as Steward of Hampton Court and Windsor Castle, and more routine Council and administrative duties, including the organization of the Chest at Chatham for sick and aged mariners, founded by Drake and Hawkins.

In 1596, having at last convinced the Council of the merit of the scheme, Howard was given the joint command with the Earl of Essex (see Devereux, Robert) of an expedition to attack the Spanish at Cadiz; he was to take precedence at sea, Essex on land. After many delays, the impressive fleet of four English squadrons and a fifth Dutch squadron, totalling some 120 vessels, with Howard aboard the *Ark Royal*, sailed from Plymouth on 3 June. The Lord Admiral proceeded with his usual caution, but after Essex's impetuous landing without waiting for the battle at sea to be over, Howard too landed and played an important part in the capture and sacking of the town. In council with his subordinate commanders, who included Ralegh, Sir Francis Vere (q.v.), Lord Thomas Howard, and Sir George Carew, the Lord Admiral subsequently overruled the young Earl's proposals, firstly to remain in Cadiz, and secondly to lie in wait for the Spanish treasure ships off the Azores. As a result a coolness sprang up between the two men which soon flared into enmity, and this was not improved when in 1597 the Queen created Howard Earl of Nottingham. In the feud which followed Essex was eventually placated by an appointment as Earl Marshal, which gave him precedence over Nottingham, whereupon the latter took offence and retired to his house in Chelsea, one of several residences which he maintained at this stage in his career and where on several occasions he entertained the Queen. A few weeks later the quarrel appears to have been patched up, although both men retained a good deal of bitterness. It was Nottingham who stepped between Essex and the Queen when the young Earl drew his sword during a quarrel over the choice of a new Lord Deputy of Ireland.

In the summer of 1599 there was a serious invasion scare, and in the absence of Essex in Ireland, Nottingham was appointed by the Queen as Lord Lieutenant and Captain General of England. Amid panic and confusion he mobilized an army of 20–30,000 men and dispatched a fleet of twenty-three ships to intercept the anticipated Spanish fleet, which never came. In February 1601 he took charge of the precautions at court during the Essex uprising and was one of the commissioners at Essex's subsequent trial. Since the death of Burghley (see Cecil, William) in 1598 Nottingham had been the senior member of the Privy Council; he worked closely with Sir Robert Cecil (q.v.) at this period and was at some stage drawn into the secret correspondence with James VI of Scotland (q.v.) over the succession. When Elizabeth lay dying, at the end of March 1603, it was to Nottingham that she managed to convey her reply, 'our cousin in Scotland', on his insistence that she made clear her intention.

Lady Nottingham's death a few weeks previously had been a source of great grief both to the Earl and to the Queen. (There is considered to be little truth in the story that she had failed to deliver to Elizabeth a jewel entrusted to her by the condemned Essex; the deep melancholy into which Elizabeth fell after Lady Nottingham's death was probably brought on by a combination of grief and the realization of her own imminent death.) In early September, less than six months after losing his first wife, Nottingham married the high-spirited nineteen-year-old Lady Margaret Stewart, sister of the Earl of Moray and granddaughter of the former Regent of Scotland (see Stewart, Lord James); their marriage was the source of much court gossip, especially when the new Lady Nottingham bore her elderly husband no less than five children, only two of whom, however, survived infancy. A great sorrow in Nottingham's last years was the sudden death of his eldest son and heir, William Howard, in 1615.

Continued in the office of Lord Admiral by the new King, Howard was still, in the early years of the reign, a powerful political influence. The most important task entrusted to him by James was his embassy to Spain in 1605; he sat as a commissioner in the Gunpowder Plot trial (see Fawkes, Guy, in *Lives of the Stuart Age*) in 1606 and also on a number of other commissions. But as a friend of Ralegh and father-in-law of Lord Cobham (see Brooke, Henry), his position became somewhat vulnerable, especially after the rupture with his cousin, Henry Howard, Earl of Northampton, prime mover in the campaign against Ralegh and a member of the new inner circle or power group on whom James tended to lean. Deprived by the peace with Spain of his substantial income from privateering, Nottingham received grants from the King and the patent to license sellers of wine; in the last decade of his life he was obliged to sell some lands in order to meet his debts. In the findings of the commission appointed in 1618 to investigate abuses in the Navy, no blame was attached to the Lord Admiral, but the following year he was at last persuaded to relinquish the office in return for a substantial pension. He retired to his house at Haling, near Croydon, where he died on 14 December 1624, at the age of eighty-eight.

An able leader of men, whose rank and office commanded confidence, Charles Howard of Effingham is chiefly remembered for the part he played in the defeat of the Spanish Armada.

Robert W. Kenny, *Elizabeth's Admiral: The Political Career of Charles Howard, Earl of Nottingham, 1536–1624* (1970).
John K. Laughton (ed.), *From Howard to Nelson* (1899).
Robert Southey, *English Seamen* (Chicago, 1895).

*Portraits:* oil, full-length, by unknown artist: National Portrait Gallery, London (engraving, 1602, by William Rogers, in Segar, *Honor Military and Civil*: N.P.G.); miniature, by Nicholas Hilliard, 1605: National Maritime Museum, Greenwich; oil, by Daniel Mytens, *c.* 1620: N.M.M. Nottingham is also depicted in the Somerset House Conference group, by unknown artist, 1604: N.P.G. (copy at N.M.M.).

257

**Howard, Henry** (1517–1547), Earl of Surrey, courtier, soldier, and poet.

Henry Howard was the eldest son of Lord Thomas Howard, later Duke of Norfolk (see Howard, Thomas, 3rd Duke), and Elizabeth, his second wife, daughter of the Duke of Buckingham (see Stafford, Edward, 3rd Duke of Buckingham). Born at Hunsdon, Norfolk, in the spring of 1517, he received the courtesy title of Earl of Surrey when his father succeeded to the dukedom of Norfolk in 1524.

His early childhood was spent at the family estates in Norfolk and Suffolk; then shortly before his thirteenth birthday Surrey was sent to Windsor to share in the education of Henry Fitzroy (q.v.), Duke of Richmond, the bastard son of Henry VIII (q.v.) by Elizabeth Blount, to whom Norfolk was godfather. The next two years were the happiest of his life; in view of the King's impending marriage to Anne Boleyn (q.v.), the Howards were much in favour at court, and there was talk of Surrey's marriage to the Princess Mary (see Mary I). In April 1532, however, he was married to the Lady Frances de Vere, fourteen-year-old daughter of the Earl of Oxford; the couple separated immediately after the wedding ceremony and did not live together until nearly two years later.

In October the same year Surrey and Richmond accompanied the King and Anne Boleyn to France; it was during this tour, which lasted several months, that Surrey, influenced by his meeting with the Florentine refugee poet Alemmani and by reading the work of Petrarch and Molza, one of the first translators of the *Aeneid*, began to experiment with the Italian-style metres with which he and the elder Sir Thomas Wyatt (q.v.) were later to revolutionize English poetry. Shortly after their return to England, Richmond married Surrey's sister Mary. Surrey settled at the family estate of Kenninghall, Norfolk, with his wife, where his eldest son, Thomas (see Howard, Thomas, 4th Duke), was born in March 1536. This otherwise happy period in Surrey's life was however overshadowed by the bitter quarrel between his parents concerning Bess Holland, the Duke's mistress, and the impending rise of the Seymour family to favour. In May 1536 he was present at the trial and execution of Anne Boleyn, but did not attend the privately-performed marriage of the King to Jane Seymour (q.v.). In July, when news reached him of Richmond's death, Surrey became ill with grief.

In October 1536 he joined his father in putting down the Pilgrimage of Grace, but the following year he was imprisoned briefly at Windsor after striking the Earl of Hertford (see Seymour, Edward) in the face when the latter charged him with having favoured the Catholic rebels in the uprising. For the next few years Surrey lived partly the life of a country gentleman, partly that of a courtier, and at the wedding celebrations of the King and Anne of Cleves (q.v.) he excelled himself in a display of jousting. In 1540 his second son, Henry, was born. When Henry VIII took Catherine Howard (q.v.), Surrey's cousin, as his fifth wife in July 1540, the family fortunes were once more in the ascendant. For a brief period in 1543, however, he was imprisoned for damage caused in an outburst of hooliganism with his friend Thomas Wyatt the younger (q.v.).

Surrey served in the Scottish campaign of 1542 and as Field Marshal in France from 1544 to early 1546 when, his reputation having suffered on account of the English losses at Boulogne, he was replaced by his old rival, the Earl of Hertford. On returning to England he found that his father had accepted the Seymour position as virtually unassailable and was busy trying to end the feud by a series of marriage alliances (including marrying Surrey's sister, the widowed Duchess of Richmond, to Admiral Sir Thomas Seymour (q.v.), and his two elder sons to two of Hertford's daughters). Surrey told his father he would not countenance such marriages for his sons, and he had a violent scene with his sister. He played into the hands of his enemies at court by incorporating the arms of Edward the Confessor on his escutcheon and by asserting, in a conversation that was overheard, that the Howards would be the best Regents for the heir to the throne, Prince Edward (see Edward VI). Henry VIII's personal investigation convinced him that it was unsafe to allow Surrey and his father to upset the arrangements for the minority of Henry's son, when he came to the throne. On 1 December 1546 Surrey was arrested at Whitehall and was taken to the Tower; his father, arrested at Kenninghall, joined him there a few days later.

The Duchess of Richmond and Bess Holland were among those who gave evidence against them, the former alleging that her brother had advised her to become the King's mistress; at last the Duke himself, to save his own skin, informed against his son in an admission of their common guilt. Surrey made an unsuccessful attempt to escape from the Tower. At his trial at Guildhall he was found guilty of high treason and condemned to death; he was beheaded on Tower Hill on 19 January 1547, barely thirty years old. His remains, buried at All Hallow's, Barking, were in 1614 reinterred by his second son Henry, Earl of Northampton, in the family vault at Framlingham. The Surrey estates and

personal possessions were seized by Hertford and others. Norfolk, although also condemned to die, was saved by the death of Henry VIII before the sentence could be carried out.

None of Surrey's poetry was published until ten years after his death, when forty poems appeared in the collection usually referred to as *Tottel's Miscellany* (1557); in the same year his translation, *Certain Bokes of Virgiles Aenaeis* (Books II and IV of the *Aeneid*), introduced blank verse into English poetry for the first time. Some of the shorter poems are thought to have been written during his confinement at Windsor; the translation of Virgil was probably undertaken a little earlier, in the period 1535–6, following his return from France. Like Wyatt, whom he acknowledged as his master, Surrey owed much to the influence of Petrarch; he joined with the former in introducing into England the sonnet form which was later taken up by Philip Sidney (q.v.), Edmund Spenser (q.v.), and William Shakespeare (q.v.). A number of his love poems were addressed to the 'Fair Geraldine', Elizabeth, the nine-year-old daughter of the Earl of Kildare.

The poetical work of Surrey heralded a new flowering of English poetry. In comparison with the impact he made on the literature of the age, his tempestuous and unhappy career is of little importance. Arrogant and obsessed by aristocratic family pride, he brought about his own downfall.

The *Works of Surrey* have been edited by F. Nott in two volumes (1815–16), and for the Aldine Poets by James Yeowell (1866). His translation of the *Aeneid* was reprinted in 1814.

E. R. Casady, *Henry Howard, Earl of Surrey* (New York, 1938).
Hester W. Chapman, *Two Tudor Portraits* (1960, reprinted 1973).

*Portraits*: three drawings, by Holbein, *c.* 1532–5, *c.* 1535, and *c.* 1540 respectively: Royal Collection, Windsor; drawing, by Holbein, *c.* 1540: Pierpont Morgan Library, New York; oil, by Holbein, *c.* 1540: Museu de Arte, São Paulo; oil, attributed to William Scrots: Duke of Norfolk Collection, Arundel Castle; oil on panel, after Scrots: National Portrait Gallery, London; other versions at Knole, Parham, Castle Howard, and Arundel Castle; monument: Framlingham Church, Suffolk. N.B. Several drawings by Holbein are inscribed as 'Thomas, Earl of Surrey', but these are generally agreed to be of Henry Howard.

**Howard, Thomas** (1443–1524), Earl of Surrey and 2nd Duke of Norfolk, soldier and statesman.

Thomas Howard was the son of Sir John Howard, a loyal supporter of Edward IV and Richard III (for both see *Lives Before the Tudors*), who was created Duke of Norfolk in 1483. He was educated at Ipswich grammar school and entered the royal service as page to the Earl of March and later to Edward IV. After spending two years at the court of the Duke of Burgundy at Dijon, in order to study military techniques, he returned to England and fought for Edward against Warwick at Barnet in 1471. The following year he married a rich heiress, Elizabeth, daughter of Sir Frederick Tilney of Ashwell Thorpe, Norfolk, and widow of Sir Humphrey Bourchier, son of Lord Berners. In 1475 he took up residence at Ashwell Thorpe, and became Sheriff for Norfolk and Suffolk the following year. He was knighted by the King in January 1478, and in June 1483, when his father was created Duke of Norfolk, he became Earl of Surrey, a Knight of the Garter, and a Privy Councillor.

Fighting in support of Richard at the Battle of Bosworth Field in August 1485, where Norfolk was killed, Surrey was badly wounded and taken prisoner. Henry VII (q.v.) seized the Norfolk estates, but spared Surrey's life, although his title and that of his dead father were attainted. Subsequently Surrey accepted the Tudor right to the throne, and in January 1489 he was released from the Tower and restored to his earldom and part of his estates, but not to the dukedom.

Surrey was now entrusted with the maintenance of order in Yorkshire and on the Scottish border, where he forced James IV (q.v.) to retreat. In 1501 he was appointed Lord Treasurer, and he negotiated the marriage of Henry's daughter Margaret Tudor (q.v.) to the Scottish King, accompanying the Princess to Scotland and giving the bride away on behalf of Henry at the wedding on 8 August 1503.

In 1507 Surrey's wife died. Two years later he married Agnes Tilney, a cousin of his first wife; she was to survive him by more than twenty years and to bring tragedy to the Howard family through her lack of proper supervision of their granddaughter, Catherine Howard (q.v.), before her marriage to Henry VIII (q.v.).

Surrey was much trusted by Henry VIII and was an important member of the King's Privy Council; in 1510 he was appointed Earl Marshal. The next few years were unfortunately marred by Surrey's acute jealousy of Thomas Wolsey (q.v.), with whom he entered into a long and bitter struggle.

At the age of seventy, Surrey was still a great military commander, and it was in reward for his tremendous victory over James IV at Flodden in September 1513 that he was created Duke of Norfolk and granted a number of estates in Norfolk and Suffolk. In 1517 he proved his military skill still further by successfully putting down the rising of the London apprentices.

While despising Wolsey's social origins and disliking his policies, Norfolk nevertheless was forced to uphold them in public, as when he had the task of escorting another of the King's sisters, Mary Tudor (q.v.), to France for her marriage with Louis XII. In 1515 he was required to attend on Wolsey at Westminster Abbey when the latter was invested with the cardinal's hat. The King, however, continued to put his trust in the Duke, and it was a mark of his confidence that when Henry left for France for the Field of the Cloth of Gold in 1520 he left his kingdom in the hands of Norfolk.

In 1521 he was required to fulfil a most unpleasant duty, being appointed Lord High Steward to preside at the trial of his friend, the Duke of Buckingham (see Stafford, Edward), on trumped-up charges of treason against the King. It was recorded that Norfolk passed sentence of death on Buckingham with tears streaming down his face.

After this date Norfolk made only an occasional appearance at court, and on 21 May 1524 he died at Framlingham Castle, Suffolk. He was buried at Thetford Priory, but his remains were later translated to the Howard chapel at Lambeth. A long biographical inscription once at Thetford has been preserved and is the major source of information concerning his life; the original tomb was destroyed in the Dissolution of the Monasteries.

G. Brenan and E. P. Statham, *House of Howard* (2 vols; 1907).

M. J. Tucker, *The life of Thomas Howard, earl of Surrey and 2nd duke of Norfolk* (The Hague, 1964).

Polydore Vergil, *Anglicae Historiae*, ed. D. Hay (Camden Society, 3rd Series, lxxiv, 1950).

*Portrait*: oil, by unknown artist: Duke of Norfolk Collection, Arundel Castle.

**Howard, Thomas** (1473–1554), Earl of Surrey and 3rd Duke of Norfolk.

The eldest son of the 2nd Duke of Norfolk (see Howard, Thomas, 2nd Duke), Thomas was born in 1473. By his marriage, in 1495, to the Princess Anne, daughter of Edward IV (see *Lives Before the Tudors*), he became a brother-in-law of Henry VII (q.v.), who married Anne's sister, Elizabeth. The Lady Anne Howard died in November 1511, leaving no surviving issue, and the following year Howard married Elizabeth, daughter of the Duke of Buckingham (see Stafford, Edward).

In 1511, together with his brother, Sir Edward Howard, he was sent by the King to capture the Scottish naval commander, Andrew Barton, a mission which they accomplished successfully. Howard became Lord Admiral in 1513, and in September that year he led the van of the English army at the battle of Flodden. He was created Earl of Surrey in February 1514.

Lord Deputy of Ireland in 1520, he was soon afterwards recalled to command the force which ravaged the coast of Brittany and Normandy in 1522. An appointment succeeding his father as Lord Treasurer followed, and in 1523 he turned his attention to devastating the Scottish border and compelled the Duke of Albany (see Stewart, John) to retreat. On his father's death, in May 1524, he succeeded to the title as 3rd Duke of Norfolk.

Now the most powerful nobleman in England, cunning and self-seeking, he led the opposition to Thomas Wolsey (q.v.) and took Henry's side in the matter of his divorce from Catherine of Aragon (q.v.) in order that the King should marry his niece, Anne Boleyn (q.v.). Appointed President of the Council in 1529, Norfolk influenced the King to rid himself of Wolsey; in 1533 he became Earl Marshal.

His position weakened by the fate of Anne Boleyn in 1536, Norfolk now had to contend with a new royal servant, Thomas Cromwell (q.v.), with whom he and Stephen Gardiner (q.v.), representing the conservative viewpoint, were in bitter opposition. In the middle of the long struggle for power which followed, Norfolk was dispatched to the north of England to deal with the rising known as the Pilgrimage of Grace. On his return he campaigned fiercely against Cromwell, now Lord Privy Seal, and in 1540 he was quick to take advantage of the King's growing dislike of his new wife, Anne of Cleves (q.v.), whom he had married at the insistence of Cromwell, and introduced another niece, Catherine Howard (q.v.), as a rival for Henry's affections.

In June 1540 Cromwell was arrested and executed, the Norfolk-Gardiner faction having at last succeeded in discrediting him and his policy in the King's eyes. Norfolk's own position was again weakened, however, by the execution of Catherine Howard on a charge of adultery, and although he was to achieve further military successes in Scotland (1542) and in France (1544), in the next few years he was gradually ousted from power by the Earl of Hertford (see Seymour, Edward). Jealousy between Hertford and the Howard family finally erupted in December 1546, when the Earl of Surrey (see Howard, Henry), Norfolk's son, was arrested on a charge of treason, and Norfolk as an accessory to the crime. Both were condemned to death; Surrey was executed in January 1547, but the King died before the sentence on Norfolk could be carried out. The new King, Edward VI (q.v.), did not send Norfolk to the scaffold but held him in the Tower for his entire reign.

In August 1553, following the accession of Mary I (q.v.), Norfolk was released from captivity and restored to his dukedom. One of his first official duties was to preside as Lord High Steward at the trial of the Duke of Northumberland (see Dudley, John).

His last military campaign took place in January 1554, when he was dispatched to Kent in order to suppress the rebellion of Sir Thomas Wyatt the younger (q.v.), but failed to control his men in the face of the rebels.

Norfolk died on 25 August 1554; his grandson (see Howard, Thomas, 4th Duke), son of the executed Earl of Surrey, succeeded to the dukedom. The Duchess of Norfolk survived her husband for four years; since the early 1530s she and her husband had been in bitter dispute concerning the Duke's mistress, Bess Holland, and at one time the Duke had considered a divorce. His wife had lost no opportunity for revenge, which included giving evidence against him at the trial.

G. Brenan and E. P. Statham, *House of Howard* (2 vols; 1907).

*Portrait*: oil, by Holbein, 1538–9: Royal Collection, Windsor.

# Howard, Thomas (1536–1572), Earl of Surrey and 4th Duke of Norfolk.

Born on 10 March 1536, Thomas Howard was the son of the Earl of Surrey (see Howard, Henry) who was executed in January 1547. After his father's death Thomas was removed from his mother's care by the Council and entrusted to the tutorship of John Foxe (q.v.), the Protestant martyrologist, with whom he formed a lifelong friendship. His father's title was restored to him on the accession of Mary I (q.v.), and in August 1554 he succeeded his grandfather as Duke of Norfolk and Earl Marshal.

Norfolk was much in favour at the court of Mary, but was then too young to play an important role in public affairs. He was also well received by Elizabeth I (q.v.), who persuaded him, after much hesitation, to take command of the English forces during the Scottish campaign of 1559–60. He became a Privy Councillor in 1562.

His domestic life in early years was much saddened by the death of three wives: Mary, daughter of the Earl of Arundel, by whom he had one son; Margaret, daughter of Lord Audley of Walden, by whom he had one daughter and two sons; and Elizabeth, widow of Baron Dacre, who died in September 1567 leaving no issue.

A vain and somewhat weak man, Norfolk was easily swayed by others; he was jealous of the position and influence at Elizabeth's court of the Earl of Leicester (see Dudley, Robert) and Sir William Cecil (q.v.; later 1st Baron Burghley), and in 1565 he quarrelled openly with the former in the presence of the Queen.

In 1568 he presided over the commission which sat at York to enquire into the dispute between Mary, Queen of Scots (q.v.) and the Scottish lords. He had at that time recently lost his third wife and was receptive to the suggestion that he should marry Mary. Together with the Earl of Arundel and a number of other digruntled Catholic lords, he plotted the overthrow of Cecil and allowed himself to be drawn into plans for an uprising of the northern lords. He was arrested and confined in the Tower from September 1569 to August 1570. Released following the failure of the northern rebellion, he soon afterwards became involved in the Ridolfi plot (see Ridolfi, Roberto di), which embodied both the plan for a Spanish invasion of England that would restore Catholicism and that for Norfolk's marriage to the Queen of Scots.

Discovery of this plot led to the arrest of Norfolk and his fellow conspirators. He stood trial for high treason in January 1572, when he also forfeited his title and honours. Elizabeth was reluctant to order his execution, but she finally signed the order and Norfolk was taken to the scaffold on 2 June that year. He died protesting that he had never been a Papist.

In his lifetime the Duke contributed generously towards the completion of Magdalene College, Cambridge.

Norfolk and Mary Stuart never met; the letters that passed between them in the years 1569–70 have been printed in the Hardwicke State Papers (*Miscellaneous state papers from 1501 to 1726*, edited by Philip Yorke, 2nd Earl of Hardwicke, 2 vols, 1778).

G. Brenan and E. P. Statham, *House of Howard* (2 vols; 1907).

Francis Edwards, *The Marvellous Chance: Thomas Howard, 4th Duke of Norfolk, and the Ridolfi Plot* (1968).

Antonia Fraser, *Mary Queen of Scots*, chapter 21 (1969).

Neville Williams, *Thomas Howard, 4th Duke of Norfolk* (1964).

*Portraits:* oil, by Hans Eworth, 1563: private collection (copy at Knole (National Trust)); oil, attributed to van der Muelen, 1565: Earl of Carlisle Collection (copies at Arundel Castle (Duke of Norfolk Collection) and Audley End); oil, *called* 4th Duke of Norfolk, by unknown artist: National Portrait Gallery, London.

## Howard, Lord Thomas (1561–1626), 1st Earl of Suffolk and 1st Baron Howard de Walden, admiral and statesman.

The second son of the Duke of Norfolk (see Howard, Thomas, 4th Duke) by his second wife, Margaret, daughter and heiress of Baron Audley of Walden (see Audley, Thomas), Thomas Howard was born on 24 August 1561. He was educated at St John's College, Cambridge. His father was attainted and executed on a charge of treason in June 1572, and not until twelve years later, in 1584, was Thomas restored in blood as Lord Thomas Howard. By that time he had married and lost his first wife, by whom he had no children, and had in 1583 taken a second bride, Catherine, daughter of Sir Henry Knevet and widow of Richard Rich, eldest son of Lord Rich; this beautiful, but domineering woman not only bore him seven sons and three daughters, but saw to it that she enriched herself when, in later life, he held high office.

In the fight against the Spanish Armada of 1588 Howard commanded a ship as a volunteer; he was knighted at sea by his cousin, Lord Admiral Howard (see Howard, Charles), for his exceptional valour in the battle off Calais. In 1591 he was given command of the squadron that was to sail to the Azores in order to intercept the Spanish treasure ships on their way back to Spain. Sailing in the *Defiance*, with Sir Richard Grenville (q.v.) as his second-in-command in the

*Revenge*, and about twelve other ships, Howard left Plymouth in May. He was caught unawares by the main Spanish fleet at Flores at the end of August, when, after fighting against overwhelming odds, the greater part of the English squadron retreated, leaving the *Revenge* to face the attackers single-handed; Grenville, wounded in the ensuing battle, died a few days after his crew had surrendered. The revictualling squadron sent out from England failed to reach Howard, who brought his fleet home at the end of September with very few spoils. Criticized in several quarters, and by Sir Walter Ralegh (q.v.) in particular, for his action in abandoning Grenville, Howard was vigorously defended by the Lord Admiral.

In May 1596 he was given command of the third of five squadrons under the Lord Admiral and the Earl of Essex (see Devereux, Robert) in the expedition that successfully attacked the Spanish at Cadiz, and the following July he sailed as second-in-command to Essex on the ill-fated 'Islands Voyage', on which he is said to have tried very hard to smooth over the stormy relations between Essex and Ralegh.

Much in favour at court as a result of his courageous and loyal service, Howard was made a Knight of the Garter after the Cadiz voyage; in 1597 he was created Baron Howard de Walden. He subsequently became Lord Lieutenant of Cambridgeshire and the Isle of Ely, and in the crisis concerning a possible Spanish invasion in the summer of 1599 he served as Admiral of the fleet sent to keep a look-out for the enemy. As Constable of the Tower he was among those who, with the Lord Admiral, besieged Essex in his house on the night of 7 February 1601, after the Earl's unsuccessful rebellion; he sat as one of the peers in Essex's subsequent trial. In

December Howard was appointed as Acting Lord Chamberlain of the Household. By that date both he and the Lord Admiral had been drawn into the small circle who were party to the secret correspondence then being conducted between Sir Robert Cecil (q.v.) and James VI of Scotland (q.v.) concerning the succession.

Shortly after James's accession to the English throne in March 1603, Howard became a Privy Councillor and Lord Chamberlain of the Household; in July he was created Earl of Suffolk. That same year he inherited the family estate at Audley End, where he began to build an immense house with two great courtyards; it was to be one of the largest mansions in the country. He played an important part in the discovery of the Gunpowder Plot of 1605 (see Fawkes, Guy, in *Lives of the Stuart Age*), and in the next decade he held a series of commissions and the Lord Lieutenancies of Dorset, Cambridgeshire, and Suffolk. In July 1614 he became Chancellor of the University of Cambridge, where he lavishly entertained the King the following year. That same month, on his appointment as Lord High Treasurer of England, he resigned from the post of Chamberlain.

Suffolk held office as Lord High Treasurer until July 1619. Together with his cousin, the elderly Lord Admiral, now Earl of Nottingham, he tried to block the rise to power of the royal favourite, Buckingham (see Villiers, George, 1st Duke, in *Lives of the Stuart Age*). In the autumn of 1618 grave irregularities were discovered at the Treasury and Suffolk, accused of embezzling funds and jewels and extorting money from the King's subjects, was suspended from office; his wife also was indicted for extorting money. After a hearing in the Star Chamber in October–November 1619, Suffolk, who was popularly believed to have acted under the influence of his wife, was ordered to be held in the Tower separately from the Countess at the King's pleasure, fined £30,000 and required to pay back all the money wrongfully obtained; they were in fact imprisoned only ten days and the fine was subsequently reduced to £7,000.

In 1620 Suffolk was once more received into royal favour, and the following year he was appointed High Steward of Exeter. He died in London on 28 May 1626 and was buried at Saffron Walden.

G. Brenan and E. P. Statham, *House of Howard* (2 vols; 1907).

Henry Howard, *Memorials of the Howard Family* (1834).

*Portraits:* oil, by unknown artist, *c.* 1600: Naworth Castle, Cumberland (Earl of Carlisle); oil, by unknown artist, *c.* 1605: National Portrait Gallery, London; oil, full length, by unknown artist, *c.* 1614: National Maritime Museum, Greenwich; oil, by unknown artist: Knole (The Lord Sackville); oil, full length, posthumous, by B. Rebecca: Audley End, Essex; engraving, by R. Elstracke: location not known. (N.B. According to Dr Strong, the full-length portrait at Woburn of a man in Garter robes has been wrongly identified as Suffolk.)

**Howard, Lord William** (?1510–1573), 1st Baron Howard of Effingham, diplomatist, Lord High Admiral of England, 1554–1573.

Born in about 1510, Lord William was the second son of the Duke of Norfolk (see Howard, Thomas, 2nd Duke) and his second wife, Agnes Tilney. He was educated at Trinity College, Cambridge, under Stephen Gardiner (q.v.), and soon afterwards attended at court. He was given his first mission, to Scotland, in 1531. The young Howard was in favour with Henry VIII (q.v.) and was subsequently sent on other embassies to Scotland (1535 and 1536) and to France

(1537 and 1541). He lost his wife, Katherine Boughton, in 1535, and a few months later married Margaret, daughter of Sir Thomas Gamage of Coity, who was to bear him two sons, Charles Howard (q.v.), later 2nd Baron Howard of Effingham, and William; he had other issue, including one daughter from his first marriage.

In 1541 Howard and his wife were found guilty of misprision of treason in connection with shielding the immoralities of their kinswoman, Queen Catherine Howard (q.v.), but were later pardoned. In May 1544 Howard took part in the invasion of Scotland under the Earl of Hertford (see Seymour, Edward), and later that year he was with the King at the capture of Boulogne. In October 1552 he was appointed Governor of Calais, a post which he relinquished on being made a Privy Councillor the following autumn and chosen to succeed Lord Clinton as Lord High Admiral in March 1554.

Early in 1554 Howard received the Spanish ambassadors at Tower Wharf and accompanied them to Durham Place. He was made a Knight of the Garter, and in March the same year, following his action in closing Ludgate against the rebellious Thomas Wyatt (see Wyatt, Sir Thomas, the younger), he was created Baron Howard of Effingham, the manor of Effingham having been granted to him three years previously by Edward VI (q.v.). Because of his devotion to the Princess Elizabeth, later Elizabeth I (q.v.), and his outspoken remonstrances against the harshness of her treatment, Howard aroused the suspicions of Mary I (q.v.) and her advisers, and as a result he at one time contemplated resignation. In 1558, however, Mary appointed him as Lord Chamberlain.

On the accession of Queen Elizabeth, Howard was continued in the office of Lord Chamberlain and was sent to France as one of the negotiators for the Treaty of Cateau-Cambrésis, signed in April 1559. Although highly favoured by Elizabeth, he was not a man of great wealth. The lands he had inherited from his father had been added to over the years by royal grants and by the purchase of certain estates in Surrey; nevertheless in 1567 Howard complained of poverty as the result of expenses incurred in his long service of the crown. It was said that had he owned more property he would undoubtedly have been given an earldom. After 1570 his powers began to decline, and when in 1572 he at last relinquished the office of Lord Chamberlain, he was made Lord Privy Seal, an office that had ceased to carry much responsibility, purely in order that he should continue to receive some income. Howard died in January 1573 and was buried in Reigate Church.

G. Brenan and E. P. Statham, *House of Howard* (2 vols; 1907).

Henry Howard, *Memorials of the Howard Family* (1834).

**Howard de Walden, 1st Baron** (1561–1626), see Howard, Lord Thomas.

**Howard of Effingham, 1st Baron** (?1510–1573), see Howard, Lord William.

**Howard of Effingham, 2nd Baron** (1536–1624), see Howard, Charles.

**Hudson, Henry** (d. 1611), Arctic navigator and explorer, see *Lives of the Stuart Age*.

# J

**James IV** (1473–1513), King of Scotland, 1488–1513.

James was born on 17 March 1473, the eldest son of James III and Margaret of Denmark (for both see *Lives Before the Tudors*). He succeeded to the throne of Scotland at the age of fifteen, following a revolution of the nobility and the murder of his father, James III, at the Battle of Sauchieburn, near Stirling, on 11 June 1488. He was crowned at Scone on 26 June the same year. For a time Archibald Douglas, 5th Earl of Angus, acted as the King's guardian, but James soon took an active part in controlling his kingdom and showed himself to be an energetic and able leader. His vigorously pursued policy of clemency, moderation and unification won him popular support in Scotland, and he was able without much difficulty to crush those lords who rebelled against him during the early years of his reign; by 1493 he had extended his royal authority to the north and west and had brought the Isles under the crown.

In 1491 James entered into a truce with Henry VII (q.v.) which was to last for five years. Relations between Scotland and England had been very uneasy up to this point, for James was distinctly less Anglophile than his father and more intent on making Scotland a power to be reckoned with in Europe, while Henry was secretly negotiating on the one hand with certain Scots lords to have James kidnapped, and on the other with Angus to persuade him to influence the Scots King against going to war against England; there were also a number of naval skirmishes in which English ships privateering in Scottish waters were captured by the Scots. The situation was complicated in the autumn of 1495 by the arrival in Scotland of Perkin Warbeck (q.v.), pretender to the English throne, whom James received at Stirling at the request of Margaret, Duchess of Burgundy (q.v.), and helped financially. In September 1496 James broke the truce with England by sending a small invading force across the Border in support of Warbeck; there was, however, little serious fighting and poor support for the pretender among the northern English, and in the following summer James, disillusioned, withdrew his army. A new seven-year truce with England was negotiated in September 1497.

Anglo-Scottish relations were further strengthened in 1503 by the marriage of the King to Margaret Tudor (q.v.), the eldest daughter of Henry VII; incorporated in the marriage treaty was a treaty of 'perpetual peace'. The real significance of this union was that in 1603 James's great-grandson, James VI of Scotland (q.v.), would succeed to the English throne, the first in a line of Stuart kings of England.

Initially James had been reluctant to accept Henry's offer of the hand of his daughter, being deeply in love with Margaret Drummond, one of his mistresses, with whom it was rumoured that he had contracted a secret marriage. Through his liaison with earlier mistresses he had already fathered a number of illegitimate children, including Alexander Stewart, born in about 1493, who was made Archbishop of St Andrews, and James Stewart, born in about 1499, later created Earl of Moray. In 1500 Margaret Drummond died of poisoning, which left the King grief-stricken, but free to undertake the proposed English marriage. Negotiations were completed, and the thirteen-year-old Margaret Tudor arrived in Scotland in the summer of 1503. The wedding ceremony took place at the Abbey of Holyrood on 8 August. Six children were born to James and his Queen, but only one survived, a son, the future James V (q.v.), born in 1512.

James had never ceased to feel guilty about his father's death, and all his life he wore a penitential iron chain, to which from time to time he added extra links. Having succeeded in pacifying his subjects in all corners of the kingdom, he now turned his attention to improving their living standards. Legislation was introduced to encourage trade, industry, and agriculture; the first printing press in Scotland was set up in 1507 under his auspices; in the field of education he introduced the first compulsory education act and was associated with the founding of the University of Aberdeen (the third in Scotland, and the first in the British Isles to have a faculty of medicine).

James was himself a gifted linguist, and even spoke some Gaelic; he was extremely devout in religious matters; and among his numerous other interests were dentistry, surgery, alchemy, architecture, and shipbuilding. The palaces of Stirling, Falkland, and Linlithgow were much embellished during his reign, and work on the Palace of Holyroodhouse, at Edinburgh, started in readiness for his marriage, continued throughout his reign. In his determination to make Scotland a maritime power James also spent lavishly on his navy, and especially on the construction and equipment of the *Great Michael*, the largest warship of the age, which was launched in 1511.

Success and popularity at home gained James the prestige he sought in the eyes of the European powers, but he failed in his ambition to unite them in a crusade against the Turks. After 1509 the Scottish King's position was considerably weakened as a result of mounting conflict with his belligerent brother-in-law, now Henry VIII (q.v.). Although bound by treaty to England, James had never cancelled the 'Auld Alliance' with France; consequently when the so-called Holy League, which had been formed in 1511 to combat French power in Italy, was enlarged to include England a year later, he found himself under pressure to help the encircled Louis XII. James renewed the former alliance and so moved one step nearer to the now inevitable war with England.

Henry invaded France at the end of June 1513. James responded by sending his navy to the assistance of the French, and on 22 August the Scots, under the command of their King, crossed into northern England, capturing several castles. The English army, led by the Earl of Surrey (later the 2nd Duke of Norfolk; see Howard, Thomas, 2nd Duke), marched north to meet them, and battle was joined on 9 September at Flodden Edge, near Branxton. James, charging on foot with his spearmen, was killed early in the fighting; his army was utterly defeated, and the cream of Scots manhood in their thousands, the 'Flowers of the Forest', including most of his nobles and members of virtually every leading family in the kingdom, perished on the battlefield with him.

Because the corpse of the King was not recovered after the battle of Flodden, for a long time the myth persisted among the Scots that he would return. His body was in fact taken to England, for Henry VIII requested papal permission to bury it in St Paul's, James having been excommunicated for breaking his treaty; but for some reason that has never been explained no funeral or burial took place.

James was succeeded by his infant son, James V. One of his natural sons, Alexander Stewart, Archbishop of St Andrews, died with him at Flodden; a posthumous son, born in April 1514, survived for less than two years.

Generally considered to be the ablest and most popular of the Stewart kings of Scotland, it has been said of James IV that he had all the qualities of a Renaissance prince without the caution. Under his guidance peace and prosperity prevailed at home and there was a remarkable flowering of scholarship and the arts; but international ambition led him into rash expenditures and actions which culminated in the disaster of Flodden.

Caroline Bingham, *The Stewart Kingdom of Scotland* (1974).
R. L. Mackie, *King James IV of Scotland* (Edinburgh, 1958).

*Portraits*: oil, by unknown artist: Scottish National Portrait Gallery, Edinburgh; oil, by Mytens, early seventeenth century: S.N.P.G.; oil, seventeenth century copy of contemporary portrait: Colonel William Sterling of Keir; illumination, James IV at his devotions, from *Book of Hours* of James IV: Österreichische Nationalbibliothek, Vienna; oil, *called* James IV, by Holbein: National Gallery of Scotland, Edinburgh.

**James V** (1512–1542), King of Scotland from 1513 to 1542.

James was born at Linlithgow, West Lothian, on 10 April 1512, the only surviving son of James IV (q.v.) and Margaret Tudor (q.v.). He succeeded to the throne of Scotland at the age of seventeen months, following the death of his father at the Battle of Flodden on 9 September 1513, and was crowned in the Chapel Royal at Stirling on 21 September the same year.

Throughout his minority James V was a pawn in the internal power struggle between the pro-French and pro-English factions of the Scottish nobility. His mother had been appointed as his guardian under the will of James IV, but in 1514 she forfeited her regency by marrying the Earl of Angus (see Douglas, Archibald, 6th Earl), the leader of the 'English' party, and the Duke of Albany (see Stewart, John) arrived from France to be made Regent in July the following year. Albany secured the custody of James and his baby brother, the Duke of Ross (who was born after his father's death and who survived for only a few more months), while Margaret was escorted to Edinburgh, from where, having failed in a plan to abduct her children, she fled to England.

For the next few years James was kept at Stirling Castle, in the care of Lord Erskine. There he was served with much affection by the poet Sir David Lindsay, later Master of the Household, and he received his first formal lessons in French and Latin from Gavin Dunbar, the future Archbishop of Glasgow.

Meanwhile in 1517 Albany left Scotland for France, in order to renew the Franco-Scottish alliance. During his four-year absence a new power struggle broke out between the Earls of Angus and Arran (see Hamilton, James, 1st Earl), which culminated in bitter street fighting in Edinburgh in the spring of 1520 and a victory for Angus. Margaret returned to Scotland, but complicated matters by pressing for a divorce from Angus and continually shifting her support from one side to another. When Albany finally left Scotland for good in the spring of 1524, she and Arran regained control of the King and a few months later declared that the twelve-

year-old James had attained his majority and was fit to govern. Margaret's position was insecure, however, as she had lost the support of her brother Henry VIII (q.v.) because of her plan to divorce her husband, whom Albany, having returned briefly to Scotland in 1521 and 1523, had banished to France. Angus now returned to Scotland, with Henry's approval, and in a *coup d'état* in November 1525 took possession of the King.

There were several abortive attempts to rescue James, who remained a prisoner of the pro-English Douglas régime for the next two and a half years. During this time he was isolated from his former household and his education was neglected. He determined to escape and at the end of May 1528, disguised as a groom, he evaded his captors and reached Stirling, from where he took control of his kingdom.

With his mother and her third husband, Lord Methven, as his counsellors, James began his rule by driving Angus over the border into England. He then made a truce with Henry VIII and

set to work to restore law and order within his kingdom; in this, with the exception of some trouble in the Highlands and the Isles, he was largely successful. Like his father, James V soon became popular with his subjects, especially with the poorer classes; he liked to go among them in the disguise of a tenant farmer. He also followed his father in leading a far-from-celibate youth, enjoying numerous affairs both with simple country girls and young women of noble birth. His favourite mistress was Margaret, daughter of Lord Erskine, who bore him a son, Lord James Stewart (q.v.), the future Earl of Moray, who became Regent of Scotland in the reign of James's grandson, James VI (q.v.). The young King fathered at least eight other children by his various mistresses.

Scotland was by this time again the key to the balance of power in Europe, and several states offered James the hand of a princess in marriage: Henry VIII offered his daughter, Mary (see Mary I); the Pope his niece, Catherine de' Medici (q.v.); Charles V (q.v.) his sister, Mary of Hungary. In the end James chose to adhere to the French alliance, which had reserved for him a French princess. He was offered, and accepted, Marie de Bourbon, daughter of the Duc de Vendôme, with a handsome dowry, but disappointed with her mis-shapen appearance when they met, he repudiated her and insisted on marrying the delicate Princess Madeleine, daughter of François I. The wedding took place at Notre Dame in Paris on 1 January 1537. Six months later, on 7 July, only a few weeks after their return to Scotland, Madeleine died.

On his return from France James learned that his mother was scheming to divorce Lord Methven and remarry Angus; he also discovered other plots for the return of the exiled Angus to Scotland. He dealt with both severely, quashing the proposed divorce proceedings and ordering his mother to return to her husband, and sentencing to death two members of the Douglas family, Lady Glamis, Angus's sister, and his brother-in-law, for conspiracy against him. His action against Lady Glamis aroused much ill-feeling among the nobility, who were becoming increasingly alienated from their King.

In 1538, having preserved a decent period of mourning, James took a second French bride, the widowed Marie de Guise (q.v.). Their marriage was performed by proxy in May, and solemnized in the cathedral of St Andrews the following month. Marie was to bear James two sons, who died in 1541, and a daughter, Mary, the future Queen of Scots (q.v.).

By his two marriages James committed Scotland to the support of the papacy and France. He also handsomely enriched his own depleted exchequer, not only through the generous dowries paid by the French King, and by persuading the Pope to impose a tax, the 'Three Teinds' (three-tenths), on the prelates of Scotland 'for the protection and defence of the realm', but also by himself levying a 'Great Tax' of £10,000 a year, ostensibly for the endowment of the newly-founded College of Justice, though most it went to the crown. The unpopularity he incurred by these and other taxation measures levied against the nobility did not deter the King from a bout of extravagant spending on the royal household, his various palaces, and the crown jewels; he had been much influenced by the splendours of the French court and sought to enhance the image of the Scottish crown accordingly.

Meanwhile mutual suspicion was leading Scotland and England to the verge of conflict. Henry VIII, now that he was excommunicate, feared that the Franco-Scottish alliance would result in a religious war against England; in order to resist a possible Scots invasion, he began massing troops along the Border. James in turn feared English aggression. Both sides next played for time, Henry by inviting James to meet him at York in the autumn of 1541, James by agreeing to do so but not turning up, with the result that the English King returned to London in a furious temper and resolved to attack.

James's health was by this time beginning to fail, probably as a result of a hunting accident several years earlier. The sudden death of his two sons in April 1541 had affected him deeply; also he was increasingly aware that he could no longer command the universal loyalty of his nobles, a number of whom had come under the influence of the new Reformation doctrines and had embraced Protestantism, which meant that they would be unwilling to bear arms against England; others, remembering Flodden, were equally reluctant to do so.

In the autumn of 1542 an English force commanded by the Duke of Norfolk (see Howard, Thomas, 3rd Duke) crossed the border. James, his army already greatly weakened by disaffection of the nobles, immediately marched south and encamped at Fala Muir, where news was brought to him that Norfolk had retreated due to the lack of provisions and mutiny among the ranks. Eager to take advantage of the situation, the King gave orders to advance into England; his commanders, however, refused to obey; the army disbanded, and James had no choice but to return to Edinburgh. With the help of his supporters he managed to raise a second army of some 10,000 men, who were marched to Lochmaben in readiness for an attack across the Solway.

There James was taken ill, but he insisted that the invasion should go ahead as planned. While he remained at Lochmaben Castle, the army under the King's appointed commander, Oliver Sinclair, crossed into England during the night of 24 November. The following morning the Scots were totally routed by the English in a marshy area known as Solway Moss; many of the soldiers simply ran away or surrendered without putting up a fight.

News of the outcome of Solway Moss caused James to suffer a complete mental breakdown. In his despair he left Lochmaben and rode aimlessly from Edinburgh to Tantallon, then on to Linlithgow to visit the Queen, who was soon expecting her third child, and from there Falkland, where finally he took to his bed. A few days later he learned that on 8 December his wife had given birth to a daughter; he told the messenger who brought the news, 'It cam wi' a lass and it'll pass wi' a lass' – meaning the union of the crown and the house of Stewart. For the next few days the King lay with his face turned to the wall, and on 14 December, surrounded by a small group of courtiers, he died. He was buried at Holyrood, and was succeeded by his one-week-old daughter, Mary, Queen of Scots.

James V has been called 'a good poor man's King'; when he died he was still popular with the common people but was hated by his nobles. His failure was due largely to a mistrust of the nobility and a desire to take too much power, and too much money, into his own hands. His vindictive attitude towards the nobles and his support of France and the papacy alienated many of his subjects.

Caroline Bingham, *James V, King of Scots* (1971).

*Portraits*: several oils, by unknown artists: Scottish National Portrait Gallery, Edinburgh; oil on panel, by unknown artist, *c.* 1540: Royal Collection, Windsor; oil, with Marie de Guise, by unknown artist: Major Michael Crichton-Stuart of Falkland and the National Trust for Scotland; other versions at Chatsworth (illustrated) and Hardwick Hall, Derbyshire); miniature, by William Essex, after unknown artist, 1847: S.N.P.G.

## James VI of Scotland, later James I of England (1566–1625), King of Scotland from 1567, King of England 1603–1625.

James was born at Edinburgh Castle on 19 June 1566, the only son of Mary, Queen of Scots (q.v.) and her second husband, Lord Darnley (see Stewart, Henry).

James was baptized at Stirling Castle on 17 December 1566, according to the rites of the Roman Catholic Church. Less than two months later, on 9 February 1567, his father was murdered, and soon afterwards the Queen of Scots married the Earl of Bothwell (see Hepburn, James). The young prince had already been entrusted to the care of the Earl of Mar (see Erskine, John) and his wife, and he and his mother saw one another rarely. After the summer of 1567 they were never to meet again, for Mary, forced by the rebel Scottish lords first to be separated from Bothwell and then to abdicate in favour of her baby son, was imprisoned at Lochleven, from where she eventually escaped and fled to England in May 1568.

Immediately after his mother's abdication thirteen-month-old James was proclaimed King of Scotland; a few days later, on 29 July 1567, he was crowned as James VI. During his long minority the kingdom was ruled by four successive Regents – the Earls of Moray, Lennox, Mar, and Morton respectively – in an atmosphere of violent feuding and intrigue, while for the first few years of his life the young monarch, victim of a continual tug-of-war between Protestant and Marian factions, endured a bleak, loveless upbringing at Stirling at the hands of the formidable Lady Mar. These two factors combined to produce in James an emotional instability which was to dog him all his life and which showed itself in an extreme timidity in boyhood, a lifelong hatred of violence, and some rather more detrimental effects in later years. Never a robust child, James was slightly built, with weak, spindly legs and one foot which turned outwards (the result of an attack of rickets as a child), which gave him a somewhat uncouth appearance and a clumsy gait; but eventually he overcame these defects by his passion for horse-riding, hunting, and other forms of sport.

At the age of four, the King's formal education was placed in the care of George Buchanan (q.v.), who as James's senior tutor proved to be an even harsher taskmaster than Lady Mar; for the next ten years Buchanan, assisted by Peter Young and other scholars, instilled into their apt and intelligent pupil an immense amount of learning, principally in classical and biblical studies, but also in French and history. His religious education was in conformity with the strict, Calvinist-inspired doctrines of the Scottish Protestant Church. A library was assembled for him and added to a collection of French books, mainly poetical and romantic works, left behind at Stirling by his mother.

From the outset James showed considerable literary talent. At eight years old he was able to translate freely from French into Latin; at sixteen he was writing poetry. One of his youthful efforts, *Essays of a Prentise in the Divine Art of Poesie* (published in 1584) was the forerunner of a number of other scholarly works, which included several lengthy translations from the French. Pedantic, and by far the most intellectual

of all the Stewarts, James's learning was later to earn him the nickname of 'the British Solomon' and rather unfairly 'the wisest fool in Christendom'.

In January 1570 the first of James's Regents. the Earl of Moray (see Stewart, Lord James) was assassinated, and civil war broke out. Bitter fighting ensued between the 'Queen's party' and the Regency, with the former seizing and holding Edinburgh Castle; the conflict was to last for three years. During this period the Earl of Lennox (see Stewart, Matthew), the young King's grandfather, became Regent in July 1570, but was killed in September 1571; when he was succeeded by the Earl of Mar, James was placed under the governorship of the new Regent's brother, Sir Alexander Erskine. Mar died in office in October 1572. The subsequent firmer administration of the Earl of Morton (see Douglas, James) managed not only to put an end to the fighting but also to restore some solidarity to the kingdom; however, the new Regent's policy of leaning towards England and away from France led inevitably to renewed feuding among the Scottish lords and, in 1578, to Morton's fall from power, whereupon the twelve-year-old James was persuaded to take nominal control of the government.

James did not find it easy to manage the feuding nobles, and Morton was re-established in power by consent of the Scottish Parliament later the same year. However, his influence over the King was supplanted by that of Esmé Stuart (q.v.), a Franco-Scottish cousin of James, who arrived in Scotland in September 1579, and with whom the young King fell deeply in love. Stuart, an emissary from Mary's Guise relations, had the double purpose of regaining Franco-Scottish understanding and converting James to Catholicism. He swiftly took

273

advantage of the King's romantic attachment and, together with James Stewart (q.v.; later Earl of Arran), plotted the overthrow of the Regent Morton, who was impeached and executed in 1581 on the charge of implication in Darnley's murder fourteen years earlier. James then elevated his cousin to the title of Duke of Lennox; but the latter's further objectives were disrupted on 22 August 1582, when a group of Presbyterian supporters led by the Earl of Gowrie (see Ruthven, William), kidnapped the King and held him prisoner for nearly a year, during which time they forced him to send Lennox back to France.

In June 1583 James escaped from his captors and managed to reach St Andrews, where he proclaimed himself King and, at the age of seventeen, took full control of his kingdom. The problems he faced were numerous: in Scotland, the religious question and the related warring factions of the nobility, who controlled the Parliament; Mary's project to return and to rule jointly with James; while abroad there was the ever-important matter of asserting James's claim to succeed to the English throne after Elizabeth I (q.v.).

James was a Protestant by upbringing, yet throughout his reign he was to vacillate between Protestant and Catholic interests, shrewdly playing the one off against the other in his attempt to be a 'universall King'. The action of Gowrie and his associates at first set him against the Presbyterians, and in 1584 James had himself re-affirmed as head of the Church of Scotland, a victory, albeit short-lived, for episcopalianism over the ultra-Protestant faction. At the same time he toyed with negotiations with the great Catholic powers of Europe and with his mother. In these early years he was much influenced by his chief adviser,

Sir John Maitland (q.v.), later 1st Baron Maitland of Thirlestane, whom he appointed first as Secretary of State and later as Chancellor of Scotland. Maitland believed in compromise with the Presbyterians and an alliance with England, and gradually James, himself convinced of the overwhelming need for security of his kingdom, and with his sights firmly set on the succession to the English throne, moved towards a *rapprochement* with Elizabeth; in July 1586 he signed an alliance with England in return for a financial subsidy and Elizabeth's guarantee to respect his rights. Much hard bargaining went into this alliance, and James was not prepared to sacrifice it for his mother's life, with the result that Mary's execution in February 1587 produced only the most formal of protests from her son.

In 1589 James was married to the fourteen-year-old Princess Anne of Denmark (see *Lives of the Stuart Age*), daughter of Frederick II of Denmark and Norway. The wedding ceremony was performed in Oslo, where James had joined his bride after her ship had been marooned by storms on her way to Scotland; they spent the winter in Denmark and arrived back in Scotland on 1 May 1590. Although James was not greatly interested in the opposite sex, the union was not initially an unhappy one, and during the first sixteen years seven children were born, three of whom – Henry Frederick, Elizabeth (for both see *Lives of the Stuart Age*) and Charles (see Charles I in *Lives of the Stuart Age*) – survived infancy. The Scottish tradition of taking royal children away from their mother at birth alienated Anne from her husband in the early years; her Lutheran upbringing and subsequent Catholic sympathies also caused difficulties, and she was much criticized by the Scots for her frivolity and extravagance. In later years there was a gradual parting until towards the end of the Queen's life they were living in separate quarters. Their eldest son, Prince Henry Frederick, died in 1612, and Anne herself in 1619.

In the decade following his return to Scotland in 1590, the major domestic problem with which James had to contend was that of the Kirk and its opposition to episcopacy, led by the zealous Andrew Melville (q.v.), the successor to John Knox (q.v.). At the same time there were the scandal of the North Berwick witchcraft trials, which broke in 1590, and the sinister activities of the 'Wizard Earl' of Bothwell (see Hepburn, Francis Stewart) who threatened the King's person and eventually achieved Maitland's dismissal. The gulf that had developed between the Presbyterian ministers and the crown widened still further when the King refused to discipline the northern Catholic lords; in particular the clergy were angered by his leniency towards the Marquess of Huntly, who murdered the 'Bonnie' Earl of Moray in 1592, and by the pardon he gave to the lords implicated in the treasonable 'Spanish blanks' intrigue when this was discovered the same year.

Presbyterianism was restored briefly under the Maitland-sponsored 'Golden Act' of 1592, but in 1596 the extremists within the Kirk overstepped the mark by preaching against the Queen and by asserting the supremacy of ministers over the crown, whereupon James took swift action to regain control of the General Assembly. Maitland was not restored to power, and thereafter James appointed no supreme advisers; a committee of eight, known as the Octavians, set up to handle the King's dwindling finances, lasted less than a year.

The northern earls were brought to heel also in 1596, and in the period of comparative stability that followed James put in writing his reply to the Kirk's attack on the sovereign's right to head the Church, stressing, in his *Trew Law of Free Monarchies*, first published anonymously in 1598, his belief in the principle of the divine right of kings. He also published in 1598 a book of advice, dedicated to his eldest son, entitled the *Basilikon Doron*, in which he explained his standards as a king and his views on Church interference in state affairs. A tract, printed the previous year, on *Demonologie* reflected the King's obsessional interest in witchcraft.

Presbyterian resentment flared up again in 1600, when the two young Gowrie brothers, still harbouring bitterness over the earlier treatment of their father, made an abortive attempt to capture James; the conspirators were killed and for the remainder of the reign there were no further threats to the King's life. In fact, having won over the ultra-Protestant faction and tamed the Kirk and the nobility, James was now seen to be making a successful job of governing Scotland.

Now, more than ever, his ambition was fixed on succession to the English throne. He had in 1596 christened his eldest daughter Elizabeth, as a gesture to the English Queen; less openly he began to solicit the goodwill of the Pope and to woo the English Catholics with promises. A more devious and dangerous ploy was his involvement with the Earl of Essex (see Devereux, Robert). Fortunately for James, he delayed committing himself irretrievably to participation in Essex's proposed rebellion. After the latter's execution for treason in February 1601, Sir Robert Cecil (q.v.; later 1st Earl of Salisbury), Elizabeth's Secretary of State, opened a secret correspondence with James in which he advised him how to proceed if he were to persuade the Queen to name him as her rightful successor. Through his letters Cecil virtually trained James in the art of government and kingship, with the result that when Elizabeth died on 24 March 1603 the transfer of sovereignty was achieved remarkably smoothly.

Proclaimed at Whitehall James I of England, the new King set out for London as soon as news reached him; he was to revisit Scotland only once, in 1617. Almost immediately, without the consent of Parliament, he proclaimed himself 'King of Great Britain'. This was the first of a series of acts of over-confidence and extravagance which did little to endear him either to the English Parliament or to the common people, who disliked his broad Scots accent and found his manners coarse and his appearance unattractive. They were further offended by his liking for handsome and expensive young men, and distrusted his ambition to unite England and Scotland.

James soon made himself unpopular with both the Catholics and the Puritans. Although he brought the war with Spain to an end in 1604 and suspended the penals laws against Catholics, he did not, as they hoped, repeal the recusancy laws; much plotting ensued, one of the results of which was the Gunpowder Plot of November 1605 (see Fawkes, Guy, in *Lives of the Stuart Age*). The King also disappointed the Puritans by his rejection of the Millenary Petition at the Hampton Court Conference of 1604, and although he commissioned a new translation of the Bible – the Authorized Version, which was published in 1611 – his 'No bishop, no King' pronouncement expressed his definite alignment with the Church of England. He supported Richard Bancroft (q.v.), Archbishop of Canterbury, over the question of the authority of ecclesiastical courts, and in 1616 he dismissed the Lord Chief Justice, Sir Edward Coke (see *Lives of the Stuart Age*) for his opposition to Church interference in the legal system.

In the King's relations with Parliament finance was the key. Because of his extravagance James was always short of money, and Parliament, struggling to assert its power over the monarchy, was in a strong position. In the first Parliament of the reign (1604–11) a legal action known as Bate's Case recognized the crown's right to levy customs duties without parliamentary approval; but in 1611 the Commons rejected the Great Contract, an idea of Robert Cecil, now Earl of Salisbury, whereby the crown would forgo its ancient feudal rights in return for an annual grant of £200,000. The 1614 Parliament (the 'Addled Parliament') was equally blind to the King's need for money for foreign policy and court expenses and, seeing only his lack of economy, also refused him funds, so that he was forced to resort to other methods of money-raising, which included marriage negotiations with Spain on behalf of his eldest son, Prince Henry, Prince of Wales. The fact that the King was lazy and so blatantly preferred the pleasures of the chase to the more tedious business of attending to state administration did not improve the situation.

Nevertheless, with the able and experienced Salisbury holding the reins as chief minister, the first nine years of the reign were comparatively stable. Then, following Salisbury's death in 1612, James appointed as Secretary his current favourite, the young Scotsman Robert Carr (see *Lives of the Stuart Age*), later Earl of Somerset, who was to bring discredit to the court through his involvement in the scandal surrounding the murder of Sir Thomas Overbury (see *Lives of the Stuart Age*). By 1614 James was much under the influence of the Spanish ambassador, Diego Sarmiento, later Count Gondomar, with whom he was busy negotiating for the marriage of his second son, Prince Charles (now heir to the throne, following the death of Prince Henry) to the Infanta Maria; the project was distasteful to the English people and eventually came to nothing, but Gondomar's influence was so strong that in 1618 he persuaded the King to agree to the execution of Sir Walter Ralegh (q.v.).

In 1616 James took up a new favourite, George Villiers, later Duke of Buckingham (see Villiers, George, 1st Duke, in *Lives of the Stuart Age*), who was to exert an extraordinary influence over the King in his declining years. James had tried ineffectively to mediate in the conflict between Spain and the Netherlands; on the outbreak of the Thirty Years War a hostile Parliament made him equally powerless either to help his son-in-law, Frederick V (see *Lives of the Stuart Age*), the Elector Palatine who had married his daughter Elizabeth, or to mediate with the Catholic powers. Finally Charles and Buckingham formed an alliance with the Commons, from which the King was totally excluded, to push forward an aggressive policy; in 1624 they had his financial adviser, the Earl of Middlesex (see Cranfield, Lionel, in *Lives of the Stuart Age*) impeached, and forced James to declare war on Spain.

Disappointed, weary, and no longer master of his own kingdom, James was taken ill after a hunting expedition and died on 27 March 1625 at Theobalds, the country residence which he had purchased from the Earl of Salisbury in 1607 in exchange for Hatfield. He was buried at Westminster Abbey.

It is generally acknowledged that James was a good King of Scotland, but not much of a success as King of England owing to his tactless expression of authoritarian views of the divine right of kings, and an inherent laziness in state matters. He neither understood the English people nor appealed to them as the Tudors had done. Basically a man of peace and learning, he was a clever man, but undignified, more like a don than a monarch. Through his inability to see that the policies that had worked so well in Scotland went against the tide of public and political opinion in England, James aroused the hostility of Parliament and sowed the seeds of dissent that were to erupt into civil war during the reign of his son, Charles I. His Stuart heredity and the traumas of his childhood were responsible for his unstable personality, the weakness of which became more marked in later years, resulting in an over-estimation of his power, impaired judgment, and unwise emotional attachments. (It is, however, by no means certain that James was a homosexual.) His place in history rests upon his union of the two kingdoms and his long maintenance of peace. (*Note*: The period of his life as James I of England, 1603–25, is dealt with in more detail in *Lives of the Stuart Age*.)

The *Political Works of James VI*, first published in 1616, have been edited by C. H. McIlwain (Cambridge, Mass., 1918). His correspondence with Robert Cecil has been edited by John Bruce for the Camden Society, vol. lxxviii (1861), and was also published as *The Secret Correspondence of Sir Robert Cecil with James I*, edited by Lord Hailes (Edinburgh, 1766). The *Poems of James VI of Scotland*, edited by J. Craigie, were published in two volumes by the Scottish Texts Society (1955–8).

R. Ashton, *James I by his contemporaries* (1969).
Caroline Bingham, *The Making of a King* (1969).
Antonia Fraser, *King James VI of Scotland, I of England* (1974).
D. Mathew, *James I* (1967).
A. G. R. Smith (ed.), *The Reign of James VI and I* (1973).
H. G. Stafford, *James VI of Scotland and the throne of England* (New York, 1940).
T. Thomson, *The Historie and Life of King James the Sext* (1825).
D. H. Willson, *King James VI and I* (New York, 1956).

*Portraits*: oil, by van Brounckhorst, 1574: Scottish National Portrait Gallery, Edinburgh; copies attributed to Lockey: National Portrait Gallery, London, and Hardwick Hall (National Trust); oil, by unknown artist, *c.* 1585: last recorded in Count van Rechteren Limpurg-Almelo Collection; oil, half length, by unknown artist, *c.* 1587: Royal Collection, Hampton Court; oil, half length, by unknown artist: S.N.P.G.; oil; full length, attributed to J. de Critz: Loseley Park (J. R. More-Molyneux); oil, attributed to de Critz: National Maritime Museum, Greenwich; oil, by unknown artist after de Critz: N.P.G.; oil, by unknown artist: N.P.G.; miniature, by Hilliard, *c.* 1603–8: Royal Collection, Windsor; miniature, by Hilliard, *c.* 1609–14: British Museum, London; oil, full length, by van Somer, 1618: Royal Collection, Holyroodhouse; miniature by Hoskins after van Somer, *c.* 1618: V. & A.; oil, full length, in robes of state, by van Somer, *c.* 1620: Royal Collection, Windsor; oil, in Garter robes, by Mytens, *c.* 1621: N.P.G.; other versions at Oxford, Cambridge, Edinburgh, and elsewhere; statue by Colt: Hatfield House (Marquess of Salisbury).

**Jane Grey, Lady** (1537–1554), Lady Jane Dudley, Queen of England by assumption for nine days in 1553.

Jane Grey was born early in October 1537 at Bradgate, Leicestershire, the eldest surviving daughter of Henry Grey, 3rd Marquess of Dorset and later Duke of Suffolk, and his wife, Frances, daughter of the Duke of Suffolk (see Brandon, Charles) and Mary Tudor (q.v.). On her mother's side Jane was therefore a great-granddaughter of Henry VII (q.v.), and thus cousin to Edward VI (q.v.) and his sisters, the Princess Mary (see Mary I) and the Princess Elizabeth (see Elizabeth I), and after them in direct line for succession to the English throne.

Jane had an unhappy childhood. Her parents treated her harshly, and she found her only solace in studying. She was provided with excellent tutors, including John Aylmer (q.v.), future Bishop of London, and wrote Greek and Latin at a very early age. Jane's exceptional learning was referred to by Roger Ascham (q.v.) in his *Scholemaster*.

At the age of nine Jane was sent to live with Katherine Parr (q.v.), the Queen Dowager, at Chelsea. When shortly afterwards Thomas Seymour (q.v.), the Lord High Admiral, married Katherine and joined the establishment, he was quick to see the value of Jane as a pawn in his scheme to overthrow his brother, Edward Seymour (q.v.), 1st Duke of Somerset and Protector of the Realm. By offering to arrange a marriage between Jane and Edward VI, the Lord High Admiral persuaded her father, Dorset, to agree to her becoming his ward. She returned to Bradgate briefly in September 1548 after the death of Katherine Parr, but the determined Thomas Seymour won her back on payment of £500 and a renewed assurance that a marriage contract with the King would be forthcoming. Dorset, in return, agreed to support whole-heartedly his friend's sinister plans. In the event, after Seymour's arrest and imprisonment in the Tower in January 1549, Dorset not only gave damaging evidence against him but soon switched his allegiance to John Dudley (q.v.), Earl of Warwick and later 1st Duke of Northumberland. Meanwhile Jane re-turned reluctantly to Bradgate and to her classical studies.

In October 1551 the title of Duke of Suffolk was conferred on Jane's father, and from that time she attended frequently at court. Negotiations were under way for her marriage to Somerset's heir, Edward Seymour, Earl of Hertford, but they had not been finalized. Northumberland, who had assumed power following his overthrow of the Protector, was confronted with the crisis over the succession to the throne. The young King's health had been visibly failing from January 1553, and Northumberland was now intent on securing his position through appro-priate family alliances. These included the marriage of Lady Jane Grey to his fourth son, Lord Guildford Dudley, which took place, with royal approval, on 21 May at the Dudleys' London house. After the wedding Jane was compelled to reside with her husband's parents, but her marriage proved so miserable and she disliked her Dudley parents-in-law so much that she suffered a nervous breakdown.

Edward himself was responsible for the 'Device' excluding his half-sisters in favour of Lady Jane, and Northumber-land identified himself with the project. The document was signed and witnessed on 21 June by the Council, and all but one of the Judges; the signatures of the Judges, however, were obtained only after pressure on the part of Northum-berland.

Edward VI died on 6 July 1553, but his death was kept secret for three days. Although she must have had some inkling of what was going on, when the Council sent to inform her on 9 July that she was Queen, Jane's first reaction was to faint. Recovering, initially she would not accept, but then she allowed herself to be persuaded, and her proclamation was issued the following day. She was not quite sixteen years old.

For the next nine days the young Queen was lodged in the Tower. Little state business was transacted during this time, and Jane resolutely refused the Dudley family's demands that her husband should be declared King.

Meanwhile the Princess Mary had learned of her brother's death and was gathering her supporters. She had the general public behind her, especially in London, and within a short time many members of the Council met together and revoked their former approval of Jane on the grounds that they had been coerced; on 19 July the Lord Mayor of London was authorized to proclaim before a jubilant throng that Mary was Queen. Northumberland's followers deserted; even Jane herself was not unwilling to relinquish the crown that she had never wanted, when advised to do so by her father.

She and her father were committed to the Tower, but Suffolk soon received a pardon. Lady Jane and her husband were arraigned for high treason at Guildhall on 14 November; she pleaded guilty, and they were both sentenced to death. The Queen, however, intervened to suspend the sentence, as she wished to save her young cousin's life. But when at the beginning of 1554 Suffolk rashly lent his support to Wyatt's rebellion (see Thomas Wyatt the younger) against the Queen's marriage to Philip II of Spain (q.v.), Jane's fate – and that of her innocent husband – was sealed.

Lady Jane Grey was beheaded at the Tower on 12 February 1554. Her husband, not being of royal blood, had been beheaded on Tower Hill an hour before, and on her way to the block Jane is said to have met the procession bringing Lord Guildford's headless body back for burial.

There was much sympathy and compassion for the pathetic girl who had been but a tool in the hands of first, her guardian and later, her father-in-law. Nevertheless, her execution could be justified on political grounds since, as a Protestant, she represented a potential danger to Mary and the English Catholics.

The *Letters of Lady Jane Grey* have been edited by Douglas Geary and published at Ilfracombe (1951). See also *The Literary Remains of Lady Jane Grey* [with a memoir], edited by N. H. Nicolas (1895).

Hester W. Chapman, *Lady Jane Grey* (1962).
R. Davey, *The Nine Days' Queen* (1909).

A. K. Jordan, *Edward VI* (2 vols; 1968–70).
J. G. Nichols (ed.), *The Chronicle of Queen Jane and of Two Years of Queen Mary* (Camden Society, xlviii, 1850).

*Portraits:* oil on panel, by Master John, *c.* 1545: National Portrait Gallery, London; oil, by unknown artist: Sir Hugh Wontner; oil on panel, unknown girl *called* Lady Jane Grey, *c.* 1555–60: N.P.G.; oil, three-quarter-length, by unknown artist, not earlier than end of seventeenth century: The Lord Hastings; engraving, by W. and M. van de Passe, in *Herwologia*, 1620.

**Jane Seymour** (?1509–1537), third Queen consort of Henry VIII (q.v.).

Jane Seymour was born probably in 1509, the eldest daughter of ten children of Sir John Seymour of Wulfhall, Savernake, Wiltshire, and his wife, Margery, daughter of Sir John Wentworth of Nettlested, Suffolk. On her mother's side she was descended, albeit distantly, from Edward III.

Little is known of Jane's early life. She grew up at Wulfhall and in the family circle must have learned the usual feminine accomplishments of music and needlework. Her more formal education was probably entrusted to the family priest; all her life Jane retained a deep-rooted religious faith. The Seymours at this time were moving up in the social scale. Sir John was made a Knight Banneret for his services at Tournai and attended frequently at court. Two of Jane's elder brothers, Edward Seymour (q.v.) and Thomas Seymour (q.v.), had high ambitions and by the time she was twenty both were in the service of prominent courtiers, Edward as Master of Horse to the Duke of Richmond and Thomas in the employ of the warrior-poet, Sir Francis Bryan. Jane herself entered the royal service in about 1529 as maid-of-honour to Catherine of Aragon (q.v.), who was then still Queen; she later acted in a similar capacity to Anne

Boleyn (q.v.), the second wife and consort of Henry VIII.

The King is believed to have fallen in love with Jane soon after his marriage to Anne; by 1535 the affair was well known at court and was beginning to be a source of much resentment and anger on the part of the Queen. The Seymour family must have been fully aware of the King's interest by September 1535, when Henry honoured them with a three-day visit at Wulfhall.

Jane was not beautiful, but she had intelligence and an unassuming, reserved nature quite the opposite to Anne's flamboyant temperament. Flattered by the King's attentions and the jewels he showered upon her, she was also very much influenced by her brothers, who saw in their sister's royal favour the opportunity to further their own careers, and urged her to respond. Nevertheless Jane behaved throughout the courtship with the utmost discretion, refusing (as Anne had also done initially) to become the King's mistress until he was free to marry her. When Anne found Jane's presence at court no longer bearable, early in 1536, Henry cleverly installed her brother Edward (whom he had appointed a Gentleman of the Privy Chamber) and his wife in the Palace of Greenwich, so that she could live with them and he could visit her by means of a secret passage; however, he is said only to have seen her in the company of others. While Anne was awaiting trial Jane stayed with Sir Nicholas Carew at his house a few miles outside London; the King visited her there in the afternoon of the day on which sentence was passed.

On 17 May 1536, two days before Anne's execution, Archbishop Cranmer (q.v.) pronounced the King's marriage to be invalid and issued a dispensation for him to marry Jane without the publication of banns. They were betrothed on

the day following Anne's death and were married privately at York Place on 30 May.

Of all Henry's wives, Jane seems to have been the one with whom he was most in love, next to Catherine of Aragon. During the seventeen months of their marriage she managed not only to bring about a reconciliation between the King and his daughter, the Princess Mary (see Mary I), but also to give him what he most desired – a legitimate male heir. The only known occasion on which Henry showed real anger towards her was during the Pilgrimage of Grace, when the Queen pleaded with him to reinstate the monasteries; he warned her that if she meddled in affairs of state she would risk the same fate as Anne Boleyn.

Jane was never crowned. The ceremony had to be postponed on account of the plague at Westminster in the autumn of 1536, and by the following summer the Queen's pregnancy was so far advanced that it was considered too much of a risk.

She gave birth to her son, the future

Edward VI (q.v.), at Hampton Court on 12 October 1537. The baby was healthy, and there was great rejoicing throughout the realm. Twelve days later, on 24 October, Jane died of puerperal fever. Henry went into mourning (which he did for none of his other wives) and ordered that she should be buried in St George's Chapel at Windsor, where in due course his own body was to be laid beside hers. Too overcome with grief to attend the funeral on 12 November, he retired to a solitary place; the Princess Mary was chief mourner.

During her short reign Jane was popular at court and with the English people. Only the religious reformers whose views she opposed had anything derogatory to say of her; Martin Luther (q.v.) once called her 'an enemy of the Gospel', whereas Cardinal Reginald Pole (q.v.) found her 'full of goodness'. In the King's eyes her greatest achievement was that she had given him the long-desired male heir to the throne. Had events turned out differently, however, the probability is that in time Henry would have fallen out of love with her and discarded her as he did his other wives.

After Jane's death the ambitious Seymour family continued to rise in the royal favour. Her sister Elizabeth married Cromwell's son; Edward became the Duke of Somerset and later Protector of the young King Edward; Thomas was appointed Lord High Admiral. Both brothers were to end their lives at the hand of the executioner in the next reign.

H. St Maur, *Annals of the Seymours* (1902).
W. Seymour, *Ordeal by Ambition: an English family in the shadow of the Tudors* (1972).

*Portraits:* oil, by Holbein, 1536: Mauritshuis, The Hague (similar portrait, same date: Kunsthistorisches Museum, Vienna); drawing, by Holbein: Royal Collection, Windsor; watercolour miniature, by Holbein, 1536: private collection; oil, attributed to Holbein: Duke of Buccleuch Collection (but authenticity of sitter is uncertain); oil, by van Leemput, after Holbein (copy of group painting originally in Privy Chamber at Whitehall showing Henry VII, Elizabeth of York, Henry VIII, and Jane Seymour): Royal Collection, Hampton Court.

## Jewel, John (1522–1571), Bishop of Salisbury.

Born on 24 May 1522, the son of John Jewel of Berrynarbour, North Devon, John was educated at Barnstaple school and Merton College, Oxford, where his tutor in biblical studies was John Parkhurst, later Bishop of Norwich. Parkhurst subsequently influenced him to move to Corpus Christi College, and he became a fellow of that college in 1542.

While at Oxford Jewel came under the influence of Peter Martyr, the Florentine reformer who had been appointed Regius Professor of Divinity in 1547. He took his B.D. in 1552 and shortly before the accession of Mary I (q.v.) was made public orator of the university, in which capacity he delivered a congratulatory address to the Queen. He acted as notary to Thomas Cranmer (q.v.) and Nicholas Ridley (q.v.) at their disputation in 1554, but soon afterwards gave up his Protestantism and signed a series of Catholic articles, although he did not believe in them. Suspected, Jewel fled first to London and then to Frankfurt, where he issued a statement acknowledging his weakness and withdrawing his recantation; the Queen deprived him of his fellowship.

Jewel spent the next few years on the Continent, in company with other Protestant exiles. At Frankfurt he sided with Richard Cox (q.v.) in his campaign against John Knox (q.v.); he then joined Peter Martyr in Strasbourg and went with him to Zurich. Later he made a tour of Italy, spending some time at Padua. Returning to England on the accession of Elizabeth I (q.v.), Jewel set himself to defend the Established Church against the Romanists. He was chosen as one of the Protestant disputants at the Westminster conference of 1559, and in the following year was consecrated Bishop of Salisbury. He became a doctor of divinity at Oxford in 1565. Although at heart a Puritan, Jewel saw clearly that the controversy over what he called 'the scenic apparatus of divine worship' was unimportant compared with the need for preaching the Gospel and spreading the Word. His challenge to the Romanists to prove their doctrines was taken up by Henry Cole and Thomas Harding, and Jewel's most important piece of writing during the resultant long controversy was the *Apologia pro Ecclesia Anglicana*, published in Latin in 1562 and translated into English by Lady Ann Bacon, mother of Francis Bacon (q.v.), two years later; subsequently, in answer to Harding's counter-attacks he published his *Reply* (1565) and *Defence of the Apology* (1570). Later Jewel became more antagonistic towards the Puritans; an attack on Thomas Cartwright (q.v.), written in 1571, was published after his death.

All his life a patron of learning, Jewel built the cathedral library at Salisbury, and his palace there became a training ground for boys of academic promise but little money; among his protégés was the future author of *The Laws of Ecclesiastical Polity*, Richard Hooker (q.v.).

Active to the very last day, Jewel is said in his later years to have worn himself out with a ceaseless round of preaching in the diocese. He died at Monckton Farleigh on 23 September 1571 and was buried in Salisbury cathedral. In 1609 Archbishop Bancroft (q.v.) ordered copies of his *Apologia* to be placed in the churches, chained to the lectern; the work exerted a considerable influence on the Anglo-Roman controversy and was regarded as the first methodical statement of the position of the Anglican Church.

Jewel's writings were published in a folio edition by Thomas Fuller in 1609; later editions are his *Works*, edited by J. Ayre (Parker Society, Cambridge, 1845–50) and the Oxford edition in eight volumes edited by Jeff (1848).

J. E. Booty, *John Jewel as apologist of the Church of England* (1963).

W. M. Southgate, *John Jewel and the problem of doctrinal authority* (Cambridge, Mass., 1962).

F. O. White, *Lives of the Elizabethan Bishops of the Anglican Church* (1898).

*Portraits*: oil, by unknown artist, sixteenth century: National Portrait Gallery, London; versions at Corpus Christi College and Merton College, Oxford; one formerly at Bishop's Palace, Salisbury, destroyed by fire 1964.

'**Joan of Kent**' (d. 1550), see Bocher, Joan.

**Jonson, Ben** (1572–1637), dramatist and poet, see *Lives of the Stuart Age*.

# K

**Katherine Parr** (1512–1548), sixth Queen consort of Henry VIII (q.v.).

Born in 1512, Katherine was the daughter of Sir Thomas Parr, an official in the Royal Household. After her father's death in 1517 she was brought up by her mother; she was well educated, being accomplished in several languages, including Latin and Greek.

By the time she was singled out by the King as his sixth wife, in 1543, Katherine had already been twice married. Her first husband was Edwin Borough, about whom little is known except that he died in about 1529. She then married John Neville, son of Lord Latimer, a widower with two children, who had been implicated in the Pilgrimage of Grace but had escaped punishment, being in the King's favour; he died in 1542 or 1543, where-

upon Katherine agreed to marry Sir Thomas (later Lord) Seymour (q.v.). This union was overruled by the King, who wished to marry her himself.

Katherine and Henry were married on 12 July 1543. Kind-hearted and yet shrewd, she managed the King far more tactfully than his previous wives. She maintained friendly relations with his three children, watching over their education and eventually succeeding in persuading Henry to restore to Mary (see Mary I) and Elizabeth (see Elizabeth I) the rank of princess which he had taken from them on the grounds that they were bastards. Her beneficial influence extended to interceding for the victims of religious persecution under the Six Articles, but Henry in his last years was irascible and easily angered by her differences of opinion with him on religious matters; according to John Foxe (q.v.), Katherine on one such occasion escaped arrest on a charge of heresy only narrowly through her clever flattery of the King. In 1544 during Henry's absence abroad she acted as Regent.

Henry died on 28 January 1547, and soon afterwards Katherine accepted the hand of her former suitor, now Baron Seymour of Sudeley. He was the brother of the Protector, the Duke of Somerset (see Seymour, Edward), who initially opposed the marriage but was later reconciled to it by Edward VI (q.v.).

Katherine died at Sudeley Castle in Gloucestershire on 7 September 1548, having given birth to a daughter the week before.

M. A. Gordon, *Life of Queen Katherine Parr* (1952).
A. Martienssen, *Queen Katherine Parr* (1973).

*Portraits:* oil, by W. Scrots, *c.* 1545: National Portrait Gallery, London; oil, by unknown artist: Sudeley Castle, Gloucestershire; miniature, by unknown artist: Sudeley Castle.

## Ket or Kett, Robert (d. 1549), rebel.

The date of Ket's birth is not known. He was of Norman ancestry, the family name appearing in some early records as Le Chat. He and his brother William were prosperous tradesmen and landowners in Norfolk, where in 1549 Robert held the manor of Wymondham and several other properties.

Discontent had been smouldering in the area for some time as a result of the action of Sergeant John Flowerdew, a local landowner, who had stripped the priory church (which had been bought by the parishioners after the Dissolution of the Monasteries) of bells and lead from the roof whose purchase had been organized by the Kets. Consequently a feud had arisen between the Flowerdews and the Kets, and when local rioters began throwing down fences round land that had been enclosed, each party bribed men to throw down the other's fences. Ket, leading the reprisals on Flowerdew's fences at the beginning of July, thus found himself at the head of the rioters and, joined by his brother, marched them towards Norwich, throwing down fences as they went.

News of the revolt spread rapidly, and within a few weeks no fewer than 16,000 men had joined Ket and were encamped on Mousehold Heath, outside the city. Here, beneath the now-celebrated tree known as the Oak of Reformation, Ket maintained strict discipline, setting up courts and instructing his chaplains to hold services each morning. A petition was sent to the King, but the Council's reply of 21 July and offer of a pardon did not satisfy Ket, who now led an attack on Norwich. A force under the command of William Parr, Marquess of Northampton, was sent to raise the siege, which it did, but the city was captured by Ket at the beginning of August.

On 23 August the Earl of Warwick (see Dudley, John) reached Norwich with a force of some 12,000 men, and after fierce fighting took possession of the city the following day. On the 25th, the rebels moved forward from their camp stronghold to the low-lying fields of Dussindale; while they were there, exposed and cut off from their lines of communication, Warwick launched a vicious attack on them. Only after some 3,500 of their number had been slain did the rebels surrender; the Ket brothers fled on horseback, but were captured in a barn the following day, taken to London, and lodged in the Tower. At their trial at Westminster on 25 November both pleaded guilty to a charge of treason; Robert was hanged in chains from Norwich Castle and William from the steeple of Wymondham church.

At first it had been feared in London that Ket's rebellion was inspired by Catholics wishing to place the Princess Mary (see Mary I) on the throne; in fact it was an agrarian uprising which had nothing at all to do with religion. Speculation has been raised as to what the outcome might have been had the Duke of Somerset (see Seymour, Edward) taken the command at Norwich, as had originally been the intention, instead of Warwick.

J. Clayton, *Robert Kett and the Norfolk Rising* (1912).
S. T. Bindoff, *Ket's Rebellion* (Historical Association pamphlet, 1949).
F. W. Russell, *Kett's Rebellion in Norfolk* (1859).

## Knollys, Sir Francis (?1514–1596), statesman.

The elder son of Robert Knollys,

usher to Henry VII (q.v.) and to Henry VIII (q.v.), Francis Knollys was born in about 1514. He is believed to have been educated at Oxford. In 1538 the King granted to him in fee the paternal estate of Rotherfield Greys, near Henley-on-Thames, Oxfordshire, appointing him at the same time a gentleman-pensioner at the court. In this capacity Knollys was in attendance at the arrival in England in 1539 of the royal bride, Anne of Cleves (q.v.).

In 1542 Knollys entered Parliament as Member for Horsham. He served under the Protector Somerset (see Seymour, Edward) in the invasion of Scotland in September 1547 and was knighted by Somerset at Roxburgh. Because Knollys's strong Protestant convictions made him popular with the young Edward VI (q.v.) and his sister, the Princess Elizabeth, later Elizabeth I (q.v.), he was frequently at court. During the reign of Mary I (q.v.), however, he wisely withdrew to the Continent, settling first in Frankfurt and then in Strasbourg.

On the accession of Elizabeth, Knollys became a Privy Councillor, Vice-Chamberlain of the Royal Household and Captain of the Halberdiers. His wife, Catherine Carey, daughter of William Carey and Mary Boleyn, and thus a cousin of the Queen, was made a woman of the Privy Chamber. Through his friendship with Elizabeth and with her Secretary of State, Sir William Cecil (q.v.), Knollys was given a number of responsible state duties. In 1563 he was Governor of Portsmouth. From May 1568 until February 1569 he was placed in charge of the fugitive Mary, Queen of Scots (q.v.), first at Carlisle Castle and later at Bolton Castle in Yorkshire. He was on good terms with the Scottish Queen and tried conscientiously to convert her to his own strongly-held Puritan beliefs. As a solution to the problem of what Elizabeth should do about Mary, Knollys put forward the suggestion that she might be married to his wife's nephew, George Carey, son of Lord Hunsdon.

From 1562 onwards, when he sat as Member for Oxfordshire, Knollys was an active spokesman in Parliament, invariably supporting government policy while maintaining a fiercely independent attitude on religious matters. He lost no opportunity to champion the cause of Puritanism. A warm supporter of Thomas Cartwright (q.v.), he condemned Archbishop John Whitgift (q.v.) for his persecution of the Puritans. He was in conflict with Whitgift also over the Archbishop's theory of the divine right of bishops, and in 1591 declared that he would sooner retire from political office than lose his freedom to express hostility to the bishops' claims.

In July 1572 Knollys was appointed Treasurer of the Royal Household, an office which he was to hold until his death. He was made a K.G. in 1593. The last years of his life were clouded by domestic unhappiness, chiefly on account of the affair between the Earl of Leicester (see Dudley, Robert) and his daughter, Lettice, widow of Walter Devereux, 1st Earl of Essex, and the waywardness of his grandson, Lettice's son Robert, 2nd Earl of Essex (see Devereux, Robert). Lady Knollys had died in 1569, having borne him seven sons and four daughters. Sir Francis himself died on 19 July 1596. He was buried at Rotherfield Greys.

**Knox, John** (?1514–1572), Scottish reformer and historian.

Knox was born, probably in about 1514, in the neighbourhood of Haddington, East Lothian, and was the son of William Knox, a farmer. His ancestors had fought under the standard of the Earls of Bothwell, forbears of James Hepburn (q.v.) the 4th Earl, who was the husband of Mary, Queen of Scots (q.v.).

Knox received his early education probably from the priests and monks of Haddington, before going on to the local grammar school. He then studied under John Major at the University of St Andrews, but it is not known whether he graduated. He took holy orders and became an apostolic notary. In 1544 he acted as tutor to the sons of local gentry, through whom he came under the influence of the Scottish reformer George Wishart (q.v.). He accepted the Protestant doctrine and thereafter devoted himself to the cause of religious reform. At first he moved from place to place in order to escape arrest, but after Wishart had been burned at the stake for heresy he took refuge in the Protestant stronghold of St Andrews castle.

In 1547 Knox emerged as the spokesman of the Scottish Protestant movement, following a sermon he was persuaded to preach in the town of St Andrews, and from this moment onwards he regarded himself as called by God to the preaching office; however, in June the same year, after the siege of St Andrews castle, he was taken prisoner and spent the next nineteen months in the French galleys. On his release in 1549 he went to England, where the Protestant reform movement was fast gaining ground under Edward VI (q.v.) but badly needed preachers. He was sent to the north, and held appointments at Berwick-on-Tweed and at Newcastle. It was here that he met Marjory Bowes, daughter of the captain of Norham castle, whom he later married.

By this time Knox had acquired a great reputation both as a preacher and as an advocate of the most extreme form of Protestantism. In 1551 he was appointed

one of six chaplains to the King. Other preferments were offered, but refused, partly out of his mistrust of the Duke of Northumberland (see Dudley, John); nevertheless his influence left its mark, largely through his success in getting Thomas Cranmer (q.v.) to insert in the Second Prayer Book of Edward VI the famous 'Black Rubric' which laid down that kneeling at the communion did not imply adoration.

On the accession of Mary I (q.v.) in 1553, Knox fled to Switzerland, where he met with encouragement and inspiration from John Calvin (q.v.), Henry Bullinger, and Theodore de Beza. He went on to Frankfurt-am-Main to become pastor to a group of English Puritan refugees. In 1555, having been expelled from Frankfurt following trouble with Richard Cox (q.v.) over the use of the prayer book, he made a brief visit to England, where he married. He then spent nine months in Scotland preaching secretly in the houses of his supporters, but in 1556 returned to his beloved Geneva as pastor to the English congregation there. From that city, which he called 'the most perfect school of Christ on earth since the days of the Apostles', Knox issued a stream of works addressed to his faithful flock at home. The publication of his *First Blast of the Trumpet against the Monstrous Regiment of Women* in 1558 gave offence to the newly-enthroned Queen Elizabeth (q.v.).

In May 1559 Knox was recalled to Scotland to champion the Protestant cause, now imperilled by the intervention of French troops in support of the Queen Regent, Marie de Guise (q.v.), and her family. For a time things looked black for the Scottish Protestants, but early in 1560 Knox at last succeeded in persuading William Cecil (q.v.) that for political as well as religious reasons England should give them support, and Elizabeth agreed to send troops to this end. Within a short time the Protestant victory was assured, both French and English troops were withdrawn, and Knox was preaching in St Giles's cathedral, Edinburgh.

From now on, until his death in 1572, Knox was the greatest, if the most controversial, figure in the Scottish Reformation. The *Confession of Faith*, which he and five other ministers hurriedly drew up at the request of the Scottish Parliament in August 1560, was adopted as the national creed. The *First Book of Discipline*, however, which appeared in 1559, and embodied a constitution for the new church as well as an elaborate educational system that went far beyond the confines of ecclesiastical polity, was never ratified for financial reasons. He was both a fearless advocate and a powerful orator; appointed minister of Edinburgh, he preached at the coronation of James VI (q.v.) and at the opening of Parliament in 1567, and also

at the funeral of his friend the Regent Moray (see Stewart, Lord James) in 1570. In 1564 he incurred the displeasure of Mary, Queen of Scots (q.v.) by marrying without royal assent Margaret Stewart, daughter of Lord Ochiltree, a distant relative of the Queen. His first wife had died in 1560, having borne him two sons.

Knox's last years were coloured by his bitter hatred of Mary and by the struggle between supporters of the Queen and the Regency. He had contemplated a peaceful retirement to Geneva but was overtaken by a paralytic stroke; nevertheless, on hearing the news of the St Bartholomew's Day massacre in August 1572, he spoke forcibly from the pulpit of St Giles's and was also present at the installation there of his successor, James Lawson. He died in Edinburgh on 24 November 1572.

His most important literary work, the *History of the Reformation of Religion within the Realme of Scotland*, which contained an account of the return of Mary Stuart to Scotland and of Knox's interviews with her, first appeared in 1587. Its best edition is considered to be that contained in the *Works of John Knox*, edited by Laing in six volumes (1846–64).

P. Lorimer, *John Knox and the Church of England* (1875).
T. McCrie, *Life of John Knox* (2 vols; 1831).
J. D. Mackie, 'John Knox', in J. Hurstfield (ed.), *The Tudors* (Historical Association, 1973).
Lord Eustace Percy, *John Knox* (1937).
Jasper Ridley, *John Knox* (1968).
Elizabeth Whitley, *Plain Mr Knox* (1972).

*Portrait*: engraving by unknown artist, in Beza, *Icones*, 1581.

**Kyd, Thomas** (?1558–1594), dramatist and poet.

The son of a London scrivener, Francis Kyd, Thomas Kyd was baptized at the church of St Mary Woolnoth, Lombard

Street, on 6 November 1558. At the age of seven he was sent to the Merchant Taylors' School, where he was a contemporary of Edmund Spenser (q.v.). He is not thought to have attended university, but instead to have entered his father's profession as a scrivener. This, however, he soon gave up in favour of literature.

In about 1590, Kyd seems to have entered the service of a lord (possibly Ferdinando, Lord Strange, who was the patron of a company of actors). By that date he already had a reputation as a tragic poet, principally through the immense popularity of his blank-verse drama *The Spanish Tragedy* which, although not entered on the Stationers' Register until 1592, may well have been acted in London as early as 1585. It was definitely played a number of times by Lord Strange's Men in 1592 and subsequently revived by both the Admiral's Men and the Chamberlain's Men; Ben Jonson (see *Lives of the Stuart Age*) was commissioned to write additions to it in 1602. (Another play, *The First Part of Ieronimo*, which tells of events leading up to those of *The Spanish Tragedy*, but which was not printed until 1605, has been attributed to Kyd but was probably not written by him, although he may have been the author of an earlier version.)

Kyd's first published book, a translation from the Italian of Torquato Tasso's *Householders Philosophie*, appeared in 1588. He is known to have written one pamphlet, if not two, on contemporary murders; these were published by his brother in 1592. His translation from the French of a Senecan tragedy entitled *Pompey the Great his fair Cornelias Tragedie*, first printed in 1594, is the only play apart from *The Spanish Tragedy* known definitely to have been written by Kyd. He may have been the

author of *The Tragedy of Solyman and Perseda*, printed in 1599. He probably wrote a pre-Shakespearian *Hamlet* (now lost), and undoubtedly had a hand in a number of anonymous plays of the period, including possibly *Arden of Feversham*.

An intimate friend of the dramatist Christopher Marlowe (q.v.), with whom he shared lodgings from about 1591 onwards, when they were both engaged on writing plays for the same theatrical company, Kyd was a member of the exuberant circle of young wits that included Robert Greene, Thomas Nashe, and Thomas Lodge (qq.v.), men who spent much of their time drinking and brawling in the London taverns. Early in May 1593 Kyd came under suspicion of treasonable activities and was arrested. Incriminating papers denying the deity of Jesus Christ were found in his room, but he managed to convince the authorities that they belonged to Marlowe. Subsequently, after Marlowe's death a few weeks later, when again arrested and on this occasion tortured, Kyd gave even more damaging evidence of his dead friend's atheistical opinions. He himself died in a state of poverty, and probably in considerable debt, towards the end of December 1594.

One of the most popular tragic poets of his age, Thomas Kyd was the first to introduce the Senecan theme of revenge into Elizabethan drama. Both in construction of plot and in characterization, particularly that of Hieronimo in *The Spanish Tragedy*, he broke new ground and anticipated the work of later dramatists. A collected edition of his plays by F. S. Boas was published in 1901 (reprinted with supplement, Oxford, 1955).

P. W. Edwards, *Thomas Kyd and Early Elizabethan Tragedy* (1966).
A. Freeman, *Thomas Kyd, Facts and Problems* (1967).

# L

**Lambarde, William** (1536–1601), antiquary, jurist, and diarist, author of the first English county history.

William Lambarde was born on 18 October 1536, son of John Lambarde, a wealthy City draper and sheriff of London. Details of his early education are obscure. He entered Lincoln's Inn in 1556 and was called to the bar in 1567. Appointed a Justice of the Peace for Kent in 1579, he held a number of high offices, including those of Deputy to the Alienations' Office (1589), Master in Chancery (1592), Deputy Keeper of the Rolls (1597), and Keeper of the Records in the Tower of London (1601). He was elected a bencher of Lincoln's Inn in 1597.

Parallel with his career as a barrister and J.P., Lambarde devoted much time

to the scholarly pursuits which have earned him one modern historian's praise as 'the prince of legal antiquaries'. His first published work, *Archaionomia*, a collection of Anglo-Saxon laws, appeared in 1568. A handbook for justices of the peace, *Eirenarcha* (1582), and *The Duties of Constables . . . and other Low and Lay Ministers of the Peace* (1583) both ran into several editions. Another work prompted by his interest in the English legal system, *Archeion, or a Discourse upon the High Courts of Justice in England,* although completed and presented in manuscript form to Sir Robert Cecil (q.v.) in 1591, was not published until 1635. *Ephemeris*, the diary Lambarde kept as a J.P., has been edited and published by Conyers Read.

Lambarde was not a native of Kent, but from his father he inherited Westcomb Manor at East Greenwich; he founded and endowed the College of the Poor of Greenwich. He married three times, each of his wives holding property in the county, and lived for some years at Ightham and Halling. An enthusiastic topographer of his adopted county, he achieved great success with the *Perambulation of Kent*, which appeared in 1576 (second edition 1596). The projected *Alphabetical Description of the Chief Places of England and Wales* was however abandoned after years of research when he learned that William Camden (q.v.) was engaged on *Britannia*. (Published posthumously in 1730, the *Description*'s authorship has been much disputed by historians.)

As Keeper of the Records in the

Tower of London, Lambarde prepared the *Pandecta Rotulorum*, a complete catalogue of documents in the Tower, and on 4 August 1601 he was granted a private audience of the Queen for the purpose of presenting this manuscript to her; she is said to have praised his work and to have called him her 'good and Honest Lambarde'. Shortly afterwards, on 19 August, Lambarde died at Westcomb. His monument, placed originally in the parish church of East Greenwich, was later removed by his descendants to the church of St Nicholas at Sevenoaks, Kent.

Wilbur Dunkel, *William Lambarde, Elizabethan jurist* (1965).

Conyers Read (ed.), *William Lambarde and local government: his 'Ephemeris' [etc.]* (1962).

Retha M. Warnicke, *William Lambarde, Elizabethan antiquary* (1973).

*Portraits*: oil, by unknown artist, 1570–5 (original lost, seventeenth century copies: National Portrait Gallery, London, and Mrs Campbell, née Lambarde); engraving by George Vertue, 1729 (from portrait once in Cotton Library, destroyed by fire): Mrs Campbell.

**Lane, Sir Ralph** (d. 1603), first Governor of Virginia.

Ralph Lane is believed to have been the second son of Sir Ralph Lane of Horton, Northamptonshire, and Maud, daughter of William, Lord Parr of Horton, a cousin of Queen Katherine Parr (q.v.). An equerry of the Queen, Lane appears to have been involved in maritime affairs as early as 1571, when he was commissioned by Elizabeth I (q.v.) to search certain Breton ships suspected of carrying illegal cargoes. In correspondence with Lord Burghley (see Cecil, William) he put forward a number of schemes, including proposed expeditions to the coasts of Morocco and Spain, but these came to nothing, and in 1583 Lane was sent to Ireland to supervise some fortifications; he remained there for two years, serving eventually as sheriff of Co. Kerry.

In April 1585 his thirst for overseas adventure was at last gratified, and he sailed from Plymouth in the expedition led by Sir Richard Grenville (q.v.) for the purpose of establishing a colony in North America; Lane was appointed to take charge of this new settlement. Unfortunately the venture was marred by bitter quarrels between Lane and Grenville, and when, two months after landing the colonists on the island of Wokokan, off the coast of Virginia, Grenville sailed for home to fetch supplies and reinforcements, Lane, in anticipation of the charges the former would make against him, wrote a letter to Sir Francis Walsingham (q.v.) in which he denounced Grenville for intolerable behaviour.

After Grenville's departure the colony of one hundred men moved to Roanoke (now in North Carolina) and from there explored as far north as Chesapeake Bay. The colonization proved to be a dismal failure. They were desperately short of supplies and encountered much suspicion and hostility on the part of the natives; morale had become so low that in the following June, when Sir Francis Drake (q.v.), on his way home from the West Indies, anchored off the coast and offered them a passage, Lane and his men eagerly seized upon the chance to get away. They were not to know that only a few days later a ship fitted out by Sir Walter Ralegh (q.v.) with supplies for the colony would arrive and find them gone, or that it would be followed two weeks later by Grenville himself, accompanied by considerable reinforcements. Lane and his companions, sailing home with Drake, reached Portsmouth on 28 July 1586. It has been said that they brought with them the first tobacco and potatoes to be introduced in England.

During the preparations for the threatened Spanish invasion in 1587 and 1588 Lane was employed on strengthening the coastal defences, principally in Norfolk, where he also acted as muster master. He also became muster master for the expedition to Portugal under Drake and Sir John Norris (q.v.) in 1589, and the following year he served in a similar capacity in the expedition led by Sir John Hawkins (q.v.). In January 1592 he was sent to Ireland, where he served in the army for the next two years. Knighted in October 1593, and severely wounded in the following spring, he nevertheless remained in Ireland and from 1595 onwards resided at Dublin as muster master. He was appointed Keeper of Southsea Castle, Portsmouth, at about this time, but probably carried out his duties there through a deputy. Lane died in Dublin in October 1603. The lack of records of a wife or children suggest that he was probably unmarried, but he is known to have been active in seeking favours and offices both for himself and for his nephews.

Richard Hakluyt, *The Principall Navigations* (1589; ed. W. Raleigh, 12 vols, Glasgow, 1903–5).

T. Harriot, *A Briefe and True Report of the New Found Land of Virginia* [with a preface by Ralph Lane] (1588).

D. B. Quinn, *The Roanoke Voyages, 1584–90* (Hakluyt Society, 1955).

**Lasco, John à, or Laski, John** (1499–1560), Polish reformer.

John à Lasco was born at the castle of Lask, Poland, in 1499, son of Jaroslaw, Baron of Lask, who claimed descent from Henry de Lacy, 3rd Earl of Lincoln. He and his two brothers were educated by their uncle, Archbishop Laski, and later at the university of Bologna. John was ordained in 1521 and two years later travelled to Basle, where he met Erasmus (q.v.) and was in contact with Ulrich Zwingli (q.v.) and other reformers of the time. Eventually he settled in Erasmus's house, paying the household expenses and buying a reversion to the great humanist's library.

Towards the end of 1525 he returned to Poland, and although now an enthusiastic supporter of the new doctrines he accepted benefices, including the bishopric of Vesprim, out of deference to his uncle. In March 1538 he became Archdeacon of Warsaw, but shortly afterwards, having angered the Archbishop and others by his refusal to give up a woman he had secretly married, à Lasco resigned all his benefices and fled to Germany. He spent some time at Emden as pastor of a congregation of reformers, where he became known as a Calvinist of extreme views, especially on the sacrament. For the next few years he travelled through western Europe, preaching the new doctrines.

In 1547 he formed a friendship with John Hooper (q.v.), and through him and the foreign Protestants who had settled in London, à Lasco became known to the reformers in England. Thomas Cranmer (q.v.) invited him to attend a conference of various Protestant sects, and he spent the winter of 1548–9 at Lambeth. He returned to London in May 1550 and was appointed superintendent of the church of foreign Protestants in Austin Friars, which he organized on Presbyterian lines.

John à Lasco's influence at the court of Edward VI (q.v.) was considerable; it can be discerned in the Second Prayer Book and in the views expressed by Cranmer. Hooper also was much influenced by the Polish reformer, who had taken his part in the controversy over vestments in 1550. With Martin Bucer (q.v.), however, whom he visited at Cambridge the same year, à Lasco differed on the question of the real Presence.

Following the accession of Mary I (q.v.) in 1553, à Lasco embarked at Gravesend with some of his congregation for Poland. After a hazardous journey, which included a year spent in Germany, he finally reached his destination in December 1556. He was appointed secretary to the King. In Poland during the last years of his life he worked ceaselessly for the union of the reformed churches, but was no more successful in achieving his object than he had been in England or Germany, although he did much to prepare the way. He died at Calish, Poland, on 13 January 1560, after a long illness, leaving his family in impoverished circumstances.

H. Dalton (translated by H. J. Evans), *John à Lasco: his earlier life and labours* (1886).

**Latimer, Hugh** (?1485–1555), Bishop of Worcester, martyr.

Hugh Latimer was born at Thurcaston, Leicestershire, probably in 1485, the son of a yeoman farmer, and was educated at Clare College, Cambridge. He took his B.A. and became a fellow of his college in 1510, and took his M.A. in 1514. It is not known exactly when he took holy orders, but in 1524, on the day Latimer became a bachelor of divinity, he preached a sermon attacking the doctrine of Melanchthon. Among the audience was Thomas Bilney (q.v.), who afterwards called on Latimer; the latter has recorded how at the time he was 'as obstinate a Papist as any was in England' and how Bilney made him 'smell the word of God' and forsake 'the school-doctors and such fooleries'.

Latimer always used this kind of forceful, racy language, and he soon began to achieve a reputation for his preaching and for his wit. The Bishop of Ely, suspecting him of Lutheran tendencies, forbade him to preach in the university or diocese in 1525; and when Latimer then spoke from the pulpit of the Augustinian monastery, which was immune from episcopal authority, he was summoned before Thomas Wolsey (q.v.), but on disowning any connection with Lutheranism, was given licence to preach throughout the kingdom.

He was in trouble again in December 1529, when he preached his two famous sermons 'on the cards', in which he used the allegory of men winning salvation by playing trump cards. Controversy broke out in the university and added to Latimer's increasing unpopularity there due to his voiced disapproval of pilgrimages and other voluntary works, and also the knowledge that he took the King's side in the matter of the divorce from Catherine of Aragon (q.v.). Henry VIII (q.v.) invited him to preach at Windsor in Lent 1530 and, impressed by Latimer's sermon and by a letter Latimer had written to him concerning the free circulation of the Bible, the King appointed him one of the royal chaplains. He soon wearied of court life, however, and in 1531 he accepted the living of West Kineton (sometimes referred to as West Kington) in Wiltshire.

Latimer now became ever more outspoken in his preaching. He called the bishops and clergy of England thieves, and the Virgin Mary a sinner; he denounced the worship of saints and denied purgatory and hell-fire. He was cited to appear before the Bishop of London, and was brought before Convocation in March 1533, at first refusing to sign certain articles but later accepting them and confessing that he had erred in discretion as well as in doctrine. Through his support of Henry's marriage with Anne Boleyn

(q.v.) he had friends at court and was thus protected from his enemies; following the consecration of Thomas Cranmer (q.v.) as Archbishop of Canterbury and the King's repudiation of papal authority, Latimer was in a much stronger position. Together with Cranmer and Thomas Cromwell (q.v.), he advised the King on legislative matters connected with the Church.

In 1535 he became Bishop of Worcester, but resigned his see four years later in opposition to the Act of the Six Articles. During his period as bishop Latimer had worked ceaselessly to further Puritanism in his diocese; he had given orders that every priest was to have an English Bible; he stripped the statue of the Virgin in Worcester Cathedral of jewels and ornaments; he preached at the execution of the friar John Forest, who was burned for denying the royal supremacy. On resigning his see Latimer was held prisoner for a year and then released, but forbidden to visit or preach in London, the two universities, or his old diocese.

Little is known of the next few years of his life, but in 1546 he was brought before the Council on account of his connection with the preacher Edward Crome, and committed to the Tower. His trial had not taken place by the time of Henry's death, and he was among those released by general pardon on the accession of Edward VI (q.v.).

He refused to return to his bishopric, in spite of a special request from the Commons, but embarked on a preaching programme more effective than ever, drawing huge crowds both in London and in the provinces. One of his most celebrated sermons was that known as 'the Plough', in which he attacked the non-resident bishops, pointing the contrast with the devil as 'the most diligent preacher . . . never out of his diocese . . . ever at his plough'.

Shortly after the accession of Mary I (q.v.) Latimer was summoned to appear before the Council at Westminster. He declined to take the opportunity of a few hours' notice in which to escape and, together with Cranmer and Nicholas Ridley (q.v.), was sent to Oxford to defend his views before the university divines. He and Ridley were condemned as heretics and burned in Oxford on 16 October 1555. His words to Ridley as they were led to the stake have been much quoted by historians: 'Be of good comfort, Master Ridley, we shall this day light such a candle by God's grace in England as I trust shall never be put out.'

Latimer's sincere, aggressive and down-to-earth preaching probably did more towards establishing the Reformation in England than that of any of the other Protestant leaders of his day. His courage of the last years, in spite of broken health, and the manner of his death were an inspiration to thousands of English men and women.

His works have been edited by G. E.

Corrie and published in two volumes by the Parker Society (Cambridge, 1844–5).

R. M. and A. J. Carlyle, *Hugh Latimer* (1899).
A. G. Chester, *Hugh Latimer: Apostle of the English* (Philadelphia, Penn., 1954).
H. S. Darby, *Hugh Latimer* (1953).
R. Demaus, *Hugh Latimer* (1869).
C. M. Gray, *Hugh Latimer and the sixteenth century: an essay in interpretation* (1950).

*Portraits:* oil, by unknown artist, 1555: the Deanery, Canterbury; oil on panel, by unknown artist, 1555: National Portrait Gallery, London; another version at Balliol College, Oxford; engraving by Willem and Magdalena van de Passe, in *Herwologia*, 1620.

**Leicester, 1st Earl of** (?1532–1588), see Dudley, Robert.

**Leland or Leyland, John** (?1506–1552), antiquary.

Born in London in about 1506, John Leland came from a family of Lancashire origin. He was educated at St Paul's School and later at Christ's College, Cambridge, where he took his B.A. in 1522, and at All Souls, Oxford. He subsequently completed his studies in Paris, adding French, Italian, and Spanish to his knowledge of Latin and Greek, and shortly after his return to England he entered holy orders.

In 1525 Leland became a tutor in the household of the Duke of Norfolk (see Howard, Thomas, 3rd Duke). He wrote a number of Latin panegyrics on Henry VIII (q.v.) and his courtiers with the result that before 1530 he was appointed as the King's library keeper. Soon afterwards he became a royal chaplain, and in June 1530 he was granted the rectory of Peuplingues, near Calais; he does not appear to have resided there, and in 1536 was granted a special dispensation relieving him of this obligation, presumably on account of his duties as 'King's antiquary'.

When Henry VIII appointed Leland to this newly-created office in 1533, he commissioned him to search the libraries of all the cathedrals, abbeys, priories, and colleges of England for records of antiquity. Leland devoted a full six years to this task, conscientiously visiting every manor in the country and not only making notes of the antiquities and history of each place, but also writing down descriptions of them. He had already completed a survey of English writers, and his intention now was to compile a definitive work on the 'History and Antiquities of this Nation'. He outlined his aims in an address to the King entitled *A New Year's Gift* soon after his return to London in 1545.

In the meanwhile Leland sought preferment in the Church through Archbishop Thomas Cranmer (q.v.), and in April 1542 he was granted the rectory of Haseley in Oxfordshire; he was also given a canonry at King's College (later Christ Church), Oxford, and a prebend at Salisbury Cathedral. Although greatly distressed by the Dissolution of the Monasteries in 1536 (he had begged Thomas Cromwell (q.v.) to be allowed to salvage their manuscripts for the royal library, a request that was only partially followed up), Leland had championed the King's supremacy in the Church of England in a treatise dedicated to Henry under the title *Antiphilarchia,* written soon after the completion of his antiquarian tour.

Leland spent the next few years mainly in London, arranging his vast collection of research material. The work proved too arduous, with the result that he over-taxed his brain and became incurably insane in 1550, when the Privy Council ordered him to be placed in the custody of his brother, the elder John Leland. He died without regaining his reason on 18 April 1552.

John Leland was the earliest of the modern English antiquaries, and his work was freely drawn on by later writers, including William Camden, Raphael Holinshed, and John Stow (qq.v.). Bishop John Bale, author of the first national bibliography, acknowledged his indebtedness to Leland in the second edition of his work, published in 1557.

Most of Leland's manuscripts have been preserved at the Bodleian Library, Oxford. His *Itinerary* was first published at Oxford in nine volumes (1710–12), and the *Collectanea* in six volumes (1715), both by Thomas Hearne. There is a later edition of the *Itinerary* by L. T. Smith (5 vols; 1906–8). A full bibliography of his work is contained in the Burton biography listed below.

Johan Ball (ed.), *The Laboryouse Journey and Serche of Johan Leylande for Englande's Antiquities* (1549).
Edward Burton, *The Life of John Leland* (1896).
E. G. R. Taylor, 'Leland's England and Camden's England', in H. C. Darby (ed.), *The Historical Geography of England before 1800* (Cambridge, 1936).

**Lennox, Countess of** (1515–1578), see Douglas, Lady Margaret.

**Lennox, 1st Duke of** (?1542–1583), see Stuart, Esmé.

**Lennox, 4th (12th) Earl of** (1516–1571), see Stewart, Matthew.

**Leonardo da Vinci** (1452–1519), painter, sculptor, architect, and engineer, one of the greatest of the universal men of the Renaissance.

Born in 1452, the illegitimate son of a Florentine notary, Leonardo grew up in his father's house at Vinci, where he received a good education. Recognizing the boy's artistic talent at an early age, his father apprenticed him to the sculptor Andrea del Verrochio, in whose workshop he was given a sound training in painting, sculpture, and mechanical arts. In 1472 Leonardo was accepted into the painters' guild of the city. He remained with Verrochio for a further five years, and in Florence, working as an independent painter, until 1481. In that year he was commissioned to paint a large *Adoration of the Magi* for the monks of near-by S. Donato a Scopeto, which he began but never finished.

By 1482 Leonardo had set his sights on the brilliant court of Lodovico Sforza, Il Moro, Duke of Milan, to whom he offered his services as a painter, sculptor, and engineer. He was to spend the next seventeen years in Milan, until Sforza's fall from power in 1499. During this period he maintained his own workshop of apprentices and students, and was kept busy on a variety of artistic projects; these included designs for court festivals, military fortifications, and also architectural and engineering schemes. The remarkable versatility of his genius won admiration in all quarters. To these years belong the *Lady with an Ermine* and the *Virgin of the Rocks*, as well as the monumental *Last Supper*, painted on the wall of the refectory of Sta. Maria delle Grazie; so do the sketches for the bronze equestrian statue in honour of Francesco Sforza, the founder of the dynasty, on which Leonardo worked spasmodically for twelve years, but which never got beyond the clay model stage. It was while in Milan that Leonardo began to record his observations and make sketches in a series of notebooks, with a view to writing treatises on the four subjects that interested him most: painting, architecture, mechanics, and human anatomy.

Following the French invasion of Milan in 1499 and the fall of the dynasty, Leonardo left that city and returned, via

Mantua and Venice, to Florence, where he was greeted with much acclaim. His second Florentine period, interrupted only by a few months in Rome in 1502–3, when he served as a military engineer at the court of Cesare Borgia, was to last until 1506. Much of this time he devoted to intensive scientific studies and to perfecting his skill as an anatomist. For three years he worked on a great mural depicting the Battle of Anghiari in the Palazzo Vecchio, but this, like its complementary painting of the Battle of Cascina, which the city's other leading artist (and Leonardo's great rival), Michelangelo, had been commissioned to do, was never finished. Leonardo also worked at this time on a series of the Madonna and Child with St Anne, and on a standing Leda. One of the few commissions he actually finished was the portrait of the wife of a Florentine official, famous for its enigmatic smile, painted in about 1500–4 and known as the *Mona Lisa*, or *La Gioconda*.

In 1506 Leonardo returned to Milan under the patronage of the Governor of the King of France in that city. His duties were those of an architectural adviser. He did little painting there in the next six years, but his scientific studies, especially in anatomy, were continued. A major commission to sculpt the tomb of Trivulzio, Marshal of the French Army, got no further than the preliminary sketches. In 1513 he moved to Rome, but was disappointed that no major commissions came his way; Bramante was then busy on St Peter's and Michelangelo, Raphael, and a new generation of artists were also fully employed, but most of Leonardo's time was spent on botanical observation, scientific and technical experiments, and mathematical studies. He was also working at this period on what was to be his last painting, that of St John the Baptist. Three years later, at the age of sixty-five, he accepted an invitation from François I, the young King of France, and left Italy for good.

Officially styled as the King's 'first painter, architect and mechanic', Leonardo spent the next two years at the Château of Cloux, near the royal residence at Amboise. There he busied himself with plans for a royal palace and garden, sketches for court festivals, and other designs, but did no further painting; he was chiefly concerned with editing his scientific studies. He died at Cloux on 2 May 1519 and was buried in the near-by church of Saint-Florentine. The church was later devastated during the French Revolution, and the grave has never been located.

Space does not permit here anything like an adequate assessment of Leonardo's genius and intellectual force, which was centuries ahead of his age, anticipating much later discoveries in the fields of science and aeronautics. As a painter, he excelled in the art of expression and, with his mastery of light and shadow, broke through the traditions that had hitherto existed. Because of the diversity of his talent, he failed to complete many of his projects, but the drawings he did for them, and his notebooks, are of immense interest and importance. He never visited England, but the influence he exerted on all contemporary artists, and the interest he stimulated in the new studies of science, botanical observation, and mathematics was widespread and long-lasting. It has been said of Leonardo that he ushered in the High Renaissance.

His paintings the *Mona Lisa* and *St John the Baptist*, and versions of the *Madonna and Child with St Anne*, *The Annunciation*, and the *Virgin of the Rocks* are at the Louvre, Paris; a cartoon of the *Madonna and Child with St Anne* and another version of the *Virgin of the Rocks* are at the National Gallery, London; the

*Lady with an Ermine* is at the Muzeum Narodowe, Cracow, Poland; other works by Leonardo are at the Uffizi Gallery (Florence), the Vatican Museum (Rome), the Hermitage (Leningrad), Alte Pinakothek (Munich), and the National Gallery of Art, Washington, D.C. The finest collection of his drawings is in the Royal Collection at Windsor; notebooks and other drawings are preserved in Paris, Florence, Milan, Venice, and the British Museum, London.

The treatise on painting, for which Leonardo made copious notes but which he never actually wrote, was first published by his pupil and heir, Francesco Melzi, in 1651; *Leonardo's Treatise on Painting,* edited by A. P. McMahon (2 vols; 1956) contains a facsimile edition of it, together with an English translation. Recent editions of his works are *The Notebooks of Leonardo da Vinci,* by E. McCurdy (2 vols; 1955) and *The Literary Works of Leonardo da Vinci,* by Jean P. Richter (2 vols; 3rd ed. 1970).

Kenneth Clark, *Leonardo da Vinci: An Account of his Development as an Artist* (2nd ed. 1952).
Kenneth Clark and Carlo Pedretti, *A Catalogue of the Drawings of Leonardo da Vinci in the Collection of Her Majesty the Queen at Windsor Castle* (3 vols; 2nd ed. 1968).
Cecil Gould, *Leonardo, The Artist and the Non-Artist* (1975).
M. Pomilio and A. Ottino (eds), *The Complete Paintings of Leonardo da Vinci* (1967).
Arthur E. Popham, *The Drawings of Leonardo da Vinci* (1945).
M. Philipson (ed.), *Leonardo da Vinci: Aspects of the Renaissance Genius* (1966).
P. R. Ritchie-Calder, *Leonardo and the Age of the Eye* (1970).

*Portrait:* chalk-drawing, self-portrait: Palazzo Reale, Turin.

**Leslie or Lesley, John** (1527–1596), Bishop of Ross, historian of Scotland.

Born on 29 September 1527, the illegitimate son of a parson at Kingussie, Inverness-shire, John Leslie was educated at the universities of Aberdeen, Paris, and Poitiers. He taught canon law at King's College, Aberdeen, from about 1554, and took holy orders in April 1558.

In January 1561 Leslie was among the learned men of Aberdeen who disputed with John Knox (q.v.) and other reformers at Edinburgh. A few months later, following the death of François II, the husband of Mary, Queen of Scots (q.v.), Leslie was commissioned by the Scottish Catholic nobles to visit the widowed Queen in France and to try to persuade her to return to Scotland. He was received by Mary at Vitry on 15 April and, although the Queen did not immediately fall in with his proposals, she commanded him to remain in attendance. From that moment Leslie was to remain utterly loyal to Mary. Soon after her return to Scotland in August 1561 he became her chief ecclesiastical adviser. Professor of canon law at King's College, Aberdeen, in 1562, he was appointed a judge of the court of session in 1565 and also a Privy Councillor; in 1566 he became Bishop of Ross.

After Mary's forced abdication in 1567, and her escape to England the following May, Leslie did his best to defend her interests before the commissioners who met at York in October 1568 to examine the charges brought against her. He then joined the captive Queen at Tutbury and a few months later was appointed by her as ambassador to the court of Queen Elizabeth (q.v.), for the purpose of seeking her liberty and restoration to the throne of Scotland.

Leslie was now virtually the sole means of communication between Mary and her supporters. He began actively to intrigue on her behalf, both with foreign powers and with the Scottish Catholic nobility. In London in 1569 he issued under an assumed name a tract entitled *A Defence of the Honour of the Right Highe, Mightye and Noble Princess Marie, Queen of Scotlande . . . with a Declaration as well of her Right, Title and Interests to the Succession of the Crowne of Englande*; it was immediately suppressed, but was later reprinted in Liège and Rouen.

Early in 1570 Leslie was charged with being implicated in the rebellion of the northern earls and was imprisoned for several weeks before being acquitted. He then became involved with a Florentine businessman living in London, Roberto di Ridolfi (q.v.), in a plot to depose Elizabeth, place Mary on the English throne, and marry her to the Catholic Duke of Norfolk (see Howard, Thomas, 4th Duke); in October 1571, after others in the plot had been arrested and had exposed the conspiracy, Leslie was imprisoned in the Tower. He made a series of confessions that were used as evidence in the trial of Norfolk for treason and was himself held prisoner until late 1573, when he was released only on condition that he left England. He immediately set about seeking the aid of the continental powers for Mary's cause, but without success.

At Rome in 1578 Leslie published his major literary work, a Latin history of Scotland from the death of James I (see *Lives Before the Tudors*). Written from a Catholic viewpoint, *De origine, moribus et rebus gestis Scotorum* was drawn partly from the work of Hector Boece and John Major. It was translated into Scots by a Benedictine monk, Father James Dalrymple, in 1596 and has been edited by E. G. Cody and W. Murison and reprinted by the Scottish Text Society (2 vols; 1888–95).

From 1579 onwards Leslie lived in France, as Suffragan and Vicar-General of the diocese of Rouen. As a reward for his efforts in encouraging the citizens of that town to hold out against their besiegers in 1591, Leslie was nominated by Pope Clement VIII to the bishopric of Coutances, in Normandy. Unable to travel to his see because of the civil war in France, he ultimately settled at an Augustinian monastery at Guirtenburg, near Brussels, where he died on 31 May 1596.

E. G. Cody, Introduction to *Leslie's History of Scotland* (Scottish Text Society, 2 vols, 1888–95).
David M. Lockie, 'The Political Career of the Bishop of Ross, 1568–80', *University of Birmingham Historical Journal*, iv (1953), pp. 98–145.

*Portrait*: engraving, by unknown artist: location unknown.

**Lever or Leaver, Thomas** (1521–1577), Puritan divine.

Thomas Lever was born at Little Lever, Lancashire, in 1521. He was educated at St John's College, Cambridge, taking his B.A. there in 1542 and his M.A. three years later. In 1543 he was elected a fellow and in 1548 college preacher.

A friend of Roger Ascham (q.v.) at Cambridge, Lever soon became the leader of the more extreme group of reformers in the university. He was ordained in 1550 and invited more than once to preach at court in the presence of Edward VI (q.v.). In December the following year he was appointed by royal mandate as Master of St John's, where in 1552 he took his degree as Bachelor of Divinity. After the King's death he supported the cause of the Lady Jane Grey (q.v.); when this failed and Mary I (q.v.) was proclaimed as Queen, Lever escaped to the Continent. He travelled first to Zurich, and then to Geneva, where he attended the services and lectures given by John Calvin (q.v.). In 1556 he became minister to the English congregation at Aarau.

The accession of Elizabeth I (q.v.)

299

made his return to England possible, and in 1559 Lever was appointed Rector and Archdeacon of Coventry. He married the same year a widow with three children, who was to bear him a son, Sampson, in July 1560. He was appointed Master of Sherburn Hospital at Durham in 1563, and the following year was promoted to a stall at Durham Cathedral, but this was taken from him four years later on account of his most persistent nonconformity. A talented preacher, Lever continued to preach in a black gown both at Coventry and in London, and in 1571 he was cited to appear before the ecclesiastical court for breaches of church discipline. In June 1577 he was ordered by his bishop to suppress the 'prophesyings' which he had encouraged in his archdeaconry.

Thomas Lever died at Ware, Hertfordshire, in July 1577, while travelling from London to Sherburn. He was buried at Sherburn Hospital, beneath a memorial stone inscribed 'Preacher to King Edward VI'. His *Sermons*, first published in 1550, were reissued by Arber Reprints in 1871.

**Leyland, John** (?1506–1552), see Leland, John.

**Linacre or Lineacre, Thomas** (?1460–1524), physician and classical scholar.

Thomas Linacre was born probably at Canterbury in about 1460. Little is known of his origins or early life except that he studied at Oxford, where he became a fellow of All Souls in 1484. He may have been a nephew or other relation of William de Selling, Prior of Canterbury, whom he accompanied to Italy in 1485.

Selling had been sent as ambassador to Rome by Henry VII (q.v.), but it seems that they parted company, possibly at Bologna, and Linacre went to Florence with the Italian classical scholar Poliziano. There he shared his studies with the two sons of Lorenzo de' Medici, one of whom later became Pope Leo X. Some time later he went to Rome, where it is thought that the scholar Barbarus may have influenced him to study medicine. In 1495 he spent some time in Venice, staying with Aldus Manutius, the founder of the Aldine Press, before going on to the University of Padua to study for his M.D. Having obtained his degree in medicine in August 1496, Linacre returned to England and, on the strength of it, was given an M.D. at Oxford. He soon made a name for himself as a lecturer on medical subjects in the university, and he may also have lectured there, as well as at Cambridge, on Greek. He was revered as much for his classical scholarship as for his knowledge of medicine, and his friends included Thomas More (q.v.), John Colet (q.v.) and William Grocyn (q.v.); when Erasmus (q.v.) paid his first visit to England in 1499, he was quickly drawn into this intimate circle.

In about 1500 Linacre entered the royal service as a tutor to Prince Arthur (q.v.). The Prince died not long afterwards, but his brother, on accession to the throne as Henry VIII (q.v.) in 1509, appointed him one of the royal physicians. Linacre then left Oxford and settled in London, where his distinguished medical practice included Thomas Wolsey (q.v.), William Warham (q.v.), Richard Foxe (q.v.), Erasmus, and the university friends already mentioned.

It is not known exactly when he was ordained, but during the next ten or eleven years Linacre was given many ecclesiastical benefices; in accordance with the custom of the period he did not take up residence in these places, but sold the livings to other clergy and so amassed considerable wealth. He used his fortune to further the study of medical knowledge by founding lectureships at Oxford and Cambridge, and in 1518 he founded the Royal College of Physicians, of which he was the first president.

In about 1520 he retired from medical practice to devote himself to literary work, principally his Latin translations of Galen, the Greek physician. Linacre's last appointment, in 1523, was that of tutor to the five-year-old Princess Mary (later Mary I, q.v.), for whom he composed a Latin grammar. He died on 20 October 1524 and was buried in St Paul's Cathedral, London.

One of the great scholar-physicians of the Renaissance, Linacre is sometimes described as a humanist; he differed however from the Oxford humanists with whom he associated in that his chief interest was medicine rather than theology.

J. N. Johnson, *The life of Linacre*, ed. R. Graves (1835).
W. Osler, *Thomas Linacre* [Linacre Lecture] (Cambridge, 1908).

*Portrait*: N.B. The picture hitherto believed to be of Linacre (school of Matsys, in the Royal Collection at Windsor, and also a copy of it at the Royal College of Physicians, London) is not now considered to be of this sitter.

**Lodge, Thomas** (?1558–1625), romantic writer, dramatist, and poet.

The second son of Sir Thomas Lodge, Lord Mayor of London, and his first wife, Anne, daughter of Sir William Laxton, Thomas was probably born at West Ham in about 1558. He was educated at Merchant Taylors' School, London, and at Trinity College, Oxford, and in 1578 entered Lincoln's Inn. Lodge soon abandoned law for literature, however, and began to lead a somewhat wild,

dissolute life, supporting himself largely by hack writing and translation. His first published work was *A Defence of Plays*, an unlicensed pamphlet written in reply to Stephen Gosson's attack on drama and published in 1580. When Gosson subsequently wrote an attack on his character, Lodge published *An Alarum against Usurers* (1584), exposing the dangers to extravagant young gentlemen from the moneylenders, who lured them into debt; he was almost certainly writing from his own experience. Together with this tract he published his first romance, *The Delectable Historie of Forbonius and Priscilla*, and a work in verse, *The Lamentable Complaint of Truth over England*.

In about 1588 Lodge sailed on a freebooting expedition to the Azores (Terceira) and the Canaries, and in 1591 he sailed to South America, but neither of these adventures brought him the profits he sought. It was on the trip to Terceira that Lodge wrote his second and best known romance, *Rosalynde*, in the style of 'Euphues', which became the source for Shakespeare's *As You Like It* (see Shakespeare, William); it was published in 1590. Lodge's earlier work, *Scillaes Metamorphosis*, first printed in 1589 and reissued in 1610 as *Glaucus and Scilla*, was the first romantic treatment in verse of a classical subject, and the prototype for Shakespeare's *Venus and Adonis*.

A second romance entitled *Robert, Second Duke of Normandy* was published in 1591, *Euphues Shadow* in 1592, and *Life of William Longbeard* in 1593. By this time Lodge's work was attracting notice, and he was much praised by Edmund Spenser (q.v.) and Robert Greene (q.v.). A collection of verse under the title of *Phillis*, containing sonnets and lyric poems, appeared in 1593, and the following year Lodge published two plays, *The*

*Wounds of the Civill War* and, written in collaboration with Greene, *A Looking Glasse for London and England*. In 1595 he published *A Fig for Momus*, a collection of epistles and satires modelled on Horace. The romance *A Margarite of America*, which Lodge had written during his voyage to South America in 1591, appeared in 1596. Among his other work at this date were several pamphlets, of which *Wits Miserie, and the Worlds Madnesse* (1596) is of the most interest for its denunciation of the vices prevalent at that period.

At this stage of his career Lodge became a Roman Catholic. He also took up the study of medicine, graduating at Avignon in 1600 and becoming an M.D. at Oxford in 1603. He practised for a few years in London and later in the Netherlands, where he fled to escape the measures taken against Catholics following the Gunpowder Plot of 1605 (see Fawkes, Guy, in *Lives of the Stuart Age*). By 1609 he was back in London and in practice there as a physician. Apart from two medical works, *A Treatise of the Plague*, which was published in 1603, and a manual entitled *The Poore Mans Talentt*, which was not in fact printed until 1881, Lodge's literary activities in the last years of his life consisted mainly of translations; these included selections from the work of Luis de Granada (1601), *The Famous and Memorable Workes of Josephus* (1602), *The Workes, both Morrall and Natural, of Lucius Annaeus Seneca* (1614), and *A learned Summary upon the famous Poeme of William of Saluste, lord of Bartas, translated out of the French*, published in 1625. Lodge died in London some time before 12 October of that year, when his second wife, Jane, was granted administration of his effects.

Thomas Lodge was a versatile writer, who excelled both as a lyric poet and as a follower of the 'Euphues' style. His *Complete Works* have been edited, with a memoir, by E. W. Gosse (4 vols; Glasgow, 1883).

C. J. Sisson (ed.), *Thomas Lodge and Other Elizabethans* (1933).

**Lok, Michael** (?1532–?1615), traveller and translator.

The younger son of Sir William Lok, a well-established London merchant, and his second wife, Catherine, daughter of William Cooke of Salisbury, Michael Lok was born in about 1532. He received a good education, presumably in London, and did not leave school until the age of thirteen, when his father sent him to France and Flanders to learn languages and train as a merchant.

In 1552 Lok left Flanders for Spain. While in business there and in Lisbon he saw at first hand the lucrative trade carried on by Spain with the Indies, and this stimulated his own desire to travel. During the next twenty-four years he visited most of the known lands of Christendom and also captained a ship on numerous voyages to the Levant. He was an able linguist, and wherever he went he studied not only every aspect of the trading potential but also the history; on his own admission he spent £500 on books, charts, and instruments.

In the course of his travels Lok made the acquaintance of Martin Frobisher (q.v.) and was infected by him with enthusiasm for a voyage to search for a North-West Passage in 1576, for which Lok provided the bulk of the supplies and equipment at his own expense. In 1577 he became Governor of the newly-formed Cathay Company for a term of six years, but after the failure of Frobisher's two subsequent voyages of 1577 and 1578 to find either the Passage or gold, Lok was financially ruined and was obliged to petition the Council for relief for his wife and fifteen children. (His first wife, Joan, daughter of William Wilkinson, a sheriff of London, had died in 1571, leaving him eight children, and he subsequently married Mary (or Margaret), widow of Caesar Adelmare, who had borne him seven more.) He was allowed £430, having stated in the petition that he had paid out some £7,500 on the three voyages. Lok was later imprisoned in the Fleet on a charge brought by William Borough (q.v.) of the non-payment for a ship supplied to Frobisher for his 1578 voyage; he continued to petition the Council, and as late as 1614–15 was still being pressed for a debt relating to stores for that last voyage.

It is not recorded when he was released, but in 1587–8 Lok is known to have been in Dublin. In 1592 he was appointed by the Levant Company as Consul at Aleppo for a four-year term; the contract, however, was cancelled at the end of two years, allegedly through the intrigues of a man named Dorrington, who was in the employ of Sir John Spenser, an alderman of London. Although Lok claimed full payment of his salary for four years, it is not known whether or not he received it. Certainly to the end of his long life he was in financial difficulties; as late as 1614–15, at the age of eighty-three, he was contesting an action relating to the unpaid debts of the Cathay Company. He probably died in 1615 or soon after.

The moving spirit behind Frobisher's three voyages to the North-West, Michael Lok was, in the words of G. R. Elton, 'half visionary and half speculator'. He translated into English part of Peter Martyr Anglerius's *De Orbe Novo* (1516); it was published as *Historie of the West Indies* in 1613.

Two memorials by Lok containing autobiographical details are printed in *Calendar of State Papers (Colonial): East Indies*, 1576 and 1577.

**Lovell, Francis** (1454–?1487), 1st Viscount Lovell, Lord Chamberlain to Richard III, see *Lives Before the Tudors*.

**Lovell, Sir Thomas** (d. 1524), statesman, Speaker of the House of Commons.

The fifth son of Sir Ralph Lovell of Barton Bendish, Norfolk, and his wife Anne, daughter of Robert Toppe, Thomas Lovell was probably related to the 1st Viscount Lovell (see Lovell, Francis, in *Lives Before the Tudors*). Little is known of his early life except that he was entered at Lincoln's Inn.

A staunch supporter of Henry Tudor, Earl of Richmond, later Henry VII (q.v.), Lovell was attainted in the first Parliament of Richard III (see *Lives Before the Tudors*). He fought for Henry at Bosworth in 1485, and in the first Parliament of the new reign the attainder was reversed. In October the same year he was made Chancellor of the Exchequer for life.

Elected Member of Parliament for Northamptonshire on 7 November 1485, Lovell was the following day chosen as Speaker of the House of Commons, an office which he held until 1488. He fought against Lambert Simnel (q.v.) in

1487 and was knighted after the Battle of Stoke. In 1489 he became Constable of Nottingham Castle, and in 1502 President of the Council. He was made a Knight of the Garter in 1503.

The Chancellor's chief usefulness to Henry VII was in the accumulation of wealth for the crown, which was achieved through the system of extortions devised by Lovell and Sir Reginald Bray (q.v.), and carried out by others, principally the much-hated Sir Richard Empson and Edmund Dudley. On the accession of Henry VIII (q.v.) Lovell continued as Chancellor of the Exchequer, becoming in addition Constable of the Tower. He was High Steward of the universities of Cambridge (1509) and Oxford (1509–24).

Sir Thomas Lovell withdrew from public life in 1516 and retired to his home at Elsing, near Enfield, Middlesex, where he died on 25 May 1524. He had been twice married, but left no issue.

*Portrait:* painted plaster cast, after bronze relief by Pietro Torrigiano, *c.* 1518, in Westminster Abbey: National Portrait Gallery, London.

**Luther, Martin** (1483–1546), German reformer.

Martin Luther was born at Eisleben, near Mansfeld, on 10 November 1483, the son of a miner. Both at home and in the local Latin school he was subjected to harsh discipline, and in his fourteenth year was sent to Magdeburg to continue his education. From 1501 to 1505 he studied at the University of Erfurt, but in July 1505 suddenly gave up the idea of becoming a lawyer and entered the Augustinian monastery at Erfurt.

Luther was ordained in 1507 and embarked on a career as a theological teacher. At Wittenburg University in 1508–9, where he lectured on Aristotle's *Ethics*, he came under the influence of Johann Staupitz, the Vicar-General of the Augustinian order, whom he later succeeded as Professor of Biblical Theology. During 1512–13, after a long spiritual struggle with himself, he developed his theory of justification by faith, and the new doctrine was reflected in his lectures. In October 1517 he attacked Tetzel's sale of indulgences by posting his ninety-five theses on the church door at Wittenburg, thus provoking a major controversy. Accusations of heresy were made against him by Tetzel and Eck, but he refused to recant. His attack on papal authority in 1519 resulted in a Bull of Condemnation, but this merely incited the reformer to publish several new treatises and to burn the papal decree in public in December 1520. National and religious zeal mounted, stimulated by Luther's three pamphlets, *The Liberty of a Christian Man*, *To the Nobility of the German Nation* and *On the Babylonish Captivity of the Church of Christ*, all of which appeared in 1520.

In January 1521 the Pope issued a Bull of Excommunication, calling on the Emperor Charles V (q.v.) to execute it forthwith. Instead, the Emperor bowed to the views of the Elector of Saxony and the majority of the Diet, and Luther was summoned to Worms to appear before the Diet in April that year.

Before the Diet Luther again refused to recant and was ordered to leave the city. The Elector of Saxony gave him protection at the castle of Wartburg, where the reformer remained until early 1522, producing more controversial writings and working on a German translation of the New Testament, which was published in September 1522. Under the Edict of Worms, signed by the Emperor in May 1521, Luther and his adherents were banned from the empire, but this ruling became increasingly difficult to enforce as the evangelical movement gained in strength.

In 1524–5 Luther's opposition to the Peasants' War lost him popularity with the masses but gained a number of princely supporters. At the Diet of Speyer in 1529, however, the Catholics won a resolution enforcing the Edict of Worms in Catholic territories and forbidding further religious innovation in the Lutheran states, as well as prohibiting the Zwinglian and Anabaptist reformed faiths. From the Appellation and Protestation of the Lutherans against this decision the name 'Protestant' is derived.

A further blow to the Lutheran reformation was the controversy with the Swiss reformer, Ulrich Zwingli (q.v.), over the doctrine of the Lord's Supper. Luther believed in the bodily presence of Christ in the bread and wine, and when summoned by the Landgrave of Hesse to Marburg in October 1529 to meet his opponent in an attempt to settle their differences, he argued fiercely for three days in support of the literal interpretation of the words, 'This is my body.' By this time Luther had lost the support of Erasmus (q.v.) and some of the older humanists; in 1525 he had published his *De Servo Arbitrio* ('On Unfree Will') in reply to Erasmus's *De Libero Arbitrio*. Among the younger exponents of the new learning Martin Bucer (q.v.) and Melanchthon were loyal to the Lutheran movement; the latter's confession of the Lutheran faith made before the Diet of Augsburg in 1530 became the basic creed of the Lutheran Church.

In his last years, while continuing to work for the vindication of the Reformation, Luther relaxed a little in his views, and negotiations with Bucer and the south German reformers led to the Wittenberg Concord of 1536. Although throughout his life he remained antagonistic towards the Anabaptist movement, he was impressed by the views of John Calvin (q.v.), the Genevan reformer, and maintained cordial relations with Zwingli's successor, Henry Bullinger. Much of his time was spent on revision of the Old Testament translation which he had completed in the period 1523–32, and also on that of his earlier New Testament; by the date of his death the Luther Bible, his most important constructive contribution to the Reformation, had run into well over 350 editions.

Luther died on 18 February 1546 while on a visit to his birthplace, Eisleben, steadfastly maintaining in his dying words adherence to the doctrine which he had taught. He was laid to rest in Wittenberg church, in the presence of his family (the wife he had married in 1525, and their three sons and two daughters) and a large gathering of notables and followers. Melanchthon pronounced the funeral oration.

In England Lutheran views began to circulate in the early 1520s, winning an eager response from the universities, especially among the younger dons at Cambridge. The source of the English Protestant movement can be traced to the group (nicknamed 'Little Germany') which held discussion meetings at the White Horse tavern in Cambridge. Meanwhile, in reply to Luther, Henry VIII (q.v.) put out his *Assertion of the Seven Sacraments*, probably written with the assistance of John Fisher (q.v.) and Thomas More (q.v.), for which the Pope gave him the title 'Defender of the Faith'. In 1521 Wolsey (q.v.) presided over a ceremonial burning of the books of Luther and his associates in St Paul's Churchyard, London. A number of so-called 'heretics', followers of his doctrine, were later burned at the stake.

J. W. Allen, essay on Luther in *The Social and Political Ideas of Some Great Thinkers of the*

*Renaissance and the Reformation*, ed. F. J. C. Hearnshaw (1925).

R. Friedenthal, *Luther* (1967).

H. G. Koenigsberger (ed.), *Luther: A Profile* (1973).

J. MacKinnon, *Luther and the Reformation* (4 vols; New York, 1928–30).

P. Smith, *Life and Letters of Martin Luther* (Boston, 1914).

*Portraits*: drawing, by Cranach, *c*. 1533: Duke of Buccleuch Collection; oil, by unknown artist: Bodleian Library, Oxford; oil, by unknown artist: Balliol College, Oxford.

**Lyly, John** (?1554–1606), dramatist and author of the novel *Euphues*.

Born in about 1554, John Lyly was a native of the Weald of Kent. He studied both at Oxford and at Cambridge, taking his B.A. at Magdalen College, Oxford, in 1573 and his M.A. two years later. On completing his studies he went to London, in the hope of finding a place at court. He succeeded in securing the patronage of the Earl of Oxford (see Vere, Edward de), who employed him as his secretary, and in the winter of 1578–9 Lyly wrote the first part of his *Euphues* romance; entitled *Euphues, the Anatomie of Wit* and written in an elaborate, artificial style, it won immediate acclaim on publication early in 1579, when Lyly was hailed as a writer of 'a new English'. The second part of his novel, *Euphues and his England*, was published the following year.

Lyly's spectacular literary success brought him to the notice of Lord Burghley (see Cecil, William), who gave him employment in his household until, in 1582, he came under some suspicion of dishonesty and turned to playwriting as a career. His plays *Campaspe* and *Sapho and Phao*, performed first at the Blackfriars Theatre by a company of child actors called Oxford's Boys and later at court, were published in 1584. Appointed Vice-Master of Paul's Boys, a company which frequently performed before the Queen,

together with the Children of the Chapel, Lyly next embarked on a series of plays to be presented at court. The dating of his work is necessarily conjectural: *The Woman in the Moone*, believed to have been his earliest comedy and to have been performed in 1583, was not published until 1597; *Gallathea* was probably written and produced in 1584 (published in 1592); *Endimion*, considered to be his best, written in 1586–7 (published 1591); *Love's Metamorphosis* and *Midas* written in 1589 (published in 1592 and 1601 respectively); *Mother Bombie* written in 1589–90 (published in 1594). All of these plays, with the exception of *The Woman in the Moone*, were in prose. After the disbanding of Paul's Boys in 1590, Lyly wrote a number of other entertainments for performance at court. He cherished the ambition of becoming Master of the Revels in succession to Edmund Tilney, but because the latter outlived him the appointment never came his way.

In 1589 Lyly entered the Martin Marpelate controversy with a tract defending the bishops entitled *Pappe with a Hatchet*. He was returned to Parliament that year as Member for Hindon, and between 1589 and 1601 was to represent in turn Hindon, Aylesbury, and Appleby. Overshadowed by writers such as Christopher Marlowe (q.v.), William Shakespeare (q.v.), Thomas Kyd (q.v.), and others, during these years Lyly's popularity at court dwindled and his appeals for financial assistance met with little response, in spite of his having contributed some verses praising the Queen to Henry Lok's *Ecclesiasticus*, published in 1597. In the last years of his life Lyly devoted his energies to preparing for publication several of his plays. He died in London in November 1606.

John Lyly was the most popular English writer of the 1580s. The peculiar style in which his novel *Euphues* was written, relying heavily on the use of antithesis and alliteration, and containing many allusions to history, philosophy, mythology, and natural history, exerted a considerable influence on the writers of the period, especially Robert Greene (q.v.) and Thomas Lodge (q.v.), and gave rise to the term 'euphuism'. Lyly also broke new ground in the use of prose dialogue in his comedies written for the Elizabethan theatre. Some of his plays contain fine lyrics; these first appeared in the edition of collected plays printed by Edward Blount (q.v.) in 1632. *The Complete Works of John Lyly*, edited by R. Warwick Bond, were published in three volumes (Oxford, 1902).

George K. Hunter, *John Lyly, The Humanist as Courtier* (1962).
J. Dover Wilson, *John Lyly* (1905).

# M

**Machiavelli, Niccolò** (1469–1527), Florentine statesman, political theorist, and writer.

Niccolò Machiavelli was born at Florence on 3 May 1469, the son of a jurist. Little is known of his early years or education. He entered public life in 1494 (the year of Charles VIII's invasion and the expulsion of the Medici from Florence) and held various offices in the restored republic. His chief occupation, apart from a number of diplomatic missions, was the organization of a Florentine militia. Following the collapse of the republic and the return of the Medici in 1512, Machiavelli was suspected of conspiracy against the Medici, put to the rack, and subsequently exiled. His political life over, he retired with his wife, whom he had married in 1502, and children to a farmhouse near San Casciano.

Deprived of official emoluments, Machiavelli could now barely afford to keep his family, and he turned to writing as a source of income. By the end of 1513 he had completed *Il Principe* ('The Prince'), a treatise on the art of government which he attempted to dedicate to Lorenzo de' Medici and in which he put forward the view, couched in idealistic terms, that a strong and ruthless prince should free Italy by expelling all foreigners. For the sake of achieving peace and a prosperous Italy, he held that any means, however unscrupulous, were justified, even if they meant terrorism and deceit. In Machiavelli's opinion, the evil acts of the ruler were fully justified by the evil acts of those he ruled.

Although the first printed translation of this treatise did not appear in England until 1639, manuscript editions were in circulation much earlier; there are references to Machiavelli in the work of the Elizabethan dramatists, and his theories were said to have influenced the policies of Thomas Cromwell (q.v.), Lord Burghley (see Cecil, William), and the Earl of Leicester (see Dudley, Robert). The name 'Machiavelli' soon became a synonym for a cunning and unscrupulous politician, and 'Machiavellism' came to denote political intrigue and duplicity. The hostility of English writers of the day to Machiavelli led to a popular misconception of his theories; the source of this was an attack made upon the Italian by a French Huguenot writer, Innocent Gentillet, which appeared in an English translation in 1602.

Machiavelli's other great political work, the *Discorsi sopra la prima deca di Tito Livio*, in the form of comments on the history of Livy, was written between 1513 and 1519. It was not published until after his death, although the author read extracts from it to a select audience. At about this time he was restored to a certain degree of favour, being consulted by Leo X and Giulio de' Medici on the matter of self-government for Florence and later commissioned to write a history of that state. His real public career was, however, finished, and although during the next few years the Medici employed his services on the occasional minor diplomatic mission, Machiavelli had to be content with devoting the rest of his life to literary pursuits. The *Arte della guerra* ('Art of War') was completed in 1520, and from that date onwards he worked at his history of Florence. He also wrote a series of comedies, including the brilliant *Mandragola*, considered to be the most powerful play of the Italian Renaissance.

In the last year of his life Machiavelli was employed on official business by Pope Clement VII, but the opportunity for renewed service to the state was short-lived. He died in Florence on 20 June 1527.

Machiavelli's theories on the modern state marked the end of medieval thought and the beginning of a new concept of politics as a science. The extent of his influence in England has been much argued by historians.

The best English editions of his major works are *Il Principe*, translated by E. Dacres (1639); the *Discorsi*, translated by L. J. Walker (2 vols; 1950); and the *Florentine Historie*, translated by Thomas Bedingfield (1595).

Mario Praz, 'Machiavelli and the Elizabethans', *Proceedings of the British Academy* (1928).
Felix Raab, *The English face of Machiavelli: a changing interpretation, 1500–1700* (Toronto, 1964).
R. Ridolfi, *The Life of Niccolò Machiavelli*, translated by C. Grayson (1963).
L. A. Weissberger, 'Machiavelli and Tudor England', *Political Science Quarterly*, xlii (February 1927).

*Portraits:* oil, by Santi di Tito: Palazzo Vecchio, Florence; oil, by unknown artist: Galleria Doria, Rome; bust, Florentine school, sixteenth century: Palazzo Vecchio.

## Machyn or Machin, Henry (?1498–?1563), diarist.

Henry Machyn was born probably in 1498. He called himself a 'citizen and merchant taylor of London' and lived in the parish of Trinity the Little by Queenhithe. He was married; a daughter, Catherine, was baptized on 27 September 1557. His brother Christopher was also a merchant tailor in the City.

Machyn kept a diary from July 1550 until August 1563. The earliest entries are devoted to accounts of funerals, the furnishing of which seems to have been at that time his principal occupation. The first public event noted is a reference to the committal of Stephen Gardiner (q.v.) to the Tower, and from that entry onwards the diary contains some valuable descriptions of public events interspersed with the records of funerals. Machyn was particularly diligent in writing of events connected with the religious struggles of the day; as a devout Catholic he welcomed the restoration of the old religion under Mary I (q.v.). Pageantry also inspired him, and he was the first English writer to describe the Lord Mayor's Show.

The diary comes to an abrupt end in August 1563 with an account of the outbreak of plague in London, and it seems likely that Machyn himself became a victim of the dreaded disease.

Historians have drawn on Machyn's diary as a valuable and unique contemporary source. John Strype used the manuscript when writing his *Annals* and highly commended the diarist's diligence. The original manuscript is now in the Cotton MSS collection at the British Museum, and the diary has been edited by J. G. Nichols and published by the Camden Society (1848).

## Magellan, Ferdinand (*c.* 1480–1521), seaman, discoverer of the strait named after him, and virtually the first circumnavigator of the world (in fact he died before the voyage was completed).

Fernão Maghalhães was born into the Portuguese nobility, the son of Rui de Maghalhães and Alda de Mesquita. As a boy, Magellan entered the royal service as page to the Queen. In 1505 he enlisted under Francisco de Almeida, whose expedition to check Muslim power in Africa and India left Lisbon on 25 March. Between 1505 and 1516 Magellan participated in a number of Portuguese naval and military expeditions to Africa, India, and the Orient, including the battle for control of Malacca and the siege of Azamor, in which he was wounded. He was accused of some irregular conduct after the battle of Azamor, for which reason the Portuguese King repeatedly refused his request for higher rank. Finally in 1516, after being informed that he might offer his services elsewhere, Magellan went to Spain, reaching Seville on 20 October 1517.

Joined by the Portuguese cosmographer, Rui Faleiro, Magellan (who had renounced his nationality and henceforward used only the Spanish version of his name) travelled to the court at Valladolid to offer his services to the King, later the Emperor Charles V (q.v.). Their proposal was to sail westwards in order to prove that the rich 'Spice Islands' lay to the west of the line of demarcation drawn up by the Pope in 1494, and thus in the Spanish rather than the Portuguese hemisphere. The scheme was granted royal assent in March 1518, when Magellan and Faleiro jointly were appointed to command an expedition to open up an all-Spanish route to the Moluccas. Magellan was convinced that he would find the strait that earlier seamen had sought to lead them from the Atlantic to the southern ocean and so avoid the Cape of Good Hope, which was controlled by the Portuguese.

There were delays caused by an unsuccessful attempt by Portuguese agents to sabotage the expedition. But on 20 September 1519 Magellan sailed from Sanlúcar aboard his flagship *Trinidad*,

accompanied by 270 men of nine different nationalities. At the last moment Faleiro was prevented from participating because of a mental illness. They reached Tenerife six days later, and on 3 October set sail for Brazil. On 13 December the fleet sailed into what is now the bay of Rio de Janeiro and then southwards to the estuary of the Rio de la Plata in search of the elusive strait. On 31 March they reached the Puerto San Julian (latitude 49°20S), where Magellan had to quell a mutiny led by his Spanish captains. He dealt with this ruthlessly, executing one of the ringleaders and leaving another ashore when on 24 August 1520 he set sail southwards again. On 21 October he rounded the Cabo Vírgenes and with only three of his ships remaining (one had been wrecked and another had deserted), at approximately 52°50S Magellan entered the narrow passage that would later bear his name.

On 28 November the three vessels, *Trinidad, Concepción*, and *Victoria*, entered what they called the 'Sea of the South' (the Pacific). In spite of severe deprivations such as scurvy, and so lacking in provisions that they were reduced to gnawing the leather off the yardarms of their ships, Magellan determinedly drove his crew on across the ocean. At first they sailed up the Chilean coastline, but on 18 December set a north-westerly course and did not make landfall again until 6 March 1521, when they dropped anchor at Guam in the Marianas and tasted their first fresh food for ninety-nine days. Probably with a view to revictualling and establishing a base before visiting the 'Spice Islands', Magellan decided to follow a west-southwesterly course when he left the Marianas on 9 March; this brought him to the islands later called the Philippines. Here the natives were at first friendly and willing to be converted; but on Mactan

Island they became hostile, and Magellan was killed there on 27 April 1521.

After his death the *Trinidad* and the *Victoria* eventually reached the Moluccas, under the command of Juan Sebastián de Elcano, who had originally been master of the *Concepción*; of these the *Victoria* alone, leaking but laden with spices, and with only seventeen surviving crew members, returned to Spain. Sailing homeward on the Cape route, Elcano arrived back on 8 September 1522, the first European to provide firm evidence that the earth was round.

Ferdinand Magellan was the first navigator to cross the Pacific from east to west and the first to disprove the hitherto accepted idea that the East Indies lay within a few days' sailing from the New World: at the time of his death he had brought his fleet close to them, having made an ocean crossing which lasted for three months. Death robbed him of the honour of being the first to circumnavigate the world, but his achievement lies in the fact that he conceived and directed the great enterprise.

Two contemporary accounts of Magellan's voyage have been printed: that of Antonio Pigafetta, who sailed on it, in *Magellan's Voyage Around the World by Antonio Pigafetta*, edited by J. A. Robertson (2 vols; 1906), and *The First Voyage Round the World by Magellan*, which includes accounts by other members of the expedition in addition to Pigafetta's, published by the Hakluyt Society, vol. lii (1874).

E. F. Benson, *Ferdinand Magellan* (1929).
F. H. H. Guillemard, *The Life of Ferdinand Magellan and the First Circumnavigation of the Globe, 1480–1521* (1890, reprinted 1971).

*Portrait*: oil, by unknown artist: Uffizi Gallery, Florence.

**'Maid of Kent'** (?1506–1534), see Barton, Elizabeth.

**Maitland, John** (?1545–1595), 1st Baron Maitland of Thirlestane, statesman, Chancellor of Scotland and chief adviser to James VI (q.v.).

Maitland was born in about 1545, the second son of Sir Richard Maitland of Lethington, nobleman, lawyer, and poet, and younger brother of William, 'Secretary Maitland' to Mary, Queen of Scots (q.v.). John was educated probably at Haddington grammar school and later at St Andrews University; like his father, whose patriotism and social opinions he inherited, he was trained in law. He is usually known as 'Maitland of Thirlestane', as distinct from his brother William, who is referred to as 'Maitland of Lethington'.

Maitland's first official appointment was that of Commendator of the Priory of Coldingham in February 1567; two months later, he succeeded his father as Keeper of the Privy Seal of Scotland. As a supporter of Mary, Queen of Scots, he took part in various skirmishes on her behalf, and on the fall of Edinburgh Castle to the Earl of Morton (see Douglas, James) in May 1573, he was taken into custody and held first at Edinburgh and later at Tantallon; he did not regain political power until after Morton's fall. In 1581 Maitland was given back his estates but not the office of Privy Seal. No longer a Marian supporter, to outside opinion he was nevertheless still connected with his brother's reputation, which he had to live down.

In January 1583, Maitland married Janet Fleming, daughter of the 4th Baron Fleming, who was related to the powerful Hamilton clan. He was recalled to court by James in August 1583 and at the end of that month was made a Privy Councillor. The following April he was knighted and formally appointed as Secretary, the first step on the ladder to becoming the King's chief adviser and

Lord Chancellor, which he achieved in 1587.

Maitland's great influence with James earned him the dislike and jealously of many of the Scottish nobles, especially that of the Earl of Bothwell (see Hepburn, Francis Stewart); he was the first Chancellor of Scotland who was not a lord or a bishop. After the fall from power of the Earl of Arran (see Stewart, James, Earl of Arran) and later of the King's favourite, the Master of Gray (see Gray, Patrick), Maitland was in firm control. He shared James's Erastian views and his dislike of extremism; his policy towards the Kirk was therefore one of compromise. During the negotiations for the league between Scotland and England, he at first advocated delay while negotiating at the same time with France, but once he realized that the Guise family were intriguing with Spain, he saw that the English alliance was the best possible way of strengthening the power of the Scottish crown. He aroused much hostility in the session of 1587 by his statute of annexation and by his proposal for the admission of lairds to Parliament.

In 1589 he accompanied James to Scandinavia for his marriage to the Princess Anne of Denmark (see *Lives of the Stuart Age*). To mark the occasion of Anne's coronation, in May 1590 Maitland was raised to the peerage as Baron Thirlestane. He later incurred the enmity of the Queen by his refusal to relinquish Musselburgh, which Anne regarded as part of her marriage gift from the King.

Bothwell, implicated in the North Berwick witchcraft trials of 1590–1, now began a bitter feud against Maitland and succeeded eventually in toppling the latter from power. In December 1591 there took place the first of a series of raids by Bothwell on the King's person and on Maitland. In February 1592 James

Stewart, the 'Bonnie' Earl of Moray, was murdered by the Marquess of Huntly, and when the King persisted in his policy of leniency towards Huntly and the northern Catholic lords, even after the 'Spanish blanks' affair at the end of the year, the gulf between crown and Kirk widened more than ever. By that time James had yielded to pressure to dismiss Maitland from court.

Following his withdrawal to Lethington in March 1592, the King at first used to ride over to Maitland's home to ask for his advice, but gradually James came to feel that he no longer required a chief minister, even that his former Chancellor constituted a political liability. He therefore signed a patent appointing Maitland as ambassador to France; in fact the appointment was never taken up, for Maitland, already in fear of his life, did not dare to leave Scotland for fear of what might happen to his property in his absence.

The Chancellor's last act of constructive statesmanship was to convince James of the wisdom of repairing the breach with the Kirk; he was responsible for the 'Golden Act' of 1592, which acknowledged the legal authority of presbyteries. A Maitland-sponsored act of abolition, requiring everyone in Scotland either to embrace the 'true' religion by 1 February 1594 or go into exile, was, however, rejected by the Scottish Parliament. Before ill-health finally overtook him, Maitland warned the King of the danger from the Queen's party who were trying to obtain custody of the infant Prince Henry. He died on 3 October 1595.

Maitland's great achievement was that he taught the King how to govern; he was not, as Chancellor, successful in financial affairs. Although James subsequently reversed Maitland's conciliatory policy towards the Kirk, by that time the foundations had been laid for an administration of Scotland that was not composed, as hitherto, solely of nobles. This in turn prepared the ground for the Stuart rule of the seventeenth century.

James VI wrote a sonnet expressing his grief at Maitland's death.

M. Lee, *John Maitland of Thirlestane and the Foundation of the Stewart Despotism in Scotland* (Princeton, 1959).

*Portraits:* oil, by unknown artist: Dowager Countess of Lauderdale; miniature, by unknown artist, c. 1590: National Portrait Gallery, London.

**Mar, Earl of** (?1531–1570), see Stewart, Lord James.

**Mar, 1st (18th) Earl of** (d. 1572), see Erskine, John.

**Marbeck, John** (d. ?1585), musician and theologian.

Few details are known of John Marbeck's life. He was a lay clerk at St George's Chapel, Windsor, where in 1541 he was appointed as organist. A Reformist from an early age, he was in 1543 arrested for possessing heretical writings and imprisoned in the Marshalsea. He was tried at Windsor in July 1544, condemned, and sentenced to be burned at the stake; the following day, however, Bishop Stephen Gardiner (q.v.) obtained a pardon for him (it was said on the grounds of his great musical talent) and he was freed. Wisely he refrained from further display of his religious convictions until after the accession of Edward VI (q.v.), when in 1550 he published his *Concordāce*, the earliest concordance of the English Bible. Later the same year he issued *The Boke of Common Prayer noted*, an adaptation of the plain chant to the first Prayer Book of Edward VI, the work for which he is most remembered.

Marbeck continued his musical and theological studies for the next thirty years at least. He is known still to have been organist at St George's in 1565 and, according to John Foxe (q.v.), was alive in 1583. Several theological works by him were published in the years 1574 to 1584. Marbeck is believed to have died at Windsor in about 1585.

**Margaret** (1446–1503), Duchess of Burgundy, daughter of Richard, Duke of York (see Richard, 3rd Duke of York (1411–60), in *Lives Before the Tudors*) and Cecily Neville, and sister of Edward IV (see *Lives Before the Tudors*).

Margaret was born at Fotheringay Castle, Northamptonshire, on 3 May 1446. Negotiations for her marriage to Charles, eldest son of Philip, Duke of Burgundy, began in 1466, and after a period of suspension were renewed the next year when Charles became Duke of Burgundy on the death of his father. Margaret gave her formal consent to the union at a Council held on 1 October 1467; a treaty was concluded in the following January and the alliance was announced to Parliament on 17 May 1468.

She set out for Flanders on 18 June and was received at Sluys with great pomp and pageantry. The marriage took place at Damme on 3 July, amid festivities that lasted for nine days. The link between Burgundy and the house of York was a turning-point in European history, although its importance was not fully realized until two years later, when Edward IV sought refuge in the Netherlands. Margaret strove continually for a reconciliation between Edward and his brother Clarence (see George, Duke of Clarence, in *Lives Before the Tudors*).

The Duke was killed at Nancy in January 1477, leaving Margaret a childless widow. Apart from a short visit to

England in 1480, she spent the rest of her life in the Netherlands. The dowry given to her by Edward was confiscated on the accession of Henry VII (q.v.), and Margaret plotted vigorously against him. Her court became a Yorkist centre, and she received and encouraged the two imposters, Lambert Simnel (q.v.) and Perkin Warbeck (q.v.), but was forced to apologize to Henry on this account in 1498.

From about 1470 onwards Margaret was a patron of William Caxton (q.v.), who translated the *Recuyell of the Historyes of Troye* while in her service. In 1500 she stood as godmother to the future Emperor Charles V (q.v.). She died at Mechlin in 1503 and was buried in the church of the Cordeliers there.

*Portrait*: oil, after van der Goes, sixteenth century: Society of Antiquaries, London.

**Margaret, The Lady** (1443–1509), see Beaufort, Margaret.

**Margaret Tudor** (1489–1541), Queen of Scotland.

The eldest daughter of Henry VII (q.v.), Margaret was born at Westminster on 29 November 1489. As early as 1495 her father tried to negotiate her marriage with James IV of Scotland (q.v.), but the matter was not satisfactorily settled until the end of 1502. Margaret left for Scotland in June 1503 and was married to James at Edinburgh on 8 August; she was crowned in March 1504. Two sons and a daughter, born between 1507 and 1510, died in infancy, but in 1512 she gave birth to a son, the future James V (q.v.).

Throughout her married life the meagre dowry wrung out of Henry VII was a cause of much bitterness and intrigue, both on a personal and a political level, and the financial haggling continued into the reign of Margaret's brother, Henry VIII (q.v.). The campaign waged by the Scots in 1513 that culminated in the Battle of Flodden had as its part origin a legacy disputed between Margaret and her brother, the King of England.

After James IV was killed at Flodden in September 1513, Margaret became Regent and sole guardian of her infant son, now James V. When the Duke of Albany (see Stewart, John), the next heir to the Scottish throne after Margaret's two sons, returned to Scotland in 1514 at the invitation of Parliament, conflict broke out between the two opposing factions, the one favouring an alliance with England and the other, under the leadership of Stewart, an alliance with France. This situation was further complicated by rivalry between the Earls of Arran and Angus, representing the Hamilton and Douglas families respectively; when Margaret married the Earl of Angus (see Douglas, Archibald, 6th Earl) later that year, she angered Arran and other Scottish nobles, who in July 1515 deprived her of the regency and guardianship in favour of Albany. Margaret fled to England, where she gave birth to a daughter, Margaret Douglas (q.v.), who was later to become the Countess of Lennox, mother of Lord Darnley (see Stewart, Henry), and grandmother of James VI of Scotland (q.v.; later James I of England).

In 1516 Margaret went to the court of Henry VIII in London, while Angus, against her wishes, returned to Scotland, where he made peace with Albany and had his estates restored to him. The feud between the two rival families continued, and during the next few years there was almost constant warfare on the border between the Scots and the English. When Margaret returned to Edinburgh in 1517 to find that promised access to her son and money from rents were denied her, she began to intrigue and play with both sides. Quarrelling with Angus over his infidelity and money matters, she pressed for a divorce, and when that course met with opposition from Henry VIII, she allied herself with Albany to the extent that he was accused of supporting her divorce with the aim of marrying her. First Angus and then Albany was forced to withdraw to France, while Margaret constantly changed sides and fought for the possession of the Scottish King's person.

She obtained her divorce from Angus in 1527 and immediately married Henry Stewart, the second son of Lord Avondale, who was created Lord Methven. After the fall of Angus in 1528 the Queen Mother and her husband became the chief influence in the counsels of James V, who had been declared fit to govern with the advice of his mother and a council in 1524, though confined by Angus from 1526 to 1528. Peace negotiations with England were opened, but Margaret revealed certain secrets to Henry VIII which led to her being accused by James of spying and taking bribes. Henry also treated her coldly, but she continued to bother him with various complaints, and interceded with him on behalf of her daughter, Lady Margaret Douglas, who had incurred the King's displeasure by her betrothal to Lord Thomas Howard, in 1536. Her attempt to secure a divorce from Henry Stewart was unsuccessful, and in 1537 she was overtaken trying to escape to England. The last few years of Margaret's life were not happy; she died at Methven Castle on 18 October 1541 and was buried in the church of St John, Perth.

M. A. E. Green, *Lives of the Princesses of England*, vol. v (6 vols; 1849–55).
Bruce Seton, 'The distaff side: a study in matrimonial adventure in the fifteenth and sixteenth centuries', *Scottish Historical Review*, xvii (1919).

Anon., 'Tudor Intrigues in Scotland', *Scottish Review*, xxiv (1894).

*Portraits*: oil, full length, by Mytens: Royal Collection, Holyroodhouse, Edinburgh (copies Warwickshire County Council and Queen's College, Cambridge); oil on panel, unknown lady *called* Margaret Tudor, attributed to Jean Perréal, *c*. 1520: National Portrait Gallery, London.

**Marie de Guise** (1515–1560), also known as Marie de Lorraine, Queen consort of James V of Scotland (q.v.) and Regent for her daughter, Mary, Queen of Scots (q.v.), 1554–60.

Marie was born on 22 November 1515, the eldest child of Claude, Duc de Guise. On 4 August 1534 she married her first husband, the Duc de Longueville, who died in 1537. Shortly afterwards the French King offered her as a bride to James V of Scotland, whose first wife had just died. While negotiations were proceeding for this marriage, Henry VIII (q.v.), who had just lost his third wife, Jane Seymour (q.v.), also made a bid for Marie's hand; however, François I stood by his original offer to the Scottish King, and it was agreed that the marriage should take place in the summer of 1538.

The ceremony was performed by proxy in Paris in May 1538, and the following month, on Marie's arrival in Scotland, the union was solemnized at the cathedral of St Andrews. David Beaton (q.v.), the future Cardinal, who officiated at the nuptial Mass, was to enjoy the patronage and friendship of Queen Marie throughout her lifetime; he became one of the King's most trusted counsellors and was a staunch supporter of the 'auld alliance' of Scotland and France.

Following the brief power struggle between Beaton and the Earl of Arran (see Hamilton, James, 2nd Earl), in which the latter was successful, the influence of Marie de Guise in Scottish affairs was at its lowest ebb. Her two sons died in infancy in 1541. She was given the custody of her daughter, the young Queen of Scots, (born in December 1542, just six days before the death of James V), but in the next five years had little influence in state affairs. Matthew Stewart, 4th (12th) Earl of Lennox, unsuccessfully sought her hand in marriage. After the defeat of the Scots by the English at Pinkie Cleugh in September 1547, Marie's influence and that of the French party increased. In July 1548 she was able to send the young Queen to France to be educated at the court of Henri II and Catherine de' Medici (q.v.), while at home she prepared to take over the regency from Arran. In September 1550 she went to France for a year to visit her daughter.

In April 1554 Arran was persuaded to resign, and Marie de Guise became Regent of Scotland. In order to strengthen the French alliance, she offered Mary as a bride to the Dauphin, later François II. Religious toleration was at first her policy, but pressure from France led her towards the suppression of Protestantism. In 1559 her offensive against the Calvinists gave rise to a rebellion at Perth, which spread rapidly. Arran, who had been made Duke of Châtelherault in 1548, returned to Scotland to lead the rebel cause. In October 1559 Marie de Guise was driven out of Edinburgh by the Protestant lords; she fortified herself at Leith, while the rebels, proclaiming that her regency was at an end, appointed Châtelherault in her place.

Edinburgh was recaptured, but after reinforcements sent from France in April 1560 were intercepted off the coast by the English, Leith was besieged. By this time Marie de Guise was a sick woman. She took refuge in Edinburgh Castle and, as she lay dying of dropsy, pleaded for the support of the nobles for her daughter. She died on 11 June 1560. Her coffin was several months later transported to France, where in March 1561 she was buried at the church of the Convent of St Pierre in Rheims.

The indomitable Marie de Guise was a practical woman of considerable political acumen. Her chief aim was to conserve her daughter's inheritance; she was not primarily concerned with either the independence of Scotland or the religious conflict. Once she realized that her objects would be best served by alliance with France and the suppression of Protestantism, however, she worked unremittingly towards that end. In the event, neither she nor her daughter Mary was able to arrest the Protestant movement in that country.

The correspondence of Marie de Guise has been printed in two editions: *Foreign Correspondence* (Balcarres Papers), edited by Marguerite Wood in two volumes, Scottish Historical Society, 3rd series, iv and vii (1923, 1925); and *Scottish Correspondence 1543–60*, edited by A. I. Cameron, Scottish Historical Society, 3rd series, x (1927).

E. M. H. M'Kerlie, *Mary of Guise-Lorraine, Queen of Scotland* (1931).

*Portraits*: oil, attributed to Corneille de Lyon: Scottish National Portrait Gallery, Edinburgh; oil, by unknown artist: Hardwick Hall, Derbyshire (copy by H. Munro: S.N.P.G.); drawing, by unknown artist: British Museum, London.

## Marlowe, Christopher (1564–1593), dramatist.

The second child and eldest son of a Canterbury shoemaker, John Marlowe, and his wife Catherine Arthur of Dover, Christopher Marlowe was baptized on 26 February 1564. He attended King's School, Canterbury, where he became a Queen's Scholar on 14 January 1579. The following year he won a Parker Scholarship to Corpus Christi College, Cambridge, where he took his B.A. in 1584, and remained in residence – with some periods of absence – for a further three years, with a view to taking his M.A. and possibly taking holy orders. It was soon apparent, however, that drama and poetry were of more interest to him than divinity.

There was some difficulty over the granting of his master's degree in July 1587 because Marlowe had absented himself from Cambridge in order to visit the Catholic seminary at Rheims founded by Cardinal William Allen (q.v.). After reassurance from the Privy Council that 'Christopher Marley' had been employed 'in matters touching the benefit of his country', the degree was awarded. Marlowe had in fact been engaged by Sir Francis Walsingham (q.v.) to spy out the situation at Rheims, which was attracting increasing numbers of English students who wished to train as Catholic priests; he probably first came to the notice of the Secretary of State through the patronage of one of the latter's kinsmen, Thomas Walsingham of Scadbury, near Chislehurst, Kent, or through Nicholas Faunt, his school fellow at King's, who had become Sir Francis's secretary.

The dating of Marlowe's early work is uncertain, but it is believed that he completed *Tamburlaine the Great* before leaving Cambridge in 1587; the play was first performed, by the Lord Admiral's Men, in two parts, at the end of that year. Marlowe had probably already translated Ovid's *Elegies* and the first book of Lucan's *Pharsalia*. Both at Canterbury and at Cambridge he had frequent opportunities to observe and participate in dramatic performances and 'revels'. A tempestuous, brilliant, and ambitious young man with grand ideas, he moved from Cambridge to London in about 1587–8, intent on making his mark in the theatre. He was also prepared to live by his wits, and this included continuing employment in Walsingham's 'secret service', as well as some heavy drinking and brawling in the taverns of the City.

Within a short time Marlowe was much in demand by the owner-managers of the London playhouses and actors like Edward Alleyn (q.v.), who sought to play his leading roles. The London stage had never before seen anything on such a scale as *Tamburlaine*, the triumphant story of the Scythian shepherd robber's conquest of Damascus and Babylon and of his love for Zenocrate, the daughter of the Soldan of Egypt. Its exotic setting and powerful blank verse were new departures in Elizabethan drama, and the play proved so popular that a sequel was called for. (Published anonymously in 1590, *Tamburlaine* was the only work of Marlowe's to be printed during his lifetime.) Other plays followed in rapid succession. The *Jew of Malta*, in which Barabas was a caricature of Niccolò

Machiavelli (q.v.), is believed by some to have been written in 1589–90 and by others to have been the dramatist's last work (it was not published until 1633). Also immensely popular, this play later inspired William Shakespeare (q.v.) to write *The Merchant of Venice*, in which the character of Shylock is said to be based on Marlowe's Barabas. *Edward II*, published in 1594 and considered to be Marlowe's best play, was probably written in 1591; its composition may or may not have preceded that of *The Tragicall History of Doctor Faustus*, which was first entered on the Stationers' Register in 1601 and was published in 1604. Of his two minor dramas, *The Massacre at Paris* was performed early in 1593 and *The Tragedy of Dido, Queen of Carthage*, probably written at Cambridge, appeared in 1594 as the joint work of Marlowe and Thomas Nashe (q.v.). The splendid poem *Hero and Leander* was unfinished when Marlowe was killed in May 1593; it was evidently written in competition with Shakespeare's *Venus and Adonis*, for the patronage of the Earl of Southampton (see Wriothesley, Henry), while the London theatres were closed on account of plague during 1592–3. It is not known when Marlowe wrote his exquisite lyric, 'The Passionate Shepherd to his Love', beginning 'Come live with me, and be my love', for which he is chiefly remembered by English readers today. First published in 1599 in *The Passionate Pilgrim* and reprinted in *England's Helicon* the following year, it inspired Sir Walter Ralegh (q.v.) to reply in the well-known lines, 'If all the world and love were young'; among other contemporary poets who took up the theme were Richard Barnfield and Nicholas Breton (q.v.).

Marlowe's brilliant success so young inevitably won him enemies as well as friends in London, and among the most vicious attacks on him was one by the pamphleteer and poet Robert Greene (q.v.). William Shakespeare, Marlowe's junior by a couple of months, and just emerging as a dramatist himself, commented with admiration on his great 'learning'. The few documentary records that survive of the dramatist's life concern only disturbances and fights and brushes with the law, as in September 1589, when he was involved in a quarrel between the poet Thomas Watson and a man called William Bradley; Marlowe and Bradley, fighting in Hog Lane (between Finsbury Fields and Shoreditch), were separated by Watson, who entered the fray himself and struck Bradley a blow which killed him on the spot. Both Marlowe and Watson were taken to Newgate prison and appeared before the Judges of Assize at the Old Bailey on 3 December. Marlowe was thirteen days in prison before being released on bail; he received a pardon, but Watson was held in Newgate until the following February. A similar incident (although no one was killed) involving Marlowe and another man took place at the Chequers Inn, Canterbury, in the autumn of 1592. Marlowe was at that time still engaged in espionage work for Walsingham; probably he is the 'Marlin' who carried letters from France to Sir Robert Cecil (q.v.), later 1st Earl of Salisbury.

From 1591 onwards Marlowe shared a room in London with his friend and fellow-dramatist, Thomas Kyd (q.v.), where they were both engaged in writing plays for the same theatrical company. Early in May 1593 Kyd fell under suspicion of atheistical writing; on being arrested and his room searched, papers were found which were said to deny the deity of Jesus Christ. He said that they were Marlowe's; later, under torture, he incriminated his friend still further.

Meanwhile on 18 May a warrant was issued for the arrest of Marlowe, who was brought to London from the home of Thomas Walsingham near Chislehurst, in Kent. The Privy Council treated him with surprising leniency, requiring him only to 'give his daily attendance on their lordships until he shall be licensed to the contrary'. Subsequently further information was given by the false intelligence-man-turned-informer, Richard Baines, concerning Marlowe's atheistic opinions, but no further restrictions were placed upon his movements.

On 30 May Marlowe went down to Deptford, a Kentish suburb to the southeast of London, to spend the day with Ingram Frizer, Robert Poley, and Nicholas Skeres, all three questionable characters and members of the Thomas Walsingham circle. Frizer invited the party to dine at Eleanor Bull's tavern, and after some hours of drinking and talk they remained to take supper at the inn. A dispute arose between Marlowe and Frizer over the bill, during the course of which Marlowe drew Frizer's dagger. Frizer, acting in self-defence, inflicted a wound above the dramatist's right eye which killed him instantly; undoubtedly they had all been drinking heavily. Two days later, on 1 June, the coroner's inquest found that Frizer had indeed acted in self-defence and Marlowe was buried in the parish church of St Nicholas at Deptford. The circumstances surrounding the dramatist's death, in particular the unusual leniency of the Council towards him after his arrest, have puzzled several generations of scholars. Some of Marlowe's contemporaries held the view that the official story of the quarrel over the tavern bill covered a more sinister explanation.

Generous tributes were paid to Marlowe by his contemporaries in the field of literature, among them Thomas Nashe, Michael Drayton (q.v.), George Peele (q.v.), George Chapman (q.v.), the publisher Edward Blount (q.v.), John Marston, and Ben Jonson (for the last two, see *Lives of the Stuart Age*). Shakespeare, who was then just coming to maturity as a playwright and who had been Marlowe's greatest rival, included a remembrance of the dead poet in *As You Like It*.

During the six years of his writing career, Christopher Marlowe, by virtue of the originality, power, and lyrical quality of his work – most especially his talent for the 'mighty line', as Jonson called it – dominated the English stage. Up to that time, dramatic blank verse had retained a wooden inflexibility. He also gave the lead to Shakespeare and the Jacobean dramatists in their preoccupation with the psychological inner conflict of their heroes. No one did more than Marlowe in his short lifetime to stimulate the growth of the dramatic form in English literature.

The standard edition of his works, published in six volumes under the editorship of R. H. Case, 1930–3, is being replaced by the Revels edition of the *Works of Christopher Marlowe*, several volumes of which have already appeared. The best text is that edited by Fredson Bowers (Cambridge, 1974). For a list of early editions and critical studies see S. A. Tannenbaum, *Christopher Marlowe: A Concise Bibliography* (1937; and supplement, 1947). Later critical studies include Harry Levin, *Christopher Marlowe: The Overreacher* (1954) and J. B. Steane, *Marlowe: A Critical Study* (1964).

Certain scholars believe that Marlowe may have been part-author of *Titus Andronicus* and other plays by Shakespeare. For a discussion of this theory, see Calvin Hoffman, *The Man who was Shakespeare* (1955).

F. S. Boas, *Christopher Marlowe: A Biographical and Critical Study* (1940).

J. L. Hotson, *The Death of Christopher Marlowe* (1925).

P. H. Kocher, *Christopher Marlowe: A Study of his Thought, Learning and Character* (1946).

A. L. Rowse, *Christopher Marlowe* (1964).

*Portrait:* oil, by unknown artist, 1585: Corpus Christi College, Cambridge.

**Marston, John** (1576–1634), satirist and dramatist, see *Lives of the Stuart Age*.

**Mary I** (1516–1558), Queen of England from 1553, the first woman to rule England in her own right.

Mary was the third and only surviving child of Henry VIII (q.v.) and his first wife, Catherine of Aragon (q.v.). Born at Greenwich Palace on 18 February 1516, she was put in the charge of the Countess of Salisbury (see Pole, Margaret) at an early age.

The Princess's education was supervised initially by her mother, and later by Thomas Linacre (q.v.) and Juan Luis Vives, the Spanish humanist. Mary was an intelligent and studious pupil: in addition to the usual accomplishments of music and embroidery, she acquired a knowledge of astronomy, mathematics, geography, Latin and Greek; she read the works of Erasmus (q.v.) and Thomas More (q.v.) and spoke fluently in French and Spanish, as well as a little Italian.

From babyhood she was a valuable pawn in international politics. As England needed allies, so Mary was betrothed: at the age of two, to the Dauphin of France, and when that was broken off, at the age of six to the Emperor Charles V (q.v.). Charles jilted her for a better match with Isabella of Portugal, and while fresh betrothal plans were conceived for her, in 1525 Mary was made Princess of Wales and given her own court at Ludlow Castle. There, under the care of the Countess of Salisbury and John Dudley (q.v.), later Duke of Northumberland but at that time the Princess's chamberlain, Mary spent two of the happiest years of her life. Up to this time her father had always made a great fuss of her; he called her the 'pearl of my kingdom', and she was often at court. In the spring of 1527 she was brought to Greenwich to be betrothed to François I of France, and afterwards she took part in a pageant performed to entertain the foreign ambassadors, an occasion on which Henry demonstrated in public the pride and love he bore for his daughter.

The happy times were almost at an end. Within a few months it became general knowledge that Anne Boleyn had captured the King's heart and that Henry was contemplating a divorce from Catherine in order to be free to marry again. There followed a series of events which disrupted Mary's life in the cruellest way. During the next three years, while the King's 'secret matter' was the talk of Europe, the Princess saw less and less of her parents. Then, in 1531, when Henry finally separated from his wife, Mary was forbidden either to see or write to her mother. She never saw her again.

Worse was to come. François broke off the proposed marriage, and in 1533, the year in which her mother's marriage was declared null and void, the King married Anne Boleyn. On the birth of the Princess Elizabeth (see Elizabeth I) later that year, Mary was deprived of her title of Princess of Wales and declared illegitimate; an Act of Parliament cut her out from succession to the throne. Her court was disbanded, the Countess of Salisbury, her close friend and governess, dismissed, and Mary herself was sent to live at Hatfield in the household of the baby Princess, to whom she was to act as lady-in-waiting.

Mary openly sympathized with her mother and, despite the dangers, corresponded with her secretly. She refused to give up the title of Princess and at first resisted all the pressures put on her by the King and Thomas Cromwell (q.v.) to acknowledge her own bastardy. Henry, influenced by Anne and infuriated by what he called Mary's 'Spanish pride', subjected his daughter to one humiliation after another. But Mary regarded the new Queen as her most dangerous enemy; at one time she was convinced that Anne was planning to poison her. It is hardly surprising that her health suffered under the strain.

There were demonstrations of sympathy both for Catherine and for Mary, and she, like her mother, had an influential friend to whom she could turn for advice and consolation – Eustace Chapuys, the Imperial Ambassador. He devised a scheme to have her kidnapped and taken to Spain, but before this could be implemented, Mary was removed to Hunsdon, in Hertfordshire, where she fell seriously ill.

Catherine of Aragon died on 7 January 1536, and in May that year Anne Boleyn was executed. Henry now offered to pardon Mary if she would acknowledge that his marriage to her mother had been 'incestuous and unlawful'. Mary, taking the advice of her cousin, Charles V, at last yielded, thus admitting her own bastardy, an action which she much regretted later.

The King kept his word and gave his daughter a household and finances in keeping with her position. Renewed efforts were made to find a suitable marriage for her, but these proved fruitless. 'The Lady Mary', as she was called (she was not allowed to use the title of Princess), now had a valuable friend at court in Jane Seymour (q.v.), Henry's third wife. She was the first lady of the land after the Queen, and Jane interceded for her on many occasions. When the baby Prince Edward (see Edward VI) was born, Mary was made one of his godparents; at Jane's funeral a few days later she was the chief mourner.

Although allowed back at court, she was still considered as illegitimate, and it was not until after the King's marriage to Katherine Parr (q.v.) that by Act of Parliament (1544) the title of Princess was restored and she and her half-sister Elizabeth were granted succession to the throne after Edward and any other legitimate children that might still be born to Henry.

During the reign of her half-brother Edward VI, who succeeded on Henry's death in January 1547, Mary courageously resisted all attempts put on her by the Council to make her conform to the new Protestant Church of England. These were relatively quiet years for her, and for the most part she spent them studying and doing good works, dividing her time between the various properties settled on her by her father –

Hunsdon, Copt Hall in Essex, Kenninghall and Framlingham in Norfolk. Genuinely fond of her young brother, she skilfully enlisted the support of Charles V in order to continue to celebrate Mass in the old form without quarrelling with the King and so endangering her life.

Early in July 1553 news reached her that the King was desperately ill. She was on her way to London to visit him, when she learned that Edward had died on 6 July, that Northumberland had proclaimed his newly-acquired daughter-in-law, the Lady Jane Grey (q.v.), as Queen, and that troops were being sent to intercept her. Mary swiftly turned tail and fled to Norfolk, where she rallied her own supporters and proclaimed herself as Queen. It was soon clear that the country was behind her; on 19 July the Lord Mayor of London proclaimed to a jubilant crowd that Mary was the rightful Queen. Northumberland was arrested and Lady Jane Grey imprisoned in the Tower, and a few days later Mary herself rode in triumph into London.

The reign began quietly enough. At thirty-seven, the new Queen showed that she had inherited not only her father's reddish hair but many of his other characteristics, especially his decided opinions and forceful manner; at first she seemed to favour moderation and went carefully. Taking up temporary residence in the Tower, as was customary for a new sovereign before her coronation, she immediately released all those Catholics who had been imprisoned there during the reigns of Henry VIII and Edward VI, among them Stephen Gardiner (q.v.) and the Duke of Norfolk (see Howard, Thomas, 3rd Duke). She also released the father of Lady Jane Grey and some others who had been arrested for bearing arms against her. Northumberland and his confederates were brought to trial in August; out of seven, only he and two others were executed.

Inexperienced in government, Mary relied heavily on Stephen Gardiner and on advice from Charles V. Her greatest aim was to restore Catholicism in England, and with this in mind she determined to marry Charles's son, the future Philip II of Spain (q.v.), who was eleven years her junior. When the first Parliament of the reign met in October 1553, there was no difficulty about repealing Edward's Act of Uniformity; the nobles, however, many of whom had acquired lands and wealth as a result of Henry's Dissolution of the Monasteries, vigorously opposed an enforcement of Catholic orthodoxy. The Commons sent a deputation imploring the Queen to marry an Englishman instead of Philip. 'My marriage is my own affair,' she is said to have retorted with true Tudor stubbornness, and in anger she speeded up the preparations for the ceremony.

Mary's coronation took place at Westminster on 30 November. Her union with Philip of Spain had been concluded by proxy the previous month, and once this became generally known, discontent and conspiracy mounted in various parts of the country. Early in 1554 a formidable rebellion led by the younger Sir Thomas Wyatt (q.v.), son of the poet, started in Kent and advanced rapidly on London. Mary, in an inspired and courageous speech at Guildhall, roused Londoners to resist; the rebels were duly quelled, and Wyatt and his supporters executed. But following her marriage to Philip at Winchester on 25 July 1554, violence again erupted and feelings were much inflamed by the circulation of seditious anti-Spanish pamphlets of Protestant origin.

In November 1554 the exiled Reginald Pole (q.v.), now a cardinal, returned to England as Papal Legate in order to receive the country back into the Roman Catholic Church. He was welcomed by the Queen and appointed Archbishop of Canterbury. On 30 November he solemnly absolved the government and country from their apostasy; within a short time he was virtually running the government. Under his guidance, Parliament repealed the earlier anti-papal legislation of Henry VIII and Edward VI, re-enacted the old heresy laws, and passed some new – and far more severe – treason laws. The first martyr, John Rogers (q.v.), was burned in February 1555, and in the ensuing three years nearly 300 heretics were sent to their death at the stake, earning their sovereign the nickname of 'Bloody Mary'.

Hatred of Mary and of her husband was apparent in every corner of the kingdom as a result of the vicious persecution. The King's Spanish courtiers were insulted, and many went home; Philip, following a recall to Brussels by his father to take over the government of the Low Countries in the late summer of 1555, used every possible excuse to prolong his absence. He returned in March 1557 with the sole purpose of getting England to declare war on France; this achieved, three months later he left for the Continent. Mary never saw him again.

She was broken-hearted and in ill-health. During the first year of their marriage Mary had fallen passionately in love with her fair-haired, Hapsburg husband. She longed above all else to give birth to a Catholic heir to the throne; in November 1554 she had announced happily that she was with child, but it had proved a false pregnancy; the truth was that she had an ovarian tumour and symptoms of dropsy.

In January 1558 she suffered a severe blow in the loss of Calais, England's last stronghold on the Continent, which made her more unpopular than ever. Lonely and depressed, in April Mary again deluded herself into believing that she was pregnant, but this time she did not make any public announcement. Inevitably, her disappointment at yet another false pregnancy was intense, and that autumn the Queen slipped gradually into her last illness. An old, pain-ridden woman at the age of forty-two, her brain was seized with strange fancies as the fatal disease gained ascendancy. She fretted about her successor to the throne; she asked for Philip, but he, pleading pressure of state business, sent a representative instead to press the Queen to acknowledge the Princess Elizabeth as her heir. Too weary at the last to do anything but accede, and miserable in the knowledge that everything she had struggled for would now be undone, Mary died early in the morning of 17 November 1558. She was buried in Westminster Abbey.

Of Mary's conduct as Queen the most charitable comment that can be made is that it was governed by excessive religious zeal. She was more merciful to those who plotted treason against her than to the Protestants who adhered to their religious beliefs. Blame for the Marian persecutions must rest largely on the Queen, on Cardinal Pole, and bishops like Gardiner and Bonner (see Bonner, Edmund). She was not cruel or merciless by nature, but rather a woman who desperately wanted love, children, and a happy family life, all of which were denied to her. More Spanish than English, Mary antagonized the growing English nationalism of the period by her marriage to a Spaniard and by restoring England to the Roman Catholic Church; these were her two gravest mistakes and her downfall. A convinced reactionary, she wanted to put the clock back where it had long ceased to be.

F. Madden, *Privy Purse Expenses of the Princess Mary, daughter of King Henry the Eighth, afterwards Queen Mary* [with a memoir] (1831).

H. F. M. Prescott, *A Spanish Tudor: The Life of 'Bloody Mary'* (rev. ed. 1953).

J. Ridley, *The Life and Times of Mary Tudor* (1974).

B. M. I. White, *Mary Tudor* (1935).

*Portraits:* drawing, by Holbein, *c.* 1535–40: Royal Collection, Windsor; oil on panel, by Master John, 1544: National Portrait Gallery, London; electrotype of medal by Jacopo de Trezzo, *c.* 1555: N.P.G.; oil, by Antonio Mor, probably 1554: autograph versions at Prado, Madrid, Castle Ashby (Marquess of Northampton), and Isabella Stewart Gardner Museum, Boston, U.S.A.; oil, by unknown artist: Royal Collection, Windsor; miniature, oil on wood, by unknown artist, after Mor: N.P.G.; oil miniature, by unknown artist: Kunsthistorisches Museum, Vienna; oil on panel, with Philip, by unknown artist, 1557: Woburn Abbey (Duke of Bedford); miniature, by Hans Eworth: Duke of Buccleuch and Queensbury; oil, half length, by Eworth, 1554: location unknown (formerly Lord Latimer Collection); oil, by Eworth, 1554: Society of Antiquaries, London; oil, by Eworth, 1557: private collection, New York; oil, three-quarter length, by Eworth: Colonel J. C. Wynne-Finch; miniature, oil on wood, by unknown artist after Mor: N.P.G.; numerous other versions elsewhere.

## Mary, Queen of Scots (1542–1587), Queen of Scotland, 1542–67.

Mary was the third and only surviving child of James V (q.v.) and his French wife, Marie de Guise (q.v.), whose two sons had died in infancy in 1541, and the great-granddaughter of Henry VII (q.v.). She was born at Linlithgow on 8 December 1542. When the news of her birth was brought to her father, already in despair after the defeat of the Scots at Solway Moss, he is said to have remarked, 'It cam wi' a lass, it'll pass wi' a lass', meaning the union of the crown and the house of Stewart; he then turned his face to the wall to die.

James's death on 14 December made Mary Queen of Scotland at the age of six days. Her minority was thus of unprecedented length. Initially the Earl of Arran (see Hamilton, James, 2nd Earl; later Duke of Châtelherault), after a brief power struggle with Cardinal David Beaton (q.v.), Archbishop of St Andrews, was appointed Governor or Regent. Almost immediately Henry VIII (q.v.) began to negotiate for Mary's marriage to his son, Prince Edward, later Edward VI (q.v.); he tried unsuccessfully to secure control of her, but under the Treaties of Greenwich it was agreed that Mary would be sent to the English court at the age of ten, and that in the meanwhile she was to remain in the care of her mother. She was crowned at Stirling Castle in 9 September 1543.

After the defeat of the Scots by the English at Pinkie Cleugh in September 1547, the influence of Marie de Guise greatly increased; in July 1548 she won permission to send Mary to France to be educated at the court of Henri II and Catherine de' Medici (q.v.). When Arran resigned the regency in April 1554, Marie de Guise was appointed in his place.

Mary grew up under the influence of the French court and the powerful Guise family in an atmosphere of luxury and gaiety; educated in French and in the Roman Catholic religion, she developed into a tall, slender beauty with a taste for music and poetry, and very much more a Frenchwoman than a Scot. On 24 April 1558 she was married to the sickly Dauphin of France, later François II; in secret documents signed before the ceremony she bequeathed her kingdom to that of France, should she die without issue. When Henri II died the following year, she became briefly Queen consort of France; but the premature death of François in 1560, probably before their marriage had been consummated, left Mary a widow at the age of eighteen.

Meanwhile, in England, where Elizabeth I (q.v.) had come to the throne in 1558, the Catholics regarded the Queen as illegitimate and looked on Mary, Queen of Scots as their lawful sovereign through her descent from Margaret Tudor (q.v.), daughter of Henry VII. Before his death Mary's father-in-law had claimed the English throne on her behalf and encouraged her and François to quarter the arms of England with their own. Elizabeth refused to acknowledge Mary as heir and not unnaturally viewed the Queen of Scots' return to her kingdom with hostility.

Mary had little choice but to return to Scotland; Marie de Guise had died in 1560, and at the French court her jealous mother-in-law was making life intolerable. Arriving at Leith on 19 August 1561, however, she soon discovered that her French upbringing had scarcely fitted her to cope with her native kingdom, where the Reformation under John Knox (q.v.) was in full swing and the feuding nobility maintained a constant state of turbulence. She took the advice of her Protestant half-brother, the Earl of Moray (see Stewart, Lord James), and promised a conciliatory policy in religious matters, insisting only upon her personal right to celebrate Mass within the court; privately she told the Pope that she meant to restore Catholicism to Scotland. Determined to capture the English throne, she refused to ratify the Treaty of Edinburgh unless Elizabeth would acknowledge her succession; a meeting between the two Queens, proposed for September 1562, was postponed by Elizabeth and never took place.

Mary's next objective was marriage. She refused the Earl of Arran (see

Hamilton, James, 3rd Earl) and various other foreign suitors; negotiations begun with a view to her marrying Don Carlos, son of Philip II of Spain (q.v.), were broken off in 1564 when he became insane. Then Elizabeth curiously nominated her own favourite, the Earl of Leicester (see Dudley, Robert). Early in 1565, however, Mary fell in love with her cousin, Lord Darnley (see Stewart, Henry), son of the Earl of Lennox (see Stewart, Matthew). She married him on 29 July 1565, and in so doing antagonized not only her own subjects but also Elizabeth, who viewed with displeasure Mary's choice of another Tudor descendant. In August that year the Queen of Scots drove Moray and other rebellious lords across the border after their revolt known as the Chaseabout Raid.

Having lost the support of Moray, the Queen now turned increasingly to her French secretary, David Riccio (q.v.), for advice. The latter was much disliked at court, where those who had sympathized with Moray's rebellion but not actively participated in it now banded together in a plot to get rid of the man whom they regarded as a foreign usurper. Darnley, already resentful that Mary had not granted him the crown matrimonial, and incensed by the clever suggestion put to him that Riccio was his wife's lover and that the child she was carrying was not his own, readily co-operated in the conspiracy. Riccio was murdered in the presence of the Queen on the evening of 9 March 1566 at Holyroodhouse, and Mary was held prisoner by the Earl of Morton (see Douglas, James) and his followers. Surprisingly, she did not miscarry, but escaped with Darnley to the castle of Dunbar, from where, with the help of the Earl of Bothwell (see Hepburn, James) and other supporters, she returned in triumph to Edinburgh. On 19 June she gave birth to a son, the future James VI of Scotland (q.v.; later James I of England).

For some time previously Mary had been aware of Darnley's shortcomings; her attitude towards him now was one of contempt and revulsion, coupled with the suspicion that he had aimed at her life. Their relations were not in any way improved by the birth of their son, and in the autumn of 1566 she seriously contemplated a divorce. It has long been disputed whether Mary was then involved in an adulterous liaison with Bothwell (the Casket Letters supposedly written to him by the Queen are considered to be of dubious authenticity); but it is certain that she had been assured by those close to her that some 'outgait' would be devised to free her from the Darnley marriage. It is also possible that by early 1567 Mary knew herself to be pregnant again; it was common knowledge that she had not cohabited with Darnley for some time, and it may have been in an attempt to cover up the truth that she now brought

her husband to convalesce, after an illness thought to be syphilis, at a house at Kirk o' Field, on the outskirts of Edinburgh, promising to resume marital relations with him as soon as he had recovered; Antonia Fraser, in her biography of Mary, believes, however, that she may have conceived as late as April. At any rate the house at Kirk o' Field was blown up on the night of 9 February, and Darnley was murdered attempting to escape after the explosion.

There is no proof that Mary was a party to the crime, but her behaviour in the next few months was somewhat strange: popular opinion suspected Bothwell of the deed and the Queen of foreknowledge of it, yet she showered favours on the Earl, allowed him to abduct her and carry her off to Dunbar; on 15 May she married him in the Chapel of Holyroodhouse, in accordance with Protestant rites. By this marriage she forfeited not only the last remaining support of her own subjects, but that of the rest of Europe.

On 15 June 1567 Mary and Bothwell were confronted by their enemies at Carberry Hill, near Musselburgh. The opposing force was led by Morton, who refused Bothwell's suggestion that the issue should be decided by single combat. Dejection and lack of enthusiasm among the Queen's party forced Mary's surrender. She gave in on condition that Bothwell was allowed to escape; she herself was escorted into Edinburgh as a prisoner to the accompaniment of angry shouts from the citizens of 'Burn the whore! Burn the murderess!' At Morton's suggestion she was not put to death, but imprisoned on the island of Lochleven, where a few weeks later she miscarried of twins. On 24 July she signed papers of abdication in favour of her one-year-old son James.

Mary made one last attempt to regain

the throne. Escaping from Lochleven on 2 May 1568, she revoked her abdication and rallied her supporters to meet the force led by her half-brother, the Earl of Moray, who was now Regent. She was utterly defeated at Langside, near Glasgow, on 13 May and fled to England four days later, throwing herself on the mercy of Elizabeth. The English Queen, using a number of excuses connected with the murder of Darnley, refused to send her back to Scotland, but held her cousin in captivity, in various places, for the next eighteen years.

During her long imprisonment Mary's great solace was her religion. She occupied herself with embroidery and writing poetry, but her health suffered as a result of lack of physical exercise, and her beauty faded rapidly. At first she devoted all her energies to securing her release, but when this proved fruitless she resorted to conspiracy. As the one hope of the English Catholics who sought to get rid of Elizabeth as Queen, Mary was at the centre of practically every plot to that end. She agreed to the plan for her marriage to the Duke of Norfolk (see Howard, Thomas, 4th Duke), and was aware of the plot of Roberto di Ridolfi (q.v.) which was linked to it; she also conspired with Francis Throckmorton (q.v.) in the scheme devised by the Duc de Guise for an invasion of England by the Catholic powers of Europe. In July 1586 the interception by Sir Francis Walsingham (q.v.) of correspondence between the captive Queen of Scots and Anthony Babington (q.v.), in which Mary gave her approval to a plot in which Elizabeth would be assassinated, finally brought about her tragic end. On 21 September she was taken from Chartley to Fotheringay Castle, where her trial began on 15 October; ten days later the commissioners meeting at the Star Chamber in Westminster passed sentence of death on her, deeming that so long as Mary lived the safety of Elizabeth would remain in peril.

James VI lodged only the most formal of protests; even so, Elizabeth refused for a long time to sign her cousin's death warrant. Finally she did so, and Mary was beheaded in the Great Hall at Fotheringay on 8 February 1587, going to her death with great dignity. Elizabeth afterwards maintained that she had never intended the execution to take place. Buried at first at Peterborough, the body of the Queen of Scots was in 1612 taken to its final resting-place in a sumptuous tomb in Westminster Abbey built at the command of her son, then James I of England.

Aptly described by Elizabeth as 'the daughter of debate', Mary, Queen of Scots, a controversial figure during her lifetime, is still the subject of furious argument. A romantic and tragic character to some, to others she is a schemer and adultress. In the words of Caroline Bingham, she 'accepted the challenge of a difficult inheritance, played a dangerous political game, made several disastrous mistakes and lost'.

Mary's own account of her life, dictated to her secretary, Claude Nau, during her captivity, has been edited by J. Stevenson and published in English (Edinburgh, 1883). The collected edition of her letters, *Lettres, Instructions et Mémoires de Marie Stuart*, is by A. Labanoff (7 vols; Paris, 1844); a selection of these have been edited and translated by W. B. Turnbull in *Letters of Mary Stuart* (1845). A further volume of Mary's writings is P. Stewart Mackenzie, *Queen Mary's Book* (1905).

Antonia Fraser, *Mary, Queen of Scots* (1969).
M. Tannenbaum, *Marie Stuart: Bibliography* (3 vols; 1944).
See also Chapter 8 of Caroline Bingham, *The Stewart Kingdom of Scotland, 1371–1603* (1974).

*Portraits*: drawing, by unknown artist, 1552: Musée Condé, Chantilly; drawing, by François Clouet, *c.* 1560: Bibliothèque Nationale, Paris; drawing, the '*Deuil Blanc*' portrait, by F. Clouet, *c.* 1560: B.N.; (paintings of this type at National Portrait Gallery, London; Scottish National Portrait Gallery, Edinburgh; in the Royal Collection; and elsewhere); miniature, by unknown artist, *c.* 1560–5: Uffizi Gallery, Florence (a later version at Mauritshuis, The Hague); double portrait with Darnley, by unknown artist: Hardwick Hall (National Trust); oil, by unknown artist: N.P.G.; oil, double portrait with James VI: The Duke of Atholl; medal, by Sacopo Primavera, 1572: British Museum, London (electrotypes at S.N.P.G. and N.P.G.); miniature, *c.* 1575–80, by unknown artist: St Mary's College, Blairs, Aberdeen; oil, by unknown artist after Hilliard: The Marquess of Salisbury; oil, by unknown artist after Hilliard, *c.* 1610: N.P.G.; oil, full length, by unknown artist: St Mary's College, Blairs, Aberdeen; tomb effigy by Cornelius and William Cure: Westminster Abbey, London. N.B. There are numerous other versions in circulation, but many are false. See L. Cust, *Notes on the Authentic Portraits of Mary, Queen of Scots* (1903) and Roy Strong, *Tudor and Jacobean Portraits*, vol. i (1969), pp. 219–23.

**Mary Tudor** (1496–1533), Queen of France, Duchess of Suffolk.

Mary was the second daughter of Henry VII (q.v.) and Elizabeth of York (q.v.), and was born probably in early March 1496. Under the Treaty of Calais of December 1507 she was betrothed to the Prince of Castile, the future Emperor Charles V (q.v.). The marriage was to have taken place when Charles reached the age of fourteen, but when that time came the Prince's grandfather, the Emperor Maximilian I, had set his sights elsewhere and cunningly withdrew from the contract. Mary's brother, now Henry VIII (q.v.), immediately conceived another politically advantageous match for her. With the aid of Thomas Wolsey (q.v.) he made peace with France and forced Mary, then eighteen years old, to marry the frail fifty-two-year-old Louis XII of France.

Mary had already fallen in love with the Duke of Suffolk (see Brandon, Charles), and she agreed to marry the French King only on the condition that were he to die she should be free to marry whom she chose.

The marriage was celebrated at Abbeville on 9 October 1514, and on 5 November the same year Mary was crowned Queen of France. Less than two months later, on 1 January 1515, Louis died, leaving her in a vulnerable position alone in France. Dreading another political marriage forced on her either by Henry or by the new King of France, François I, Mary persuaded Suffolk to break his promise to Henry not to marry her without his consent, and they were married secretly in Paris, probably at the end of February 1515. Henry was furious with Suffolk, but after Wolsey had interceded for him the King was ultimately placated by the promise of large sums of money (part of Mary's dowry from Louis) and the gift of all her jewels and plate, and the marriage was solemnized publicly at Greenwich on 13 May 1515.

Mary was the King's favourite sister, and his anger over the marriage did not last; although she and Suffolk lived for the most part a happy and private life, she was often at court. She bore her husband three children: a son, born in 1516, who died young, and two daughters, one of whom, Frances, born in 1517, was to marry Henry Grey, 3rd Marquess of Dorset, and to become the mother of Lady Jane Grey (q.v.).

In 1520 Mary was present at the Field of the Cloth of Gold when a treaty was made with François I restoring to her the greater part of her remaining dowry. Her relations with Henry deteriorated after 1527, however, when she sided with Catherine of Aragon (q.v.) in the matter of the divorce. She refused to see the King's mistress, Anne Boleyn (q.v.), whose sister Mary had been one of her ladies-in-waiting, and had the courage to stand up to Henry in 1532 when he wanted her to accompany him and Anne to a meeting with François I.

Mary died at Westthorpe, Suffolk, on 24 June 1533, and was buried in the Abbey of Bury St Edmunds.

M. C. Brown, *Mary Tudor, Queen of France* (1911).
M. A. E. Green, *Lives of the Princesses of England*, vol. v (6 vols; 1849–55).

*Portrait*: oil, Mary with Charles Brandon, Duke of Suffolk, by unknown artist: the Duke of Bedford Collection, Woburn Abbey.

**Medici, Catherine de'** (1519–1589), see Catherine de' Medici.

**Melville, Andrew** (1545–1622), Scottish Presbyterian leader and scholar.

Andrew Melville was born at Baldovie, Forfarshire, on 1 August 1545, the youngest child of Richard and Gills Melville. His father was killed at the Battle of Pinkie, and following the death of his mother shortly afterwards, Andrew was brought up by his eldest brother Richard and his wife. The whole family was devoted to the reformed religion, and three of his brothers, Richard, James, and John, entered the ministry.

Melville was educated at Montrose grammar school and at St Mary's College, St Andrews, which he entered in 1559, graduating in 1564. He had learned Greek at Montrose and may also have had private tuition from George Buchanan (q.v.) while at St Andrews. Between 1564 and 1566 he studied at the University of Paris, where he came under the influence of Peter Ramus. By 1566, when he left Paris for Poitiers in order to study law, he was fluent in Greek, Latin, and Hebrew, and had a knowledge of mathematics and philosophy. At Poitiers, he became regent in the College of St Marceon, but fell under suspicion as a Protestant during the siege of the town by the Huguenots in 1568, and the following year he went to Geneva; he was welcomed by the Protestant reformer, Theodore Beza, and given a teaching position at the Genevan academy.

In 1573 Melville published his first volume of Latin verse. Then, responding to appeals from Scotland to return and devote himself to raising the standard of education there, he resigned from the academy and travelled via Paris to Edinburgh, armed with a testimonial from Beza to the General Assembly. He turned down a post in the household of the Regent, the Earl of Morton (see Douglas, James), for which Buchanan recommended him, and spent the next three months at Baldovie, supervising the studies of his nephew James.

In the autumn of 1574 he was appointed as Principal of the University of Glasgow, a post which he held until 1580, when he became Principal of St Mary's College at St Andrews. In both these posts, and in the part he played in the formation of the new University of Aberdeen in 1575, Melville introduced educational reforms on Continental lines, including the promotion of Greek studies and philosophy, and as a result attracted an influx of students from abroad, many of whom later returned to Europe to teach in the growing number of Reformed institutions.

Soon after his return to Scotland, Melville took over the leadership of the Reformed Church, which had been left in abeyance following the death of John Knox (q.v.) in 1572. He was determined to stamp out all remaining forms of episcopacy, to establish presbyteries, and to preserve the independence of the Church from state control. In February 1584 he was brought before the Privy Council on a charge of treason in a sermon preached the previous June; when he protested and demanded to be tried by an ecclesiastical court, he was ordered to be imprisoned for contempt. Friends helped him to escape to Berwick, from where he went to London and attempted to enlist support at the English court for the Scottish Presbyterian movement. He was back in Scotland the following year, and in 1592 the *Second Book of Discipline* (1581), which had been largely his work, was incorporated in the 'Golden Act' of religious settlement.

By 1596 however the tide was turning against Presbyterianism. Melville strongly resisted the King's attempts to go back on his charter. Telling James that he was merely 'God's sillie vassal' (i.e. God's simple servant), he expressed his views concerning the supremacy of the Kirk over the State, the 'two Kingdoms' he told James existed in Scotland. But the King, skilfully using his powers over the Assembly in regard to their meetings, succeeded eventually in getting the Kirk to accept episcopy, which was a blow to the Melvillian theocracy. In 1605 a crisis occurred when the General Assembly met in Aberdeen in defiance of royal orders, and Melville was amongst those ministers summoned to London in August 1606 to appear before the Council. He spoke in favour of a new assembly, but ruined his case by a satirical Latin poem on the Anglican ritual and a derisory remark about the Archbishop's robes, which he termed 'Romish rags'; the post of Principal of St Mary's College was declared vacant and he was sent to the Tower.

Although Melville sent an apology to the King in 1608, his release was effected only in April 1611, when he was offered the chair of biblical theology at the university of Sédan, France. He remained at Sédan until his death in 1612.

Andrew Melville is considered to have been too rigid a theorist and too outspoken in his views to be a good leader. Through his insistence on a hierarchy of courts rather than bishops, under his leadership the Scottish Reformed Church acquired its Presbyterian character. His greatest achievement was undoubtedly the reform of the Scottish universities, which won him international recognition and brought foreign students to Scotland for the first time. As a Latin poet Melville has been ranked next to Buchanan.

T. McCrie, *Life of Andrew Melville* (2 vols; Edinburgh, 1819; rev. ed. 1899).

*Portrait*: engraving, by unknown artist: Scottish National Portrait Gallery, Edinburgh.

**Mildmay, Sir Walter** (?1520–1589), Chancellor of the Exchequer.

The youngest son of Thomas Mildmay of Chelmsford and his wife Agnes, Walter Mildmay was born in about 1520. He was educated at Christ's College, Cambridge, but left without taking a degree to accept employment under his father in the Court of Augmentation. He became one of the two Surveyors-General of that Court in 1546, when he entered Gray's Inn.

Knighted in February 1547, Mildmay was appointed revenue commissioner the same year. He soon proved himself to be an able financier. During the reign of Edward VI (q.v.) he held commissions to examine the mint accounts, to levy the King's debts, and to supervise the receipt by the crown of plate, jewellery and other resources from the dissolved monasteries. He had entered Parliament as Member for Lostwithiel as early as 1545 and was to represent Lewes in 1547, Maldon in 1552, Peterborough in 1553, and Northamptonshire from 1557 until his death. Although a Calvinist, Mildmay was towards the end of the reign of Mary I (q.v.) given the appointment of Treasurer of the forces sent to relieve Calais.

On the accession of Elizabeth I (q.v.) Mildmay became Treasurer of the Royal Household. His influence grew steadily, and among other commissions he was in 1560 directed to supervise the issue of a new coinage. In April 1566 he succeeded Sir Richard Sackville as Chancellor of the Exchequer, being at the same time appointed auditor of the Duchy of Lancaster. He had married Mary, sister of Sir Francis Walsingham (q.v.), and as the latter's brother-in-law and a friend of Sir William Cecil (q.v.), held a powerful position in the Privy Council and in Parliament. In 1572 he helped to prepare evidence against the Duke of Norfolk (see Howard, Thomas, 4th Duke). In 1586 he went to Fotheringay to inform Mary, Queen of Scots (q.v.), of her forthcoming trial, in which he participated as one of the commissioners. The suggestion put forward on several occasions that he should act as ambassador to Scotland came to nothing, due largely to his ill-health. Mildmay died at Hackney on 13 May 1589 and was buried in St Bartholomew's Church in the City.

Sir Walter Mildmay was greatly interested in education. He founded Emmanuel College at Cambridge, and was a governor of Chelmsford School and a benefactor to Christ's Hospital, London, Christ's College, Cambridge, and other educational institutions.

S. E. Lehmberg, *Sir Walter Mildmay and Tudor Government* (1964).

**Moray, 1st Earl of** (?1531–1570), see Stewart, Lord James.

**More, Sir Thomas** (1478–1535), statesman and author.

Born in Cripplegate, London, on 6 February 1478, Thomas More was the eldest son of John More and his first wife, Agnes Graunger; his father was then a rising lawyer of Lincoln's Inn, later to be knighted and made a judge of the King's Bench. As More himself later said, he came of 'no famous family but of honest stock'.

Thomas received his early education at St Anthony's School in Threadneedle Street, in the City, and at the age of twelve he was placed in the household of the Lord Chancellor and Archbishop of Canterbury, John Morton (q.v.), where he remained for about two years. In 1492 he went to Oxford, probably to Canterbury College (later Christ Church), and came under the influence of exponents of the 'new learning', William Grocyn (q.v.) and Thomas Linacre (q.v.). At the university More studied Latin, French, music, and theology, but did not begin Greek until a few years later, after he had returned to London; he also developed literary talents, experimenting in poetry and drama.

In 1494 his father sent More to the Inns of Court. Initially he was at New Inn, but in about 1496 he transferred to Lincoln's Inn, where he was called to the bar and became brilliantly successful in a short space of time. More now underwent a spiritual crisis, in which he contemplated entering the priesthood; for some years he lived, without taking vows, among the monks of Charterhouse, sharing as much as possible of their religious devotions. In 1503 he finally decided against taking holy orders, but the routines of early rising, prayer, and fasting, as well as wearing a hair shirt, were continued for the rest of his life.

During these early years in London More became intimate with John Colet (q.v.), through whom he was introduced to the Dutch humanist, Desiderius

Erasmus (q.v.), when the latter visited England in 1499. More was to become Erasmus's closest friend, and it was through the Dutchman that he was drawn into the circle of scholars who were seeking to resuscitate original Latin, Greek, and Hebrew texts. Under their influence More took up the study of Greek, with Grocyn and Linacre as his tutors; he was to prove one of the most ardent humanists of the group.

In 1504 he was elected to Parliament, and towards the end of that year, or early in 1505, he married Jane Colt, daughter of a gentleman farmer of Netherhall in Essex. Barely seventeen at the time of her marriage, Jane bore her husband a son and three daughters. More was at this period translating from the Latin the life of the early Italian humanist, Giovanni Pico della Mirandola. At his house in Bucklersbury, alongside the Thames, in the City, he played host to the eminent scholars of the day, including Erasmus, who stayed with More in 1505 and again in 1509. On the first of these visits the two men competed with one another in

translating the works of Lucian, the Greek satirist; during the second Erasmus wrote his *In Praise of Folly* and likened the More household to Plato's Academy on a Christian footing.

The death of Henry VII (q.v.) in April 1509 improved More's prospects. Under the new monarch, Henry VIII (q.v.), his talents as a lawyer and negotiator were soon to be noticed and rewarded. In 1509 he represented a number of London companies in important negotiations with the Antwerp merchants, and the following year he was elected an Under-Sheriff of the City, an office which he held for the next seven years.

In 1511 More's wife died. He remarried a few weeks later, Alice Middleton, a widow seven years older than himself, with a son and daughter of her own; she was to prove a good mother to his children and a competent, if somewhat unsympathetic, wife. At about this time the More household moved from Bucklersbury to Crosby Place in Bishopsgate Street. As a Justice of the Peace and a Reader at Lincoln's Inn, More was immersed in his public and legal work during the next few years; he was also working on his *History of Richard III*, in both a Latin and an English version. Another preoccupation was his growing fear of where the policies of Henry VIII and Thomas Wolsey (q.v.) would lead.

In May 1515 he was sent on a mission to Flanders with Cuthbert Tunstall (q.v.), the future Bishop of London, and while he was abroad he began to write his literary masterpiece, *Utopia*. Written in Latin for the benefit of his humanist friends, and published at Louvain in December 1516, it was a forthright attack on the evils of society disguised in the witty fantasy of the 'Isle of Nowhere', a mythical island in the New World. It was greeted with acclaim throughout the cultivated world of Europe.

During the next few years More urged on the return to humanist, especially Greek, studies advocated by Erasmus. His letter to the university authorities at Oxford, of March 1518, repelling reactionary tendencies there, was a brilliantly argued case for the place of humanistic learning in society.

Meanwhile he was being drawn into the royal service. In May 1517 he had helped to quell a riot of London apprentices, and in the autumn of that year he favourably impressed the King by his handling of negotiations with the French at Calais and Boulogne. When Henry insisted that he became a Privy Councillor in 1518, More had no choice but to obey; he resigned from the office of Under-Sheriff and pledged himself to further the causes of peace and reform to which, at that moment, both the King and Wolsey appeared to be inclined.

More rose rapidly in the King's estimation. He was present with Henry at the Field of the Cloth of Gold in 1520 and in that year and 1521 he took part in important negotiations with Charles V and the Hansa merchants in Calais and Bruges. Already Master of the Court of Requests, he was knighted and appointed Under-Treasurer of the Exchequer in May 1521. The execution of the Duke of Buckingham (see Stafford, Edward, 3rd Duke of Buckingham) that year gave him a warning of the brutal side of Henry's character and also of the King's desperation over the lack of a male heir. He acted as adviser when Henry wrote his *Assertion of the Seven Sacraments* in reply to Martin Luther (q.v.) and subsequently took up the quarrel on the King's behalf, writing, under the pseudonym of Gulielmus Rosseus, a bitter attack entitled *Responsio ad Lutherum* (1523).

In April 1523 More became Speaker of the House of Commons, where he made an eloquent plea for freedom of debate and speech. Wolsey was forced to bully Parliament into voting the funds for Henry's war with France. In a mood of despondency about the political, economic, and religious situation, More had the previous year started to write *The Four Last Things*, a meditation on death, doom, pain, and joy, which he was never to finish.

At about this date More moved his family to Chelsea. The Great House which he had built there included a chapel and a library where he hoped to be able to pursue his philosophical, literary, and devotional occupations undisturbed. In 1524 he was appointed High Steward of Oxford University, and of Cambridge the following year. In 1525 he was made Chancellor of the Duchy of Lancaster. Among the foreign guests he welcomed at Chelsea at this period was the painter, Hans Holbein the younger (q.v.), a friend of Erasmus, who executed portraits of the More family.

Far from being able to pursue his literary work, as he rose higher in the royal service More found himself at the King's beck and call at all hours, frequently required to bear urgent dispatches to and from the royal hunting palaces and Wolsey's London residences, or retained by Henry to discuss all manner of subjects until the early hours. In 1527, when the King first broached the question of a possible divorce from Catherine of Aragon (q.v.), More tried not to be drawn into it; but soon the issue became unavoidable.

In the summer of 1527 More accompanied Wolsey on his unsuccessful mission to try to persuade the French to declare war on Charles V (q.v.). Two years later, he went with Cuthbert Tunstall, then Bishop of London, to

Cambrai, where they succeeded in getting England included in the peace treaty between France and the Emperor. Wolsey, in disgrace on account of his failure to obtain a divorce for the King and his foreign policy, now in ruins, was dismissed; he surrendered the Great Seal on 19 October 1529, and six days later More became Lord Chancellor in his place.

As Chancellor, More carried out his legal duties with the utmost integrity and speed. Increasingly, however, in the next two years he found himself out of sympathy both with the King's determination to secure a divorce and with the anti-clerical movement in Parliament. He regarded Catherine as Henry's true wife and he decided to stand by her and the old faith; furthermore, he was not willing for a national Parliament to overrule the spiritual supremacy of the Pope. Although obliged to voice the opinion of the universities of Oxford and Cambridge favourable to the divorce, More declined to sign the letter sent by the English prelates and nobility to the Pope in 1530 urging him to grant the King's request. He tried to resign in February 1531, when the clergy acknowledged Henry as Supreme Head of the Church in England, but the King would not let him go until More pleaded ill-health; he finally relinquished his office on 16 May 1532.

During the next two years More lived very modestly, devoting all his energies to writing his controversial works for the old faith. He had been commissioned by Tunstall in 1528 to refute the writings of the English reformers, and in the years 1529–33 he published seven works on the subject, the best known being A Dialogue concerning Heresies (1528) and the Apology (1533). His most scathing attacks were directed against William Tyndale (q.v.), whose translations of the New Testament had begun to circulate in England

in 1526; when Tyndale replied with his Answer unto Thomas More's Dialogue in 1530, More counter-attacked with a Confutation (1532).

His refusal to attend the coronation of Anne Boleyn (q.v.) in June 1533 was courageous, for More must have known only too well the danger of incurring the King's wrath, especially now that Henry had a new adviser, Thomas Cromwell (q.v.), who was bent on subjecting the English Church to the authority of the crown. Within the next few months the campaign against him was mounted. An attempt was made to implicate More in the case against Elizabeth Barton (q.v.), the Maid of Kent, who had made prophecies against the King's divorce, and his name was included on her bill of attainder; but after More produced a letter he had written warning the Maid not to interfere in state matters, his name was struck out.

On 30 March 1534 Parliament passed the Act of Succession, requiring an oath to the succession of the children of Anne Boleyn. Summoned before the commissioners at Lambeth to take the oath on 13 April, More said that while he would accept Parliament's right to deal with the succession, he could not in conscience take an oath which repudiated the papal supremacy, nor would he acknowledge the Princess Elizabeth (see Elizabeth I) as legitimate. He was committed to the Tower a few days later, charged with high treason, and brought to trial at Westminster Hall on 1 July 1535. While in prison awaiting trial More wrote his masterpiece, A Dialogue of Comfort against Tribulacion. Efforts by his favourite daughter, Margaret, to persuade him to change his mind, and thus to save his life, were unsuccessful.

At the trial More defended himself ably, but was convicted on the questionable evidence of the Solicitor General, Sir

Richard Rich (q.v.), and sentenced to a traitor's death, subsequently changed by the King to death by beheading. The execution took place at Tower Hill on 6 July, when, on being led to the scaffold, More told the spectators that he was dying 'in the faith and for the faith of the Catholic Church, the King's good servant but God's first'. Europe was shocked at his death, and when the news reached Erasmus, he spoke of his old friend as a man 'whose soul was more pure than any snow, whose genius was such that England never had and never again will have its like'.

A resolute, disciplined man of high principles and steadfast faith who deliberately chose to follow the dictates of his conscience, even when this meant certain death, Thomas More was canonized in May 1935. Although his life and writings bore the stamp of medievalism, he was at the same time a reformer and humanist, but without the greed for riches of the 'new men'. He was a convinced persecutor of heretics, out of his fear that they would overthrow the old faith and order, but never quite the fierce persecutor alleged by John Foxe (q.v.); by the time the majority of persecutions took place, More's power had already dwindled and he was on the point of resignation. Popular among his contemporaries for his qualities of kindliness, hospitality, honesty, good humour, and ready wit, he was not only a man of genius but a saint.

Utopia, first published in 1516 and translated into English by Ralph Robinson in 1551, rapidly became one of the most popular works of the age; it was also translated into several European languages. The first folio English Works appeared in 1557, with a dedication to Queen Mary (see Mary I); editions of More's Latin works were published in Basle (1563), Louvain (1565), and Frankfurt (1689). William Roper, who had married More's daughter Margaret in about 1525, wrote his personal recollections of his father-in-law, which were printed in Paris in 1626 (see below), while More's great-grandson, Cresacre More, also wrote a biography, published in 1631. In the last years of the reign of Elizabeth I (q.v.) an anonymous group of English dramatists, who probably included Henry Chettle (q.v.), Thomas Heywood (see Lives of the Stuart Age), and, in a later revision, Thomas Dekker (see Lives of the Stuart Age) and William Shakespeare (q.v.), wrote a play, Sir Thomas More, based on the principal events in his life, but it was not performed.

The Complete Works of St Thomas More is in preparation at Yale University Press; at the time of writing (1976) fourteen volumes have been published. Two recent bibliographical studies are: R. W. Gibson and J. M. Patrick, St Thomas More: A Preliminary Bibliography of His Works and of Moreana to the Year 1750, published in 1961, and F. and M. P. Sullivan, Moreana: Materials for the Study of Saint Thomas More (5 vols; 1964–71). A convenient edition of Utopia is published in the Everyman's Library series, No. 461 (1910; revised edition 1951).

R. W. Chambers, Thomas More (1935).

Cresacre More, The Life and Death of Sir Thomas More (St Omer or Douai, 1631; edited by J. Hunter, London, 1828).

W. Roper, The Life, Arraignement and Death of ... Syr Thomas More (Paris, 1626; Everyman edition, 1963).

E. M. G. Routh, Sir Thomas More and his Friends (1934).

F. Seebohm, The Oxford Reformers (1867; Everyman edition, 1938).

Portraits: oil, by Hans Holbein the younger, 1527: Frick Collection, New York (several copies by unknown artists: National Portrait Gallery, London); drawing, by Holbein, for above portrait: Royal Collection, Windsor; oil, by

Rowland Lockey, 1593, copy of group painting of Sir Thomas More and his descendants by Holbein in 1527–8: N.P.G. (another version at Nostell Priory (Lord St Oswald) and a miniature by Lockey now in the collection of the Rev. and Mrs. J. E. Strickland, Jersey). For a full discussion of More portraits, see S. Morison and N. Barker, *The Likeness of Thomas More* (1963).

## Morley, Thomas (?1557–1603), organist and madrigal composer.

Little is known of Thomas Morley's early life, except that he studied under William Byrd (q.v.), probably while the latter was organist at Lincoln Cathedral. He may have become a Catholic under the influence of Byrd. From 1583 to 1587 Morley was Master of the Children at Norwich Cathedral. In 1588 he was admitted a Bachelor of Music at Oxford University. Soon afterwards he moved to London, where by 1589 he held the post of organist at St Giles, Cripplegate. In 1591 he became organist at St Paul's Cathedral.

Unlike Byrd, Morley did not adhere for long to the Catholic faith. When exactly he defected is uncertain, but in 1591 it is known that he was in the Netherlands engaged on espionage among the English Catholic exiles there. He nearly lost his life while on this mission, but eventually arrived home with valuable information for use against the Catholic party in England.

The following year, 1592, Morley was made a Gentleman of the Chapel Royal. He was to hold this appointment for the rest of his life, becoming in turn epistoler and gospeller. He also retained his post at St Paul's.

At about this time Morley became interested in the new vogue for madrigals, which had reached England from Italy. He began to compose his own songs, lightening the Italian style to suit English taste. In 1593 he published a collection of twenty-five canzonets for three voices; further songs for five and six voices appeared in 1597. In the meantime Morley's first set of madrigals (twenty-two in all) came out in 1594, and a collection of twenty *balletti* (ballads), modelled on the work of the Italian composer Gastoldi, in 1595. His text-book, dedicated to Byrd, entitled *A Plaine and Easie Introduction to Practicall Musicke* appeared in 1597. The following year he brought out a selection of English versions of Italian madrigals.

The monopoly held by William Byrd and Thomas Tallis (q.v.) for the printing and sale of music had by this time expired, and in September 1598 Morley was granted a licence for twenty-one years to print ruled music paper and song books in English, Latin, French, and Italian.

Ill-health was now beginning to overtake him, and he produced only one more volume of original compositions, *The First Booke of Ayres* (1600). Nevertheless he was able to edit the important collection of twenty-five madrigals written by various composers in praise of Oriana (generally thought to be Elizabeth I (q.v.)); entitled *The Triumphes of Oriana*, it appeared in 1601. Two years later both the Queen and Morley were dead.

Morley was at this time living in the parish of St Helen's, Bishopsgate, but illness forced him to lead a more and more solitary life. He resigned from the Chapel Royal probably towards the end of 1602. The exact date of the composer's death is not known, but it is believed to have occurred in September or early October. This conjecture is based on the fact that his widow was granted administration of his estate at the end of that month.

Thomas Morley was the first of the great English madrigalists. His compositions are of two distinct styles: that of the earlier, presumably Catholic, period, in which he was much influenced by Byrd, and the later Italianate madrigal style. To the first belong a number of fine Latin motets that have survived in manuscript. As a composer of the lighter type of canzonet or madrigal, Morley was unsurpassed. Among his most popular songs are the well-known 'Now is the month of maying' and 'It was a lover and his lass'. His textbook *A Plaine and Easie Introduction to Practicall Musicke*, which has been edited by R. A. Harman (1952), is a valuable source for musical history in England. Some examples of Morley's church music, and also pieces for the virginal, have survived in various printed and manuscript collections. The madrigals have been published in *The English Madrigal School*, volumes 1–4 and 32, edited by E. H. Fellowes (1913–24).

E. H. Fellowes, *The English madrigal composers* (2nd ed. 1948).

**Morton, 4th Earl of** (?1516–1581), see Douglas, James.

**Morton, John** (?1420–1500), statesman, Archbishop of Canterbury, and cardinal.

The eldest of five sons of Richard Morton and his wife Elizabeth, daughter of Richard Turburville, John Morton is believed to have been born in 1420, either at Milborne St Andrew or Bere Regis in Dorset. His father's family came from Nottingham.

Morton received his early education at the Benedictine Abbey at Cerne, before going to Balliol College, Oxford, to study law; there he also took holy orders. In 1446 he was one of the Vice-Chancellors, or commissaries, of that university. Probably at about that time he moved to London, where he practised as a lawyer, chiefly in the Court of Arches, and Henry VI (see *Lives Before*

*the Tudors*) made him a Privy Councillor and Chancellor of the Duchy of Cornwall. In the next few years Morton was granted a large number of ecclesiastical preferments, but did not reside in any of them. During the Wars of the Roses he supported the Lancastrians; after fighting in the Battle of Towton he escaped to Flanders, and on the accession of Edward IV (see *Lives Before the Tudors*) was declared a traitor and attainted. In the ten years he remained abroad, he attended Queen Margaret (see Margaret of Anjou in *Lives Before the Tudors*) and played an important role in achieving the coalition of certain disaffected Yorkists with the Lancastrians that was to drive Edward from the throne.

Morton returned to England with the Lancastrian party in September 1470, but after the decisive Battle of Tewkesbury he became reconciled with the Yorkists. Edward IV, on regaining his throne, reversed Morton's attainder and appointed him as Master of the Rolls. In 1474 the King sent him on an embassy to Hungary, and the following year he was one of the negotiators of the Treaty of Pecquiny with Louis XI of France. Morton was well rewarded for his services, both financially and by the grant of a number of prebends and archdeaconries. On his appointment as Bishop of Ely in 1479, he gave up the post of Master of the Rolls in order to devote himself to his religious duties; he also became tutor to the Prince of Wales (see Edward V in *Lives Before the Tudors*).

In 1483, after Richard of Gloucester (see Richard III in *Lives Before the Tudors*) had seized the throne, Morton was imprisoned first in the Tower and later at Brecon Castle, where he helped the Duke of Buckingham (see Stafford, Henry, 2nd Duke, in *Lives Before the Tudors*) to plan his abortive uprising of October that year. As the intermediary

337

between Buckingham and Sir Reginald Bray (q.v.) he gained the ear of the Countess of Richmond (see Beaufort, Margaret), mother of Henry Tudor, later Henry VII (q.v.), and may have been the first to suggest to her the marriage between Henry and Elizabeth of York (q.v.), Edward IV's daughter, as a means of ending the Yorkist-Lancastrian feud. After escaping from Brecon to Ely, and then to Flanders, he warned Henry Tudor that the Duke of Brittany would betray him to Richard III, and advised him to seek refuge at the French court.

On Henry's accession to the throne in 1485 Morton was summoned back to England. He became one of the King's most trusted councillors. Archbishop of Canterbury in 1486, Lord Chancellor in 1487, and a cardinal in 1493, he was, next to Henry, the most powerful man in the kingdom. As Head of the Church he determined to remedy the many abuses among the clergy and in the monasteries, and to this end the Archbishop embarked on a series of visitations. In order to fill the King's empty exchequer he and Bray together developed a system that was nothing less than extortionate when it came to extracting revenues due to the crown; Morton's 'Fork', or 'Crutch', of which he was traditionally the inventor, instructed commissioners levying benevolences to tell the wealthy that they could afford to contribute more and to accuse the thrifty or less well-off of concealing their riches.

One of the Cardinal's chief interests was building. During his period of office Morton made extensive repairs to many episcopal residences and other church properties; he built himself a palace at Hatfield (where Hatfield House now stands) and restored the bridge at Rochester, Kent; the canal he cut through the Fens in order to bring that part of the country into cultivation, known as 'Morton's Dyke', was to remain in use for over 200 years.

Archbishop Morton died on 15 September 1500 at Knole, in Kent. He had been Chancellor of Oxford University for the last five years of his life. Of all the advisers to Henry VII, he had been probably the most valuable; certainly he was the closest friend to the King. He had also borne the brunt of the unpopularity of the financial measures imposed on Henry's subjects. N.B. It is now generally believed that Sir Thomas More (q.v.), and not Morton, was the author of both the Latin and the English versions of *The History of Richard III*.

C. Jenkins, 'Cardinal Morton's Register', in R. W. Seton-Watson (ed.), *Tudor Studies* (1924).
R. I. Woodhouse, *The Life of John Morton, Archbishop of Canterbury* (1895).

**Mountjoy, 4th Baron** (d. 1534), see Blount, William.

**Mountjoy, 8th Baron** (1563–1606), see Blount, Charles.

# N

**Napier or Neper, John** (1550–1617), mathematician, see *Lives of the Stuart Age*.

**Nashe or Nash, Thomas** (1567–1601), dramatist and satirist.

Born at Lowestoft in 1567, the son of a minister or preacher, William Nashe, and his second wife, Margaret, Thomas Nashe was educated at St John's College, Cambridge, where he matriculated as a sizar in October 1582 and took his B.A. in 1586. He made a hurried tour through France and Italy, and some time before 1588 settled in London, resolved to make a livelihood by his pen.

He soon became intimate with Robert Greene (q.v.), Christopher Marlowe (q.v.), Thomas Lodge (q.v.), and other contemporary writers, and in 1589 he published his first work, *The Anatomie of Absurditie*, and also a preface to Greene's *Menaphon*, in which he launched a satirical attack on recent English literature. Next Nashe plunged into the Martin Marprelate controversy, his hatred of Puritanism unleashing a talent for sarcasm and brilliant abuse that was to become characteristic of his work. Under the pseudonym 'Pasquil' he is believed to have written *A Countercuffe given to Martin Junior* (August 1589), *The Returne of the renouned Cavaliero Pasquil of England* (October 1589), *The First Parte of Pasquils Apologie* (1590), and possibly also some of the other attacks on the Martinists; he was definitely the author of *An Almond for a Parrat*, published in 1590, but not, as was at one time thought, of *Pappe with an Hatchet*, which came from the pen of John Lyly (q.v.), with whom Nashe was associated in the controversy.

At about this time Nashe acquired the patronage of Sir George Carey, and for some months during a period of plague in London he lived at the latter's home in Surrey. All his life he was short of money, and he later made determined efforts to secure the patronage of both the Earl of Southampton (see Wriothesley, Henry) and Ferdinando Stanley, 5th Earl of Derby. Nashe's personality, however, resulted in his not retaining any one patron for very long. He wrote a preface to the unauthorized edition of Sidney's *Astrophil and Stella* (see Sidney, Sir Philip) in 1591, and accompanied it with a dedication to the poet's sister, the Countess of Pembroke, but the book was withdrawn from publication and re-issued minus Nashe's preface. In 1593 he is said to have worked as a hack writer in the employ of the printer John Danter.

By this time Nashe had become involved in his friend Greene's feud with the Harvey brothers. Richard Harvey had attacked Nashe's preface to *Menaphon*, and in 1591 Nashe replied to him in *A wonderful, strange, and miraculous Astrologicall Prognostication*; this was followed in 1592 by *Pierce Pennilesse his Supplication to the Divell*, in which Nashe satirized both Richard and Gabriel Harvey. In the ensuing exchange of pamphlets with Gabriel Harvey, Nashe wrote *Strange Newes of the Intercepting certaine Letters* (1593) and *Have with you to Saffron-Walden* (1596); eventually the controversy was brought to an end by order of the Archbishop of Canterbury in 1599.

In 1593 Nashe had published some religious reflections entitled *Christes Teares over Jerusalem*, in which he attacked contemporary society and warned that 'sinful' London would share the fate prophesied by Christ for Jerusalem. In *The Terrors of the Night* the following year he attacked demonology. Also in 1594 he published a tale of adventure, *The Unfortunate Traveller, or the Life of Jacke Wilton*, which was dedicated to the Earl of Southampton. Like most of his fellow writers of the age, Nashe tried his hand at poetry and at writing for the stage, but in his comedy *The Isle of Dogs* (1597) he attacked, and made personal reflections on current abuses in the state to such an extent that the theatre was closed and he was imprisoned in the Fleet for several months; the play has not survived. His masque *Summer's Last Will and Testament*, written in 1592 and first published in 1600, is extant and contains some fine lyrics. Nashe's last work, *Lenten Stuffe* (1599), in praise of the red herring, was written to repay hospitality and a loan he received at Yarmouth, where he is believed to have died some time during 1601, aged only thirty-four.

An eccentric personality, Thomas Nashe was the most original and inventive of prose writers, and so occupied a unique place in Elizabethan literature. His picaresque novel *The Unfortunate Traveller* was the first of its kind in England. For the complete writings see *The Works of Thomas Nashe*, edited by R. B. McKerrow (5 vols, 1904–10; revised edition by F. P. Wilson, 1958).

E. G. Harman, *Gabriel Harvey and Thomas Nashe* (1923).

*Portrait*: woodcut, in *The Trimming of T. Nashe Gentleman*, by Gabriel Harvey, 1597: British Museum, London.

**Norfolk, 2nd Duke of** (1443–1524), see Howard, Thomas, 2nd Duke.

**Norfolk, 3rd Duke of** (1473–1554), see Howard, Thomas, 3rd Duke.

**Norfolk, 4th Duke of** (1536–1572), see Howard, Thomas, 4th Duke.

**Norris, Sir John** (?1547–1597), military commander, known in later life as 'Black John'.

The second son of Henry, Baron Norris of Rycote, and his wife Marjorie, daughter of Lord Williams of Thame, John Norris was born in about 1547. His grandfather, Henry Norris, had been executed in 1536 as one of the alleged lovers of Anne Boleyn (q.v.).

The military life attracted John Norris at an early age, and after leaving university in 1571 he served under Admiral Coligny in France. Two years later he held a captaincy under Walter Devereux, 1st Earl of Essex, in Ireland. In the summer of 1577 he and his brothers crossed to the Low Countries to fight on behalf of William of Orange (q.v.) against the Spanish; John distinguished himself in this campaign both at Rymenant in August 1578 and at Steenwyk in February 1580. He remained in Friesland until March 1584, when he returned to England.

In July 1584 Norris was appointed Lord President of Munster. He served in that capacity until May the following year, when, on hearing that the Spaniards were besieging Antwerp, he transferred his powers to his brother Thomas in order to go to the aid of his former allies; he was appointed to command the army sent to Holland under the terms of a treaty concluded on 10 August between Queen Elizabeth (q.v.) and the States General. He was joined in December by another force under the superior command of the Earl of Leicester (see Dudley, Robert). Jealousy and dissension between the two men, combined with Leicester's inept leadership, rendered the campaign fruitless. Knighted after the victory at Grave in April 1586, in which he received a severe wound in the breast, Norris was recalled at the end of that year. The Queen treated him coolly as a result of his differences with Leicester, and in the autumn of 1587 Norris was again sent to the Low Countries, where he served for a few months under Lord Willoughby de Eresby (see Bertie, Peregrine). By the beginning of 1588, however, he was needed in England.

During the preparations against the threatened Spanish Armada that summer, Norris acted as marshal of the military camp at Tilbury, under Leicester; he was also in charge of preparations in Kent, with particular responsibility for the fortifications at Dover. He took no active part in the fighting against the Armada, but afterwards, in October, Norris was sent as ambassador to the States General to thank them for their help in defeating the Spaniards and to discuss further measures to be taken.

In April 1589 Norris was given the joint command with Sir Francis Drake (q.v.) of the expedition whose aim was to destroy enemy shipping off the coasts of Spain and Portugal. He landed near Corunna and burned part of the town, thus warning the Spaniards of the intended attack on Lisbon. The expedition was a dismal failure, partly owing to the difficulty in mounting the operation but chiefly to the lack of co-ordination between the two commanders. They returned home in July, having accomplished very little.

In 1591–2 and again in 1593 Norris served in Brittany in Henri IV's campaign against the Catholic League. Together with the Duc d'Aumont, he seized the fortress of Crozon in November 1593, but was badly woun-

ded in the fighting. Because of disagreements with his French counterparts, Norris lost his command the following May, but he remained at Brest until the end of that year.

In 1595 Norris, who was still in effect Lord President of Munster, was summoned to Ireland to assist the Lord Deputy, Sir William Russell, in putting down the rebellion of the Earl of Tyrone (see O'Neill, Hugh). He and Russell had never been good friends, and Norris's task was now made more difficult by his suspicion that the Lord Deputy was secretly thwarting his efforts. After failing to get O'Neill to come out into the open, negotiations were begun and a hollow peace was signed at Dundalk in 1596. It was soon obvious that Tyrone had no intention of surrendering, but was playing for time; there was talk of recalling both Russell and Norris. In May 1597 Russell was replaced as Lord Deputy by Lord Burgh, and in June Norris, whose health was failing, retired to Munster. He died in the arms of his brother Thomas at Mallow on 3 July.

One of the most skilful military commanders of his day, John Norris achieved popularity by his successes in the Low Countries and Brittany, but in the last years of his life his reputation was marred by the futility of his Irish command and incessant wrangling with those with whom he served.

R. Bagwell, *Ireland under the Tudors* (3 vols; 1885–90).

*Portrait:* engraving, 1793, by unknown engraver, after unknown artist: location not known.

**North, Sir Thomas** (?1535–?1601), soldier and translator of Plutarch.

The youngest son of Edward North, 1st Baron North, and his first wife, Alice Squyer, Sir Thomas North was born in about 1535. He is believed to have studied at Peterhouse, Cambridge. He entered Lincoln's Inn as a student in 1557, where he was influenced by a group of lawyers interested in translations and soon afterwards turned his attention wholeheartedly to literature. His first work, *The Diall of Princes*, based on the Spanish and French editions of the *Meditations* of Marcus Aurelius by Antonio de Guevara, was published in December that year. Following the death of their father in 1564, Thomas appears to have been to some extent financially dependent on his elder brother Roger, now 2nd Baron North, whom he accompanied on a mission to France in 1574.

North's translation from the Italian of *The Morall Philosophie of Doni* was published in 1570. In 1579 he issued his greatest work, a translation of Plutarch's *Lives* taken from the French of Amyot. Dedicated to the Queen, and vividly written, the book became immensely popular; it was much used as source material by William Shakespeare (q.v.) for his Roman plays. Additions from several other authors were included in a

second edition (1595), and the work ran into several later editions up to 1676. There is a modern edition by C. F. T. Brooke, in two volumes (1909).

Parallel with his literary career, North took part in a number of military exploits. He fought in Ireland in 1582 and again in 1596–7. During the years 1585–7 he was in the Low Countries, supporting the Dutch against the Spanish. In 1588, under threat of the Spanish Armada, he trained a company of militia at Ely. Knighted in 1591 and a J.P. for Cambridgeshire the following year, North was in 1601 granted a pension by the Queen. He is believed to have died soon afterwards.

Sir Thomas North has been called the first great master of English prose. Probably the most famous of the Elizabethan translators, his influence on contemporary writing was considerable.

Frances Busby, *Three Men of the Tudor Time* [includes a biography of Sir Thomas North] (1911).

H. H. Davis, 'The military career of Thomas North', *Huntingdon Library Quarterly*, xii (1949), pp. 315–21.

**Northumberland, 1st Duke of** (?1504–1553), see Dudley, John.

**Norton, Thomas** (1532–1584), lawyer, poet, and co-author of the tragedy *Gorboduc*.

Born in London in 1532, Thomas Norton belonged to a family who were connected with the Grocers' Company; his father, Thomas Norton, was a wealthy citizen of the City, and his mother was Elizabeth, the daughter of Richard Merry of Northall. Norton may have been educated at Cambridge. He followed his father into the Grocers' Company and when still a youth entered the service of the Protector Somerset (see Seymour, Edward) as amanuensis. He was admitted as a student at the Inner Temple in 1555 and shortly afterwards married Margaret, a daughter of Archbishop Thomas Cranmer (q.v.).

While diligently pursuing his legal studies, Norton now began to devote more of his time to literary work. He had already published a translation from the Latin of a letter from Peter Martyr to Somerset in 1550, as well as some early verses. In 1559, under the influence of his wife's stepfather, the Calvinist printer Edward Whitchurch, he translated the *Institutions of the Christian Religion* of John Calvin (q.v.); it was published in 1561 and ran into several editions. At the same period Norton was collaborating with Thomas Sackville (q.v.) on a play, *The Tragedie of Gorboduc*, which was performed at the Inner Temple on Twelfth Night, 1561, and printed in 1565. Written in blank verse, *Gorboduc* was the earliest English tragedy.

Norton was also an active campaigner in Parliament for sterner measures against the Catholics. He was elected as Member for Galton in 1558, and for Berwick in 1562, and was to represent London in the Parliaments of 1571, 1572, and 1580. From 1581 onwards, in his capacity of official censor of the Queen's Roman Catholic subjects, he personally examined and put to the torture many Catholics; these activities earned him the nickname of 'rackmaster'.

Some time before 1565 Norton's first wife had died, whereupon he had married her cousin, Alice Cranmer. By 1582 this lady had become hopelessly insane and was never to regain her reason. Norton himself, through his increasing Puritan views, early in 1584 suffered a short term of imprisonment in the Tower for his opposition in Parliament. This seriously affected his health, and he died at his house at Sharpenhoe on 10 March 1584.

'Notes on Thos. Norton, M.P.', *Archaeologia*, xxxvi (1855), pp. 97–119.

**Nottingham, 1st Earl of** (1536–1624), see Howard, Charles.

**'Nun of Kent'** (?1506–1534), see Barton, Elizabeth.

## O

**O'Donnell, Hugh Roe** (?1571–1602), Lord of Tyrconnel, Irish rebel chieftain.

The eldest son of Sir Hugh MacManus O'Donnell, who had succeeded to the Lordship of Tyrconnel in 1566, Hugh Roe O'Donnell was born in about 1571. The old-established O'Donnell family was split into two factions, one side favouring an alliance with England, the other, like Sir Hugh's branch, siding with the rebellious O'Neills. The wary Sir Hugh, however, tried to go along with both sides and made protestations of loyalty to the English government which were not entirely believed, and in 1587 Sir John Perrot had the young Hugh kidnapped as hostage for his father's loyalty, taken to Dublin Castle and imprisoned. Early in 1591 Hugh escaped, but was soon recaptured. He escaped a second time at the end of the year, when his father surrendered the chieftainship in Hugh's favour.

In 1592 O'Donnell formally submitted to the government, but secretly intrigued against the English, applying to Spain for assistance. In 1595 he marched into Connaught and destroyed Sligo Castle; he invaded Connaught again in January 1597, but was forced by O'Conor Sligo to retreat across the Erne river. The following summer he went to the assistance of Tyrone (see O'Neill, Hugh), and took part in the defeat of the English army at Yellow Ford on 14 August. He forced O'Conor Sligo to submit in 1598. His cousin, Sir Niall Gary O'Donnell, who had objected to Hugh's election as chieftain of the O'Donnells, now moved against him,

having deserted to the English on the promise of the grant of Tyrconnel; he successfully wrested Lifford and Donegal from Hugh. The siege of Donegal was still in progress when news reached Hugh Roe O'Donnell of the arrival of the Spanish troops at Kinsale; he immediately marched southwards to join Tyrone. Their joint attack, launched on 23 December, resulted in a victory for the English army under Mountjoy (see Blount, Charles), whereupon O'Donnell handed over authority to his brother, Rory O'Donnell, and himself embarked for Spain with the object of trying to persuade Philip III to send a further expeditionary force to aid the Irish rebels. He was unsuccessful in this mission and withdrew to Simancas, where he died on 10 September 1602, having been poisoned by a native of Galway.

L. O'Clery (O'Cleirigh), *Life of Hugh Roe O'Donnell* (Irish Texts Society, xlii, 1948).
P. Walsh, 'Historical Criticism of the Life of Hugh Roe O'Donnell', *Irish Historical Studies*, i (1939), pp. 229–50.

**Oldham, Hugh** (d. 1519), Bishop of Exeter, and founder of Manchester Grammar School.

A native of Lancashire, son of an attorney, the exact date and place of Hugh Oldham's birth are not known. He was educated in the household of the 1st Earl of Derby (see Stanley, Thomas, in *Lives Before the Tudors*) and at Queen's College, Cambridge. He subsequently became chaplain to 'the Lady Margaret' (the Countess of Richmond and Derby;

see Beaufort, Margaret), through whose interest he entered the royal service and from whom he received numerous benefices.

'A man of more devotion than learning', according to Godwin, Oldham was an able administrator. He rose swiftly in the Church to become a figure of national importance, and in January 1503 he was among those chosen to lay the foundation stone of Henry VII's chapel in Westminster Abbey. In recognition of his services he was transferred in 1504 to the bishopric of Exeter, an office which he held until his death.

As Bishop of Exeter, he was involved in the long dispute with Archbishop Warham (q.v.) concerning the prerogatives of the Archbishop with regard to the probate of wills and the administration of the estates of intestates, a dispute which had finally to be settled by the King. Oldham's poor opinion of the monks and his outspoken views on this subject also led to quarrels with the Abbot of Tavistock. His advice to his friend Bishop Richard Foxe (q.v.) resulted in the foundation of Corpus Christi College, Oxford, to which Oldham contributed 6,000 marks. In August 1515 he founded a grammar school at Manchester for the 'bringing up of children in good learning and manners'. He died on 25 June 1515, and was buried in Exeter Cathedral.

Francis Godwin, *Catalogue of the Bishops of England* (1643).
J. A. Graham and B. A. Phythian, *The Manchester Grammar School* (1965).

*Portrait*: oil, three-quarter length, by unknown artist: Corpus Christi College, Oxford.

**Oliver, Isaac** (?1556–1617), miniature painter.

Isaac Oliver is believed to have been born at Rouen, France, in about 1556

and brought to England by his Huguenot parents, Peter and Typhan Oliver, after the capture of Rouen by the Guises in 1562. Although in later life he frequently signed as 'Olivier' or 'Ollivier', he was regarded as an Englishman by his contemporaries. It is recorded that his father, a goldsmith by trade, was living in Fleet Lane, in the City of London, in 1571, with his wife and son Isaac, and that later that year the family was living in the parish of St Sepulchre's. There seems little doubt that he was the Isaac Oliver of Rouen who married Sara Gheeraerts, daughter of the painter Marcus Gheeraerts the elder, on 9 February 1602 at the Dutch church of Austin Friars, London. He may also have been related to Nicasius Russel, jeweller to James I (see James VI of Scotland), to whose son he stood as godfather.

Isaac became a pupil of Nicholas Hilliard (q.v.), whom he followed (and later rivalled) in miniature painting; although he used the effect of shadowing to build up his portraits, in contrast to Hilliard's linear technique, their work has sometimes been confused. Oliver soon won acclaim not only for his miniatures, but also for his larger portraits and religious and classical pictures. He is believed to have spent some time abroad from about 1588, probably in order to study Italian art with a view to painting historical miniatures; he is known to have been in Venice in 1596.

In 1604, after the accession of James to the English throne, Oliver was appointed as limner to Queen Anne (see Anne of Denmark in *Lives of the Stuart Age*). He painted James and all his family, and also many of the court and nobility of the day; of Queen Elizabeth (q.v.), to whom his master Hilliard was official limner, there is one (unfinished) miniature extant by Oliver, now at the Victoria and

Albert Museum, London. Among his other well-known paintings are a full-length study *called* Sir Philip Sidney (q.v.), now in the Royal Collection at Windsor, and a group picture of the three sons of the 2nd Viscount Montague, which is now in the possession of the Marquess of Exeter at Burghley House (copy in Earl Spencer collection).

Oliver lived for some time in the district of Blackfriars, London, where following his death on 2 October 1617 he was buried in the parish church of St Anne's. He was married twice, if not three times; in his will he made his wife Elizabeth his executrix and mentioned his eldest son, Peter, also a miniature painter, and other sons not yet of age. To Peter he left all his painting equipment and portraits, finished and unfinished; these included a large unfinished limning of *The Enthronement of Christ*. Some of his works were later completed by his son.

Isaac Oliver's work is more realistic than that of Hilliard. Probably because of his Flemish affiliations, he painted with less refinement and less fantasy than his master, but was by no means his inferior.

Erna Auerbach, *Tudor Artists* (1954).
G. Reynolds, *Nicholas Hilliard and Isaac Oliver* (Victoria and Albert Museum Handbook, 1947).

*Self-portraits:* miniatures: National Portrait Gallery, London, and Royal Collection; drawing: Fitzwilliam Museum, Cambridge; engravings: Duke of Portland and Earl Gosford Collections. Another *supposed* self-portrait is in the possession of H.M. the Queen of the Netherlands.

**O'Neill, Hugh** (*c.* 1540–1616), 3rd Baron of Dungannon and 2nd Earl of Tyrone, Irish rebel known as 'The Great Earl'.

The second son of Matthew O'Neill, 1st Baron of Dungannon and the illegitimate son of Con O'Neill, 1st Earl of Tyrone, Hugh O'Neill was born in about 1540. The O'Neills were the most powerful family of Ulster, but split into rival factions. When Hugh's father was murdered by supporters of Shane O'Neill (q.v.) shortly after the latter's succession as chieftain in 1559, it was thought safer for his son to be sent to England; the young O'Neill therefore grew up and was educated at the home of the Sidney family at Penshurst and in London. In 1562, following the murder of his elder brother, he became Baron of Dungannon.

In 1567 Turlough Luineach O'Neill became chieftain of the O'Neills on the death of Shane, and the following year Dungannon returned to Ireland. Gradually, by co-operation with the English government, he consolidated his position, and in 1587 he was invested with his grandfather's title and estates. His wife died in January 1591 and a few months later O'Neill caused a sensation by eloping with Mabel, daughter of Sir Nicholas Bagenal, former Marshal of the English army in Ireland. In 1593 he replaced Turlough as chieftain of the O'Neills.

Tyrone now began to intrigue with the Irish rebels and the Spaniards against the English government. His rebellion of 1595 was put down, but he refused to abide by his undertaking to submit and after three years of negotiations reopened hostilities in 1598. His victory at the Yellow Ford in August that year triggered off general support for 'the O'Neill' throughout Ulster, Connaught, and Leinster, but although he received the approval of Pope Clement VIII and was reinforced by 4,000 Spanish troops at Kinsale, in Munster, Tyrone suffered a major defeat there at the hands of Mountjoy (see Blount, Charles) in December 1601, finally surrendering on 30 March 1603, a few days after the death of the Queen.

In spite of rather lenient treatment by James I (see James VI of Scotland), Tyrone was dissatisfied with his loss of prestige and secretly intrigued once more with Spain. In 1607, together with other northern Irish chieftains, he secretly embarked on a ship bound for Spain. After a storm had forced them to land in the Netherlands, the refugees fled to Rome, where Tyrone was to live as an outlaw for the rest of his life. He died in that city on 20 July 1616.

The defeat of Tyrone at Kinsale finally clinched the subjugation of Ireland by the English.

Camden, William, *Britannia*, enlarged edition by R. Gough (3 vols; 1789).
C. P. Meehan, *The Fate and Fortunes of Hugh O'Neill, Earl of Tyrone and Rory O'Donnell, Earl of Tyrconnel* (Dublin, 1868; rev. ed. 1886).
Cyril Falls, *Elizabeth's Irish Wars* (1950).
S. O'Faolain, *The Great O'Neill* (1943).
T. Stafford, *Pacata Hibernia* (2 vols; Dublin, 1810; London, 1896).

**O'Neill, Shane** (*c.* 1530–1567), 2nd Earl of Tyrone, Irish rebel chieftain, known as 'The Proud'.

The eldest legitimate son of Con O'Neill, 1st Earl of Tyrone, Shane O'Neill was born in Ireland in about 1530. On the death of his father he challenged the rights of inheritance granted to his illegitimate brother Matthew, and determined to raise a faction against him; having succeeded his father as chieftain in 1559, he had his supporters murder his rival. Queen Elizabeth I (q.v.), however, refused to acknowledge Shane's claim to the chieftainship or his title, preferring instead the son of the murdered man, young Hugh O'Neill (q.v.), who was brought to England to be educated; her action incited the Irish claimant to rebellion.

After a three-year period of skirmishes with the English army in Ireland, a compromise was reached and eventually O'Neill agreed to negotiate with Elizabeth. He went to England in January 1562 and formally submitted to her authority, in return for which he was acknowledged as Captain of Tyrone; but after his return to Ireland he soon went his own way again, and hostilities were reopened. Four years of savage warfare followed, during which O'Neill won complete control over Ulster, defeating the Antrim Scots (the MacDonnells) in 1565. So confident was he that his uprising would be successful that he appealed to Rome, to Mary, Queen of Scots (q.v.), and to France for support. This forced the Lord Deputy, Sir Henry Sidney (q.v.), to take action in the form of a great march through Ulster; but before his forces could engage with those of O'Neill, the latter was defeated by his old enemies, the O'Donnells of Tyrconnel, at Farsetmore. O'Neill subsequently took refuge with the MacDonnells, who at first made him welcome but later took their revenge for his earlier attacks by brutally hacking him to pieces on the evening of 2 June 1567. His head is said to have been pickled and sent to Sidney at Dublin Castle, where it was exhibited on a pole.

Shane O'Neill was a primitive character, who drank heavily and fought savagely. Of all Elizabeth's Irish opponents, he was the most formidable.

Richard Bagwell, *Ireland under the Tudors* (3 vols; 1885–90).
E. J. B. Barrett, *The Great O'Neill* (Boston, 1939).
Cyril Falls, *Elizabeth's Irish Wars* (1950).

**Ormonde, 10th Earl of** (1532–1614), see Butler, Thomas.

**Oxenham, John** (d. 1580), sea captain.

Believed to be a Plymouth man, John Oxenham, described by the Spaniards in 1576 as a man of about forty, was probably born in about 1530–5. He almost certainly came from a Devonshire family of some standing, but unfortunately no records have survived to throw light upon his parentage or early life.

He is known to have sailed with Francis Drake (q.v.) from Plymouth in May 1572 on the expedition that attacked Nombre de Dios in Panama and captured a mule train laden with treasure crossing the Isthmus. It was during this voyage that Drake and Oxenham vowed to sail one day in the Pacific, or 'Great South Sea'.

Oxenham conceived the idea of gaining control of the Isthmus, intercepting the unarmed Spanish treasure ships in the Pacific, and then withdrawing with the plunder to the Caribbean; and soon after his return he began to make preparations for such an expedition. The plans were discussed with Drake, who, although he himself had been advised to lie low for a while, may well have subscribed towards the voyage. The Hawkins family (see Hawkins, John and Richard) probably also took a share, along with several others, including one John Willes, to whom there is a reference in the Plymouth archives.

Accompanied by a certain John Butler, probably the Irishman known to the Spaniards at Panama as 'Captain John' and much feared by them, Oxenham set sail from Plymouth in 1576 and reached the Isthmus later that year. He took only fifty men, but relied on an alliance made with the local Cimaroons (negroes who had escaped from Spanish slavery and who roamed the area) on the previous expedition. With their help, he successfully carried out the first part of his plan and kept control of the Isthmus until well into the second half of 1577. But while he was crossing the Isthmus to collect the treasure, the Spaniards discovered his ships and stores, which they destroyed. Within a short time Oxenham, Butler, and all but a handful of their men were captured. Most of the ordinary seamen were hanged; a few became slaves in the Spanish galleys. Oxenham and his officers were imprisoned at Lima and brought before the Inquisition. In 1580, having been subjected to an *auto da fé* parade and 'reconciliation' with the Catholic Church, they were hanged.

There is evidence in the Spanish archives that England had the intention of gaining permanent control of the Isthmus. After the failure of John Oxenham's brilliant exploit, however, no further moves were made. It has been speculated that Drake, before setting out on his great voyage of circumnavigation in December 1577, may have made a secret plan with the Queen to link up with Oxenham on the Isthmus. Only on reaching the Peruvian coast would he have heard of the expedition's fate.

Richard Hakluyt, *The Principall Navigations* (1589; ed. W. Raleigh, 12 vols, Glasgow, 1903–5).
I. A. Wright, *Documents concerning English Voyages to the Spanish Main, 1569–1590* (Hakluyt Society, 2nd ser., lxxi, 1932).

**Oxford, 17th Earl of** (1550–1604), see Vere, Edward de.

# P

**Paget, William** (1505–1563), 1st Baron Paget of Beaudesert, statesman.

Said to have been born in humble circumstances at Wednesbury in 1505, the son of William Paget, a sergeant-at-mace in the City of London, William Paget was nevertheless descended from an old Staffordshire family. He was educated at St Paul's School in London and, with the support of the Boleyn family, at Trinity Hall, Cambridge, during the mastership of Stephen Gardiner (q.v.). On leaving the university he entered the Gardiner household and was sent by his employer to complete his studies in Paris. Undoubtedly through Gardiner's influence, from 1529 he was employed by Henry VIII (q.v.) on several diplomatic missions to the Continent.

Knighted in 1537, Paget was two years later appointed as secretary to the King's new bride, Anne of Cleves (q.v.). In 1540 he became clerk to the Privy Council. The following year he undertook the delicate mission of explaining to the French court the sudden fall of Catherine Howard (q.v.); on his return he was made a Privy Councillor and, in 1543, one of the Secretaries of State. In the last years of Henry's reign he was on close terms with the King and, together with Edward Seymour (q.v.), Earl of Hertford, one of his chief advisers. In 1547 he entered Parliament as Member for Staffordshire.

A party to the breaking of Henry's will, in the first days of the reign of the young Edward VI (q.v.) Paget proposed a protectorate in the Council and em-erged as a firm supporter of Hertford, now Duke of Somerset. His friendship with the Protector was rewarded by a K.G. and appointments as Comptroller of the Royal Household and Chancellor of the Duchy of Lancaster, followed in 1549 by an elevation to the peerage as Baron Paget of Beaudesert. Continued loyalty to Somerset, however, led him into opposition to the Earl of Warwick (see Dudley, John; later Duke of Northumberland) and, in October 1551, to arrest and imprisonment on an absurd charge of conspiring against Warwick's life. He was deprived of the Garter, officially on the grounds of his insufficient birth (but in fact so as to make room for Warwick's son, Lord Guildford Dudley), and fined £6,000 for using his high offices for personal enrichment. By the end of the reign he had managed cleverly to extricate himself from his difficulties and was again in favour.

After Edward's death in July 1553, Paget joined the Council of Queen Jane (see Jane Grey, Lady), probably under compulsion, since he lost no time in supporting the proclamation of Mary I (q.v.) in London and was one of those who escorted her into the City. He became a Privy Councillor and High Steward of the University of Cambridge, was restored to the Garter, and in 1556 was appointed Lord Privy Seal. As a proponent of the Queen's marriage to Philip II of Spain (q.v.), Paget was high in favour; and after Gardiner's death he was the leading secular minister.

On the accession of Elizabeth I (q.v.)

in 1558, Paget relinquished the office of Lord Privy Seal and retired from the Council. He died at West Drayton House, Middlesex, on 9 June 1563, when he was succeeded by his son Henry, the eldest of four sons borne to him by his wife Anne, daughter of Henry Preston of Westmorland.

S. R. Gammon, *Statesman and Schemer: William, 1st Lord Paget, Tudor Minister* (1973).

*Portraits:* oil, attributed to the Master of the Stätthalterin Madonna, probably 1549: National Portrait Gallery, London; oil, by unknown artist: the Marquess of Anglesey.

**Parker, Matthew** (1504–1575), Archbishop of Canterbury.

Born on 6 August 1504 at Norwich, Matthew Parker was educated at Corpus Christi College, Cambridge, where he took his B.A. in about 1524–5. Ordained in 1527, he was in the same year elected a fellow of Corpus Christi, having refused the opportunity of joining the college newly founded by Cardinal Thomas Wolsey (q.v.). At Cambridge Parker was a popular preacher and a member of the group of reformers who met at the White Horse Inn to discuss the new religious ideas. He was not a controversialist, however, preferring to devote his time to the study of early Church history.

In 1535 Parker was appointed chaplain to Queen Anne Boleyn (q.v.) and was made Dean of the College of St John the Baptist at Stoke-by-Clare, Suffolk. He spent the next nine years there, following his studies and training young secular priests; it was during this time, probably the happiest of his entire life, that he became betrothed to a remarkable woman, Margaret Harlestone, of Mattishall, Norfolk; he was to marry her in June 1547, as soon as the law on celibacy of the clergy had been amended. Ap-

pointed Master of Corpus Christi College in 1544, Parker became Vice-Chancellor of the University the following year. He quarrelled with Stephen Gardiner (q.v.), then Chancellor of Cambridge University, over the performance of a play at the College which cast aspersions on the papacy, and thus forfeited Gardiner's good opinion of him; he also made a valiant stand against the spoliation of university revenues by the crown. In 1549, happening to be in Norfolk at the time of the rebellion led by Robert Ket (q.v.), Parker preached a courageous sermon to the rebels advising them against lawlessness and disorder. He became a close friend of the German Protestant reformer, Martin Bucer (q.v.), who was invited to England by Archbishop Thomas Cranmer (q.v.) at the end of that year and was appointed Regius Professor of Divinity at Cambridge. In 1552 Parker was installed as Dean of Lincoln.

As a married priest, and one who had espoused the cause of the Lady Jane Grey (q.v.), Parker was deprived of all his preferments on the accession of Mary I (q.v.), and he lived in retirement throughout her reign. When Elizabeth I (q.v.) came to the throne his name was put forward by his old Cambridge friend, William Cecil (q.v.), as the right choice for Archbishop of Canterbury, the man who had not gone into exile and become infected with extreme Continental ideas – in fact a moderate. Parker, who would have preferred a return to university life, accepted the office with some reluctance; he was consecrated at Lambeth on 17 December 1559.

The new Archbishop strove hard to establish uniformity within the Church, the *via media* favoured by the Queen as against Rome on one side and Geneva on the other. As a scholar, Parker emphasized the antiquity of the English Church, and encouraged antiquarian studies reaching back to Anglo-Saxon times. He reduced Cranmer's Articles of Religion from forty-two to thirty-nine, and in 1565 issued his celebrated 'Advertisements' in which he laid down regulations of service but compromised with the growing Puritan faction over the wearing of vestments.

From 1563 to 1568 Parker worked on a revised translation of the scriptures, which was intended to counteract the popularity of the Geneva Bible issued by the Calvinists in 1560; this was published in 1568, and it became known as the 'Bishops' Bible'. The Thirty-Nine Articles were issued in 1571. Thereafter, faced with increasing hostility from the Earl of Leicester (see Dudley, Robert) and his party, the disobedience of many of his own clergy, and a growing weariness with the duties of carrying out, and taking the blame for, unpopular measures ordered by the Queen, the Archbishop withdrew more and more from public life. He devoted much of his time to the editing of the manuscripts of the early English chroniclers such as Aelfric, Gildas, Asser, Matthew Paris, and Walsingham, and the *Flores Historiarum*. A great collector of books and manuscripts and a generous benefactor both to the University of Cambridge and to individual printers, engravers, and transcribers, Parker's own work, *De Antiquitate Ecclesiae et Privilegiis Ecclesiae Cantuariensis cum Archiepiscopis ejusdem 70* (1572), stated the Anglican position as to the antiquity of its Church and tradition.

A gentle, modest man who disliked the trappings of public office, and who had worn himself out in the loyal service of his Queen and his Church, Matthew Parker died on 17 May 1575. He was buried in Lambeth Church, where his grave was desecrated by the Puritans in 1648. His correspondence was published by the Parker Society in 1853. A manuscript donated by the Archbishop to Corpus Christi College is known as the 'Parker Chronicle'.

W. F. Hook, *The Lives of the Archbishops of Canterbury*, vol. ix (12 vols; 1860–76).
W. P. M. Kennedy, *Archbishop Parker* (1908).
F. J. Shirley, *Elizabeth's First Archbishop* (1948).
John Strype, *The Life and Acts of Matthew Parker* (1711; reprinted in 3 vols, Oxford, 1821).

*Portraits:* oil, by unknown artist: Corpus Christi College, Cambridge; oil, by unknown artist, 1559: Courtauld Institute, London.

**Parr, Katherine** (1512–1548), see Katherine Parr.

**Parry, William** (d. 1585), conspirator.

Originally known as William ap Harry, William Parry was the son of Harry ap David of Flintshire and his second wife, Margaret, daughter of the Archdeacon of St Asaph's. The date of his birth is not known; his father, a man of means, who died in about 1566, was said to have had fourteen children by his first marriage and sixteen by his second.

Educated at Chester grammar school, William made several attempts to escape, and eventually succeeded in reaching London, where he lost no time in marrying a wealthy widow, Mrs Powell, and in entering the service of the Earl of Pembroke (see Herbert, William). On the Earl's death in 1570, Parry was accepted into the royal service and, also at about this date, his first wife having died, he married Catherine Heywood, another widow; in 1571 he was involved in litigation concerning her estates.

A wealthy and somewhat profligate young man-about-town, Parry had rapidly squandered both his own and his wives' money; in order to escape his creditors he applied to Lord Burghley (see Cecil, William) to be taken on as a spy on the Continent. He made several journeys abroad, endeavouring to ingratiate himself with the exiled English Catholics, so as to report back to Burghley. Still pursued by creditors at home, on a return visit to England he was sentenced to death for violently assaulting one of them, but received a pardon from the Queen and, in 1582, permission to travel abroad again.

By this time Parry was playing a dangerous double game. Although secretly he had become a Catholic, he continued to pretend to Burghley that he was consorting with the exiled recusants in order to search out their secrets and report them. Meanwhile he read, and was influenced by, the writings of Cardinal William Allen (q.v.); in Paris he was in contact with Charles Paget and Thomas Morgan, agents of Mary, Queen of Scots (q.v.).

Returning to England in January 1584, he had an interview with the Queen and managed to convince Elizabeth (q.v.) that his only purpose in dealings with the Pope and agents of the Queen of Scots had been to discover details of the plots against her own life; pardoned, he was given a seat in Parliament, but immediately got into trouble for opposing an anti-Catholic bill and was released from prison only at the Queen's command.

As short of money as ever, Parry now resumed his espionage activities. To an accomplice named Edmund Neville he proposed a plot for the Queen's assassination, which was promptly betrayed by him to one of Elizabeth's courtiers, and so to the Queen, whereupon Parry was arrested, examined three times by Sir Francis Walsingham (q.v.) and, partly on evidence supplied by Neville and partly on his own admission to Elizabeth a few weeks earlier, found guilty of compass-

ing the Queen's death. He was hanged at Westminster on 2 March 1585.

There is some doubt about William Parry's guilt. He may have spoken to Neville of the Queen's assassination simply in order to extract some admission which could be used against him, in which case Parry was guilty only of so doing without ministerial authority; whether he ever intended to go through with the assassination is a matter for speculation. What seems certain is that the instigator of the so-called 'Parry Plot' was nothing more than a vain, weak character, puffed up with his own importance and driven by extravagance and debt into double dealing.

An official account of the Parry plot was printed as *A True and Plaine Declaration of the Horrible Treasons practised by W. Parry, the Traitor, against the Queenes Majestie* (1585; rev. ed. 1679; it was re-printed in Holinshed's *Chronicles* (2nd ed., vol. iii (1587), pp. 1382 ff.).

L. Hicks, 'The strange case of Dr William Parry', in *Studies*, xxxvii (1948), pp. 343–62.
Conyers Read, *Sir Francis Walsingham*, vol. iii (Oxford, 1925).

## Parsons or Persons, Robert (1546–1610), Jesuit and controversialist.

Robert Parsons was born at Nether Stowey, Somerset, the sixth of eleven children of a country blacksmith. After receiving his early education at Stogursey and Taunton, he went up to Oxford, where he studied first at St Mary's Hall and then at Balliol. He became a fellow of Balliol and took a teaching post at the University.

Parsons left Oxford in 1575 after a quarrel with his colleagues, and on account of his known Roman Catholic sympathies. Although he had taken the Oath of Supremacy, in his heart he had always been a Catholic and, leaving England, he spent some months in

Louvain, before going on to Padua and then to Rome, where he entered the Society of Jesus on 4 July. He was ordained in 1578.

From 1579 onwards he worked with William Allen (q.v.) to organize Roman Catholic resistance in England to the Protestant régime that had been established under Elizabeth I (q.v.). It may have been Parsons who conceived the idea of sending Jesuit priests to England in 1580. Allen appointed him as leader of the mission, which consisted of Parsons, Edmund Campion (q.v.), and seven others. They travelled together, mostly on foot, as far as Rheims, where they split up. Parsons reached England on 16 June and had a meeting at Southwark with a synod of Catholic priests from London. He joined Campion at his lodgings in Chancery Lane in July, but they decided for safety reasons to leave the city and tour the country separately. Before parting they were persuaded by a Catholic named Thomas Pounde to put in writing their reasons for coming to England, which might be published in the event of their arrest, and Campion gave Pounde a letter addressed to the Privy Council. Parsons then set out on a tour of Northampton, Derby, Worcester, and Gloucester, preaching, hearing confession, saying Mass, and administering the sacraments as he moved from house to house, reconciling and converting to Catholicism. He returned to London in October and eventually made his headquarters at Bridewell, which became a clandestine meeting place for Catholic priests. His claim that the Jesuit mission had met with considerable success alarmed the government. A secret printing press was set up, first at Barking and later at Stonor, near Henley in Oxfordshire, which produced a pamphlet by Parsons entitled *A Brief Discourse containing certain Reasons why Catholics refuse to go to Church*, and also the *Decem Rationes* ('Ten Reasons') pamphlet of Campion that caused a sensation when it was distributed before a church service at St Mary's, Oxford, in June 1581.

For a short time after Campion's arrest, Parsons went into hiding in Sussex. Then he left England for the Continent, reaching Rouen on 30 August. There he remained for the following six months, engaging in various political intrigues, which included negotiations for the sending of a Jesuit mission to Scotland, and issuing a stream of pamphlets under his own name and various pseudonyms. He also founded a school for English boys at Eu, near Dieppe; this was later moved to St Omer and eventually became Stonyhurst College in England.

In June 1582 Parsons went to Spain in an attempt to assist the negotiations then taking place between the papacy and Philip II (q.v.) for the invasion of England. He was back in France by May the following year, when he met William Allen at Rheims. Then, after a brief visit to Pope Gregory XIII in Rome, he went to Flanders to advise the Duke of Parma concerning the number of English Catholics in that country. Throughout 1584 he worked closely with Allen in Paris, organizing the movements of English Catholics and involving himself in a number of political intrigues aimed at the overthrow of Elizabeth and the restoration of Catholicism; Allen subsequently made him responsible for the direction from abroad of the whole Jesuit mission in England. His *Christian Directorie* was published in 1585.

In September 1585 Parsons accompanied Allen to Rome. Ostensibly the latter's purpose was to discuss the finances of the seminary at Rheims, while Parsons wished to take his final

353

vows; their true mission was to convince the new Pope, Sixtus V, of the immense importance of the Spanish 'Enterprise' against England. (Sixtus did not believe in it.) Parsons remained at the English College in Rome for three years, continuing to direct the Jesuits in England, and writing incessantly and sending a constant stream of advice to Philip II concerning the planned invasion. In May 1587 he took his last vows, and the following year he became Rector of the English College. Among other concerns, he was instrumental in securing a cardinal's hat for Allen.

As soon as news reached him of the failure of the Armada, Parsons went to Spain. He was to spend nearly nine years there, founding English seminaries at Valladolid, Seville, and Madrid, and urging Philip to make another attack on England. But his continual intriguing abroad aroused much discontent among the English Catholics, and when Parliament made it a treasonable offence to possess a copy of his *Conference about the next Succession*, published in 1594, which upheld the Pope's power to depose, many of them repudiated altogether the doctrine Parsons advocated. Another source of dispute was the high-handed manner in which he appointed George Blackwell (q.v.) as archpriest in 1598.

Parsons spent his last years in Rome, as deeply involved as ever in sundry political intrigues. He died there on 15 April 1610 and was buried beside Cardinal Allen in the church of the English College.

Robert Parsons was the ablest and most uncompromising of the English Catholic exiles. He regarded the Queen as a heretic whom the community had a right to overthrow, and he favoured armed intervention by the Catholic powers of Europe as a means of restoring Catholicism to England. As Christopher Morris has written, he was 'the real power behind Cardinal Allen and behind all plots against Elizabeth, and he had a genius not only for political organization, but also for political thought'. The historian J. A. Froude called him a 'politician in priest's disguise'.

A prolific writer, Parsons was one of the foremost of Elizabethan masters of prose; his *Christian Directorie*, suitably edited by an Anglican cleric, was used even by Protestants. A resumé of his writings will be found in the appendix to *The History of the Jesuits in England, 1580–1773*, by E. L. Taunton (Philadelphia, 1901).

L. Hicks, 'Letters and Memorials of Father Robert Parsons, S.J. [1578–88]', *Catholic Record Society*, xxix (1942).
Christopher Morris, *Political Thought in England: Tyndale to Hooker* (1954).
J. H. Pollen, 'The Memoirs of Father Robert Parsons', *Catholic Record Society Miscellany*, ii (1905) and iv (1907).

*Portrait*: engraving, by unknown artist, 1622: British Museum, London.

## Paulet, Pawlet, or Poulet, Sir William (?1485–1572), 1st Marquess of Winchester, statesman.

The eldest son of Sir John Paulet of Basing, near Basingstoke, Hampshire, a commander at the Battle of Blackheath in 1497, William Paulet is believed to have been born in 1485.

Sheriff of Hampshire in 1512 and in several later years, Paulet was knighted some time before 1525. He quickly gained the confidence of Henry VIII (q.v.) and by 1526 was a Privy Councillor. He also held a number of minor official posts and represented Hampshire in the Reformation Parliament of 1529–36. In 1532 he was appointed Comptroller of the Royal Household. He played a prominent part in putting down the Pilgrimage of Grace in 1536, being rewarded for his services by the grant of Netley Abbey, near Southampton, promotion to the office of Treasurer of the Royal Household in 1537, and, two years later, an elevation to the peerage as Baron St John of Basing. He continued high in favour to the end of the reign, becoming Chamberlain of the Royal Household in 1543, Great Master in 1545, and Lord President of the Council a year before the King's death.

Nominated by Henry as one of the Council of Regency for Edward VI (q.v.), St John was for a few months Keeper of the Great Seal under the Protector Somerset (see Seymour, Edward). Not long afterwards, however, he switched his allegiance to the Earl of Warwick's party (see Dudley, John; later Duke of Northumberland) in seeking to overthrow the Protector. In 1550 he was made Lord Treasurer in place of Somerset and, at the same time, Earl of Winchester. On the final fall of the Protector, he was created a Marquess. Six weeks later he acted as Lord Steward at Somerset's trial.

Opposed to the proclamation of the Lady Jane Grey (q.v.) as Queen, Winchester proclaimed Mary I (q.v.) at Baynard's Castle on 19 July 1553. He was confirmed in all his offices by Mary and in addition made Lord Privy Seal. Except in the matter of the Queen's Spanish marriage, in which he acquiesced only with reluctance, he loyally and vigorously carried out her wishes, giving much support to Bishop Stephen Gardiner (q.v.) in the House of Lords.

In spite of his advanced years, Winchester was continued in the office of Lord Treasurer on the accession of Elizabeth I (q.v.). A man who disliked extremes, at the beginning of her reign he maintained good relations with Sir William Cecil (q.v.); but later, having seen the way in which Cecil's foreign

policy was going, the Lord Treasurer sided with those who intrigued against the Secretary of State. He died in harness, a very old man, at Basing House, the magnificent seat which he had built, on 10 March 1572. By his wife, Elizabeth, daughter of Sir William Capel, he had four sons and four daughters; before he died he claimed that he had lived to see no less than 103 direct descendants.

Asked in his old age how it was that he had managed to retain the office of Lord Treasurer through three very different reigns, Winchester gave the reply, 'By being a willow, not an oak'.

*Portrait:* oil, by unknown artist: National Portrait Gallery, London: other versions at Knole, Penshurst, Hardwick Hall, Syon House, and elsewhere.

## Peele, George (*c.* 1558–1596), poet, playwright, and actor.

The son of James Peele, a citizen and salter of London, and at one time clerk to Christ's Hospital, George Peele was born in about 1558. He was educated at Christ's Hospital and at Broadgates Hall (Pembroke College) and Christ Church, Oxford, where he graduated as B.A. in 1577 and as M.A. two years later. Peele achieved some notoriety at Oxford, not only as a poet and translator of one of the plays of Euripides, but also on account of his gay social life. His poem *The Tale of Troy,* an epitome of Homer's *Iliad,* although not printed until 1589, was probably written while at the university.

On moving from Oxford to London, Peele began to lead the dissipated, Bohemian life that was to be his style for the next seventeen years. In September 1579 he was turned out of his father's house within the precincts of Christ's Hospital by the governors because of his riotous living, but this did not deter him; nor did marriage, which he entered into some time before 1583, although his wife brought him certain lands. In 1583 he returned to Oxford to assist in the presentation of two plays by Gager at Christ Church. His own *Arraignment of Paris*, a pastoral verse drama written expressly to flatter Queen Elizabeth (q.v.), may have been performed at court before this date; a new departure, in that it was written in a variety of metres, the play was printed in 1584.

A successful actor as well as a playwright, Peele was a member of the Lord Admiral's company and, later, of the Queen's Men. He also devised and produced a series of pageants for the City of London, of which *Device of the Pageant Borne Before Woolstone Dixi* is the earliest surviving complete Lord Mayor's Show (1585), and *Descensus Astraeae* (1591) the only other example preserved. His drinking (and brawling) companions included fellow-writers Thomas Nashe, Thomas Kyd, Christopher Marlowe, Thomas Lodge, and Robert Greene (qq.v.).

Peele was an experimental, versatile, and prolific writer. His numerous works fall into three categories: plays, pageants, and the kind of commendatory or miscellaneous verse which he wrote to earn money. He undoubtedly had a hand in many other popular dramas of the period, but only four have been definitely attributed to him, in addition to *The Arraignment of Paris: Edward I* (1593) and another historical play, *The Battle of Alcazar*, based on the life of the adventurer Thomas Stukeley (q.v.), printed in 1594; *The Old Wives' Tale*, a burlesque of the supernatural (1595); and a biblical drama, *The Love of King David and Fair Bethsabe* (1599). Many fine lyrics are contained in the plays. Among his poems were *Polyhymnia* (1590), the *Eclogue Gratulatory* (1589) to the Earl of Essex (see Devereux, Robert), and *Honour of the Garter* (1593) to the Earl of Northumberland.

Sickness, said to have been the pox, together with continual financial anxieties brought on by the way he lived, dogged Peele for the last two years of his life. The exact date of his death is not known, but it is believed to have occurred in 1596.

Much praised by his contemporaries, George Peele was one of the most important and most versatile of the pre-Shakespearian dramatists. His *Dramatic and Poetical Works*, edited by A. Dyce, were first published in three volumes in 1828–39; they were reissued, with a *Life*, together with the works of Robert Greene, also edited by Dyce, in 1861. There is a later edition, *The Works of George Peele*, in two volumes, edited by A. H. Bullen (1888).

J. A. Symonds, *Shakespeare's Predecessors* (1884).

**Pembroke, 1st Earl of** (?1501–1570), see Herbert, Sir William.

**Percy, John** (1569–1641), Jesuit priest, see Fisher, John, in *Lives of the Stuart Age*.

**Persons, Robert** (1546–1610), see Parsons, Robert.

**Philip II** (1527–1598), King of Spain from 1556, and joint sovereign of England with Mary I (q.v.) from 1554 to 1558.

Born at Valladolid on 21 May 1527, Philip was the only son of the Holy Roman Emperor Charles V (q.v.) and Isabella of Portugal. Groomed from an early age for his future role, Philip was given his own household at the age of seven, with a university professor to supervise his studies and a grandee to instruct him in fencing, hunting, and jousting. His mother died when he was twelve, and from 1543 onwards, whenever Charles V went abroad Philip, created Duke of Milan, acted as Regent of Spain.

In 1543 Philip contracted the first of his four marriages, to the Infanta Maria of Portugal; she died in childbirth in 1545. His father urged him to marry again, and eight years later the twenty-six-year-old Philip reluctantly agreed to the commencement of negotiations for his union with Mary I of England; she was eleven years his senior and, as a child, had been for a short time betrothed to Charles.

On 13 July 1554 Philip embarked at Corunna on board the *Espiritu Santo*; he reached Southampton on the 19th. His first meeting with the Queen took place four days later, and on 25 July they were married at Winchester Cathedral amid great spendour and ceremonial. Philip was styled joint sovereign with Mary 'of England and France, Naples, Jerusalem, and Ireland, Defenders of the Faith, Princes of Spain and Sicily, Archdukes of Austria, Dukes of Milan, Burgundy, and Brabant, etc.'

The marriage was extremely unpopular with the English people, and there were many ugly demonstrations against Philip and his Spanish courtiers. So far as their personal relations went, it was observed that Philip treated his unwanted bride with deference and great kindness; the passion was all on her side. Nevertheless they spent happy times at Hampton Court in the year they were together, for both had retiring natures. Philip frequently amused himself with hunting expeditions and interfered little in state affairs. Although at the time he was much blamed for the Marian persecutions, in which some 300 heretics and rebels were burned at the stake, in fact it was he who continually urged moderation on the Queen and her Council.

In November 1554 Mary had announced that she was with child, but by the

following May it was clear that she had been mistaken; this was the first of her false pregnancies, now known to have been caused by an ovarian tumour and early symptoms of dropsy.

That summer Philip learned that the Emperor, his father, intended to abdicate and would begin by relinquishing to him the sovereignty of the Low Countries. Using the excuse that he was needed in Brussels, on 29 August he embarked at Greenwich for Flanders, the Queen having accompanied him to say a tearful goodbye.

In Brussels on 25 October Philip formally accepted the throne of the Low Countries; a few months later he became King of Spain. Mary, alarmed by rumours of his licentious escapades, sent letters imploring him to return; Philip, however, pleading pressure of state business, prolonged his absence for a full eighteen months. When he did return, in March 1557, it was with the object of urging England to declare war on France, and once this was achieved he was off again. Mary accompanied him as far as Sittingbourne, where he left her on 5 July. They were never to see one another again. When Mary entered the last stage of her fatal illness, in the autumn of 1558, and Philip was asked to come, he sent the Count of Feria in his place. By the time news of his wife's death reached him, Philip was too grief-stricken by the loss of his father to pay much attention to it.

Early in 1559 he made, through an ambassador, a tentative proposal of marriage to Queen Elizabeth I (q.v.), whom he had met – and allegedly flirted with – at Hampton Court four years earlier. Elizabeth haughtily rejected his terms, and for most of their respective reigns they were bitter adversaries, while at the same time retaining great respect for each other.

The war with France came to an end that year, and under the peace treaty of Câteau-Cambrésis Philip contracted to marry Elizabeth of Valois, daughter of Henri II of France. He married her by proxy (the Duke of Alva standing in for him) in Paris later that summer; she was to bear him two daughters before her death in 1568. In 1570 Philip married his fourth and last wife, Anne of Austria, daughter of the Emperor Maximilian II; she died in 1580, leaving one surviving son, the future Philip III.

Philip returned to Spain from the Netherlands in 1559 and never again left the Iberian Peninsula, preferring to rule his empire from Madrid and later from his palace at El Escorial, where he lived an austere and dedicated existence. For the first twenty years of his reign, he worked hard to preserve peace with his Western European neighbours, while at the same time fighting a major naval war in the Mediterranean with the Ottoman Empire. From 1568 he was faced with growing rebellion in the Netherlands, which was increasingly supported by England and France. In 1580 he con-

quered Portugal, which alarmed the rest of Europe. Spain was then at her greatest, both in extent and influence.

By the 1580s Philip had become convinced that the Catholic religion and Spanish authority in the Netherlands could not be sustained unless he took action against England and France. He therefore equipped the Armada, which eventually sailed on its mission to defeat England, with the assistance of Spanish troops from the Netherlands, in the summer of 1588. It failed dismally, due to a combination of factors: the shrewd preparations made by Lord Burghley (see Cecil, William), the seamanship of Sir Francis Drake (q.v.), and adverse weather conditions. Philip's support of the Catholic League against the Huguenots in France also failed, and under the Peace of Vervins in 1598 he was forced to accept Henri of Navarre as Henri IV of France. Yet from Philip's point of view it was not total failure, for although England and the northern Netherlands remained Protestant, it was Spanish intervention that had forced Henri of France to become a Catholic, and thus not only had a great Catholic victory been won both in that country and in the southern Netherlands, but the spread of heresy in Spain and Italy had been halted. And when Philip died, ten years later, Spain was still at the height of her power.

The King's last years were poisoned by a morbid suspicion of his most loyal servants and by growing intrigue and faction at the Spanish court. He aged rapidly and became virtually a recluse in his favourite room, nothing more than a cell, at El Escorial. After an agonizing last illness, in which his body practically rotted away, Philip died at El Escorial on 13 September 1598. Champion of the Counter-Reformation, he was in his seventy-second year and had reigned over Spain for forty-two years.

The official papers of Philip's reign relating to England will be found in *Calendar of State Papers (Spanish), 1558–1603* (4 vols; 1892–9), edited with introductions by Martin A. S. Hume.

L. Cabrera de Cordova, *Felipe Segundo, Rey de España* (4 vols; Madrid, 1876–7).
H. Forneron, *Histoire de Philippe II* (4 vols; Paris, 1881–2).
E. Grierson, *King of Two Worlds: Philip II of Spain* (1974).
M. A. S. Hume, *Two English Queens and Philip* (1908).
M. A. S. Hume, *Philip II of Spain* (1897).
Peter Pierson, *Philip II of Spain* (1976).
W. H. Prescott, *History of the Reign of Philip II* (1855).
W. T. Walsh, *Philip II* (New York, 1937).

*Portraits*: oil, by Titian, 1551: Prado, Madrid; oil, by Titian, 1553: Prado (copy at Palazzo Barberini, Rome); oil, by unknown artist, after Titian, mid-1550s: Galeria Palatina, Pitti Palace, Florence; electrotype of medal by Jacopo de Trezzo, 1555: National Portrait Gallery, London; oil on panel, with Mary, 1557: Woburn Abbey (Duke of Bedford); oil, by unknown artist, Spanish school, 1560: National Maritime Museum, Greenwich; miniature, by unknown artist after Titian, *c*. 1580: N.P.G.; oil, by unknown artist, *c*. 1580: N.P.G.; oil, by J. P. de la Cruz, *c*. 1598: El Escorial; miniature, oil on wood, by unknown artist, possibly eighteenth century: N.P.G.; numerous others elsewhere (England and on the Continent).

## Pole, Sir Edmund de la (?1472–1513), Earl of Suffolk, claimant to the English throne.

The second and eldest surviving son of the 2nd Duke of Suffolk (see Pole, John de la, 2nd Duke of Suffolk, in *Lives Before the Tudors*) and his wife Elizabeth, sister of Edward IV (see *Lives Before the Tudors*), Edmund de la Pole was born in about 1472. He had not reached his majority when his father died in 1491, and because of the attainder against his brother, the Earl of Lincoln (see Pole, John de la, Earl of Lincoln, in *Lives Before the Tudors*), a supporter of Lambert Sim-

nel (q.v.), in whose cause he had died at the Battle of Stoke in 1487, Edmund was not allowed to inherit the dukedom; instead he came to an agreement with Henry VII (q.v.) whereby two years later he took the title of Earl of Suffolk in return for the restoration of part of the forfeited estates and an annual revenue paid by the King.

For the next few years Suffolk remained at court under the watchful eye of the King and his advisers. Then, in the summer of 1499, he became discontented and fled to the Continent without licence; he went first to Guisnes, near Calais, where he had consultations with Sir James Tyrrell (q.v.), and then to St Omer. Henry, alarmed at his departure and its implications, swiftly sent messengers to fetch the Earl back, and although he agreed to go with them and was once more received at court, from that time onwards – and especially after the execution of Edward, Earl of Warwick, in November – Suffolk became increasingly suspicious of the King's intentions towards the house of York. In the early autumn of 1501, having heard that the Emperor Maximilian was willing to help a member of the family of Edward IV regain the English throne, he absconded for the second time and went to visit the Emperor in the Tyrol. Fortified by the promise of men and money to support his claim, Suffolk settled temporarily in Aix-la-Chapelle, while in England his brother, Lord William de la Pole, Sir James Tyrrell, and other Yorkist friends in the plot were rounded up and imprisoned; in December 1502 Suffolk himself was declared an outlaw. The Emperor's promises proved empty, for in the summer of that year Maximilian signed a treaty with England under which, in return for £10,000, he agreed not to harbour any English rebels; and Suffolk was obliged to live on borrowed money at Aix, which was outside the Emperor's jurisdiction. There he was surrounded by loyal supporters, but also spied on by those working for Henry: following the death of his eldest son, Prince Arthur (q.v.), in 1502, the English King worried more than ever about the continuance of the Tudor dynasty, and he was anxious to have Suffolk, the latest Yorkist claimant to the throne, safely in his grasp. Attainted by Parliament, along with his brothers William and Richard, in January 1504, Suffolk lived a miserable life at Aix until Easter that year, when, leaving his brother Richard behind as hostage, he set out for Friesland to join the Duke of Saxony. He was seized *en route* by the Duke of Gueldres, who had previously guaranteed him a safe conduct, and eventually, after much negotiation, was handed over to the Emperor's son, Philip of Castile, who surrendered him to Henry in March 1506 on the understanding that his life would be spared.

For the remainder of the reign Suffolk was held prisoner in the Tower. Exempted from the general pardon on the accession of Henry VIII (q.v.), he was sent to the block in 1513. His brother Richard, having extricated himself from the Earl's creditors at Aix, persuaded the French King to recognize him as the rightful King of England, but was killed fighting for France at the Battle of Pavia in 1525. Suffolk, who had married Margaret, a daughter of Richard le Scrope, Lord Scrope, left no male issue.

**Pole, John de la** (?1464–1487), Earl of Lincoln, see *Lives Before the Tudors*.

**Pole, John de la** (1442–1491), 2nd Duke of Suffolk, see *Lives Before the Tudors*.

**Pole, Margaret** (1473–1541), Countess of Salisbury.

Daughter of George, Duke of Clarence (see *Lives Before the Tudors*), and Isabel, daughter of Warwick the 'Kingmaker' (see Neville, Richard, in *Lives Before the Tudors*), Margaret Pole was born at Castle Farley, near Bath, in August 1473. She was married by Henry VII (q.v.) in about 1491 to Sir Richard Pole, a landed gentleman of Buckinghamshire whom the King made a K.G. and a squire of his bodyguard. Pole died in 1505, leaving his widow with five children, one of whom was the future Cardinal Reginald Pole (q.v.).

Henry VIII (q.v.), on his accession, wished to atone for the execution by his father of Margaret's brother, Edward, Earl of Warwick; in 1513 he created her Countess of Salisbury, granting her the lands of the earldom in fee. In 1521 she was appointed as governess to the Princess Mary (see Mary I), but on the King's marriage to Anne Boleyn (q.v.) in 1533 she refused to give up the Princess's jewels to the new Queen and was dismissed from her post.

The Countess returned to court after the fall of Anne, but her position was jeopardized by her son Reginald's book *Pro Ecclesiasticae Unitatis Defensione* ('In Defence of Ecclesiastical Unity'), at which Henry took great offence and which determined him to destroy the entire Pole family. Margaret's two sons, Sir Geoffrey Pole and Henry, Baron Montague, were arrested in the autumn of 1538; Montague was executed, together with the Marquess of Exeter, in December. The Countess herself was examined and held in custody while her house was searched; in March 1539 she was taken to the Tower and in May the same year was included in an attainder passed by Parliament on most members of the Pole family and many others. The attainder was not immediately enforced, and at one time it was believed that the

Countess would be released from the Tower; but in April 1541, when news reached the King of the uprising in Yorkshire led by Sir John Neville, it was resolved that she should die. She was beheaded on East Smithfield Green, within the precincts of the Tower, on 27 May.

See the titles listed under Cardinal Reginald Pole.

## Pole, Reginald (1500–1558), cardinal and Archbishop of Canterbury.

Born at Stourton Castle, near Stourbridge, Staffordshire, in March 1500, Reginald Pole was a son (probably the third son) of Sir Richard Pole and his wife Margaret (see Pole, Margaret; later Countess of Salisbury). His father died when he was five years old and he was carefully brought up by his mother and educated at the expense of Henry VIII (q.v.) at the Charterhouse school at Sheen and at Magdalen College, Oxford, where his studies were directed by Thomas Linacre (q.v.). In 1521 he was sent to Italy to complete his education at Padua university; there he came into contact with the great Italian scholars of the day and also corresponded with the Dutch humanist Erasmus (q.v.), through whom he met the Polish reformer John à Lasco (q.v.). He returned to England in 1527 but, taking a dislike to life at court, soon retired to Sheen to pursue his studies. The King, fully aware of Pole's potentially hostile Yorkist claim to the throne by his descent, and anxious to keep on good terms with his cousin, granted him a number of minor ecclesiastical offices and revenues.

Although at this time high in favour with the King, Pole foresaw only too well the crisis that loomed ahead over Henry's determination to secure a divorce from Catherine of Aragon (q.v.), of which he personally disapproved, and in 1529 he obtained leave to go to Paris.

While there he was required by the King to seek the opinion of the university on his 'great matter', and when this proved favourable, thanks to the influence of François I, Pole was recalled to England. Henry, realizing the need to keep Pole on his side in the quarrel with Rome, urged him to accept first the bishopric of Winchester and then the archbishopric of York, but Pole felt unable to do so on those terms. An interview with the King, in which Pole was tactlessly outspoken, ended in a violent quarrel, but this was patched up in 1532 when Pole, having pleaded for permission to go abroad on the grounds that when the matter came before Parliament he would be bound to speak according to his conscience, was finally allowed to leave England. He returned to Padua, where once more he immersed himself in theological studies.

During the next three years Henry made several abortive attempts to get Pole onto his side, but reconciliation became impossible when in 1536, at the suggestion of the Emperor Charles V (q.v.), Pole sent to the King a long treatise in which he attacked Henry's policy of royal supremacy and defended the spiritual authority of the Pope; this was published (without Pole's consent) under the title of *Pro Ecclesiasticae Unitatis Defensione* ('In Defence of Ecclesiastical Unity'). To the fury of the English King, Pope Paul III made Pole a cardinal and sent him as a legate to the Low Countries, where he tried unsuccessfully to urge France and Spain to join together in invading England; in retaliation, Henry set a price on the Cardinal's head and executed several members of the Pole family, including his mother, the Countess of Salisbury, and his brother Henry, Lord Montague.

In August 1541 Pole was appointed Governor of the Patrimony of St Peter. Settling at Viterbo, he gathered round him an intimate circle of humanists, which included the Italian poetess, Vittoria Colonna, and those who, like himself, were liberal in outlook and eager to achieve compromise between the Catholic and Lutheran doctrines. In 1542 he was appointed as one of three Papal Legates to open the Council of Trent, but as the Council did not meet for three years, Pole used the waiting period to write his treatise, *De Concilio*. When the Council at last met, in December 1545, Pole was one of the two presiding Legates; his reforms, however, were rejected in favour of stricter orthodoxy, and from that moment the Cardinal's influence began to wane. Nevertheless, on the death of Paul III in 1549, Pole, with the backing of Charles V, was very nearly elected as Pope; the Italian and French cardinals refused to endorse his candidacy, however, and the choice fell on Julius III. In 1552, on the adjournment of the Council of Trent due to the military situation in Europe, Pole retired to a monastery on the shores of Lake Garda.

On the accession of Mary I (q.v.) the Pope immediately commissioned Pole as Legate to the new Queen. In England it was suggested in some quarters that the Cardinal, who was then still in deacon's orders, should marry Mary, but Charles V, pressing his son's suit, saw to it that Pole did not arrive until after the Queen's marriage to Philip II (q.v.) had taken place, the reason given being that the country was not yet in a sufficiently settled state to receive a Papal Legate.

Pole landed in England on 20 November 1554. Ten days later he formally absolved Parliament and the country from their break with Rome and received them back into the Catholic Church. Next he set about reorganizing the Church, refounding the monasteries and making plans to prevent the future accession of the Princess Elizabeth (see Elizabeth I). On 20 March 1556 he was ordained as a priest and the following day – the actual day on which Thomas Cranmer (q.v.) was burned at Oxford – Pole was consecrated as Archbishop of Canterbury. For the next two years he virtually ran the government, busying himself in both Church and secular affairs and seeming to approve, if not to activate, Mary's vigorous persecution of the Protestants. In 1557 Pope Paul IV, then at war with Spain, cancelled Pole's legatine authority and denounced him as a heretic. Utterly demoralized, Pole fell ill and died in London just twelve hours after the Queen, on 17 November 1558.

A sincere and single-minded champion of the Catholic Church, Reginald Pole gravely underestimated the task of reconciling England with Rome. How far he personally was responsible for the burning of the Protestant 'heretics' has long been a matter of dispute: it has been said that he hated extreme measures but that he did not dare to oppose the Queen, that he shirked his duty in not putting a stop to the burnings, that on the other hand the persecutions increased after Pole had become Mary's supreme adviser. On the credit side it must be said that under the influence of the Italian humanists, Pole clearly saw the need for reform in the Church and strove towards that end.

An edition of Pole's *De Concilio* was published in Venice in 1562; the *Pro Unitatis Ecclesiasticae Defensione*, first published in Rome in 1536, was reprinted at Ingolstadt in 1587. His correspondence has been edited in five volumes by A. M. Quirini (Brescia, 1744–57), and a further 349 of the Cardinal's letters will be found in the *Calendar of State Papers, Venetian*, vol. v.

L. Beccatelli, *The Life of Cardinal Reginald Pole*, translated by B. Pye (1776).
Martin Haile, *Life of Reginald Pole* (1910).
W. Schenk, *Reginald Pole, Cardinal of England* (1950).
K. B. McFarlane, *Cardinal Pole* (1924).

*Portraits*: oil, by unknown artist, after 1536: Lambeth Palace, London; oil, by unknown artist, after 1556: National Portrait Gallery, London; other versions at Magdalen College and Corpus Christi College, Oxford, and at Hardwick Hall (National Trust).

**Poulet, Sir William** (?1485–1572), see Paulet, Sir William.

**Poynings, Sir Edward** (1459–1521), soldier and statesman, Lord Deputy of Ireland under Henry VII (q.v.).

Born in Southwark towards the end of 1459, Edward Poynings was the only son of Robert Poynings and his wife Elizabeth, daughter of the Judge William Paston, and grandson of Robert de Poynings, 5th Baron Poynings. His father, who had been sword-bearer to the rebel Jack Cade (see *Lives Before the Tudors*), was killed in battle at St Albans in February 1461. Edward was brought up by his mother, who inherited her

husband's property in Kent and subsequently remarried.

In October 1483 Poynings was leader of a rising in Kent against Richard III (see *Lives Before the Tudors*) intended to support Buckingham's insurrection (see Stafford, Henry, 2nd Duke, in *Lives Before the Tudors*). He escaped to the Continent and joined Henry Tudor, Earl of Richmond (later Henry VII), with whom in August 1485 he landed at Milford Haven. He was made a knight banneret by the new King and a Privy Councillor a few months later. In the following year Poynings was given command of a force sent to the Netherlands to aid the Emperor Maximilian, whose subjects had risen in rebellion. When this mission had been successfully accomplished, he joined Henry before the siege of Boulogne. In 1493 he was appointed Governor of Calais.

Meanwhile the King had become concerned about the situation in Ireland, traditionally a Yorkist stronghold; two claimants to his throne, Lambert Simnel (q.v.) and Perkin Warbeck (q.v.), had both obtained effective support there. Determined to subject the country to English rule, he made his younger son, the future Henry VIII (q.v.), Viceroy of Ireland, appointing Poynings as the Prince's deputy.

Poynings landed in Ireland in October 1494. He subdued the treasonable Earl of Kildare, but abandoned his invasion of Ulster and in December summoned a Parliament at Drogheda to pass statutes (later known as Poynings's Law) requiring all Irish legislation to be confirmed by the English Privy Council and making all laws passed in England prior to 1494 valid in Ireland. When Warbeck invaded Ireland in the following summer, Poynings led the attack against the pretender, forcing him to flee to Scotland. By 1496 the Yorkist following in Ireland had been virtually destroyed and Henry, alarmed at the cost of Poynings's administration – in particular his method of subsidizing Irish chieftains – decided to recall the Lord Deputy.

During the last years of Henry's reign Poynings was actively employed at home and abroad. He was appointed Warden of the Cinque Ports and Comptroller of the Royal Household, both offices being continued to him by Henry VIII, who also made him a Knight of the Garter. From 1511 onwards he was frequently in the Netherlands on diplomatic missions of one sort and another; in 1513 he was present at the capture of Thérouanne and Tournai, and in 1520 at the historic meeting of the French and English monarchs at the Field of the Cloth of Gold, in the preparations for which he had taken an active part.

Sir Edward Poynings died at Westenhanger, Kent, in October 1521. He was survived for a few years by his widow, Isabel (or Elizabeth), daughter of Sir William Scot, Marshal of Calais, but their only son had predeceased him and his estates passed to the Earl of Northumberland.

R. D. Edwards and T. W. Moody, 'The History of Poynings' Law, 1495–1615', *Irish Historical Studies*, ii (1941), pp. 415–24.

# R

**Radcliffe or Ratclyffe, Sir Thomas**
(?1526–1583), 3rd Earl of Sussex, statesman.

The eldest son of Sir Henry Radcliffe,
2nd Earl of Sussex, by his first wife,
Elizabeth, daughter of the Duke of
Norfolk (see Howard, Thomas, 2nd
Duke), Thomas Radcliffe was born in
about 1526. He was educated at
Cambridge and in 1561 admitted as a
member of Gray's Inn. After 1542, when
his father succeeded to the earldom, he
was known as Viscount Fitzwalter.

Knighted by Henry VIII (q.v.) for his
part in the expedition to France of 1544,
Fitzwalter held a command at the Battle
of Pinkie Cleugh in September 1547. He
was employed on various diplomatic
missions both by Edward VI (q.v.) and
by Mary I (q.v.). At the beginning of her
reign Mary created him Baron Fitzwalter. He helped to suppress the Wyatt
rebellion of 1554 (see Wyatt, Sir
Thomas, 'the younger'), participated in
the negotiations for the Queen's marriage to Philip II of Spain (q.v.), and in
1556 was appointed Lord Deputy of
Ireland. He succeeded his father as Earl of
Sussex the following year.

In Ireland Sussex proved to be a
competent and vigorous administrator.
He was continued in office on the
accession of Elizabeth I (q.v.), who in
1560 gave him the title of Lord
Lieutenant of Ireland. From 1559 to 1562
he engaged in a campaign to subdue the
rebellious Irish chieftain Shane O'Neill
(q.v.), which ended however in an
unsatisfactory (and only temporary)
compromise. He was rather more

successful in Limerick, where he defeated
the opponents of the pro-English
chieftain Conor O'Brien, and also in the
province of Leinster, where, in accordance with the Queen's wishes, he
established English settlements at Offaly
and Leix. Ill-health and the failure to
subdue O'Neill led Sussex to ask to be
relieved of his post, this being finally
allowed in 1564.

On returning to England, Sussex
became associated with the governmental faction opposed to the Queen's
favourite, the Earl of Leicester (see
Dudley, Robert). Appointed Lord
Lieutenant of the North in 1569, he
effectively put down the rebellion of the
northern earls in 1569–70. He was
appointed a Privy Councillor towards
the end of 1570 and, supporting the series
of proposals that Elizabeth should marry
first the Archduke Maximilian, then the
Duc d'Anjou, and later his brother,
François, Duc d'Alençon (q.v.), in consequence fell foul of Leicester. This conflict, coupled with his own ill-health,
proved too much for him, and after a
long illness Sussex died at his house in
Bermondsey on 9 June 1583. He had been
twice married, but left no heir and was
succeeded in the earldom by his brother
Henry.

*Portraits:* oil, by unknown artist, c. 1565: Baron
Fitzwalter (other versions in National Portrait
Gallery, London; Knole, Sevenoaks, Kent;
Hardwick Hall, Derbyshire; and elsewhere);
tomb effigy: Boreham Church, Essex.

**Ralegh, Sir Walter** (?1554–1618),
soldier, seaman, writer, courtier, ex-

plorer, and colonizer. (Of some seventy-three known contemporary spellings of his surname, Ralegh was the one he himself most used; the 'Raleigh' favoured by some modern writers happens to be one version that he is believed never to have employed.)

Ralegh was born probably in 1554, at Hayes Barton, near Budleigh Salterton, Devonshire, where his father, Walter Ralegh of Fardell, had established his residence. He was the latter's fifth son, or rather his second son by his third wife, Katherine Champernowne. The Raleghs were an old-established Devon family. Walter's father had mercantile interests, owning at least one ship based at Exeter. On his mother's side Walter was related to most of the local gentry; the Champernownes were a distinguished seafaring family, Katherine's brother, Sir Arthur Champernowne, being a Vice-Admiral of Devon. By her previous marriage Katherine had three sons, one of whom, Humphrey Gilbert (q.v.), Walter's senior by about thirteen years, was to achieve fame as a navigator and explorer.

Little is known of Ralegh's formative years. In 1568 he enrolled as a commoner at Oriel College, Oxford, but left without taking a degree. From the early spring of 1569 until some time in 1572 he served in France as a volunteer in the force raised by his cousin, Sir Henry Champernowne, to assist the Huguenots against the Catholics. According to his own record, he was present at the Battles of Jarnac and Moncontour in March and October 1569; but since he makes no mention of the St Bartholomew Massacre, it is believed that he left France shortly before August 1572. By the end of that year he was back at Oxford, where one of his closest friends was Richard Hakluyt (q.v.), the future geographer.

In 1575 Ralegh became a member of the Middle Temple in London, but he devoted more of his attention to drama and poetry than to the law. By 1577 he had moved to Islington, where he had two servants and described himself as 'of the Court'. He probably used his half-brother's friendship with the poet George Gascoigne (q.v.) to obtain an introduction to the Earl of Leicester (see Dudley, Robert) and thus an entry into the royal service. In 1576 Gascoigne had published Humphrey Gilbert's *Discourse* on a North-West Passage, while Ralegh composed an eighteen-verse poem commending Gascoigne's satire, *The Steele Glas*, also published that year.

In 1578 Ralegh joined Gilbert in fitting out an expedition to the coast of North America; he was given command of the Queen's ship, the *Falcon*. A seven-ship fleet sailed on 19 November, but owing to lack of discipline and poor equipment it broke up a few weeks later, when all vessels except the *Falcon* either returned to England or resorted to piracy. Ralegh set course for the West Indies, but he too was forced by lack of supplies to turn back after he had reached the Cape Verde Islands, arriving in Plymouth in May 1579.

The next few months were marked by quarrels at court, for which Ralegh was twice called before the Privy Council and committed briefly to prison. In July 1580 he was appointed by Lord Grey of Wilton, the Lord Deputy of Ireland, to command a force of one hundred men raised in the City of London for service against the Irish rebels in Munster. At Smerwick that November, on Grey's orders, he took part in the massacre of the Irish, Italian, and Spanish garrison that followed. After a winter stationed at Cork, Ralegh at last received permission to take possession of Barry Court and Barry Island. He fought his way out of an ambush laid for him by the Seneschal of Imokelly and was rewarded by an appointment as one of three commissioners to administer Munster during the absence in England of the Earl of Ormonde (see Butler, Thomas). In this capacity he made a daring capture of Lord Roche of Bally, who was suspected of aiding the rebels.

In December 1581 his company was disbanded, and Ralegh was sent by Grey with dispatches to London. There the self-confident young man succeeded in establishing himself in the eyes of the Council, and in spite of protests from Grey, as an authority on Irish affairs. He lost no time in joining the court at Greenwich, where he swiftly rose to favour. The incident described for the first time some eighty years later by the historian Thomas Fuller, in which Ralegh chivalrously threw down his cloak 'in a plashy place' for Queen Elizabeth I (q.v.) to walk on, is typical of the ambitious, extravagant young courtier; his rapid advancement was viewed with increasing jealousy by the court, and in particular by the now ageing Leicester. As the Queen's new favourite, rich rewards came Ralegh's way: estates in Munster in recognition of his Irish service; the lease of part of Durham House, in the Strand, London, with a monopoly of wine licences and of the export of broadcloth; a knighthood; the offices of Warden of the Stannaries (Cornish tin mines) and Lord Lieutenant of Cornwall. In 1584 he was elected Member of Parliament for Devon, and in 1587 the Queen made him Captain of the Guard. By this time Ralegh was a wealthy man, having been granted by the crown most of the properties formerly belonging to the conspirator Anthony Babington (q.v.).

Throughout the 1580s Ralegh devoted much of his time to a project to

colonize the New World. At first he worked with Gilbert, who had a patent for exploration and colonization that lasted from 1578 until 1584. Ralegh built a ship, the *Bark-Ralegh*, of 200 tons, to accompany the expedition. Then the Queen forbade them to depart. She relented subsequently, although only so far as Gilbert was concerned, and the expedition finally set sail in June 1583. It took possession of Newfoundland; then the flagship foundered, and later, on the way home, Gilbert went down in the *Squirrel*.

Ralegh immediately acquired by charter the powers and privileges that had previously been given to Gilbert. In the next three years he was to invest heavily in a project to colonize Roanoke Island (now in North Carolina). The Queen again refused to let her favourite courtier leave, so that Ralegh had to remain at court while his cousin, Sir Richard Grenville (q.v.) sailed with a fleet of ten vessels to take Ralph Lane (q.v.), as governor of the new colony, together with a distinguished company, to Roanoke. The project was an abject failure, and in 1586 the colonists were brought back to England by Sir Francis Drake (q.v.); the valuable experience gathered, written up by Thomas Harriot (q.v.), provided information for the ultimate foundation of Jamestown.

As Lord Lieutenant of Cornwall Ralegh was responsible for preparing the English defences there against the threatened Spanish invasion of 1588. He does not appear to have fought actively against the Armada, but had the Spanish fleet made a landing on the Irish coast, he and Grenville were to have gone to Ireland to intercept them.

In the summer of 1589 Ralegh went to Ireland, not to fight the Spaniards but because he was under some kind of cloud at court. Leicester had died the previous September, and a new, young favourite, the Earl of Essex (see Devereux, Robert), had captivated the ageing Elizabeth, with the result that jealousy between the two courtiers developed and later became of political importance. The young Earl had challenged Ralegh to a duel but, forbidden by the Privy Council to fight, had joined Drake's expedition in defiance of the Queen's wishes; when shortly afterwards Essex was restored to royal favour, Ralegh took his departure.

In Ireland Ralegh met and discussed poetry with Edmund Spenser (q.v.), whose estates bordered on his own. Each paid tribute to the other in verse, and Ralegh, impressed with what Spenser had so far written of The Faerie Queene, persuaded the poet to accompany him back to England in December 1589; he was instrumental in getting the first three books published the following year.

Because of his spectacular rise to favour Ralegh had made many enemies; although in 1590 the Queen temporarily showed him her appreciation during Essex's brief disgrace following his secret marriage, he never regained his old ascendancy. Nevertheless, after promising him participation as Vice-Admiral in Lord Thomas Howard's expedition to the Azores in 1591, Elizabeth yet again at the last moment refused to let him go; his place was taken by his cousin, Sir Richard Grenville, in the ill-fated Revenge. Ralegh subsequently published an anonymous pamphlet entitled Report of the Truth of the Fight about the Iles of Azores (1591).

Ralegh's personal fortunes now took an upward turn. Towards the end of the same year he secretly married a maid-of-honour to the Queen, Elizabeth, daughter of Sir Nicholas Throckmorton (q.v.), whom he had seduced some months earlier; their first son, Damerei, was born the following March. In January one of his great ambitions – the acquisition of the manor of Sherborne, in Dorset – was at last achieved. The Queen, still unaware of his marriage, gave him command of an expedition which was to intercept the Spanish treasure fleet, but yet again the opportunity for action was to be denied him, for Elizabeth changed her mind, appointed Sir Martin Frobisher (q.v.) in his stead, and ordered that Ralegh should accompany the fleet for only fifty or sixty leagues and then return.

When he sailed at the beginning of May, rumours were fast increasing about his liaison with 'Bess' Throckmorton; though he denied it, it would be only a matter of time before the Queen knew of their secret marriage. By the 18th, when he returned, Elizabeth knew of it; six weeks later Ralegh and his wife were sent to the Tower for their breach of trust and attempt to brazen it out.

In September that year the fleet which Ralegh should have commanded returned to Dartmouth with a prize cargo valued at £141,000. Riots and pilfering broke out when the returning officers and men learned of Ralegh's imprisonment, and necessitated his presence. The Queen released him, with a keeper, to go to the West Country to restore order and, together with Sir Robert Cecil (q.v.), to oversee the distribution of the spoils. Although Ralegh offered the Queen the bulk of the prize money, not for some years did she forgive his offence; she never forgave her former maid-of-honour, his wife.

Released from the Tower but banished from court, Ralegh spent the next few years in retirement at Sherborne, where he consoled himself with his official business in Cornwall and Devon and personal interests such as building, planting, breeding racehorses, and raising falcons. His first son had not survived, but a second boy, Walter known as Wat, was born in 1593. Although he continued in his offices as Lieutenant of Cornwall and Warden of the Stannaries, and sat in Parliament during the winter and spring of 1592–3, when he argued in favour of renewed action against Spain, Ralegh was bitter at his continued exclusion from court; restless and frustrated, he constantly sought a new means to recapture the Queen's favour.

By the end of 1593 he was planning an expedition to Guiana, in South America, in the heart of the Spanish colonial empire, where he hoped to succeed, as the Spaniards had failed, in finding the fabulous El Dorado, city of gold. A reconnaissance expedition was sent in 1594, and on 6 February 1595 Ralegh himself embarked with four ships from Plymouth; his patent from the Queen commissioned him not only to discover and conquer new lands but to 'offend and enfeeble the King of Spain'.

Ralegh spent some time exploring the coast of Trinidad, where he attacked the Spaniards and captured Antonio Berrio, who had led earlier Spanish expeditions in search of El Dorado. He then headed up the Orinoco River, making friends with the native Indians en route; dissuaded by the native chieftain from pressing on to Guiana at the onset of the rainy season, he then returned to England, promising to return the following year.

He was not given a favourable reception on his arrival home in August. The samples of ore he brought back were declared to be worthless, and Ralegh was even accused of never having gone to Guiana at all, but of hiding in a remote part of Cornwall. Furious, he wrote an account of his travels, *The Discoverie of the Large, Rich and Bewtiful Empyre of Guiana*. Published in 1596, it was an immediate success and ran into several editions before 1602, including translations into Latin, German, and Dutch, but neither restored its author to favour nor convinced the Queen of the value of a colonial empire.

Ralegh now became involved in the renewed agitation for a revival of war with Spain; he was also reconciled with Essex. At last, early in 1596, Elizabeth agreed to mount an expedition under Essex and Lord Admiral Howard (see Howard, Charles) to attack Cadiz; Ralegh was given command of one of the four squadrons. On 3 June the English fleet set sail, Ralegh aboard his brand-new flagship *Warspite*; two weeks later they stood off Cadiz, ready to attack on 20 June as planned. At the last moment Ralegh managed to persuade the joint commanders to call off a troop landing and to delay the attack until the ships could go in the following dawn; he was given the honour of leading the assault. In the last stages of a fierce three-hour sea battle he was wounded in the leg and so was unable to participate in the storming of the city after the Spanish galleons had cut their cables and gone aground. The spoils were far less than had been anticipated, as the Spanish commander set fire to his fleet rather than let the English take the vessels. Nevertheless the action gave a great boost to English prestige in Europe and increased war-weariness in Spain.

The Queen, disappointed at the trifling spoils from the Cadiz expedition, delayed another year before restoring Ralegh to favour; but at last, in June 1597, he was reinstated as Captain of the Guard. By that time he had reached an understanding with Cecil and Essex and was working with them to mount an expedition to Ferrol and the Azores, in order to forestall Philip II (q.v.) in his avowed determination to avenge Cadiz. When the English fleet sailed on 10 July, Ralegh, as Rear Admiral, once more aboard the *Warspite*, was in command of the third squadron. Fierce gales forced them back to port a few days later, and they did not sail again until the middle of August, when fresh storms decided them to forgo Ferrol and proceed straight to the Azores in order to intercept the Spanish plate fleet. The expedition was a dismal failure, marred by quarrels between the commanders over Ralegh's impulsive action in landing men to attack Fayal without permission from Essex, and culminating in their missing the Spanish treasure ships altogether. They arrived home to find England in a state of alarm, and another Spanish armada heading for the Cornish coast; fortunately, however, the same strong winds that had helped them home from Finisterre forced the Spaniards back to port, with heavy losses, and the danger of invasion passed.

Immediately after the Azores voyage Ralegh was ill, probably through physical exhaustion. He soon recovered

and devoted much of his time to attendance at Parliament, lavish building work at Sherborne, his work as Warden of the Stannaries, and plans for another expedition to Guiana, which came to nothing. Although in 1600 he was appointed Governor of the island of Jersey, he did not succeed either in winning back the Queen's confidence or in his ambition to become a Privy Councillor or Vice-Chamberlain. On the surface the quarrel with Essex had been patched up, but relations between them rapidly deteriorated again, in the face of the latter's unsteady behaviour. At this period in his life Ralegh enjoyed the friendship of Robert Cecil, whose son William was received at Sherborne as companion to young Wat Ralegh. Following the execution of Essex in 1601, however, Ralegh enviously and unwisely moved away from Cecil.

On the accession of James I (see James VI of Scotland) in March 1603, Ralegh was deprived of his office of Captain of the Guard and ordered to leave Durham House. The new sovereign, in pursuance of his policy of peace with Spain, ordered that all privateering, from which Ralegh still derived an income, was to cease. Ralegh's enemies now began more seriously to plot his ruin. In July he was arrested on suspicion of involvement with Lord Cobham (see Brooke, Henry) and others in the conspiracy against the King known as the Main Plot. Sent to the Tower to await trial, he was deprived of his Governorship of Jersey and of the Lieutenancy of Cornwall. At his trial on 17 November the Attorney General, Sir Edward Coke (see *Lives of the Stuart Age*) spoke for the prosecution and at the last moment produced written evidence from Cobham that sealed Ralegh's fate; found guilty of high treason, he was sentenced to death. A last-minute reprieve, in December, commuted the sentence to imprisonment, and he was taken back to the Tower, where he was to spend the next thirteen years. One of his chief concerns was the welfare of his wife and son, and he fought hard against the forfeiture of his beloved Sherborne to the crown, made possible only because of a clerical error in his conveyance of the estate to Wat in 1602; eventually the King agreed to compensate Lady Ralegh with £400 a year for life.

Ralegh was given an apartment in the Bloody Tower and allowed his own servants to attend him; in the early years his wife and son Wat spent much of the time with him, until an outbreak of plague made Lady Ralegh rent a house on Tower Hill where, in the winter of 1604–5, she gave birth to another son, Carew.

Apart from constant appeals to the King for his release, the prisoner occupied himself largely with writing his monumental *History of the World*, of which he completed only one volume, from the Creation to the year 130 B.C., which was published in 1614. The work gave offence to the King. Ralegh also wrote a number of essays on various subjects, and he valued the patronage of Prince Henry Frederick (see *Lives of the Stuart Age*), from whom he hoped for great things in the future. The Prince's death in November 1612 was a major blow to Ralegh; had he lived, Ralegh would in all probability have been released that Christmas and have recovered Sherborne, which the King had promised to his son, who, it was said, intended to give it back to its former owner.

In the event Ralegh was released (but not pardoned) in March 1616, in order to prepare for a second expedition to Guiana in search of gold. He had to promise the King to keep the peace with Spain and to return to England even if he

failed. He sold almost all his remaining property to raise money to finance the expedition, which sailed from Plymouth on 12 June 1617, with Wat as captain of his father's flagship, the *Destiny*. It was ill-fated from the outset, first by weather conditions, which held Ralegh up in Ireland, and then by sickness which took a severe toll of his men and left him personally so weak that he was unable to lead the expedition up the Orinoco river to seek the gold mine he was convinced existed. Lawrence Keymis, his lieutenant, took his place, with Wat as his captain. While they went up-river Ralegh cruised along the coast of Trinidad, keeping watch for the Spanish fleet. Meanwhile Keymis, in defiance of Ralegh's orders, launched an attack on the town of San Thomé, in which Wat was killed; no gold mine was discovered, and on 2 March some 150 survivors out of an expeditionary force of 400 rejoined their fleet. Ralegh, grief-stricken, was harsh with Keymis, as a result of which the latter committed suicide; several of his captains now deserted and others sailed straight for home; even some of the crew of the *Destiny* mutinied, not daring to return to England, and Ralegh had to promise to land the mutineers in Ireland before returning to Plymouth.

It was unfortunate for Ralegh that James was trying to negotiate a Spanish marriage alliance for his son, the future Charles I (see *Lives of the Stuart Age*), at the very time that news was received of the expedition's outcome. Gondomar, the Spanish ambassador, immediately reminded the King of his promise to deliver Ralegh to Madrid to be hanged, but after opposition had been voiced in the Council, it was decided to give him a hearing in London. A proclamation was issued on 9 June denouncing the 'hostile invasion of the town of S. Thomé' and stating that Ralegh had maliciously infringed the peace and friendship between England and Spain.

He was not arrested on arrival in Plymouth on 21 June. His wife urged him to escape, but Ralegh played for time on the way to London, feigning illness so that he could write his *Apology*, or defence against the charges made. Then on the night of 9 August he attempted to reach Tilbury, from where he would sail to the Continent, but was betrayed by Sir Lewis Stukely and arrested at Greenwich; while a case was prepared against him, he was lodged in the Tower. After a hearing before the commissioners on 22 October, he was taken before the Justices of the King's Bench on the 28th; the original death sentence of 1603 was invoked, with the concession that he was to be beheaded instead of hanged, drawn, and quartered. The execution was carried out early the following morning, 29 October, at Old Palace Yard, Westminster. Ralegh was afterwards buried in St Margaret's, Westminster.

Sir Walter Ralegh has been portrayed both as a romantic hero and as an unscrupulous schemer. Disliked and distrusted by most of his contemporaries, at least up to his trial in 1603, he remains one of the most interesting, if enigmatic, of the Elizabethans, ahead of his time in his ideas on colonial empire, intellectually gifted, restless, possessed of a vivid imagination, a persuasive pen, and a brilliant, but bitter, tongue. His enemies wrongly accused him of atheism, and the Queen, although she liked his company, never had sufficient confidence in him to grant him the power he sought.

Only some thirty pieces of his poetry are extant, the most important being a fragment entitled 'Cynthia, Lady of the Sea', addressed to the Queen. Ralegh is portrayed as the 'Shepheard of the Sea' in Spenser's *Colin Clouts come home againe*.

Ralegh's writings have been edited by Thomas Birch as *The Works of Sir Walter Ralegh* (8 vols; Oxford, 1829). Other modern editions are *The Discoverie . . . of Guiana,* edited by V. T. Harlow (1928); *The Poems of Sir Walter Ralegh*, edited by Agnes Latham (2nd ed. 1951); and *The History of the World* (selections), edited by C. A. Patrides (1971). See also T. N. Brushfield, *A Bibliography of Sir Walter Raleigh* (2nd ed. Exeter, 1908).

J. Adamson and H. F. Folland, *The Shepherd of the Ocean: An Account of Sir Walter Ralegh and his Times* (1969).

E. Edwards, *The Life of Sir Walter Ralegh* (2 vols; 1868). (Volume ii contains most of Ralegh's extant letters.)

Robert Lacey, *Sir Walter Ralegh* (1973).

A. L. Rowse, *Ralegh and the Throckmortons* (1962).

W. Stebbing, *Sir Walter Raleigh* (Oxford, 2nd ed. 1899).

J. Winton, *Sir Walter Ralegh* (1975).

*Portraits:* watercolour on card, by N. Hilliard, *c.* 1585: National Portrait Gallery, London; oil, attributed to the monogrammist H (? Hubbard), 1588: N.P.G.; oil, by unknown artist, *c.* 1590: Colonial Williamsburg, U.S.A.; oil, full length, with his son, by unknown artist, 1602: N.P.G.; engraving, by S. van de Passe: in *History of the World* (3rd ed. 1617).

## Rastell, John (1475–1536), lawyer, printer, and playwright.

Born in Coventry in 1475, John Rastell was trained as a lawyer. He entered Lincoln's Inn, was called to the bar, and soon acquired a considerable practice in London. In 1510 he set up his own printing press, specializing at first in legal books and later in plays; the printing office was later moved to a house in St Paul's Churchyard.

Rastell was a man of many parts. In addition to his legal and printing career, he was interested in politics and sat in Parliament as Member for Dunheved, Cornwall, from 1529 to 1536. He was in later life an agent for Thomas Cromwell (q.v.). In 1517 he invested in an expedition to found a settlement in the 'New Found Lands', but this had to be abandoned because of mutiny among the crew. A more enduring pastime was Rastell's connection with a number of dramatic ventures, which included the design and production of pageants and plays, some of them on a stage built in the garden of his house at Finsbury Fields, and also the printing not only of his own original plays, but also of those of other contemporary playwrights, including John Heywood (q.v.), who was his son-in-law. Several of the pageants devised by Rastell were performed at court, where he was probably introduced by Sir Thomas More (q.v.), to whose sister Elizabeth he was married.

Towards the end of his life Rastell fell on hard times. A staunch Catholic, he became involved in religious controversy and in 1536 was thrown into prison, suspicion attaching to him on account of his relationship to More. He is believed to have died in prison later that year, in such poor circumstances that he could leave his wife only the house he had settled on her at the time of his marriage. Rastell's son William was to follow his father into the law and to become a judge in the reign of Elizabeth I (q.v.).

The interludes written by John Rastell and issued by his press include *The Nature of the Four Elements* (1519) and *Of Gentylness and Nobylyte* (c. 1527). He was probably the author of another interlude printed in about 1527, *Calisto and Melibea*, taken from the novel by Fernando de Rojas, *La Celestina*. Apart from the many legal works printed by Rastell, he was responsible for More's *Life of Pico*, a Latin grammar by Thomas Linacre (q.v.), and the only known copy of Henry Medwall's *Fulgens and Lucres*, the earliest English secular play that is extant.

**Ratclyffe, Sir Thomas** (?1526–1583), see Radcliffe, Sir Thomas.

**Recorde, Robert** (?1510–1558), mathematician.

Robert Recorde was born of good family at Tenby, Pembrokeshire, probably in 1510, and admitted as a scholar at Oxford in about 1525. In 1531 was elected a fellow of All Souls College. Some years later Recorde moved to Cambridge, where he read, and probably also taught, mathematics and medicine, graduating as M.D. in that university in 1545. He subsequently returned to Oxford to teach arithmetic and mathematics, but although he acquired a reputation for immense learning, his reception there was not altogether favourable and he soon left again, this time for London.

Recorde practised as a physician and may have been physician to Edward VI (q.v.) and Mary I (q.v.). In 1549 he was appointed Comptroller of the Mint at Bristol, and in May 1551 the King made him General Surveyor of the Mines and Money, in which office he served both in England and in Ireland. Most of his time was devoted to his mathematical skills, but he was also a gifted physician and a learned antiquary. He was almost certainly a champion of the Protestant reformation. He was the first writer in English on arithmetic, geometry, and astronomy; he introduced algebra into England; in the field of astronomy he was one of the early followers in this country of the system of Copernicus (q.v.); he was the first to use the sign = to indicate equality.

His principal works were *The Grounde of Artes*, on arithmetic, published in 1546; *The Urinal of Physick* (1547); a four-volume work on geometry, *The Pathway to Knowledge* (1551–1602); *The Castle of Knowledge*, on astronomy

(1551); and *The Whetstone of Witte*, on algebra (1557). Recorde's mathematical works were regarded as standard authorities until the end of the sixteenth century.

Recorde died in King's Bench Prison at Southwark in 1558, having probably been imprisoned for debt and accused of improper dealings at the Mint.

F. R. Johnson and S. V. Larkey, 'Robert Recorde's mathematical teaching and the anti-Aristotelian movement', *Huntington Library Bulletin*, vii (1935).

*Portraits*: oil, by unknown artist, early seventeenth century: Faculty of Mathematics, Cambridge University; woodcuts in Recorde's *Urinal of Physick* and *Pathway to Knowledge*.

## Riccio or Rizzio, David (*c.* 1533–1566), secretary to Mary, Queen of Scots (q.v.).

There are two theories concerning Riccio's birth, which took place probably in 1533: one, that he was the son of a music teacher in Turin, Italy, and the other that he came from the wealthy Riccio di Solbitro family of Piedmont.

Riccio is said to have been an accomplished musician and singer. He spent some time at the court of the Duke of Savoy before accompanying the latter's ambassador, Moretta, to Scotland in 1561. At the time the Queen of Scots was seeking a singer to complete her private quartet; Riccio applied for and was given the post. In 1564 he became the Queen's French secretary.

His rapid advancement was much resented by the Scottish nobility, who regarded him as an upstart foreigner and a papal agent. He was initially on close terms of friendship with the Queen's husband, Lord Darnley (see Stewart, Henry). Afterwards, however, when Mary turned increasingly to Riccio for advice, ousting William Maitland of Lethington, the Secretary of State, Darn-

ley joined with those who plotted Riccio's murder; the conspirators included the Earl of Moray (see Stewart, Lord James), who did not, however, take an active part as he was an outlaw in England at the time, the Earl of Morton (see Douglas, James), Patrick Lindsay, 6th Baron Lindsay, Patrick Ruthven, 3rd Baron Ruthven, and his son, later the 4th Baron Ruthven (see Ruthven, William), and several others who stood for the restoration of Protestantism in Scotland.

Riccio was murdered on the evening of 9 March 1566. He was with the Queen at supper in Holyroodhouse, when the conspirators, led by Patrick Ruthven, who had been admitted to the palace by Darnley, entered the room, dragged him away, and stabbed him over fifty times; before making their escape they left Darnley's dagger in his corpse in order to implicate him in the deed. Darnley subsequently betrayed his accomplices to the Queen, and they in turn showed her written proof of his part in the plot, for which she never forgave him.

Riccio's body was for a time interred in the royal tomb at Edinburgh, but was later transferred to another resting place in the church.

P. Ruthven, *A Relation of the Death of David Rizzio* (1699; rev. ed. Edinburgh, 1890).
A. F. Steuart, *Seigneur Davie: A Sketch Life of D. Riccio* (1922).

## Rich, Barnabe (?1540–1617), soldier and writer.

Born in Essex in about 1540, Barnabe Rich was probably distantly related to Lord Chancellor Rich (see Rich, Sir Richard). He joined the army at an early age and first fought in the war with France of 1557–8. At the beginning of the reign of Elizabeth I (q.v.) he served in the Low Countries and, rising to the rank of captain, became acquainted with other soldiers of literary bent such as Thomas

Churchyard and George Gascoigne (q.v.), who in turn introduced him in London to more prominent men of letters. In 1573 Rich was sent to Ireland, where he served for virtually the rest of his life, holding a command in 1584 and later becoming an informer for the crown. From that time on, however, his leisure was devoted exclusively to writing, in which he had the encouragement of his patron, Sir Christopher Hatton (q.v.).

Altogether Rich wrote about twenty-six books, chiefly romances written in the style of Lyly's *Euphues* (see Lyly, John), but also pamphlets on military and other subjects, reports on Ireland, and personal reminiscences. The story *Apolonius and Silla* in *Rich, His Farewell to the Military Profession*, published in 1581, was used by William Shakespeare (q.v.) as his source for the plot of *Twelfth Night*.

Barnabe Rich died on 10 November 1617.

T. M. Cranfill and D. H. Bruce, *Barnaby Rich: A Short Biography* (Austin, Texas, 1953).

**Rich, Sir Richard** (?1496–1567), 1st Baron Rich, lawyer and statesman, Lord Chancellor from 1547 to 1551.

The second son of Richard Rich and his wife Joan Dingley, Richard Rich was born in about 1496 in the parish of St Lawrence Jewry, in the City of London. He may have studied at Cambridge before entering the Middle Temple, where he was autumn reader in 1529. In November that year he entered Parliament as Member for Colchester.

Although he was said to have led a dissipated youth, Rich was well trained in the law. He was also adept at looking after his own interests, constantly shifting his political and religious allegiances to gain the best advantage. In 1533 he was appointed Solicitor General and was knighted. He prosecuted in the treason trials of Bishop John Fisher (q.v.) and Sir Thomas More (q.v.), using in the former case evidence obtained on a personal visit to Fisher in prison, when he had pledged the King's word that their conversation would be confidential; at the latter trial Rich was accused directly by More of committing perjury.

From 1536 Rich assisted Thomas Cromwell (q.v.) in carrying out the dissolution of the monasteries, considerably enriching himself in the process. He subsequently deserted Cromwell, who had been both friend and benefactor to him, when the latter fell from grace, and thereafter worked with Bishop Stephen Gardiner (q.v.) in persecuting the reformers. In the case of Anne Askew (q.v.) it is recorded that Rich himself turned the screws when she was tortured on the rack.

A Privy Councillor by 1540, he was created Baron Rich of Leez, Essex, shortly after the accession of Edward VI (q.v.) in 1547. In October that year he was appointed Lord Chancellor. At first he acquiesced in the policy changes decreed by the Protector Somerset (see Seymour, Edward), but two years later Rich helped the Earl of Warwick (see Dudley, John; later Duke of Northumberland) to overthrow him. Next, at Warwick's bidding, he took part in proceedings against Gardiner and Bishop Edmund Bonner (q.v.) and in the enforcement of measures against the Princess Mary, later Mary I (q.v.). At the end of 1551 illness forced him to resign the office of Lord Chancellor. He retired to Essex, but continued to attend the Privy Council. Although, like his fellow Councillors, in 1553 he signed the declaration proclaiming the Lady Jane Grey (q.v.) as Edward's successor, after the King's death Rich went down to Essex and declared for Mary. He attended

Mary on her entry into the City, and following her proclamation as rightful Queen he was sworn in as a Councillor. In fact he took little further part in state affairs, due to ill-health.

Lord Rich died at Rochford, Essex, on 12 June 1567. By his wife Elizabeth, daughter of William Jenks, he had a family of five sons and ten daughters. He was succeeded by his eldest son, Robert.

*Portrait*: drawing, by Hans Holbein the Younger, *c.* 1541–3: Royal Collection, Windsor.

## Richmond and Derby, Countess of

(1443–1509), see Beaufort, Margaret.

## Ridley, Nicholas (?1500–1555), Bishop of London, martyr.

Ridley came from an ancient Border family, the second son of Christopher Ridley of Unthank Hall, near Willimot-iswick, Northumberland. He was educated at Newcastle and at Pembroke Hall, Cambridge, where he was financed by his uncle, Dr Robert Ridley, who taught Greek at the university. Nicholas was a

brilliant Latin and Greek scholar, and later studied philosophy and divinity, taking his M.A. and becoming a fellow of Pembroke Hall in 1524–5. From 1527 to 1530 he continued his studies abroad, at the Sorbonne in Paris and at Louvain University.

On his return to Cambridge Ridley was appointed junior treasurer of his college; in 1532 he was made chaplain to the university, and two years later a senior proctor. It was during this second period at Cambridge that he began to show leanings towards Protestantism. In 1537 he resigned his university posts to become private chaplain to Archbishop Cranmer (q.v.), whom he had probably met at Cambridge some years earlier. He took up residence at Ford in Kent, and the following year Cranmer gave him the near-by living of Herne.

Ridley was now fast becoming an able spokesman for Protestant doctrines; he took his doctorate of divinity at Cambridge, but when elected Master of Pembroke Hall in 1540, declined to reside there, preferring to remain with Cranmer to help him in his work. He became a royal chaplain and a canon of Canterbury Cathedral, where he was involved in a series of quarrels between the Catholic and Protestant clergy. The position of the Protestants had become more dangerous since the fall of Thomas Cromwell (q.v.), and in 1543 Ridley was accused of heretical teaching, but acquitted. It was at about this time that he finally abandoned the doctrine of transubstantiation, but did not make his views public.

In October 1545 Ridley was given a prebend at Westminster, and in September 1547 he was consecrated Bishop of Rochester. Throughout the reign of Edward VI (q.v.) he and Cranmer devoted their energies to promoting the English Reformation. Ridley supported the extremists' attacks on images, but preached against their denunciation of the Mass. He probably helped Cranmer to compile the Book of Common Prayer, and when this was debated in the House of Lords in December 1548 he brought his arguments against the theory of transubstantiation into the open for the first time. He also spoke in support of the bill to allow the clergy to marry. Much of his time was taken up in getting the new Prayer Book accepted in his diocese; he also tried unsuccessfully to persuade the Anabaptist Joan Bocher (q.v.) to recant. In 1549 he was appointed to the Commission of Visitors to the University of Cambridge, set up with the purpose of enforcing Protestantism there; at the end of the debate between Catholics and Protestants on the Mass, he pronounced against the doctrine of transubstantiation.

When Edmund Bonner (q.v.) was deprived of his bishopric in October 1549, Ridley succeeded him as Bishop of London. In this office he not only continued to work for the enforcement of Protestantism, ordering amongst other innovations that altars be replaced by communion tables, but by drawing the King's attention to the poverty prevalent in London, he strove to improve the conditions of the poor. He examined Stephen Gardiner (q.v.), and concurred in his being deprived of the bishopric of Winchester and imprisoned. On 16 July 1553, having previously signed the letters patent that settled the English crown on Lady Jane Grey (q.v.), he preached at Paul's Cross on the theme that the Princesses Mary and Elizabeth were both illegitimate, and that Mary's succession would be against the religious interests of the country. When Northumberland (see Dudley, John) failed in the plot to put Lady Jane on the throne, Ridley threw himself on the mercy of the new Queen, Mary I (q.v.), but on his way to see her at Framlingham was arrested and sent to the Tower; he was exempted from the amnesty and soon afterwards deprived of his bishopric.

From prison Ridley defended his religious views in writing and refused all attempts to persuade him to recant. The rebellion of Sir Thomas Wyatt the younger (q.v.) determined the Queen to get the Protestant leaders to recant, and Ridley, Cranmer, and Hugh Latimer (q.v.) together were sent to Oxford to face a public disputation; in April 1554, following a noisy debate, Ridley was declared a heretic and excommunicated. He continued to write various treatises on Protestantism, some of which, smuggled out of prison and printed abroad, found their way to England. He steadfastly refused to recant, and together with Latimer was led to the stake at Oxford on 16 October 1555. The flames were slow to consume his body and he is said to have suffered an agonizing death.

A fine scholar and a man of steadfast faith, not in sympathy with the extremists, Ridley represented all that was best in the English Reformation. His works have been edited by H. Christmas for the Parker Society, Cambridge (1841).

G. W. Bromiley, *Nicholas Ridley, 1550–1555, scholar, bishop, theologian, martyr* (1953).
M. L. Loane, *Masters of the English Reformation* (1954).
J. G. Ridley, *Nicholas Ridley* (1957).

*Portraits*: oil on panel, 1555, by unknown artist: National Portrait Gallery, London; engraving by Willem and Magdalena van de Passe, in *Herwologia*, 1620; painted version: Captain W. H. W. Ridley; engraving, by R. White, 1681: location not known.

**Ridolfi, Roberto di** (1531–1612), conspirator.

Born in Florence on 18 November 1531, Ridolfi came from a prominent family of senators and supporters of the Medici. He was educated and trained as a banker, and built up his business largely through trade with London merchants.

In about 1555 Ridolfi settled in England, where he soon became intimate with many of the influential Catholic families during the reign of Mary I (q.v.). He quickly established a reputation as a banker not only with the City merchants, but also with the government, to whom he was useful through his contacts with agents in Italy and thus with the papacy.

The accession of Elizabeth I (q.v.) does not appear to have affected Ridolfi's influence or activities, probably because William Cecil (q.v.; later 1st Baron Burghley) and his government found him of service in monetary affairs. His financial dealings brought him into the plot to marry the Duke of Norfolk (see Howard, Thomas, 4th Duke) to Mary, Queen of Scots (q.v.), with which he was in sympathy. He became a champion of the cause of the discontented Catholics in England, and, being now in the pay of both France and Spain, he acted as intermediary between the English conspirators, the Pope, the French and Spanish ambassadors in London, and the Bishop of Ross, Mary Stuart's agent. Large sums of money from abroad found their way into the hands of the English Catholics.

In October 1568 these transactions were brought to the attention of Cecil. Ridolfi was arrested and sent to Sir Francis Walsingham (q.v.) for examination; under interrogation he admitted that he had passed funds to the Bishop of Ross and the Duke of Norfolk, and that he was aware of the 'matter of the marriage betwixt the Queen of Scots and the Duke'. His house was searched, but no further charge was made against him. For a time he was able to convince the Queen's ministers that all his money dealings were part of legitimate banking business and that his negotiations with the Spanish embassy were concerned only with the matter of the Spanish treasure ships seized by England earlier in the year, negotiations on which he had been employed at Cecil's command. Within a month he was freed on payment of £1,000 bail, on condition that he stayed in his own house and did not interfere in matters of state; in January 1570 he was freed from this restriction and his bail was refunded.

Ridolfi now set to work on the plot for a Spanish invasion of England that would lead to the restoration of the old Catholic religion. Lists were drawn up of the English Catholic peers who would rise and help the Spaniards to overthrow Elizabeth and her government and put Mary Stuart on the English throne. To this was added, with the approval of the Queen of Scots, the original plan for her marriage to Norfolk. Early in 1571 Ridolfi left England for the Continent to explain his scheme in person to the Duke of Alva, the Pope, and Philip II of Spain (q.v.). He met with a lukewarm reception from Alva in the Netherlands, but the Pope and Philip were more encouraging. Philip undertook that if Elizabeth were assassinated, Alva and his army would invade England.

By this time, however, the English ministers knew of the plot. Charles Baillie, Ridolfi's messenger, had been arrested at Dover carrying cipher letters from Ridolfi to Norfolk and the other conspirators, and had made a confession. Further letters sent by Ridolfi from Rome via the Spanish ambassador in London never reached their destination: the recipients, Norfolk and others, had already been arrested. Alva refused to invade, and Ridolfi, his plan having completely failed, was unable to return to England. He had, however, inveigled Norfolk to his end.

He spent the rest of his life in Florence, where he became a senator and died on 18 February 1612.

Francis Edwards, *The Marvellous Chance: Thomas Howard, 4th Duke of Norfolk and the Ridolfi Plot* (1968).

**Rizzio, David** (*c.* 1533–1566), see Riccio, David.

**Rogers, John** (?1500–1555), Protestant martyr.

John Rogers was born at Ashton, near Birmingham, probably in 1500, and was educated at Pembroke Hall, Cambridge, graduating as a B.A. in 1526. In 1532 he became Rector of Holy Trinity in the City of London, but resigned this living two years later to become chaplain to the English merchants in Antwerp. Here Rogers came under the influence of William Tyndale (q.v.) and was converted to Protestantism. Shortly before Tyndale's arrest Rogers took charge of his incomplete translation of the Old Testament. After Tyndale's death he carried on with the work, using the Coverdale version (see Coverdale, Miles) for the untranslated books, and Tyndale's New Testament (which had been published in 1526), and adding an original preface, marginal notes, and a title page which he signed with the pseudonym 'Thomas Matthew'. The book was printed in Antwerp and sold in England by Richard Grafton; it became known as 'Matthew's Bible' and was used as a basis for the Great Bible of 1539–40.

While in Antwerp Rogers married Adriana de Weyden, who bore him eleven children. They spent some years at Wittenberg, where Rogers was minister of a Protestant congregation, but in 1548 following the accession of Edward VI (q.v.) he returned to England with his family, who were naturalized a few years later by special Act of Parliament. He now published a translation of Melanchthon's *Considerations of the Augsburg Interim*. He was given the livings of St Margaret Moyses and St Sepulchre in London in 1550, and the following year a prebend at St Paul's, where he was appointed divinity lecturer by the dean and chapter.

On the accession of Mary I (q.v.) Rogers preached two sermons which landed him in Newgate prison; he extolled the 'true doctrine' of Edward's reign and warned his audience against popery. He spent a year in Newgate, together with John Hooper (q.v.), John Bradford, and others, and during his imprisonment drew up a statement confessing his convinced Protestantism. He was examined by Stephen Gardiner (q.v.), and condemned to death as a heretic for denying the claims of the Church of Rome and the real presence in the sacrament. He refused to recant, even when offered a pardon at the last moment, and was burned at Smithfield on 4 February 1555.

Rogers was the first Protestant victim of the Marian persecution, and his death gave much encouragement to his followers.

J. L. Chester, *John Rogers* (1861).
M. L. Loane, *Pioneers of the Reformation in England* (1964).

**Russell, John** (?1486–1555), 1st Earl of Bedford, statesman.

The son of James Russell and his first wife, Alice, John Russell was born in about 1486. The family was an old-established one in the west of England, John being the great-grandson of Henry Russell, Member of Parliament for Weymouth, a Bordeaux wine merchant who had flourished at the beginning of the fifteenth century.

Russell is believed to have spent some of his early years travelling on the Continent before entering the royal service in 1506 as a gentleman usher to Henry VII (q.v.). Because of his proficiency in foreign languages he was soon entrusted by Henry VIII (q.v.) with a number of diplomatic missions. Knighted for his part in the expedition to France of 1513, in which he served as a captain, Russell was in attendance on the King at the Field of the Cloth of Gold in 1520. In 1522 he accompanied the force commanded by the Earl of Surrey (later the Duke of Norfolk; see Howard, Thomas, 3rd Duke) in the attack on the coast of Normandy and Brittany. He was made Knight Marshal of the Royal Household in 1532, Comptroller in 1537, and the next year a Privy Councillor. A succession of promotions and honours followed: Knight of the Garter and elevation to the peerage as Baron Russell of Chenies in 1539; High Steward of the Duchy of Cornwall; Lord High Admiral of England, 1540; High Steward of Oxford University and Lord Privy Seal in 1542.

In 1544 Russell took part in the invasion of France. He was one of Henry's executors and on the accession of Edward VI in 1547 was reappointed Privy Councillor and Lord Privy Seal. He distinguished himself in putting down the Western rebellion in 1549 and, after helping to overthrow the Protector Somerset (see Seymour, Edward), Russell was in January 1550 rewarded with an earldom, taking the title of Earl of Bedford. Although he signed the King's declaration naming the Lady Jane Grey (q.v.) as his successor, Bedford subsequently allied himself with Mary I (q.v.), by whom he was reappointed as Lord Privy Seal and made Lord Lieutenant of Devonshire. He helped to suppress the Wyatt rebellion of 1554 (see Wyatt, Thomas, 'the younger') and was joint ambassador, with Viscount Fitzwalter (see Radcliffe, Sir Thomas), to Spain for the purpose of concluding the marriage treaty between Mary and Philip II of Spain (q.v.).

John Russell, 1st Earl of Bedford, died on 14 March 1555 at his house in the Strand, London. He had amassed considerable riches during his lifetime, including the abbeys of Tavistock and Woburn, as well as extensive London properties at Covent Garden and Long Acre. He was succeeded by his eldest son, Francis.

*Portrait:* chalk drawing, by Hans Holbein the Younger: Royal Collection, Windsor.

**Ruthven, William** (?1541–1584), 4th Baron Ruthven and 1st Earl of Gowrie, conspirator.

Born probably in 1541, William Ruthven was the second son of Patrick Ruthven, 3rd Baron Ruthven, and Janet, natural daughter of the Earl of Angus (see Douglas, Archibald, 6th Earl). In April 1562 his father conceded to William and his wife, Dorothea Stewart, granddaughter of the Lord Methven whose first wife was Margaret Tudor (q.v.), certain lands in the barony of Ruthven; this may have been at the time of his marriage.

In March 1566 Ruthven joined with his father, the Earl of Morton (see Douglas, James), and others in the plot to murder David Riccio (q.v.), the French secretary to Mary, Queen of Scots (q.v.). The elder Ruthven, although supposed to be dying, led the conspirators into the royal apartment where the Queen and Riccio were at supper; both he and his son subsequently fled to England. On his father's death at Newcastle, William Ruthven succeeded to the title, but the lands had previously been forfeited as he had been denounced as a rebel. In December the same year, however, he received a pardon from the Queen and returned to Scotland.

There is no evidence of Ruthven's connection with the murder of Lord Darnley (see Stewart, Henry); it is probable that he joined those who sought revenge against the Earl of Bothwell (see Hepburn, James) for the crime. He was among the lords who confronted the Queen and Bothwell at Carberry Hill on 15 June 1567; he also fought against Mary after her escape and took part in her defeat at Langside on 13 May 1568. Appointed Provost of Perth in August 1567, Ruthven became Lord Treasurer of Scotland in July 1571. He supported Morton as Regent, and after the latter's overthrow, which had been engineered by the Duke of Lennox (see Stuart, Esmé), he was created Earl of Gowrie in an attempt to placate him. Shortly afterwards, however, he took the side of the Earl of Arran (see Stewart, James, Earl of Arran) in a dispute with Lennox over the right to bear the crown at the opening of Parliament.

Arran's appointment of Robert Montgomerie as Archbishop of Glasgow, unacceptable to the General Assembly, triggered off the 'Ruthven Raid', a coup d'état of the extreme Protestant group led by Gowrie. The young King, James VI (q.v.), induced to visit Ruthven on 23 August 1582, was kidnapped and held prisoner for nearly a year, during which time he was forced to sign proclamations against both Lennox and Arran.

After the King's escape in July 1578, Arran gained influence over James, and in February 1584 persuaded him to order Gowrie to leave Scotland. The Earl delayed his departure while devising a conspiracy, together with the other Protestant lords, for the capture of Stirling Castle. The plot was discovered, and Gowrie, arrested at Dundee, was taken to Stirling to stand trial. He confessed his part in the conspiracy, for which he was convicted of high treason and beheaded at Stirling on 2 May 1584.

Gowrie's lands were forfeited and his wife and children treated with severity until the fall from power of Arran in 1586, after which they were restored. In August 1600 there occurred the mysterious 'Gowrie Conspiracy', when the King was lured to Gowrie House at Perth by the Earl's two sons, John (now the 3rd Earl of Gowrie) and Alexander, probably in revenge for their father's execution. The purpose of this plot – whether it was to capture the King's person or to settle a debt – has never been discovered. James was rescued by his attendants and both Gowrie and his brother were killed in the attempt.

The *Papers relating to William, 1st Earl of Ruthven* were privately printed in 1867. See also S. Cowan (ed.), *The Ruthven Family Papers* (1912), which gives the family version of the Gowrie conspiracy.

W. Roughhead, *The Riddle of the Ruthvens and other studies* (Edinburgh, 1919; rev. ed. 1936).

A. F. Steuart, *Seigneur Davie: A Sketch Life of D. Riccio* (1922).

# S

**Sackville, Thomas** (1536–1608), 1st Earl of Dorset and Baron Buckhurst, statesman, dramatist, and poet.

The only son of the wealthy Sir Richard Sackville, Under-Treasurer of the Exchequer and Treasurer of the Army (later Chancellor of the Exchequer), and his wife Winifred, daughter of Sir John Bruges, Thomas Sackville was born at Buckhurst, Withyham, Sussex, in 1536. Through his father, a first cousin of Anne Boleyn (q.v.), he was related to Queen Elizabeth (q.v.). It seems probable that he was educated at Hart Hall, Oxford, and St John's, Cambridge, before being admitted to the Inner Temple. He was called to the bar, but appears to have devoted

most of his youth to literary pursuits. Sackville married in 1555 Cecily, daughter of Sir John Baker of Sissinghurst, Kent, by whom he was said to have had four sons and three daughters. He entered Parliament in 1558 as Member for Westmorland, representing East Grinstead the following year and Aylesbury in 1563. From 1560 to 1567 he was Grand Master of the Freemasons.

Already at Oxford Sackville's talent as a writer of sonnets had attracted some notice. His major literary work was undertaken while at the Inner Temple, where he collaborated with Thomas Norton (q.v.) in a blank verse drama, *Ferrex and Porrex* or *The Tragedie of Gorboduc*, for which Sackville probably wrote the last two acts; the first tragedy to be written in English, *Gorboduc* was performed at the Inner Temple in 1561. At this time he was also working on *A Myrroure for Magistrates*, a poetic work planned in the manner of Lydgate's *Falls of Princes* (see Lydgate, John, in *Lives Before the Tudors*); for the enlarged edition of 1563 Sackville wrote 'The Induction' and 'The Complaint of Buckingham', the two contributions which alone are considered to have literary merit.

Extravagant living at this period of his life led inevitably to pecuniary difficulties and disgrace, and in the years 1563–6 Sackville found it expedient to travel on the Continent. He visited France and Italy, and while in Rome was imprisoned for a short time on suspicion of spying. The death of his father in April 1566 recalled him to England, where he took possession of a considerable inheritance and rose swiftly to prominence at court. The Queen, who looked with favour on her kinsman and wished to have him close at hand, gave Sackville the manor of Knole, near Sevenoaks, Kent, three months after his return; he was not able to take possession of it until 1603, however, and in the meanwhile he leased from the crown the palace of Sheen, near Richmond. In June 1567 he was knighted and raised to the peerage as Baron Buckhurst.

For the next forty years Buckhurst devoted himself to the service of the state. He was sent as ambassador to France early in 1568 in order to negotiate with Catherine de' Medici (q.v.) for the marriage of her second son, the Duc d'Anjou, to the English Queen, and again in 1571 to congratulate Charles IX on his marriage. He became a member of the Privy Council and sat as a commissioner on a number of notable trials, including those of the Duke of Norfolk (see Howard, Thomas, 4th Duke) and Anthony Babington (q.v.). In 1586 he was appointed to convey to Mary, Queen of Scots (q.v.), at Fotheringay the confirmation of her death sentence. Following the recall of the Earl of Leicester (see Dudley, Robert) from the Low Countries towards the end of 1587, Buckhurst was sent as special ambassador to the States General, principally to inform them that Elizabeth would not provide any more money or men for their cause and to report to her on the situation there. On this occasion he incurred the Queen's displeasure by allegedly interpreting her instructions too literally (in fact she had changed her mind about continuing the war), and on his return Buckhurst was for nine months confined to his house. Restored to favour after Leicester's death, he was in 1588 appointed

Commissioner of Ecclesiastical Causes, and was made a K.G. the following year. The next three years involved him in further diplomatic activity, both in the Low Countries and in France, where in 1591 he was one of the commissioners who signed a treaty of peace; in 1598 he was for the last time in the Low Countries, for the renewal of a treaty with the United Provinces.

At home Buckhurst was well rewarded for his services. Chancellor of Oxford University in 1591, he was in 1599 appointed Lord Treasurer. As Lord High Steward in 1601, he presided at the trial of the Earl of Essex (see Devereux, Robert). On the accession of James I (see James VI of Scotland) he was confirmed in the office of Lord Treasurer for life and in March 1604 he was created Earl of Dorset. That same year he was one of the commissioners who negotiated the new treaty of peace with Spain. By this date Dorset had taken possession of Knole and was both enlarging and embellishing the house. Active to the last, he died suddenly of 'dropsy on the brain' while at the council table at Whitehall on 19 April 1608. He was buried in the Sackville chapel of Withyham church after a funeral at Westminster Abbey.

The *Poetical Works* of Thomas Sackville have been edited by the Rev. R. W. Sackville West (1859). 'Induction' and 'Buckingham', edited from the author's MSS by M. Hearsey, were published in 1936 together with a short biography.

Victoria Sackville-West, *Knole and the Sackvilles* (1922).

J. Swart, *Thomas Sackville* (1949).

*Portraits:* oil, by John de Critz the Elder, 1601: Knole, Sevenoaks, Kent (another version at National Portrait Gallery, London); see also painting of the Somerset House Conference, 1604: N.P.G. and National Maritime Museum, Greenwich.

**Sadler, Sadleir, or Sadleyer, Sir Ralph** (1507–1587), diplomatist.

Born at Hackney, Middlesex, in 1507, Ralph Sadler received a good education and at an early age became a ward of Thomas Cromwell (q.v.), who was then rising spectacularly in royal favour. Probably soon after his guardian's elevation to the peerage in July 1536, Sadler was appointed a Gentleman of the Privy Chamber. The following year he was sent by Henry VIII (q.v.) to Scotland to enquire into the complaints of the Dowager Queen Margaret (see Margaret Tudor) against the Scots and her son, James V (q.v.), and soon afterwards to France in order to ascertain the true nature of relations between the Scots King and that country. He acquitted himself so well that in 1540 he was entrusted with a mission of greater importance: to advise James against the designs of Cardinal David Beaton (q.v.) and the adoption of an ecclesiastical policy antagonistic to Rome. On his return he was appointed one of two principal Secretaries of State, together with Thomas Wriothesley (q.v.). He was knighted in 1542.

Following the Battle of Solway Moss and the death of James V in December 1542, Sadler was sent by Henry to reside in Edinburgh, for the purpose of preventing the revival of Beaton's influence; he was also to negotiate for the marriage of the young Mary, Queen of Scots (q.v.), to Prince Edward (see Edward VI). He acted as Treasurer of the Navy during the invasion of Scotland by the Earl of Hertford (see Seymour, Edward; later Duke of Somerset) in 1544.

Under the terms of Henry VIII's will, Sadler was one of the council of twelve appointed to govern and act as guardians for the young Edward VI. He accompanied Somerset to Scotland in the summer of 1547 as High Treasurer of the Army and fought at Pinkie, where he was made a Knight-Banneret for his gallantry. He spent the reign of Mary I (q.v.) in retirement from public life, but on the accession of Elizabeth I (q.v.), being a keen Protestant, he came to be used by William Cecil (q.v.) as one of his most trusted agents. Sadler played a major part in securing the alliance between England and Scotland, signed in 1560, and in 1568 he was given the office of Chancellor of the Duchy of Lancaster. Following the flight of Mary, Queen of Scots, to England, he was one of three English commissioners appointed to treat with the Scottish commissioners at York concerning 'the great matter of the Queen of Scots'. In 1570 he accompanied the Earl of Sussex (see Radcliffe, Thomas) on his expedition to put down the rebellion in the north of England on behalf of the Duke of Norfolk (see Howard, Thomas, 4th Duke) and the Queen of Scots; nominally Sadler went in the capacity of Paymaster-General, but in reality he was there to supervise and advise.

In August 1584 Sadler reluctantly took over from the Earl of Shrewsbury (see Talbot, George) as jailer of the Queen of Scots, beseeching Sir Francis Walsingham (q.v.) to relieve him of the charge as soon as possible in consideration of his advanced years. Mary was duly handed over to Sir Amias Paulet the following spring. At the age of eighty, Sadler possibly carried out his last diplomatic mission in 1587, when he is believed to have been sent as envoy to James VI (q.v.) in order to reconcile him to the execution of his mother. He died soon afterwards, on 30 May 1587, and was buried in Standon church.

*The State Papers and Letters of Sir Ralph Sadler*, edited by Arthur Clifford (2 vols; Edinburgh, 1809), are a valuable source for Anglo-Scottish relations of the period.

H. Drummond, *Our Man in Scotland: Sir Ralph Sadleir, 1507–1587* (1969).

F. S. Stoney, *Life of Sir R. Sadleir* (1877).

T. U. Sadleir, *A Brief Memoir of the Rt. Hon. Sir Ralph Sadleir* (1907).

A. J. Slavin, *Power and Profit: a study of Sir Ralph Sadler, 1507–1547* (1966).

**Salisbury, Countess of** (1473–1541), see Pole, Margaret.

**Salisbury, 1st Earl of** (1563–1612), see Cecil, Robert.

**Savile, Sir Henry** (1549–1622), scholar, see *Lives of the Stuart Age*.

**Scott or Scot, Reginald or Reynold** (?1538–1599), author of *The Discoverie of Witchcraft*.

The son of Richard Scot and grandson of Sir John Scot of Scots Hall, Smeeth, Kent, Reginald Scott was born in about 1538. At the age of seventeen he entered Hart Hall, Oxford, but left the university without obtaining a degree. He may have studied law subsequently.

Scott spent most of his life in his native county of Kent, managing the properties which he had inherited there and administering the affairs of his cousin and patron, Sir Thomas Scot of Scots Hall, Smeeth. He married in 1568 Jane Cobbe, of Cobbes Place, near Aldington, and after her death took as his second wife a widow called Alice Collyar. In 1588–9 he represented New Romney in Parliament. He may also have been a Justice of the Peace. Scott died on 9 October 1599, having three weeks earlier drawn up his own Will.

During his lifetime Reginald Scott published two books: *A Perfite Platforme of a Hoppe Garden*, the first practical treatise on the cultivation of hops, in 1574 (reprinted 1576 and 1578); and the work for which he is best known, *The Discoverie of Witchcraft*, which appeared in 1584. In the latter, written with the purpose of preventing the persecution of poor, aged and simple folk who were popularly believed to be witches, Scott boldly exposed current attitudes towards sorcery, in particular the impostures and credulity of contemporary Elizabethan society. Scott's attempt to unmask ancient beliefs aroused the fury of several other writers on the subject, including James VI of Scotland (q.v.), but in general his work was well received both at home and abroad. William Shakespeare (q.v.) used it as a source for the witches' scene in *Macbeth*. The book has been edited by Brinsley Nicholson and reprinted in 1886 and 1930, together with a short introduction.

**Seymour, Edward** (?1500–1552), 1st Earl of Hertford, 1st Duke of Somerset, and Protector of the Realm during part of the reign of Edward VI (q.v.).

Born in about 1500, probably at the Seymour family home, Wulfhall, near Savernake, Wiltshire, Edward Seymour was the second son of Sir John and Lady Margery Seymour. All that is known of his formal education is that he studied at Oxford; he may also have spent a short time at Cambridge. Singled out by his father at an early age for a life at court (the elder son, John, was a sickly boy and died young), Edward fulfilled his first royal duty when about fourteen years old, acting as page to Mary Tudor (q.v.) at her wedding to Louis XII of France, which took place at Abbeville on 9 October 1514. It seems likely that he went to Oxford the following year and may still have been studying there in 1517, when he was granted the post of Constable of Bristol Castle, in association with his father. In 1522 he accompanied

Sir John to court at the time of the visit of Charles V (q.v.). At about this date he married Katherine, daughter of Sir William Fillol.

In August 1523 Edward sailed to France with a large force under the command of the Duke of Suffolk (see Brandon, Charles). He was knighted at Roye in November that year for outstanding services on the battlefield.

Soon after his return home in 1524, Sir Edward was given his first minor court post, that of a Gentleman Usher. The following year he was appointed a member of the Commission for the Peace in Wiltshire; he also became Master of the Horse to the young Duke of Richmond, the King's natural son. It was undoubtedly in this post that he first attracted the attention of Henry VIII (q.v.).

In 1527 Sir Edward was chosen by Thomas Wolsey (q.v.) to accompany him on a mission to the French King at Amiens, and in 1532 he was present, with his father, at the meeting of Henry and François I. On the latter occasion Edward's sister Jane Seymour (q.v.) was probably in attendance on Anne Boleyn (q.v.), the newly-created Marquess of Pembroke. By this time Sir Edward was firmly established at court. He had been appointed a Squire of the Body in 1530, and in the next few years he made the most of every opportunity to acquire landed interests and positions in various parts of the kingdom.

This period of his life was, however, marred by domestic unhappiness, arising out of Katherine Seymour's adulterous behaviour. Edward suspected that the eldest son born to his wife had been conceived while he was abroad in 1523. Eventually he sent Katherine to live in a convent, where it is thought that she died some time between 1530 and 1535. In the latter year Sir Edward married again, taking Anne Stanhope, a former lady-in-waiting to Anne Boleyn, as his new wife. It was to be a happy marriage to which four sons and six daughters were born.

In September 1535 the King paid a three-day visit to Wulfhall; a month later he was entertained by Sir Edward at Elvetham, the family home in Hampshire. It was soon apparent that Henry had fallen in love with Jane Seymour, and from this time onwards the fortunes of the family were to rise spectacularly.

Shortly before the King's marriage to Jane, in May 1536, Sir Edward was appointed a Gentleman of the Privy Council, and he and his wife were lodged at Greenwich Palace; Jane was sent to live with them there, so that Henry could visit her secretly. A week after his sister's marriage Sir Edward was raised to the peerage as Viscount Beauchamp. Grants of land followed, as well as an appointment as Chancellor and Chamberlain of North Wales. Seymour also purchased other posts, including that of Governor of Jersey in July 1536. He was sworn in as a member of the Privy Council in May 1537, and within a few days of the christening of his nephew, Prince Edward, he was created an earl, taking the title of Hertford.

The next few years, following the death of Jane, were comparatively uneventful for Hertford. Then in March 1539 he was sent on a mission to inspect the defences at Calais. In August the same year the King paid another visit to Wulfhall, and a few months later both Edward and his younger brother Thomas (q.v.), who was also rising rapidly in royal favour, were among those sent to Calais to meet Henry's fourth bride, Anne of Cleves (q.v.); they also participated in the King's reception for Anne held at Shooters Hill on 3 January 1540.

In January the following year Hertford was again sent to France, this time on a complicated and fruitless mission to settle the boundaries of the English pale. Ordered home in March, during that summer he was one of three Councillors left in charge while the King and his fifth wife, Catherine Howard (q.v.), were on their royal progress in the north of England. Shortly after the Court's return he served on the commission which examined those implicated in the 'adultery' trial of the Queen.

Appointed Lord High Admiral in December 1542, Hertford relinquished this post almost immediately in favour of that of Lord Great Chamberlain. He was in regular attendance at meetings of the Privy Council throughout 1543 and was one of those who sentenced the Earl of Surrey (see Howard, Henry) to imprisonment.

In 1542 and again in February 1544 Hertford was sent to campaign on the Scottish Border; on the later occasion he replaced the Duke of Suffolk as Lieutenant-General of the North. He invaded Scotland and, following the King's instructions, in May sacked Edinburgh and the surrounding countryside. He was to return to the north in the autumn of 1545 for another round of raids on the Scots, but in the meantime Henry recalled him to London to discuss his forthcoming campaign in France.

While the King went to France in July 1544, Hertford was made one of the advisers to the Regent, Queen Katherine Parr (q.v.), but a few weeks later he was summoned to join Henry in France. Following the surrender of Boulogne, he participated in the peace negotiations, and when these were broken off he was sent with Stephen Gardiner (q.v.) to Brussels to try to persuade Charles V to resume the war against France. In less than two months, however, he was back in France, where he won a brilliant victory over the French at Boulogne in February 1545.

For the rest of 1545 Hertford was kept busy in Scotland but in March 1546 he was sent once more to France, this time to replace the Earl of Surrey at Boulogne. He remained there until the late autumn, returning briefly to England in August in order to participate in the ratification of the peace treaty.

In the last years of Henry's reign the Privy Council often met at Hertford's house near Temple Bar. It was during this period that the old rivalry between the Seymours and the Howards flared up again. Ever since the execution of Catherine Howard, which had weakened the Howard position, Hertford had been gradually ousting the Duke of Norfolk (see Howard, Thomas, 3rd Duke) from power. In December 1546 Norfolk and his son, the Earl of Surrey, were arrested and taken to the Tower, charged with treason. Hertford sat on the commission that tried Surrey at the Guildhall on 13 January and sentenced him to death; Norfolk was also sentenced, but was saved from execution by the King's death.

Henry VIII died on 28 January 1547. Hertford, named in his Will as one of the executors, rode to Hertford Castle to bring the new King, nine-year-old Edward VI (q.v.), to London. The next day it was announced that the Regency Council had unanimously agreed to appoint Hertford Protector of the Realm, contrary to the late King's wishes that no one councillor should have pre-eminence. A few days later he became Duke of Somerset, Lord High Treasurer, and Earl Marshal of England, as decreed by Henry just before his death.

For the next two and a half years Somerset acted as King in all but name. His tolerance and moderation earned him the title of 'the good Duke', but not the affection of his nephew, and by repealing the old King's heresy and treason laws he opened the way to social and religious discord. He failed dismally in all his social and economic policies. Inflation, enclosures, and other injustices to the poor led to rebellions of the peasantry in Cornwall, Devonshire, and Norfolk. In an attempt to deal with the religious question, he imposed by Act of Uniformity the first Common Prayer Book of 1549, written largely by Thomas Cranmer (q.v.). Its purpose was to bring together in one Protestant Church the various religious beliefs; to this end it avoided the central issue of the precise nature of the Mass, but failed in that by so doing it angered both the Protestants and the Catholics.

Furthermore, in political and international affairs he showed himself to be sadly lacking in foresight and acumen. His great victory against the Scots at the Battle of Pinkie Cleugh in September 1547 led only to England's involvement in a costly war with France that ended in defeat. By this time most of the Council had lost their respect for the Protector, and his principal rival for power, the Earl of Warwick (see Dudley, John; later Duke of Northumberland)

was actively plotting his downfall. Somerset's position was considerably weakened by the execution of his brother Thomas in March 1549. The inevitable palace revolution ensued, and in October that year he was taken to the Tower and deprived of office.

Released in February, pardoned and placed under house arrest, in April Somerset was reinstated to the Council, ostensibly reconciled with Warwick. There was an uneasy truce between them in the summer of 1550, but it was not long before the two men clashed again. All the while, Warwick was scheming against his rival. Finally, in October 1551 he had him arrested on trumped-up charges of treason; the Duke and his wife were imprisoned in the Tower. The trial was held at Westminster Hall on 1 December, when Somerset was found guilty of felony and sentenced to death. (The best account of his trial is contained in Edward VI's journal: see W. K. Jordan, *The Chronicle and Political Writings of King Edward VI* (1966).) He was executed on Tower Hill on the morning of 22 January 1552 and buried in St Peter's Chapel in the Tower.

How many of Somerset's family were in the Tower at the time of his death is uncertain, but it is known that both his sons by Katherine Fillol were kept imprisoned after the execution; the eldest, John, died there the following December, and Edward was released in March 1553. Anne, Duchess of Somerset, was not released until August 1553, after the accession of Mary I (q.v.).

Historians generally agree on the admirable personal and idealistic qualities of the Protector. That his liberal policies failed so utterly has usually been blamed on Edward Seymour's incompetence, especially his lack of political perceptiveness. Another of his faults was that he tended to be over-possessive with his nephew the King, whom he genuinely loved, and to assume powers above his station. He amassed a considerable fortune, largely from the spoliation of church property; this and his use of stone from St Paul's Cathedral for the building of a grandiose mansion, Somerset House, in the Strand, which he began in 1547, won him much unpopularity.

A. F. Pollard, *England under Protector Somerset* (1900).

H. St Maur, *Annals of the Seymours* (1902).

W. Seymour, *Ordeal by Ambition: an English family in the shadow of the Tudors* (1972).

*Portraits:* miniature, by Nicholas Hilliard, 1560: The Duke of Buccleuch and Queensberry; oil, by unknown artist: Longleat (The Marquess of Bath); oil on panel, *called* Somerset, by unknown artist: National Portrait Gallery, London; see also allegorical group painting of Edward VI and the Pope, by unknown artist, *c.* 1548–9: N.P.G.; other portraits at Syon House (The Duke of Northumberland), in the Ailesbury Collection, and at Sudeley Castle, Gloucestershire, are of doubtful authenticity; engraving by Willem van de Passe in *Herwologia Anglica*, 1620.

**Seymour, Jane** (?1509–1537), see Jane Seymour.

**Seymour, Lady Katherine** (1540–1568), see Grey, Lady Katherine.

**Seymour, Thomas** (?1508–1549), Baron Seymour of Sudeley, Lord High Admiral.

Born in 1507 or 1508, Thomas Seymour was the fourth son of Sir John and Lady Margery Seymour of Wulfhall, near Savernake, Wiltshire, younger brother of the Duke of Somerset (see Seymour, Edward), and elder brother of Jane Seymour (q.v.), third wife of Henry VIII (q.v.).

Virtually nothing is known of his early life, which he probably spent at Wulfhall. He was in no way academically inclined, but preferred to hunt and to hawk and to tilt; in this he was much influenced by the Seymour family friend, the courtier and diplomat Sir Francis Bryan. Unlike the rest of the family, who were kindly and placid, Thomas had an impetuous, wild, and flamboyant nature. Physically well-built and tall, he was always stylishly dressed.

The first known fact about Thomas is that he accompanied Sir Francis Bryan to France in October 1530, when the latter was sent as ambassador; it seems that Thomas went partly as a companion and partly in the capacity of courier. Little more is known of him until 1536, when his sister Jane was married to the King, from which time the fortunes of all the Seymour family were in the ascendancy. In that year Thomas was made a Gentleman of the Privy Chamber, and shortly after the birth of Jane's son, Prince Edward, he received a knighthood. By this date, as was customary with those who were close to the King, he had acquired possession of extensive lands in various parts of the country that had fallen to the crown at the Dissolution of the Monasteries.

In the autumn of 1538 Sir Thomas accompanied Sir Anthony Browne and Edmund Bonner (q.v.), later Bishop of London, to Paris to negotiate a possible French marriage for Henry VIII; the discussions proved unfruitful, however, and the mission was recalled in November the same year. His next official duty seems to have been in December 1540, when he accompanied the Lord Admiral to Calais to welcome the King's fourth bride, Anne of Cleves (q.v.), and to escort her to England. He also participated in the official reception for Anne held at Shooters Hill on 3 January 1540. On May Day that year he took part in the great tournament held at the Palace of Westminster in the presence of the King and Queen, when he had the satisfaction of triumphing over the Earl of Surrey (see Howard, Henry), who was known to regard the Seymour family as upstarts.

In June 1542 Sir Thomas was sent on a mission to King Ferdinand of Hungary, with the task of trying to enlist imperial help for Henry's intended campaign against the French the following year. He was unsuccessful and was recalled to England in January 1543. It must have been at this time that he began his courtship of Katherine Parr (q.v.), Lord Latimer's widow, but this came to an end when the King decided he would marry her.

In April 1543 Seymour was sent abroad again, this time as joint-ambassador with Dr Nicholas Wotton, Dean of Canterbury, to Mary, Queen Dowager of Hungary, Regent of the Netherlands, in the hope of enlisting the support of the Empire for a joint enterprise against France. While in Brussels, Seymour and Wotton took up the cause of the English Merchant Adventurers in Antwerp against a levy on exports. In this and in the main object of their visit they were able to reach agreement; at the end of May the Emperor and Henry agreed to go to war against France, and a few weeks later Sir Thomas was instructed to proceed to Calais.

His career as a diplomat was virtually over, and for the next few years he was to serve his King and country in a military and naval capacity. At Calais in July 1543 he was appointed marshal of the army under Sir John Wallop; for a short time during Wallop's illness he was in command of the English army in the Netherlands. In April 1544 the King appointed him Master of the Ordnance for life. Thus he was expected not only to produce the guns, shot, and powder required by the army, but to take an active part in the long-planned invasion of France, where both he and his brother

Edward fought in the campaign at Boulogne. In October Thomas was appointed a vice-admiral of the navy.

For the next fifteen months, with a brief interval as Warden of the Cinque Ports in the summer of 1545, Seymour was almost continually afloat, his chief duties being to guard the Narrow Seas and to convoy supplies to Boulogne. His failure to revictual that French town earned him a severe reprimand from the Council, but the King subsequently accepted the vice-admiral's statement that bad weather rather than lack of seamanship had been its cause.

Henry evidently recognized his brother-in-law's ability, and he seems to have been genuinely fond of him. Thomas, for his part, was a loyal servant to the King; so long as Henry was alive, he held his own turbulent temperament in check. At the end of 1545 Henry gave him a splendid house near Temple Bar in London, Hampton Place – which Thomas, by then bitten with ambition, promptly renamed Seymour Place. Seymour was present at the ceremonial ratification of the peace treaty with France in the late summer of 1546, and his last duty before Henry's death was to serve on a commission sent to France to determine the terms of the treaty as ratified. On 23 January 1547, a few days before the King's death, he was sworn in as a member of the Privy Council.

In the list of honours drawn up by Henry before he died, Seymour was given a barony, and when later in the year he acquired Sudeley Castle in Gloucestershire, he took the title of Lord Seymour of Sudeley. Other honours were to follow in rapid succession at the hand of his brother Edward, the newly-created Duke of Somerset and Protector of the Realm: in February 1547 Thomas became Lord High Admiral and a Knight of the Garter.

Ambition and self-aggrandizement now possessed him entirely, and from this time onwards Seymour, resentful at being given an inferior status to his brother, began to intrigue against the Protector, taking advantage of the latter's weaknesses and indecision. Firstly, he tried to obtain the guardianship of the young King Edward (q.v.). Unsuccessful in this, he turned his attention to the possibility of a royal marriage, and rumour linked his name both with the Princess Mary (see Mary I) and with the Princess Elizabeth (see Elizabeth I). That he ever sought a union with the former is now thought unlikely, and there is only slender (and doubtful) evidence that Seymour actually proposed to Elizabeth. In any event, his old love, Katherine Parr, now the Queen Dowager, was again free, and he lost no time in marrying her at a secret ceremony performed some time during May 1547. Knowing that his brother would be angry, Seymour next carefully ingratiated himself with the King and even induced the latter to believe that he had brought about the union, before making it public.

The Princess Elizabeth had been sent to live with Katherine Parr after her father's death, and she remained with the Seymours after their marriage. From depositions made by members of the household after Thomas Seymour's subsequent arrest, it appears that he and his wife were in the habit of indulging in some strange behaviour with their guest, which took the form of romps in the Princess's bedroom in the early morning and other frolics. Soon these got out of hand and in the early summer of 1548 Katherine, who was then pregnant, became aware of the lecherous advances being made by her husband to the innocent young girl, and she arranged for Elizabeth to leave Sudeley.

Seymour soon occupied himself with another dangerous scheme. Aware of Somerset's ambition that the King should marry his own daughter Jane and that Lady Jane Grey (q.v.) should marry his son Edward, Thomas set out to thwart both plans. The Lady Jane Grey had been living with Katherine Parr for some time before her marriage was made public, and her parents agreed that she should remain with the Seymours only on the promise by Thomas that he would arrange a marriage contract for her with the King. While Somerset was campaigning in Scotland, Seymour curried favour with Edward, inviting him to visit Katherine at Chelsea, giving him pocket money and other presents, and eventually persuading the King to support him in his efforts to regain the jewels that had once been Katherine's but which the Protector had appropriated for the crown. In other matters, such as his endeavour to get Edward to sponsor a bill in Parliament to make him Governor of the King's Person, he found that the young King had taken the advice of his tutor, Sir John Cheke (q.v.), and he was less successful. This did not deter him from his determination to overthrow the protectorate, and although a move to have Somerset's patent revoked was supported in Parliament only by Thomas and Lord Dorset, father of the Lady Jane Grey, he gained more support for a patent which would limit the Protector's powers. This bill, however, never became law.

By this time the Lord High Admiral was behaving in a most aggressive and antagonistic manner. The Board of Admiralty complained that he was not fulfilling his duties, and there were insinuations of corruption, specifically of his conniving with pirates on the western coasts. In July 1548 a confrontation took place between the brothers. Seymour was summoned before the Council; he failed to appear but apologized to his brother for his behaviour, and the Protector weakly let the matter drop.

To a certain extent Seymour was protected by his wife's rank. But when Katherine died in early September, having given birth to a daughter, he was in dire trouble. He now embarked on a series of even more foolhardy actions: he renewed his pursuit of the Princess Elizabeth, but did not succeed in seeing her; he boasted openly of his design to overthrow the Protector; besides Lord Dorset, he enlisted the support of the Marquess of Northampton and of Sir William Sharington, Vice-Treasurer of the Bristol Mint. Seymour was a wealthy man; he had also amassed a quantity of booty from his dealings with the pirates. But this was insufficient to raise and pay the 10,000 men he needed for his rebellion, and Sharington, who had been fraudulently minting coins to fill his own coffers for some time, agreed to mint money to aid the scheme.

At the beginning of 1549 Sharington's activities became known to the Council, and in a search of his home documents were discovered incriminating Seymour. Pressure was put upon the Protector, whose enemies, notably the Earl of Warwick (see Dudley, John; later Duke of Northumberland) and the Earl of Southampton (see Wriothesley, Thomas) quickly seized the opportunity to cause a rift between the brothers. When Seymour refused to appear before the Protector, the Council ordered his arrest and imprisonment in the Tower. All those who could contribute evidence, including the Princess Elizabeth and members of her household, were examined. No less than thirty-three charges were laid against him.

He was refused an open trial, and at the end of February a bill of attainder was presented in Parliament, where the Lords were unanimous in condemning him for treason but where the Commons debated it hotly for several days before consenting. In order to prevent Somerset from being moved to petition the King for mercy, the Council saw to it that no meeting took place between the brothers. The warrant for execution was signed on 17 March, and three days later Seymour was beheaded on Tower Hill. He did not make the usual confession on the scaffold, and after his death letters were found in his shoes addressed to the two Princesses, urging them to beware of the Protector, who, he said, was trying to induce the King to deprive them of their rights of succession.

Thomas Seymour's death considerably weakened his brother's position, and Warwick and his supporters were not slow to encourage those who held the view that the Protector was a murderer and unfitted to govern. As a man, perhaps the Princess Elizabeth summed up Seymour the most intelligently, commenting when told of his execution, 'This day died a man with much wit, and very little judgment.'

John Maclean, *Life of Thomas Seymour* (1869).
A. F. Pollard, *England under Protector Somerset* (1900).
H. St Maur, *Annals of the Seymours* (1902).
William Seymour, *Ordeal by Ambition: an English family in the shadow of the Tudors* (1972).

*Portraits*: oil, by unknown artist: Sudeley Castle, Gloucestershire; oil on panel, by unknown artist: National Portrait Gallery, London; other versions at National Maritime Museum, Greenwich, and Longleat (Marquess of Bath).

**Shakespeare, William** (1564–1616), poet and dramatist.

The eldest son and third child of John Shakespeare and his wife Mary, daughter of Robert Arden, traditionally Shakespeare was born at Stratford-on-Avon on

23 April 1564; in fact the date of his birth is uncertain, but it is recorded that he was baptized at Holy Trinity Church, Stratford, on 26 April that year. His father was a yeoman and a glover by trade, who had held a number of municipal offices in Stratford and rose to be an alderman in the year after his son's birth and bailiff three years later; he owned property in the town, including the two adjoining houses in Henley Street where William was born. His mother was the daughter of a wealthy small gentleman farmer of Wilmcote, not far from Stratford.

Little is known of William's education, but it is assumed that he attended the free grammar school at Stratford. The methods and Latin tags of a grammar school education are much in evidence in his plays. What he did immediately on leaving school is not known, but he may have been apprenticed to his father or some other local trader, or alternatively have found employment in an aristocratic household in the district. From about 1576 onwards the elder Shakespeare seems to have fallen on hard times; he borrowed money, had to sell some property in order to pay debts, and finally was struck off the Stratford aldermanic roll in September 1586.

Meanwhile young William was courting a woman eight years his senior, Anne, elder daughter of Richard Hathaway, a farmer at Shottery, near Stratford, who had died the previous year. On 27 November 1582 a licence was issued for Shakespeare, who was still a minor, to marry 'Anne Whatley' of Temple Grafton (the name 'Whatley' is believed to be a clerical error; Temple Grafton was possibly where she was living or where the marriage took place); it is not known precisely when or where the ceremony was performed. The

twenty-six-year-old bride was already pregnant, for a daughter, Susanna, was baptized on 26 May the following year; twins, Hamnet and Judith, were baptized on 2 February 1585.

Little is known of Shakespeare's life during the years 1585–92. He and his wife and young children continued to live in his father's home in Henley Street, Stratford, until he made the decision to seek his fortune with a company of actors in London, probably in about 1587–8. There is no evidence that the marriage was unhappy, but it is believed that Shakespeare spent much of his time frequenting the local taverns; there is an old Stratford tradition that he was involved in deer poaching activities; and information from a member of his company that he was for a time a schoolmaster in the country. He most likely became interested in drama when a number of visiting troupes of players performed in Stratford in the late 1580s, but his fascination may date from a visit to Kenilworth as a schoolboy at the time of the sumptuous entertainment staged there for Queen Elizabeth (q.v.) by the Earl of Leicester (see Dudley, Robert) in the summer of 1575. He may also have seen the cycle of mystery plays performed in Coventry by the craft guilds at this period. At any rate his enthusiasm and talent were such that when the Queen's Men played in Stratford in 1587 Shakespeare is believed to have offered his services to replace one of the company killed in a duel and subsequently to have accompanied them to London, where, again according to legend, he may at first have earned his keep by minding the horses belonging to the playgoers.

Beginning his theatrical career as an actor, Shakespeare soon turned his hand to writing for the stage, scoring a marked success with his *Henry VI* plays. But the plague years, 1592–3, constituted a serious setback, during which period he was dependant on his patron, the Earl of Southampton (see Wriothesley, Henry). Then in 1594 he became a founder member of the Lord Chamberlain's company, with whom he was to remain for the rest of his stage career. That by 1592 he was already making his name both as an actor and as a dramatist is confirmed by the attack on him as 'an upstart crow, beautified by our feathers' in the *Groats-worth of Witte*, written by Robert Greene (q.v.) in that year. According to the most generally accepted date order of the plays, it would seem that the three parts of *Henry VI*, *Titus Andronicus*, and possibly *The Taming of the Shrew*, had been written before the enforced closure of the London theatres during the plague years. There is a theory that Shakespeare travelled in Italy during 1592–3, but it is more generally believed that he remained in England, cultivating important friends and experimenting with non-dramatic work. In April 1593 he

published the poem *Venus and Adonis*, with a dedication to his young patron; another poem, *The Rape of Lucrece*, published in May the following year, was also dedicated to Southampton, in exceptionally warm terms. The *Sonnets*, mostly written during these years but not published until 1609, are believed by many scholars to have been addressed to Southampton, but this is still the subject of much controversy. (The dedication to 'Mr W.H.' was not Shakespeare's but that of Thomas Thorpe (q.v.), the publisher.) Dr A. L. Rowse has identified the 'dark lady' of Shakespeare's infatuation in the sonnets as Emilia Lanier, the discarded mistress of Lord Chamberlain Hunsdon, the patron of Shakespeare's company. In May 1594 there was a performance of *A Midsummer Night's Dream* at Southampton House, to celebrate the wedding of the mother of Shakespeare's patron, Mary, Countess of Southampton, to Sir Thomas Heneage; the play was probably written specially for the occasion.

On the reopening of the playhouses at the end of 1594, Shakespeare emerged as one of the leading members of the Lord Chamberlain's Men, a company which had as its principal actor Richard Burbage (q.v.). As part of the Christmas festivities that year Shakespeare and another member of the company were summoned to Greenwich to play before the Queen; this was the first of many court performances. *Richard III, Romeo and Juliet*, and *Richard II* date from this period. *The Merry Wives of Windsor*, probably written at the royal command, may have had its first performance at a Garter Feast at Windsor.

By this date Shakespeare was lodging in the parish of St Helen's, Bishopsgate, in the City of London. John Aubrey (see *Lives of the Stuart Age*) informs us that Shakespeare went into the country each year, probably to spend the summer at Stratford, where his son Hamnet died in August 1596. In May 1597 Shakespeare bought New Place, a large house in Stratford, as a permanent home for his wife and daughters, while in London he moved to Southwark, where the Burbage brothers were building their theatre, to be known as The Globe.

Shakespeare was now a prosperous man. He used his wealth to benefit the family fortunes, and in spite of his successes in London he never lost touch with Stratford. He visited his native town frequently and in later years bought or acquired leases of several other properties there. In October 1596, probably at his son's instigation, John Shakespeare was granted a coat of arms by the College of Arms, which established the family as members of the gentry. The elder Shakespeare died in 1601; his wife, the dramatist's mother, in 1608.

In 1599 Shakespeare became a member of a syndicate composed of the Burbage brothers and five others from the Lord Chamberlain's company, who were to share in the expenses and profits of The Globe playhouse. With the new theatre in mind, he worked harder than ever at his playwriting; *Henry V, Much Ado About Nothing, Julius Caesar, As You Like It, Twelfth Night,* and *Hamlet* are believed to have been written in the years 1598–1601.

On the accession of James I (see James VI of Scotland) the Lord Chamberlain's Men changed their name to the King's Men. Shakespeare was then at the height of his powers, both as a dramatist and as an actor; he was also making considerable sums of money from his financial interest in The Globe. Seven of his plays were included in the eleven performed as part of the revels of 1604–5. *Othello, King Lear, Macbeth,* and *Anthony and Cleopatra*

all had their first productions during these years, Richard Burbage playing most of the leading roles. A good-natured rivalry existed between Shakespeare and his fellow-dramatist, Ben Jonson (see *Lives of the Stuart Age*), whose plays Shakespeare welcomed to his company, himself performing in *Every Man in his Humour.* There is a tradition that a group of poets and playwrights, including Shakespeare, Jonson, John Donne, Francis Beaumont, and John Fletcher (for the last three, see *Lives of the Stuart Age*), met regularly at the Mermaid Tavern in Bread Street.

In 1609 Shakespeare joined with Burbage and five others in buying the lease of the Blackfriars Theatre; henceforth the King's Men played there as well as at The Globe. For some time in about 1612–13 Shakespeare was in lodgings in Cripplegate; in March 1613 he invested in the gatehouse at Blackfriars Priory, convenient for winter performances. *Henry VIII* was produced at The Globe that year, and it is said that Shakespeare himself spoke the prologue. But after The Globe was destroyed by fire in June 1613, he must have sold his share in the theatre, for he was not financially involved in the new Globe. At about this date Shakespeare began gradually to retire from the theatre, spending more and more of his time at Stratford, until during the last year or two of his life he took up permanent residence in his native town. He was buried in the parish church of Holy Trinity there on 25 April 1616, having died two days earlier, on his birthday, 23 April. A monument sculpted by Gheerart Janssen was erected some time before 1623.

Shakespeare's will left the bulk of his estate to his daughter Susanna, and his 'second best bed' to his wife. His widow died in 1623, and his last surviving descendant, Susanna's daughter, Elizabeth, Lady Barnard, in 1670. The will, bearing three signatures by him, is at the Public Record Office, London.

Some of the thirty-eight plays Shakespeare wrote were printed, both in 'good' and 'bad' quartos, during his lifetime, but the first collected edition, known as the First Folio, was not published until 1623; further folio editions appeared in 1632, 1663 (with a second version in 1664), and 1685. There have been numerous critical editions since the early eighteenth century, and some modern editions are still in progress. Shakespeare's work has been translated into all the world's languages, and he is generally considered to be one of the greatest writers of all time.

The most popular dramatist of his age, and ever since, William Shakespeare was first and foremost a man of the theatre: actor, dramatist, producer, sharer in the company and eventually its part-owner. The inspiration of the theatre brought out his finest poetry, and his genius produced the finest poetic drama of the English language. Shakespeare's influence on literature has been universal; his work has also provided an extraordinary inspiration in other arts, such as music, opera and painting.

There is a vast bibliography, but space does not permit the inclusion here of more than a few standard titles. The most recent biographical study is S. Schoenbaum, *William Shakespeare: A Documentary Life* (1975); see also P. Quennell, *Shakespeare* (1963) and A. L. Rowse, *William Shakespeare* (1963) and *Shakespeare the Man* (1973). The standard work is E. K. Chambers, *William Shakespeare: A Study of Facts and Problems* (2 vols; 1930). W. Ebisch and L. L. Schucking, *Shakespeare Bibliography* (1931, with supplement 1937) has been continued by G. R. Smith, *A Classified Shakespeare Bibliography, 1936–1958* (1963); *Shakespeare Survey* (London) and *Shakespeare Quarterly* (New York) publish annual listings of recent studies.

*Portraits:* Three only have a claim to authenticity: oil, by unknown artist, *c.* 1610 (The Chandos Portrait): National Portrait Gallery, London; engraving, by Martin Droeshout, in the First and subsequent Folios: impression from the third state: N.P.G.; tomb effigy, by Gheerart Janssen, *c.* 1620: Holy Trinity Church, Stratford-on-Avon. See D. Piper, *O Sweet Mr Shakespeare I'll have his Picture* (N.P.G., 1964) and M. H. Spielmann, *The Portraits of Shakespeare* (1906–7).

**Shaxton, Nicholas** (?1485–1556), Bishop of Salisbury.

Born in about 1485 in the diocese of Norwich, Nicholas Shaxton studied at Cambridge, graduating there as B.A. in 1506. He was elected a fellow of Gonville Hall and was president of Physick's Hostel, which was attached to Gonville, in 1512–13. In 1520 he became a university preacher, taking his B.D. the following year. His name appears in the records among those who met at the White Horse inn to discuss the new views on religion which were then circulating.

In 1530 Shaxton was appointed a member of the committee of Cambridge divines to discuss the King's marriage with Catherine of Aragon (q.v.); it is recorded that he was favourable to the views of Henry VIII (q.v.). He became almoner to Anne Boleyn (q.v.) and under her patronage rose rapidly in the Church, being appointed Treasurer of Salisbury Cathedral in 1533, a canon of Westminster in 1534, and Bishop of Salisbury in 1535, when he acknowledged the King as supreme head of the Church in England. In 1539, however, together with Bishop Hugh Latimer (q.v.), he resigned his see over the question of the Six Articles. After a period of confinement, he was set free but prohibited from preaching. Shaxton spent the next few years in obscurity, until in 1546, having held a parochial charge at Hadleigh, in Suffolk, he was summoned to London to answer for maintaining false doctrine on the sacrament. Arraigned for heresy at the

Guildhall, together with Anne Askew (q.v.) and two others, Shaxton was condemned to be burned at the stake. At the last moment he recanted, but was made to preach at Anne's burning on 16 July that year. The King subsequently gave him the post of Master of St Giles's Hospital at Norwich.

For the remainder of his life Shaxton was consistent in publicly repenting of his former 'errors', even during the Protestant rule of Edward VI (q.v.), when he was required to surrender the post of Master of St Giles's to the King. In the reign of Mary he was appointed as suffragan to Thomas Thirlby, Bishop of Ely. He died at the beginning of August 1556.

**Shrewsbury, Countess of** (1520–1608), see Hardwick, Elizabeth.

**Shrewsbury, 6th Earl of** (?1528–1590), see Talbot, George.

**Sidney, Sir Henry** (1529–1586), Lord Deputy of Ireland and President of Wales.

Henry Sidney was born, probably in London, on 20 July 1529, the only son of Sir William Sidney, a distinguished soldier who had fought in the Battle of Flodden in 1513 and had become a favoured courtier to Henry VIII (q.v.).

At a very early age Henry Sidney was himself introduced to court life, being chosen as a companion to the future Edward VI (q.v.). Sir William had in 1538 been appointed tutor, chamberlain, and steward to the young Prince. Henry soon won Edward's confidence and friendship, and he, in return, when he became King, showed his gratitude to the Sidneys through the grant of lands, including Penshurst in Kent (which became the family seat) to the father, and by conferring a knighthood on Henry in

1550. When the latter contracted a brilliant marriage to Mary Dudley, daughter of the Duke of Northumberland (see Dudley, John), his future prospects seemed bright indeed.

In spite of the close connection between the Sidneys and the Dudleys, Sir Henry did not play an active role in the conspiracy over Lady Jane Grey (q.v.), and consequently was one of the first to receive a pardon from Mary I (q.v.) on her accession. He professed conformity to the religion of the new reign; in 1552 he was sent on a mission to France, and by 1554 was sufficiently high in royal esteem to be among the group of courtiers who escorted Philip II of Spain (q.v.) to England for his marriage to the Queen. In April 1556 Sidney was appointed Vice-Treasurer of Ireland and took up his duties in that country, leaving behind his wife and baby son and heir, Philip Sidney (q.v.), who had been born in November 1554. When he returned four years later, Elizabeth I (q.v.) had been on the throne for a year, and he was to make an equally swift readjustment to the new conditions of royal service.

In Ireland Sidney served under his brother-in-law, Thomas Radcliffe, later 3rd Earl of Sussex, who was then Lord Deputy and a vigorous administrator. He took part in the latter's expedition into Ulster and acted as Lord Justice when Radcliffe returned to England temporarily on the death of Queen Mary in 1558.

Shortly after his own arrival back in England in 1559, Sir Henry was appointed President of the Council of Wales and of the Marches, an office which he was to hold for the rest of his life. He was subsequently entrusted with missions to France and to Scotland, and in 1564 he was made a Knight of the Garter.

In 1565 the Queen appointed Sidney

Lord Deputy of Ireland. The situation there was fraught with savage guerilla warfare on the part of the native chieftains, whose power had to be broken before the Anglican Church and civil administration could be established; it was feared that premature enforcement of the Acts of Supremacy and Uniformity might drive the inhabitants of the Pale into an alliance with the native Irish, and possibly even with Spain. Sidney took decisive action from the outset: he restored Calvagh O'Donnell to leadership of the clan and, in spite of inferior forces, made a magnificent march through Ulster in which he garrisoned the town of Derry and crushed the powerful rebellion of the chieftain Shane O'Neill (q.v.), which had been gaining momentum since 1559. He was unable, however, completely to pacify the other chieftains, but he managed to persuade some of them, including the rebellious Butlers, to submit to authority, and by delaying the introduction of anti-Catholic legislation in the Irish Parliament he avoided the risk of a combined rebellion against Elizabeth's religious policy in Ireland. In this policy he had the support of William Cecil (q.v.; later Baron Burghley). Trouble then broke out in the south, in Munster, where Gerald Fitzgerald, 15th Earl of Desmond, was carrying on a bitter feud with the Earl of Ormonde (see Butler, Thomas), and tyrannizing the whole region. Sidney swiftly intervened, sent Desmond to the Tower and, in an attempt to break the power of the chieftains, set up presidents in Munster and Connaught. This resulted in an uprising, led by James Fitzmaurice Fitzgerald, in 1569, of the whole of Munster, which was eventually suppressed by Ormonde and Humphrey Gilbert (q.v.).

In 1570 Sidney carried an act through Parliament for the establishment of schools with English masters; but the policy of plantations was forcibly resisted by all the Irish lords, and trouble continued. Sidney felt that the Queen had failed to provide him with adequate forces for his task and in 1571, exasperated and dispirited, he resigned. He spent the next four years at home, devoting his time to his family and to the administration of Wales. He now had three sons – Philip, Robert, and Thomas – and one daughter, Mary, who would later marry the Earl of Pembroke.

The Irish situation deteriorated still further during this time, and in the summer of 1575 Sir Henry was sworn a member of the Privy Council and reappointed Lord Deputy. He arrived back in Ireland at the beginning of September to fulfil what he himself called a 'thankless charge'. The proper enforcement of authority was much hampered by lack of funds, and in an attempt to solve this aspect of the problem Sidney imposed a tax on landholders (cess). This was unpopular among the gentry of the Pale, and when certain landowners refused to pay the cess, Sidney imprisoned them in Dublin Castle; the situation was complicated by the Queen's wish that Ormonde, a favourite of hers, should be exempt from the tax. To this Sidney would not agree, whereupon Ormonde proceeded to spread the story in England that Sir Henry was guilty of corruption, that he was merely enriching himself in Ireland and would soon be recalled. At this stage Philip Sidney, who had spent several months with his father in 1576, wrote a masterly defence of Sir Henry's policies entitled *Discourse on Irish Affairs*; he described him as 'an honest servant, full of zeal in his prince's service and not without well grounded hopes of good success'.

The Queen, however, was not impressed. Convinced that Sidney was guilty of excessive expenditure, in February 1578 she summoned him to London. It was typical of Sir Henry that in his anxiety to leave Irish affairs in as good an order as possible – which he did, settling disputes between the chieftains by making them landowners and establishing English presidents in the provinces – he delayed his departure and did not reach England until September. Following a friendly but cool reception, it was made clear to him that he could no longer be of service to Elizabeth in Ireland. Later, in 1582, there was some talk of his reappointment, but this came to nothing and in the event Sidney spent the last years of his life in comparative obscurity, dividing his time between the affairs of Wales, which he governed from Ludlow Castle, and his home at Penshurst.

In the spring of 1586 he caught a chill after travelling by barge from Bewdley to Worcester and died at Ludlow on 5 May. He was buried at Penshurst. His three sons were at the time all serving in the Netherlands. When Philip applied for leave to settle family affairs and to comfort his mother, herself in poor health, his request was turned down by the Queen, an unjustified last gesture towards a loyal servant.

N. Canny, *The Elizabethan Conquest of Ireland* (1976).

A. Collins (ed.), *Letters and Memorials of State* . . . *written and collected by Sir Henry Sidney* . . . *Sir Philip Sidney and his brother Sir Robert Sidney* . . . *transcribed from the originals at Penshurst Place in Kent* . . . *and his Majesty's office of papers and records* (2 vols; 1746).

C. Falls, *Elizabeth's Irish Wars* (1950).

D. B. Quinn, *The Elizabethans and the Irish* (Ithaca, N.Y., 1966)

A. L. Rowse, *The Expansion of Elizabethan England* (1955).

*Portraits*: oil, by unknown artist, full length, 1573: Petworth Collection; oil, by unknown artist, half length: National Portrait Gallery, London; oil, by unknown artist (head and shoulders version of Petworth portrait): Penshurst (Viscount De L'Isle); oil on paper, by unknown artist, head and half shoulders: N.P.G. N.B. An earlier portrait (1565–6) by A. van Brounckhorst has not been identified. A second portrait at Penshurst may not be of Sir Henry.

**Sidney, Sir Philip** (1554–1586), poet, statesman, and soldier.

Philip Sidney was born at Penshurst, Kent, on 30 November 1554, the eldest son of Sir Henry Sidney (q.v.) and his wife, Lady Mary Dudley, daughter of the Duke of Northumberland (see Dudley, John). Philip II of Spain (q.v.) was one of his godfathers. From an early age he was destined for a career at court, where both his parents came into high favour following the accession of Elizabeth I (q.v.), and his uncle, Robert Dudley (q.v.; later Earl of Leicester), was the Queen's favourite.

After a childhood spent mostly at Penshurst (his father being Vice-Treasurer of Ireland and his mother at court), at the age of ten Philip entered Shrewsbury School. There he formed a lifelong friendship with his fellow pupil, Fulke Greville (q.v.). In February 1568 he went to Christ Church, Oxford, where he studied for three years but left the university without taking a degree. Among his friends and contemporaries at Oxford were William Camden (q.v.), Richard Hakluyt (q.v.), Walter Ralegh (q.v.), Henry Savile (see *Lives of the Stuart Age*) and Edmund Campion (q.v.).

In May 1572, equipped with servants, horses, and liberal funds from his father, young Sidney set out on a grand tour of the Continent planned as part of his further education. During this time he perfected his knowledge of foreign languages and, through meetings with most of the leading statesmen of Europe, acquired a first-hand knowledge of the political issues of the day. He was in Paris on the day of the St Bartholomew

massacre, and there also he came under the influence of the distinguished Protestant scholar, Hubert Languet, who was to become his mentor. He went on to visit Germany, Austria, Hungary, and Italy, before returning to England in 1575.

Sidney came home full of Protestant idealism. He was a handsome young man, learned, athletic, and imbued with all the social graces, 'the flower of England' as he was later described. That summer he was present at the magnificent entertainment at Kenilworth Castle offered to the Queen in the course of her royal progress by Philip's uncle, now Earl of Leicester. In the following spring, 1576, he received his first court appointment, becoming cup bearer to the Queen in succession to his father, who had been reappointed Lord Deputy of Ireland. It was at about this time that he formed a close friendship with Walter Devereux, 1st Earl of Essex, who expressed the wish that Philip might marry his daughter Penelope, the 'Stella' to whom Sidney was later to address his famous series of

sonnets; however, the two young people did not meet until several years later. In any case, Sidney was too occupied with his career to think of an early marriage; already he was deeply interested in the cause of the Protestant activists in the Netherlands, and in February 1577, still only twenty-two years old, he was given his first diplomatic mission, ostensibly to carry the Queen's condolences to the German Emperor Rudolf II and the Elector Palatine Louis VI on the deaths of their fathers, but secretly also to sound out the German princes on the possible formation of a Protestant league which would protect England against the menacing power of Catholic Spain. While abroad he took the opportunity to visit other continental statesmen, including Don John of Austria; and in Prague he met again his old university acquaintance, Edmund Campion, now in exile.

The formal part of his mission accomplished, Sidney applied himself so enthusiastically to the question of a Protestant league that the Queen, fearing that he would commit England to a policy contrary to her wishes, hurriedly recalled him; however, the letter of recall was followed almost immediately by one directing him to visit William of Orange (q.v.), an opportunity which Sidney eagerly seized. In the course of his visit to Gertruidenberg, the young diplomat stood as godfather to the second child of William and his wife, Charlotte de Bourbon, named Elizabeth in honour of the English Queen; he was also commissioned by Orange to offer to the Queen the union of Holland and Zeeland with the crown of England, which would have constituted an important first step towards the projected Protestant League. The Queen, however, took the view that in discussing such matters Sidney was exceeding the terms of his embassy; not only did the scheme come to nothing, but he was not to be entrusted with another official post for eight years.

Nevertheless, after his return to England in June 1577, Sidney continued to be active in diplomatic and political circles. He entertained foreign visitors and kept up a correspondence with the leading continental statesmen; he wrote a spirited *Discourse on Irish Affairs* in defence of his father's policies in Ireland; and in 1579, probably influenced by Leicester and Sir Francis Walsingham (q.v.), he sent a private letter to the Queen advising her against her proposed marriage with the Duc d'Alençon (q.v.; later Duc d'Anjou). This last action led to his withdrawal from court under a cloud, and in the twelve months of retirement that followed Sidney turned to literature as a major outlet for his talents and energies. He had previously written a pastoral play, *The Lady of May*, which was presented to the Queen in 1578, and now he began work on a heroic prose romance, the *Arcadia*, for the amusement of his sister, the Countess of Pembroke; it was not intended for publication and although he started, but never finished, a radical revision of the work in 1584, Sidney is said to have expressed a dying wish that it should be destroyed. (In fact the incomplete revised version was printed in 1590, four years after the author's death, and the original text much later.)

The Sidney circle at this time was composed chiefly of Fulke Greville, Edward Dyer, Gabriel Harvey, Daniel Rogers, and Edmund Spenser (q.v.). When Spenser's *Shepheardes Calender* appeared in 1579, it carried a dedication to 'the noble and virtuous gentleman, most worthy of all titles both of learning and chivalry, Mr Philip Sidney'. Sidney had the wish to see a literature take shape in English which might be comparable to that in Italian. He advanced this not only by his own writings in verse and prose, but also by his patronage of other writers.

Reconciled with the Queen early in 1581, Sidney attended Elizabeth on her royal progresses and distinguished himself spectacularly in court tournaments, but was repeatedly denied the important post and the active service for which he yearned. In 1581 and again in 1584–5 he sat as a Member of Parliament, representing the county of Kent.

Some time in 1582 Sidney fell in love with Penelope Devereux, daughter of his old friend, the Earl of Essex. She had been introduced at court the previous year by her guardian, the Countess of Huntingdon (who was Sidney's aunt), and a few months later had been married, against her will, to Robert Rich, 3rd Baron Rich. Although their names had been linked some years earlier, they had not previously met, and Sidney soon found himself deeply attracted to the beautiful and vivacious young woman. How far she encouraged his attentions is not known, but it seems that the ardour was largely one-sided, for long before her marriage Penelope had herself fallen in love with Charles Blount (q.v.), later Earl of Devonshire and 8th Baron Mountjoy, whom she was to marry in 1605 after her divorce from Rich. Nevertheless the relationship was to last for two years, during which time Sidney composed the celebrated series of sonnets, *Astrophil and Stella*, expressing in a witty and romantic style his great passion and his moral struggle to overcome it. Like the *Arcadia*, these sonnets were not intended for publication and were printed only after Sidney's death (first edition 1590), so that their chronological sequence remains uncertain. His eloquent *Defense of Poesie* (later entitled *Apologie for Poetrie*), first published in 1595, was probably written at about this time, since it was partly a reply to an attack on the theatre by an ex-playwright turned cleric, Stephen Gosson, which appeared in 1579 under the title *The School of Abuse*. Sidney's work was one of the most important critical statements of the time, setting standards for the new literature then taking shape, partly under his influence and inspiration.

Various proposals had been made for Sidney's marriage, including one for his union with the sister of William of Orange, but these had come to nothing. Now, in September 1583, aged nearly twenty-nine years, he married Frances Walsingham, daughter of the Secretary of State. In spite of the romantic passion he bore for his 'Stella', there is a likelihood that this was a love match, besides corroborating his political attachment to the forward policies of Walsingham. Some of Sidney's contemporaries were even confused as to whether 'Stella' was in fact Penelope or Frances. The Queen was displeased at the match and continued to deny Sidney the opportunity to serve the State; it was well known that the knighthood conferred on him in January 1583 had been granted not for his own merit but purely in order that he might stand proxy for his friend Prince Casimir, the German Calvinist, at the latter's investiture with the Order of the Garter.

The long-sought-after public office was not given until July 1585, when Sidney was appointed joint Master of the Ordnance with his uncle, Ambrose Dudley, Earl of Warwick. In the intervening years he was, however, far from inactive: with Walsingham and others he was involved in schemes to use the Portuguese pretender, Don Antonio, against Spain; and he also concerned himself with the affairs of the Protestant Scottish lords. At about this time Sidney began to revise *Arcadia*, and he is believed to have met and formed a relationship with the Italian philosopher and astronomer Giordano Bruno when the latter came to England in 1583.

Sidney had long been interested in exploration and the discovery of the New World. As early as 1576 he had invested in the voyages of Martin Frobisher (q.v.), and in 1582 Hakluyt had dedicated his *Divers voyages touching the discoverie of America* to him. This interest was now rekindled through his friendship with the mathematician and astrologer John Dee (q.v.) and the proposal by Sir Walter Ralegh to colonize Virginia. The desire for active service was still very strong, and in the late summer of 1585, Sidney took a decision to accompany Sir Francis Drake (q.v.) on an expedition against the Spaniards.

By this time Elizabeth had at last been forced to assist the Dutch against the imminent danger of being overwhelmed by Spain, and preparations were made to send a force under the Earl of Leicester. As soon as she learned of Sidney's proposed expedition, the Queen offered him service under Leicester and made him Governor of Flushing, with command of a company of cavalry. He took up his duties in November and spent the next eleven months waging ineffective campaigns against the Spaniards with inexperienced troops.

On 22 September 1586, in a hard-fought engagement to prevent the Spaniards from sending supplies to the town of Zutphen, Sidney charged three times through the enemy lines before being struck by a musket ball just above the knee; out of bravado he had discarded the armour to protect his thighs, and the bone was shattered. His friend and biographer, Fulke Greville, has described how he rode his horse from the field and, although bleeding copiously, gave his bottle of water to another mortally wounded soldier. He was carried to

Arnhem, in the hope that he might recover, but the wound became infected and he died on the afternoon of 17 October.

Philip Sidney's death, at the age of thirty-one, was marked by Protestant and Catholic alike throughout Europe. His body lay in state for eight days at Flushing before being conveyed to London, where he was buried at St Paul's Cathedral amid much pomp and ceremony. He was survived by his wife Frances and a baby daughter, Elizabeth, who later married the 5th Earl of Rutland. Nearly every English poet, including Spenser, composed an elegy in praise of the Protestant hero knight, and many universities throughout Europe issued commemorative volumes. To those who mourned he was a heroic figure, a Christian knight, the embodiment of virtue and the ideal gentleman of the age, a reputation that has not diminished since his death. Spenser wrote of him that 'He only like himself, was second to none', and Camden that he was 'the great glory of his family, the great hope of mankind, the most lively pattern of virtue, and the glory of the world'.

Too committed to be an outstanding diplomat, Sidney's fame rests on a romantic personal history, the heroic manner of his death, and on his literary work. The *Defense of Poesie* ranks among the finest examples of Elizabethan literary criticism, while the *Astrophil and Stella* sonnets inspired the sonnet sequences of the 1590s. *Arcadia* represents the best prose fiction of the sixteenth century and exerted an extraordinary influence on other writers, including William Shakespeare (q.v.). Amongst Sidney's other works is an unfinished paraphrase of the Psalms of David, completed by his sister and first printed in 1823.

*The Complete Works of Sir Philip Sidney* have been edited by A. Feuillerat

and published in four volumes (Cambridge, 1922–6). The *Correspondence of Sir Philip Sidney and H. Languet* has been edited and translated from Latin in two editions: by S. A. Pears (1845) and by W. A. Bradley (Boston, 1912). The Sidney papers, *Letters and Memorials of State . . . written and collected by Sir Henry Sidney . . . Sir Philip Sidney and his brother Sir Robert Sidney . . . transcribed from the originals at Penshurst Place in Kent . . . and his Majesty's office of papers and records*, have been edited by A. Collins in two volumes (1746). Modern critical editions of his work are *Poems*, edited by W. A. Ringler, Jr. (1962) and *The Countess of Pembroke's Arcadia (The Old Arcadia)*, edited by Jean Robertson (1973).

F. S. Boas, *Sir Philip Sidney* (1955).
J. Buxton, *Sir Philip Sidney and the English Renaissance* (1954).
Fulke Greville, *The Life of the Renowned Sir Philip Sidney* (1652; ed. by Nowell Smith, 1907).
M. W. Wallace, *Sir Philip Sidney* (1915).

*Portraits*: oil, by unknown artist, 1577: Earl of Warwick Collection; two other versions: location not known of one (formerly Duke of Bedford Collection), the other at Longleat (Marquess of Bath); later copies at Penshurst (Viscount De L'Isle) and National Portrait Gallery, London; drawing or tracing, three-quarter length, by G. Vertue after J. de Critz the Elder, 1585; private collection; several versions of this type, probably by de Critz, at Knebworth (Lady Hermione Cobbold), Penshurst (Viscount De L'Isle), Hall i' th'Wood Museum, Boston, Blickling Hall (National Trust), and Knole (Lord Sackville); watercolour, unknown man *called* Sir Philip Sidney, attributed to George Perfect Harding, 1818: N.P.G.; numerous other unsubstantiated portraits elsewhere. N.B. The portraits known to have existed by A. Abondio and N. Hilliard have never been traced. The full length portrait by Isaac Oliver, engraved as Sidney by Vertue, in the Royal Collection at Windsor, may be of another sitter.

## Simnel, Lambert (?1475–1525), imposter.

Lambert Simnel was born at Oxford in about 1475, the son of Thomas Simnel, a tradesman in that town. Intelligent and handsome, his education was undertaken by a local priest, Richard Symonds, who first conceived the idea of putting the young boy forward as Richard, Duke of York (see *Lives Before the Tudors*), the younger son of Edward IV (see *Lives Before the Tudors*), one of the two Princes who had been murdered in the Tower, about whom the Yorkists were spreading rumours to the effect that they were still alive. Later, when another rumour was circulated that the young Earl of Warwick, son of the Duke of Clarence (see George, Duke of Clarence, in *Lives Before the Tudors*), had died in the Tower, Symonds decided that he could more effectively impersonate Warwick.

In 1487 Simnel was taken by Symonds to Ireland where the Yorkists had many followers, and with the support of the Earl of Kildare, the Archbishop of Dublin, the Lord Chancellor, and many other sympathizers, 'Warwick' was crowned as Edward VI in Dublin Cathedral on 24 May. Plans were made for the Irish rebels to land in England, and the Earl of Lincoln (see Pole, John de la, Earl of Lincoln, in *Lives Before the Tudors*) and Lord Lovell (see Lovell, Francis, in *Lives Before the Tudors*) arrived in Dublin with 2,000 German mercenaries sent by Margaret, Duchess of Burgundy (q.v.), to support their cause. They landed in Lancashire on 4 June, but met with little support. Marching towards London, they met the King's army at Stoke-on-Trent on 16 June and were totally defeated after a fierce battle. Several of the Yorkist leaders were killed, and Simnel, together with Symonds, was taken prisoner.

Henry VII (q.v.) treated Simnel with great leniency, recognizing that he had been a tool in the hands of the Yorkists, and while Symonds the priest was imprisoned for life, the boy was taken into the

royal service as a scullion and later rose to be royal falconer. He subsequently joined the household of Sir Thomas Lovell (q.v.), and is said to have died in 1525.

B. Scott Daniell, *The Boy They Made King* (1959).

**Skelton, John** (?1460–1529), poet and satirist.

Nothing is known of John Skelton's birthplace or early life, although he is believed to have been of Norfolk origin. He studied at Cambridge, and possibly also at Oxford; both English universities, and also the University of Louvain, created him 'poet laureate' (then an academic distinction for rhetoric). Skelton's literary talent, notably his translations from the Greek and Latin, brought him to the notice of the court and led in 1489 to his appointment as court poet. His early work included several elegies on members of the royal family and the nobility, as well as a satire on the court of Henry VII (q.v.), *The Bowge of Court*, which was printed by Wynkyn de Worde. In spite of his outspokenness, Skelton continued in the royal favour, becoming 'scolemaster' to the young Duke of York, later Henry VIII (q.v.), a few years later. Such was his reputation as a poet and scholar that the great Dutch humanist, Desiderius Erasmus (q.v.), on his visit to England in 1499 called Skelton 'the incomparable light and glory of English letters'. He took holy orders in 1498 and four years later was appointed Rector of Diss, in Norfolk.

Skelton resided at Diss from about 1502 until 1512. It is clear from local records that, contrary to the tradition that has persisted of his buffoonery as a preacher and his alleged co-habitation with a woman by whom he had a number of children, though he did not marry her, Skelton fulfilled his duties as an orthodox cleric responsibly during this time. It was while at Diss that he developed the vigorous and often jocular poetic style of short rhyming lines now known as 'Skeltonics'. Among his work at this period were the poems *Phylup Sparowe* and *Ware the Hawke*, and a series of verses written in honour of Henry VIII's accession.

From 1512, when the King bestowed on him the title of *orator regius*, Skelton lived in London, where he entertained the court with a flow of satirical, political and abusive poems. To this period belong *A ballad of the Scottysshe Kynge*, written after the Battle of Flodden in 1513; *The Tunning of Elynour Rumming*, a coarse but humorous poem about a drunken alewife; *Magnyfycence*, a morality play and political satire combined, written in 1516 but never staged; and his celebrated political and clerical satires, *Speke Parrot* (1521), *Colyn Cloute* and *Why come ye nat to courte* (both 1522), all three of which were directed against the growing influence of Cardinal Thomas Wolsey (q.v.) and what the poet saw as dangers in the spread of humanism. There is some foundation for the story that Wolsey took his revenge by forcing Skelton into sanctuary at Westminster, but in the last years of his life the poet confined his writing to lyrical and allegorical themes. He died at Westminster on 21 June 1529 and was buried in the chancel of St Margaret's Church.

The bitter invective characteristic of his work was unpopular with the later Tudors, and Skelton's reputation declined during the second half of the sixteenth century; it is only recently that his poetic talent has been fully appreciated. Skelton praised himself in an allegorical poem, *The Garlande of Laurell*, published in 1523; in it he is crowned among the great poets of the world. The standard edition of his work is that by Alexander Dyce (2 vols; 1843). A translation of the Greek historian Diodorus Siculus, one of the few examples of Skelton's early scholarship that have survived, was published in 1956.

H. L. R. Edwards, *Skelton, The Life and Times of an Early Tudor Poet* (1949).
P. Green, *John Skelton* (1960).
A. R. Heiserman, *Skelton and Satire* (1962).
M. Pollet, *John Skelton* (1962).

*Portrait*: engraving, frontispiece to *The Garlande of Laurell*, 1523: British Museum, London.

**Smith, Sir Thomas** (1513–1577), statesman, scholar, and author.

The eldest son of John and Agnes Smith, Thomas Smith was born at Saffron Walden, Essex, on 23 December 1513. He was educated at the local grammar school and at Cambridge, where in 1530 he became a fellow of Queens' College. He graduated as M.A. in 1533 and in 1538 was appointed public orator at the university. In 1540 he went to the Continent to pursue his studies, visiting Paris and Padua, where he graduated as D.C.L. On his return to Cambridge in 1542 he was incorporated as L.L.D. and, together with his friend John Cheke (q.v.), Smith played a leading role in the campaign to reform Greek pronunciation. In 1544 he was appointed Regius Professor of Civil Law at Cambridge and also Vice-Chancellor of the University.

As a staunch supporter of Protestantism, Smith rose swiftly to prominence in the reign of Edward VI (q.v.). In 1547 he entered the service of the Protector Somerset (see Seymour, Edward) and after holding several minor offices, including that of Provost of Eton, he was in April 1548 sworn in as one of the principal Secretaries of State. He was knighted later that year, following the first of a number of missions on the Continent. Loyal to Somerset to the last, he was on the latter's overthrow removed from his seat on the Council and the office of Secretary of State and also deprived of his Cambridge professorship; after a few months' imprisonment in the Tower he was released in March 1550, when, apart from accompanying Northumberland (see Dudley, John) to France the following year, he lived for the most part at Eton. Thanks to his friendship with Stephen Gardiner (q.v.), Smith was protected from molestation during the reign of Mary I (q.v.); he lived quietly in retirement, having in 1554 resigned from the post of Provost of Eton.

On the accession of Elizabeth I (q.v.), Smith again came into prominence. Appointed to serve on a number of commissions at home at the beginning of the reign, in 1562 he was sent by the Queen as ambassador to France, where a delicate situation had arisen because of hostilities between the Guise party and the Huguenots. Sir Nicholas Throckmorton (q.v.), the other English ambassador, was at the time in prison following the English attack upon Le Havre. Jealousy between the two men led to violence and a threat to Smith's life, but in the event their joint actions culminated in the signature of the Peace of Troyes, signed in April 1564.

Smith remained in France for a further two years, returning to England in May 1566. He spent the next five years in retirement in Essex until, in March 1571, he was readmitted to the Privy Council. In the following year he was reappointed Secretary of State. He accompanied the Queen on her progress in 1575, but ceased to attend the Council in the spring of the following year, when his health began to fail. He died at Theydon Mount, Essex, on 12 August 1577.

Generally considered to be one of the most upright statesmen of the age, Sir Thomas Smith was also a great classical scholar, rivalled in this field only by his friend Cheke. In addition to his several tracts on the reform of Greek and English, on the marriage of the Queen, on Roman coinage, and other subjects, he translated some of the Psalms and Songs of David. Smith's major work, *De Republica Anglorum*, written in France but not published until after his death, in 1584, is a detailed survey of Tudor government and the only contemporary account. It ran into eleven editions before 1640 and was translated into Latin, Dutch, and German. The best modern edition is by L. Alston (Cambridge, 1906). Twice married, Smith had an illegitimate son who accompanied him on his various missions to France. Some scholars hold the view that he and not John Hales (q.v.) was the author of *A Discourse of the Common Weal of this Realm of England*. Some of Smith's correspondence has been printed in *The Compleat Ambassador* by Sir Dudley Digges (1655).

Mary Dewar, *Sir Thomas Smith: A Tudor Intellectual in Office* (1964).
D. B. Quinn, *Sir Thomas Smith, 1513–1577, and the Beginnings of English Colonial Theory* (1945).
John Strype, *The Life of the Learned Sir T. Smith* (1698; standard ed., Oxford, 1820).

## Smithson or Smythson, Robert

(1535–1614), architect.

Member of a family of mason-architects, three generations of whom flourished in the late sixteenth and early seventeenth centuries, Robert Smithson was employed by Sir John Thynne in the building of Longleat House, Wiltshire, in the years 1568–80. In about 1578 he made improvements to Wardour Castle, also in Wiltshire.

In 1580 Smithson began work on Wollaton Hall, Nottinghamshire, the first of the great Elizabethan mansions to be designed and built by one man. A splendid example of Elizabethan Renaissance architecture, it was original in that it was not built around an open courtyard, as were many great houses of the period, but rose like a high and flamboyant tower with projecting round turrets at the four corners, the façade richly decorated with mouldings and huge windows.

Smithson's next house may have been Worksop Manor, designed for the Earl of Shrewsbury (see Talbot, George) at the time when he was married to 'Bess' Hardwick (see Hardwick, Elizabeth). Following the Earl's death in 1590 Smithson was engaged by the Countess on the design and building of Hardwick Hall, Derbyshire. The construction was completed in three years and the Hall decorated and furnished by 1597.

The leading architect of the Elizabethan age (architecture being then a new profession), Robert Smithson undoubtedly had a hand in many other contemporary mansions in the Midlands. He died in 1614 and was buried at Wollaton, where his tomb describes him as 'architector and surveyor unto the most worthy house of Wollaton with divers others of great account'.

Mark Girouard, *Robert Smythson and the Architecture of the Elizabethan Era* (1966).

**Somerset, 1st Duke of** (1500–1552), see Seymour, Edward.

**Southampton, 1st Earl of** (1505–1550), see Wriothesley, Thomas.

**Southampton, 3rd Earl of** (1573–1624), see Wriothesley, Henry.

**Southwell, Robert** (1561–1595), Jesuit martyr and poet.

Born towards the end of 1561, Robert Southwell was the third son of Richard

Southwell of Horsham St Faith, near Norwich; the family was distantly related to the Cecils and the Bacons, and Robert's father was the illegitimate son of Sir Richard Southwell, who had played a prominent part in the dissolution of the monasteries under the direction of Henry VIII (q.v.) and Thomas Cromwell (q.v.).

Kidnapped by a gipsy woman while in his cradle, but soon recovered, Southwell spent his childhood in the family circle. At the age of sixteen he was sent to the English College at Douai and subsequently moved to Rome, where in October 1578 he was accepted as a candidate for the Jesuit order. After two years as a novice in Tournai, Southwell returned to Rome, where he took holy orders and became Prefect of Studies at the English College. He was determined to take part in the mission to England, in spite of the severe laws against Jesuits and fully aware that it would lead to martyrdom. In the summer of 1586 his wish was granted; together with Henry Garnett, he landed in England in July and, under the assumed name of Cotton, began moving about the country making converts and comforting the persecuted Catholics.

From the outset Southwell's activities were known to the government, and he was closely watched. In 1589 he became chaplain to Anne Howard, Countess of Arundel, who concealed him at her house in the Strand. From this hiding place he issued letters and tracts for the encouragement of his fellow Catholics. Most of his writings were circulated surreptitiously in manuscript, but one, *An Epistle of Comfort*, written in 1591, was secretly printed abroad.

On 20 June 1592 Southwell was arrested while celebrating Mass at the house of a Catholic friend, Richard Bellamy. Imprisoned and brutally tortured over a length of time, he was put on trial in February 1595, charged with treason, and condemned to death. He was hanged at Tyburn on 21 February.

It was during his three years' imprisonment that Southwell wrote much of his poetry, the theme of which is spiritual love; the best known is his delightful poem, 'The Burning Babe'. His main work, a narrative of the last events in the life of Christ spoken by St Peter, entitled *St Peter's Complaynt*, was published after his death in 1595. Among his other writings were a collection of poems under the title of *Maeconiae* 1595) and a *Fourefold Meditation of the Four Last Things*, published in 1606; a full bibliography will be found at the end of the article in *D.N.B.* Southwell's work was highly praised by Ben Jonson (see *Lives of the Stuart Age*).

M. Bastian, *Robert Southwell* (1931).
Christopher Devlin, *The Life of Robert Southwell* (1956).
P. Janelle, *Robert Southwell the Writer* (1936).

*Portrait*: engraving, by W. J. Alais, 1872, after C. Weld, after unknown artist, at the end of his life: location not known.

**Speed, John** (?1552–1629), historian and cartographer.

Believed to have been born in about 1552 at Farringdon or Farndon, Cheshire, John Speed was brought up in the tailoring trade by his father, also John Speed, a freeman of the Merchant Taylors' Company. John was himself admitted to the freedom of the Company in September 1580, and shortly afterwards, in 1582, he married and settled with his wife Susanna in a tenement leased from the Merchant Taylors at Moorfields, London; they were to have twelve sons and six daughters.

Speed first began to draw maps of the counties of England in his spare time. His interest in history and genealogy brought him into contact with Sir Fulke Greville (q.v.), on whose recommendation he was in 1598 given a post in the Custom-House. Through Greville he subsequently became a member of the Society of Antiquaries, where he met the historian William Camden (q.v.), the antiquary Sir Robert Bruce Cotton (q.v.), and others who helped him in his historical researches and encouraged him to write the *Historie of Great Britaine*, published in 1611 as a continuation of his collection of maps.

As early as 1598 Speed had presented some of his maps to the Queen, and in 1600 he had given others to the Merchant Taylors' Company. The first to be printed was a copy of Norden's map of Surrey, used in the first edition of Camden's *Britannia* (1607). Between 1608 and 1610 Speed published a series of fifty-four maps of England and Wales; these maps, together with descriptive matter, were incorporated into his *Theatre of the Empire of Great Britaine*, published in 1611, and closely followed by the *Historie*. Both volumes ran into several editions, as did Speed's *Gene-*

*alogies recorded in Sacred Scripture*, which also appeared in 1611, and a later theological work, *A Cloude of Witnesses . . . confirming . . . God's most Holie Word*, published in 1616.

By 1625 Speed was complaining that increasing blindness prevented him from working on a continuation of the *Historie*. His wife died in March 1628, by which time his own health was also rapidly failing; he died on 28 July 1629, aged seventy-seven, and was buried in St Giles's, Cripplegate.

Although John Speed's *Historie* earned him much praise from his contemporaries and established him as the first of the English historians, as distinct from the earlier chroniclers, it was later severely criticized by James Spedding, editor of the works of Francis Bacon (q.v.), for its use of old materials and the repetition of 'almost all the old blunders'. Nevertheless, Conyers Read considers him the most readable of the Elizabethan historians. Speed's maps, on the other hand, are of immense historical value; some of them are extant and at the British Museum, London. The third edition of his collection was published in 1631 under the title *A Prospect of the Most Famous Parts of the World*.

*Portraits*: engraving, by Soloman Savery, used in *A Prospect of the Most Famous Parts of the World*, 1631, and *Historie of Great Britaine*, 1632; painted version of this engraving: Bodleian Library, Oxford; oil, *called* John Speed, by unknown artist: National Portrait Gallery, London.

**Spenser, Edmund** (?1552–1599), poet, author of the allegorical poem, *The Faerie Queene*.

Born in London in about 1552, Edmund Spenser was the son of John Spenser, a gentleman tradesman in the cloth business whose family was connected with the Spencers of Althorp, and his wife Elizabeth. The family was not rich, and Edmund attended as a 'poor boy' the newly-founded Merchant Taylors' School, where he came under the influence of Richard Mulcaster, then headmaster, whose views on English literature were far ahead of his time. From 1569 to 1574 he studied as a 'sizar' at Pembroke Hall, Cambridge, obtaining his B.A. in 1573 and his M.A. in 1576. While still a student he contributed translations from Petrarch and Du Bellay to an anti-Catholic tract, *The Theatre for Worldlings*, published in 1569. At Cambridge Spenser wrote his *Hymnes in honour of Love and Beautie*, but these were not published until 1596.

In 1578, through his university friend, the poet Gabriel Harvey, Spenser obtained a post in the household of the Earl of Leicester (see Dudley, Robert). He began work on *The Faerie Queene*, and in 1579 published *The Shepheardes Calender*, dedicated to Sidney. Enthusiastically received by Spenser's contemporaries, the *Calender* announced the appearance of a new poet of the first order. Its success brought Spenser to the notice of the court. In 1580 he was appointed as secretary to Lord Grey de Wilton, a friend of the Sidney family, who was about to take office as Lord Deputy of Ireland.

Spenser was to spend the next nineteen years in Ireland. He was appreciative of the landscape of Munster, which figures in his verse, and was granted a sinecure post in the province, where from about 1584 he deputized for his old Cambridge literary friend Lodowick Bryskett as clerk of the lords president. In 1586 he became one of the 'undertakers' for the settlement of Munster, acquiring in about 1588 the castle of Kilcolman in the county of Cork. He settled there, probably with his family (he had married in 1579 Machabyas Chylde, by whom he had one son and one daughter), intending to devote himself to his literary work, principally *The Faerie Queene*; this was to consist of twelve books, each one an adventure of a different knight of Gloriana (Queen Elizabeth). Spenser had in 1586 written *Astrophil*, a pastoral elegy lamenting the death of Sidney, and was to compose a further elegy on his mentor entitled 'The Ruines of Time'; this was included in a collection of his *juvenilia* and minor verse entitled *Complaints* and published in 1591.

At Kilcolman Spenser became acquainted with Sir Walter Ralegh (q.v.), whose estate adjoined his own. The two poets wrote complimentary verses to each other, and Ralegh persuaded Spenser to accompany him back to England in December 1589 in order to present the first three books of *The Faerie Queene* personally to Queen Elizabeth (q.v.). He was well received at court, where Ralegh was high in favour with the Queen, and with his friend's assistance he saw his work through the press; *The Faerie Queene* (Books I-III) was duly published in 1590, with a dedication to Elizabeth and sundry verses in praise of Lord Burghley (see Cecil, William) and other courtiers. Spenser hoped thereby to win preferment, but his old patron, Leicester, was dead, and Burghley had been offended by his earlier work, *Prosopopoia, or Mother Hubberd's Tale*, which had attacked the proposed marriage between the Queen and the Duc d'Alençon (q.v.). Nevertheless the Queen granted Spenser a generous pension, which was said to have been halved by her Lord Treasurer. Back in Ireland, Spenser wrote *Colin Clouts come home againe*, an allegorical poem commemorating his visit to London and dedicated to Ralegh. In 1591 his collection entitled *Complaints* was published; this contained a satire on court favour, which Spenser had added to *Mother Hubberd's Tale*.

In 1594 Spenser married his second wife, Elizabeth Boyle. Their courtship and marriage are commemorated in his sonnet sequence *Amoretti* and marriage ode *Epithalamion*, published together the following year. He completed the second three books of *The Faerie Queene*, taking them to London to be printed in 1596, together with the *Fowre Hymnes* (the two 'In Honour of Love' and 'In Honour of Beauty' written while at Cambridge, with two new ones of 'Heavenly Love' and 'Heavenly Beauty' added). While in London Spenser lived at the house of his friend, the Earl of Essex (see Devereux, Robert), where in between supervising these publications he wrote *Prothalamion*, to celebrate the double marriage of two daughters of the Earl of Worcester, published in 1596, and also a prose account entitled *View of the Present State of Ireland*, which was not printed until 1633.

Spenser returned to Kilcolman in 1597, but in the following October he was forced to flee, with his wife and four children, to Cork, after the castle had been burned during an insurrection. Greatly distressed, and said to be destitute, Spenser arrived in London bearing official letters on the current state of Ireland. He died in lodgings in King Street, Westminster, on 13 January 1599, and was buried in Westminster Abbey, the expenses of his funeral being borne by the Earl of Essex.

Edmund Spenser was considered by his contemporaries to be the greatest of the English poets; he was honoured as having glorified England and the English language in *The Faerie Queene*, in the same way that Virgil had glorified Rome and the Latin tongue in the *Aeneid*. The nine-line stanza form in which Spenser wrote his long allegorical poem was copied by the Romantic poets of the late eighteenth and early nineteenth centuries.

The standard edition of Spenser's works is that by E.A. Greenlaw *et al.*, *The Works of Edmund Spenser: A Variorum Edition* (10 vols; 1932–49).

Alexander C. Judson, *The Life of Edmund Spenser* (1945).

**Stafford, Edward** (1478–1521), 3rd Duke of Buckingham.

The eldest son of the 2nd Duke of Buckingham (see Stafford, Henry, in *Lives Before the Tudors*) and his wife Catherine Woodville, whose sister was the wife of Edward IV (see *Lives Before the Tudors*), Edward Stafford was born at Brecknock Castle, Wales, on 3 February 1478. He was five years old in November 1483, when his father was beheaded for leading an insurrection against Richard III (see *Lives Before the Tudors*) and his estates forfeited. The attainder was reversed by Henry VII (q.v.) in 1485, and Edward was made a ward of the King's mother, the Countess of Richmond (see Beaufort, Margaret). An arrogant young courtier, he liked to boast of his royal descent (on his father's side) from Edward III (see *Lives Before the Tudors*), and in certain quarters his name was widely supported as a claimant to the throne, especially when the death of Prince Arthur (q.v.) in 1502 left only Prince Henry, later Henry VIII (q.v.), as heir to the dynasty. A Knight of the Garter in 1499, the following year he married Alianore, eldest daughter of Henry Percy, 4th Earl of Northumberland; she was to bear him a son and three daughters, all of whom were destined to make influential marriages.

Buckingham came into prominence early in the reign of Henry VIII. A Privy Councillor in 1509, he accompanied the King to the Field of the Cloth of Gold in June 1520 and to his meeting with the Emperor Charles V (q.v.) at Gravelines the following month. His wealth and family connections made him the object of bitter hatred on the part of the lowborn Thomas Wolsey (q.v.), whom Buckingham and his fellow nobles, especially those who had been excluded from high office, openly despised. The King himself, desperate for a male heir, was jealous of the Duke's position and suspicious of his intentions, and when in late 1520 Wolsey received an anonymous letter containing allegations of treason against Buckingham, Henry swiftly took proceedings, personally examining the witnesses. The unsuspecting Duke was summoned to London early in April 1521 and committed to the Tower. He stood trial on 13 May on trumped-up charges of having listened to prophecies of Henry's death and his own succession and of having expressed his intention to kill the King. It was clear that Henry was determined that Buckingham should die, and the peers, presided over by the Duke of Norfolk (see Howard, Thomas, 2nd Duke), not daring to go against the King's wishes, duly pronounced him guilty. His execution at Tower Hill on 17 May aroused much popular sympathy.

See the introduction by J. S. Brewer to *Letters and Papers, Foreign and Domestic of the Reign of Henry VIII*, vol. ii, part i (21 vols; 1862–1910).

**Stafford, Sir Edward** (?1552–1605), diplomatist.

Born in about 1552, Edward Stafford was the eldest son of Sir William Stafford of Grafton and Chebsey, Staffordshire, and his second wife, Dorothy, daughter of Henry Stafford, 1st Baron Stafford. His mother was Mistress of the Robes to Queen Elizabeth (q.v.), and it was probably through her influence that Edward entered the royal service.

In May 1578 Stafford was sent by Elizabeth to Catherine de' Medici (q.v.) to protest against the intention of her son, the Duc d'Anjou (see Alençon, François, Duc d') to accept sovereignty of the Netherlands. The following year he was chosen to carry out the delicate negotiations for a possible marriage between the Queen and Alençon, which involved him in a number of journeys to and from France. His efforts pleased Elizabeth, who knighted him for his services and in 1583 appointed him as resident ambassador in that country.

By this date Stafford had lost his first wife, who had borne him a son and two daughters, and had married the notorious Douglas, sister of Lord Howard of Effingham (see Howard, Charles); the widow of Lord Sheffield, she had dared to have an affair with the Queen's favourite, the Earl of Leicester (see Dudley, Robert), by whom she had had a son. Stafford engaged the young Richard Hakluyt (q.v.) to act as chaplain and tutor to his household in Paris.

During the seven years he remained at his post in France Stafford conducted himself as a loyal Protestant and servant of the crown, courageously refusing to allow his house to be draped during the feast of Corpus Christi in 1584 and spurning the guard offered to him by the Duc de Guise on the 'Day of Barricades' (12 May 1588). In February 1588 the ambassador was consulted by Henri III as to the Queen's willingness to mediate with the Huguenots. When news reached him of the defeat of the Spanish Armada in the summer of that year, he immediately wrote and had printed and circulated at his own expense a pamphlet to counter the false news of Spanish success issued by the Spanish ambassador.

On his return to England at the end of 1588 there were rumours that Stafford would be appointed Secretary of State and Chancellor of the Duchy of Lancaster, as promised to him by the Queen; neither of these posts materialized, and he had to be satisfied with an appointment to the Pipe Office and the post of Remembrancer of First Fruits. In 1592 Stafford received an M.A. at Oxford and also became a bencher at Gray's Inn; the following March he was elected as Member of Parliament for Winchester. He served on a commission for the relief of maimed soldiers and seamen during that Parliament and was re-elected to represent Stafford in 1597–8 and 1601, and Queenborough in 1604. He was granted £60 a year by James I (see James VI of Scotland) out of exchequer lands as compensation for not getting the post of Chancellor of the Duchy of Lancaster. Stafford died on 5 February 1605 and was buried in St Margaret's, Westminster.

The correspondence of Sir Edward Stafford (at the Public Record Office, the British Museum (Cottonian MSS), and Hatfield) is a major source for diplomatic history of the period. Some letters have been printed in *Collection of State Papers . . . left by William Cecil, Lord Burghley*, edited by S. Haynes and W. Murdin (2 vols; 1740–59) and in *Miscellaneous State Papers from 1501 to 1726*, edited by Philip Yorke, 2nd Earl of Hardwicke (2 vols; 1778).

On the difference of opinion among modern historians concerning Stafford's integrity, see Conyers Read, 'The Fame of Sir Edward Stafford', in *American Historical Review*, xx (1915), pp. 292–313, and xxv (1930), pp. 560–6; A. F. Pollard in *English Historical Review*, xvi (1901), pp. 572–7; J. E. Neale in *English Historical Review*, xliv (1929), pp. 203–20.

**Stafford, Thomas** (?1531–1557), rebel.

The ninth child and second surviving son of Henry Stafford, 1st Baron Stafford, and his wife Ursula, daughter of Sir Richard Pole, Thomas Stafford was born in about 1531; on his mother's side he was the grandson of Margaret Pole (q.v.), Countess of Salisbury, and nephew of Cardinal Reginald Pole (q.v.).

After receiving a private Protestant education, Stafford travelled to the Continent in 1550 and spent the next three years in Italy. In 1553 he visited Poland, where he influenced the King and Queen to write letters on his behalf to Queen Mary I (q.v.), urging her to restore Stafford to the dukedom of Buckingham, forfeited on the attainder of his grandfather, the 3rd Duke (see Stafford, Edward). When this had no effect, Stafford came out into the open as a fierce opponent of the Queen's proposed marriage to Philip II of Spain (q.v.) and, returning to England, he supported the abortive uprising led by Henry Grey, Duke of Suffolk, father of the Lady Jane Grey (q.v.), in January 1554; for a short time afterwards he was imprisoned in the Fleet, but on regaining his liberty in March he fled to France.

For the next few years Stafford involved himself deeply in the intrigues of the English exiles in France, not only plotting to overthrow the Queen but declaring himself to be, after Mary, the next rightful heir to the throne, being of royal descent, both on his father's and his mother's side; this led to a bitter quarrel with a fellow exile, Sir Robert Stafford (who was not his brother, as is sometimes stated). His activities were known to the English ambassador in France, and it was believed that the French King, in an attempt to use Stafford as a pawn in what was seen as the inevitable conflict between the two countries, was aiding and abetting his plans; it seems likely that Henri II provided the two ships in which Stafford and his followers embarked from Dieppe in April 1557.

After landing at Scarborough, where he seized the Castle on 25 April, Stafford denounced the Queen's marriage and, warning that a Spanish army was assembling to invade the country, urged the population to rise in his support. He was defeated and captured before any real fighting had taken place and was sent to London to be tried for high treason. Stafford was hanged and quartered at Tyburn on 28 May 1557.

**Stanley, Sir William** (d. 1495), Lord Chamberlain to Henry VII, see *Lives Before the Tudors*.

**Stewart or Stuart, Henry** (1545–1567), Lord Darnley, second husband of Mary, Queen of Scots (q.v.), and father of James VI of Scotland (q.v.; later James I of England).

Born at Temple Newsam, Yorkshire, on 7 December 1545, Henry Stewart was the second but eldest surviving son of the Earl of Lennox (see Stewart, Matthew) and the Lady Margaret Douglas (q.v.).

Darnley was educated privately, under the supervision of a Scottish priest, John Elder. His intellectual capacity was not very high, but he was an accomplished lutenist and, like his father, excelled at physical exercises; in later life he was to show himself to have a morally weak character.

He was still very young when his mother, abandoning her earlier aim of securing the English throne for herself after Elizabeth I (q.v.), began to intrigue for Darnley's marriage to the recently widowed Mary, Queen of Scots. The Lennox home in Yorkshire was at this period the centre of Catholic intrigue and was closely watched by Elizabeth's spies. Should the Queen die childless, the Catholics were determined to put Darnley on the throne, and with this in mind the Countess of Lennox in 1560

sent him to France so that Mary should become acquainted with him and understand that the English throne could be hers if she married him. The mission was not immediately successful, however; Mary was more interested in Don Carlos of Spain than a mere fifteen-year-old – blond, tall, and handsome though he was. And when the plan was revealed prematurely to the Queen in 1562, Lennox was sent to the Tower, while Darnley and his mother were confined at the house of Sir Richard Sackville at Sheen. All three were released soon afterwards, however, and once more received at court.

In February 1565 Darnley was permitted to join his father in Scotland, possibly because Elizabeth now wished to prevent the proposed marriage between the Queen of Scots and the Earl of Leicester (see Dudley, Robert). On this occasion Mary was captivated by her cousin; by the end of April it was clear that she intended to marry him. The match was largely brought about by the Queen's secretary, David Riccio (q.v.),

who had great influence over her; he and Darnley were initially close friends. It is possible that a secret marriage took place as early as March 1565; on the 15th of that month Darnley was created Earl of Ross, and later Duke of Albany. His attack of measles caused the Queen much anxiety, but on 29 July she and Darnley were married in the chapel of Holyrood, according to Catholic rites.

From the outset Darnley had been hated by the Protestant Scottish lords because of his religion; it now became obvious to them, and to Mary, that he had many shortcomings, not least of these being his addiction to drink and disreputable company and an inability to keep his mouth shut politically. Wisely, the Queen refused him the crown matrimonial and instead turned increasingly to Riccio for advice in state affairs.

Riccio, as a Catholic and a foreigner, was much hated, especially by those who sympathized with the Earl of Moray (see Stewart, Lord James). This group now combined with Darnley's Catholic friends to plot Riccio's murder. The participation of Darnley was secured by promise of their support to obtain for him the crown matrimonial, as well as by clever insinuation that Riccio was the Queen's lover. Darnley became intensely jealous, to the point that he believed the child Mary was carrying to be Riccio's and not his.

On the evening of 9 March 1566, while the Queen was at supper at Holyroodhouse, attended by Riccio, Darnley admitted the conspirators and led them to her room; included among them were the Earl of Morton (see Douglas, James), Patrick Lindsay, 6th Baron Lindsay, Patrick Ruthven, 3rd Baron Ruthven, and his son, later the 4th Baron Ruthven (see Ruthven, William). Riccio was dragged from the room and stabbed over fifty times, the other lords taking care to leave Darnley's dagger in the corpse in order that he should be implicated in the deed.

Darnley afterwards betrayed those who had taken part in the plot. Mary, not wishing to do anything that would affect the legitimacy of her unborn child, was reconciled briefly with her husband, and they escaped together to the castle of Dunbar. When she was shown written proof of his agreement to take part in the murder, however, she could not forgive him; after the birth of her son, the future James VI, she turned increasingly to those who hated Darnley and were determined to get rid of him. His position thus became impossible, so that Darnley himself made plans to leave Scotland. He was at Stirling for the baptism of James on 17 December, but did not attend the ceremony; soon afterwards he left for Glasgow, where he intended to take a ship to foreign parts, but before he could leave he became ill with what is thought to have been syphilis.

In January the Queen persuaded him to return to Edinburgh to convalesce, promising to resume marital relations after his recovery. He was lodged in a house at Kirk o' Field, just outside the city. On the night of 9 February 1567 the house was blown up; Darnley's body and that of his page were found early the next morning in the garden, obviously strangled, and unmarked by the explosion. The Earl of Bothwell (see Hepburn, James) was thought to be the man responsible for the murder plot, which was probably committed with the full knowledge of the Queen, who was by that time in love with, and possibly pregnant by, the Earl; she was to marry him three months later.

Darnley was buried in the chapel at Holyrood. Through his son he was the ancestor of the Stuart and ensuing sovereigns of Great Britain. To this day the apportionment of responsibility for his death remains in debate.

G. Chalmers, *Life of Mary, Queen of Scots* (1818). R. H. Mahon, *The Tragedy of Kirk o' Field* (1930).

*Portraits*: oil, three-quarter length, by Hans Eworth, 1555: The Lord Bolton; oil, with his brother Charles, by Eworth, 1562: Royal Collection, Holyroodhouse (another smaller version, 1563, at Windsor); oil, three-quarter length, attributed to Eworth, *c.* 1565: The Lord Bolton; miniature, by unknown artist: Mauritshuis, The Hague; Darnley memorial picture, 1568: Holyroodhouse (another version in Duke of Richmond Collection, Goodwood, Sussex); electrotype, from tomb of his mother, Margaret, Countess of Lennox, in Westminster Abbey: National Portrait Gallery, London (plaster cast: Scottish National Portrait Gallery, Edinburgh).

**Stewart, Lord James** (?1531–1570), Earl of Mar and of Moray, half-brother of Mary, Queen of Scots (q.v.), and Regent of Scotland 1567–70.

Lord James Stewart was the natural son of James V (q.v.) and Margaret, daughter of Lord Erskine, who at the time of his birth was married to Robert Douglas of Lochleven. Born probably in 1531, little is known of his childhood. He was well provided for by his father, and in 1538 was made Commendator of the Priory of St Andrews, one of the wealthiest monastic foundations in Scotland. He took up residence there, while remaining in close touch with his mother, and later studied at St Andrews University. During this time he was converted to Protestantism by John Knox (q.v.).

In 1542 Stewart had supported the bid of Marie de Guise (q.v.) for the Regency following the death of James V; he continued to support her in 1554 when she actually became Regent and was one of the commissioners sent to France in February 1558 to negotiate the marriage treaty of the young Mary, Queen of Scots. By this time, incited by Knox, the Protestant lords were banding together in a group (later known as the 'Lords of the Congregation'), of which Stewart became a prominent member; when Marie de Guise launched her offensive against the Calvinists he and the Duke of Châtelherault (see Hamilton, James, 2nd Earl of Arran) led the rebellion against her which drove the Regent out of Edinburgh. Stewart, however, was disappointed in his hope of achieving the regency on account of his illegitimacy, and the new council was headed by Châtelherault.

After the death of Mary's French husband, François II, in December 1560, Stewart went to France to visit his half-sister and to urge her, on behalf of the moderate Protestant party, to adopt a policy of conciliation in religious matters when she returned to take up the rule of her kingdom. They reached an understanding, and soon after the Queen's arrival in Scotland in August 1561, Stewart became a member of her Privy Council; in January the following year he was given the earldom of Moray, but had to keep this secret temporarily because of claims to some of the Moray lands by the house of Huntly. In the meantime, as a wedding present, he was given other lands and the title of Earl of Mar. He married on 8 February 1562, in a ceremony performed by Knox at St Giles, Edinburgh, Agnes Keith, daughter of the Earl Marischal; three children were to be born to them, of whom only two daughters survived.

Moray worked for an arrangement between Mary and Elizabeth I (q.v.) that would settle the succession and assure the supremacy of Protestantism in Scotland; increasingly in the next few years he incurred the Queen of Scots' disfavour by his support of Knox. He refused to approve Mary's marriage to Lord Darnley (see Stewart, Henry) and in August 1565 led the revolt against the Queen's authority which became known as the Chaseabout Raid. Outlawed, Moray was driven across the border into England. He was one of the conspirators in the murder of David Riccio (q.v.) on 9 March 1566, although, being an outlaw at Newcastle at the time, he took no active part in it, returning to Edinburgh the following day to receive the Queen's pardon. He was also probably involved in the plot to murder Darnley, but again not actively, since he left Edinburgh the previous day for St Andrews, where his wife had suffered a miscarriage. Early in March 1567 he returned to court, but when he became aware of the Queen's intention to marry the Earl of Bothwell (see Hepburn, James), he left for France, where he remained for the next three months.

On Mary's abdication in July that year, Moray returned to Scotland. On 22 August he was appointed Regent for the infant James VI (q.v.). After her escape from Lochleven, Moray's forces decisively defeated the Queen of Scots' forces at Langside on 13 May 1568, when Mary fled to England. He found it difficult to consolidate his position as Regent, however, the Scottish nobility being divided between those who supported the pro-English Protestant policies which Moray represented and those who followed the Queen; the Hamiltons, and Châtelherault in particular, resented his appointment as Regent and accused him of aiming at the throne.

On 23 January 1570, while riding through Linlithgow, Moray was assassinated by James Hamilton of Bothwellhaugh. His death plunged Scotland into three years of civil war.

James Stewart, Earl of Moray, is sometimes spoken of as the 'Good Regent'. Whether or not he was scheming to obtain the throne for himself, he managed to retain the goodwill of England, and especially that of William Cecil (q.v.; later 1st Baron Burghley); through his efforts the success of the Scottish Reformation was ensured.

M. Lee, *James Stewart, Earl of Moray, a Political Study of the Reformation in Scotland* (New York, 1953).

*Portraits:* oil, by Hans Eworth, 1561: Darnaway Castle, Moray; oil, copy by H. Monro, 1925: Scottish National Portrait Gallery, Edinburgh.

### Stewart, James, of Bothwellmuir (d. 1595), Earl of Arran.

James Stewart was the second son of Andrew Stewart, 2nd Baron Ochiltree, and Agnes, daughter of John Cunningham of Caprington; his sister Margaret was the second wife of John Knox (q.v.). The date of his birth is not known. He was well educated, probably with the intention of his entering the Church. An adventurous young man, however, he decided to become a soldier and served in Holland against the Spaniards. He returned to Scotland in 1579 and in October the following year was appointed a Gentleman of the Chamber to James VI (q.v.); he was also put in charge of his cousin, the 3rd Earl of Arran (see Hamilton, James, 3rd Earl), who was insane. He allowed himself to be used by the Duke of Lennox (see Stuart, Esmé) in accusing the Earl of Morton (see Douglas, James) of the murder of Lord Darnley (see Stewart, Henry) some fourteen years earlier; as a reward for his services he was recognized as head of the Hamiltons and on 22 April 1581 was granted the earldom of Arran, in spite of the fact that the 3rd Earl was still alive.

In July 1581 Arran married Elizabeth, elder daughter of John Stewart, 4th Earl of Atholl, having seduced her from her second husband.

Jealousy now arose between Arran and Lennox, and although this was temporarily smoothed over, Arran was merely biding his time. After the Ruthven Raid he succeeded in getting into the Gowrie stronghold, but was arrested in his attempt to rescue the King. When James escaped the following year, Arran was made Provost of Stirling; in 1584 he became Chancellor of Scotland and Provost of Edinburgh, which marked the climax of his career.

By his policy of crushing the Protestants by large-scale forfeitures, Arran made many enemies. His influence with Queen Elizabeth (q.v.) was undermined by the Master of Gray (see Gray, Patrick), who persuaded her to send the banished Protestant lords back to Scotland in order to plot Arran's overthrow. In 1586, after implication in the murder of Francis Russell, 2nd Earl of Bedford, and the discovery of a plot to assassinate Gray, Arran was declared a traitor, deprived of his earldom, and banished.

He returned to Scotland in 1592 as Captain James Stewart, and during the next few years, while he lived in comparative obscurity, there were various abortive intrigues for his return to power. Towards the end of 1595 he was attacked and murdered while riding through Clydesdale by Sir James Douglas of Parkhead, a nephew of Morton; his corpse was left to rot on the ground or as prey to wild animals, while his head was carried through the country on a spear by his triumphant murderer.

Details of the papers of Captain James Stewart appear in the 10th Report of the Historic Manuscripts Commission.

Caroline Bingham, *The Stewart Kingdom of Scotland, 1371–1603* (1974).

G. Donaldson, *Scotland, James V to James VII* (1965).

J. D. Mackie, *History of Scotland* (1964).

**Stewart, John** (1481–1536), Duke of Albany, Regent of Scotland, 1515–24, during the minority of James V (q.v.).

John Stewart was a grandson of James II of Scotland (see *Lives Before the Tudors*), being the only son of Alexander Stewart, Duke of Albany, by his second wife, Agnès de la Tour d'Auvergne et de Boulogne. His father died in 1485, and thereafter John was brought up in France by his mother. All his life he considered himself to be a Frenchman, whereas the Scots thought of him as a native of Scotland.

Little is known of his early years. In 1505 Albany married his cousin Anne, Comtesse de la Tour d'Auvergne. He seems to have been on intimate terms with the French King, François I, and to have held a number of official appointments at his court, including that of Admiral of France. His services as a foreign diplomat resident in France were sometimes used by James IV (q.v.).

After the death of James IV at the Battle of Flodden in September 1513, many of the Scottish nobles were opposed to Margaret Tudor (q.v.) as Regent for her infant son, James V; they therefore wrote to Albany, as the nearest blood relative of the young King, urging him to return to Scotland to take over the government. He accepted their invitation somewhat reluctantly, and arrived in Scotland in May 1515.

Margaret Tudor had by this date forfeited her regency by her marriage to the Earl of Angus (see Douglas, Archibald, 6th Earl) and was living at Stirling Castle with the three-year-old James V and her second, posthumous son by James IV, the baby Duke of Ross. Albany, having failed to win her alliance, stormed Stirling in August 1515 and forced her to surrender both the royal children and the castle. He entrusted James and his brother to the care of John Erskine, 5th Baron Erskine at Stirling, while he himself took up residence at Holyroodhouse. Following an unsuccessful attempt to abduct the children, Margaret fled to England.

Albany was soon able to establish his authority in Scotland, in spite of the fact that his enemies implied that, like his father, he had designs on the throne and constituted a danger to the King; an attempt to pin on him responsibility for the death of the infant Duke of Ross was soon quelled, and so was a rebellion led by Alexander Home, 3rd Baron Home, in conjunction with Angus and the Earl of Arran (see Hamilton, James, 1st Earl), in 1516. In November that year the Scottish Parliament confirmed the divorce of Albany's father from his first wife, in order to declare the Regent as heir to the throne. He then obtained their consent to his return to France for six months, in order to negotiate a Franco-Scottish alliance and to attend to family affairs. He left in June 1517 and in fact remained abroad for over four years.

In Albany's absence a power struggle erupted between Angus and Arran, culminating in a bitter contest for the possession of Edinburgh in the spring of 1520. When the Regent returned in November 1521, having negotiated the Treaty of Rouen, under which François I agreed to the marriage of one of his daughters to James V, he banished Angus to France and won the short-lived support of the Queen Dowager. When it was rumoured that he was aiding Margaret in her attempt to obtain a divorce from Angus because he wished to marry her himself, however, Albany is said to have replied that he greatly preferred his French estates to the crown of Scotland, and that one wife was quite enough. Margaret subsequently betrayed his plans for the invasion of England to which, in the face of the projected attack on France by Henry VIII (q.v.) and Charles V (q.v.), Scotland was bound under the terms of the 'Auld Alliance'.

The Scots themselves, remembering Flodden, were reluctant to do more than defend their country against English aggression, and taking advantage of a truce offered by England, Albany went to France in October 1522 to seek reinforcements. He returned in September 1523 with troops and money supplied by François, but once again he found the Scots reluctant to cross the Border, and after a brief foray he was forced to withdraw.

His prestige greatly damaged by these two abortive military campaigns, Albany again obtained leave of absence, this time on condition that if he did not return within four months he would forfeit his regency. He sailed from Dumbarton on 20 May 1524. Margaret Tudor, assisted by Arran, took the opportunity to regain control of the young King and to have him declared fit to govern; in July James was 'erected' as sovereign and Albany's regency was formally annulled.

Albany never returned to Scotland. He lived for another twelve years, most of which were spent in Italy, where he accompanied François I on his campaign against Charles V. He used his influence with Pope Clement VII to obtain a divorce for Margaret in 1527, possibly in the mistaken belief that this would weaken the English interest in Scotland. During the years 1530–3 he was sent on several missions to Rome, where he negotiated the marriage of his wife's niece, Catherine de' Medici (q.v.), to Henri, Duc d'Orléans (later Henri II of France). He did not live to see the outcome of his negotiations for the marriage of James V to a French princess, but died on 2 June 1536. His wife had died in 1524; they had no children,

although Albany is said to have had a natural daughter by a mistress in Scotland.

The failure of John Stewart, Duke of Albany, as Regent was due almost entirely to his preference for life in France and to his frequent absences from Scotland. In his first period of office he successfully restored law and order to the Borders, but left before his work was fully accomplished. His greatest talent was his ability as a negotiator, and he believed implicitly in the Franco-Scottish alliance.

M. W. Stuart, *The Scot who was a Frenchman* (1940). See also titles listed under James V.

**Stewart, Matthew** (1516–1571), 4th (12th) Earl of Lennox, Regent of Scotland, grandfather of James VI (q.v.).

Born on 21 September 1516 at Dumbarton Castle, Matthew Stewart was the son of John Stewart, 3rd Earl of Lennox, and Anne, daughter of John Stewart, 1st Earl of Atholl. He succeeded to the title when his father was murdered after the Battle of Linlithgow in 1526, and together with one of his brothers, was brought up in France by a kinsman, Robert Stuart d'Aubigny; in 1537 he was naturalized as a French subject.

After the death of James V (q.v.) in 1542, Lennox was persuaded by Cardinal David Beaton (q.v.) and the French party to return to Scotland in order to assist in the overthrow of the Earl of Arran (see Hamilton, James, 2nd Earl). The inducement was that he would be put forward as Arran's rival as the next heir to the throne after the Princess Mary, later Queen of Scots (q.v.); also mentioned was the possibility of his marriage to the Queen Dowager, Marie de Guise (q.v.).

Arran at first refused Lennox's offer of money and troops in order to resist an

English invasion, but came to terms after the latter had assembled a force which seized the Queen Dowager and the infant Princess and took them to Stirling. Following the invasion led by the Earl of Hertford (see Seymour, Edward) in 1544, Arran was forced to accept the influence of Beaton and Marie de Guise; the proposed marriage of the young Mary, Queen of Scots, to Prince Edward, later Edward VI (q.v.), was no longer advocated. Lennox suspected the Beaton-Arran rapport, however, and, disappointed at his failure to secure the hand of Marie de Guise, he looked to England for a new alliance. Bent on self-advancement, he let it be known to Henry VIII (q.v.) that his services (i.e. in promoting the Anglo-Scottish marriage) might be bought in return for the hand of the Lady Margaret Douglas (q.v.), the King's niece, and the governorship of Scotland in place of Arran.

Lennox obtained his naturalization as an English subject on 10 July 1544, the day on which he and the Lady Margaret were married. Considerable lands were granted to him in England, and they made their home at Temple Newsam, Yorkshire, which in the reign of Elizabeth I (q.v.) was to become the centre of Catholic intrigues. It was a successful union; husband and wife were working for the same ends, the Countess being, however, the stronger personality and the greater schemer.

In 1545 Lennox assisted Hertford in his second invasion of Scotland; for his part in what came to be known as this 'Rough Wooing' he forfeited his Scottish estates. In September 1547 he routed the Scots at the Battle of Pinkie Cleugh.

The Earl and Countess were greatly in favour during the reign of Mary I (q.v.), but came under the suspicion of Elizabeth after her accession. In 1562, when their plan to marry Lord Darnley (see Stewart, Henry), their eldest surviving son, to the recently widowed Mary, Queen of Scots (q.v.), was revealed prematurely to the English Queen, Lennox was sent to the Tower, the Countess and Darnley being confined at the house of Sir Richard Sackville at Sheen. A cleverly phrased letter of flattery to the Queen from the Countess secured their release soon afterwards, when they were all three once more received at court.

In September 1564 Lennox was permitted to return to Scotland, where he was restored to his title and estates and in 1565 appointed Lieutenant of the Western Counties. After his son's marriage to the Queen of Scots he remained in Scotland but had little political influence. His arrogant manner antagonized the nobility and lost him the favour of the Queen. In the aftermath of the murder of David Riccio (q.v.), to which he was a party, Lennox warned Mary of Darnley's intention to leave the country, but he was unable to prevent the estrangement between them from becoming a public scandal. On the acquittal of the Earl of Bothwell (see Hepburn, James), whom Lennox had accused of Darnley's murder, he fled to England.

Following the imprisonment of the Queen of Scots at Lochleven and the assassination, in January 1570, of the Earl of Moray (see Stewart, Lord James), who was Regent to James VI (q.v.), Lennox, the young King's grandfather, was elected as the next Regent. Much fighting ensued between the King's party and the supporters of the Earl of Huntly and the Hamiltons, and on 4 September 1571, in a surprise attack on Stirling led by William Kirkaldy of Grange, Lennox was shot in the back; he died the same day and was buried in the royal chapel at Stirling.

William Fraser, *The Lennox* (2 vols; 1874).

**Stow, John** (?1525–1605), chronicler and antiquary.

Born in the parish of St Michael, Cornhill, London, in about 1525, John Stow was a tailor by trade, having probably followed his father in this occupation. In November 1547 he was admitted as a freeman of the Merchant Taylors' Company. He seems to have made a success of his tailoring business and to have become prosperous by 1560, when he began to devote the bulk of his time to the collection of rare books and manuscripts. Self-educated, he developed a passion for antiquarian studies that was to consume his entire fortune and cause him to end his life in poverty.

Stow's first published work was an edition of *The Woorkes of Geffrey Chaucer* (see Chaucer, Geoffrey, in *Lives Before the Tudors*), which appeared in 1561; for several years afterwards he continued his annotation of Chaucer's text, and these further studies were printed by Stow's friend Thomas Speght in 1598. An original work, *Summarie of Englyshe Chronicles*, published in 1565, was attacked by the rival chronicler, Richard Grafton (q.v.); nevertheless, it ran into a number of editions, each one fully revised and brought up to date, which ultimately confirmed Stow as the more reliable historian.

In 1568 and again in the two following years Stow came under suspicion of adhering to the old Catholic faith; his house was searched, and he was examined by the Council and charged with possessing popish books and other dangerous writings, but escaped without punishment. His friendship with Archbishop Matthew Parker (q.v.), whom he assisted in editing a number of medieval chronicles, remained unimpaired, and with the latter's help he published Matthew of Westminster's *Flores Historiarum* in 1567, Matthew

Paris's *Chronicle* in 1571, and Thomas Walsingham's *Chronicle* in 1574. Stow's major contribution to English history, *The Chronicles of England*, was first published in 1580; it was reissued in 1592 and subsequently as *The Annales of England faithfully collected out of the most authenticall authors, records and other monuments of antiquitie, from the first inhabitation untill this present yeare 1592* (popularly known as the *Annals*). In both editions Stow made extensive use of the work of Raphael Holinshed (q.v.), but without acknowledgment; he was at the same time engaged on the preparation for the press of the second edition of Holinshed's *Chronicles*, which was published in 1587.

The next period of Stow's life was largely devoted to the compilation of his *Survey of London*, which he published in 1598; the result of lengthy research and many perambulations through the various wards, it contained detailed information on the origins, growth, and customs of the city. Stow's enthusiasm for topography and antiquities brought him to financial ruin, however, and in the last years of his life he was dependent on charity from the Merchant Taylors' Company and other benefactors. He died in London on 6 April 1605 and was buried in the church of St Andrew Undershaft, Leadenhall Street, where his widow Elizabeth erected a fine effigy in his memory.

John Stow is reckoned to be the most accurate of all the chroniclers and historians of the sixteenth century. His great *Survey of London*, invaluable for its description of contemporary London, was brought up to date by John Strype in two volumes (1720); the standard edition is by C. L. Kingsford (2 vols; Oxford, 1908). The best edition of the *Annals* is considered to be that of 1605.

See the 1615 edition of the *Annals*, edited by Edmund Howe; a memoir by John Strype in the 1720 edition of the *Survey of London*; the Everyman edition of the *Survey* (1955); and C. M. Clode, *Memorials of the Merchant Taylors' Company* (1874).

*Portrait*: engraving, by J. T. Smith, 1791, after the monument in St Andrew Undershaft: location not known.

### Stuart, Arabella or Arbella (1575–1615), claimant to the throne.

Arabella was the daughter of Charles Stuart, Earl of Lennox, younger brother of Lord Darnley (see Stewart, Henry), and Elizabeth, daughter of Sir William Cavendish and 'Bess of Hardwick' (see Hardwick, Elizabeth). Born in the autumn of 1575, she was, after James VI of Scotland (q.v.), next in succession to the throne of England after the death of Elizabeth I (q.v.).

Both Arabella's parents died young, and from 1582 she was brought up largely by her maternal grandmother, now Countess of Shrewsbury. She became a favourite companion of the imprisoned Mary, Queen of Scots (q.v.),

whose gaoler was the Earl of Shrewsbury (see Talbot, George).

From babyhood Arabella was the centre of intrigue. Both her Shrewsbury and her Lennox grandmothers tried in vain to secure for her the earldom of Lennox following her father's death; while for those who refused to accept James as Elizabeth's successor, she was the rightful heir to the English throne. There were various plans for Arabella's marriage, all of which met with suspicion on the part of the Queen, and from 1590 onwards the Countess of Shrewsbury kept the young girl closely guarded at Hardwick. After at least two attempts at escape, she was transferred to the care of the Earl of Kent.

James I on his accession received her at court and treated her favourably, but she was prohibited from marrying. An attempt to flee to Scotland resulted in her arrest, but in 1610 Arabella was secretly married to William Seymour; he was a grandson of Edward Seymour, Earl of Hertford (son of the Protector) and of Lady Katherine Grey (q.v.), and thus of royal descent. For their disobedience, the King had them both imprisoned, Arabella at Lambeth and Seymour in the Tower.

Arabella was later transferred to the care of the Bishop of Durham, and in June 1611 she managed to escape and board a ship bound for Calais. At the same time her husband escaped from the Tower and was also on his way to France, when Arabella was recaptured and confined in the Tower. There she was to spend the rest of her short life, sinking deeper and deeper into melancholic moods verging almost on insanity, until her death in September 1615. She was buried in the tomb of Mary, Queen of Scots, in the chapel of Henry VII at Westminster Abbey.

E. T. Bradley, *The Life and Letters of Arabella Stuart* (1889).
P. M. Handover, *Arabella Stuart* (1957).

*Portraits:* oil, by unknown artist, 1577: Hardwick Hall; oil, by monogrammatist C.V.M., 1589: Hardwick Hall (copy in Duke of Portland Collection; oil on panel, by M. Gheeraerts, 1605: Scottish National Portrait Gallery, Edinburgh; oil, unknown lady *called* Arabella Stuart: National Portrait Gallery, London; oil, full length, by unknown artist, traditionally of Arabella: Department of the Environment, London; numerous other (non-authenticated) portraits elsewhere.

**Stuart, Esmé** (?1542–1583), 6th Seigneur d'Aubigny and 1st Duke of Lennox, favourite of James VI of Scotland (q.v.), of whom he was a distant cousin.

Esmé Stuart was the only son of John Stuart (or Stewart), 5th Seigneur d'Aubigny, who was the youngest son of John Stewart, 3rd (11th) Earl of Lennox, by his wife Anne de la Quelle. Born in about 1542, Esmé was brought up in France and succeeded his father as Seigneur d'Aubigny in 1567. At about this date he is known to have been engaged on an embassy in the Low Countries. In the autumn of 1579, at the instigation of the Guise family, he was sent to Scotland, ostensibly to congratulate the young King, but with the double purpose of regaining Franco-Scottish understanding and converting James to Catholicism. In fact he had an ulterior personal motive, that of establishing his own position in the line of succession and his rights to the Lennox title; within a few weeks of his arrival he confidently assured the French ambassador that he would be made Earl of Lennox and declared successor to the throne in the event of the King dying childless.

Handsome and accomplished, the Frenchman charmed the King by his courteous manners. To the astonishment and dismay of the Scottish court, James, totally unused to affection or reverence, responded by forming a passionate attachment for his cousin. In November 1579, less than two months after his arrival, he gave Stuart the Abbey of Arbroath, one of the forfeited properties of the Hamilton family; in March the following year he bestowed on him other lands and the lordship of Lennox (Lord Robert Stewart having been persuaded to relinquish the title).

Lennox's swift rise in the King's affections greatly alarmed the Scottish ministers, who condemned James for 'consorting with atheists and papists', whereupon Lennox in June 1580 publicly declared that he had been converted to Protestantism. More honours followed: in September 1580 he was given the custody of Dumbarton Castle, and the following month he became Lord Chancellor and First Gentleman of the Royal Chamber. Already he was plotting the overthrow of the one man who now blocked his path to supreme power – the Regent, the Earl of Morton (see Douglas, James). His chosen accomplice in this plot was James Stewart (q.v.; later Earl

423

of Arran), who in early January 1581 had Morton brought before the Privy Council and accused of complicity in the murder of Lord Darnley (see Stewart, Henry) fourteen years earlier.

After Morton's execution in June the same year, Lennox's influence over the King reached its zenith. Rewarded with the title of Duke of Lennox, he felt himself safe and dropped his conciliatory manner towards the Kirk. The King's passion was at its most intense; he was sometimes seen to clasp and kiss his French cousin in public. Rumours and suspicions abounded. The Kirk thought that in spite of his alleged conversion Lennox had remained a Catholic, and would try to reinstate Mary, Queen of Scots (q.v.); Mary, for her part, feared that he would betray her interests and throw in his lot with the Protestants. Inevitably, also, rivalry for power erupted between Lennox and James Stewart, now Earl of Arran. In order to allay the Kirk's suspicions in view of the religious accusations made against him, Lennox signed the 'Negative Confession' condemning Catholic belief and practice; but this did not prevent him from secretly receiving agents of the Duc de Guise, who hoped to win his support for a scheme in which England would be invaded by Philip II of Spain (q.v.) and Mary returned to Scotland to rule jointly with her son.

In August 1582 Lennox's power was brought abruptly to an end by a *coup d'état* organized by an extreme Protestant group under the leadership of the Earl of Gowrie (see Ruthven, William), who seized the King and held him captive, forcing him to issue a proclamation against both Lennox and Arran. After protesting his innocence in religious affairs, Lennox was ordered to quit the country. He left Scotland on 21 December 1582 and travelled south to London, where on 14 January he had an audience with Queen Elizabeth (q.v.). He was so plausible in affirming his Protestantism that even she was taken in, and the attempts of Sir Francis Walsingham (q.v.) through a spy to discover Lennox's true religious sympathies were also unsuccessful.

From London Lennox travelled to Paris, where a few months later, on 26 May, he died, maintaining to the end that he had been converted to Protestantism. He left instructions that his heart was to be embalmed and sent to James, to whom he entrusted the care of his children. He had two sons and three daughters by his French wife, Catherine de Balsac d'Entragues. The eldest son, Ludovic, was later in 1583 taken to Scotland to be educated as the King's protégé.

Esmé Stuart, Duke of Lennox, was the first in a series of favourites of James VI, and the King's 'first love'. Yet it was his religious sentiments and his dominance over the King in political affairs at a time of large-scale Catholic plotting in Europe, rather than the emotional attachment, that turned the Scottish nobility against him.

See the bibliography under James VI.

*Portraits:* oil, by unknown artist: Scottish National Portrait Gallery, Edinburgh; drawing, by unknown artist: British Museum, London.

**Stuart, Henry** (1545–1567), see Stewart, Henry, Lord Darnley.

**Stukeley or Stucley, Sir Thomas** (d. 1578), adventurer.

Rumoured to be an illegitimate son of Henry VIII (q.v.), Thomas Stukeley was in fact the third son of Sir Hugh Stukeley and his wife Jane, daughter of Sir Lewis Pollard; the family name is spelled in various ways. He was born in about 1520, but no records have survived of his early years.

Stukeley is believed to have been in the service of the Duke of Suffolk (see Brandon, Charles) until the latter's death in 1545, when he joined the Earl of Hertford (see Seymour, Edward; later Duke of Somerset). He was employed by Somerset on various missions between England and France, and on the Protector's fall from power he fled to the court of Henri II in France.

In 1552 Henri sent Stukeley to Edward VI (q.v.) with a secret mission to obtain information he needed for an attack on Calais. Stukeley betrayed the French King's intention to the English government, but was himself betrayed by Northumberland (see Dudley, John) and imprisoned in the Tower. On his release he fled to the Continent to escape his creditors and entered the service of the Duke of Savoy. He accompanied the Duke to England at the end of 1554 and was allowed six months in which to settle his debts; in the following year he married a rich heiress, Anne, daughter of Sir Thomas Curtis. Because of the debts still unpaid he was forced to escape overseas once again. He served under the Duke of Savoy in the Battle of St Quentin in August 1557.

Stukeley now turned to privateering as a source of income. He put forward a plan to found a colony in Florida and persuaded Queen Elizabeth (q.v.) to provide one of the six ships he needed, but this was merely a cover for piracy. For the next few years he roamed the high seas, robbing vessels of all nations until, at the request of several foreign powers, Elizabeth had him arrested.

Stukeley was given a pardon, and in 1566 he was allowed to go to Ireland; ostensibly he was sent to assist his friend Shane O'Neill (q.v.) in Ulster against the Scots. However, the Queen was well aware that Stukeley had been corresponding with Philip II of Spain (q.v.)

and that he had ulterior motives. In June 1569 he was arrested on a charge of treason and imprisoned at Dublin Castle but he was released in October for lack of evidence. He escaped to Spain, where Philip offered him a handsome pension; from his court Stukeley now began seriously to plot and intrigue against Elizabeth.

Stukeley had the capacity to win people's confidence at the first meeting, but he almost always lost it again. He left the Spanish court in 1571 for Rome and on his way there fought courageously in the Battle of Lepanto; his gallantry there restored him to the favour of Philip II. During the next six years Stukeley was active all over the Continent, drumming up support for the invasion of Ireland. He eventually won the confidence of Pope Gregory XIII (q.v.), but smartly diverted the papal troops supplied for the 'English enterprise' to assist the King of Portugal in the invasion of Morocco. He lost his life in the Battle of Alcazar on 4 August 1578.

Z. N. Brooke, 'The Expedition of Thomas Stukeley in 1578', *The Month*, xxviii (1913), pp. 330–7.

J. H. Pollen, 'The Irish Expedition of 1579', *English Historical Review*, ci (1903), pp. 69–85.

**Suffolk, Duchess of** (1496–1533), see Mary Tudor.

**Suffolk, 1st Duke of** (?1484–1545), see Brandon, Charles.

**Suffolk, Earl of** (?1472–1513), see Pole, Sir Edmund de la.

**Suffolk, 1st Earl of (of the Howard family)** (1561–1626), see Howard, Lord Thomas.

**Surrey, Earl of** (1443–1524), see Howard, Thomas, 2nd Duke of Norfolk.

**Surrey, Earl of** (1517–1547), see Howard, Henry.

**Surrey, Earl of** (1473–1554), see Howard, Thomas, 3rd Duke of Norfolk.

**Surrey, Earl of** (1536–1572), see Howard, Thomas, 4th Duke of Norfolk.

**Sussex, 3rd Earl of** (?1526–1583), see Radcliffe, Sir Thomas.

# T

**Talbot, George** (?1528–1590), 6th Earl of Shrewsbury.

The only son of Francis Talbot, the 5th Earl, George Talbot was born probably in 1528 and succeeded to the title on his father's death in September 1560. He shared the 5th Earl's inclination for military life, and in 1547 took part in the invasion of Scotland led by the Protector Somerset (see Seymour, Edward). His first marriage, to Gertrude, daughter of the Earl of Rutland, produced four sons and three daughters; in February 1568, two years after her death, Shrewsbury became the fourth husband of 'Bess of Hardwick' (see Hardwick, Elizabeth), by whom he had no children. It proved to be a marriage beset by domestic quarrels.

In 1569 Shrewsbury was chosen by Queen Elizabeth (q.v.) to act as keeper in charge of Mary, Queen of Scots (q.v.), a task which he discharged for fifteen years. He treated Mary as a sovereign and honoured guest in his houses at Tutbury, Chatsworth, Sheffield Castle, and elsewhere, but won only recriminations from all sides. Mary constantly complained of her imprisonment; the Queen's ministers were suspicious of Shrewsbury's leniency towards his charge; and Bess made accusations against her husband concerning his relationship with Mary, which she was subsequently made to withdraw before the Privy Council. The relationship with his wife deteriorated to such an extent that Shrewsbury at one time asked for a divorce; however, a formal reconciliation was eventually achieved under pressure from the Queen.

Throughout his career Shrewsbury was completely trusted by Elizabeth. When the Duke of Norfolk (see Howard, Thomas, 4th Duke) was arrested for his part in the Ridolfi plot (see Ridolfi, Roberto di), Shrewsbury was appointed High Steward of England and acted as one of the judges in Norfolk's trial. In June 1572, following the latter's execution, Shrewsbury became Earl Marshal.

In September 1584 Mary was taken out of Shrewsbury's custody, but he could not escape the additional duties of attending her trial at Fotheringay in October 1586. The following February he was present at her execution.

Shrewsbury died on 18 November 1590. The Talbot papers of the Tudor period have been edited by E. Lodge in *Illustrations of British History* (3 vols; 1791, revised 1838).

*Portraits:* oil, by unknown artist, 1580: Hardwick Hall (National Trust), and one almost identical in Duke of Portland Collection, Welbeck Abbey; watercolour, by unknown artist: National Portrait Gallery, London; also Shrewsbury appears in *Procession of Knights of the Garter*, 1576, by Marcus Gheeraerts the Elder: British Museum, London.

**Tallis, Thomas** (?1505–1585), organist and composer.

Tallis is believed to have been a native of Leicestershire, born about 1505–10. His first known position was at the Abbey of the Holy Cross, Waltham, Essex, as master of the choristers or organist. On the dissolution of the Abbey in 1540 he received a small compensation and went first to Canterbury, where he obtained a post as lay clerk at the cathedral. Not long afterwards he was appointed one of the Gentlemen of the Chapel Royal and settled in London. In 1552 he married; from his will it is clear that both Tallis and his wife Joan were Anglicans.

Tallis became organist of the Chapel Royal some time before 1572, when his former pupil and protégé, William Byrd (q.v.), arrived in London to share the duties with him. The close personal and professional association between the two men lasted for the rest of Tallis's life and had a great impact on the musical world. In January 1575 Queen Elizabeth (q.v.) granted them a licence for the printing, publishing, and sale of music and music paper, a monopoly which they enjoyed for the next twenty-one years. The first work issued under their joint imprint was a collection of *Cantiones Sacrae* (1575), dedicated to the Queen and containing sixteen motets by Tallis and eighteen by Byrd. Apart from five anthems to English words included in the collection printed by John Day in 1563, no other work by Tallis was published during his lifetime.

Tallis had a house at Greenwich, where he spent the closing years of his long life. He died there on 23 November 1585 and was buried in the parish church (now destroyed), where an epitaph commemorated the fact that he had been a member of the Chapel Royal during four reigns. Unlike Byrd, Tallis was a conforming Anglican, and he provided the liturgy of the Church with musical settings, services and hymns which established a lasting tradition for the English Church.

'The father of English cathedral music', as he has been rightly styled, Tallis represented the reaction from the excessively complicated compositions that were fashionable before the Reformation. He re-invigorated and inspired the English school founded by Christopher Tye (q.v.) and raised it to the high standard it was to maintain until the death of Orlando Gibbons (see *Lives of the Stuart Age*). Tallis was among the first to write music to English words for use in accordance with the rites of the Anglican Church, and some of his earliest compositions, arrangements in harmony of the plainsong and responses of the English church service, including the beautiful *Venite* for four voices, were published for the first time in John Barnard's *First Book of Selected Church Music* (1641). His *Litany* has been described as 'one of the finest pieces of ancient church music extant'.

Tallis's genius as a composer was many-sided. His skill as a contrapuntalist is borne out in the canon *Miserere nostri*, while his magnificent forty-part motet, *Spem in alium*, stands out as an almost unique achievement. He also wrote a number of original English anthems. The popular hymn tune known as 'Tallis's Canon' is an adaptation of one of eight tunes he wrote for inclusion in Archbishop Parker's *Whole Psalter*, published in 1576.

A great quantity of Tallis's music has survived. Some has been printed in *Tudor Church Music*, vol. 6 (ed. Carnegie, 1928); a full list of his manuscript and printed works will be found in Grove's *Dictionary of Music and Musicians* (5th ed. 1954).

J. S. Bumpus, *A history of English cathedral music, 1549–1889* (2 vols; 1908).

E. H. Fellowes, *English cathedral music from Edward VI to Edward VII* (1942).

W. Shaw, *From Tallis to Tomkins: a survey of church music c. 1550–c. 1650* (Church Music Society Occasional Papers, xxii, 1953).

*Portrait:* engraving, by Vandergucht, 1730: British Museum, London.

**Tarleton or Tarlton, Richard** (d. 1588), actor, ballad writer, and jester.

He was born at Condover, Shropshire, and was of humble origin and little education. According to one source, he spent his youth tending his father's swine; another theory is that he was a water-bearer and later an apprentice in the City of London. In later life he and his wife Kate were London innkeepers, with taverns in Gracechurch Street and Paternoster Row.

Tarleton seems to have been well into middle age before he emerged as the leading comic actor and jester of the day. Probably he first came into contact with players and musicians through his innkeeping activities. He first appears in the records in 1570 as a writer and singer of ballads; in 1576 a book of English verse entitled *Tarlton's Toyes* was registered at the Stationers' Company.

By this time the comedian's popularity was spreading, especially on account of his so-called 'happy unhappy answers' and the rustic jig which he is said to have introduced to London. His performances attracted the attention of the Earl of Leicester (see Dudley, Robert), who brought him to the notice of Queen Elizabeth (q.v.). Soon he became the Queen's favourite jester, the only person who was able, as he himself put it, to 'undumpish' her when she was in a bad mood. On one occasion, however, he overstepped the mark by directing some jests against Leicester and Sir Walter Ralegh (q.v.), which incurred her temporary displeasure. Early in 1583 he became one of the Queen's Men and was to be that company's leading comic actor for the remaining five years of his life.

During his last years Tarleton won tremendous popularity as a jester, principally on account of his talent for improvising doggerel verse to themes suggested by the audience. He also wrote a number of short pieces, all of which have been lost; these were much praised by Tarleton's contemporaries and included *The Seven Deadlie Sinns*, which was performed at court in 1585. It is possible that Shakespeare may have been influenced by him in creating the role of Bottom in *A Midsummer Night's Dream*, and that Tarleton may also have been the original model for the court jester, Yorick, described in *Hamlet*, as well as 'Pleasant Willy' in *Tears of the Muses* by Edmund Spenser (q.v.).

Towards the end of his life Tarleton lived at Holywell Street, Shoreditch, in conditions of extreme poverty. By all accounts he led a dissipated life; his wife, Kate, who pre-deceased him, was known to be a 'loose' woman. Tarleton himself died at the house of a woman of bad repute, in Shoreditch, on 5 September 1588.

Richard Tarleton's popularity was so widespread that long after his death publications appeared bearing his name, and a number of inns were named after him. Among the jest-books published after his death, the majority of which are thought to be spurious, were *Tarlton's Newes out of Purgatorie* (c. 1590) and the more celebrated *Tarlton's Jests*, published originally in three parts (1592–1600), of which the earliest extant edition is that of 1611; it was re-issued by J. O. Halliwell-Phillips, for the Shakespeare Society (1844).

L. B. Campbell, 'Richard Tarlton and the Earthquake of 1580', *Huntington Library Quarterly*, iv (1941), pp. 293–301.
John Day, *The Isle of Gulls* [with a memoir of Tarleton] (1606; reprinted 1831).
W. J. Lawrence, 'On the Underrated Genius of Dick Tarleton', in *Speeding up Shakespeare: Studies of the Bygone Theatre and Drama* (1937).

*Portrait:* drawing, by John Scottowe: British Museum, London (Harleian MSS No. 3885, f. 19).

429

**Thorne, Robert** (d. 1527), merchant and geographical writer.

The son of Nicholas Thorne, member of an Anglo-Portuguese syndicate to whom in 1502 Henry VII (q.v.) had granted letters patent for exploration in the North-West, but whose venture had failed, Robert Thorne was brought up in the family mercantile business, probably in Bristol. He may have been the Robert Thorne of that city who was among those appointed as commissioners for the office of Admiral of England in 1510.

Thorne spent a considerable part of his life in Seville, where he had charge of the family business. From there in 1527 he addressed letters to Henry VIII (q.v.) and to the English ambassador in Spain, urging the exploration of the Indies by the north-eastern or north-western route; he accompanied his letters with a map, which was later incorporated in Hakluyt's *Divers Voyages* (see Hakluyt, Richard).

Robert Thorne died in Seville in 1527, shortly after dispatching his letters. He had for many years been enthusiastic about overseas expansion and was one of the first Englishmen to make a significant contribution towards convincing the King that exploration was in his interests and in the interests of English trade. In 1525 the Thorne family business had contributed generously towards the expedition of Sebastian Cabot (q.v.) to South America.

Thorne's two letters, which urged Englishmen to beat the Spaniards and the Portuguese by taking short cuts to the Indies via the north-eastern or north-western route, or even across the Pole, were printed by Hakluyt in his *Principall Navigations*, first published in 1589.

**Thorpe, John** (*c.* 1563–*c.* 1655), architect and surveyor.

Born in about 1563, the son of Thomas Thorpe, a Northamptonshire mason, John Thorpe moved in about 1583 to London, where he was at one time resident in the parish of St Martin's-in-the-Fields.

He became a Clerk of the Queen's Works and in this capacity was at various dates employed at Whitehall, Hampton Court, Greenwich, the Tower, Eltham Palace, and Richmond. From about 1600 he seems also to have been a successful surveyor, being frequently commissioned to survey crown property. Thorpe's folio book of plans and drawings (now in the Soane Museum) consists mainly of buildings that he surveyed and is not regarded as evidence that he designed any of them.

The houses which Thorpe is believed to have built, or at least to have had some part in building, include Kirby Hall, Northamptonshire, constructed in 1570–5 for Sir Humphrey Stafford; Longford Castle, Wiltshire, begun in 1580; Holland House, Kensington (the first design), built in 1606–7 for Sir Walter Cope; Rushton Hall, Northamptonshire; and Audley End, Essex. He may also have worked on alterations for Sir Richard Sackville at Buckhurst, near Withyham, Sussex, and also at Knole, near Sevenoaks, Kent, and at other great mansions in the south of England.

J. Summerson (ed.), *The Book of Architecture of John Thorpe* (Walpole Society, 1966).

**Thorpe, Thomas** (?1570–?1635), stationer, publisher of the *Sonnets* of William Shakespeare (q.v.).

The son of an innkeeper in Barnet, a few miles north of London, Thomas Thorpe was in 1584 apprenticed to Richard Watkins, a printer and stationer of London, for a period of nine years. In 1594 he duly took up the freedom of the Stationers' Company and found employment in the City as a stationer's assistant.

In 1600, having acquired the unpublished manuscript of a translation by Christopher Marlowe (q.v.) of the *First Book of Lucan* (Lucan's *Pharsalia*), he proceeded, with the help of his friend and fellow stationer Edward Blount (q.v.), to publish it. Between 1603 and 1624 he issued a number of other publications, including plays by George Chapman (q.v.) and Ben Jonson (see *Lives of the Stuart Age*) and, in 1609, the work for which he is best known, Shakespeare's *Sonnets*.

How Thorpe acquired the *Sonnets* is not known, but copies had been in circulation in manuscript form for some time among the poet's friends; one may have been surreptitiously obtained for him by the patron of the volume, 'Mr W.H.', probably William Hall, a fellow stationer, who had earlier procured for Thorpe a poem by the Jesuit martyr Robert Southwell (q.v.). Thorpe entered the *Sonnets* in the Stationers' Register on 20 May 1609. The book was printed for him by George Eld and sold through two bookselling agents; as was customary, Thorpe, as owner of the 'copy', provided the dedication, which he signed 'T.T.'

Thomas Thorpe does not appear to have owned his own press, but to have had his books printed by others. For a short time he had premises for selling books in St Paul's Churchyard, but otherwise seems to have had no fixed abode. In 1635 he was granted a room in an almshouse at Ewelme, where he probably died.

## Throckmorton or Throgmorton, Francis (1554–1584), conspirator.

Francis Throckmorton was the son of Sir John Throckmorton of Feckenham, Worcestershire, and his wife Margery, daughter of Robert Puttenham, and nephew of Sir Nicholas Throckmorton (q.v.). Unlike the latter, Sir John had not embraced Protestantism, and both Francis, born in 1554, and his brother Thomas, were brought up as zealous Catholics.

Educated at Hart Hall, Oxford, where he matriculated in 1572, Francis was admitted to the Inner Temple, London, in 1576. He appears to have got into bad odour with the authorities, probably on account of his religious practices, for in February 1579 he and his father were called before the Privy Council and given into the custody of the Dean of St Paul's, Alexander Nowell. His cousin, Arthur Throckmorton, son of Sir Nicholas, pleaded for Francis's release, which was granted on the 25th of that month; on that same day Francis received a licence to marry. Sir John, who had been Master of the Requests under Mary I (q.v.), was in even greater trouble with the Council a few months later, being deprived of his public offices and heavily fined. He died not long afterwards, and Francis, together with his brother Thomas, left England in 1580 for a prolonged tour of the Continent.

Everywhere they went they met exiled English Catholics and learned of projects for the restoration of the old religion in England. In Paris they saw Charles Paget and Thomas Morgan, agents of Mary, Queen of Scots (q.v.) and became involved in the plan devised by the Duc de Guise, and financed by Pope Gregory XIII (q.v.) and Philip II of Spain (q.v.), for the invasion of England and the overthrow of Elizabeth (q.v.); this was to be supported by an uprising of the English Catholics.

In 1583 Francis returned to London and took a house at Paul's Wharf, from where he organized a communications network between Morgan in Paris and Bernardino de Mendoza, the Spanish

431

ambassador to the English court. Sir Francis Walsingham (q.v.) already knew of the existence of a conspiracy, but had no firm proof. He engaged a spy in the French embassy, who duly reported that Throckmorton was an agent of the Queen of Scots and was in the habit of visiting the ambassador's house at night. Walsingham had him watched, and early in November 1583 Throckmorton was caught in the act of writing a cipher letter to Mary, and was arrested. He managed to get rid of a casket of incriminating documents, which he sent by a maidservant to Mendoza, but when his house was searched and all his papers seized, a list of Catholic noblemen prepared to participate in the rebellion, and also a plan of harbours suitable for the landing of invasion forces, were discovered.

Under examination by the Council, Throckmorton denied all knowledge of the papers and refused to confess. From a window in the Tower, where he was held, he threw a playing card on which he had scribbled a note assuring Mendoza that he would never denounce his Catholic friends and that he had denied that the discovered documents were written in his hand. Put to the rack a few days later, he maintained his position, but when tortured a second and third time he made a full confession of all that he knew of the conspiracy, thoroughly implicating the Queen of Scots as having written encouraging letters to the Spanish ambassador concerning it. Several of those involved managed to escape to the Continent, including Francis's brother, Thomas; but Henry Percy, 8th Earl of Northumberland, who had been arrested, committed suicide while confined in the Tower.

At his trial at Guildhall on 21 May 1584, Throckmorton said that the confession had been extricated from him under torture and was false. Found guilty

and not only condemned to death, but ordered to repeat his confession, he appealed to the Queen for forgiveness, blaming youthfulness for his rash conduct and acknowledging his just sentence. It was of no avail; he was executed at Tyburn on 10 July.

As a result of the so-called Throckmorton Plot, Mendoza, the Spanish ambassador, who had been deeply involved in it, was expelled from England. An official account of the conspiracy was published by the government under the title *A Discoverie of the Treasons practised and attempted against the Queenes Majestie and the Realme by F. Throckmorton* (1584); it has been reprinted in the *Harleian Miscellany* (various editions).

Conyers Read, *Sir Francis Walsingham*, vol. ii (1925).
A. L. Rowse, *Ralegh and the Throckmortons* (1962).

## Throckmorton or Throgmorton, Sir Nicholas (1515–1571), statesman and diplomat.

Nicholas Throckmorton was born in 1515, probably at the family home at Coughton in Warwickshire, the fourth son of Sir George Throckmorton and Catherine, daughter of Lord Vaux of Harrowden; through his mother he was distantly related to Queen Katherine Parr (q.v.).

As a boy Nicholas became a page in the household of Henry Fitzroy, Duke of Richmond, bastard son of Henry VIII (q.v.). Richmond died in 1536, at a time when the Throckmorton family, being staunch Catholics, were temporarily out of favour with the King; Sir George had been somewhat too outspoken in opposing Henry's divorce. Their fortunes revived with the King's marriage to Katherine Parr in July 1543, when Nicholas was appointed a server-in-waiting to the new Queen. Influenced by the Reform movement at court, he and three of his brothers became militant Protestants. All four fought in France in 1543–4, Nicholas as captain of a hundred light horsemen; as a reward for his services he became Master of the Horse and was given generous grants of lands. In 1545 he entered the House of Commons as member for Maldon; he sat in five subsequent Parliaments almost continuously until 1563.

On Henry VIII's death he continued to serve the Queen Dowager; as a member of her household Throckmorton came into frequent contact with the young Princess Elizabeth (see Elizabeth I), who at that time lived with her stepmother. He fought under William, Lord Parr of Horton, in Scotland and must have been present at the Battle of Pinkie Cleugh in September 1547, since he had the honour of bringing news of the English victory to the young King Edward VI (q.v.). From this date he was very much in favour with Edward; the King gave him a knighthood and many other favours, including the post of Under-Treasurer of the Mint.

In 1549–50 he served again in France, during the siege of Boulogne. At about this time he married Anne, daughter of Sir Nicholas Carew of Beddington, Surrey. By 1553, having exchanged his post at the Mint for an annuity, he had a retinue of twenty-five and was on the threshold of a brilliant career at court, his prospects marred only by the jealousy of the Duke of Northumberland (see Dudley, John).

On the death of Edward VI in July 1553, the Throckmorton brothers are said to have sent a warning message to the Princess Mary (see Mary I), for which in due course they were well rewarded. Sir Nicholas had signed the document giving the throne to Lady Jane Grey (q.v.), but within a few days of the

proclamation of Mary he changed his allegiance; a formal pardon was granted to him in October. Early in 1554, however, he was sent to the Tower for alleged complicity in the Wyatt rebellion (see Wyatt, Thomas, the younger) against the Queen's marriage to Philip II of Spain (q.v.). Arraigned for high treason at Guildhall on 17 April, he conducted his own case with such skill that the jury took the unprecedented step of acquitting him. Nevertheless, he was not released from the Tower until January the following year.

At the beginning of 1556 Throckmorton's name was connected with a conspiracy to rob the Exchequer and start another rebellion. Taking no chances, in June he fled to France. He remained in exile until the New Year 1558, by which time his services in supplying intelligence of French preparations for an attack on England and his participation in the Battle of St Quentin the previous August had secured him a pardon at home.

Disappointed on the accession of

Elizabeth, when the only office that came his way was that of Chief Butler, Throckmorton developed an intense jealousy of William Cecil (q.v.; later 1st Baron Burghley). Then in May 1559 the Queen appointed him as ambassador to France, ostensibly to confirm the Treaty of Château-Cambrésis, which had brought to an end the Hapsburg-Valois wars but allowed the French to keep Calais. In reality he had a delicate mission, for Elizabeth wanted especially to get Calais back and to gain intelligence about the activities of the Guises in Scotland, where the Regent, Marie de Guise (q.v.), was in open conflict with the Lords of the Congregation. Secretly Throckmorton also had instructions to effect the escape of James Hamilton, Earl of Arran and Duke of Châtelherault (see Hamilton, James, 2nd Earl), who was held as a hostage by the French.

In France Throckmorton established a good relationship with the young Mary, Queen of Scots (q.v.), who was married to the Dauphin, François. When Henri II of France died in July and was succeeded by François, Mary became Queen of France; the Guise family were now all-powerful and determined to uphold the French faction in Scotland. Throckmorton advised Elizabeth to strike while the iron was hot and take Calais, but she was reluctant to force the issue; meanwhile he managed to get Arran out of France. In October he returned to London on a brief visit, regarded by the Duc de Guise as a preliminary to war. Towards the end of the year Elizabeth did send forces to help the Scottish Lords of the Congregation; in February 1560 she signed the Treaty of Berwick, with the object of expelling the French from Scotland. When the French were finally defeated in July, Throckmorton was rewarded with the office of Chamberlain to the Exchequer; he

nevertheless returned as ambassador to France. He displeased the Queen by some candid remarks, written to Cecil, on her relations with Robert Dudley (q.v.; later Earl of Leicester), but Elizabeth undoubtedly found him useful in France, where the situation was changed by the sudden death of François II in December. Throckmorton reported all he knew of Mary's intentions to return to Scotland and also his secret conversations with Lord James Stewart (q.v.; later Earl of Mar and of Moray), half-brother of the young Queen of Scots. The English government, however, refused his request for a safe-conduct for Mary through England.

Throckmorton now became deeply involved with the Huguenots in the first War of Religion in France. Seeing in this conflict the chance for England to recapture Calais, he urged Elizabeth and Cecil to commit themselves to the Protestant cause. As a result of his pressure, in September 1562 the Queen signed the Treaty of Hampton Court with the Huguenot leaders, promising the support of English troops. In October English troops captured Le Havre, which angered Catherine de' Medici (q.v.); she refused Throckmorton a safe conduct to leave Orleans, where he was forced to remain in close consultation with the Huguenots. In December he was captured at the Battle of Dreux, but the peace negotiations following the assassination of the Duc de Guise shortly afterwards gave him the chance to slip back to England. He was back in Le Havre in February 1563, when plague spread through the town in June and seriously undermined the English garrison, which surrendered to the French on 28 July.

His next mission was to the French court at Rouen, to participate in the negotiations for a peace treaty between the two countries. Catherine de' Medici, regarding Throckmorton as responsible for the English attack on Le Havre, had him arrested, and he spent the next ten months in confinement at St Germain. In the meanwhile a new ambassador to France, Sir Thomas Smith (q.v.), arrived; he was Cecil's man, whereas Throckmorton was Dudley's, and there were bitter complaints from Sir Nicholas that Smith and Cecil were not making sufficient efforts to obtain his release. At one stage Elizabeth gave Throckmorton sole responsibility for the negotiations at Fontainebleau, only to disapprove later of the arrangements, so that he remained a prisoner; in the final discussions leading to the Peace of Troyes, Throckmorton and Smith participated jointly, but not without incident – a drawn dagger and a threat to Smith's life on the part of Sir Nicholas.

Under the Treaty of Troyes (April 1564), Throckmorton was released. He returned to England in poor health and even more opposed to Cecil than before. In April 1565 he was sent to Scotland with instructions to try to prevent or delay the marriage of the Queen of Scots to Lord Darnley (see Stewart, Henry) by proposing Robert Dudley, now Earl of Leicester, as an alternative candidate; but Mary was firmly resolved. On his return to court Sir Nicholas advised Leicester on a stratagem in order to find out whether Elizabeth would marry him herself, but this also was unsuccessful.

In July 1567 Throckmorton was sent again to Scotland, to mediate between the Lords of the Congregation and the Queen of Scots, imprisoned at Lochleven. He was refused access to Mary, and the meetings with the Lords were endlessly delayed; finally, after talks with William Maitland of Lethington, he was able to report to Elizabeth that Mary would not be put to any violent death.

On his return to court, Throckmorton and Leicester remained very close. Through their mutual hostility towards Cecil they were drawn into the secret intrigue for the marriage of Mary, Queen of Scots, to the Duke of Norfolk (see Howard, Thomas, 4th Duke); the aim was to overthrow Cecil and to resolve the uncertainty with regard to the succession. When the conspiracy was uncovered in September 1569, all those implicated, except Leicester, were arrested. For a short time Throckmorton was held in the Tower. Under examination he admitted to having conferred with Norfolk and Leicester on the subject of the marriage, but said that he had believed good might come of it for Queen Elizabeth and for England. Although his loyalty to the Queen was unquestioned, and he was released shortly afterwards, Throckmorton's public career was virtually finished. He had been, as Dr A. L. Rowse has put it, 'the ablest intelligence-man of his time'. In February 1571 he was taken ill while at supper at Leicester's house and died a few days later. He was buried in the parish church of St Katherine Cree in Aldgate.

Sir Nicholas Throckmorton left a widow and a young family of six sons and one daughter. Of these, Arthur, the second son, who succeeded to his father's estate, was to keep a remarkable diary, the discovery of which in recent years has thrown new light on the secret marriage of his sister, Elizabeth Throckmorton, with Sir Walter Ralegh (q.v.) and the birth of their first child.

A. L. Rowse, *Ralegh and the Throckmortons* (1962).

*Portraits:* oil, by unknown artist, *c.* 1562: National Portrait Gallery, London; oil, by unknown artist, 1562: E. E. Y. Hales Collection; watercolour, by George Perfect Harding: N.P.G.; tomb effigy, by unknown artist: St Katherine Cree, Aldgate, London; engraving, by P. Fourdrinier, 1724, after unknown artist: location not known.

**Tichborne, Chidiock** (?1558–1586), conspirator and poet.

Born in Southampton in about 1558, Chidiock Tichborne was the son of Peter Tichborne and his wife Elizabeth, daughter of Henry Middleton. The Tichborne family had been established in England since before the Norman Conquest.

Little is known of Chidiock's life until 1583. Both he and his father were ardent Papists whose activities aroused the suspicion of Sir Francis Walsingham (q.v.). They were in communication with the Spanish court and other Catholic groups on the Continent, and Chidiock probably made several unauthorized trips abroad: he met Anthony Babington (q.v.) in France in 1580, and in 1583 Walsingham had him interrogated about certain 'Popish relics' which he had brought back to England, having been absent without permission. In 1586 one of the family servants gave information to Walsingham's agents concerning the 'Popish practices' observed by the Tichbornes.

As one of the admirers of Babington, Tichborne had pledged himself to join the projected uprising of the English Catholics; in the spring of 1586 he was easily persuaded by the priest John Ballard to participate in the more serious plot being organized on the Continent which involved the invasion of England and the assassination of Queen Elizabeth (q.v.). In June that year he agreed to be one of six who would be responsible for killing the Queen. He worked closely with Babington and on 30 July helped his leader to decipher the long letter from Mary, Queen of Scots (q.v.), approving of their plans.

When Ballard was arrested on 4 August and the other conspirators fled with Babington to St John's Wood, Tichborne was unable to go with them because of a leg injury; he was arrested on 14 August and sent to the Tower. He was tried, together with the others, on 13 and 14 September, and after some hesitation pleaded guilty; like his fellows, he was sentenced to be hanged and quartered. While confined at the Tower waiting for the day of execution, he wrote a moving letter to his wife Agnes and also some beautiful stanzas beginning with the words, 'My prime of youth is but a frost of cares', for which he is chiefly remembered.

At the public execution on 20 September, when he was the fifth of the conspirators to be hanged, Tichborne aroused the pity of the spectators by a great speech, before being brutally hanged and disembowelled while still alive.

See the titles listed under Babington, Anthony.

**Tindale, William** (?1495–1536), see Tyndale, William.

**Travers, Walter** (?1548–1635), Puritan divine.

Walter Travers was born in Nottingham about 1548, the eldest son of Walter Travers, a local goldsmith. He matriculated and took his master's degree at Christ's College, Cambridge; in 1569 he was elected a senior fellow of Trinity. In about 1572 he left the university and went to Geneva. John Whitgift (q.v.), at that time Master of Trinity College, later said that had Travers not left when he did, he would have expelled him for nonconformity.

Already Travers strongly favoured reform within the Church of England, and this opinion was greatly strengthened in Geneva through his friendship with Theodore de Beza, Calvin's successor. He began to write the *Ecclesiasticae Disciplinae*, which was published in 1574 and translated into English by Thomas

Cartwright (q.v.); it appeared anonymously, but was immediately ascribed to Travers's authorship.

He returned to England briefly and took his D.D. at Oxford in July 1576 but, declining to subscribe, he was unable to obtain a licence to preach. Early in 1578 he joined Cartwright in the Low Countries and was ordained by him at Antwerp in May that year.

Two years later Travers was back in England again as domestic chaplain to Lord Burghley (see Cecil, William) and tutor to his son, Robert Cecil (q.v.; later 1st Earl of Salisbury). On the recommendation of Burghley and John Aylmer (q.v.), Bishop of London, he was next appointed afternoon lecturer at the Temple in London. In this office he was said by Thomas Fuller (see *Lives of the Stuart Age*) to 'refute in the afternoon what Richard Hooker [q.v.; then the Master] had said in the morning'. In 1583, when appointed to succeed Alvey as Master of the Temple, Travers refused to be re-ordained according to the rites of the Church of England, and the appointment was not confirmed. All his life he remained a staunch nonconformist; he acted as chief advocate for the Puritans at the Lambeth conference of September 1584; and even after 1586, when a prohibition was issued against him, he continued to hold meetings at his own house.

In 1591 Travers was given the chair of divinity at St Andrews University, and a few years later, in December 1595, through his patron Burghley he was appointed Provost of the newly-founded Trinity College, Dublin. He resigned this post for health reasons in 1598 and returned to England, where he was reputed to have spent his last years in poverty – although some doubt has been cast on this statement since he died on 14 January 1634 a comparatively wealthy man, leaving legacies to nieces and nephews as well as bequests to Emmanuel and Trinity Colleges, Cambridge, and to Trinity College, Dublin.

S. J. Knox, *Walter Travers: paragon of Elizabethan puritanism* (1962).

**Tudor, Henry** (1457–1509), see Henry VII.

**Tudor, Jasper** (?1431–1495), Earl of Pembroke and Duke of Bedford, see *Lives Before the Tudors*.

**Tudor, Margaret** (1489–1541), see Margaret Tudor.

**Tudor, Mary** (1496–1533), see Mary Tudor.

**Tunstall, Cuthbert** (1474–1559), prelate, successively Bishop of London and Bishop of Durham.

Cuthbert Tunstall was born in Yorkshire in 1474, the natural son of Thomas Tunstall of Thurland castle, Lancashire. His mother was the daughter of Sir John Conyers, whom Thomas Tunstall took as his second wife several years after the boy's birth.

He was educated at Balliol College, Oxford, and Trinity College, Cambridge, and subsequently studied abroad, spending six years at Padua. At Oxford, where he became a friend of Thomas More (q.v.), William Grocyn (q.v.), and Thomas Linacre (q.v.), Tunstall acquired a reputation for his learning in mathematics. He later studied law, as well as Greek and Hebrew, and became a fellow of Trinity. He was praised by Erasmus (q.v.), and while in Italy met some of the leaders of the Renaissance, returning to England in 1505.

Tunstall was ordained in 1509, by which time he had already been given

437

several preferments; others followed, and he was a prebendary of Lincoln in 1514, and Archdeacon of Chester the following year. Archbishop Warham (q.v.) appointed him as his chancellor, and for the next seven years Tunstall was employed on various diplomatic missions at home and abroad by Henry VIII (q.v.). He became Master of the Rolls in 1516, and in 1521 was sent on an embassy to Charles V (q.v.). He was at the Diet of Worms in Germany that year, and did not care for what he saw of the Lutheran movement; all his life Tunstall was to adhere to the traditional doctrines of Roman Catholicism.

Back in England, he was appointed Dean of Salisbury in 1521, Bishop of London in 1522, and Keeper of the Privy Seal in 1523; he thus became one of the most important officers of the crown, both in civil and in ecclesiastical matters. His diplomatic skills continued to be employed in negotiations with Charles V in 1525 and in arranging the treaty of Cambrai in 1530. Within his diocese he embarked on a determined campaign to

root out the revival of Lollardy which had sprouted under the influence of the Lutherans; he had earlier refused a request from William Tyndale (q.v.) to become his chaplain, and in 1526 he prohibited copies of all heretical books, including the Tyndale New Testament, even to the extent of buying up all available copies and having them burned.

In 1530, following the fall of Thomas Wolsey (q.v.), Tunstall was appointed to the see of Durham. He was to hold this bishopric until 1552, when he was deprived of office by Northumberland (see Dudley, John); he was reinstated by Mary I (q.v.) in 1553, only to lose it again under Elizabeth I (q.v.) in 1559. He was also made President of the Council of the North, in which capacity he spent much time negotiating with the Scots. In Parliament in 1539 he participated in the debates on the Six Articles. Adhering firmly to the old dogmas, Tunstall was at first reluctant to accept the royal supremacy, but was eventually persuaded to do so by Henry VIII; he showed his dislike of the religious policy of Edward VI (q.v.) by voting against the First Act of Uniformity in 1549, which led to his being put under house arrest and subsequently imprisoned in the Tower and deprived of his bishopric.

Reappointed Bishop of Durham in 1553, he was at Gravesend with the Queen to welcome Reginald Pole (q.v.) back to England, and he also participated in Mary's coronation. He assisted at the trial of John Hooper (q.v.) and other Protestant bishops. On Elizabeth's accession, however, he stubbornly refused to take the oath of royal supremacy and would not participate in the consecration of Matthew Parker (q.v.) as Archbishop of Canterbury. The Queen deprived Tunstall of his bishopric, and he was confined at Lambeth, where he died on 18 November 1559.

Tunstall was the author of the first printed work on arithmetic to appear in England. Entitled *De Arte Supputendi*, it was dedicated to his friend Thomas More, but was not translated into English.

G. H. Ross-Lewin in W. E. Collins (ed.), *Typical English Churchmen* (2 vols; 1902).
L. Baldwin Smith, *Tudor prelates and politics* (1953).
C. Sturge, *Cuthbert Tunstal: churchman, scholar, statesman, administrator* (1938).

*Portrait:* engraving, by P. Fourdrinier, 1724, after unknown artist: location not known.

## Turner, William (*c.* 1520–1568), Dean of Wells, physician and botanist.

Born at Morpeth, Northumberland, in about 1520, William Turner was educated at Pembroke Hall, Cambridge, under the patronage of Thomas Wentworth, 1st Baron Wentworth. At the university, where he became the friend and protégé of Nicholas Ridley (q.v.), then Master of Pembroke, Turner developed his interest in medicine and natural history. In 1538, while still at Cambridge, he published his *Libellus de re Herbaria*, which attracted attention as an essay on a science hitherto unknown at the university.

A forthright Protestant, Turner left Cambridge in 1540 and spent some time preaching in various parts of the country and making observations on bird and plant life. After a brief period of imprisonment for preaching without a licence, he went to the Continent, where he pursued his nature studies. Returning to England on the accession of Edward VI (q.v.), he was appointed chaplain and physician to the Protector Somerset (see Seymour, Edward). In November 1550 he was made Dean of Wells; he was ordained as a priest by Ridley in 1552.

Deprived of his deanery in 1553, Turner spent the reign of Mary I (q.v.) on the Continent; he visited Italy, Germany, Switzerland, and the Netherlands, all the while collecting specimens and material for his future work. It was during his Marian exile that he made the acquaintance of the Swiss naturalist Conrad Gesner, whose ideas Turner was later to introduce to England through his masterpiece, the three-volume *Herball*, written abroad but eventually published, with revisions and additions, in England in the years 1551 to 1568. During his exile Turner also wrote a number of controversial religious books which were printed on the Continent; these were forbidden to be read in England.

Turner was restored to his deanery under Elizabeth I (q.v.), but in 1564 was suspended on account of his nonconformity. He appears to have spent the last years of his life in his house at Crutched Friars, London, where he died on 7 July 1568.

The pioneer of natural history in England, William Turner not only named many plants (such as 'goatsbeard' and 'hawkweed') but also studied their medicinal usage. He is believed to have introduced lucerne into England. His *Avium praecipuarum*, published in 1544, was the first English treatise on birds.

G. E. Fussell, 'William Turner, the father of English botany', *Estate Magazine,* xxxvii (1937), pp. 367–70.
C. E. Raven, *English Naturalists from Neckam to Ray* (1947).

## Tusser, Thomas (?1524–1580), agricultural writer and poet.

Born in about 1524 at Rivenhall, near Witham, Essex, the fourth son of William and Isabella Tusser, Thomas was sent at an early age as a chorister to Wallingford College in Berkshire. Because he was ill-treated and unhappy there, his family managed, through the influence of friends, to have him transferred to St Paul's Cathedral, where he became a chorister under John Redford. He went subsequently to Eton and then to Cambridge, first to King's College and later to Trinity Hall, but illness forced him to leave the university without a degree and he entered the service of Lord Paget (see Paget, William) as a musician.

Tusser spent ten happy years at court in Paget's service, before leaving (against his patron's advice) to get married and settle at Cattiwade in Suffolk as a farmer. There he introduced into the neighbourhood the cultivation of barley and wrote his *Hundreth Good Pointes of Husbandrie*, a collection of agricultural and domestic hints interspersed with wise and humorous maxims on general behaviour, the whole written in doggerel verse. First published by Tottel in 1557, it became immensely popular; a new edition, entitled *Five Hundreth Points of Good Husbandrie*, was published in 1573, and altogether the book ran into some twenty editions before 1640.

After the death of his wife, Tusser married again and settled at West Dereham in Norfolk, under the patronage of Sir Robert Southwell. On the latter's death he obtained a singing post at Norwich Cathedral, but ill-health forced him back into farming, this time in Essex. The venture having proved unsuccessful, Tusser moved with his family to London, but left the City on account of the plague in 1573–4 for Cambridge. He was back in London by 1580, when the records show that he was in financial difficulties. He died a prisoner for debt on 3 May that year, and was buried in the church of St Mildred in the Poultry.

Tusser's autobiography written in verse was prefixed to the 1573 edition of his *Husbandrie*; modern editions are by W. F. Mavor (1812), the English Dialect Society (1879), E. V. Lucas (1931) and Dorothy Hartley (1931). (The Hartley edition includes other writings by Tusser.)

**Twyne or Twine, John** (?1507–1581), schoolmaster, antiquary, and author.

The son of William Twyne of Bullingdon, Hampshire, John Twyne was born there in about 1507. He was educated at Oxford, where he graduated from New Inn Hall as a Bachelor of Civil Law in 1525, having also attended lectures at Corpus Christi College.

Either just before or soon after leaving university Twyne married Alice, daughter of William Piper (or Peper), a prominent citizen of Canterbury. He moved to Canterbury in about 1525–6 and took up a post as 'supreme Moderator' of the free grammar school in the town.

From 1532 onwards he lodged at St Augustine's Abbey, and although so far as is known he did not share the Archbishop's 'advanced' views, in 1534 he was employed by Thomas Cranmer (q.v.) to read a 'lecture of heresy' twice weekly at Sandwich. At the time of the surrender of St Augustine's to the crown in 1538 he managed to rescue some of the Abbey's printed manuscripts and books; these were eventually given by his grandson, Brian Twyne, to Corpus Christi College, and are now in the Bodleian Library at Oxford.

In 1541 the school was reconstituted by Henry VIII (q.v.) as King's School, and Twyne became its first Headmaster. According to the records he was successful in his career and 'grew rich', buying a number of properties in Canterbury and the surrounding district and leasing other former Abbey estates from the crown. A freeman of Canterbury in 1538, he became Sheriff in 1544 and Alderman in 1553; in January that same year he was elected to represent the town in Parliament. This was the time of the extreme

Protestant régime of the Duke of Northumberland (see Dudley, John), and Twyne, who clung to the old ideas, was imprisoned for a short time in the Tower for his views; he was however re-elected as Member of Parliament on his release and was elected Mayor of Canterbury in 1554, the year of the accession of Mary I (q.v.).

When Sir Thomas Wyatt the younger (q.v.) raised a rebellion in Kent to protest against the Queen's proposed marriage to Philip II of Spain (q.v.), Twyne swiftly raised a hundred local horsemen to resist the uprising; in 1558 Mary came personally, with Cardinal Reginald Pole (q.v.) to Canterbury to thank the Mayor for his loyalty.

By this date Twyne had already written the greater part (if not all, apart from the finishing touches) of his *De Rebus Albionicis, Britannicis atque Anglicis*, a work which was to be published after his death by his son Thomas and to earn him the praise of the antiquary John Leland (q.v.), and William Camden (q.v.), author of *Britannia*. Twyne's book is now accepted as firm evidence that there must have existed in Canterbury in the first half of the sixteenth century a small group of independent-thinking antiquaries who rejected the previously-accepted theories of British ancient history based on the work of Geoffrey de Monmouth. A literary conversation-piece, it purports to tell what took place at a supper party held in about the year 1530 between John Foche, the last Abbot of St Augustine's, John Dygon, the monk who later became the last Prior, Nicholas Wotton, who was to be the first Dean of Canterbury, and the author himself. Wotton and Dygon have just returned from escorting the Spanish humanist scholar Juan Luis Vives to Oxford, and are reporting back to the Abbot. In the course of their discussion some revolutionary views are put forward, including one that Britain was earlier inhabited by the descendants of Albion, and not by Brutus and the Trojans, and another that the second great colonizers of this island were the Phoenicians. The book ran into several editions and was published in an English translation by Philemon Holland in 1610. None of Twyne's other known works have survived.

Towards the end of his life Twyne became an eccentric, and he was not infrequently in trouble with the Canterbury authorities. In 1560 he was ordered not to meddle with any public offices in connection with the town or city and to 'utterlie abstaine from riott and dronkynnes'. Whether or not for this reason, he ceased to be Headmaster of King's School in 1561. Allegations of 'filthy and unseemly talk' were made against him the following year; he was also said to be a magician, with a devil in the shape of a great black dog that would dance about the house. Furthermore, his addiction to 'popish religion' landed him in trouble with the Privy Council. This did not prevent him, in 1576, from complaining to Lord Burghley (see Cecil, William) that Archbishop Parker (who had died the previous year) was continually pursuing him and trying to rob him of his keepership of woods at Littlebourne.

Twyne spent his retirement peacefully at the rectory of Preston-by-Wingham, which he had leased. He had a large collection of Romano-British coins, pottery, and glass, and was interested in a number of archaeological excavations in the county. After the death of his wife Alice, he married Margaret Carpenter in 1568. His three sons by his first marriage all went to King's School: Thomas, who published his father's work in 1590, later became a physician; Lawrence achieved recognition as a translator; and John is said to have written verse. John Twyne senior died on 28 November 1581, at the age of seventy-four. He was buried in St Paul's Church, Canterbury, under a commemorative brass which recorded his academic career and his part in the defence of the realm during the Wyatt rebellion.

It is not known exactly how much importance Twyne's contemporaries attached to his views. He is, however, outstanding as one of the most original antiquaries of the sixteenth century. The first to come out in print against Brutus, in his inspired guess about the Phoenician invasion of Britain John Twyne was some two hundred years ahead of his time.

D. L. Edwards, *A History of the King's School, Canterbury*, chapter VI (1957).
T. D. Kendrick, *British Antiquity* (1950), pp. 105 ff.

**Tye, Christopher** (?1497–1573), musician.

Born probably in 1497 in East Anglia, Christopher Tye is thought to have been a chorister at King's College, Cambridge, from about 1511. He was granted a degree as Bachelor of Music in 1536, and left the university in about 1541 to become master of the choirboys at Ely Cathedral. In 1545 he proceeded to the degree of Doctor of Music, also at Cambridge; three years later, undoubtedly through his friendship with Dr Richard Cox (q.v.), who had been elected Chancellor of Oxford University in 1547, Tye was incorporated as Mus.D. in that university also.

By 1553, when he published his *Actes of the Apostles*, to be sung as part-songs and played on the lute, Tye referred to himself as a Gentleman of the Chapel Royal. This does not necessarily mean that he had given up his post at Ely; he most likely combined his duties there and

at the Chapel Royal with those of music instructor to the young Edward VI (q.v.), to which reference is made in a play by Samuel Rowley. The Reformation was already seen to be influencing church music, with the result that some of the finest composers, who had been accustomed to the traditional free style of composition, were tempted to give up the struggle. Tye himself appears to have left Ely towards the end of 1561. He had been ordained by Cox in November that year and was granted the living of Doddington, to which were added subsequently the rectories of Newton-cum-Capella and Wilbraham Parva. He retired with his wife and family to Doddington and died there in the early part of 1573.

Some of the compositions written by Tye for the musical setting of his versification of the *Acts of the Apostles* have been adapted as hymn tunes; for instance 'Winchester' is nowadays well known as the tune of the Christmas carol, 'While shepherds watched their flocks by night'. Of his other compositions, two Masses only survive from his Latin church music, but there are numerous English anthems, psalm settings, and other sacred works composed for instrumental ensembles. Christopher Tye, like the organist and composer Thomas Tallis (q.v.), lived and worked during the period of transition from the Roman to the Anglican liturgy.

*Grove's Dictionary of Music and Musicians* (5th edition, 9 vols, 1954; paperback edition, 10 vols, 1976).
D. W. Stevens, *Tudor Church Music* (New York, 1955).

**Tyndale or Tindale, William** (?1495–1536), translator of the Bible.

Tyndale's origins are not certain, but it is thought that he was born at Slimbridge, Gloucestershire, in about 1495.

He came from yeoman stock and had two brothers; little else is known of his family except that for some reason they were also known by the name of Hychins.

Using the name of Hychins, William entered Magdalen Hall, Oxford, in 1510. He took his B.A. and M.A. there, but was attracted by the reputation founded at Cambridge by Erasmus for the study of Greek and theology, and in 1518 he moved to that university with the idea of reading the New Testament in the original Greek. He was ordained towards the end of 1521, when, probably for financial reasons, he left Cambridge and joined the household of Sir John Walsh at Old Sodbury, Gloucestershire, as chaplain and tutor. He remained in this post for two years, but made such a habit of airing his modern theological views at Sir John's table and spending his leisure hours preaching in the neighbourhood, to the fury of the local clergy, that he was summoned before the chancellor of Worcester, William of Malvern, on suspicion of heresy. He was cleared of the charge, but by this time he had decided to translate the New Testament into the vernacular as an antidote to the corruption he saw in the Church. He left Gloucestershire for London hoping to obtain the help of Cuthbert Tunstall (q.v.), Bishop of London; disappointed by Tunstall, he found employment in the house of a wealthy merchant, Humphrey Monmouth. In London Tyndale came under the influence of Lutheran ideas and also formed a firm friendship with John Frith (q.v.), the future martyr. It was probably by Monmouth and his fellow merchants, who were supporters of Lutheranism in England, that Tyndale was financed to go to Hamburg in 1524, in order to finish his translation and to get the New Testament printed in English, with a view to gradually infiltrating copies into England.

In Germany Tyndale visited Martin Luther (q.v.) at Wittenberg and then, with his assistant, an English friar called William Roye, he completed his work on the New Testament and took it to Peter Quentel, a printer in Cologne, who agreed to produce it in a quarto volume, with marginal notes and references. The printing was well advanced when, through indiscretions of Roye, word reached the municipal authorities; the senate put a stop to further printing, and warnings were sent to England to watch the ports. Tyndale and Roye escaped with their sheets to Worms, where a new version was printed very quickly, in an octavo edition, but without the references and notes. Copies reached England early in 1526, but were suppressed by the Bishops; Archbishop Warham (q.v.) even went so far as to buy up copies on the Continent in order to destroy them. Tyndale himself was ordered to be seized at Worms, but he was given sanctuary at Marburg by the Landgrave of Hesse.

At this stage he adopted Zwinglian views (see Zwingli, Ulrich) and became an active pamphleteer on the subject. His *Parable of the Wicked Mammon* and *Obedience of a Christian Man,* which set out the major principles of the Reformation, were both published at Marburg in 1528; but the approval of Henry VIII (q.v.), which Tyndale had won by upholding the authority of the King in the state, was soon lost on publication of the *Practyse of Prelates* (1530), for while in this he strongly criticized Roman Catholicism, he also opposed the King's divorce.

Tyndale now began work on a translation of the Old Testament. In 1529 when on his way from Antwerp to Hamburg he was shipwrecked off the Dutch coast and lost his manuscripts; helped by Miles Coverdale (q.v.) he started afresh. After the death of Thomas Wolsey (q.v.), Antwerp became a safer place for the Protestant exiles, and Tyndale returned there to issue his translation of the Pentateuch from the original Hebrew, a language which he had taught himself, probably while at Marburg. This new publication again angered the orthodox Anglican bishops and laid Tyndale open to the charge of heresy.

From Antwerp Tyndale conducted his famous controversy with Thomas More (q.v.). After reading Tyndale's New testament in 1528, More had written his *Dialogue concerning heresies and matters of religion*; Tyndale replied with an *Answer unto Sir Thomas More's Dialogue* (1530); More returned to the attack with a *Confutation*, and the argument dragged on.

Henry VIII now tried to persuade Tyndale to return to England, and when he refused, the King tried first to have him kidnapped, and then to get the Emperor to surrender him. Tyndale left Antwerp for two years, and on his return in 1533 he went to live at the house of the English merchants in the town, where he worked on the revision of his translations. In May 1535 a young Englishman, Henry Phillips, who had hoodwinked him by professing to be a student of the new faith, betrayed Tyndale to the Imperial guards; he was arrested and imprisoned for eighteen months at Vilvorde Castle, near Brussels, before being brought to trial. Despite great efforts on the part of the English merchants and of his old friend Thomas Cromwell (q.v.) to secure leniency, Tyndale was condemned as a heretic; on 6 October 1536 he was strangled at the stake before being burned.

Although he spent many years out of England, Tyndale was one of the major forces in the English Reformation. He greatly influenced the thinking of the Puritans through his writings, which were both sound and scholarly. The translation of the Bible, on which his fame now largely rests, and which consists of the New Testament, the Pentateuch, and Jonah, has been endorsed by later scholars as accurate; it formed the basis for the Authorized Version of 1611.

Tyndale's *Works* have been edited by H. Walter for the Parker Society (3 vols; 1848–50).

W. E. Campbell, *Erasmus, Tyndale and More* (1949).
R. Demaus, *William Tyndale* (1871).
S. L. Greenslade, *The Work of William Tindale* (1938).
M. L. Loane, *Masters of the English Reformation* (1954).
J. F. Mozley, *William Tyndale* (1937).

*Portraits*: oil, half length, *called* William Tyndale, by unknown artist, probably late seventeenth or early eighteenth century: National Portrait Gallery, London; oil, head and shoulders, *called* William Tyndale, by unknown artist: N.P.G.; other versions at Hertford College, Oxford, and at the British and Foreign Bible Society.

**Tyrconnel, Lord of** (?1571–1602), see O'Donnell, Hugh Roe.

**Tyrone, 2nd Earl of** (*c.* 1530–1567), see O'Neill, Shane.

**Tyrone, 2nd Earl of** (*c.* 1540–1616), see O'Neill, Hugh.

**Tyrrell, Sir James** (d. 1502), supposed agent in the murder of the Princes in the Tower (see Edward V and Richard, Duke of York in *Lives Before the Tudors*).

The eldest son of William Tyrrell of Gipping, Suffolk, and his wife Margaret, James was a grandson of Sir John Tyrrell (d. 1437), Speaker of the House of Commons. A staunch Yorkist, he was knighted after the Battle of Tewkesbury in May 1471. He sat as a Member of Parliament for Cornwall in December 1477, and fought for Richard, Duke of Gloucester, later Richard III (see *Lives Before the Tudors*) in the war with Scotland, becoming a Knight-Banneret on 14 July 1482.

After the accession of Richard, Tyrrell was appointed Master of the Royal Henchmen and Master of the Horse. He was given various other commissions under Richard, including the office of Steward of the Duchy of Cornwall and an appointment as one of the Chamberlains of the Exchequer. Henry VII (q.v.) on his accession also showed Tyrrell favour by granting him a number of posts in Wales, as well as the post of Governor of Guisnes Castle, near Calais. He came under suspicion, however, in 1499, when the Yorkist claimant to the throne, the Earl of Suffolk (see Pole, Edmund de la), fled to Guisnes; in 1501, after Suffolk had fled the kingdom for a second time, Tyrrell was tricked into surrendering Guisnes Castle and imprisoned in the Tower charged with having harboured a traitor. He was beheaded on Tower Hill on 6 May 1502, after supposedly confessing to the murder of young Edward V and Richard, Duke of York.

Sir James Tyrrell's involvement in the murder of the two Princes in the Tower, as recounted by Sir Thomas More (q.v.) in his *History of Richard III*, has naturally not been conclusively proved. More, however, was the most truthful of men, and although his account of these concealed events may be wanting in some details, he had several sources of information very close to them. (See also his *Edward V*.) Richard's guilt is corroborated by the Howard family tradition, as stated in Lord Henry Howard's *Defensative of Supposed Prophecies*.

P. M. Kendall, *Richard III*, Appendix I (1955).
P. M. Kendall (ed.), *Richard III: The Great Debate* (1965), pp. 104–6 and 191–6.

# U

**Udall, Nicholas** (?1505–1556), school-master, reformer, dramatist, and trans-lator.

Nicholas Udall was born at Southamp-ton, probably in December 1505, and was educated at Winchester and Corpus Christi College, Oxford, where he became a lecturer and fellow. Because of his suspected Lutheran views he did not receive his M.A. until 1534.

Udall became a schoolmaster in 1529. Two years later he probably held a teaching post in London, for it is known that he won favour at court in 1533 through some 'ditties and interludes' which he wrote for the masques that were performed at the coronation celebrations of Anne Boleyn (q.v.). The following year, 1534, Udall published his first translation, *Floures for Latine Spekynge Selected and Gathered out of Terence, and the same translated into Englysshe*. Shortly afterwards he was appointed Headmaster of Eton College.

Udall was a severe disciplinarian. One of his pupils at Eton, Thomas Tusser (q.v.), the agricultural writer and poet, later recorded that he had been severely flogged by the Headmaster 'for fault but small or none at all'. Far more enjoyable no doubt were the traditional plays of Terence and Plautus performed by the boys, under the direction of the Headmaster, every November in celeb-ration of the feast of St Andrew.

In 1541 Udall came under suspicion after some silver images and other plate had been stolen from the College by two of the scholars with the assistance of the Headmaster's servant. On examination it appeared that he had had no part in the theft, although he did admit a moral offence with one of his pupils. Deprived of his headship, he was sent to the Marshalsea Prison by the Privy Council, but on his release not long afterwards he was soon in favour again at court, and in the next few years he received several preferments in the Church.

From about 1542 to 1545 Udall was living in London and working as a translator. In 1542 he issued his version of the *Apophthegmes* of Erasmus (q.v.). He was much encouraged in this enthusiasm for the Reformation by Katherine Parr (q.v.), who became Queen in 1543. She employed him to supervise a translation into English of Erasmus's paraphrase of the New Testament; the first volume of this work, to which Udall contributed a translation of the Gospel of St Luke, appeared in 1548. The following year he was employed by the government of Edward VI (q.v.) to write a reply to the rebels of the West Country who were demanding that the old religion be restored. Udall fulfilled this task forth-rightly and with vigour. He translated Peter Martyr's discourse on the Lord's Supper in 1550, and Thomas Gemini's *Anatomia* in 1552. Meanwhile, in 1551 he had been given a prebend at Windsor.

Udall was now acquiring a reputation as a writer and producer of plays, and when Mary I (q.v.) came to the throne in 1553 he was one of the few Protestants who were retained in favour at court; he also became a tutor in the household of Stephen Gardiner, Bishop of Winchester (q.v.). There are records of a number of performances at court in which Udall was concerned at this date, and as a mark of her esteem for his talent, the Queen – disregarding altogether his past record – in 1554 appointed him Headmaster of Westminster School.

Although he is known to have written a number of plays, only one is extant – *Ralph Roister Doister*, generally considered to be the first real English comedy. Some historians have taken the view that this was written much earlier and performed by the boys of Eton during the playwright's headship there; but it is now accepted that the play was probably written in about 1553–4 as a Christmas entertainment for some of Udall's London pupils, and first performed by the boys of Westminster School in 1554.

The Tudor schoolboy was encouraged to act in classical plays, and out of the schools' successful Latin performances there grew a demand, first for translations from the classics, and later for original English plays. Nicholas Udall was the first and most famous of several schoolmasters who catered for this need; in *Ralph Roister Doister*, which showed the influence of Terence and Plautus, he followed classical principles but used English characters and colloquial English idiom. With this play English comedy came into its own, leaving behind the old medieval morality plays and farces. An early copy of the play is in Eton College Library, and W. D. Cooper has edited it for the Shakespeare Society (1847).

Another play known to have been written by Udall is *Ezechias*, which was performed in front of Queen Elizabeth (q.v.) in 1564. Also attributed to him are *A New Enterlude called Thersytes* (c. 1537); *Respublica* (a Christmas interlude, 1553); *Jacke Jugeler*, called 'a new Enterlude for chyldren to playe', which was published in 1562; and *A Newe Mery and Wittie Comedie or Enterlude ... upon ... Jacob and Essau*, printed in 1568. None of these has survived.

*Cambridge History of English Literature*, vol. 5 (1907–15).
M. Lyte, *History of Eton College* (1911).

# V

**Vere, Edward de** (1550–1604), 17th Earl of Oxford, courtier, poet, and dramatist.

The only son of John de Vere, 16th Earl of Oxford, and his second wife, Margaret, daughter of John Golding, Edward de Vere was born at Castle Hedingham, Essex, on 12 April 1550, and given the title of Lord Bulbeck. His father kept a company of actors who gave regular entertainments at Castle Hedingham, and the young de Vere grew up among scholars and poets. He studied at Queen's College, Cambridge, matriculating there as an 'impubes' fellow-commoner in November 1558.

He succeeded to the earldom on the death of his father in 1562. As a ward of William Cecil (q.v.), later Lord Burghley, Oxford received further education at Cecil House under the tutorship of Lawrence Nowell, before going on to St John's College, Cambridge, to complete his studies. He took a degree there in August 1564 and his M.A. at Oxford two years later. In 1567 he was admitted as a member of Gray's Inn, where he met the poet and dramatist George Gascoigne (q.v.), whose plays were then being performed at the Inn and to whom the Earl was related by marriage. It is probable that Oxford was writing poetry and plays himself at this period.

An impulsive, hot-tempered and wayward youth, he became an embarrassment to his guardian on account of the violent quarrels he had with the Cecil household; in July 1567 there was a nasty incident in which a servant died and a jury had to be persuaded to return the verdict that the man had run himself on the young Earl's sword.

In the spring of 1570 Oxford served on the Scottish border under Thomas Radcliffe (q.v.), 3rd Earl of Sussex. On his return he established his residence at Vere House, in the City of London, and took his seat in Parliament in April 1571. In December that year he married Anne Cecil, Burghley's eldest daughter. At court during the next few years, he was high in the favour of Queen Elizabeth (q.v.), but became estranged both from his wife and from Burghley; the rift between the two men arose over the prosecution of the Duke of Norfolk (see Howard, Thomas, 4th Duke), who was Oxford's cousin. Burghley repeatedly refused the Earl's requests for service in the Navy, and in July 1574 Oxford

suddenly left the court without the Queen's consent and went to Flanders. He was brought back and eventually, having been granted permission to travel, he set out for France and Italy, returning to England the following year. His wife had given birth to a daughter in July 1575, and Oxford raised scandalous doubts over the child's parentage. The couple were temporarily reconciled and three more children, two daughters and one son, who did not survive, were to be born to them. In the meanwhile some of Oxford's lyrics appeared in an anonymous collection *A Hundred Sundrie Flowres*, published in 1573, together with others by Gascoigne.

As time went on Oxford became more and more eccentric. In the literary sphere he was involved with John Lyly (q.v.), whom he employed as secretary, and the latter's dramatic activities with the boys' companies. At about this time the Earl, together with some of his friends, secretly became a Catholic. His extravagant mode of living and constant quarrels with fellow courtiers incurred the Queen's displeasure. In 1579, after he had insulted Sidney by calling him a 'puppy', Elizabeth forbade a duel, and in 1582 Oxford was confined for a short time in his own house following a duel with Thomas Knyvet, a Gentleman of the Privy Chamber, in which both men were wounded. By the summer of the following year he was restored to royal favour, and in 1586, having sold most of his estates to pay his debts, he was granted an annuity of £1,000 by the Queen, to support his status. He maintained a company of actors, taken over from the Earl of Warwick in 1580, which regularly provided entertainment at court. In the summer of 1588, during preparations against the Spanish Armada, the Earl had a ship fitted out at his own expense and is believed to have taken part in the early part of the sea battle.

Two of Oxford's daughters had died in 1587, and in June 1588 his unhappy wife succumbed to a fever while at the Palace of Greenwich. Following her death the Earl became for a while a recluse, devoting himself almost entirely to literary pursuits. He married again in 1591, his second wife being one of the Queen's maids-of-honour, Elizabeth, daughter of Sir Thomas Trentham; she was to bear him one son, Henry, born in February 1593. They made their home at Stoke Newington, in Middlesex, where the Earl collaborated with William Stanley, 6th Earl of Derby, in writing anonymous plays and musical entertainments for their respective companies of actors; Oxford's Men were amalgamated with Worcester's in 1602.

On the accession of James I (see James VI of Scotland) Oxford was appointed to the Privy Council and also continued to receive his annuity and other benefits. He died at Stoke Newington on 24 June 1604 and was buried in Hackney church.

The neurotic, unstable but talented Earl was best known to his contemporaries as a courtier and for his patronage of men of letters such as Lyly. Only in the twentieth century has he emerged as a strong contender for the authorship, or part-authorship, of Shakespeare's plays. On this question see P. Allen, *The Story of Edward de Vere as William Shakespeare* (1932) and *Talks with Elizabethans revealing the Mystery of 'William Shakespeare'* (1947); Hilda Amphlett, *Who was Shakespeare?* (1955, reprinted 1970); J. T. Looney, *'Shakespeare' identified in Edward de Vere, the Seventeenth Earl of Oxford* (1920). None of Oxford's drama has survived, but some twenty-three lyrics have been identified as his.

P. Allen, *Anne Cecil, Elizabeth and Oxford* (1934).

B. M. Ward, *The Seventeenth Earl of Oxford, 1550–1604* (1928).

*Portraits:* oil, by unknown artist, 1575: The Duke of Portland Collection on loan to the National Portrait Gallery, London; engraving, by Brown, after Harding, after unknown artist: location not known.

## Vere, Sir Francis (1560–1609), soldier.

The second son of Geoffrey Vere and grandson of the 15th Earl of Oxford, Francis Vere was born in 1560, probably at Crepping Hall, Essex. His father died when he was about eight years old, and Francis and his brothers were brought up at Kirby Hall, near Hedingham, where they first learned military skills from Sir William Brown, who had seen many years of service in the Low Countries. Well before he was twenty, Francis had determined upon a military career.

His first venture was a visit to Poland with a Captain Francis Allen, possibly to serve in the Polish army. In the summer of 1585 he volunteered to serve under the Earl of Leicester (see Dudley, Robert) in the Netherlands, where a few months later he attached himself to the cavalry commanded by Lord Willoughby de Eresby (see Bertie, Peregrine). After taking part in engagements with the enemy at Axel, Doesburg, and Zutphen, Vere was given the captaincy of 150 men in the Bergen-op-Zoom garrison. A brilliant and daring young officer, he distinguished himself first in the siege of Sluys in June-August 1587, and then in October at Bergen-op-Zoom, where he was knighted by Willoughby, who by this time had replaced Leicester as commander of the English forces in the Low Countries. He returned briefly to England that winter, but by February 1589 was back in action as Willoughby's second-in-command; following the latter's resignation a few months later, Vere took over as acting commander.

The first operation under his command was the relief of Rheinsberg, which was successfully accomplished in the autumn of 1589. The next five years saw a series of exploits, ranging from the capture of Breda from the Spanish in December 1589 to the taking of Deventer and Nijmegen in 1591, and culminating in the great siege and capture of Groningen, in the north, in July 1594. From 1593 Vere was in the pay of the States General, an arrangement that had the approval of Queen Elizabeth (q.v.).

In the spring of 1596 it was decided to strike at Spain elsewhere than in the Netherlands, and Vere, with one thousand of his veterans, sailed for England to join the expedition to Cadiz led by Lord Howard of Effingham (see Howard, Charles) and the Earl of Essex (see Devereux, Robert). Almost immediately he became involved in the rivalry that existed between the various commanders, and in particular he quarrelled with Sir Walter Ralegh (q.v.); the order was finally made that Ralegh was to have precedence at sea, Vere on land. In storming Cadiz Vere had a steadying influence on the impetuous Essex; he played a leading part in the capture of the town and shared the glory that greeted the expedition on its return to England.

The following year, 1597, Vere sailed with Essex on the disastrous expedition to the Azores. In the quarrels that arose between Essex and Ralegh he sided with the former, and on their return to England he defended Essex before the Queen. Soon afterwards Vere returned to the Netherlands, where in January 1598 he helped Prince Maurice to capture Turnhout. In May that year he was chosen by the Queen to negotiate a new treaty with the States General, and in the autumn he received a special mark of royal favour in his appointment as Governor of Brill.

From the early spring of 1599, when he took up his governorship, until 1604, when he retired from service in the Netherlands, Vere waged an incessant and brilliant campaign against the Spaniards, scoring outstanding victories at Bommel (1599) and at Nieuwpoort (summer 1600). The sieges of Leiden and Antwerp followed, and in July 1601 Vere took a heroic defensive stand at Ostend, which was to hold out for over two years. Vere himself was recalled from that town in order to take a command in the field in March 1602, when together with Prince Maurice he laid siege to Grave, near Nijmegen, where he was seriously wounded. He was continued in his governorship of Brill on the accession of James I (see James VI of Scotland) in 1603, but when England signed a treaty with Spain the following year he retired from active service. Granted a substantial pension by the States General, Vere took up residence on his estate at Kirby Hall, where he began to write his *Commentaries*, narrative accounts of his various campaigns, intending them only for private circulation. In June 1606 he was appointed Governor of Portsmouth and the isle of Portsea, and in October the following year he married a sixteen-year-old girl, Elizabeth Dent.

Vere lived to see the recognition of the independent United Provinces under the truce with Spain of April 1609. On 28 August the same year he died suddenly in London and was buried in Westminster Abbey. He left no issue. During the last years of his life he had contributed generously towards the library at Oxford recently founded by his friend Sir Thomas Bodley (q.v.).

One of the most accomplished soldiers of his day, Sir Francis Vere was very highly regarded by his contemporaries as a military strategist and leader of men. He was, however, completely outshone at court by men like Drake and Ralegh. Vere's *Commentaries*, first published in 1657, have been reprinted in Edward Arber, *An English Garner* (8 vols, 1877–96; 10 vols, 1903).

C. R. Markham, *The Fighting Veres* (1888).

*Portrait*: oil, by unknown artist: National Portrait Gallery, London.

**Vergil or Virgil, Polydore** (?1470–?1555), historian, chiefly remembered for his *Anglicae Historiae* ('History of England').

Vergil was born at Urbino, Italy, and educated at the universities of Padua and Bologna. His *Proverbiorum Libellus*, published in Venice in 1498, was dedicated to the Duke of Urbino, to whom he was secretary; the first collection of Latin proverbs ever printed, it anticipated the *Adagia* of Erasmus (q.v.) by two years. In 1499 Vergil brought out the work on which his reputation was largely to rest during his lifetime: *De Inventoribus Rerum*, a study of the origins of all things relating to human activity. The enlarged edition of this work (1521) was placed on the *Index Expurgatorius* because of its references to pagan customs in the origin of the Christian religion.

In 1502 Vergil joined his kinsman, Cardinal Castellensis, in England as Deputy Collector of Peter's Pence, and through his influence obtained a succession of ecclesiastical appointments: the living of Church Langton in Leicestershire, prebendaries of Hereford, Lincoln, and St Paul's, London, and the archdeaconry of Wells. Almost all the rest of his life was spent in England, where he was naturalized in 1510.

In 1514 he travelled to Rome in an

unsuccessful attempt to secure a cardinal's hat for Thomas Wolsey (q.v.), but the following year, after the interception of an outspoken letter against Wolsey and Henry VIII (q.v.), he was imprisoned in the Tower for several months and deprived of his post as Collector. On his release he devoted all his time to writing. His *Gildas* (1525) and *Liber de Prodigiis* (1526) both achieved considerable popularity.

Vergil worked for almost thirty years on his history of England, which was first suggested to him by Henry VII (q.v.). The first edition of *Anglicae Historiae* (twenty-six books), in Latin, was printed in Basle in 1534. A twenty-seventh book, covering the reign of Henry VIII down to 1537, was added to the third edition in 1555. The chief value of the work lies in the section covering the period 1450–1537, and it is an especially valuable source for the reign of Henry VII.

Some time around 1551 Vergil returned to Italy. He is believed to have died at Urbino in 1555.

Denys Hay, *Polydore Vergil, Renaissance historian and man of letters* (1952).

**Verulam, Baron** (1561–1626), see Bacon, Francis.

**Walsingham, Sir Francis** (?1532–1590), statesman, Secretary of State to Elizabeth I (q.v.).

The only son among six children of William Walsingham, a London barrister, and his wife Joyce, daughter of Sir Edmund Denny, Francis Walsingham was born in about 1532, probably at Footscray, Kent, where his parents owned a country house. His father died while Francis was a baby, and soon afterwards his mother married Sir John Carey, who was the brother-in-law of Anne Boleyn's sister, Mary, and who brought Francis up as a zealous Protestant.

In 1548 Francis was sent to King's College, Cambridge. He left two years later without a degree, but having absorbed a great deal of the enlightened teachings there of John Cheke (q.v.), then Provost of King's, Martin Bucer (q.v.), and other Reformers. All his life Walsingham was to retain an uncompromising adherence to the Protestant faith.

He spent the next two years travelling on the Continent, perfecting his knowledge of French and Italian; by 1552 he was back in England and a member of Gray's Inn. When Mary I (q.v.) came to the throne the following year, however, Walsingham soon headed for the Continent again, probably on account of his Puritan sympathies, but also, it is believed, because he may have been involved in the conspiracies of the Duke of Northumberland (see Dudley, John) and Sir Thomas Wyatt the younger (q.v.). He travelled to Italy, Germany, and Switzerland, where he made contact with many of the English Protestant exiles; most of his time was spent in Italy, where he studied law at the University of Padua and was much influenced by his observation of the new statecraft of Niccolò Machiavelli (q.v.) in practice.

Back in England in 1559–60, he entered Parliament three years later as Member for Lyme Regis. In 1562 he married a widow, Anne Carleill, who died two years later without bearing him any children; in about 1566–7 he married again, this time Ursula St Barbe, widow of Sir Richard Worsley of Appuldurcombe, who was to give birth to two daughters: one of them died young and the other, Frances, later made two brilliant marriages, firstly to Sir Philip Sidney (q.v.) and secondly, after his death, to the Earl of Essex (see Devereux, Robert).

Through his family Walsingham had influential friends. He was known to be hard-working and proficient in languages, and it may have been this last quality which brought him to the notice of Queen Elizabeth. In 1570, probably on the advice of Lord Burghley (see Cecil, William), who for the past two years had been using his services to obtain information concerning foreign spies in London, the Queen appointed Walsingham as her ambassador to France, his mission being to negotiate the proposed marriage between her and the Duc d'Anjou; this in fact was nothing more than a diplomatic ploy in the wider campaign to draw France into a defensive alliance against Catholic Spain.

Walsingham loyally subordinated his own sympathies (which lay with the Huguenots) to those of the Queen; the negotiations with Catholic Anjou were distasteful to him, and he was much relieved when they were allowed to lapse. In April 1572 the defensive Treaty of Blois, negotiated by Walsingham and Sir Thomas Smith (q.v.), was concluded, but in August that year relations with France were ruptured by the St Bartholomew's Day Massacre. Walsingham felt himself partly responsible, since it was through his diplomacy that Huguenot influence at the French court had increased to the extent that Catholic fear and hatred could no longer be contained; the massacre also further embittered him against Catholicism.

In December 1573 he was recalled to London and appointed to the Privy Council as Secretary of State, a post which he was to hold until his death. He was employed chiefly on foreign affairs, but shared with Burghley the supervision of the central administration. Burghley encouraged Walsingham to establish his highly efficient secret service, on which he is said to have spent almost his entire private fortune; he employed more than fifty agents in foreign courts and numerous spies in London and other parts of England, including at one time the young Christopher Marlowe (q.v.). Walsingham's zealous Protestantism, coupled with patience and ingenuity, helped him to expose a number of plots against Elizabeth, including not only the Ridolfi Plot (see Ridolfi, Roberto di), but also the conspiracies of William Parry (q.v.), Francis Throckmorton (q.v.), and Anthony Babington (q.v.); his discovery of an incriminating letter from Mary, Queen of Scots (q.v.) to Babington finally brought the Scottish Queen to the block in 1587.

Walsingham's hatred for Catholicism led him to support several projects for English expansion overseas at the expense of Spain and Portugal. He contributed generously to the voyages of Martin Frobisher (q.v.), Francis Drake (q.v.), Humphrey Gilbert (q.v.), and others, and spared no effort to persuade the Queen to sanction their expeditions. Richard Hakluyt (q.v.) dedicated his *Principall Navigations* to him.

Apart from his determination to get rid of Mary, Queen of Scots, at home Walsingham's persecution of English Catholics was efficient but not fanatically cruel. Although he used Machiavellian methods and often countenanced torture or death when state authority was endangered, these were methods customary at that time, and in fact, rather than make martyrs of his victims, he preferred to hold them in detention; at one time he developed a project to populate a colony in America with them, but this came to nothing.

In foreign affairs Walsingham was often outspoken to the Queen, who, although she trusted his loyalty, invariably neglected his advice, including that to discontinue her negotiations to marry the Duc d'Alençon and, in 1587, to make adequate preparations to meet the Spanish Armada. On several occasions Elizabeth sent him on missions that conflicted with his views: dutifully he went to the Low Countries in 1578, to France in 1581, to Scotland in 1583. He was rewarded for his loyal service with a knighthood in 1577 and an appointment as Chancellor of the Order of the Garter the following year; in 1587 he was made Chancellor of the Duchy of Lancaster. Over the years he also received other favours in land and in money, but all his wealth was swallowed by the cost of maintaining his secret service and settling the debts left by his son-in-law, Philip Sidney, in 1586.

Some time after his return from France in 1573 Walsingham had sold his estate at Footscray and settled at Barn Elms, Surrey; he was to represent Surrey in Parliament from 1576 for the rest of his life. In London he maintained a fine mansion at London Wall and later at Seething Lane. His pursuits were intellectual rather than physical, for owing to the ill-health he suffered almost all his life Sir Francis was unable to enjoy sports; among his interests were the universities of Oxford and Cambridge (he founded a Divinity lecture at the former) and patronage of the art of letters. When he died on 6 April 1590, Burghley acknowledged the great loss suffered by 'the Queen's Majesty and her realm and I'; Philip II of Spain (q.v.), on reading a report from a Spanish agent in England that 'Secretary Walsingham has just expired, at which there is much sorrow', made a note in the margin, 'There, yes! But it is good news here.'

Sir Francis Walsingham was a man of many talents, but his outstanding gift was that of service to his Queen and country. His linguistic ability and diplomatic skills, and in particular his efficient organization of espionage activities, contributed much to the execution of Elizabeth's foreign policy and ensured the security of her crown.

Walsingham's official papers are at the British Museum and the Public Record Office, London, and in the archives at Hatfield House. His correspondence covering the period of his service as ambassador in France (1570–3 and 1581) has been printed in the *The Compleat Ambassador*, edited by Sir Dudley Digges (1655). Other letters will be found in Thomas Wright, *Queen Elizabeth and her Times* (2 vols; 1838). His diary, 'The Journal of Sir Francis Walsingham' (from December 1570 to April 1583) has been edited by C. T. Martin, *Camden Society Miscellany*, vi (1871).

Conyers Read, *Mr Secretary Walsingham and the Policy of Queen Elizabeth* (3 vols; Oxford, 1925).

*Portraits:* oil on panel, probably by J. de Critz the Elder, *c.* 1585: National Portrait Gallery, London; oil on panel, after J. de Critz: N.P.G.; other versions: King's College, Cambridge, Lord Petre, Knole, Sudeley Castle, Gloucestershire, and elsewhere; engraving: *Herwologia*, 1620.

**Warbeck, Perkin** (?1474–1499), pretender to the English throne.

Warbeck's origins have been much debated, and it has not been proved whether he was an illegitimate Yorkist prince, or the son of Margaret, Duchess of Burgundy (q.v.) and the Bishop of Cambrai, or merely (as he himself stated under examination) the son of a humble citizen of Tournai.

According to Warbeck's own account, he was born in Flanders, the son of John Osbeck (or Werbecque) and his wife, Catherine de Faro. He spent his boyhood in Antwerp and Middelburg, and then joined the household of Sir Edward Brampton, a Yorkist supporter, as page to the latter's wife, travelling with them to Portugal. He spent about a year in that country, partly in the service of a Portuguese knight, before joining a Breton merchant, Pregent Meno, with whom he sailed to Ireland in 1491. From this date onwards his life is well documented.

Perkin was a handsome, rather conceited boy. When he landed at Cork dressed in his master's splendid silk garments and was hailed by the Irish as the Earl of Warwick, at first he strongly denied this, but it took little persuasion on their part subsequently to get him to impersonate Richard, Duke of York (see *Lives Before the Tudors*), the younger of the two Princes murdered in the Tower. With the encouragement of the Earls of Kildare and Desmond, he was taught English and suitably regal manners.

The following year Charles VIII of France conceived the idea of using Warbeck in his quarrel with Henry VII (q.v.), and invited him to France. The scheme misfired because of the Treaty of Etaples, and Warbeck had to leave the country. He went to Flanders, where Margaret, Duchess of Burgundy, welcomed him as her 'nephew' and put the finishing touches to his grooming as a Yorkist 'prince'. Shortly afterwards Warbeck went to Vienna, where the Emperor Maximilian I acknowledged him as Richard IV, rightful king of England, and on his return the Netherlands became a centre for the conspiracy against Henry VII. The King learned of the plot through the treachery of Sir Robert Clifford, who had been one of Warbeck's supporters, and as a result of this leak of information a number of prominent men in England who had become involved in the conspiracy, including Sir William Stanley (see *Lives Before the Tudors*), the Lord Chamberlain, were executed.

In June 1495 Warbeck landed a force of some 1,500 men, provided by Maximilian, at Deal, but was forced to withdraw. A similar fiasco at Waterford in Ireland sent him on to Scotland, where he was well received by James IV (q.v.). The Scottish King was instrumental in his marriage to the daughter of the Earl of Huntly, and in 1496 James provided Warbeck with a small force with which to invade Northumberland, but this was not successful and the pretender withdrew once more to Ireland. The following year he tried to take advantage of a rebellion which had broken out in Cornwall over taxation proposed to meet the King's expenses in quelling the Scottish invasion, but his arrival on 7 September 1497 was mistimed; the rebellion was over, and although Warbeck advanced as far as Taunton, he met with strong resistance and on 21 September deserted his followers for the sanctuary of Beaulieu. A week later he surrendered to the King and made a full confession of his imposture.

At first Warbeck was held in honourable confinement in the Tower, but following an escape attempt in June 1498 he was more severely imprisoned. He tried to escape again the following year, together with the Earl of Warwick, and for this he was hanged on 23 November 1499.

S. D. Chastelain, *L'imposture de Perkin Warbeck* (Brussels, 1955).

J. Gairdner, essay on Perkin Warbeck, appendix to *History of the life and reign of Richard the Third* (1898; reprinted 1972).

*Portrait*: drawing, probably contemporary: town library, Arras, France.

## Warham, William (?1450–1532), lawyer and Archbishop of Canterbury.

Warham was a native of Hampshire, born probably in 1450, and educated at

Winchester and New College, Oxford, of which he became a fellow in 1475.

Warham's early career was spent at Oxford, where he directed the school of civil (Roman) law. In 1488 he moved to London to practise as an advocate in the Court of Arches, and was soon one of the foremost lawyers in the country. He was sent on a number of important missions abroad: to Rome on business for the Bishop of Ely in 1490; to Antwerp to settle a mercantile dispute in 1491; to Flanders again in 1493 in an unsuccessful attempt to persuade Margaret, Duchess of Burgundy (q.v.) to give up support of Perkin Warbeck (q.v.).

In September 1493 he took holy orders, being ordained as a sub-deacon. By this time he had won the trust of Henry VII (q.v.), and many preferments followed. Master of the Rolls in 1494, Warham was responsible two years later for negotiating the marriage between Arthur, Prince of Wales (q.v.), and Catherine of Aragon (q.v.), and in the next few years he handled a number of important diplomatic missions for the King.

Parallel with his success in legal and diplomatic spheres, Warham rose swiftly in the Church. In 1502 he was consecrated Bishop of London and became Keeper of the Great Seal; in 1504 Archbishop of Canterbury and Lord Chancellor. In 1506 he was appointed Chancellor of Oxford University, a post which he held until his death.

After 1509, a spectacular year in which he married Henry VIII (q.v.) and Catherine of Aragon, and, a fortnight later, on 24 June, crowned the King in Westminster Abbey, Warham's prominence began to wane. Under the new monarch he no longer enjoyed the position of confidence he had occupied under Henry VII, and he was not in sympathy with either the new policies or the new men,

such as Thomas Wolsey (q.v.), on whom Henry VIII relied. The relations between Warham and Wolsey are far from clear, but as a representative of the old order it seems that the Archbishop stuck rigidly to his views and that Wolsey lost no opportunity to humiliate him. In 1515, the year in which Wolsey became a cardinal, Warham resigned the post of Lord Chancellor and thereafter appeared rarely on state occasions, an exception being the Field of the Cloth of Gold in 1520, at which he was present.

From the moment the King's divorce was mooted, Warham's dislike of Henry and his policies hardened. Yet, as his much-quoted favourite expression, *ira principis mors est* ('the wrath of the ruler means death'), showed, he greatly feared the King. Appointed one of the counsellors to assist Catherine in the proceedings, he did little for her, being reluctant to risk incurring Henry's displeasure; in 1530 he signed the letter to the Pope urging him to annul the marriage, and subsequently accepted Henry as supreme head of the Church of England with the saving clause, 'so far as the law of Christ allows'. The King's subsequent proposal to the Pope that Warham should try the divorce suit was never implemented.

By this time the Archbishop was old and weary, and much dispirited by the proceedings of the Reformation Parliament of 1529 and the continual attacks on the church. Henry's demand for the submission of the clergy was, however, more than he could take, and disregarding the fate which he knew would await him, he made it known that at the next session in the House of Lords he intended to move the repeal of all the acts passed by Parliament since 1529. It was a valiant plan for a last-ditch stand, but one which was never put into action, for his health was already failing and before the session opened Warham was dead.

He died on 22 August 1532 and was buried in a splendid tomb in Canterbury cathedral. The contents of his library were bequeathed to Winchester College and to New College and All Souls College, Oxford, but he left very little money. According to Erasmus (q.v.), who had been a friend of Warham's, the Archbishop, although a frugal liver himself, had been very generous with gifts of money and sumptuous entertainment during his lifetime.

It is of interest that this firm opponent of Church Reform should have been connected with the humanist movement. There is a sympathetic portrait of Warham by Erasmus in *Ecclesiastes*.

W. F. Hook, *Lives of the Archbishops of Canterbury*, vol. vi (12 vols; 1860–76).

*Portraits*: drawing, by Holbein, 1527: Royal Collection, Windsor; oil, by Holbein, 1527: Musée du Louvre, Paris; copies at Lambeth Palace and National Portrait Gallery, London; miniature and three pencil and wash drawings, all by unknown artists: New College, Oxford; tomb: Canterbury Cathedral.

**Warwick, Earl of** (?1504–1553), see Dudley, John.

**Webster, John** (?1580–?1625), dramatist, see *Lives of the Stuart Age*.

**Weelkes, Thomas** (?1570–1623), organist and composer.

There is no documentary material relating to Thomas Weelkes's early life. That he was born in about 1570 has been deduced from a reference to his 'yeeres yet unripened' in his first published work of 1597–8. It is believed that he may have been the 'Thomas Wikes' who was a chorister at Winchester College in 1583–4.

Weelkes was an organist, first at Winchester Cathedral, from about 1598 to 1601, and later at Chichester Cathedral. He probably took up his appointment at Chichester towards the end of 1601 or the beginning of 1602. In the latter year he obtained the degree of Bachelor of Music at Oxford, and he married soon afterwards.

By this time he had already published several sets of madrigals: one volume containing compositions for three, four, five, and six voices, in 1597; a book of *Balletts and Madrigals* in 1598; and two volumes, one for five voices and the other for six, considered to be his finest work, in 1600. After this date he produced only one other book of secular compositions, *Ayeres or Phantasticke Spirites*, for three voices, in 1608, devoting the remainder of his creative activity to sacred works. Altogether he wrote ten Anglican services, but none of these has survived in its entirety. He also composed forty-one anthems, of which about twenty-five are more or less complete. Most of his other compositions for the organ, viols, and virginal are fragmentary.

In his 1608 book of madrigals Weelkes stated that he was a Gentleman of the Chapel Royal. He was at this date still living in Chichester, where there are records of his being charged with drunkenness and other misdemeanours. He died in London on 30 November 1623.

Thomas Weelkes is one of the most original of the English madrigal composers of the late sixteenth century. His output far exceeded that of his contemporaries, and nearly a hundred of his madrigals are extant. The bulk of these were written in the period 1597–1600. They cover a wide range, from those written in the light-hearted Italian style to the more serious, such as 'Thule' and the magnificent 'O Care, Thou Wilt Dispatch Me'. His church music is much more restrained, and among the finest examples of his work in this field are the anthems 'O Jonathan', 'When David heard, O my son Absalom', and 'O Lord, Arise'.

Weelkes's madrigals have been published in volumes 9–13 of *The English Madrigal School*, edited by E. H. Fellowes (1913–24). See also *Tudor Church Music*, edited by P. C. Buck and others (10 vols; 1923–30) and *Early English Organ Music*, edited by Margaret Glyn, volume i (1939).

D. Brown, *Thomas Weelkes: A Biographical and Critical Study* (1969).
E. H. Fellowes, *English Cathedral Music from Edward VI to Edward VII* (1942).
E. H. Fellowes, *English Madrigal Composers* (2nd ed. 1948).
C. E. Welch, *Two Cathedral Organists: T. Weelkes 1601–1623 and T. Kelway 1720–1744* (1957).

**Wentworth, Paul** (1533–1593), Puritan parliamentary leader.

The third son of Sir Nicholas Wentworth and younger brother of Peter Wentworth (q.v.), Paul was born in 1533. Through his marriage to Helen, widow of William Tyldesley, he acquired the lease of Burnham Abbey, Buckinghamshire, which had been granted to Tyldesley at the Dissolution. In January 1563 Wentworth was returned as Member of Parliament for Buckingham. He played a prominent part in the debate on the petition addressed in 1566 to Queen Elizabeth (q.v.) by the House of Commons requesting her to marry and to name her successor, to which the Queen returned an evasive reply. From 1572 to 1583 he represented Liskeard, Cornwall, when during the session of 1581 he again incurred the Queen's disapproval by carrying a motion which recommended a general fast and the preaching of a sermon before each meeting of the Commons; the House, submitting to the royal view, then dropped the procedure, and Wentworth was pardoned.

In 1590 he requested a further lease on Burnham Abbey. This was granted on the grounds of Wentworth's 'long and dutiful service', with special reference to his custody at Burnham of the late Duke of Norfolk (see Howard, Thomas, 4th Duke) prior to the latter's removal to the Tower to stand trial in 1569.

Paul Wentworth died in 1593 and was buried in Burnham church.

W. L. Rutton, *Three Branches of the Family of Wentworth* (1891).

**Wentworth, Peter** (?1530–1596), Puritan parliamentary leader.

Born in about 1530, the eldest son of Sir Nicholas Wentworth, chief porter of Calais, who had been knighted by Henry VIII (q.v.), Peter Wentworth was descended from the Wentworth family of Nettlestead, Suffolk. His first wife was a cousin of Queen Katherine Parr (q.v.); after her death he married Elizabeth, sister of Sir Francis Walsingham (q.v.). In 1557 he inherited from his father the estate of Lillingstone Lovell, near Buckingham. He was returned as Member of Parliament for Barnstaple in 1571, and was to sit in six Parliaments over a period totalling twenty-two years, representing in turn Barnstaple, Tregony, and Northampton.

As a Member for Parliament and a Puritan Wentworth was an active and vociferous campaigner. In 1571 he attacked Sir Humphrey Gilbert (q.v.) for 'fawning' on the court, and later in the same session he served on the committee that rejected the Thirty-Nine Articles and argued forcibly that the House had the right to discuss church matters in defiance of the Queen's order to the contrary. In the session of Parliament that opened in February 1576, in which several hitherto extinct boroughs had been revived for the express purpose of preventing a Puritan majority, he made a memorable speech on the liberties of the House, bitterly condemning the interference of the crown. Examined by a committee of the House, he was afterwards imprisoned for several weeks in the Tower. Wentworth was sent to the Tower a second time in March 1587, for a speech that again challenged the Queen's absolute rights in ecclesiastical affairs. In 1593 he offended Elizabeth (q.v.) by a further petition asking her to name her successor. On this occasion he was held permanently in the Tower, having especially antagonized the Queen by his support of Edward Seymour, Baron Beauchamp, as the heir to the throne, in *A Pithie Exhortation to her Majesty for establishing her Successor to the Crowne*; he wrote the manuscript during his imprisonment in answer to the case put forward for the Infanta of Spain, but it was not printed until 1598, after his death. A martyr to the principle of the freedom of speech, Peter Wentworth died in the Tower on 10 November 1596.

J. E. Neale, 'Peter Wentworth', *English Historical Review*, xxxix (1924), pp. 36–54, 175–205.
W. L. Rutton, *Three Branches of the Family of Wentworth* (1891).

**Whitgift, John** (*c.* 1530–1604), Archbishop of Canterbury.

Born at Grimsby in about 1530, the son of a wealthy merchant, John Whitgift was educated at St Anthony's School in London, at Queens' College, Cambridge, and later at Pembroke Hall, where as a promising pupil he attracted the attention of Nicholas Ridley (q.v.), then non-resident Master. He rose swiftly to a position of prominence in the university, being elected a fellow of Peterhouse in 1555, Master of Pembroke and Trinity in 1567 and, that same year, Vice-Chancellor and Regius Professor of Divinity. Ordained in 1560, he became chaplain to Richard Cox (q.v.), Bishop of Ely, and in 1567 chaplain to the Queen. Whitgift became Dean of Lincoln in 1571, when he was granted a special dispensation to hold at the same time a prebend of Ely, the post of Master of Trinity, and the rectory of Teversham.

In 1572 he was appointed Prolocutor of the Lower House of Convocation. His *Answere to a Certen Libel Instituted, An Admonition to the Parliament*, published that year, was a powerful defence of the Anglican Church against the advocates of Presbyterianism. Bishop of Worcester from 1577 to 1583, and Vice-President of the Marches of Wales from 1577 to 1580, Whitgift was in 1583 appointed to succeed Edmund Grindal (q.v.) as Archbishop of Canterbury.

As Archbishop, Whitgift held the respect and trust both of the Queen and of Burghley (see Cecil, William). In 1586 he became the first ecclesiastic to be appointed by Elizabeth to her Privy Council. Faced with the urgent need to

strengthen and restore discipline in the Church, he strove unremittingly to achieve conformity, instructing his chaplains to uncover the secret Presbyterians and those Puritans responsible for the Martin Marprelate tracts of 1588–9. He was, however, determined to avoid creating Puritan martyrs, and once a certain conformity had been established he relaxed his rule and even treated many of the Puritans with sympathy: included among these was Thomas Cartwright (q.v.), with whom he had been involved in long-drawn-out conflict since the days when he was Vice-Chancellor at Cambridge. Urged by the Cambridge divines to pronounce in favour of the Calvinist doctrines, in 1595 Whitgift called a conference at Lambeth and subsequently issued the Lambeth Articles, which made considerable concessions to the Calvinist theology. This was much disapproved of by the Queen, and the Articles were held in abeyance.

Whitgift was called by the Queen to minister to her as she lay dying in March 1603. In January the following year he participated in the Hampton Court Conference, supporting the King (see James VI of Scotland) in his refusal to sanction doctrinal changes in the Church, but upholding the request of the Puritans for a new translation of the Bible. The Archbishop died on 29 February 1604 and was buried in the parish church at Croydon, where he had during his lifetime founded a hospital and a free school.

The *Works* of John Whitgift (chiefly his *Answer* to the *Admonition to the Parliament* and later writings against Cartwright) have been edited for the Parker Society by John Ayre (3 vols; 1851–3).

V. J. K. Brook, *Whitgift and the English Church* (1957).

P. M. Dawley, *John Whitgift and the English Reformation* (New York, 1954).
W. F. Hook, *The Lives of the Archbishops of Canterbury*, vol. v (12 vols; 1860–76).
George Paule, *The Life of the most revered prelate J. Whitgift* (1612).

*Portraits:* oil, half length, by unknown artist, c. 1583: Lambeth Palace, London; oil, three-quarter length, by unknown artist, c. 1598: two versions, one at University Library, Cambridge, the other at Whitgift's Hospital, Croydon; oil, by unknown artist, probably early seventeenth century: National Portrait Gallery, London; engraving, by C. van de Passe, 1620: location not known.

## Whittingham, William (?1524–1579), Dean of Durham.

William Whittingham was born at Chester, probably in 1524, and was educated at Brasenose College, Oxford, remaining at the university to become a fellow of All Souls in 1545 and Senior Student and M.A. of Christ Church in 1548.

In about 1550 Whittingham left Oxford and spent three years travelling in France, Germany, and the Low Countries. At Louvain University he became proficient in French and married a lady of extreme Protestant views. He returned to England in 1553, but not for very long: being a staunch Protestant it was dangerous for him to remain in the country after the accession of Mary I (q.v.). He fled to Frankfurt and joined John Knox (q.v.) in agitating for a Prayer Book more extreme than the Second Prayer Book of Cranmer (q.v.). When Knox was expelled from that city, Whittingham followed him to Geneva, where he became first an elder, then deacon, and ultimately minister in succession to Knox.

During the five years he spent in Geneva, Whittingham was engaged on the translation of the New Testament into English (the first English Bible to be divided into chapters and verses), and also, with the help of Miles Coverdale (q.v.) and others, on the Geneva Bible, known as the 'Breeches Bible', which was published in 1560; this was to become the standard Bible in English homes for many years. He was also responsible for selecting the tunes for what was known as the Genevan-English Order, the Prayer Book which included metrical versions of the Psalms and the Ten Commandments.

Whittingham did not return to England immediately after Elizabeth I (q.v.) came to the throne, but remained in Switzerland to supervise the publication of the Geneva Bible. By 1560 however he had entered the service of two brothers, Ambrose Dudley, Earl of Warwick, and Lord Robert Dudley (q.v.), later Earl of Leicester. He accompanied Warwick to France as his chaplain in 1562 at the defence of Le Havre, and as a reward for his valiant service there was given the deanery of Durham.

Whittingham was an extreme Protestant, unsympathetic to the middle course steered by Elizabeth. He tried to introduce Genevan principles at Durham; he removed certain images and church ornaments; on one occasion he even locked his own bishop out of the cathedral. In 1572 he adamantly refused the office of Secretary of State. Charges of adultery and drunkenness were later brought against him, but none was proved; in 1578 the question of his ordination was raised, and it was said that he had never been properly ordained. In fact this was quite true: he had been merely 'ordered' as minister in Geneva; but before any final decision on the matter was arrived at, the Dean died at Durham on 10 June 1579.

Modern historians have cast some doubt on the authorship of the work commonly attributed to Whittingham, *A brief discourse of the troubles at Frankfurt 1554-1558*, although it is generally conceded that he wrote at least part of it. The edition by E. Arber (1908) contains a short life.

M. A. E. Green, 'The life and death of Mr William Whittingham', in *Camden Society Miscellany, vi* (1870).

S. L. Greenslade, 'William Whittingham, dean of Durham 1524-78', *Durham University Journal,* viii (1946).

**Wilbye, John** (1574-1638), madrigal composer, see *Lives of the Stuart Age*.

**William** (1533-1584), Prince of Orange, usually known as 'William the Silent'. Son of the Count of Nassau-Dillenburg, William was born at Dillenburg Castle, Nassau, Germany, on 24 April 1533. He spent his childhood in the Lutheran environment of the family home. Later, at the insistence of the Emperor Charles V (q.v.), he was sent to Breda and Brussels to be brought up as a Catholic and educated to take possession of the vast family estates which he had inherited in the Netherlands in addition to the principality of Orange.

Popular with Charles V and his court in Brussels, the young Prince was made a member of the Council of State on the accession of Philip II of Spain (q.v.). When Philip finally left the Low Countries to return to Spain in August 1559, he appointed William as *Stadhouder* (governor and commander-in-chief) of Holland, Zeeland, and Utrecht.

During the next six years resentment mounted among the nobles of the Low Countries, who felt they were not being allowed their rightful share in the government of the country. The religious issue was not at first of paramount importance, but as Protestantism and the influence of the humanist Desiderius Erasmus (q.v.)

spread and it became clear that Philip would tolerate nothing short of orthodox Catholicism, hatred of their religious persecutors, and in particular Cardinal Granvelle, increased. By 1561 William was the leading member of a group who protested openly against the encroachment on their liberties.

Philip was prevailed upon to recall Granvelle in March 1564, but the persecutions went on unabated, and on 31 December the same year William argued forcibly in the Council of State that princes did not have the right to rule over the consciences of their subjects and that it was not possible to enforce religious unity. Sympathizing with the group of nobles who came to be known as 'Les Gueux' ('The Beggars'), he managed to persuade them to petition the Regent, Margaret, Duchess of Parma, to relax the anti-heresy laws rather than resort to violence. He was too late; although some moderation was effected, in August 1566 hysterical Calvinist mobs broke into and desecrated the Catholic churches. Philip's response was to send the Duke of Alva to crush the rebellion, whereupon William fled temporarily to the family estates at Dillenburg. When summoned to appear before the Court of Troubles set up by Alva, he sent a written 'Justification'; all his possessions within the Netherlands were confiscated.

William now saw that his fortunes were inextricably bound up with those of the Low Countries, and, having by this time openly reverted to the Protestantism of his childhood, he took up arms and led his supporters into what has come to be called the Eighty Years War against the Spanish oppressors. He did not, however, accept the more extreme Calvinist doctrines, and it was not until 1573 that he joined the Reformed Church.

In the early campaigns William was out-manoeuvred by Alva, but in 1572 a successful expedition by the 'Sea Beggars', exiles from the Low Countries, who captured the port of Brielle in Zuid-Holland, gave the impetus to a popular uprising. For the next four years William organized a heroic resistance against the Spanish tyranny, while his agents in France, Germany, and England endeavoured to raise support for his cause. Among those who were active on his behalf was Sir Philip Sidney (q.v.), who visited William at Gertruidenberg in 1577, but it was not until after the Prince's death that an English force was sent to aid the Dutch. The support William had hoped for from France also failed to materialize. After the temporary collapse of Spanish power in the Netherlands in 1576, it seemed that a general union of all the provinces might be achieved, but its success was jeopardized by the intolerance of the Calvinists, which led to the southern provinces pledging their support to Spain. In 1579 the seven northern and central regions united under the Union of Utrecht. William's position was, however, considerably weakened when, in March 1580, Philip outlawed him and offered a reward for his assassination. An attempt was made on his life at Antwerp in 1582; a few months later, when the Spaniards under the Duke of Parma began advancing from the south, William retreated to Delft and established his headquarters in a former convent, now called the *Prinsenhof*. He was shot there by a Catholic emissary of Philip on 10 July 1584 and, the family seat being in enemy hands, was buried in the New Church at Delft.

William of Orange was the great protagonist in the long struggle of the Dutch against their Spanish oppressors. That he failed in his lifetime to achieve the national unity and religious freedom to which he had dedicated himself was due largely to the divisive interests of his supporters and in particular to the intolerant attitude of the Calvinists with whom he had been forced into an alliance. Nevertheless he was the founder of the independent United Provinces, and thus of the later Kingdom of the Netherlands, which today is ruled by his direct descendants. He was married four times: from 1551 to 1558 to the Countess Anne of Egmond-Buren; after her death, in 1561 to Anna of Saxony, whom he divorced ten years later; in 1575 to Charlotte of Bourbon-Montpensier, who died in 1582; and in 1583 to Louise de Coligny. Two of William's sons, Prince Maurice and Prince Frederick Henry, in turn succeeded him as *Stadhouder* of the United Provinces.

The nickname 'William the Silent' is said to have had its origin in a remark made by the Prince's adversary, Cardinal Granvelle, who used the old Dutch adjective *schluwe*, meaning 'sly' or 'secretive', which was wrongly translated into the Latin *taciturnus* and so came to be rendered in English as 'silent'.

The correspondence of William, Prince of Orange, has been published in Dutch and French editions: *Correspondentie van Willem den Eerste, Prins van Oranje, 1551–1561*, edited by N. Japikse (The Hague, 1934); *Guillaume le Taciturne: Correspondance*, edited by L. P. Gachard (6 vols; Brussels, 1847–66).

P. J. Blok, *Willem de Eerste, Prins van Oranje* (2 vols; Amsterdam, 1919-20).

N. A. Robb, *William of Orange* (2 vols; 1962–6).

C. V. Wedgwood, *William the Silent* (1944; rev. ed. 1960).

F. Rachfahl, *Wilhelm von Oranjen und der niederländlische Aufstand* (4 vols; Halle and The Hague, 1906–24).

*Portrait:* oil, by Adriaan Thomasz Key, 1581: Mauritshuis, The Hague.

**Williams, Sir Roger** (?1540–1595), soldier.

Born at Penrhos, Monmouthshire, in about 1540, Roger Williams came from an old-established, but not wealthy, family. He was well educated, possibly in part at Oxford, and at an early age entered the household of Sir William Herbert (q.v.), 1st Earl of Pembroke, as a page. According to his own statement, he was first attracted to the military life while in Pembroke's employ and is said to have taken part with his master in the storming of St Quentin in 1557.

In the spring of 1572 Williams joined a force of volunteers under Thomas Morgan which went to support the Dutch in their revolt against the Spaniards at Flushing; he subsequently served under Humphrey Gilbert (q.v.) in the unsuccessful attempt to take Goes later that year. In 1577 he joined the English army under Sir John Norris (q.v.) in the Low Countries, where for the best part of seven years he acted as the latter's lieutenant.

Petitioning the Queen in 1584 for a higher military post, Williams let it be known that the Spaniards had tried to lure him to fight on their side. He was eventually given a command in the force dispatched to the Low Countries the following year under the Earl of Leicester (see Dudley, Robert). Wounded at Doesburg, Williams served throughout the campaign with great valour and took part in the fighting at Zutphen in September 1586 in which Sir Philip Sidney (q.v.) was fatally wounded. He was knighted by Leicester for his services. The following summer he was besieged at Sluys, which he surrendered to the Duke of Parma at the beginning of August; Leicester gave him the unpleasant task of breaking news of this defeat to the Queen.

In the summer of 1588 Williams was

appointed Master of the Horse at the camp at Tilbury which was set up to prepare for the threatened Spanish invasion. As soon as that danger had passed, he returned to the Low Countries, where Lord Willoughby de Eresby (see Bertie, Peregrine) had taken over command of the English forces. He returned home with Willoughby in March 1589 and accompanied him to Dieppe that autumn, with a force sent to aid Henri of Navarre in his struggle against the Catholic League. He was to spend the rest of his military career in France fighting for Navarre's cause.

In 1590 Williams published *A Briefe Discourse of Warre*, a book that contained much personal reminiscence and was also highly critical of the English military authorities; in it the author maintained that success in war depended on proper discipline, adequate finance and, above all, a good commander. He dedicated the work to the Earl of Essex (see Devereux, Robert), who was shortly afterwards to arrive with a new force in Normandy, and with whom Williams joined in besieging Rouen. The two men became intimate friends, and when Essex was recalled in January 1592 Williams took over as commander. He subsequently distinguished himself in valiant combat against the Spanish at Rue and was highly commended for this action by Navarre.

Williams spent most of the remaining years of his life in France, but from time to time brought news from the Continent to England. Taken ill on one of these visits, he died in London on 12 December 1595 and was buried in St Paul's with full military honours; Essex, to whom Williams left his personal property, was one of the chief mourners.

In addition to the *Discourse*, which has been reprinted in Edward Arber, *An English Garner* (8 vols, 1877–96; 10 vols,

1903), Williams wrote an account of the campaign in the Netherlands; entitled *The Actions of the Lowe Countries*, it was first published in 1618 and has been reprinted in *Somers Tracts*, volume i of the standard edition by Walter Scott (13 vols; 1809–15). On the French wars, see *News from Sir Roger Williams*, published in London, 1591.

L. V. D. Owen, 'Sir Roger Williams and the Spanish Power in the Netherlands', *Army Quarterly*, xxxiv (1937), pp. 53–66.

**Willoughby de Eresby, Baron** (1555–1601), see Bertie, Peregrine.

**Wilson, Thomas** (?1525–1581), statesman and scholar.

Thomas Wilson was born in about 1525, the son of Thomas Wilson of Strubby, Lincolnshire, and his wife, Anne Cumberworth. He has sometimes been confused with several other Thomas Wilsons who were his contemporaries.

Wilson was educated at Eton, and in 1541 he was elected a scholar at King's College, Cambridge. At Cambridge, where he took his B.A. in 1545–6 and his M.A. in 1549, he came under the influence of Sir John Cheke (q.v.), Sir Thomas Smith (q.v.), and Roger Ascham (q.v.), leaders of the revival in Greek studies. The Duchess of Suffolk appointed him as tutor to her two sons, Henry and Charles Brandon, both of whom later became Dukes of Suffolk.

In 1551 a treatise written by Wilson entitled *The Rule of Reason* was published by Richard Grafton. His next publication, the *Arte of Rhetorique*, which bears no printer's name and of which the earliest known copy is dated 1553, was sub-titled 'for the use of all such as are studious of eloquence, sette forth in Englishe by Thomas Wilson'; it was dedicated to John Dudley, eldest son of the Duke of Northumberland (see Dudley, John). Denouncing the use of 'strange inkhorn terms' and of French or Italian idiom in English prose, it is believed to have influenced many contemporary writers, including Shakespeare.

Wilson enjoyed the patronage of the Dudley family, including (much later) the Earl of Leicester (see Dudley, Robert). Therefore when Northumberland fell from power in 1553, soon after the publication of the *Arte of Rhetorique*, he prudently sought refuge on the Continent, travelling to Padua and to Rome. In March 1558 he was summoned back to England in the name of Mary I (q.v.) and Philip II of Spain (q.v.). On his failure to return, he was arrested and charged before the Inquisition with writing books on logic and rhetoric and with being a heretic. During the riots that broke out in Rome on the death of Pope Paul IV, Wilson managed to escape and settled at Ferrara, when he received his LL.D. in November 1559; this was incorporated at Oxford in 1566 and at Cambridge in 1571.

In 1560 he returned to London and was admitted as an advocate in the Court of Arches; he also became Master of Requests and Master of St Catherine's Hospital in the Tower. In the Parliament of 1563–7 he sat as Member for Michael Borough, Cornwall, and in 1567 was sent on a commercial mission to Portugal. In the autumn of 1571 Wilson conveyed the Duke of Norfolk (see Howard, Thomas, 4th Duke) to the Tower and was responsible for examining his servants, as well as those concerned in the Ridolfi plot (see Ridolfi, Roberto di). The following year he was elected as Member of Parliament for Lincoln.

During these years Wilson was busy translating *The Three Orations of Demosthenes*, first published in 1570, and writing his *Discourse uppon Usurye by way of Dialogue and Oracions*, dedicated to Leicester and published in 1572.

He was entrusted with his first major diplomatic mission in the autumn of 1574, when he was sent to the Netherlands; he remained there until March the following year, and in October 1576 returned to the Netherlands on a second mission. The purpose behind these activities was to negotiate a *modus vivendi* between the new Spanish governor, Don John of Austria, and the Dutch insurgents, but Wilson, swiftly realizing the impracticability of such an agreement, urged an understanding with William of Orange (q.v.); he also negotiated the proposed marriage between Queen Elizabeth (q.v.) and François, Duc d'Alençon (q.v.; later Duc d'Anjou).

On his return to England he became a Privy Councillor; in November 1577 he was appointed Secretary of State and in 1580 lay Dean of Durham. The chief authority on Portuguese matters in the Council, he was however overshadowed there by the brilliant Sir Francis Walsingham (q.v.). Wilson attended his last Council meeting in May 1581; he died on 16 June the same year at St Catherine's Hospital, where he was buried the following day. He had been twice married: firstly to Jane, daughter of Sir Richard Empson, by whom he had no issue; and secondly to Agnes, sister of Admiral Sir William Wynter (q.v.), by whom he had one son and two daughters.

Thomas Wilson was the first English translator of Demosthenes, but he made the greatest impact on the Tudor literary scene with his *Arte of Rhetorique*, which stimulated the development of an English prose free from foreign idiom; it has been edited by G. H. Mair (1909). The *Discourse uppon Usurye* has been edited with a valuable introduction by R. H. Tawney (1925).

W. S. Howell, *Logic and Rhetoric in England 1500–1700* (New York, 1961).

*Portrait*: oil on panel, by unknown Flemish artist, 1575: National Portrait Gallery, London.

**Wiltshire and Ormonde, Earl of** (1477–1539), see Boleyn, Sir Thomas.

**Winchester, 1st Marquess of** (?1485–1572), see Paulet, Sir William.

**Winter, Sir William** (d. 1589), see Wynter, Sir William.

**Wishart, George** (?1513–1546), Scottish reformer and martyr.

There is some uncertainty about George Wishart's birth, which took place in about 1513; he was either the son or nephew of Sir James Wishart of Pittarrow, near Montrose, who was Lord Justice Clerk in the period 1513–24. Educated probably at Fordun school, he later graduated in arts at King's College, Aberdeen; he may have completed his studies on the Continent.

For about four years from 1534 he held a teaching post at Montrose grammar school, where he is said to have taught the New Testament in Greek. For this reason he was impeached by David Beaton (q.v.), then Abbot of Arbroath, in 1538; summoned on a charge of heresy, Wishart fled to England, and later, in about 1539–40, to the Continent. He visited first Germany and then Switzerland, where he came under the influence of Henry Bullinger, successor to Ulrich Zwingli (q.v.). Bullinger was at this time drawing up the First Helvetic Confession, which Wishart subsequently translated into English.

On his return to England in 1541–2 he became a tutor at Corpus Christi College, Cambridge. In July 1543, however, he seized the opportunity of returning to Scotland with the representatives who had travelled to London to negotiate with Henry VIII (q.v.). He took a house near to the church at Montrose and began to preach. Crowds flocked to hear him. In 1545 he went to Dundee, where he preached on the Epistle to the Romans; when a prominent local citizen challenged him in the names of Marie de Guise (q.v.) and the Earl of Arran (see Stewart, James, Earl of Arran), he is said to have come down from the pulpit threatening God's vengeance for interference with His messenger.

Wishart next went on to preach in the western part of Scotland, returning to Dundee when plague struck the town. During his second stay in Dundee an attempt was made on his life. Wishart now prophesied his own early death and the triumph of the Reformation in Scotland. He preached in Perth and from there went on to Leith, where John Knox (q.v.) heard him for the first time and decided to become his disciple. There was another attempt on his life near Montrose, and after Christmas Wishart went to Lethington and Haddington, taking Knox with him; when he found his audiences greatly diminished, due to the influence of Patrick Hepburn, 3rd Earl of Bothwell, he spoke vehemently against his opponents. Invited to spend the night at Ormiston House, the home of John Cockburn, Wishart was seized there that evening by Bothwell. He refused Knox's offer to accompany him, advising him to return to his pupils and saying that 'ane [one] is enough for a sacrifice'.

He was taken by his captors to Edinburgh Castle and given into the custody of Archbishop Beaton, who placed him in strict confinement in the Castle of St Andrews. Tried before a convocation of bishops and other clergy on 28 February, Wishart was convicted of heresy and burned at the stake, with the utmost cruelty, on 1 March 1546.

George Wishart was the first popular preacher of the Reformation in Scotland. His martyrdom marked the start of a movement towards reform which was to gather momentum under his successor, John Knox.

An account of Wishart's trial appears in the *Book of Martyrs* of John Foxe (q.v.), first published in Basle (1559). The reformer's only known writing is a translation of the First Helvetic Confession, which was first published after his death, probably in 1548, and reprinted in the *Wodrow Miscellany* under the editorship of David Laing (1844).

W. Cramond, *The Truth about George Wishart, the Martyr* (1898).

John Knox, *History of the Reformation* (various editions).

C. Rogers, 'Memoir of George Wishart, the Scottish martyr', *Transactions of the Royal Historical Society*, iv (1876), pp. 260–363.

D. P. Thomson, *George Wishart: The Man who roused Scotland* (1952).

*Portrait:* oil, by unknown artist, 1543: Scottish National Portrait Gallery, Edinburgh.

**Wolsey, Thomas** (?1473–1530), cardinal, Archbishop of York, and statesman, Lord Chancellor of England from 1515 to 1529.

Thomas Wolsey came from a family of Suffolk butchers and was the eldest child of Robert and Joan Wolsey of Ipswich. The year of his birth is uncertain, but it is generally assumed to be 1473. An intelligent and academically inclined child, Thomas was educated at Magdalen College, Oxford, which he entered at an exceptionally young age

and where he was known as the 'boy bachelor', having taken his B.A. when only fifteen. Some time before 1497 he became a fellow of his college, and on 10 March 1498 he was ordained. The following year he obtained the position of Bursar of Magdalen, but exchanged it for the post of Dean of Divinity a year later, the tradition being that he was forced to resign for having appropriated funds for the building of the college tower without authority. At the same time he acquired a number of benefices as far apart as Suffolk, Somerset, and Kent. In 1501 he was made one of the domestic chaplains to Henry Deane, Archbishop of Canterbury.

In 1503 Wolsey took the post of chaplain to Sir Richard Nanfan, Deputy Governor of Calais, having been recommended to him by Deane, and Nanfan in his turn recommended Wolsey to Henry VII (q.v.), with the result that on Sir Richard's death in 1507, Wolsey became a royal chaplain. The following year he was entrusted with a secret mission to visit the Emperor Maximilian I in Flanders, in connection with the King's proposal to negotiate a marriage with Margaret of Savoy. As a reward for his services Henry appointed Wolsey Dean of Lincoln in February 1509.

At the start of the reign of Henry VIII (q.v.) a few weeks later, Wolsey was not automatically reappointed royal chaplain, probably because the influential Countess of Richmond (see Beaufort, Lady Margaret) held no great opinion of his ability. However, he soon attracted the attention and confidence of the young monarch, and in November that year he was appointed as Royal Almoner and a member of the King's Council. Wolsey very quickly acquired the taste for power and wealth. He set about making himself indispensable to the King and had no difficulty in persuading Henry to let him shoulder the tedious burdens of state affairs. He had no particular religious vocation, and no doubt it was purely with a view to removing any obstacle to his higher ecclesiastical advancement that he became a Doctor of Divinity at Oxford in 1510.

After the fiasco of the war against France in 1512, Wolsey successfully organized the campaign of the following year in which the English armies scored great victories at Thérouanne, Tournai, and in the Battle of the Spurs. In 1514 he negotiated the peace treaty with France and a separate marriage treaty between Henry's sister, Mary Tudor (q.v.), and the ailing Louis XII. It was a diplomatic triumph which brought Wolsey into sudden eminence, and he was not unrewarded. Immediately after the surrender of Tournai Henry had given him the bishopric of that city; now, in February 1514, the King appointed him to the vacant see of Lincoln. In September the same year he resigned the bishopric on being made Archbishop of York, but because the previous Archbishop, Christopher Bainbridge (q.v.), had died in suspicious circumstances, the cardinal's hat on which Wolsey had set his sights was withheld; it was granted only in November 1515 after personal representations to Pope Leo X by Henry and the King of France, and a letter from Wolsey himself. A few weeks later, on 24 December, the new Cardinal became Lord Chancellor of England in succession to Archbishop William Warham (q.v.).

With one eye already on the papacy, Wolsey now saw himself in the role of 'arbiter of Europe', and for the next fourteen years he completely dominated Henry's foreign policy, making decisions with only the barest reference to

Parliament. He masterminded the meeting of the English and French monarchs at the Field of the Cloth of Gold in June 1520, but not long afterwards committed England to the support of the Emperor Charles V (q.v.) in the latter's war against France, causing much resentment at home by the heavy taxation he imposed in order to finance this campaign; in 1528 he dragged England into a conflict with the Emperor. Wolsey continued to play off François against Charles until the peace signed at Cambrai between France and Spain in 1529 not only took him by surprise, but left England isolated.

By this time the Cardinal had become the most universally hated man in the country. His authority in the Church stemmed from his appointment as *legatus a latere* in 1518; his powers were subsequently increased by a series of papal bulls until early in 1524 Pope Clement VII made him a legate for life, with authority that far exceeded any previous legatine powers. Wolsey not only exercised these powers in the most ruthless manner, but he pocketed the wealth that accrued from them. Although aware that the Church was in need of reform, he failed completely to reform it, and his suppression of some twenty-nine monasteries was carried out primarily to obtain money for his own purposes. Wolsey acted with the utmost severity towards other members of the clergy, while he himself practised the most glaring plurality, holding and obtaining revenue from a large number of benefices in most of which he never set foot; these included the archbishopric of York and also the Abbey of St Albans, the richest in England. He was also guilty of accepting bribes and of breaking the rule of celibacy, having as early as 1511 entered into a liaison with the daughter of a Thetford innkeeper by the name of Lark. She was to bear him a son and a daughter, and while the boy was still in his teens the Cardinal saw to it that he too secured many rich benefices within the Church.

Possessed of a fine legal brain, although not trained as a lawyer, Wolsey's judicial activities were more commendable. He greatly increased the work of the Court of Chancery and influenced the development of a system of equity jurisdiction at that court. He also extended the jurisdiction of the Court of the Star Chamber, making use of it to discipline those nobles who considered themselves above the law and seeing to it that the poor obtained justice. By keeping the exercise of judicial power tightly in his own hands, however, he antagonized the members of the legal profession, who much resented the Chancellor's encroachment into the field of common law. His policy on enclosures, in which he sought to champion the rights of the poor by sending out several commissions to tear down illegally erected hedges and to restore open fields, was largely ineffective and

succeeded only in arousing the enmity of the country landowners.

Wolsey enjoyed pomp and ceremony. He lived on a lavish scale, and his several residences were even more splendid than those of the King. Soon after becoming Chancellor in 1515 he authorized a massive rebuilding of York Place, Westminster. He also acquired the manor of Hampton, where he proceeded to build the palace of Hampton Court; this he subsequently gave to Henry VIII (while retaining the right to live there) in an attempt to regain favour following the failure of his 'amicable loan' scheme of 1525. He had two other magnificent country houses, The More and Tyttenhanger.

While the Cardinal appears to have held few religious convictions and to have shown no particular enthusiasm for the 'new learning', he did found a college at Oxford for the training of secular clergy, Cardinal College (which later became Christ Church), and also a smaller one in his native town of Ipswich. It was for this purpose that he obtained the King's permission to dissolve certain monasteries, and he took a genuine interest in both foundations.

On two occasions during his period of office, in 1521 and 1523, Wolsey tried – and failed – to get himself elected as Pope. In 1529, when with the King's 'great matter' pending his election would have been the most useful, he precipitately set in motion his plans once again on hearing a false rumour of the death of Pope Clement VII. In the event, Clement was to outlive the Cardinal.

It was Wolsey's failure, in the years 1527-9, to persuade the Pope to annul Henry's marriage to Catherine of Aragon (q.v.) that brought about his fall from power. Contemporary opinion, and Catherine herself, maintained that the Cardinal had originated the 'great matter' of the divorce, but Wolsey on his deathbed stated that he had tried many times to dissuade the King 'from his will and appetite'. Historians have since argued that when the divorce was first mooted, Wolsey may not have known about Henry's attraction to Anne and that he hoped, therefore, in the interests of the balance of power, ultimately to arrange a French marriage for him; others have pointed out that the Cardinal would not have wished to see Anne as Queen because of her close relationship to his enemies, the Howards. The truth must be that Wolsey realized only too well the dilemma in which he was involved and, not unaware that his own continuance in power depended upon a successful outcome, he tried desperately both to serve his King and to fulfil his own ambition.

In May 1527 the Cardinal sat with Archbishop Warham in a secret and collusive court to examine the King concerning the validity of his marriage to his brother's widow; at the last moment, however, he shrank from the responsibility of pronouncing a decision. There followed two years of fraught diplomatic moves on the part of all those concerned: first Wolsey's abortive visit to France in the hope of obtaining the necessary authority from his fellow-cardinals while the Pope was temporarily in captivity; then his series of representations, through agents, to the Pope after his release; Clement's continual prevarication; Henry's appeal to the Pope behind Wolsey's back; Catherine's vain efforts to enlist the support of both Charles V and the Pope, while learning to her cost just how formidable and ruthless an opponent the Cardinal could be.

In the summer of 1528 the Pope dispatched Cardinal Campeggio from Rome with authority to hear and determine the case jointly with Wolsey. There followed another period of procrastination, engineered by the Italian, during which time it was noticeable that the King, angry and impatient, had begun to lose confidence in Wolsey. The proceedings of the new legatine court were opened at Blackfriars on 31 May the following year, but were unexpectedly adjourned by Campeggio at the end of July. They were never resumed, for in the meanwhile Spain and France had ended their conflict and were about to sign the peace of Cambrai, and the Emperor had put pressure on the Pope to revoke the case to Rome. Wolsey's usefulness to his monarch was over.

Events now moved fast to bring the Cardinal down. His enemies on the Council – principally the Dukes of Norfolk and Suffolk (see Howard, Thomas, 3rd Duke, and Brandon, Charles, respectively), Sir Thomas Boleyn (q.v.) and Sir Thomas More (q.v.) – lost no time in persuading the King to rid himself of the man who had failed to secure the divorce he so desperately wanted. Writs were issued to summon a new Parliament; on 9 October the Lord Chancellor was indicted at Westminster Hall on a *praemunire* charge of having exceeded his legatine authority; on the 18th he was forced to surrender the Great Seal, and three days later he signed a confession of guilt. Stripped of his many offices and preferments and ordered to leave York House (which soon afterwards became the King's Palace of Whitehall), he retired to his house at Esher. In the Parliament that met on 3 November Wolsey was arraigned on forty-six charges, but was ably defended by his solicitor, Thomas Cromwell (q.v.). The King dealt generously with his former servant, refusing either to send him to prison or to give an undertaking not to employ him again; and in February 1530 Henry not only restored Wolsey to the archbishopric of York, but gave him more than adequate financial provision.

On 5 April 1530 the Archbishop set out for York. He made deliberately slow progress and attracted much unfavourable comment en route on account of his lavish living style; word was sent ahead to prepare for a splendid enthronement on 7 November. In the meanwhile Wolsey was unable to resist the temptation to meddle in politics; the suspicions of King and Council were aroused, some incriminating correspondence with the French and Spanish ambassadors was intercepted, and on 4 November the former Chancellor was arrested at Cawood and charged with high treason. On the way back to London to face trial, Wolsey was taken ill at Leicester Abbey, where he died on 29 November and was buried close to Richard III (see *Lives Before the Tudors*) in what came to be known as 'tyrants' grave'.

A man of high intellect and great administrative ability, and the only English statesman of the pre-Reformation period to have risen from humble origins, Thomas Wolsey achieved painfully little in his years of service to the crown. He had the capacity for hard work, but his arrogance and personal vanity, as well as an almost insatiable greed for wealth and power, an overbearing manner, and a lack of morals, combined eventually to bring about his downfall. His influence on the judiciary alone has won commendation from historians. His opportunist foreign policy and efforts towards peace in Europe resulted only in the isolation of England from the great continental powers, and he left the Church in an appallingly vulnerable and unreformed state. Because he was the promoter of the King's divorce, Wolsey has been held responsible for the ensuing break with Rome and called the architect of the Reformation. Among his most vicious contemporary critics were the poet John Skelton (q.v.), the scholar Alexander Barclay (q.v.) and the historian Polydore Vergil (q.v.). The modern historian G. R. Elton has written of Wolsey as 'the most disappointing man who ever held great power in England and used it for so long with skill and high intelligence'.

G. Cavendish, *The Life and Death of Cardinal Wolsey* (1641; ed. R. S. Sylvester, Early English Text Society, 1959).

A. F. Pollard, *Wolsey* (1929; new ed. 1953).

Neville Williams, *The Cardinal and the Secretary* (1975).

*Portraits:* oil on panel, by unknown sixteenth-century artist: National Portrait Gallery, London; drawing, by J. le Boucq: Bibliothèque d'Arras, France.

**Wotton, Sir Henry** (1568–1639), poet and diplomat, see *Lives of the Stuart Age*.

**Wriothesley, Henry** (1573–1624), 3rd Earl of Southampton, patron of William Shakespeare (q.v.).

The son of Henry Wriothesley, 2nd Earl of Southampton, and his wife, Mary Browne, daughter of the 1st Viscount Montagu, Wriothesley was born at Cowdray, Sussex, on 6 October 1573. The headstrong 2nd Earl was at that time in the custody of his father-in-law, having only a few months previously been released from the Tower; he had been involved in certain conspiracies of the Catholic lords and had been betrayed by the Bishop of Ross (see Leslie, John), the agent of Mary, Queen of Scots (q.v.), from whom he had sought advice as to whether or not to obey Queen Elizabeth (q.v.).

Shortly after his son's birth Southampton was restored to full liberty, and for the first six years of his life young Harry and his elder sister, Mary, spent a normal, happy, and luxurious childhood at the several Wriothesley and Montagu family residences in Hampshire. By 1579, however, their parents were at loggerheads, the Countess charged with adultery and banished from her husband's presence. At about this time the Earl was again in trouble with the authorities on account of his Catholic activities, and it was probably a combination of inherited fragile health (consumption) and domestic and political strains that led to his death on 4 October 1581, at the age of only thirty-six. His son and heir, now the 3rd Earl of Southampton, was within two days of his eighth birthday.

As a ward of Lord Burghley (see Cecil, William), Master of the Wards and Lord Treasurer, the young Earl went to live at Cecil House, London; there he met, among others, Burghley's son, Robert Cecil (q.v.) and the young Earl of Essex (see Devereux, Robert). In October 1585 Southampton was sent to St John's College, Cambridge, to complete his education; he took his M.A. there in 1589. While at the university he formed a close friendship with another of Burghley's wards, Roger Manners, the young Earl of Rutland. There too he probably first developed a liking for drama, an interest which he continued when he returned to London, where he had been admitted as a member of Gray's Inn in February 1588; several plays were performed at the Inns of Court from about 1594, and most of the young gentlemen about town were regular patrons of the playhouses on the outskirts of the City.

When Southampton reached the age of sixteen, Burghley began to put pressure on him to marry; the bride he had in mind was his own granddaughter,

Lady Elizabeth Vere. The young Earl, however, was not at all interested in marriage; disappointed at having been too young to take part in the campaign against the Armada of 1588, he was at this time fired with two ambitions only: military achievement and the patronage of literature. But his refusal of the lady in question was to prove costly, for when the Earl came of age Burghley was to extract a huge fine from him, and in the meantime he made no further effort towards the proper administration of the Southampton estates; it also brought Southampton into disfavour with the whole Cecil family.

It was at about this time that Southampton was presented at court, where he was befriended by Essex and rose swiftly to prominence. A number of literary men, possibly over-estimating the wealth which he was about to inherit when he came of age in 1594, now sought his patronage: William Shakespeare, who in 1593 dedicated *Venus and Adonis* to him and, the following year, *Lucrece*; Barnabe Barnes, who included a sonnet addressed to Southampton in his collection *Parthenophil and Parthenophe*, also published in 1593; Thomas Nashe (q.v.), whose *Unfortunate Traveller, or the Life of Jack Wilton* appeared in 1594 with a dedication to the Earl. In later years there would be many others. Of all these Shakespeare was the first to make a bid for patronage, and Southampton became his only patron; it is likely that the two men had become acquainted as early as 1591–2, probably on one of the Earl's visits to the playhouse. The question of whether Shakespeare's *Sonnets*, the bulk of which were written between the years 1593 and 1596, were addressed to his patron or to someone else, has been the subject of much controversy and remains unsolved.

Southampton came of age in October

1594. At this time he became involved in the unsavoury episode of the Danvers brothers, friends and neighbours of his in Hampshire, who had murdered Henry Long; after hiding the wanted men at Titchfield, he organized their escape to France. No disciplinary measures were taken against the Earl, but since Burghley soon afterwards extracted from him the enormous fine for his refusal to marry Lady Elizabeth, there may have been some kind of deal.

In 1595 Southampton was much at court, and there was talk of his ousting Essex as the Queen's favourite. By the end of that year, however, he was out of favour, probably on account of the attention he was paying to Elizabeth Vernon, one of the Queen's maids-of-honour. He was living extravagantly and running up vast debts. He longed for military action, but was denied permission by the Queen to accompany Essex on his expeditions to Calais and Cadiz in 1596. In the summer of the following year he was allowed to take part in the 'Islands Voyage' to the Azores, aimed at intercepting and destroying the Spanish treasure fleet on its way back from South America. It was a disastrous expedition which lost Essex all the prestige he had won at Cadiz, but Southampton, in command of the *Garland*, won some glory for his attack and capture of a Spanish frigate; he was knighted by Essex for his part in the campaign.

In 1598 Southampton accompanied Robert Cecil to France and was given permission to travel on the Continent for two years. He returned briefly a few months later to marry Elizabeth Vernon, who was pregnant; the wedding was a secret one, but when the news leaked out the Queen was furious and ordered the Earl's return. He delayed for as long as possible, but was back in London at the beginning of November, and was confined for a few weeks in the Fleet prison; during this time his daughter, christened Penelope, was born. It was probably at about this date that he became a Protestant.

In the spring of 1599 Southampton accompanied Essex to Ireland, but the Queen, angered by Essex's having appointed the Earl as General of the Horse without her permission, stripped him of his command. He returned with Essex in September that year, but did not accompany him to Nonsuch. Shortly afterwards the Earl and Countess of Southampton took up residence at Essex House, where they became involved in the plans to rescue Essex from his confinement at York House. Southampton returned briefly to Ireland to serve under Mountjoy (see Blount, Charles), but withdrew soon afterwards to the Netherlands; he was forbidden by the Queen to engage in a duel with Lord Grey. By the end of 1600 he was back in London, where Essex had by that time been released and was recruiting his supporters; Southampton became one of the most active participants in the plan to overthrow the Cecil government. Their preparations for a coup were incited by an attack on Southampton by Grey early in January 1601, and on the evening of 7 February the Earl and his friends persuaded the players at The Globe to revive their production of Shakespeare's *Richard II*, including the controversial deposition scene; this was aimed at inciting the public to join the revolt, planned for the following morning.

Arrested with Essex after the fiasco of the rebellion, Southampton stood trial with the former at Westminster Hall on 19 February. His defence, that he had had no knowledge of the revolt but had intended only to protect his friend from his private enemies, was not accepted, and both he and Essex were condemned to death. Essex was executed on 25 February, but the sentence on Southampton was subsequently commuted to one of life imprisonment in the Tower, on the intervention of Sir Robert Cecil.

On the accession of James I (see James VI of Scotland), Wriothesley (he had been deprived of his earldom under the attainder) received a full pardon and was restored to his place at court. On 9 July 1603 he was installed as a Knight of the Garter; later the same month he was restored as Earl of Southampton. In August the King granted him the lucrative 'Farm of the Sweet Wines', and a month later the post of Captain of the Isle of Wight. Once again high in royal favour, Southampton was much sought after as a patron by the literary men of the day, and the next few years produced a spate of dedications by hopeful authors. In 1605 a son and heir, James, to whom the King stood as godfather, was born, and a second son, Thomas, three years later; two daughters, Elizabeth and Mary, were born in 1609 and 1611. Thanks to the financial provisions made by the King, Southampton lived in splendid style, with a large retinue of servants, dividing his time between Southampton House in Holborn, London, when he was in attendance at court or Parliament, his country estates of Titchfield and Beaulieu, and the official residence of Carisbrooke Castle on the Isle of Wight. On several occasions he entertained the King at Beaulieu.

During the early years of the reign Southampton benefited from the close friendship of Robert Cecil, but after the latter's death he became involved in a struggle for power between the Protestant faction, of which he was one of the leaders, and the house of Howard. Although in 1619 he was, through the influence of the royal favourite, Buckingham (see Villiers, George, 1st Duke,

in *Lives of the Stuart Age*), at last made a member of the Privy Council, there soon developed a wide rift between the two men. The Earl's growing opposition to Buckingham brought him into disfavour with James, who abruptly dissolved the 1621 Parliament and put Southampton into confinement for a short period. At this time the King was also displeased with the way in which the Virginia Company, of which the Earl was Treasurer, was being managed; but when Virginia became a Crown Colony in 1624 he was again in royal favour.

In August 1624 Southampton and his elder son sailed for the Netherlands, having volunteered for service in the struggle of the United Provinces against Spain. On 5 November young Lord Wriothesley succumbed to the contagious fever that was spreading through the armies in their winter quarters. Five days later, on 10 November, while on the way home with his son's body, Southampton himself died of a 'lethargy' (probably a heart attack brought on by grief and exhaustion) at Bergen-op-Zoom. Father and son were buried together in the family tomb at Titchfield on 28 December.

The impact of Henry Wriothesley, 3rd Earl of Southampton, on the Elizabethan age rests chiefly on his patronage of Shakespeare; there is strong evidence to support the theory that the poet's *Sonnets* were addressed to the Earl. Unstable and reckless in his youth, when he was a member of the Essex circle, Southampton became in later life an upright and respected statesman and member of the Jacobean court. His interest in colonial expansion, and in America particularly, made him a generous sponsor of voyages of exploration to the New World; in his last years he was an active member of the Virginia Company. Born into one of the leading

475

Catholic families of England, he alienated some of his contemporaries by his conversion to Protestantism.

G. P. V. Akrigg, *Shakespeare and the Earl of Southampton* (1968).

A. L. Rowse, *Shakespeare's Southampton: Patron of Virginia* (1965).

C. C. Stopes, *The Life of Henry, Third Earl of Southampton* (Cambridge, 1922).

*Portraits:* miniature, by Nicholas Hilliard, 1594: Fitzwilliam Museum, Cambridge; oil, full length, by unknown artist, *c.* 1595–1600: Welbeck Abbey (Duke of Portland); oil, by John de Critz the Elder: Boughton (The Duke of Buccleuch and Queensberry); miniature, by Nicholas Hilliard, *c.* 1605–10: location unknown; oil, by Daniel Mytens, 1618: Althorp (The Earl Spencer); oil, after Mytens: National Portrait Gallery, London; miniature, by Peter Oliver: National Museum, Stockholm; oil, three-quarter length: Woburn Abbey (The Duke of Bedford).

**Wriothesley, Thomas** (1505–1550), 1st Earl of Southampton, statesman.

Born on 21 December 1505, Thomas Wriothesley was the eldest son of William Wriothesley, then York Herald, and his wife Agnes, daughter of James Drayton of London. His grandfather, Sir John Writh (or Wriothesley), had been the third Garter King-of-Arms, and several other members of the family served as heralds. The name should be pronounced 'Risley'.

Thomas was educated at Cambridge, where he is believed to have studied under Stephen Gardiner (q.v.), the future Bishop of Winchester. He left the university without a degree and accompanied Gardiner on a mission to the Continent. On his return young Wriothesley obtained employment at the court of Henry VIII (q.v.), probably in a clerical capacity and as a King's Messenger, or bearer of dispatches. In 1530 he was appointed a Clerk of the Signet, and it was at about this time that he attracted the notice of the rising Thomas Cromwell (q.v.) and was brought into his service. From December 1532 onwards his duties frequently took him abroad, primarily in connection with the King's 'great matter'. In 1534 he was admitted as a member of Gray's Inn and in 1536, probably as a reward for his hard work in connection with the divorce, Wriothesley was given the post of 'Graver' of the Tower and also the office of Coroner and Attorney in the King's Bench.

As a further reward for his devotion to the royal service, Wriothesley received substantial grants of lands from the dissolved monasteries, principally those of Titchfield and Beaulieu, and also Quarr Abbey in the Isle of Wight. He had a few years earlier settled in Hampshire, having married Jane, daughter and heiress of William Cheney of Chesham Bois, and a half-sister of Gardiner's nephew. They were to have three sons (of whom only the third, Henry, born in 1545, survived infancy) and five daughters.

In the autumn of 1538 Wriothesley was sent on a mission to the Netherlands to ask, on Henry's behalf, for the hand of the Duchess of Milan; this was an attempt to delay the imminent coalition between France and Spain, and it came to nothing. Soon afterwards Cromwell made his fatal mistake of proposing Anne of Cleves (q.v.) as a suitable bride for the King. In the aftermath of that hated union and Cromwell's sudden fall from power, Wriothesley was called upon to give evidence as to the non-consummation of the marriage; he was subsequently one of the commissioners sent to Anne to obtain her consent to the annulment.

Following his master's execution in July 1540, Wriothesley continued in the royal service and gradually came more into line with Gardiner's more conservative policy; it is possible that he had earlier been secretly working with the Bishop to bring Cromwell down. When the Howards fell from favour as a result of Queen Catherine's disgrace (see Catherine Howard), Wriothesley was not slow to seize the advantage. By 1542 he had become one of the King's leading advisers and, in the words of an observer, 'almost governed everything'. His greatest efforts at this period were directed towards the restoration of the imperial alliance, culminating in a joint Anglo-Spanish invasion of France in 1544. For his services in this connection, in 1544 he was created Baron Wriothesley of Titchfield; in May the same year he succeeded Thomas Audley (q.v.) as Lord Chancellor. He acted as one of the advisers to Queen Katherine Parr (q.v.) during Henry's absence in France that summer, and in April 1545 he was made a Knight of the Garter.

During the last three years of the reign Wriothesley was the most influential of all the King's advisers. His rigorous persecutions of the Protestants, the punishments he pronounced in the Star Chamber, and in particular his personal racking of Anne Askew (q.v.), earned him much notoriety. One of his last duties to Henry was the drafting of accusations against Surrey (see Howard, Henry) and Norfolk (see Howard, Thomas, 3rd Duke).

Henry VIII died at the end of January 1547, and under his will Wriothesley was appointed both an executor and a member of the Privy Council until the young King Edward VI (q.v.) attained his majority. On 5 February he was created Earl of Southampton, and a fortnight later he carried the sword of state at the coronation. He soon clashed with the Protector, the Duke of Somerset (see Seymour, Edward), over policy, and in March he was deprived by Somerset of the Great Seal, on a trumped-up charge of having issued a commission without consulting his fellow executors. There had long been hostility between the two men, and although Southampton subsequently agreed to go along with Somerset's proposed Protestant reforms and was restored to the Council, he secretly joined with the Earl of Warwick (see Dudley, John) in plotting the Protector's overthrow. Only when this had been achieved, in October 1549, did Southampton see that Warwick had double-crossed him and that he intended to legislate for an even more rapid advance into Protestantism.

Under great strain and in frail health (he was suffering from consumption), Southampton continued for a few months to attend at court, even after his exclusion from the Council by Warwick in February 1550. He died on 30 July that year, at the age of forty-five, and was buried at St Andrew's, Holborn; his remains were later transferred to the family tomb at Titchfield. In his will, Southampton provided generously for his family and friends and left several small bequests to the young King.

The zeal with which Thomas Wriothesley carried out the duties imposed on him by each of his masters in turn – first Cromwell and then Henry VIII – earned him the dislike and distrust of many of his contemporaries. During the final three years of the reign he was the King's most influential Councillor. Having under Cromwell secretly adhered to the Catholic doctrine, in the last years of his life he moved, with Henry, towards the Protestant position.

*Portrait:* oil, by unknown artist: Palace House, Beaulieu, Hants (Lord Montagu of Beaulieu).

**Wyatt, Sir Thomas** (?1503–1542), 'the Elder', statesman and poet.

Thomas Wyatt was the son of Sir Henry Wyat, or Wiat, and was born at Allington Castle, near Maidstone, Kent, probably in 1503. Sir Henry, who came from a Yorkshire family, was a staunch Lancastrian and had been imprisoned and put to the torture under Richard III (see *Lives Before the Tudors*). He held several offices at the court of Henry VIII (q.v.) and purchased Allington in about 1493. The name is usually spelled as Wyatt.

Thomas was admitted to St John's College, Cambridge, when about twelve years old. He took his B.A. there in 1518, and M.A. in 1522. From a very early age he was in the royal service, acting as server to the King in 1516 and Keeper of the King's Jewels in 1524. It is recorded that he won distinction in a court tournament at Christmas 1525. Henry employed him on a number of foreign missions during the following decade; these included embassies to the King of France and to the Pope. In 1528–30 he was High Marshal at Calais.

Wyatt's father having been associated with Sir Thomas Boleyn (q.v.) at Norwich Castle, Thomas must have been acquainted with the family from his childhood. When Anne Boleyn (q.v.) first returned from France to live at the English court, in about 1522, he became one of her most ardent admirers and almost certainly her lover. (It was said that he confessed his intimacy with her to the King and even warned Henry against marrying Anne; this seems unlikely, however, as he continued high in royal favour.) In 1536 he was sent to the Tower for a short time, probably with a view to getting him to incriminate the Queen in the adultery proceedings brought against her, but he was released a month later.

In the autumn of 1536 Wyatt took part in the suppression of the Leicestershire rising. Appointed Sheriff of Kent in 1537 and knighted for his services to the crown in March the same year, he was soon afterwards sent abroad as ambassador to the Emperor Charles V (q.v.), at whose court he remained until 1539. Edmund Bonner (q.v.), the future Bishop of London, sent a letter to Thomas Cromwell (q.v.) accusing Wyatt of disloyalty to the King's interests, but so long as Cromwell remained in power these allegations were ignored. After his recall in 1539, Wyatt was given responsibility for negotiations with Charles V the following year. When Cromwell fell in the summer of 1540 the accusations were renewed, and Wyatt's enemies also charged him with having conducted a treasonable correspondence with Cardinal Reginald Pole (q.v.). Imprisoned in the Tower in January 1541, he was released the following March only after the intercession of Queen Catherine Howard (q.v.); he confessed his guilt and, at the Queen's request, promised to take back the wife (Elizabeth, daughter of Lord Cobham) whom he had married in about 1520 but from whom he had been separated for some fifteen years. (Their only surviving son was Thomas Wyatt the younger (q.v.), conspirator and leader of the 1554 rebellion.)

Having been granted a full pardon, Wyatt now received several further marks of royal favour. One of these was the office of Knight of the Shire for Kent. In the summer of 1542 he was sent to Falmouth to meet the ambassadors of Charles V on their arrival in England. During a heatwave on the journey he fell ill and never recovered. He died at Sherborne, Dorset, on 11 October 1542. His friend and fellow-poet, the Earl of Surrey (see Howard, Henry), commemorated him in two sonnets and a well-known epitaph beginning 'Wyat resteth here, that quick could never rest'.

Thomas Wyatt was, together with Howard, a pioneer of the sonnet form in England. He was the first poet to end his sonnets with a couplet (this was not done by the French or Italians), a practice which was later followed by Shakespeare (q.v.). His work, none of which was published during his lifetime, falls into two categories: the sonnets, rondeaux and lyric poems, for which he is best known; and the satires, which owed much to the Italian influence. Of the thirty-one sonnets he wrote, ten are translations from Petrarch.

The earliest of his published works was a book of 'Penitential Psalmes', which was issued in 1549 as *Certayne Psalmes . . . drawen into Englysche meter by Sir Thomas Wyat Knyght*. The love poems, a number of which express his feeling for Anne Boleyn, are thought to date from before his first imprisonment in 1536. About ninety-six of Wyatt's poems were included by Tottel in 1557 in a collection of *Songes and Sonettes* (commonly known as *Tottel's Miscellany*). Among the best known are 'They flee from me', 'Forget not yet', and 'To his lute'.

The *Works* have been edited by G. F. Nott (1816) and the *Collected Poems* by J. Daalder (1975); the *Songs and Sonettes* by E. Arbor (1870); the *Poems* by A. K. Foxwell (2 vols; 1913).

E. K. Chambers, *Sir Thomas Wyatt . . . and collected studies* (1933).

H. A. Mason, *Humanism and Poetry in the Early Tudor Period* (1959).

K. Muir, *Life and Letters of Sir Thomas Wyatt* (1963).

Patricia Thomson, *Sir Thomas Wyatt and his background* (1964).

*Portraits*: drawing, by Holbein, c. 1535 (and copy of it by Zuccaro): Royal Collection, Windsor; two oils, both by unknown artists after Holbein, sixteenth century: National Portrait Gallery, London; other versions in Earl of Romney Collection and Bodleian Library, Oxford.

**Wyatt, Sir Thomas** (?1521–1554), 'the Younger', soldier and conspirator.

Born at Allington Castle, near Maidstone, Kent, probably in 1521 (the exact date is not known), Wyatt was the only son of Sir Thomas Wyatt the elder (q.v.), statesman and poet, and his wife Elizabeth, daughter of Lord Cobham. The Duke of Norfolk (see Howard, Thomas, 3rd Duke) was his godfather.

Little is known of Thomas's youth, except that he was brought up as a Catholic. Since his parents were at loggerheads and his father spent most of his time either at court or abroad, he cannot have had a very happy childhood. There is no evidence to support the story that he once accompanied his father to Rome, where they were held to ransom by the Spaniards and threatened by the Inquisition, but managed to escape; it was said that this experience was the root of his hatred of Philip II (q.v.).

At the age of sixteen Thomas married Jane Hawte, daughter of Sir William Hawte of Bourne and Wavering, near

Boxley, Kent. They were to have ten children. Having married so young, probably because of the unhappy atmosphere in the family home, Thomas later fell in love with several other women; he is known to have fathered at least one natural child.

In October 1542 he inherited Allington on the death of his father, but was forced to sell part of the estate in order to pay the latter's enormous debt to the crown. He formed a close friendship with the Earl of Surrey (see Howard, Henry), who had been associated with the elder Wyatt but was only a few years senior to his son. Together the two high-spirited young men indulged in a campaign of hooliganism in London, breaking windows and causing other damage, for which they were brought before the Privy Council in April 1543; Wyatt was sent to the Compter prison and later to the Tower, Surrey to the Fleet.

On their release Wyatt was persuaded by Surrey to volunteer for service in France. He spent nearly seven years with the English army there, taking part in the capture of Boulogne from the French and serving as second-in-command to Surrey; he proved himself to be a brave and resourceful officer.

Following the Peace of Boulogne in 1550, which marked the end of the war with France, Wyatt returned home to Allington, where for the next few years he led the life of a country gentleman. As a Catholic, Wyatt supported the accession of Mary I (q.v.) in July 1553, but when rumours began to circulate towards the end of that year that the Queen intended to marry Philip of Spain, he allied himself with Edward Courtenay, Earl of Devon, and other noblemen from various parts of the country who had supported the rising for Lady Jane Grey (q.v.) in a conspiracy to depose Mary and place Elizabeth (see Elizabeth I) on the throne. He agreed to raise the men of Kent, while Henry Grey, Duke of Suffolk, and Sir Peter Carew made themselves responsible for Warwickshire and the West Country. It was decided that the rising would take place in March.

On 15 January 1554 the formal announcement of the Queen's intended marriage was made public. Six days later the conspiracy was betrayed by Courtenay to Stephen Gardiner (q.v.), Bishop of Winchester, which precipitated a rising in the West before the appointed date. Summoned to London, Carew took fright and fled to France. Wyatt immediately called a conference of the remaining conspirators at Allington, and it was agreed that the Kentish men would march four days later. Proclamations were issued and some 1,500 recruits assembled at Maidstone, with the promise of another 5,000 men. Marching to Rochester, they captured the castle there and made it their headquarters.

While Sir Robert Southwell, Sheriff of Kent, tried to raise a force to put down the insurgents, news reached London that the French King was preparing to invade should the conspiracy prove to be successful. The Duke of Norfolk's force was defeated at Rochester Bridge when his 'Whitecoats' defected to Wyatt, and on 30 January the rebels captured Cowling Castle. On the following day Wyatt decided to march to London; that same night he reached Gravesend with between two and three thousand men.

Emissaries from the Council arrived to negotiate, promising Wyatt a fair hearing, but the rebel leader's demands (which included custody of the Tower and of the Queen) were so excessive that a heated argument ensued and the conference was broken off. The Earl of Pembroke (see Herbert, William) replaced Norfolk, while Mary, alarmed when Wyatt reached Dartford, made a spirited appeal to the citizens of London at Guildhall, with the result that some 25,000 men volunteered to defend the crown.

On 1 February Wyatt marched from Dartford to Greenwich and on to Deptford Strand; on the 3rd, he reached Southwark. There he heard news that the Duke of Suffolk's uprising in Warwickshire had failed, which meant that he was now alone in leading the rebellion. Seeing the defences assembled on the far side of London Bridge under the Lord High Admiral, Lord William Howard (q.v.), Wyatt decided instead to cross the river at Kingston. This he achieved the following evening, and after delays caused by appalling weather conditions and with a force now numbering only some 1,500 men (many of his followers having deserted when they saw that the populace was not on their side), he reached Charing Cross. Here 10,000 loyalists were waiting and his column was cut in two. Wyatt nevertheless pressed on determinedly to Ludgate but, on being refused admission by the Lord High Admiral, he then led his men back to Temple Bar, where, after a short fierce conflict, he surrendered.

He was taken first before the Privy Council at Westminster and then to the Tower, where he was interrogated under torture in the hope of wringing from him a confession that the rebellion had been plotted in concert with Elizabeth (who was also by this time in the Tower). Lord Guildford Dudley and Lady Jane Grey were beheaded on 12 February, the Duke of Suffolk on the 23rd; and hundreds of Kentishmen, convicted of treason, were hung, drawn, and quartered in the next few weeks. Wyatt himself was not brought to trial until 14 March. He confessed his guilt, saying that he believed the Queen would be endangered by the proposed marriage,

but he never fully implicated Elizabeth. Sentenced for high treason, Wyatt was executed on 11 April; in his last speech on the scaffold he completely exonerated Elizabeth. Following the execution, his head was exhibited on the gallows at Hay's Hill and the quarters of his body at various places in London. On 17 April the head was stolen – presumably by some of his friends – and was never recovered. Wyatt's property was confiscated and given to the crown, but Elizabeth on her accession re-allocated parts of his estate to his widow and heirs.

Wyatt was too gentlemanly, too highly strung, and too imaginative to be a successful rebel leader. He had no great personal ambitions and seems to have been motivated only by the desire to save England from the domination of Spain and the effects of the Inquisition. It is unlikely that he would have instigated a rising on his own account. Although the rebellion failed, its effect on world history was far-reaching; it strengthened the growing belief of Englishmen in England as a nation and so alarmed the

Queen and her government that they were forced to tread more warily; its most important effect, however, was that Elizabeth was spared to become Queen. After their execution, public opinion, increasingly repelled by the Marian persecutions, looked on Wyatt and his followers as heroes and martyrs.

D. M. Loades, *Two Tudor Conspiracies*, (1965).
E. N. Simons, *The Queen and the Rebel* (1964).

*Portraits*: oil, by unknown artist: Dr. L. S. Fry Collection; oil, by unknown artist: National Portrait Gallery, London; engraving, by unknown engraver, *c*. 1800, after unknown artist, *c*. 1545–50: location not known.

## Wynter or Winter, Sir William (d. 1589), admiral.

William Wynter was the second son of John Wynter, a sea captain and merchant adventurer of Bristol, and his wife Alice, daughter of William Tirrey of Cork. On his father's side he was descended from two great Gloucestershire families, the Hungerfords and the Wyrrals; his mother was a granddaughter of the Earl of Desmond.

William almost certainly served his sea apprenticeship under his father, who traded with Spain and the Levant. He was still a young boy when he entered the service of the crown, probably in about 1544 at the time when Henry VIII (q.v.) made the elder Wynter Treasurer of his Navy. He is known to have taken part in the expedition sent to Leith and Edinburgh in May 1544, and to have served under Lord Lisle in the Channel the following year. In 1546 his father died, and William inherited the family estate at Lydney, Gloucestershire, built by John Wynter on lands seized by the King from the dissolved monasteries. In September 1547 he took part in the invasion of Scotland led by the Protector Somerset (see Seymour, Edward). Two

years later he served in the islands of Guernsey and Jersey.

On 8 July 1549 Wynter was appointed Surveyor of the Navy. He was to hold this post, together with that of Master of the Ordnance, to which he was appointed in November 1557, to the end of his life. He voyaged to the Levant in 1553, was in action at Conquêt in 1558, and in 1559 commanded the fleet which carried out a successful blockade of the French in the Firth of Forth; in 1563 he was at Le Havre. In 1567 he acted as one of the commissioners sent to France to demand the restitution of Calais under the treaty of Cateau-Cambrésis.

At some date that is not known Wynter married Mary, daughter of Thomas Langton and member of a well-known West Country family. Of their four sons and daughters, Edward, the eldest, and William, the youngest son, both served with Sir Francis Drake (q.v.); another son was killed during the fight against the Spanish Armada in 1588. Several of Wynter's nephews also served in the Navy at this period, including the John Wynter who commanded the *Elizabeth* in Drake's ill-fated voyage of 1578 and returned home through the Magellan Straits.

Wynter was knighted for his services on 12 August 1573. He was held in much esteem at court and, as a man of wealth, he contributed generously towards the financing of the several voyages of John Hawkins (q.v.) and Drake. But after Hawkins was appointed Treasurer of the Navy in 1577, a post which he thought should have been his, there were clashes between the two men, which culminated in Wynter accusing Hawkins to Burghley (see Cecil, William) of inefficiency and dishonesty. Nevertheless Wynter did valuable work as a member of the Navy Board and deserves much of the credit for the improvement in design and armament of Her Majesty's ships. When the Armada threatened England in the summer of 1588 he mobilized the ships of London from his house in Seething Lane near the Tower.

The fight against the Spaniards was the crowning achievement of Wynter's life. In command of his flagship, the *Vanguard*, under Lord Henry Seymour, he joined the main fleet under Lord Howard of Effingham (see Howard, Charles) off Calais on 27 July. It was his proposal to send in fireships among the enemy. On the 29th he and his sons and nephews fought brilliantly in the battle off Gravelines, which is depicted in the painting by Sir Oswald Brierley now at the National Maritime Museum, Greenwich.

Sir William Wynter died in 1589.

Joan Simon, 'They Sailed with Drake', *Gloucestershire Life* (August 1972).

# Z

**Zwingli, Ulrich** (1484–1531), Swiss reformer.

Born on 1 January 1484 at Wildhaus, near St Gall, Switzerland, of peasant stock, Ulrich Zwingli was educated at schools in Basle and Berne and then sent to study philosophy at the university of Vienna. He later returned to Basle, where he graduated in the university and took up a post as a classics teacher.

At the age of twenty-two he was ordained and elected parish priest of Glarus. Ten years later, in 1516, he moved to Einsiedeln, and began to found his preaching on 'the Gospel', taking the Bible as the only rule of faith and seeking to restore simplicity within the church. In 1518 he became people's priest at Zurich cathedral.

The Reformation is said to have begun in Zurich with a series of sermons preached there by Zwingli in 1519, on St Matthew's Gospel, the Acts of the Apostles, and the Epistles of Paul. He went on to attack the papacy, preaching against the worship of saintly images, fasting, and the celibacy of priests. In 1523 the Pope tried to get rid of Zwingli, but the council of Zurich upheld their preacher and the canton became separated from the bishopric of Constance.

The Zwinglians next won over Berne to their side, urging also constitutional reform in order to reduce the disproportionate voting power of the five Forest Cantons which were strongly opposed to the Reformation.

In April 1524 Zwingli publicly celebrated his marriage, and a few months later he published a pamphlet setting out his views on the Eucharist and denouncing the worship of images and the Mass.

Conflict with Martin Luther (q.v.) now came into the open. Zwingli had for some time been jealous of the German reformer's influence, believing that he himself had discovered the evangelical truth long before Luther; but their main divergence of opinion was over the Real Presence, Zwingli maintaining that the Communion was symbolical, commemorative of Christ's death, and not the repetition of the sacrifice. An attempt was made to get the two reformers to meet and settle their difference, but it was unsuccessful and the Protestant movement split into two camps. Civil war broke out between the opposing cantons, and in a battle fought at Kappel on 10 October 1531 Zwingli was struck to the ground. The next day he was brutally killed, and his body quartered by the local executioner and burned.

By this time Zwinglianism had spread through Europe and reached England through the continental reformers Martin Bucer (q.v.), Peter Martyr, John à Lasco (q.v.), and others. Under their influence Thomas Cranmer (q.v.) towards the end of his life came near to accepting the Zwinglian concept of the sacrament.

S. M. Jackson, *Heroes of the Reformation* (1901).
J. Rilliet, *Zwingli, Third Man of the Reformation* (1964).

# INDEX

This index contains entries for all the main characters but, for reasons of space, only the more important secondary characters, mentioned in the present volume. Figures in bold type indicate the main reference. Members of an entrant's family are not included unless they have significance in their own right; in the case of monarchs, statesmen and others who occur repeatedly throughout the text, the major references only are listed.

# CLASSIFIED INDEX